Compulsory Acquisition and Comp

Compulsory Acquisition and Compensation

by Sir Frederick Corfield QC
& R. J. A. Carnwath, *Barrister*

assisted by D. A. Richards, *Barrister*

London
Butterworths
1978

England London	Butterworth & Co (Publishers) Ltd 88 Kingsway WC2B 6AB
Australia Sydney	Butterworths Pty Ltd 586 Pacific Highway, Chatswood, NSW 2067 Also at Melbourne, Brisbane, Adelaide and Perth
Canada Toronto	Butterworth & Co (Canada) Ltd 2265 Midland Avenue, Scarborough M1P 4S1
New Zealand Wellington	Butterworths of New Zealand Ltd 77–85 Customhouse Quay
South Africa Durban	Butterworth & Co (South Africa) (Pty) Ltd 152/154 Gale Street
USA Boston	Butterworth (Publishers) Inc 19 Cummings Park, Woburn, Mass 01801

ISBN 0 406 16160 7

Printed in Great Britain by
Cox & Wyman Ltd, London, Fakenham and Reading

PREFACE

Although in recent years a number of works on the law governing compulsory acquisition and compensation have been available, it has seemed to the authors of this book that there still remains a gap to be filled, namely the provision of a reference book in which either student or practitioner can expect to find what he needs to know on any particular aspect of the subject as far as possible under a single heading, and with the minimum amount of cross-references or superfluous reading.

Although the work falls naturally into two parts—Chapters 1 to 4 dealing with procedures relating to the acquisition of land, and chapters 5 to 10 setting out the substantive law governing the assessment of compensation—it seemed helpful to deal with basic principles and their historical development in a single introductory chapter (Chapter 1). In including this chapter we have particularly had in mind the student and others coming to this branch of the law for the first time, for it is a subject that, in the years following the Second World War, has been bedevilled by acute political controversy and constant change. Indeed, every change of Government during this period has seen either a change in the basic rules governing the assessment of compensation or in the manner in which compensation reflecting any enhancement in the development value of land acquired is to be treated for tax purposes. Sometimes changes have been made under both heads, and in either case the Opposition of the day have invariably responded by pledging themselves to drastic amendment or repeal.

In these circumstances a proper grasp of basic principles is inevitably made more difficult: without such a grasp comprehension and mental retention of detail also becomes more difficult. We hope, therefore, that by outlining the post-war development of the law and the criticisms of successive legislation that have led to further change, this problem will at least be eased.

In the remainder of the work we have sought to deal as far as possible with what may be called the "modern" law, and to avoid extensive references to those parts of the older statutes which, though still applicable in certain isolated cases, have minimal significance for everyday purposes. Thus, for example, when dealing with compulsory purchase procedures we have concentrated on the procedures under the Compulsory Purchase Act 1965, and have avoided frequent references to the Lands Clauses Consolidation Act 1845.

Chapter 2 (Compulsory Purchase Procedure) deals with the powers and duties of public authorities in the compulsory acquisition of interests in land. The first section of Chapter 3 (Determination and Payment of Compensation) deals with the Lands Tribunal procedure for the determination of disputes, as between vendor and acquiring authority, either as to valuation, method of assessment, or both. The second section of that Chapter is devoted to a short review of the effect of the latest legislation in this field—the Development Land Tax Act of 1976—on the amount actually payable to the owner of the interest acquired.

Under this Act development land tax, although of general application, has particular relevance to development value realised upon sale (whether compulsory or by agreement) to public authorities, because it falls to be deducted from the compensation payable instead of being left to be collected by the Inland Revenue direct from the vendor. Since, by definition, neither the amount of the tax nor the compensation from which it is to be deducted can be assessed until the gross compensation payable has been agreed, or determined by the Lands Tribunal, it might appear to be more logical to deal with this matter at the end of the book. We have opted for inclusion in Chapter 3, however, first because it has nothing to do with the assessment of compensation as such, and secondly because a detailed consideration of the Development Land Tax Act is not within the scope of this book; our concern has been more with the procedure than with the detailed determination of the tax.

Chapter 4 (Purchase and Blight Notices) deals with the circumstances in which owners of interests in land can require the acquisition of their land by public authorities, and the procedures to be adopted. In such cases compensation falls to be determined in precisely the same way as when the acquisition is initiated by the appropriate authority in pursuance of compulsory powers; this is, of course, the subject matter of Chapters 5 to 10. To this general proposition there is one relatively minor exception in relation to purchase notices served under the Town and Country Planning Act 1971. It is therefore considered in detail in Chapter 4 in the procedural context to which it applies.

Conversely, in the case of the compulsory acquisition of certain categories of land considered in Chapter 6, the method of assessing compensation is so intertwined with the special procedures involved that it is simpler to deal with both procedure and assessment of compensation under the same head. This is particularly so in the case of an acquisition of common land. In other cases such as the acquisition of land belonging to statutory undertakers and acquisitions under the Housing Act 1957 we have accepted a degree of repetition.

Chapter 5 (Compensation for Land Taken) gives a General Introduction to the Law of Compensation designed to explain the heads under which compensation may be claimed, the basic principles upon which the law is based, a guidance note as to the format of this and succeeding chapters, and a "check list" designed on the one hand to draw attention to the head under which compensation is likely to be claimable in any particular case, and secondly, to provide a quick means of identifying the crucial issues.

The remainder of Chapter 5 deals with the assessment of compensation for interests in land acquired other than acquisitions in respect of which special provisions in regard to the assessment of compensation apply. These are dealt with in Chapter 6 (Compensation for Land Taken: Special Cases).

Chapter 7 deals with the Community Land Act 1975 in so far as it affects the assessment of compensation. For the most part its immediate impact in this regard is marginal for the relevant provisions do not come into operation until the Second Appointed Day which, at the time of going to press, is wholly indefinite, and conceivably, if there is a change of Government and the Conservatives redeem their pledge to repeal the Act, may never materialise. Three provisions affecting compensation did, however, come into effect on, or shortly after, the passing of the Act: first, there are powers to penalise those who carry out development while planning permission therefore is suspended. These provisions are considered in detail in Chapter 7. Secondly, the Act effected a relatively minor amendment to the Land Compensation Act 1961, s. 17; the effect of this amendment is therefore considered as part of the current law in Chapter 5. Thirdly, the Act provides special powers and special rules in regard to compensation in respect of new and unoccupied office premises; unoccupied office premises are therefore dealt with as a special case in Chapter 6.

Chapter 8 (Severance and Injurious Affection) deals with compensation for injurious affection in the hitherto accepted sense and concludes with a consideration of the extension to the general law effected by Part I of the Land Compensation Act 1973.

Chapter 9 deals with claims for compensation for disturbance, and similarly includes consideration of certain analogous claims for home loss, farm loss and disturbance payments under Part III of this latter Act, as well as certain other provisions of that Act for the benefit of persons displaced by compulsory acquisition.

Chapter 10 deals with the circumstances in which compensation may be payable in respect of certain limited categories of planning decisions and describes the relevant procedures and the measure of compensation in each case.

In setting out the text of this work it has seemed to us that the practitioner resorts to a reference book of this nature for one of two separate, though closely related, purposes. If the matter with which he is dealing raises either an issue with which he is unfamiliar, or a matter of doubtful interpretation, he will wish to know something of the principles upon which statutory provisions, and particularly judicial decisions, have been based, so that he can apply them to the case in hand. In such cases we believe that he (and *a fortiori*, the student) will find an analysis of principle and of the statutory provisions and leading cases more helpful than a relatively bald statement of the law supported merely by references to the appropriate statute and case law. On the other hand the latter type of approach may be all that is required by a practitioner already familiar with the subject matter and anxious merely to check a reference or point of detail.

To meet this second requirement we have, whenever the subject matter considered under the heading in question makes it appropriate to do so, inserted a summary. From these summaries it is hoped that the basic law can be immediately extracted and that the cross-references will readily enable those requiring more detailed explanation to find the appropriate paragraphs of the text without constant reference to the index.

In practice, of course, we have found it convenient, as well as more logical, to commence with an explanation of the underlying principle and, where appropriate, of its historical development; to go on to a detailed exposition, and to conclude with a summary.

We hope that the check list at the beginning of Chapter 5, together with these summaries, will serve the more experienced practitioner as a useful means of quick reference, and the student as a helpful aide-memoire.

Last, but certainly not least, we wish to express our thanks to Miss Sheila Kerr, who has deciphered, checked and typed our manuscripts only to find, on all too many occasions, that we have decided to introduce substantial alteration necessitating much retyping.

F.V.C.
R.J.A.C.
November 1977

CONTENTS

Preface   v

Table of Statutes   xiii

Table of Cases   xxvii

1 Development of the Law of Compensation upon Compulsory Acquisition   1

1 Introductory   1

2 The Lands Clauses Acts   3

3 The Acquisition of Land (Assessment of Compensation) Act 1919   4

4 Betterment   4

5 Town and Country Planning Act 1947   8

6 The Town and Country Planning Acts 1953 and 1954   10

7 The Town and Country Planning Act 1959 and The Land Compensation Act 1961   14

8 The Land Commission Act 1967   19

9 The development gains tax   21

10 The community land scheme   22

11 Historical summary   28

2 Compulsory Purchase Procedure   30

1 Introduction   30

2 A procedure under the Acquisition of Land (Authorisation Procedure) Act 1946   32

3 From confirmation to entry   66

4 Procedure under the Community Land Act 1975   74

5 Procedure under the Housing Act 1957, Part III   77

6 Procedure under the New Towns Act 1965   80

3 Determination and Payment of Compensation   83

1 Determination of compensation   83

2 Special cases   88

3 Advance payment of compensation   95

4 Interest   96

5 Deductions for tax   97

6 Deduction of development land tax   97

4 Purchase and Blight Notices   106

1 Introductory   106

2 Counter notices of objection to severance of land   108

3 Purchase notices   114

4 Blight notices   129

5 Compensation for Land Taken   158

1 General introduction to the law of compensation   158

2 Compensation for land taken: Parts II and III, Land Compensation Act 1961   163

3 Adjustments to compensation when the value of an owner's interests is affected by development of neighbouring land   217

6 Compensation for Land Taken: Special Cases   238

1 Introductory   238

2 Property for which there is no market demand: Compensation on the basis of the cost of equivalent reinstatement   239

3 Land and/or apparatus of statutory undertakers   250

4 Houses unfit for human habitation: Compensation based on site values   255

5 Minerals   273

6 Buildings of special architectural or historical interest   274

7 Commons, etc.   277

8 Extinguishment or acquisition of easements, profits à prendre and breaches of restrictive covenants   283

9 Unoccupied office premises   286

7 Compensation under the Community Land Act 1975   296

1 Introductory   296

2 The second appointed day   305

8 Compensation for Severance and Injurious Affection   314

1 Introductory   314

2 Compensation for severance and injurious affection of land held by the vendor of land compulsorily acquired   314

3 Compensation for injurious affection to land held by third parties   321

9 Compensation for Disturbance   344

1 Introductory   344

2 Compensation for disturbance in the case of acquisition of a freehold or long leasehold   346

3 Compensation for disturbance arising from the acquisition of short tenancies   365

4 Home, farm loss and disturbance payments under Part III, Land Compensation Act 1973   372

5 Other provisions for the benefit of displaced residential occupiers under Part III, Land Compensation Act 1973   390

10 Compensation in Respect of Certain Planning Decisions   393

1 Introduction   393

2 Compensation for planning decisions restricting new development   394

3 Other restrictions on development or use of land   405

Appendix: Town and Country Planning Act 1971, Schedules 8 and 18   456

Index   461

Table of Statutes

References in this Table to *"Statutes"* are to Halsbury's Statutes of England (Third Edition) showing the volume and page at which the annotated text of the Act will be found. Page references printed in bold type indicate where the Act is set out in part or in full.

PAGE

A

Acquisition of Land (Assessment of Compensation) Act 1919 . . 3, 28, 83, 85, 180
s. 1 . . . . 4, 83, 344
2 . . . . 4, 15, 163
(1)–(6) 8
12(2) 163
Acquisition of Land (Authorisation Procedure) Act 1946 (6 *Statutes* 154) 2, 3, 46, 69, 74, 90
s. 1(1) 32
(3) 273
5 . . . . 37, 47, 50
(1) 36
(2) 41, 45, 46
6(3) 48
7(1), (3) 32
8 . . . . 33, 250
(1) . . . 32, 33, 48, 49, 50, 111, 277
Sch. 1 . . . . 30, 31, 32, 37, 66, 68, 295
para. 1 32
3 . . . 33, 34, 94, 137, 206, 275
4 . . . . 35, 36, 45, 46, 75, 82
5 35
6 . . . . 36, 37, 302
7 . . . . 46, 47, 48, 302
9 . . . . 48, 81
10 . . . . . 49, 250, 251, 252
11 . . . . . 49, 50, 277, 279
12 50
13 . . . . 45, 51
15 . . 44, 51, 52, 54, 55, 56, 57, 59, 61, 62, 63, 64, 65
16 . . . . 36, 52, 65, 66, 67, 80
17 . . . . 52, 54
18 33
19 . . . . 33, 34, 68
Sch. 2—
para. 4 . . . . 106, 108
7 273
8 . . . . 173, 417
Sch. 4—
para. 4 . . . . 75, 76, 77

PAGE

Administration of Justice Act 1965 (7 *Statutes* 744)—
s. 4 88
Admiralty (Signal Stations) Act 1815 . 2
Agricultural Holdings Act 1948 (1 *Statutes* 685) . . 113, 171, 182, 331, 342, 355, 365, 366, 379, 381, 388
s. 23 367
(1) 172
24(1) 367
(2) 172, 367
25(1) 367
32 371
34(1), (2) 371
35, 36, 46, 56 371
Agriculture (Miscellaneous Provisions) Act 1968 (40 *Statutes* 8) 365, 389
s. 9–11 371
12 . . . . 367, 371, 380
(1) 371
(2) 372
Airports Authority Act 1965 (2 *Statutes* 648)—
s. 15 . . . . 338, 339, 342
Ancient Monuments Act 1931 (24 *Statutes* 254) 50, 405, 427
s. 3 429
(1) 432
6(1), (2), (5) 428
15(1) 427, 428
(2) 427
Ancient Monuments Consolidation and Amendment Act 1913 (24 *Statutes* 241) 50, 405, 427
s. 4 429
12 427
(1) 428
Ancient Monuments Protection Act 1882 (24 *Statutes* 239)—
Schedule 427
Arbitration Act 1950 (2 *Statutes* 433)—
s. 12(1)–(3) 85
(4)–(6) 84
14 86

PAGE

Arbitration Act 1950—*contd.*
s. 20 . . . . 86, 96
Artizans and Labourers Dwelling
    Act (1868) (Amendment) Act
    1879 6

B

British Transport Commission Act 1962 283

C

Caravan Sites and Control of Develop-
    ment Act 1960 (24 *Statutes* 145)—
s. 1(4) 376
Civil Aviation Act 1949 (2 *Statutes*
    514)—
s. 41(2) 330
Civil Evidence Act 1968 (12 *Statutes*
    910) 85
s. 10(3) 85
    18(1) 85
Civil Evidence Act 1972 (42 *Statutes*
    72) 85
s. 5(1) 85
Coal Act 1938 (22 *Statutes* 92) 273
s. 17 273
Coal Industry Nationalisation Act 1946
    (22 *Statutes* 143) 273
Commons Act 1876 (3 *Statutes* 874) . . 279
Commons Registration Act 1965 (3
    Statutes 919)—
s. 1, 2 278
    17, 18 278
    22(1) 49, 278
Commonable Rights Compensation Act
    1882 (3 *Statutes* 902) 49, 282
Community Land Act 1975 (45 *Statutes*
    91) 4, 6, 8, 15, 18, 20, 23, 30,
                74, 83, 159, 189, 201, 216,
                238, 252, 257, 260, 283
s. 1 . . . . .23, 191, 296
    (1) 99
    (2) 23
    2 . . . . .99, 296
    3 23
    (1) 296
    (2) 76, 191, 296
    (3) 297
    4 74
    (1) 74, 298, 299, 308
    (2) 299
    5(2) 299
    (4), (5) 253
    6(1) . .74, 186, 296, 298, 299, 300, 305
    (2) 298, 300
    (3) 300, 304
    (4) 304
    7 98
    (3) 298, 306, 310
    8–14 296
    15 . . . . .74, 142
    15(2) 74

PAGE

Community Land Act 1975—*contd.*
s. 15(3) 74, 279
    (4) 32, 74
    (5) 74, 187, 191
    16 . . . . .26, 298
    17 24
    18 . . . . .24, 298
    (3) 298
    (4) 299
    (6) 304
    19 . . . . 100, 142, 300
    (5) 301
    20 . . . . 100, 142, 300
    21 . . . . 100, 142, 304, 305
    (1), (2) 304
    (3)–(8), (10) 305
    22 . . . . . . .25, 100, 142, 296
    (1) 304
    (2) 100, 304
    (4) 304
    (6) . . .17, 142, 154, 156, 188, 303
    (7) 302
    25 . . . . . 161, 211, 235, 306, 311
    (1) 306, 307, 308, 309
    (2) 309
    (3) 306
    (4) 298, 306
    (5) 308, 309
    (6) 309
    (7) 308
    (8) 235, 307
    (9) 307, 312
    (10) 25
    26 . . . . 310, 311
    (6) 309
    27 300
    (1) 310, 311, 312
    (2)–(7) 311
    (8) 211, 312
    (10), (11) 311
    28 . . . . 286, 295
    (1) 287, 289
    (2)–(4) 287
    (5) 288
    (6) 287
    (7), (8) 289
    29 . . . . 286, 288
    (1) 293
    (2) 293, 294
    (4)–(6) 294
    30 . . . . 286, 295
    (1) 288
    31 286
    (1), (2) 295
    (3), (4) 293
    32 286
    (1), (2) 288
    33 286
    (1)–(3) 289
    (4) 289, 290
    (5), (6) 290
    (7) 291
    (8) 290
    34 286

PAGE

Community Land Act 1975—*contd.*
s. 34(1), (2) 289, 292
 (3)–(6) 292
35 . . . . 286, 289
 (1)–(3) 292
36 . . . . 286, 290
 (1), (2) 293
40 313
41 48
 (2) 187
42 24
44(2), (5) 27
47 . . . . . 205, 208, 213, 214, 310
 (3) 208, 209
 (6) 211
50 . . . . 99, 296
53 305
58(2) 300
Sch. 1 . . . . . 23, 74, 75, 296, 299
para. 1 . . . . 74, 306
 2 306
 3 . . . . 297, 306
Sch. 4 75
Pt. I 295
 para. 7 293
  10 283
  17 . . . . . 252, 253, 254
  18, 19 . . . . . 253, 254
  23 . . . . . . 187, 191
Sch. 5 298
Sch. 6—
para. 1 . . . . 24, 193
 2 26
Sch. 7—
para. 1 . . . . 301, 302
 2 . . . 300, 301, 302, 303, 305
 5 . . . . . . 300, 301, 303
 7, 8 301
 9 . . . . 300, 301
Sch. 8 285
Sch. 9 . . . . 213, 214, 310
Pt. I 205, 208
Sch. 10—
para. 3 . . . . 83, 86
 4 257
 6, 7 300
Compulsory Purchase Act 1965 (6
Statutes 281) 3, 31, 66
s. 1(1) 31, 66
 (3) 90, 93
2 . . . . 89, 94
3 66
4 . . . . . . 67, 165, 216, 240
5 . . . . 315, 369
 (1) 68, 184
 (2) 67, 83, 171
 (3) 68, 88
6 84
7 . . 93, 233, 236, 283, 314, 315, 320,
     322, 340, 366, 418
8 . . . . 35, 106, 108, 149
 (1) 108, 109
 (2), (3) 110
9 . . . . 89, 91, 93, 113

PAGE

Compulsory Purchase Act 1975—*contd.*
s. 9(1)–(4) 90
10 . . . . 33, 68, 96, 237, 274, 283,
     314, 321, 322, 330
 (1) 321
11 . . . . 111, 113, 328
 (1) 68, 70, 95, 111, 113
 (2) 68, 70, 104
 (3) 70
 (4) 71
12(1)–(4), (6) 71
13 70
14 91
 (2), (3) 90
 (4)–(7) 91
15 91
 (1) 104
 (3)–(7) 91
16 . . . . 91, 319
 (1) 91, 104
 (2), (3) 91
 (4) 91, 92
 (5) 91
 (6) 92
17(1), (2) 92
18(2)–(4) 92
 (5) 93
 (6) 92
19(1)–(5) 93
20 . . . . 68, 93, 345, 366, 367, 369
22(1)–(5) 89
23(1), (2) 93
 (3)–(5) 94
 (6) 93
25 . . . . 71, 88
26 93
28 . . . . 88, 90
30(3) 68
31 . . . . 94, 293
34 80
 (2) 108
35 31
Sch. 1 . . . . 89, 94
para. 2, 4 94
 6–8, 10 94
Sch. 2 . . . . 68, 88, 89, 184
para. 1 . . . . 88, 184
 2, 3 88
 4 . . . . 88, 89
Sch. 3 . . . . 68, 70, 113
para. 2 70
 3 71
Sch. 4—
para. 1 278
 4–6 280
Sch. 5 93
Control of Office Development Act
 1977—
s. 1 125
Countryside Act 1968—
s. 25 436
Courts Act 1971 (41 *Statutes* 285)—
Sch. 10 71
Customs Consolidation Act 1853 . . . 2

PAGE

D

Defence Act 1842 (29 *Statutes* 1092) . .   2
Defence Act 1860 (29 *Statutes* 1123) . .   5
Development and Road Improve-
    ment Funds Act 1909 (37
    Statutes 17)—
    Schedule 235
Development Land Tax Act 1976   . 22, 25,
                                        98, 313
    s. 1(1)–(3)   98
       2   98
       3, 4   98
       5   98
          (1)   98
       7(2)–(6)   99
      11   99
          (1)   99
      12 102
      13 . . . . .98, 103
      24 310
      25 . . . . .99, 310
      39 . . . . .97, 99
          (1), (2)   99
          (4) 104
          (5), (6) 105
          (10)   99
      41(1)   98
      45(2) 100
      46(3)   98
      47(1)   99
    Sch. 7   97
      para. 1 . . . . .99, 100
           2 101
           3, 4 . . . . .101, 102
           5 . . . . .102, 103
           6 102
           7 103
           8, 9 104
          10 . . . . .104, 105
          11–13 105
Distribution of Industry Act 1950 . .   2
Drainage (Ireland) Act 1842   5

E

Electric Lighting (Scotland) Act 1902—
    s. 2 185
Electric Lighting (Clauses) Act 1899
    (11 *Statutes* 862)—
    Schedule—
      para. 10 185
Electricity Act 1957 (11 *Statutes*
    1015)—
    s. 32 185
       34 185

F

Finance (1909–10) Act 1910 178
Finance Act 1965   29
Finance Act 1974   21
Finance Act 1975 (45 *Statutes*
    1770)—

PAGE

Finance Act 1975—*contd.*
    s. 29 222
    Sch. 6 222
Forestry Act 1951—
    s. 13 433
Forestry Act 1967 (14 *Statutes* 193) 446, 452
    s. 4 436
       9(1) 433
          (2)–(4) 433
      10(4) 434
      11 . . . . .405, 435
          (1) 434
          (2) 451
          (3)–(5) 434
          (6) 452
      14 434
      15(1)–(3) 433
          (5), (6) 433
      31(1) 452
      35 451
    Sch. 3 433
    Sch. 6—
      para. 1 451

G

Gas Act 1972 (42 *Statutes* 466)—
    Sch. 2—
      para. 14 109
General Turnpike Act for Scotland
    1831   5
General Rate Act 1967 (27 *Statutes*
    72) 377
    Sch. 1 288
General Rate Act 1970 (27 *Statutes*
    266) 377

H

Highways Act 1959 (15 *Statutes* 143) .   30
    s. 159 140
          (6) 140
      222(6) 235
      295(1) 335
    Sch. 1—
      para. 1, 2, 7 136
Highways Act 1971 (41 *Statutes*
    625)—
    s. 1 136
      47 136
    Sch. 6—
      para. 8 109
Highways (Miscellaneous Provisions)
    Act 1961 (15 *Statutes* 485)—
    s. 3 155
Historic Buildings and Ancient Monu-
    ments Act 1953 (24 *Statutes* 267)—
    s. 10 428
          (3) 428
      11(1), (2) 428
      12 452
          (1) 428, 430
          (2) 429, 430
          (3) 429, 451

PAGE

Historic Buildings and Ancient
  Monuments Act 1953—*contd.*
s. 12(5) 428, 429
    (6) 431, 451
   13(4) 429, 431
   22(2) 427
Schedule 428
Housing Act 1930 (16 *Statutes* 41)—
Sch. 1—
para. 4 65
Housing Act 1957 (16 *Statutes* 109) . . . 3,
            30, 32, 33, 42, 55, 56, 59, 60,
            77, 108, 221, 257, 272, 277, 345
s. 4 257
  9(1) 258
  10 . . . . 258, 271
  11 258
  12 . . . . 258, 262, 266
    (2) 258
  16 258
  17 . . . . 258, 265
  19 266
  23 . . . . 260, 271
  24 270
  25(1) 261
  27(2) 270
  29 . . . . 256, 345
  30 262
  32 270
  39(2) 258
  42 . . . . 140, 259
    (1) 77
  43 . . . . . . 108, 140, 260, 368
    (1) 77
    (2) 56, 77, 79, 140, 260
    (4) 78
    (7) 58
  44 260
  48 80
  51 . . . . 108, 260
  56 . . . . 260, 261
  57(1) 261
  59 . . . . 256, 317, 345
  60 . . . . 262, 263
    (1B), (1D) 263
  63 270
  72 260
    (4) 260
  73 260
  74 260
    (1) 260
  77 261
  96 56
  98 95
  100 270
  101 113
  169 78
    (1) 78
  189 258
    (1) 33, 258
Sch. 2 . . . . 263, 386
para. 2, 3 263
    4 269
    6 . . . . 269, 270, 272

PAGE

Housing Act 1957—*contd.*
Sch. 3—
para. 1 77
    2 78
    3 . . . . 78, 79
    4 . . . . 79, 235
Sch. 3—
para. 8 69
    10 . . . . 80, 95
  Pt. III, para. 1, 2, 4 262
Sch. 4 77
para. 1, 2 79
    3-5 80
Sch. 9—
para. 1 390
Housing Act 1969 (16 *Statutes* 496) . . . 12,
                                257, 373
s. 28, 29 138
  31 . . . . 137, 139
  32 139
  65 262
  67 . . . . 262, 264, 272
    (1), (2) 264
  68 . . . . 265, 272
    (2) 269
  69 270
  86(2) 265
  108 140
Sch. 4 . . . . 262, 263
para. 1 . . . . . . 263, 264, 269
    3 265
Sch. 5 . . . . 265, 272, 386
para. 1 . . . . . 265, 266, 268, 271
    2 . . . . 265, 272
    3 . . . . 265, 266, 267
    5 . . . . 265, 266, 269
Sch. 6—
para. 2 265
    3 269
Housing Act 1974 (44 *Statutes* 405) . . . 128
s. 12 299
  13(1) 299
  18(1) 372
  85(3) 128
  92 129
  101(1), (2) 129
  104(2) 128
  108 . . . . 77, 260
    (1) 260, 263
    (2) 263
  130 140
    (4) 260
Sch. 9 263
Sch. 13 372
para. 38 . . . . . . 372, 373, 379
    40 389
Sch. 15 . . . . 140, 260
Housing Finance Act 1972 (42
  Statutes 557)—
s. 80 372
Housing Repairs and Rents Act 1954
  (16 *Statutes* 87)—
s. 50(1) 33

PAGE

Housing (Slum Clearance Compensation) Act 1965 (16 *Statutes* 447)—
s. 1 265
Housing Town Planning &c., Act 1909 5
Hull Docks Act 1844 4

I

Inclosure Act 1845 (3 *Statutes* 702) 49
s. 11 49
Inclosure Act 1852 (3 *Statutes* 820)—
s. 22 282
Inclosure Act 1854 (3 *Statutes* 837) 282
Income and Corporation Taxes Act 1970 (33 *Statutes* 17) 299
s. 341 299
Interpretation Act 1889 (33 *Statutes* 434)—
s. 1 268
23 3
26 34
38(1) 41

L

Land Commission Act 1967 (36 *Statutes* 451) 19, 25, 29
Land Commission (Dissolution) Act 1971 (41 *Statutes* 1563) . . . 20, 29, 72
Land Compensation Act 1961 (6 *Statutes* 238) . . 6, 12, 14, 19, 23, 25, 29, 31, 72, 81, 180, 211, 312
s. 1 . . . . 31, 83, 206
(1) 35
2 . . . . 31, 206, 452
(2), (3), (5) 86
3 . . . . 31, 207, 452
4 . . . . 31, 452
(1) 87
(2) 84, 87
(3), (5), (6) 87
5 . . . 4, 15, 164, 251, 254, 312, 337, 344, 348, 383, 446, 447
(1) 177
(2) 177, 350, 382, 383
(3) 177, 218, 219, 382, 383
(4) 177, 194, 261, 382, 444
(5) . . . 239, 240, 241, 251, 309, 380
6 . . 16, 202, 219, 220, 222, 223, 227, 231, 232, 233, 236, 318, 358, 447
(1) 221, 224, 226
(3) 220, 221, 237
7 . . . 16, 17, 219, 220, 222, 224, 231, 233, 235, 237, 262, 447
8 . . . 219, 220, 225, 231, 340, 447
(1) 17, 235, 237
(2) 17, 233, 237
(3) 232, 237
(5) 17, 234, 236

PAGE

Land Compensation Act 1961—*contd.*
s. 8(6) 235, 340
(7) 17, 235
9 . 9, 17, 176, 177, 223, 350, 368, 447
10–12 447
13 . . . . 10, 159, 447
14 . . 15, 166, 189, 204, 213, 307, 309, 317, 339, 350, 447
14(1) 181
(2) 185, 302
(3) 181, 189, 197, 214
(4) 185, 190
15 . . . 15, 160, 166, 185, 189, 191, 203, 204, 205, 213, 235, 307, 309, 317, 339, 350, 383, 447
(1) 188, 191, 226, 236
(2) 190, 191
(3) 127, 195, 225, 393
(4) 195
(5) 213
16 . . . . . 15, 166, 185, 189, 192, 196, 198, 204, 213, 215, 226, 307, 309, 317, 339, 350, 447
(1) 198, 205
(2) 199, 205, 206
(3) 201, 205, 206
(4) . . . 202, 205, 206, 216, 225
(5) . . . 202, 205, 206, 216, 225
(6) 190, 201
(7) 196, 199, 201
(8) 198, 202
17 . . . . 15, 23, 192, 204, 205, 210, 213, 214, 216, 225, 296, 307, 317
(1) 206, 225
(2) 207
(3) 193, 208
(4) 208, 209, 210, 213
(5) 190, 209
(6) 209
(7) 209, 213
(9) 209
18 . . . . 15, 23, 204, 205, 209, 213, 307, 317
(1) 210
(2) 205, 211
(3) 211
(4) 210
19 . . . . . . 15, 23, 204, 213, 307
(2) 333
20 . . . . 15, 204, 210, 213
21 . . . . 15, 204, 213
22 . . . . . . 15, 204, 212, 213
(2) 206, 215
(3) 206, 207
31 . . . . 68, 112, 169
(1)–(3), (5) 84
32 . . . . 70, 96, 311, 328, 385
38 208
(1) 210
39 83
(1) 164, 197, 230
(2), (6) 221
Sch. 1 . . . . . . 202, 219, 227, 318
Pt. I 16, 220, 233, 235

PAGE

Land Compensation Act 1967—*contd.*
Sch. 1—
  para. 1 236
       2 . . . . . . 224, 236, 271
       3 . . . . 224, 236
       3A 224, 236
       4 . . . . 224, 236
       5–8 230
Sch. 2 . . . . 261, 271
  para. 1 257
       2 . . . . . 257, 265, 266, 271

Land Compensation Act 1973 (43
  Statutes 170) 5, 15, 106,
      108, 133, 159, 162, 174, 235,
      239, 271, 272, 314, 321, 323
s. 1 . . . . 329, 343
  (2) 333
  (3) 329
  (4), (5) 335
  (6) 330, 343
  (7) 330, 343
  (8), (9) 333
 2 334
  (1) 333
  (3), (4) 334
  (6) 331
 3(1) 335
  (2) 333
  (3) 334
  (4) 336
  (5) 338
 4 339
  (1), (2) 337
  (3) 338, 339, 341
  (4), (5) 337
 5 . . . . 337, 339
  (3) 338
  (4) 337
 6 339
  (1) 336
  (2) 339
  (3) 235, 340
  (4) 340
  (5) 336
 7 336
 8(1) 337
  (2) 340
  (7) 338
 9(1)–(3) 333
  (4) 336, 337, 339, 340
  (5) 329
  (6), (7) 330
 10 336
  (1) 332, 337
  (4) 332
 11 333
  (1) 333
 12 132
  (6) 336, 337
 13 336
 14(1) 335
 15 333
 16(2) 334

PAGE

Land Compensation Act 1973—*contd.*
s. 18(1) 338
 19(1) 335
  (2) 335, 337
  (3) 335
 20 . . . . 329, 338, 340, 341
  (4), (5) 341
 21 . . . . . . 329, 339, 340, 341, 342
 22 . . . . . . 136, 137, 329, 340, 341
 23 . . . . 329, 340, 341
  (1), (2) 338
 24 . . . . 338, 340, 341
 25 . . . . 340, 341
 26 . . . . 329, 338, 340, 341
 27 . . . . 329, 340, 341
  (2) 338
 28 . . . . 323, 329, 340
  (2), (3) 323
 29 . . . . . . 346, 349, 372, 388
  (1) . . . 372, 373, 374, 387, 391
  (2) 374
  (3) 373, 378
  (3A) 372, 379
  (4) 375, 380
  (5) 372
  (6), (7A) 373
  (8) 375
 30 . . . . 346, 372, 388
  (1)–(3) 377
 31 . . . . 346, 372, 388
 32 . . . . 346, 372, 388
  (1) 375, 376, 378
  (2) 378, 379
  (3) 374, 376
  (4) 375, 376, 378
  (5) 374
  (6) 376, 378
  (7) 373, 379, 387
 33 . . . . . . 346, 372, 376, 388
  (2) 376, 378
  (4) 377
  (5), (7) 376
 34 . . . . 346, 379
  (1), (2) 379
  (3) 381
  (4) 380
 35 . . . . 346, 379
  (1), (2) 381
  (3), (4) 382
  (5)–(7) 380, 382
  (8) 381, 383
  (9) 385
 36 . . . . 346, 379
  (1) 384, 385
  (2) 385
  (3) 384
  (4) 379
  (5), (6) 385
 37 . . . . . . 346, 361, 385, 388
  (1) 385
  (2) 366, 386
  (3) 387, 390
  (4), (5) 387
  (6) 388

PAGE

Land Compensation Act 1973—*contd.*

s. 37(7) 385
38 . . . . . . 346, 361, 385
(1) 387
(2) 388
(3) 386, 388
(4) 388
39 . . . . . . 166, 175, 346, 389
(1) 170, 391
(2), (3) 290
(4) 389
(5) 390
(6) 390, 391
39(7) 392
(8) 389
40 346
41 . . . . 346, 389
(1)–(5) 392
(9), (10) 392
42 346
43 . . . . 346, 391
(1) 391
(2), (3) 392
(4) 391
44 . . . . 318, 320
45 . . . . . 129, 165, 177, 349, 381
46 . . . . 355, 361, 363
(1) 361, 362, 363
(3), (4) 362
(5) 362, 363
(6) 363
(7) 388
47 . . . . 182, 247, 331, 355, 361, 367
(3) 370
48 . . . . . 182, 332, 355, 367, 379
(1) 172
50(2) 166, 170, 171, 175
51 . . . . 228, 230
(1), (4) 228
(6) 229
52 . . . . 70, 95, 100, 103
(2) 95
(4) 95, 96
(5) 96
(6) 95
(7)–(10) 96
(11) 95
53 . . . . 106, 109, 111, 144
(1), (4) 111
(5) 145
(11) 95
54 . . . . 106, 109, 111
(4), (6) 112
(7), (8) 113
55 . . . . 106, 111, 112
56 . . . . 106, 111
(2), (3) 113
57 . . . . 106, 111, 113
58 109
(2) 111
63 . . . . 96, 328, 342
64 . . . . 54, 62
65(1) 388
68 . . . . . . 17, 130, 133, 152, 156

PAGE

Land Compensation Act 1973—*contd.*

s. 68(1) 133, 134, 150
(2) 134
(3) 135
(4), (5) 134
(6) 152, 153
(10) 155
69 . . . . 17, 130, 133, 156
(1) 136
70 . . . . . . 17, 130, 133, 137,
138, 146, 156, 352
(1), (2) 137
70(3) 155
71 . . . 17, 130, 133, 135, 138, 155, 156
(1), (2) 138
72 . . . . . . 17, 130, 133, 139, 156
(1) 139
(2), (3) 140
73 . . . . . . 17, 130, 133, 140, 156
(1), (2) 140
(3) 155
74 . . . . . . 17, 130, 133, 136, 156
75 . . . . . . 17, 130, 133, 137, 156
(3) 146
76 . . . . . . 17, 130, 133, 140, 156
(1), (3) 141
(4) 142
77 143
78(1) 133, 152
(3) 151, 152
79 . . . . 144, 380
80 . . . . 148, 380
(3)–(5) 148
(6) 149
81(1)–(5) 149
87 111
(1) . . 330, 331, 334, 339, 380, 386
Sch. 3 270
**Land Compensation (Scotland) Act
1963**—
s. 22–24 350
35(1) 387
Land Drainage Act 1930 (18 *Statutes*
180)—
s. 34 316
Land Powers (Defence) Act 1958 . . 221
Landlord and Tenant Act 1927 (18
Statutes 451) 348, 350, 389
s. 1 369
(1) 369, 370
(2), (3) 370
2 369
Landlord and Tenant Act 1954 (18
Statutes 726) 132, 182, 331,
342, 355, 361, 365, 389, 401
s. 20 370
23 367
24, 25 . . . . 367, 369
26 367
27(2), (3) 370
(5) 371
30 367
(1) 182, 368, 370
(2) 370

PAGE

Landlord and Tenant Act 1954—*contd.*
s. 37 387
   (1) 370
   39 369
   (1) 367
   (2) 370
   43 367
Lands Clauses Consolidation Act
   1845 (6 *Statutes* 63) . . . 2, 3, 28, 108,
                        238, 252, 278, 344
s. 1 3
   8(4) 234
   18 . . . . 315, 369
   49–62 3
   63 . . . . 3, 177, 233, 315, 322, 340
   68 . . . 274, 321, 322, 323, 326, 327
   85 113
   89 71
   92 . . . . . . 106, 108, 145, 149
   93 . . . . 110, 145
   94 110
   99–103 278
   104–107 . . . . 278, 280
   112 319
   121 . . . . 345, 367, 369
   122 345
   123 67
Lands Clauses Consolidation Act
   1869 3
Lands Clauses Consolidation Acts
   Amendment Act 1860 (6 *Statutes*
   63) 3
Lands Clauses (Taxation of Costs)
   Act 1895 3
Lands Clauses (Umpire) Act 1883 . . 3
Lands Tribunal Act 1949 (6 *Statutes*
   191) 31, 83, 109
s. 1 85
   3 . . . . 83, 86
   (2) 88
   (4) 87
   (5) 86
Law of Property Act 1925 (27
   Statutes 341)—
s. 1(2) 33
   40 167
   84 285
   193, 194 279
   209(2) 279
Leasehold Reform Act 1967 . 132, 332, 342
Light Railways Act 1896 (26 *Statutes*
   845) 3, 277
s. 13 235
Light Railways Act 1912 (26 *Statutes*
   872) 3, 277
Local Government Act 1933 (19
   Statutes 393)—
s. 162 55
   182 122
   (1) 452
   250 . . . . 46, 79
   (2) 41, 46, 47, 50
   (3) 41, 46, 47, 50
   (4) 41, 45, 46, 47, 50

PAGE

Local Government Act 1933—*contd.*
s. 250(5) 41, 44, 45, 46, 47, 50
   254(2) 453
   290(2)–(5) 41
Sch. 12—
   para. 39 449
Sch. 16—
   para. 15, 25 453
         34 . . . . 452, 453
         35 452
         55 . . . . 205, 208
Sch. 17 452
Local Government Act 1974 (44
   Statutes 637)—
Sch. 6 413
Local Government (Miscellaneous
   Provisions) Act 1976—
s. 10 270
   13 . . . . 158, 283, 284
Local Loans Act 1875 (22 *Statutes*
   727) 32
s. 34 32

M

Magistrates' Courts Act 1952 (21
   Statutes 181)—
s. 50 87
Metropolitan Commons Act 1866 (3
   Statutes 859) 279
Metropolitan Paving Act 1817 3
Military Lands Act 1892 (29
   Statutes 1149) 3

N

National Assistance Act 1948
   (23 *Statutes* 636)—
s. 29 388
National Health Service Act 1946
   (23 *Statutes* 9) 2
National Trust Act 1907 (24 *Statutes*
   286) 48
s. 21 48
National Trust Act 1939 (24 *Statutes*
   314)—
s. 8 48
New Towns Act 1946 . . . 236, 257, 277
s. 1 257
New Towns Act 1965 (36 *Statutes*
   374) 31, 32, 75, 224, 236
s. 1 80
   (1) 80
   2 80
   3(1) 80
   6(1) 80
   7(1) 81
   8(1) 81
   10 82
   11 . . . . . 81, 139, 372, 379, 390
   12 . . . . 66, 81
   19 283
Sch. 1 . . . . 80, 139, 228
Sch. 3 81

PAGE

New Towns Act 1965—*contd.*
Sch. 3—
  para. 2 81
       4 . . . . 81, 82
Sch. 4 82
Sch. 6 81
  para. 4 113
New Towns Act 1966 224

O

Opencast Coal Act 1958 (22 *Statutes* 472)—
s. 2 185

P

Public Health Act 1925 (26 *Statutes* 146)—
s. 30 141
  (4) 141
  276 415

Q

Quia Emptores (1289–90) (27 *Statutes* 290) 280

R

Railways Act 1921 (26 *Statutes* 875) . . 3
Railways Clauses Consolidation Act 1845 (26 *Statutes* 730) 322
s. 6 322
  16 327
  77–85 273
Rating (Caravan Sites) Act 1976 (46 *Statutes* 1230)—
s. 1 377
Rebuilding of London (1666) 5
Rebuilding of London (1670) 5
Recorded Delivery Service Act 1962 (32 *Statutes* 775)—
s. 1 78
  (1) 34, 210
Rent Act 1968 (18 *Statutes* 777)—
s. 70(3) 375
  71 375
Rent and Mortgage Interest Restrictions Act 1939 263
Requisitioned Land and War Works Act 1945 (6 *Statutes* 98) 159

S

Settled Land Act 1925 (30 *Statutes* 344) 332, 336
Slum Clearance (Compensation) Act 1956 . . . . 265, 269
Small Dwellings Acquisition Act 1899 (16 *Statutes* 10) 389
Small Dwellings Acquisition Act 1923 389
Statute of Sewers 1427 5
Statute of Sewers 1531 5

PAGE

Statutory Orders (Special Procedure) Act 1945 (*Statutes* 658) . . . 3, 51, 277
s. 2(1), (2) 51
  3(2)–(5) 51
  4(2),)3) 51
  5 52
  6(1)–(4) 52
  7 52
  9 51
Streets, London and Westminster (1662) 5

T

Taxes Management Act 1970 (34 *Statutes* 1245)—
s. 55 101
Town and Country Amenities Act 1974 (44 *Statutes* 1742)—
s. 6 274
Town and Country Planning (Interim Development) Act 1943—
s. 8 436
Town and Country Planning Act 1932 . . . . 5, 436
s. 19 399
Town and Country Planning Act 1944 . . . . 4, 7, 28, 164
Town and Country Planning Act 1947 (36 *Statutes* 22) . . 4, 6, 7, 13, 17, 22, 25, 107, 161, 164, 195, 238, 317, 394, 406, 408, 420
s. 19 . . . . 10, 114
  21 440
  22 440
  (1) 440
  28(1) 439
  29 414
  31 440
  37 2
  43 . . . . 8, 11
  52 10
  58 8
  (3) 10
  62, 63 8
  64 11
  65(2) 10
  111(4) 117, 194
Sch. 3 . . . . 15, 28, 117, 126
Pt. II 29
Town and Country Planning Act 1953 . . . . 11, 394
Town and Country Planning Act 1954 . . 4, 6, 11, 13, 28, 195, 394, 400
s. 17(1) 396
  35 13
  38 440
  48 395
  60 11
Sch. 3 9
Town and Country Planning Act 1959 (6 *Statutes* 230) . . 4, 12, 14, 29, 107, 129, 161, 164
  5 107

PAGE

Town and Country Planning Act 1959—*contd.*

s. 7 6
9 . . . . .16, 219
18–21 191
31 414
37 402
43 17
Sch. 1—
Pt. I 6
Sch. 2 261
para. 4 262
Sch. 5—
para. 7 129

Town and Country Planning Act
1962 (36 *Statutes* 69)—

s. 4(4) 198
. 118 440
138(1) 135
143(1) 348

Town and Country Planning Act
1968 (40 *Statutes* 301) 71, 139

s. 19 . . . . 442, 446
30 . . . . .66, 100
37(1) 130
59 50
Sch. 3 . . . 31, 71, 107, 109, 113, 167
para. 1 . . . . 71, 72
2–5 72
6 . . . . 72, 73, 111
7 . . . . 71, 72
8 73
11, 12 73
13, 14 74
16 73
Sch. 3A 72, 107, 109
para. 1, 2 72
7, 11 110
13 95
14 88

Town and Country Planning Act
1971 (41 *Statutes* 1571) . 9, 12, 30, 76,
97, 108, 129, 252, 257

s. 1(1) 452
6 . . . . 197, 199
7 . . . . 133, 197, 199
8, 9 . . . . 197, 199
10 . . . . 133, 197, 199
10B 134
11 . . . . 197, 199
(1) 301
12 . . . . 197, 199
(2) 134
14 . . . . .76, 197, 199
15 . . . . 197, 199
(3) 134
16–19 . . . . 197, 199
20 . . . . .76, 197, 199
(1), (2) 139, 197
21 . . . . 197, 199, 404
22 . . . . . 23, 74, 217, 297, 411, 431
(1) 194, 273, 398, 399, 442
(2) . 194, 196, 409, 411, 425, 431
(3) 194, 268, 442
(5) 195, 393

PAGE

Town and Country Planning Act 1971—*contd.*

s. 23 . . . . 194, 196
(2)–(5) 398
24 402
(1)–(3) 414
(2) 426
26 399
27 . . . . 300, 402, 453
(1), (7) 300
30 186
32 304
33 . . . . 186, 393
(1) 445
34 187
35 . . . . 401, 450, 453
36 . . . . 401, 453
37 . . . . 304, 449
38, 39 401
40 185
(3) 54
41 . . . 118, 190, 302, 307, 408, 413
(1) 190
42 . . . 118, 190, 302, 307, 408, 413
(2) 190
43, 44 190
45 . . . 115, 123, 126, 127, 393, 413,
414, 432, 438, 439, 448
(1), (2) 413, 414
(3) 413, 417
(4) 413, 414, 415, 438
(5) 414
46 . . . . . 416, 417, 425, 439, 449
(1), (5), (6) 413
51 . . . . 56, 115, 116, 127, 195, 338,
393, 413, 415, 448
(1) 415
(2) 413, 415, 439
(3)–(6), (8) 415
54 . . . . 115, 118, 424
55 . . . . 115, 118, 274, 394
(1), (2) 425
56 . . . . 115, 118
(1) 424
(2) 274
57 . . . . 115, 118
58 . . . . 115, 118, 394
(1) 425, 450
(2) 275
(3) 425, 450
(4) 425
59 . . . . 115, 119, 394
60 . . . . 115, 119, 394
(1) 119, 432
(2) 119, 439
(4), (5) 432
61, 62 119
63 . . 115, 119, 185, 394, 399, 437, 439
(2) 119, 438, 439
(3) 119, 438
(4), (5) 119
64 . . . . 119, 185
67 115
(1) 408
68(2) 408

PAGE

Town and Country Planning Act 1971—*contd.*

s. 68(4), (5) 145
69(2) 145
70 . . . . 118, 185
(2) 145
71 . . . . . 118, 399, 419
(2) 145
72 . . . . 115, 408
(1) 408
(2) 145
74(4) 124
77 . . . . 118, 185
81(2) 124
82 . . . . . . 118, 399, 408, 419
83 124
86(1) 125
87 . . . . 180, 441
(1) 416
(2) 441
(3) 416, 441
(4) 441
(8) 441
(9) 445
88 . . . . 180, 303, 304
(1) 441, 443, 444, 445
(2) 441
(4), (5) 442
(6) 303
(7) 303, 442
89 180
90 . . . . 180, 394, 442
(1) 442
(2) 442
(3) 442
(4) 443, 445
(5) 442
(6) 443
(7) 442, 445
(8) 446
91–93 180
94 . . . . 180, 196
95–107 180
108 180
(1), (2) 415
109–111 180
112 . . . . 27, 188, 198
114 275
(3) 275
(6), (7) 275, 276, 277
115 . . . . 121, 275
116 . . . . 274, 276
118 283
120, 121 279
117(1), (2) 277
(4)–(7) 276, 277
127 322
(1)–(3) 321
134(2) 402
(4) 397, 401
140(1) 402
145(1) 395
(2), (3) 396
(4) 397
(5)–(7), (9) 398

PAGE

Town and Country Planning Act 1971—*contd.*

s. 145(10) 397
147 . . . . 398, 400
(1) 398, 399
(2) 399, 402
(3) 399
(4) 400
(5) 399, 400
(6) 398
148 400
(2) 400
(3) 398
149 . . . . 398, 400
149(4) 400
152(1), (2) 402
(3)–(5) 403
153(1), (5) 402
154 400
(2) 400
(4) 403
(5) 400, 401
155 401
156 404
(1) 404
(2) 422
158(1) 404
(4), (5) 422
(6) 404
159 422
(1) 404
(2) 404, 423
(3) 404, 405, 423
160 422
(1) 404, 423
(2) 424
(3) 405, 424
(4), (5) 424
(6) 423
161 405
162(2) 405
163(2) 403
164 . 126, 405, 439, 440, 446, 447, 449
(1) 416
(2) 126, 416
(3) 417
(4) 407, 417, 421
(5) 439
165 . . . . 400, 405, 411, 431, 446,
447, 449, 453
(1) 419, 420
(2) 420, 449
(3), (4) 419
166 . . . . . 405, 421, 439, 454
(1)–(3), (6) 422
167 . . . . . 405, 421, 424, 439
168 . . . . . 405, 421, 422, 439
(1) 423
(3) 424
(4) 422
169 . 127, 195, 338, 393, 405, 407, 408,
410, 421, 426, 446, 449
(1) 196, 407, 410
(2) 407, 410
(3) 407, 408, 409, 410, 426

PAGE

Town and Country Planning Act 1971—contd.
s. 169(4), (5) 408
   (6) 409, 410, 412
   (7), (8) 408
170 . . . 195, 338, 405, 446, 449, 454
   (1) 421
171 . . . . . 276, 405, 424, 446, 450
   (1)–(4) 426
172 . . . 405, 424, 426, 427, 446, 450
   (1) 426, 427
   (2), (3) 427
173 . . . . . 405, 424, 446, 450, 453
173(2) 426, 450
   (3), (4) 426
174 . . . . . . 405, 435, 446, 452
175 . . . . . . 405, 436, 446, 452
   (2), (3) 436
   (4) 436, 451
176 . . . . 394, 405, 439, 451, 453
177 . . 405, 443, 444, 446, 450, 454
   (1) 444, 445, 446
   (2) 443, 444, 445
   (3) 444
   (6) 446
178(1) 446, 447
   (2) 444, 446, 447, 448
179(1), (2) 452
180 . 10, 107, 111, 115, 119, 127, 426
   (1) 116, 407
   (2) 116
   (3) 117
   (4) 118
   (5), (6) 122
181 . . . . . 107, 111, 114, 119
   (1), (2), (4) 122
182 . . . . . 107, 111, 119, 122
   (3), (4) 122
183 . . . . 107, 111, 119
   (2) 123, 125
   (3) 123, 125, 126
   (4) 123
184 . . . . 107, 111, 124
   (2) 124
185 . . . . 107, 111, 124
   (1) 125
186 . . . . 107, 111, 119
   (2), (3) 125
   (4), (5) 126
187 . . . . 107, 111, 119
   (1) 126
   (2), (3) 127
   (5) 126
188 . . . 107, 114, 115, 125, 127, 426
   (1), (2) 116
   (3) 123
189 . . 107, 111, 115, 116, 125, 127
   (1) 116, 119
   (2) 116
   (3) 123
190 . . . . . 107, 115, 127, 426
   (1) 114, 116
   (2) 116
   (3) 125
191 . . . . 107, 115

PAGE

Town and Country Planning Act 1971—contd.
s. 191(1) 119, 138
   (2) 116, 118
192 . . . . . 17, 134, 136, 156, 303
   (1) 130, 133, 134, 135, 136, 137, 138,
          140, 143, 145, 146, 150, 152
   (2) 134
   (3), (5) 303
193 . . . . 17, 151, 188, 216, 303
   (1) 131
   (3) 143
193(4) 130
194 . . . . 17, 303
   (2) . . . 145, 148, 151, 152, 157
   (3) 150
   (4) 146, 148
195 . . . . 17, 153, 303
   (1) 145
   (2), (3) 153
196 . . . . 17, 303
   (1), (2) 144
197 . . . . 17, 276, 277, 303
198 . . . . 17, 154, 303
199 . . . . 17, 303
   (1) 151
   (2) 146, 151
   (3), (4) 149
200 . . . . 17, 151, 303
201 . . . . 17, 133, 303
   (3) 152, 154
   (6) 151, 152
202 . . . . 17, 149, 303
   (1) 145
   (2) 150
203 . . . . 17, 132, 303
   (1) 131
   (3) 131
   (4) 144
204 . . . . 17, 303
   (1)–(4) 133
205 . . . . 17, 303
   (1)–(3) 154
206 . . . . 17, 303
   (1), (2) 155
   (3) 137
   (5) 155
   (6) 156
207 . . . . 17, 303, 331
   (1) . . . 111, 131, 144, 331, 334
224 . . . . 250, 253
229(2), (3) 251
230 252
232 253
237(4) 255
238(1) 254
   (2) 251, 252, 254
   (3) 252
239 251
   (1) 251, 254
242(1), (2) 413, 415
   (3) 126
245 . . . . . . 59, 126, 413, 415
254 454
255(2), (3) 454

PAGE

Town and Country Planning Act 1971—*contd.*

s. 256 151
257 424
270 190
276 . . . . 453, 454
(1) . . . . : 432
(2) 438, 439
(5) 442, 443
278 417
282 46
287(3) 414
290 229
(1) 33, 116, 250, 273, 376, 401, 406,
410, 412, 415, 422, 423, 437
(2) 250
(4) 401, 449
(5) 423
294(4) 449
Sch. 3—
para. 3, 4 454
5, 6 455
Sch. 5 . . . . 139, 197
para. 1 . . . . 198, 205
3 135
9 135
Sch. 6 . . . . 139, 197
Sch. 7 76
para. 1 139
Sch. 8 . 8, 9, 15, 28, 29, 99, 116, 117, 120,
125, 126, 217, 235, 274, 306,
337, 393, 421, **456–458**
Pt. I 160, 195, 196, 393, 410
para. 1 . . . . 406, 409, 410, 459
Pt. II . . . 127, 160, 195, 196, 338,
393, 405, 412, 420, 448
para. 3 . . . . . . 406, 409, 410
4 410
5 411
6 . . . . 194, 411
7, 8 412
Pt. III—
para. 10 413
11 409
12 406
Sch. 9 44
Sch. 11—
Pt. I 425
para. 4 . . . . 426, 453
8 . . . . 426, 453

PAGE

Town and Country Planning Act 1971—*contd.*

Sch. 11—
para. 9 453
Pt. II 127
para. 10–12 425
Sch. 12, 13 124
Sch. 14 . . . . 395, 404
Sch. 16 . . . . 395, 454
para. 34, 35 454
Sch. 17 395
Sch. 18 . . 117, 409, 412, 422, **458–459**
para. 1 410
2 . . . . 409, 410
4 409
5 410
Sch. 19—
para. 2 . . . . 122, 123
Sch. 21—
Pt. I 190
Sch. 23 . . . . 199, 202, 205, 224, 236
Sch. 24 163
Pt. X 135
Town and Country Planning (Amendment) Act 1972 (42 *Statutes* 2134)—
s. 1 139
2 . . . . 134, 139
3, 4 139
5(1) 125
Town and Country Planning (Scotland) Act 1947 . . . . 8, 10
Town Development Act 1952 (36 *Statutes* 25) 16, 224
s. 6 257
Town Planning Act 1925 5
Transport Act 1947 (26 *Statutes* 903)—
s. 8 2
Tribunals and Inquiries Act 1971 (41 *Statutes* 248) 31, 61, 62, 79
s. 11 37

W

War Damage Act 1943 (38 *Statutes* 537) 159
s. 8 406
Water Act 1945 (39 *Statutes* 69) . . . 324
Waterworks Clauses Act 1847—
s. 6 322

Table of Cases

In the following Table references are given to the English and Empire Digest where a digest of the case may be found.

A

A and B Taxis Ltd v Secretary of State for Air, [1922] 2 KB 328, 91 LJKB 779, 127 LT 478, 38 TLR 671, 66 Sol Jo 633, CA, 17 Digest (Reissue) 486 . . . . 241, 249, 250

Adams and Wade, Ltd v Minister of Housing and Local Government (1965), 18 P & CR 60, Digest Cont Vol C 972 124

Alexandre v Cambridge City Council (1976), 31 P & CR 444, 236 Estates Gazette 423, 489, 567 . . . . 183, 369

Amalgamated Investment and Property Co Ltd v John Walker & Sons Ltd, [1976] JPL 308, 119 Sol Jo 406, 235 Estates Gazette 565 429

Anderson v Glasgow Corpn, [1974] RVR 398 387

Anisminic Ltd v Foreign Compensation Commission, [1969] 2 AC 147, [1969] 1 All ER 208, [1969] 2 WLR 163, 113 Sol Jo 55, HL, Digest Cont Vol C 282 54

Argyle Motors (Birkenhead) Ltd v Birkenhead Corpn, [1974] 1 All ER 201, [1974] 2 WLR 71, 118 Sol Jo 67, 72 LGR 147, 27 P & CR 122, [1973] RVR 617, HL, 11 Digest (Reissue) 174 325

Ashbridge Investments Ltd v Minister of Housing and Local Government, [1965] 3 All ER 371, [1965] 1 WLR 1320, 129 JP 580, 109 Sol Jo 595, 63 LGR 400, CA, Digest Cont Vol B 336 . . . . 55, 57, 58, 61, 64

Associated Provincial Picture Houses Ltd v Wednesbury Corpn, [1948] 1 KB 223, [1947] 2 All ER 680, [1948] LJR 190, 177 LT 641, 112 JP 55, 63 TLR 623, 92 Sol Jo 26, 45 LGR 635, CA, 45 Digest (Repl) 214 . . . . 55, 59

Aston Charities Trust Ltd v Stepney Corpn (1952), 3 P & CR 82 . . 243, 245, 248, 249, 250

A-G v Corke, [1933] Ch 89, [1932] All ER Rep 711, 148 LT 95, 48 TLR 650, 76 Sol Jo 593, 31 LGR 35, sub nom A-G and Bromley Rural Council v Corke, 102 LJ Ch 30, 36(1) Digest (Reissue) 452 169

A-G and Bromley Rural Council v Corke. See A-G v Corke

A-G of The Gambia v N'jie, [1961] AC 617, [1961] 2 All ER 504, [1961] 2 WLR 845, 105 Sol Jo 421, PC, 8 (2) Digest (Reissue) 855 . . . . 52, 53

A-G of Straits Settlements v Wemyss (1888), 13 App Cas 192, 57 LJPC 62, 58 LT 358, 31(1) Digest (Reissue) 284 324

B

Babij v Metropolitan Borough of Rochdale (1976), 33 P & CR 119, 239 Estates Gazette 987 171, 267

Bailey v Derby Corpn, [1965] 1 All ER 443, [1965] 1 WLR 213, 129 JP 140, 108 Sol Jo 939, 63 LGR 36, 16 P & CR 192, [1965] RVR 43, CA, 11 Digest (Reissue) 147 361

Bailey v Reading Borough Council (1977), 33 P & CR 124 171

Banham v London Borough of Hackney (1970), 22 P & CR 922 . . . . . . .69, 170, 173

Barnard v Great Western Rly Co (1902), 86 LT 798, 66 JP 568, 11 Digest (Reissue) 163, 324

Barstow v Rothwell UDC (1970), 22 P & CR 942 179

Beckett v Midland Rly Co (1867), LR 3 CP 82, 37 LJCP 11, 17 LT 499, 16 WR 221, 11 Digest (Reissue) 168 325

PAGE

Bede Distributors Ltd v Newcastle upon Tyne Corpn (1973), 26 P & CR 298: 349, 351, 353,
354, 364

Bell (John T.) & Sons Ltd v Newcastle upon Tyne Corpn, [1971] RVR 209 . . . 220, 227

Belmont Farm Ltd v Minister of Housing and Local Government (1962), 13 P & CR 417 410

Benjamin v Newham London Borough Council. *See* Newham London Borough Council v
Benjamin

Bennett v Minister of Housing and Local Government, Cmnd 5730 1974 . . 212, 213, 214

Bibby & Sons Ltd v Merseyside Council [1977] JPL 528 349

Bidder v North Staffordshire Rly Co, *Re* (1878), 4 QBD 412, CA, 19 Digest (Repl) 121, 356

Binney v Hammersmith and City Rly Co (1863), 8 LT 161, 9 Jur NS 873, 11 Digest
(Reissue) 217 . . . . 112, 121

Bird v Great Eastern Rly Co (1865), 19 CBNS 268, 34 LJCP 366, 13 LT 365, 11 Jur NS
782, 13 WR 989, 11 Digest (Reissue) 129 . . . . 316, 323

Bird v Wakefield Metropolitan District Council, [1977] JPL 179 220

Bird and Bird v Wakefield Metropolitan District Council (1976), 33 P & CR 310 . . . 223

Birmingham City Corpn v West Midland Baptist (Trust) Association Inc, [1970] AC 874,
[1969] 3 All ER 172, [1969] 3 WLR 389, 133 JP 524, 113 Sol Jo 606, 67 LGR 571, 20
P & CR 1052, [1969] RVR 484, HL, 11 Digest (Reissue) 149 . . 69, 166, 169, 240, 259,
308, 351, 366, 416

Bizony v Secretary of State for the Environment, [1975] JPL 306, 239 Estates Gazette 281 53

Blow and Blow v Norfolk County Council (1965), 16 P & CR 342 . . . . . . 416, 421

Bollans v Surrey County Council (1968), 20 P & CR 745 . . . . 418, 435, 436

Bolton Corpn v Owen, [1962] 1 QB 470, [1962] 1 All ER 101, [1962] 2 WLR 307, 126 JP 58,
105 Sol Jo 1105, 61 LGR 7, 13 P & CR 231, [1962] RVR 25, CA, 45 Digest (Repl)
325 . . . . 134, 145, 153

Bone v Staines UDC (1964), 15 P & CR 450 135

Borthwick-Norton v Collier, [1950] 2 KB 594, [1950] 2 All ER 204, 114 JP 375, 66 (pt 2)
TLR 131, 94 Sol Jo 404, 48 LGR 429, CA, 17 Digest (Reissue) 498 114

Bostock Chater & Sons Ltd v Chelmsford Corpn (1973), 26 P & CR 321 . . . 97, 344, 351,
353, 354, 360

Bosworth-Smith v Gwynnes Ltd (1919), 89 LJ Ch 368, 122 LT 15, 36(1) Digest (Reissue)
418 330

Bousefield v Chatham Corpn (1973), 27 P & CR 241 184

Bowie (Inspector of Taxes) v Reg Dunn (Builders), Ltd, [1974] STC 234, 49 TC 469, L
(TC) 2515, [1974] TR 77, 53 ATC 74 57

Bowling v Leeds County Borough Council (1974), 27 P & CR 531 . 135, 142, 143, 222, 271

Bowman, South Shields (Thames Street) Clearance Order, *Re*, 1931, [1932] 2 KB 621, 101
LJKB 798, 147 LT 150, 96 JP 207, 48 TLR 351, 76 Sol Jo 273, 30 LGR 245, 26
Digest (Repl) 694 35

Boyer (William) & Sons Ltd v Minister of Housing and Local Government (1968), 20 P &
CR 176, 113 Sol Jo 53, 67 LGR 374, Digest Cont Vol C 970 42

Bradford Property Trust Ltd v Hertfordshire County Council (1973), 27 P & CR 228 . 170

Brain and Drive Yourself Car Hire Co v LCC (1958), 9 P & CR 113 . . . . 346, 347, 349

Brand (R.A.) & Co v S Barrow & Co (1965), 109 Sol Jo 834, 196 Estates Gazette 405, CA 327

Brayhead (Ascot) Ltd v Berkshire County Council, [1964] 2 QB 303, [1964] 1 All ER 149,
[1964] 2 WLR 507, 128 JP 167, 108 Sol Jo 178, 62 LGR 162, 15 P & CR 423, 45 Digest
(Repl) 348 . . . . 62, 63

Breen's (Lord) Executors v British Waterway Board, [1977] JPL 730 319

Bresgall & Sons Ltd v London Borough of Hackney (1976), 32 P & CR 442 350

Brinklow and Croft Bros Ltd v Secretary of State for the Environment [1976] JPL 299 . 59

British Westinghouse Co Ltd v Underground Railways, [1912] AC 673, [1911–13] All ER
Rep 63, 81 LJKB 1132, 107 LT 325, 56 Sol Jo 734, HL, 17 Digest (Reissue) 126, 327

Broadleas Land, Devizes, *Re*, [1967] JPL 730 121

Broderick v Erewash Borough Council [1977] JPL 666 140

Bromilow v Greater Manchester Council (1974), 29 P & CR 517 . . . . 181, 213

Brookdene Investments Ltd v Minister of Housing and Local Government (1969), 21 P &
CR 545, 67 LGR 673, [1969] RVR 595, Digest Cont Vol C 972 120

Brown v Ministry of Housing and Local Government, [1953] 2 All ER 1385, 118 JP 143, 97
Sol Jo 797, 52 LGR 34, 3 P & CR 111, 26 Digest (Repl) 703 . . . . 33, 61

Buccleuch (Duke) v Metropolitan Water Board (1872), LR 5 HL 418, [1861–73] All ER
Rep 654, 41 LJ Ex 137, 27 LT1, 36 JP 724, 11 Digest (Reissue) 159 318

Buckingham Street Investments Ltd v Greater London Council (1975), 31 P & CR 453
166

Burke v Minister of Housing and Local Government (1956), 8 P & CR 25 53

PAGE

Burlin v Manchester City Council (1976), 32 P & CR 115 . . . . .96, 447
Burman v St Albans Corpn (1961), 12 P & CR 360 406
Burrow v Metropolitan Rly Co (1884), Times, 22nd November 354, 356
Burson v Wantage RDC (1974), 27 P & CR 556 . . . . .70, 166
Buxton v Minister of Housing and Local Government, [1961] 1 QB 278, [1960] 3 All ER
  408, [1960] 3 WLR 866, 124 JP 489, 104 Sol Jo 935, 59 LGR 45, 12 P & CR 77, 45
  Digest (Repl) 340 52

C

Caledonian Rly Co v Colt (1860), 3 Macq 833, 3 LT 252, 7 Jur NS 475, 11 Digest
  (Reissue) 162 . . . . 318, 326
Caledonian Rly Co v Walker's Trustees (1882), 7 App Cas 259, [1881–5] All ER Rep 592,
  46 LT 826, 46 JP 676, 30 WR 569, HL, 11 Digest (Reissue) 165 324
Camden London Borough Council v Secretary of State, [1975] JPL 661 43
Camrose (Viscount) v Basingstoke Corpn, [1966] 3 All ER 161, [1966] 1 WLR 1100, 130
  JP 368, 110 Sol Jo 427, 64 LGR 337, [1966] RVR 459, CA, Digest Cont Vol B 699
  181, 219, 226, 227
Capital Investments Ltd v Wednesfield UDC, [1965] Ch 774, [1964] 1 All ER 655, [1964]
  2 WLR 932, 128 JP 287, 108 Sol Jo 377, 62 LGR 566, 15 P & CR 435, Digest Cont Vol
  B 340 . . . . .66, 67, 68
Cardiff Corpn v Cook, [1923] 2 Ch 115, [1922] All ER Rep 651, 92 LJ Ch 177, 128 LT
  530, 87 JP 90, 67 Sol Jo 315, 21 LGR 279, 11 Digest (Reissue) 208 . . . . 68, 84, 173
Cardigan Timber Co v Cardiganshire County Council (1957), 9 P & CR 158:   433, 434, 435, 436
Cardwell v Midland Rly Co (1904), 21 TLR 22, CA, 11 Digest (Reissue) 313 71
Carrington (Lord) v Wycombe Rly Co (1868), 3 Ch App 377, 37 LJ Ch 213 110
Caswell v Powell Duffryn Associated Collieries Ltd, [1940] AC 152, [1939] 3 All ER 722, 108
  LJKB 779, 161 LT 374, 55 TLR 1004, 83 Sol Jo 976, HL, 33 Digest (Repl) 907 . . 328
Cedar Rapids Manufacturing and Power Co v Lacorte, [1914] AC 569, [1914–15] All ER
  Rep 571, 83 LJPC 162, 110 LT 873, 30 TLR 293, 11 Digest (Reissue) 151 . . . 3, 218
Central Methodist Church, Todmorden Trustees v Todmorden Corpn (1959), 11 P & CR 32
  245, 249
Challinor v Stone RDC (1974), 27 P & CR 244 183
Chamberlain v West End of London and Crystal Palace Rly Co (1863), 2 B & S 617, 2
  New Rep 182, 32 LJQB 173, 8 LT 149, 9 Jur NS 1051, 11 WR 472, 11 Digest (Reissue)
  116 . . . . 324, 326
Chandler's Wiltshire Brewery Co and London County Council, Re, [1903] 1 KB 569, 72
  LJKB 250, 88 LT 271, 67 JP 119, 51 WR 573, 19 TLR 268, 47 Sol Jo 319, 1 LGR 269, 11
  Digest (Reissue) 150 160
Christodoulou v Islington London Borough Council (1973), 230 Estates Gazette 233 . . 87
Church of Scotland Trustees v Helensburgh Council (1972), 25 P & CR 105 145
City of London Corpn v Secretary of State for the Environment (1971), 23 P & CR 169   194
City of London Real Property Co Ltd v War Damage Commission, [1956] Ch 607, [1956] 3
  All ER 236, [1956] 3 WLR 615, 100 Sol Jo 634; affd., [1957] Ch 274, [1957] 1 All ER
  519, [1957] 2 WLR 379, 101 Sol Jo 190, CA, 17 Digest (Reissue) 542 406
Clark v Wareham and Purbeck RDC (1972), 25 P & CR 423 . . . . 319, 320
Clarke and Wandsworth District Board of Works, Re (1868), 17 LT 549, 11 Digest (Reissue)
  173 349
Clayton v Sheffield County Borough Council (1964), 192 Estates Gazette 309 220
Clibbett (W.) Ltd v Avon County Council, [1975] RVR 131, 237 Estates Gazette 271:   360, 361
Colac (President etc) v Summerfield, [1893] AC 187, [1891–4] All ER Rep Ext 1655, 68 LT
  769, 62 LJPC 64, 11 Digest (Reissue) 180 326
Coleen Properties Ltd v Minister of Housing and Local Government, [1971] 1 All ER 1049,
  [1971] 1 WLR 433, 135 JP 226, 115 Sol Jo 112, 69 LGR 175, 22 P & CR 417, [1971]
  RVR 489, CA, Digest Cont Vol D 388 . . . . 43, 55, 56, 57, 58, 69
Coleshill and District Investment Co Ltd v Minister of Housing and Local Government,
  [1969] 2 All ER 525, [1969] 1 WLR 746, 133 JP 385, 113 Sol Jo 469, 20 P & CR 679, HL,
  Digest Cont Vol C 961 431
Collins v Basildon Development Corpn (1969), 21 P & CR 318 220
Collins v Feltham UDC, [1937] 4 All ER 189, 36 LGR 34, 45 Digest (Repl) 369 . . . 418
Colls v Home and Colonial Stores, [1904] AC 179, 73 LJ Ch 484, 90 LT 687, 53 WR 30, 20
  TLR 475, HL, 19 Digest (Rep) 135 326
Colman v Basingstoke RDC (1966), 17 P & CR 270 . . . . 284, 328

PAGE

Comley and Comley v Kent County Council, [1977] JPL 666 138
Continental Sprays Ltd v Minister of Housing and Local Government (1968), 19 P & CR
774   . . . . 42, 64
Conway v Rimmer, [1968] AC 910, [1968] 1 All ER 874, [1968] 2 WLR 998, 112 Sol Jo 191,
HL, 18 Digest (Reissue) 156   . . . . .41, 64, 85
Cooke v LCC, [1911] 1 Ch 604, 80 LJ Ch 423, 104 LT 540, 75 JP 309, 9 LGR 593, 11 Digest
(Reissue) 205   . . . . .68, 89, 90
Cooke v Secretary of State for the Environment (1973), 27 P & CR 234   . . . . 222, 317, 346
Corrie v Central Land Board (1954), 4 P & CR 276 179
Corrie v MacDermott, [1914] AC 1056, 83 LJPC 370, 111 LT 952, PC, 11 Digest (Reissue)
130   . . . . 180, 447
Cotswold Trailer Parks Ltd v Secretary of State for the Environment (1974), 27 P & CR
219   222
Cowper Essex v Acton Local Board (1889), 14 App Cas 153, [1886–90] All ER Rep 901, 58
LJQB 594, 38 WR 209, 5 TLR 395, sub nom. Essex v Acton District Local Board, 61
LT 1, 53 JP 756, HL, 11 Digest (Reissue) 160   . . . . 315, 323
Crabtree v Minister of Housing and Local Government (1965), 64 LGR 104, 109 Sol Jo 921,
17 P & CR 232, Digest Cont Vol B 698 64
Cunningham v Sunderland City Borough Council (1963), 14 P & CR 208   244

D

DHN Food Distributors Ltd v Tower Hamlets London Borough Council, [1976] 3 All
ER 462, [1976] 1 WLR 852, 120 Sol Jo 215, 74 LGR 506, 32 P & CR 240, 239
Estates Gazette 719, CA 247, 316, 347
Darlassis v Minister of Education (1954), 4 P & CR 281 43
David v London Borough of Lewisham, [1977] JPL 528 170
Davis (H. & C.), Station Road, Godalming, Re, [1971] JPL 239   121
Davy v Leeds Corpn, [1964] 3 All ER 390, [1964] 1 WLR 1218, 128 JP 541, 108 Sol Jo 561,
62 LGR 628, 16 P & CR 244, [1964] RVR 776; affd., [1965] 1 All ER 753, [1965] 1 WLR
445, 129 JP 308, 109 Sol Jo 196, 63 LGR 181, 17 P & CR 83, [1965] RVR 171, HL
218, 219, 221, 222, 227, 256
Davy (J.) Ltd v Hammersmith London Borough (1975), 30 P & CR 469, 234 Estates Gazette
685   . . . . 176, 181
Dawson v Great Northern and City Rly Co, [1905] 1 KB 260, [1904–7] All ER Rep 913, 74
LJKB 190, 92 LT 137, 69 JP 29, 21 TLR 114, CA, 8(2) Digest (Reissue) 507 . . . 173
Deasy v Minister of Housing and Local Government (1970), 214 Estates Gazette 415 . 64
Domestic Hire v Basildon Development Corpn (1969), 21 P & CR 299 220
Dorchester Road Land, Weymouth, Re, [1973] JPL 43 120
Drake and Underwood v LCC (1960), 11 P & CR 427 . . . . 353, 357, 359, 360

E

Eagle v Charing Cross Rly Co (1867), LR 2 CP 638, 36 LJCP 297, 16 LT 593, 15 WR 1016,
11 Digest (Reissue) 172   . . . . 324, 325, 326
Eales Johnson v Minister of Housing and Local Government (1958), 9 P & CR 350 . 422
Ealing Borough Council v Minister of Housing and Local Government, [1952] Ch 856,
[1952] 2 All ER 639, 116 JP 525, [1952] 2 TLR 490, 50 LGR 699, 3 P & CR 173, 45
Digest (Repl) 344   . . . . .45, 122
Eastern Counties and London and Blackwell Railway Companies v Marriage (1860), 9 HL
Cas 32, 31 LJ Ex 73, 3 LT 60, 7 Jur NS 53, 8 WR 748, 11 Digest (Reissue) 108   . 110
Eastham v Leigh London Provincial Properties, Ltd, [1971] Ch 871, [1971] 2 All ER 887,
[1971] 2 WLR 1149, 115 Sol Jo 266, 46 Tax Cas at 699, [1971] TR 33, 50 ATC 53, CA,
Digest Cont Vol D 474   100
Easton v Islington Corpn (1952), 3 P & CR 145   349
Edge Hill Light Rly Co v Secretary of State for War (1956), 6 P & CR 211   . . . 245, 250
Edwards (Inspector of Taxes) v Bairstow, [1956] AC 14, [1955] 3 All ER 48, [1955] 3 WLR
410, 99 Sol Jo 558, 36 Tax Cas at 220, [1955] TR 209, 34 ATC 198, 48 R & IT 534, HL,
28 (1) Digest (Reissue) 567   . . . . 57, 58, 241
Edwards v Minister of Transport [1964] 2 QB 134, [1964] 2 WLR 515, 108 Sol Jo 34, 62 LGR
223, 15 P & CR 144, [1964] RVR 182, CA, 11 Digest (Reissue) 160 318
Elementary Education Acts, Re, [1909] 1 Ch 55, 78 LJ Ch 281, 99 LT 862, 73 JP 22, 25 TLR
78, CA, 11 Digest (Reissue) 265   93

PAGE

Ellick v Sedgemoor District Council, [1976] JPL 434, 32 P & CR 134, 239 Estates Gazette
513 134

Elliott v Southwark London Borough, [1976] 2 All ER 781, [1976] 1 WLR 499, 120 Sol Jo
200, 74 LGR 265, 32 P & CR 256, CA 44

Elliott Steam Tug Co Ltd v Shipping Controller, [1922] 1 KB 127, 91 LJKB 294, 126 LT
158, 15 Asp MLC 406, CA, 17 Digest (Reissue) 127 327

Empire Motors (Swansea) Ltd v Swansea County Council (1972), 24 P & CR 377 . . 132

English Exporters (London) Ltd v Eldonwall Ltd, [1973] Ch 415, [1973] 1 All ER 726,
[1973] 2 WLR 435, 117 Sol Jo 224, 25 P & CR 379, 225 Estates Gazette 255 . . . 85

Enoch and Zaretzky Book & Co, Re, [1910] 1 KB 327, [1908–10] All ER Rep 625, 79 LJKB
363, 101 LT 801, CA, 22 Digest (Reissue) 510 85

Errington v Metropolitan District Rly Co (1882), 19 Ch D 559, 51 LJ Ch 305, 46 LT 443, 30
WR 663, CA, 11 Digest (Reissue) 109 273

Errington v Minister of Health [1935] 1 KB 249, [1934] All ER Rep 154, 104 LJKB 49, 152
LT 154, 99 JP 15, 51 TLR 44, 78 Sol Jo 754, 26 Digest (Repl) 695 . . . . .40, 46, 65

Essex County Council v Essex Incorporated Congregational Church Union, [1963] AC 808,
[1963] 1 All ER 326, [1963] 2 WLR 802, 127 JP 182, 107 Sol Jo 112, 14 P & CR 237,
[1963] RVR 151, HL, 45 Digest (Repl) 367 . . . . 131, 145

Eton College v Eton RDC (1959), 11 P & CR 66 279

Evans v Cheshire County Council (1952), 3 P & CR 50 . . . . 416, 417

Evans and Glamorgan County Council, Re (1912) 76 JP 468, 56 Sol Jo 668, 10 LGR 805, 11
Digest (Reissue) 328 371

F

Fairbairn Lawson Ltd v Leeds County Borough Council (1970), 222 Estates Gazette 561 . 184

Fairmount Investments Ltd v Secretary of State for the Environment, [1976] 2 All ER 865,
[1976] 1 WLR 1255, 120 Sol Jo 801, 75 LGR 33, HL 42, 43, 56, 61, 65, 79

Falkner v Somerset and Dorset Rly Co (1873), LR 16 Eq. 458, 42 LJ ch 851, 11 Digest
(Reissue) 215 110

Fergusson v London, Brighton and South Coast Rly Co (1863), 3 De G J & Sm 653, 2 New
Rep 566, 33 LJ Ch 29, 9 LT 134, 27 JP 580, 11 WR 1088, 11 Digest (Reissue) 213 . . 108

Ferrar v London Sewers Comrs (1869), LR 4 Exch 227, 38 LJ Ex 102, 21 LT 295, 17 WR
709, 11 Digest (Reissue) 159 321

Festiniog Railway Society Ltd v Central Electricity Generating Board (1962), 106 Sol Jo
112, 60 LGR 157, 13 P & CR 248, [1962] RVR 202, CA, 11 Digest (Reissue) 148 87, 241

Field v Caernarvon and Llanberis Rly Co (1867), LR 5 Eq 190, 37 LJ Ch 176, 17 LT 534, 16
WR 273, 11 Digest (Reissue) 249 70

Field Place Caravan Park Ltd v Harding (Valuation Officers), [1966] 3 All ER 247, [1966] 3
WLR 198, 130 JP 397, 110 Sol Jo 386, 64 LGR 399 [1966] RVR 447, [1966] RA 393,
CA, Digest Cont Vol B 612 377

Fitzwilliams (Earl) Wentworth Estates Co v Minister of Housing and Local Government,
[1951] 2 KB 284, [1951] 1 All ER 982, 115 JP 309, [1951] 1 TLR 878, 49 LGR 314, 1
P & CR 429, CA; affd., [1952] AC 362, 1 All ER 509, 116 JP 183, [1952] 1 TLR
521, 96 Sol Jo 193, 50 LGR 257, 2 P & CR 385, HL, 45 Digest (Repl) 367 60

Fletcher v Birkenhead Corpn, [1907] 1 KB 205, [1904–7] All ER Rep 324, 76 LJKB 218, 96 LT
287, 71 JP 111, 23 TLR 195, 51 Sol Jo 171, 5 LGR 293, CA, 19 Digest (Repl) 182 . 322

Fogg v Birkenhead County Borough Council (1971), 22 P & CR 208 137

Frank Warr & Co Ltd v LCC. See Warr (Frank) & Co Ltd v LCC

Fraser v City of Fraserville, [1917] AC 187, 86 LJPC 91, 116 LT 258, 33 TLR 179, PC, 11
Digest (Reissue) 133 218

Freeman v Middlesex County Council (1965), 16 P & CR 253 279

Fry v Essex County Council (1962), 11 P & CR 21 421

Furness Rly Co v Cumberland Co-op Building Society (1884), 52 LT 144, 49 JP 292, HL, 11
Digest (Reissue) 165 324

G

Garland v Minister of Housing and Local Government (1968), 112 Sol Jo 841, 20 P & CR 93,
67 LGR 77, Digest Cont Vol C 973 . . . . 420, 444

Gibson v Hammersmith and City Rly Co (1863), 2 Drew & Sm 603, 1 New Rep 305, 32 LJ Ch
337, 8 LT 43, 27 JP 132, 9 Jur NS 221, 11 WR 299, 11 Digest (Reissue) 252 . . . 355

Givaudan & Co Ltd v Minister of Housing and Local Government, [1966] 3 All ER 696,
[1967] 1 WLR 250, 110 Sol Jo 371, 64 LGR 352, Digest Cont Vol B 692 . . . . 44, 62

Glover v Edmonton Corpn (1953), 3 P & CR 451 . . . . 177, 178

PAGE

Glover v North Staffordshire Rly Co (1851), 16 QB 912, 20 LJQB 376, 17 LTOS 73, 15 Jur
673, 11 Digest (Reissue) 171 324

Goldsmiths' Co v West Metropolitan Rly Co, [1904] 1 KB 1, [1900–3] All ER Rep 667, 72
LJKB 931, 89 LT 428, 68 JP 41, 52 WR 21, 20 TLR 7, 48 Sol Jo 13, CA, 11 Digest
(Reissue) 202 67

Goldstyles Ltd v London County Council (1964), 15 P & CR 317 85

Gordondale Investments Ltd v Secretary of State for the Environment (1971), 23 P & CR
384, 70 LGR 158, CA, Digest Cont Vol D 387 . . . . 55, 56

Gosling v Secretary of State for the Environment, [1975] JPL 406, 234 Estates Gazette 531 . 65

General Estates Co v Minister of Housing and Local Government (1965), Estates Gazette,
17th April, 201 . . . . 120, 121

Glamorgan County Council v Carter, [1962] 3 All ER 866, [1963] 1 WLR 1, 127 JP 28, 106
Sol Jo 1069, 61 LGR 50, 14 P & CR 88, 45 Digest (Repl) 388 417

Gough and Aspatria, Silloth and District Joint Water Board, Re, [1905] 1 KB 417, [1904–7]
All ER Rep 726, 73 LJKB 228, 90 LT 43, 68 JP 229, 52 WR 552, 20 TLR 179, 48 Sol Jo
207, CA, 11 Digest (Reissue) 144 218

Gower's Walk Schools Trustees and London Tilbury and Southend Rly Co. See London
Tilbury and Southend Rly Co and Gower's Walk Schools

Granada Theatres Ltd v Secretary of State for the Environment, [1976] JPL 96 . . . 65

Grangewalk Properties Ltd v Minister of Housing and Local Government (1969) 31
October (unreported) 63

Great Western Rly Co v Swindon and Cheltenham Rly Co (1884), 9 App Cas 787, 53 LJ Ch
1075, 51 LT 798, 48 JP 821, 32 WR 957, HL, 11 Digest (Reissue) 108 71

Greenwood's Tyre Service Ltd v Manchester Corpn (1971), 23 P & CR 246 366

Gredley (Investment Developments) Co Ltd v London Borough of Newham (1973), 26 P &
CR 400 85

Green v Birmingham Corpn (1951), 2 P & CR 220 406

Green v Minister of Housing and Local Government, [1967] 2 QB 606, [1966] 3 All ER 942,
[1967] 2 WLR 192, 111 Sol Jo, 75, Digest Cont Vol B 694 64

Greenberg v Grimsby Corpn (1961), 12 P & CR 212 349

Grice v Dudley Corpn, [1958] 1 Ch 329, [1957] 2 All ER 673, [1957] 3 WLR 314, 121
JP 466, 101 Sol Jo 591, 55 LGR 493, 11 Digest (Reissue) 204 67

Griffith v Richard Clay & Sons Ltd, [1912] 2 Ch 291, 81 LJ Ch 809, 106 LT 963, CA, 19
Digest (Repl) 212 327

Grimley v Minister of Housing and Local Government, [1971] 2 QB 96, [1971] 2 All ER 431,
[1971] 2 WLR 449, 135 JP 362, 115 Sol Jo 34, 69 LGR 238, 22 P & CR 339, Digest Cont
Vol D 389 . . . . 33, 61

Grosvenor (Lord) v Hampstead Junction Rly Co (1859), 1 De G & J 446, 26 LJ Ch 731,
29 LTOS 319, 21 JP 547, 3 Jur NS 1085, 5 WR 812, 11 Digest (Reissue) 214 . . . 108

H

Halford v Oxfordshire County Council (1951), 2 P & CR 358 . . . . 418, 435

Halliwell and Halliwell v Skelmersdale Development Corpn (1965), 16 P & CR 305 . 226

Hamilton v Secretary of State for Scotland, [1972] SLT 233 . . . . 43, 54

Hammersmith and City Rly Co v Brand (1869), LR 4 HL 171, [1861–73] All ER Rep 60, 38
LJQB 265, 21 LT 238, 34 JP 36, 18 WR 12, HL, 11 Digest (Reissue) 107 . . 321, 322

Hammerton v Honey (1876), 24 WR 603, 13 Digest (Reissue) 29 278

Hanily v Minister of Local Government and Planning, [1951] 2 KB 917, [1951] 2 All ER
749, 115 JP 547, 95 Sol Jo 577, 49 LGR 769, 2 P & CR 161, CA, 11 Digest (Reissue)
243 64

Hanily v Minister of Local Government and Planning, [1952] 2 QB 444, [1952] 1 All ER
1293, 116 JP 321, [1952] 1 TLR 1304, 96 Sol Jo 328, 50 LGR 437, 3 P & CR 6, 45
Digest (Repl) 336 402

Hanks v Ministry of Housing and Local Government, [1963] 1 QB 999, [1963] 1 All ER 47,
[1962] 3 WLR 1482, 127 JP 78, 106 Sol Jo 1032, 61 LGR 76, 15 P & CR 246,
Digest Cont Vol A 657 . . . . 59, 60, 65

Harding v Metropolitan Rly Co (1872), 7 Ch App 154, 41 LJ Ch 371, 26 LT 109, 36 JP
340, 20 WR 321, 11 Digest (Reissue) 235 167

Harpurhey Conservative and Unionist Club v Manchester City Council (1975), 31 P & CR
300, 235 Estates Gazette 765 247

Harpurhey Constitutional Club Ltd v Manchester City Council (1975), 31 P & CR 300,
235 Estates Gazette 765 247

PAGE

Harrison v London Borough of Croydon, [1968] Ch 479, [1967] 2 All ER 589, [1967] 3 WLR
    100, 111 Sol Jo 255, 65 LGR 338, 18 P & CR 486, [1967] RVR 270, 11 Digest (Reissue)
    241 . . . . .83, 452
Harrison v Gloucestershire County Council (1953), 4 P & CR 99 421
Harvey v Crawley Development Corpn, [1957] 1 QB 485, [1957] 1 All ER 504, [1957] 2 WLR
    332, 121 JP 116, 101 Sol Jo 189, 55 LGR 104, CA, 11 Digest (Reissue) 149 . . 345, 346,
                                       348, 391
Harvie v South Devon Rly Co (1874), 32 LT 1, 23 WR 202, CA, 11 Digest (Reissue) 214: 108, 112
Haynes v Haynes (1861), 1 Drew & Sim 426, 30 LJ Ch 578, 4 LT 199, 7 Jur NS 595, 9 WR
    497, 11 Digest (Reissue) 208 68
Healy (or McArdle) v Glasgow Corpn (1971), 24 P & CR 134 . . . . 345, 350, 358
Herrburger Brooks v St Pancras Corpn (1960), 11 P & CR 390 358
Hewett v Essex County Council (1927), 97 LJKB 249, 138 LT 742, 44 TLR 373, 72 Sol Jo
    241, 11 Digest (Reissue) 170 . . . . 324, 325
Hibernian Property Co Ltd v Liverpool Corpn, [1973] 2 All ER 1117, [1973] 1 WLR
    751, 117 Sol Jo 466, 71 LGR 395, 25 P & CR 417, Digest Cont Vol D 584 . . . 183
Hibernian Property Co Ltd v Secretary of State for the Environment (1973), 27 P & CR 197,
    72 LGR 350, Digest Cont Vol D 387 . . . . 42, 61, 62, 79
Hickmott v Dorset County Council (1975), 30 P & CR 237; on appeal, [1977] JPL 715 . 329
Hicks v Leeds County Borough Council (1974), 27 P & CR 531 142
High Street Nos, 21/25, Chasetown, Lichfield, *Re*, [1971] JPL 535 121
Highham v Havant and Waterloo UDC, [1951] 1 KB 509, [1951] 1 All ER 173, 115
    JP 56, 95 Sol Jo 30, 49 LGR 117, 1 P & CR 281; affd., [1951] 2 KB 527, [1951] 2 All ER
    178n, 115 JP 406n, [1951] 2 TLR 87, 95 Sol Jo 514, 49 LGR 683, 2 P & CR 115,
    CA, 45 Digest (Repl) 370 . . . . 444, 445
Hillingdon Estates Co v Stonefield Estates Ltd, [1952] Ch 627, [1952] 1 All ER 853, [1952] 1
    TLR 1099, 50 LGR 587, 2 P & CR 415, 12 Digest (Reissue) 464 68
Hills (Patents), Ltd v University College Hospital Board of Governors, [1956] 1 QB 90, [1955]
    3 All ER 365, [1955] 3 WLR 523, 99 Sol Jo 760, CA, 31(2) Digest (Reissue) 969: 108, 132
Hobbs (Quarries) Ltd v Somerset County Council (1975), 30 P & CR 286: 96, 97, 344, 360, 416,
                                   418, 446, 448
Holditch v Canadian Northern Ontario Rly Co, [1916] 1 AC 536, 85 LJPC 107, 114 LT 475,
    32 TLR 294, 27 DLR 14, 20 Can Ry 101, 11 Digest (Reissue) 155 315
Holloway v Dover Corpn, [1960] 1 WLR 604, [1960] 2 All ER 193, 124 JP 305, 104 Sol Jo
    466, 58 LGR 338, CA, 11 Digest (Reissue) 151 . . . . 172, 173, 174
Holmes v Bradfield RDC, [1949] 2 KB 1, [1949] 1 All ER 381, [1949] LJR 978, 113 JP 140, 65
    TLR 195, 93 Sol Jo 183, 47 LGR 278, 45 Digest (Repl) 371 416
Hood Investment Co v Marlow UDC (1963), 15 P & CR 229 87
Hope v Secretary of State (1975), 31 P & CR 120 . . . . 44, 62
Horn v Sunderland Corpn, [1941] 2 KB 26, [1941] 1 All ER 480, 110 LJ KB 353, 165 LT 298,
    105 JP 223, 57 TLR 404, 85 Sol Jo 212, 39 LGR 367, CA, 11 Digest (Reissue) 130 . 160, 161,
                                345, 348, 350, 359
Horton v Colwyn Bay UDC, [1908] 1 KB 327, 77 LJKB 215, 98 LT 547, 72 JP 57, 24 TLR
    220, 52 Sol Jo 158, 6 LGR 211 CA, 11 Digest (Reissue) 161 327
Hoveringham Gravels Ltd v Chiltern District Council and Buckingham County Council,
    [1977] RVR 243, 31 P & CR 466 . . . . 183, 213, 214
Hoveringham Gravels Ltd v Secretary of State for the Environment, [1975] QB 754, [1975] 2
    All ER 931, [1975] 2 WLR 897, 119 Sol Jo 355, 73 LGR 238, 30 P & CR 151, [1975]
    RVR 136, CA, Digest Cont Vol D 937 . . . . 429, 430, 452
Hull Trinity House Corpn v Humberside County Council (1975), 234 Estates Gazette 915 . 168,
                                       175
Hunter v Cardiff City Council, [1971] RVR 186 . . . . 220, 267, 268
Hunter v Manchester City Council (1975), 30 P & CR 58 266
Hurley v Cheshire County Council (1976), 31 P & CR 433 . . . . 148, 153

I

Iddenden v Secretary of State for the Environment, [1972] 3 All ER 883, [1972] 1 WLR 1433,
    137 JP 28, 116 Sol Jo 665, 71 LGR 20, 26 P & CR 553, CA, Digest Cont Vol D 931 . 431
Imperial Gas Light and Coke Co v Broadbent (1859), 7 HL Cas 600, 29 LJ Ch 377, 34 LTOS
    1, 23 JP 675, 5 Jur NS 1319, 11 Digest (Reissue) 158 . . . . 318, 326
Incorporated Society of the Crusade of Rescue and Homes for Destitute Catholic Children v
    Feltham UDC (1960), 11 P & CR 158 . . . . 242, 249

PAGE

IRC v Clay, [1914] 3 KB 466, [1914–15] All ER Rep 882, 83 LJKB 1318, 110 LT 909, 30 TLR
    436, 39 Digest (Repl) 249 178
Isgood-Jones v Llanrwst UDC. *See* Jones v Llanrwst UDC
Iveagh (Earl) v Minister of Housing and Local Government, [1964] 1 QB 395, [1963] 3 All
    ER 817, [1963] 3 WLR 974, 128 JP at p 72, 107 Sol Jo 790, 851, 62 LGR 32, 15 P & CR
    233, [1963] RVR 791, CA, 45 Digest (Repl) 366 . . . . .44, 62, 63, 414

J

Jeary v Chailey UDC (1973), 26 P & CR 280, CA, Digest Cont Vol D 927 441
Jelson v Blaby District Council (1974), 28 P & CR 450 223
Jelson v Minister of Housing and Local Government, [1969] 1 QB 243, [1969] 3 All ER 147,
    [1969] 3 WLR 282, 133 JP 564, 113 Sol Jo 427, 67 LGR 543, [1969] RVR 391, CA, Digest
    Cont Vol C 979 207
Johnson (B.) & Co (Builders) Ltd v Minister of Health, [1947] 2 All ER 395, [1948] LJR
    155, 177 LT 455, 111 JP 508, 45 LGR 617, CA, 26 Digest (Repl) 702 . . . . . 36, 37
Jolliffe v Exeter Corpn, [1967] 2 All ER 1099, [1967] 1 WLR 993, 131 JP 421, 111 Sol Jo 414,
    65 LGR 401, 18 P & CR 343, [1967] RA 413, CA, 11 Digest (Reissue) 169 . . . 321
Jolly v Kine, [1907] AC 1, 76 LJ Ch 1, 95 LT 656, 23 TLR 1, 51 Sol Jo 11, HL, 36 (1) Digest
    (Reissue) 414 326
Jones v Llanrwst UDC, [1911] 1 Ch 393, [1908–10] All ER Rep 922, 80 LJ Ch 145, 103 LT
    751, 75 JP 68, sub nom. Isgoed-Jones v Llanrwst UDC, 27 TLR 133, 55 Sol Jo 125, 9
    LGR 222, 36 (1) Digest (Reissue) 455 326
Jubb v Hull Dock Co. (1846), 9 QB 443, sub nom. R v Hull Dock Co, 15 LJQB 403, 8 LTOS
    293, 10 JP 835, 11 Jur 15, 3 Ry & Can Cas 795, 11 Digest (Reissue) 146   4

K

K and B Metals Ltd v Birmingham City Council, [1976] JPL 760, 33 P & CR 135: 417, 421
Kaye v Basingstoke Development Corpn (1968), 20 P & CR 417, [1968] RVR 744, 764,
    776 . . . . 219, 223, 227
Kent County Council v Bachelor, [1976] JPL 254, 75 LGR 151, CA, Times, 7 October,
    1976 432
Kent Messenger Ltd v Secretary of State for the Environment, [1976] JPL 372 62
Kidgill v Moor (1850), 9 CB 364, 1 LM & P 131, 19 LJCP 177, 14 Ltos 443, 14 Jur 790,
    36 (1) Digest (Reissue) 477 326
King v Birmingham Corpn (1970), 21 P & CR 979 . . . . 221, 256
King v West Dorset Water Board (1962), 14 P & CR 166 328
King v Wycombe Rly Co (1860), 28 Beav 104, 29 LJ Ch 462, 2 LT 107, 24 JP 279, 6 Jur NS
    239, 11 Digest (Reissue) 213 109
Kirby v Harrogate School Board, [1896] 1 Ch 437, 65 LJ Ch 376, 74 LT 6, 60 JP 182, 12 TLR
    175, 40 Sol Jo 239, CA, 11 Digest (Reissue) 175 321
Kirby and Shaw v Bury County Borough Council (1973), 228 Estates Gazette 537 . . 169
Kitchin, *Re, ex parte* Punnutt (1880), 16 Ch D 226, 50 LJ Ch 212, 44 LT 226, 29 WR 129, CA,
    5 Digest (Reissue) 697 356
Kitchin v Leeds County Borough Council (1974), 27 P & CR 531 142
Knapp v London Chatham and Dover Rly Co (1863), 2 H & C 212, 2 New Rep 329, 32 LJ
    Ex 236, 8 LT 541, 9 Jur NS 671, 11 WR 890, 11 Digest (Reissue) 248 71
Knott Hotels Co of London Ltd v London Transport Executive (1975), 31 P & CR 295, 236
    Estates Gazette 64 283
Knott Mill Carpets Ltd v Stretford Borough Council (1973), 26 P & CR 129 354

L

LCC v South Eastern Rly Co, *See* South Eastern Rly Co v LCC
LTSS Print and Supply Services Ltd v London Borough of Hackney, [1975] 1 All ER 374,
    [1975] 1 WLR 138, 139 JP 166, 119 Sol Jo 64, 73 LGR 102, 29 P & CR 416, 233 Estates
    Gazette 147 417
Lade and Lade v Brighton Corpn (1971), 22 P & CR 737 143
Lagan Navigation Co v Lamberg Bleaching, Dyeing and Finishing Co, [1927] AC 226,
    [1926] All ER Rep 302, 96 LJPC 25, 136 LT 417, 91 JP 46, 25, LGR 1, HL, 13 Digest
    (Reissue) 341 318
Laing v Buckinghamshire County Council (1960), 11 P & CR 114 417
Laitner v Sheffield County Borough Council (1964), 192 Estates Gazette 245 220

PAGE

Lake v Cheshire County Council, [1976] JPL 434 130

Lambe v Secretary of State for War, [1955] 2 QB 612, [1955] 2 All ER 386, [1955] 2 WLR
1127, 119 JP 415, 99 Sol Jo 368, 53 LGR 481, 5 P & CR 227, CA 178

Lamplugh, *Re. See* Watch House Boswinger, *Re*

Lane v Dagenham Corpn (1961), 12 P & CR 374 . . . . 248, 250

Langley (Thomas) Group Ltd v Royal Borough of Leamington Spa (1974), 29 P & CR 358,
CA 185, 196

Lavender (H.) & Son Ltd v Minister of Housing and Local Government, [1970] 3 All ER
871, [1970] 1 WLR 1231, 114 Sol Jo 636, Digest Cont Vol C 968 . . . . 41, 43, 59, 407

Lee (Judge) v Minister of Transport, [1966] 1 QB 111, [1965] 3 WLR 553, 63 LGR 327,
[1965] RVR 427, CA, sub nom. Minister of Transport v Lee, [1965] 2 All ER 986,
129 JP 511, 109 Sol Jo 494, 17 P & CR, Digest Cont Vol B 698 348

Leeds Grammar School, *Re*, [1901] 1 Ch 228, 70 LJ Ch 89, 83 LT 499, 65 JP 88, 49 WR 120,
45 Sol Jo 78, 11 Digest (Reissue) 286 89

Legg v Inner London Education Authority, [1972] 3 All ER 177, [1972] 1 WLR 1245,
116 Sol Jo 680, 71 LGR 58 79

Lewis Executors and Palladium Cinema (Brighton) Ltd v Brighton Corpn (1956), 6 P & CR
318 360

Ley and Ley v Kent County Council (1976), 31 P & CR 439 130

Line (John) & Sons Ltd v Newcastle upon Tyne Corpn (1956), 6 P & CR 466 . . 348, 356

Link v Worcestershire County Council (1965), 16 P & CR 255 135

Livingstone v Rawyards Coal Co (1880), 5 App Cas 25, 30, 42 LT 334, 28 WR 357, HL, 17
Digest (Reissue) 89 326

Lloyd and North London Rly (City Branch) Act 1861, *Re*, [1896] 2 Ch 397, 65 LJ Ch 626, 74
LT 548, 44 WR 522, 12 TLR 432, 11 Digest (Reissue) 296 93

Lockers Estates Ltd v Oadby UDC (1970), 21 P & CR 448 145

London and South Western Rly Co, *ex parte* (1869), 38 LJ Ch 527, 11 Digest (Reissue) 218 . 88

London and South Western Rly Co v Blackmore (1870), LR 4 HL 610, [1861–73] All ER Rep
Ext 1694, 39 LJ Ch 713, 23 LT 504, 35 JP 324, 19 WR 305, 11 Digest (Reissue)
316 110

London and Westcliffe Properties Ltd v Minister of Housing and Local Government, [1961]
1 All ER 610, [1961] 1 WLR 519, 125 JP 229, 105 Sol Jo 208, 59 LGR 244, 12 P & CR
154, Digest Cont Vol A 655 36

London Corpn v Cusack-Smith, [1955] AC 337, [1955] 1 All ER 302, [1955] 2 WLR 363, 119
JP 172, 99 Sol Jo 108, 53 LGR 209, 5 P & CR 65, HL, 45 Digest (Repl) 344 . . . 114

London Corpn (as Governors of St Thomas's Hospital) v Charing Cross Rly Co (1861),
4 LT 85, 11 Digest (Reissue) 218 108

London County Council v Hackney Borough Council, [1928] 2 KB 588, 18 Digest (Reissue)
413 132

London County Council v Tobin, [1959] 1 All ER 649, [1959] 1 WLR 354, 123 JP 250, 103
Sol Jo 272, 57 LGR 113, 10 P & CR 79, CA, 11 Digest (Reissue) 131 348

London County (Devons Road, Poplar) Housing Confirmation Order 1945, *Re* (1956),
6 P & CR 133 90

London Diocesan Fund v Stepney Corpn (1953), 4 P & CR 9 . . . . 246, 249

London Tilbury and Southend Rly Co and Gower's Walk Schools Trustees, *Re* (1889), 24
QBD 326, 62 LT 306, 38 WR 343, sub nom. Gower's Walk Schools Trustees and
London Tilbury and Southend Rly Co, 59 LJQB 162, 6 TLR 120, CA, 11 Digest
(Reissue) 173 . . . . 316, 324, 327

Long Eaton Recreation Grounds Co v Midland Rly Co [1902] 2 KB 574, 71 LJKB 837, 86
LT 873, 67 JP 1, 50 WR 693, 18 TLR 743, CA, 11 Digest (Reissue) 175 . . . 324, 326

Louisville Investments Ltd v Basingstoke District Council (1976), 31 P & CR 419: 143, 146, 150,
153

Lowestoft Manor and Great Eastern Rly Co, *Re*, *ex parte* Reeve (1833), 24 Ch D 253, 52 LJ Ch
912, 49 LT 523, 32 WR 309, CA, 11 Digest (Reissue) 280 89

Loweth v Minister of Housing and Local Government (1971), 22 P & CR 125 60

Lucas (F.) & Sons Ltd v Dorking and Horley RDC (1964), 62 LGR 491, 17 P & CR 111 124

Lucey's Personal Representatives & Wood v Harrogate Corpn (1963), 14 P & CR 377 . 328

Luke (Lord) of Pavenham v Minister of Housing and Local Government, [1968] 1 QB 172,
[1967] 2 All ER 1066, [1967] 3 WLR 801, 131 JP 425, 111 Sol Jo 398, 65 LGR 393, 18
P & CR 333, CA, Digest Cont Vol C 968 43

Lyon v Fishmongers' Co (1876), 1 App Cas 662, 46 LJ Ch 68, 35 LT 569, 42 JP 163, 25 WR
165, HL, 26 Digest (Repl) 347 324

M

McCartney v Londonderry and Lough Swilly Rly Co, [1904] AC 301, 73 LJPC 73, 91 LT
    105, 53 WR 385, HL, 19 Digest (Repl) 162 326
McEwing (D.) & Sons Ltd v Renfrewshire County Council (1960), 11 P & CR 306, 1960
    SC 53, 1960 SLT 140, 11 Digest (Reissue) 136 418
Macey v Metropolitan Board of Works (1864), 3 New Rep 669, 33 LJ Ch 377, 10 LT 66, 10
    Jur NS 333, 12 WR 619, 11 Digest (Reissue) 170 324
McKay v City of London (1966), 17 P & CR 264 . . . . .49, 279
McKinnon Campbell v Greater Manchester Council, [1976] JPL 700, 33 P & CR 100 . 147, 150,
    153
McMeechan v Secretary of State for the Environment, [1974] JPL 411, 232 Estates
    Gazette 201 62
Maltglade Ltd v St Albans RDC, [1972] 3 All ER 129, [1972] 1 WLR 1230, 136 JP 707, 116
    Sol Jo 468, 70 LGR 490, 24 P & CR 32, Digest Cont Vol D 934 34
Manchester Homeopathic Clinic (Trustees) v Manchester Corpn (1970), 22 P & CR
    241 . . . . 184, 241, 242, 246, 247, 248, 249
Margate Corpn v Devotwill Investments Ltd, [1970] 3 All ER 864, 135 JP 19, 69 LGR 271,
    22 P & CR 328, 218 Estates Gazette 559, HL 200, 201
Margery v Brighton Corpn (1962), 13 P & CR 438 144
Marten v Secretary of State (1959), 10 P & CR 390 68
Martin v London, Chatham and Dover Rly Co (1866), 1 Ch App 501, 35 LJ Ch 795, 14 LT
    814, 12 Jur NS 775, 14 WR 880, 11 Digest (Reissue) 304 . . . . 68, 89
Marylebone (Stingo Lane) Improvement Act, Re, ex parte Edwards (1871), LR 12 Eq 389, 40
    LJ Ch 697, 25 LT 149, 19 WR 1047, 11 Digest (Reissue) 305 69
Marzell v Greater London Council (1975), 30 P & CR 259, Estates Gazette 621 . . . 270
Mason, Re (1934), 50 TLR 392, 78 Sol Jo 414, 26 Digest (Repl) 698 65
Mason Street Land, Southwark, Re, [1968] JPL 180 121
Mathews v Bristol Corpn (1954), 4 P & CR 401 359
Maurice v LCC, [1964] 2 QB 362, [1964] 1 All ER 779, [1964] 2 WLR
    715, 128 JP 311, 108 Sol Jo 175, 62 LGR 241, [1964] RVR 341, CA, Digest Cont Vol B
    607 53
Mercer v Liverpool, St Helens and South Lancashire Rly Co, [1904] AC 461, 73 LJKB 960, 91
    LT 605, 68 JP 533, 53 WR 241, 20 TLR 673, HL, 11 Digest (Reissue) 306 . . 69, 167
Mercer v Manchester Corpn (1964), 15 P & CR 321 135
Merediths Ltd v LCC (No. 2) (1957), 9 P & CR 258 86
Metcalfe v Basildon Development Corpn (1974), 28 P & CR 307 170
Metropolitan Board of Works v Howard (1889), 5 TLR 732, HL, 11 Digest (Reissue) 171 . 324
Metropolitan Board of Works v McCarthy (1874), LR 7 HL 243, 43 LJCP 385, 31 LT 182,
    38 JP 820, 23 WR 115, 11 Digest (Reissue) 169 325
Metropolitan Board of Works v Metropolitan Rly Co (1868), LR 3 CP 612, 41 Digest (Repl)
    41 . . . . 316, 324
Middlesex County Council v Minister of Local Government and Planning, [1953] 1 QB 12,
    [1952] 2 All ER 709, 116 JP 543, [1952] 2 TLR 651, 96 Sol Jo 712, 50 LGR 673, CA, 11
    Digest (Reissue) 243 . . . . 35, 48
Midland Bank Trust Co Ltd (Executors) v London Borough of Lewisham (1975), 30 P & CR
    268, 235 Estates Gazette 59 170
Migdal Investments Ltd v Secretary of State for the Environment, [1976] JPL 365 . . 58
Miles Lane, Tandridge, Surrey, Re, [1962] JPL 201 121
Miller v Weymouth and Melcombe Regis Corpn (1974), 27 P & CR 468, 118 Sol Jo 421,
    Digest Cont Vol D 932 65
Miller (T.A.) Ltd v Minister of Housing and Local Government, [1968] 2 All ER 633, [1968]
    1 WLR 992, 112 Sol Jo 522, 66 LGR 539, 19 P & CR 278, [1969] RPC 91, CA, Digest
    Cont Vol C 958 .40, 41, 64
Minister of Transport v Lee. See Lee (Judge) v Minister of Transport
Minister of Transport v Pettitt (1969), 20 P & CR 344 219
Ministry of Transport v Holland (1962), 61 LGR 134 132
Mogridge (W.J.) (Bristol 1937) Ltd v Bristol Corpn (1956), 8 P & CR 78 . . . . 349, 358
Morgan and London and North West Rly Co, Re, [1896] 2 QB 469, 66 LJQB 30, 75 LT 226,
    45 WR 176, 12 TLR 632, 40 Sol Jo 753, 11 Digest (Reissue) 308 . . . . 174, 175, 215
Morris v Jacombs Ltd v Birmingham District Council (1976), 31 P & CR 305, 235 Estates
    Gazette 679; on appeal, [1976] JPL 694, CA 134, 177, 219, 223
Mortimer v South Wales Rly Co (1859), 1 E & E 375, 28 LJQB 129, 5 Jur (NS) 784,
    7 WR 292 324

PAGE

Mountgarret v Claro Water Board (1963), 15 P & CR 53 83
Mountview Court Properties Ltd v Devlin (1970), 21 P & CR 689, 114 Sol Jo 474, [1970]
    RVR 451, 31(2) Digest (Reissue) 1072 63
Mountview Estates Ltd v London Borough of Enfield (1968), 20 P & CR 729 183
Moxey v Hertford RDC (1973), 27 P & CR 274 . . . . 406, 411
Munton v Greater London Council, [1976] 2 All ER 815, [1976] 1 WLR 649, 120 Sol
    Jo 147, 74, LGR 416, 32 P & CR 269, 239 Estates Gazette 43, CA. Digest Supp   167, 172
Myers v Milton Keynes Development Corpn, [1974] 2 All ER 1096, [1974] 1 WLR 696, 118
    Sol Jo 364, 72 LGR 420, 27 P & CR 518, [1974] RVR 128, CA, Digest Cont Vol D
    102 .88, 191, 203, 219, 220, 226, 236

N

National Provincial Bank v Portsmouth Corpn (1959), 11 P & CR 6 406
Newham London Borough Council v Benjamin, [1968] 1 WLR 694, 112 Sol Jo 253, 66 LGR
    372, sub nom. Benjamin v Newham London Borough Council, 19 P & CR 365, [1968]
    RVR 157, CA, 11 Digest (Reissue) 312 . . . . 315, 363, 365, 366, 369
Nielson v Camden Borough Council (1968), 19 P & CR 801 . . . . 359, 360
Noeltex Ltd v Westminster City Council, [1964] EGD 138 359
Nonentities Society Trustees v Kidderminster Borough Council (1970), 22 P & CR 224 . 244
North Eastern Housing Association Ltd v Newcastle upon Tyne Corpn (1972), 25 P & CR
    178 . . . . 220, 227
Northwood v LCC (No 2), [1926] 2 KB 411, 96 LJKB 520, 137 LT 49, 91 JP 93, 43 TLR 347,
    25 LGR 254, CA, 11 Digest (Reissue) 230 . . . . 317, 345

O

Odeon Associated Theatres Ltd v Glasgow Corpn (1973), 27 P & CR 271 183
Oppenheimer v Minister of Transport, [1942] KB 242, [1941] 3 All ER 485, 111 LJKB 702,
    166 LT 93, 106 JP 46, 58 TLR 86, 40 LGR 23, 11 Digest (Reissue) 160 . .68, 315, 316
Ostreicher v Secretary of State for the Environment (1977), Times, 6th May 39
Overland v Minister of Housing and Local Government (1957), 8 P & CR 389 398
Oxley v Keighley Corpn (1960), 11 P & CR 465 137
Oxshott Garages Ltd v Esher UDC, [1964] RVR 440 418

P

Packwood Poultry Products Ltd v Metropolitan Borough of Solihull (1975), 31 P & CR 315,
    236 Estates Gazette 283 224
Page v Gillingham Borough Council (1970), 21 P & CR 973 135
Pages Luxury Flats v Cockerill (1968) 11th December (unreported) 63
Palmer and Harvey Ltd v Ipswich Corpn (1953), 4 P & CR 5, 11 Digest (Reissue) 157 . 317
Palser v Grinling Property Holding Co Ltd v Mischeff, [1948] AC 291, [1948] 1 All ER 1,
    [1948] LJR 600, 64 TLR 2, 92 Sol Jo 53, HL, 31(2) Digest (Reissue) 1017 144
Park Automobile Co Ltd v City of Glasgow District Council (1975), 30 P & CR 491, 235
    Estates Gazette 307, 385 . . . . 182, 356
Parrish v Minister of Housing and Local Government (1961), 59 LGR 411, 105 Sol Jo 708, 13
    P & CR 32, 45 Digest (Repl) 368 63
Pearce v Bristol Corpn (1949), 1 P & CR 367 . . . . 359, 366
Penny, Re (1857), 7 E & B 660, 26 LJQB 225, 3 Jur NS 957, 5 WR 612, sub nom. R v South
    Eastern Rly Co, 29 LTOS 124 316
Penny v Penny (1868), LR 5 Eq 227, 37 LJ Ch 340, 18 LT 13, 16 WR 671, 11 Digest (Reissue)
    151 173
Pepys v London Transport Executive, [1975] 1 All ER 748, [1975] 1 WLR 234, 118 Sol Jo
    882, 29 P & CR 248, sub nom. London Transport Executive v Pepys, [1975] RVR 57,
    Ca, Digest Cont Vol D 105 87
Perezie v Bristol Corpn (1955), 5 P & CR 237 359
Performance Cars Ltd v Secretary of State, for the Environment [1976] JPL 370;
    revsd, [1977] JPL 585, CA 39, 61
Perkins v West Wiltshire District Council (1976), 31 P & CR 427, 237 Estates Gazette
    661 . . . . 143, 146
Phoenix Assurance Co v Spooner, [1905] 2 KB 753, 74 LJKB 792, 93 LT 306, 54 WR 313, 21
    TLR 557, 49 Sol Jo 553, 10 Com Cas 282, 29 Digest (Repl) 446 169

PAGE

Piggott and Great Western Rly Co, *Re* (1881), 18 Ch D 146, 50 LJ Ch 679, 44 LT 792, 29
    WR 727, 11 Digest (Reissue) 256 328
Plymouth City Corpn v Secretary of State for the Environment, [1972] 3 All ER 225, [1972] 1
    WLR 1347, 116 Sol Jo 565, 70 LGR 567, 24 P & CR 88, Digest Cont Vol D 925 . 124
Pointe Gourde Quarrying and Transport Co Ltd v Sub-Intendent of Crown Lands,
    [1947] AC 565, 63 TLR 486, PC, 11 Digest (Reissue) 139 . . . 171, 178, 218, 219, 220,
                        222, 223, 224, 226, 227, 235, 236, 237, 285, 318, 319
Polsue and Alfieri Ltd v Rushmer, [1907] AC 121, [1904–7] All ER Rep 586, 76 LJ Ch 365, 96
    LT 510, 23 TLR 362, sub nom. Rushmer v Polsue and Alfieri Ltd 51 Sol Jo 324, HL,
    36 (1) Digest (Reissue) 469 330
Powner and Powner v Leeds Corpn (1953), 4 P & CR 167 357
Poyser and Mills' Arbitration, *Re*, [1964] 2 QB 467, [1963] 1 All ER 612, [1963] 2 WLR 1309,
    107 Sol Jo 115, Digest Cont Vol A 18 44
Preece and Preece v Worcester City Corpn (1967), 18 P & CR 103 143
Priestman Collieries Ltd v Northern District Valuation Board, [1950] 2 KB 398, [1950] 2 All
    ER 129, 66 (pt 1) TLR 1215, 94 Sol Jo 421, 33 Digest (Repl) 874 177
Provincial Properties (London) Ltd v Caterham and Warlingham UDC, [1972] 1 QB 453,
    [1972] 1 All ER 60, [1972] 2 WLR 44, 136 JP 93, 115 Sol Jo 832, 70 LGR 151, 23 P & CR
    8, CA, Digest Cont Vol D 926 . . . . 198, 199

R

R v Boldero, *ex parte* Bognor Regis UDC (1962), 60 LGR 292, Digest Cont Vol A 639 . 53
R v Brown (1867), LR 2 QB 630, 36 LJ QB 322, 16 LT 827, 32 JP 54, 15 WR 988, sub nom.
    R v Midland Rly Co, *ex parte* Brown, 8 B & S 456, 11 Digest (Reissue) 139 . . 3, 318
R v Clerk of the Peace for Middlesex, *ex parte* London Electric Rly Co. *See* R v Middlesex
    (Clerk of the Peace)
R v Corby District Council, *ex parte* McLean, [1975] 2 All ER 568, [1975] 1 WLR 735, 119
    Sol Jo 354, 73 LGR 274, 29 P & CR 451, [1975] RVR 153, Digest Cont Vol D 105   374
R v Hull Dock Co. *See* Jubb v Hull Dock Co
R v Kennedy, [1893] 1 QB 533, 62 LJMC 168, 68 LT 454, 57 JP 346, 41 WR 380, 5 R 270, 11
    Digest (Reissue) 209 . . . . 173, 174
R v Middlesex (Clerk of The Peace), [1914] 3 KB 259, [1914–15] All ER Rep 685, 83 LJKB
    1773, sub nom. R v Clerk of the Peace for Middlesex, *ex parte* London Electric Rly Co,
    111 LT 579, 79 JP 7, 11 Digest (Reissue) 304 316
R v Midland Rly Co, *ex parte* Brown. *See* R v Brown
R v Minister of Housing and Local Government, *ex parte* Chichester RDC, [1960] 2 All ER
    407, [1960] 1 WLR 587, 124 JP 322, 104 Sol Jo 449, 58 LGR 198, 11 P & CR 295, 45
    Digest (Repl.) 344 120
R v Minister of Housing and Local Government, *ex parte* Rank Organisation (1958), 10 P &
    CR 9 . . . . 116, 122
R v Northumberland Compensation Appeal Tribunal, *ex parte* Shaw, [1952] 1 KB 338, [1952]
    1 All ER 122, 116 JP 54, [1952] 1 TLR 161, 96 Sol Jo 29, 50 LGR 193, 2 P & CR 361,
    CA, 30 Digest (Reissue) 267 61
R v Pearce, *ex parte* London School Board (1898), 67 LJQB 842, 78 LT 681, 14 TLR 465, 11
    Digest (Reissue) 160 318
R v St Luke's Vestry (1871), LR 7 QB 148, 11 Digest (Reissue) 157 324
R v Scard (1894), 10 TLR 545 356
R v Secretary of State for the Environment, *ex parte* Ostler, [1977] QB 122, [1976] 3 All ER 90,
    [1976] 3 WLR 288, 120 Sol Jo 332, 75 LGR 45, 32 P & CR 166, 238 Estates Gazette 971,
    CA 52, 54, 55, 65
R v Secretary of State, *ex parte* Reinisch (1971), 22 P & CR 1022 . . . . 45, 65
R v South Eastern Rly Co. *See* Penny, *Re*
Ramsden v Manchester, South Junction and Altrincham Rly Co (1848), 1 Exch 723, 12 Jur
    293, 5 Ry & Can Cas 552, 10 LTOS 464, 11 Digest (Reissue) 108 71
Ravenseft Properties v London Borough of Hillingdon (1968), 20 P & CR 483 109
Rawson v Minister of Health (1965), 17 P & CR 239 146
Reddin v Metropolitan Board of Works (1862), 4 De GF & J 532, 31 LJ Ch 660, 7 LT 6, 27
    JP 4, 10 WR 764, 11 Digest (Reissue) 216 108
Redfield Hardware Ltd v Bristol Corpn (1963), 15 P & CR 47 348
Reeve v Hartlepool Borough Council (1975), 30 P & CR 517 266
Remnant v LCC (1952), 3 P & CR 185 357
Richards v Swansea Improvement and Tramway Co (1879), 9 Ch D 425, 38 LT 833, 43 JP
    174, 26 WR 764, CA, 11 Digest (Reissue) 212 108

PAGE

Richardson v Minister of Housing and Local Government (1956), 8 P & CR 29 . . . 61
Ricket v Metropolitan Rly Co (1867), LR 2 HL 175, [1861–73] All ER Rep Ext 2164, 36
    LJQB 205, 16 LT 542, 31 JP 484, 15 WR 937, 11 Digest (Reissue) 167 . . . . 4, 323,
                                                              324, 325, 327
Ripley v Great Northern Rly Co (1875), 10 Ch App 435, 23 WR 685, 11 Digest (Reissue)
    140 317
Ripon (Highfield) Housing Order 1938, Re, [1939] 2 KB 838, 108 LJKB 768, 161 LT 109, 103
    JP 331, 55 TLR 956, 83 Sol Jo 622, 37 LGR 533, 26 Digest (Repl) 700 . . . 58, 61, 64
Roberts v Coventry Corpn, [1947] 1 All ER 308, 111 JP 165, 63 TLR 108, 91 Sol Jo 162, 45
    LGR 84, 11 Digest (Reissue) 176 349
Roberts v Dover Corpn (1962), 14 P & CR 47 . . . . 245, 248, 250
Robinson v Minister of Town and Country Planning, [1947] KB 702, [1947] 1 All ER 851,
    [1947] LJR 1285, 177 LT 375, 111 JP 378, 63 TLR 374, 91 Sol Jo 294, 45 LGR 497, CA,
    45 Digest (Repl) 366 37
Robson and Wood v Teeside County Borough Council, [1974] JPL 365, 28 P & CR 313 266
Rockingham Sisters of Charity v R, [1922] 2 AC 315, 91 LJPC 198, 127 LT 608, 38 TLR 782,
    11 Digest (Reissue) 160 318
Rought (W.) Ltd v West Suffolk County Council (1954), 4 P & CR 347 . . . . . 357, 358
Routh v Reading Corpn (1970), 217 Estates Gazette 1337 65
Routh's Trustees v Central Land Board (1957), 8 P & CR 290 87
Rowley v Southampton Corpn (1959), 10 P & CR 172 . . . . 241, 242, 248
Roy v Westminster City Council (1975), 31 P & CR 458 . . . . . . 352, 354, 356, 357
Rugby Joint Water Board v Shaw-Fox, [1973] AC 202, [1972] 2 WLR 757, [1972] 1 All ER
    1057, 136 JP 317, 116 Sol Jo 240, 70 LGR 339, 24 P & CR 256, HL, 11 Digest (Reissue)
    309 . . . . 171, 172, 174, 215, 219, 366
Rush and Tomkins Ltd v West Kent Main Sewerage Board (1963), 14 P & CR 469 . . 328
Rushmer v Polsue and Alfieri Ltd. See Polsue and Alfieri Ltd v Rushmer
Rutter v Manchester Corpn (1974), 28 P & CR 443 348

S

SJC Construction Co Ltd v Sutton London Borough Council (1975), 29 P & CR 322, 234
    Estates Gazette 363, CA 183, 285, 324
St John's Wood Working Men's Club v LCC (1947), 150 Estates Gazette 213 . . 246, 249
St Thomas' Hospital (Governors) v Charing Cross Rly Co (1861), 1 John & H 400, 30 LJ
    Ch 395, 25 JP 771, 7 Jur NS 256, 9 WR 411, sub nom. London Corpn (as Governors of
    St Thomas's Hospital) v Charing Cross Rly Co, 4 LT 13 108
Sadler v Sheffield Corpn, [1924] 1 Ch 483, 93 LJ Ch 209, 131 LT 55, 88 JP 45, 68 Sol Jo 403,
    40 TLR 259, 22 LGR 138, 19 Digest (Repl) 634 60
Saffron Walden Chalkpit Case. See Buxton v Minister of Housing and Local Government
Sainty v Minister of Housing and Local Government (1964), 15 P & CR 432 406
Salisbury (Marquis) v Great Northern Rly Co (1852), 17 QB 840, 21 LJQB 185, 18 LTOS
    240, 16 Jur 740, 7 Ry & Can Cas 175, 11 Digest (Reissue) 250 67
Scunthorpe Borough Council v Secretary of State for the Environment, [1977] JPL 653 205
Segal v Manchester Corpn (1966), 18 P & CR 112 132
Shaw v London Borough of Hackney (1974), 28 P & CR 477 184
Shearman v Folland, [1950] 2 KB 43, [1950] 1 All ER 976, 66 (pt 1) TLR 853, 94 Sol Jo 336,
    CA, 36 (1) Digest (Reissue) 337 326
Shell Mex and BP Ltd v Langley (V O), [1962] 3 All ER 433, [1962] 1 WLR 1392, 106 Sol
    Jo 650, 60 LGR 490, 9 RRC 249, [1962] RVR 517, CA, Digest Cont Vol A 1296 . 130
Shepherd and Shepherd v Lancashire County Council, [1977] JPL 106 329
Sheppard v Secretary of State for the Environment (1974), 233 Estates Gazette 1167 . 124, 125
Shulman (Tailors) Ltd v Greater London Council (1966), 17 P & CR 244 359
Sidebotham, Re, Sidebotham ex parte (1880) 14 Ch D 458, [1874–80] All ER Rep 588, 49 LJ
    Bay 41, 42 LT 783, 28 WR 715, CA, 4 Digest (Reissue) 256 52
Simeon and the Isle of Wight RDC, Re, [1937] Ch 525, [1937] 3 All ER 149, 106 LJ Ch 335,
    157 LT 473, 101 JP 447, 53 TLR 854, 81 Sol Jo 526, 35 LGR 402, 11 Digest (Reissue)
    172 322
Simpsons Motor Sales (London) Ltd v Hendon Corpn, [1964] AC 1088, [1963] 2 All ER 484,
    [1963] 2 WLR 1187, 127 JP 418, 107 Sol Jo 491, 62 LGR 1, 14 P & CR 386,
    [1963] RVR 522, HL, Digest Cont Vol A 656 67
Sinclair-Lockhart's Trustees v Central Land Board (1950), 1 P & CR 195 409
Smith v Birmingham Corpn (1974), 29 P & CR 265 . . . . 349, 354, 355

PAGE

Smith v East Elloe RDC, [1956] AC 736, [1956] 1 All ER 855, 120 JP 263, 100 Sol Jo 282, 54
  LGR 233, HL, 26 Digest (Repl) 703 . . . . 54, 55, 61, 65
Smith v Somerset County Council (1966), 17 P & CR 162 135
Smith, Stone, Knight Ltd v Lord Mayor, Alderman and Citizens of Birmingham, [1939] 4 All
  ER 116, 161 LT 371, 104 JP 31, 83 Sol Jo 961, 37 LGR 665, 11 Digest (Reissue)
  127 . . . . 247, 347
Smith and Waverley Tailoring Co v Edinburgh District Council (1976), 31 P & CR 484,
  1976 SLT (Lands Tr) 19 73
Solomon Woolfson and Solfred Holdings Ltd v Glasgow Corpn (1975), 3 P & CR 505 . 347
Somers and Somers v Doncaster Corpn (1965), 16 P & CR 323 . . . . . . 354, 357, 358
Soper and Soper v Doncaster Corpn (1964), 16 P & CR 53 173
South Eastern Rly Co and LCC's Contract, Re, South Eastern Rly Co v LCC, [1915] 2 Ch
  252, 84 LJ Ch 756, 113 LT 392, 79 JP 545, 59 Sol Jo 508, 13 LGR 1302, CA, 11 Digest
  (Reissue) 129 . . . . 3, 218
Southern Olympia (Syndicate) Ltd v West Sussex County Council (1952), 3 P & CR 60 . 416, 417
Sovmots Investments Ltd v Secretary of State for the Environment, [1977] QB 411, [1976] 1
  All ER 178, [1976] 2 WLR 73, 119 Sol Jo 612, 74 LGR 95, 31 P & CR 59; on appeal,
  [1977] QB at 445, [1976] 3 All ER 720, [1976] 3 WLR 597, 120 Sol Jo 662, 74 LGR 556,
  CA; revsd., [1977] 2 All ER 385, [1977] 2 WLR 951, 121 Sol Jo 336, HL . . 33, 36, 284
Spackman v Great Western Rly Co (1855), 1 Jur NS 790, 26 LTOS 22, 11 Digest (Reissue)
  216 112
Sparkes v Secretary of State for Wales (1974), 27 P & CR 545 132
Speyer v Westminster Corpn (1958), 9 P & CR 478 359
Sprinz v Kingston upon Hull City Council (1975), 30 P & CR 273 223
Square Grip Reinforcement Co (London) Ltd v Rowton Houses Ltd and London County
  Council (1967), 18 P & CR 258 351
Sri Raja Vyricherla Narayana Gajapatiraju Bahadur Garut v Revenue Divisional Officer,
  Vizagapatam, [1939] AC 302, [1939] 2 All ER 317, 108 LJPC 51, 55 TLR 563, 83 Sol Jo
  336, PC, 11 Digest (Reissue) 140 . . . . 179, 180, 286, 447
Steele v Midland Rly Co (1869), 20 LT 475, 11 Digest (Reissue) 214 71
Steele v Minister of Housing and Local Government (1956), 6 P & CR 386 79
Stokes v Cambridge Corpn (1961), 13 P & CR 77 . . . . 183, 284, 285
Stokes v Secretary of State for War (1950), 1 P & CR 118 412
Stretton v Great Western and Brentford Rly Co (1870), 5 Ch App 751, 40 LJ Ch 51n, 23 LT
  44, 11 Digest (Reissue) 208 89
Stubbs v West Hartlepool Corpn (1961), 12 P & CR 365 . . . . 143, 144
Summers v Minister of Health, [1947] 1 All ER 184, 176 LT 237, 111 JP 89, 45 LGR 105,
  26 Digest (Repl) 702 64
Swick v Chelsea Borough Council (1964), 108 Sol Jo 376, 190 Estates Gazette 593, CA . 66
Sydney Municipal Council v Campbell, [1925] AC 338, [1924] All ER Rep Ext 930, 133 LT
  63, 11 Digest (Reissue) 120 60

T

Tamplin's Brewery Ltd v County Borough of Brighton (1971), 22 P & CR 746 349
Taylor v Greater London Council (1973), 25 P & CR 451 . . . . 346, 347
Tiverton Estates v Wearwell Ltd, [1975] Ch 146, [1974] 1 All ER 209, [1974] 2 WLR 176, 117
  Sol Jo 913, 27 P & CR 24, CA, Digest Cont Vol D 116 65
Toogood v Bristol Corpn (1973), 26 P & CR 132 171
Tranter v Birmingham District Council (1976), 31 P & CR 327 . . . . 176, 196
Trocette Property Co Ltd v Greater London Council and Southwark London Borough
  Council (1973), 27 P & CR 256 . . . . 182, 183, 184
Trunk Roads Act 1936, and London Portsmouth Trunk Road Surrey Compulsory Purchase
  Order (No. 2) 1938, Re, [1939] 2 KB 515, 108 LJKB 555, 160 LT 554, 83 Sol Jo 458, 55
  TLR 640 47
Tull's Personal Representatives v Secretary of State for Air, [1957] 1 QB 523, [1957] 1 All ER
  480, [1957] 2 WLR 346, 101 Sol Jo 189, 55 LGR 100, CA, Digest Cont Vol A 211 . 160, 316
Turner v Secretary of State for the Environment (1973), 72 LGR 380, 28 P & CR 123, Digest
  Cont Vol D 921 . . . . 38, 53
Tynemouth Corpn and Duke of Northumberland, Re (1903), 89 LT 557, 67 JP 425, 19 TLR
  630, 11 Digest (Reissue) 144 349
Tyrford Properties v Secretary of State for the Environment, [1977] JPL 724 43

U

Upperton v Hampshire County Council (1965), 16 P & CR 333 417
Uttley v Todmorden Local Board of Health (1874), 44 LJCP 19, 31 LT 445, 39 JP 56, 11
    Digest (Reissue) 324 326

V

Vale Estates (Acton) Ltd v Secretary of State for the Environment (1970), 69 LGR 543, Digest
    Cont Vol D 922 . . . . .43, 44, 60
Vassily v Secretary of State for the Environment, [1976] JPL 364, 239 Estates Gazette 353 . 57
Vaughan (Viscount) v Cardiganshire Water Board (1963), 14 P & CR 193 . . 246, 247, 249
Venables v Department of Agriculture for Scotland 1932 SC 573, 11 Digest (Reissue)
    307 . . . . 348, 349, 354
Vyricherla Narayana Gajapatiraju v Revenue Divisional Officer, Vizagapatam. *See*
    Sri Raja Vyricherla Narayana Gazapatiraju Bahadur Garut v Revenue
    Divisional Officer, Vizagapatam

W

W and S (Long Eaton) Ltd v Derbyshire County Council (1976), 31 P & CR 99, 236 Estates
    Gazette 726, CA 168, 171, 175
Wahiwala v Secretary of State (1977), 75 LGR 651 . . . . 36, 60
Waitemata County v Local Government Commission, [1964] NZLR 689 50
Wakerley v St Edmundsbury Borough Council, [1977] JPL 455 . . . . 366, 367
Walkes-Hilliman v Greater London Council (1969), 20 P & CR 736 345
Walters, Brett and Pack v South Glamorgan County Council (1976), 32 PCR 111, 238
    Estates Gazette 733 . . . . 174, 176, 352, 353
War Secretary and Hurley's Contract *Re*, [1904] 1 IR 354, 11 Digest (Reissue) 308 . . 93
Ware v City of Edinburgh District Council (1976), 31 P & CR 488, 1976 SLT (Lands Tr)
    21 167
Warr (Frank) & Co Ltd v LCC, [1904] 1 KB 713, 73 LJKB 362, 90 LT 368, 68 JP 335, 52
    WR 405, 20 TLR 346, 2 LGR 723, CA, 11 Digest (Reissue) 129 . . . . . . .68, 323
Watch House, Boswinger, *Re* (1967), 66 LGR 6, sub nom. *Re* Lamplugh 19 P & CR 125,
    Digest Cont Vol C 977 . . . . 55, 56, 415
Webb v Minister of Housing and Local Government, [1965] 2 All ER 193, [1965] 1 WLR
    755, 129 JP 417, 109, Sol Jo 374, 63 LGR 250, CA, 47 Digest (Repl) 720 . . 60, 133
Webb v Stockport Corpn (1962), 13 P & CR 339 351
Wednesbury Corpn v Ministry of Housing and Local Government (No 1), [1965] 1 All ER
    186, [1965] 1 WLR 261, 129 JP 123, 108 Sol Jo 1012, 63 LGR 51, CA, 18 Digest
    (Reissue) 157 . . . . 41, 64
Wednesbury Corpn v Ministry of Housing and Local Government (No 2), [1966] 2 QB 275,
    [1965] 3 All ER 571, [1965] 3 WLR 956, 130 JP 34, 109 Sol Jo 630, 63 LGR 460, CA,
    Digest Cont Vol B 504 . . . . .40, 46, 55
Wellington (Duke) Social Club v Blyth Borough Council (1964), 15 P & CR 212 . . . 146
Wells v Chelmsford Local Board of Health (1880), 15 Ch D 108, 49 LJ Ch 827, 43 LT 378, 45
    JP 6, 29 WR 381, 11 Digest (Reissue) 263 89
Welsh National Water Development Authority v Burgess (1974), 28 P & CR 378, [1974]
    RVR 395, CA, Digest Cont Vol D 1021 . . . . 316, 326
Welton Station, Watford, Northants, *Re*, [1973] JPL 604 121
West Midland Baptist Association v Birmingham City Corpn, [1968] 2 QB 188, [1968] 1 All
    ER 205, [1968] 2 WLR 535, 132 JP 127, [1967] RVR 780, 796, 819, 19 P & CR 9, 204
    Estates Gazette 1023, CA 86, 165, 166, 169, 170, 171, 172, 173, 174, 240, 366
West Suffolk County Council v W. Rought Ltd, [1957] AC 403, [1956] 3 All ER 216, [1956] 3
    WLR 589, 120 JP 522, 100 Sol Jo 619, 54 LGR 473, 6 P & CR 362, HL, 11 Digest
    (Reissue) 147 360
Westminster Bank Ltd v Minister of Housing and Local Government, [1971] AC 508, [1970]
    1 All ER 734, [1970] 2 WLR 645, 134 JP 403, 114 Sol Jo 190, 21 P & CR 379, [1970]
    RVR 176, HL, Digest Cont Vol C 980 430
Wheeldon v Burrows (1879), 12 Ch D 31, 48 LJ Ch 853, 41 LT 327, 28 WR 196, CA, 19
    Digest (Repl) 49 284
Wheland v Minister of Housing and Local Government (unreported) 44
White v Public Works Comrs (1870), 22 LT 591 356

PAGE

Widden (G.E.) & Co v Kensington and Chelsea Royal London Borough Council, [1970] RVR 160 . . . . 351, 353, 357

Wilcock v Secretary of State for the Environment, [1975] JPL 150, 232 Estates Gazette 1385 . . . . 49, 64

William Boyer & Sons Ltd v Minister of Housing and Local Government. *See* Boyer (William) & Sons Ltd v Minister of Housing and Local Government

Williams v Cheadle and Gatley UDC (1966), 17 P & CR 153 135

Williams and Stevens v Cambridgeshire County Council, [1977] JPL 529 194

Wills v May, [1923] 1 Ch 317, [1923] All ER Rep 502, 92 LJ Ch 253, 128 LT 826, 67 Sol Jo 350, 19 Digest (Repl) 212 327

Wilrow Engineering Ltd and Stapleton v Letchworth UDC, [1973] RVR 221 183

Wilson v Liverpool City Council, [1971] 1 All ER 628, [1971] 1 WLR 302, 135 JP 168, 114 Sol Jo 932, 22 P & CR 282, [1971] RVR 45, CA, Digest Cont Vol D 1063 . . 219, 220

Wilson v Secretary of State for the Environment, [1974] 1 All ER 428, [1974] 1 WLR 1083, 138 JP 161, 117 Sol Jo 728, 71 LGR 442, 26 P & CR 232, Digest Cont Vol D 377: 34, 50, 62

Wilson v West Sussex County Council, [1963] 2 QB 764, [1963] 1 All ER 751, [1963] 2 WLR 669, 127 JP 243, 107 Sol Jo 114, 61 LGR 287, 14 P & CR 301, [1963] RVR 278, CA, 45 Digest (Repl) 332 417

Wilsons Brewery Ltd v West Yorkshire Metropolitan County Council, [1977] JPL 667 . 323

Wimpey & Co Ltd v Middlesex County Council, [1938] 3 All ER 781, 45 Digest (Repl) 369 418

Winders v Forestry Commission (1958), 9 P & CR 500 434

Wood v Secretary of State for the Environment, [1973] 2 All ER 404, [1973] 1 WLR 707, 137 JP 491, 117 Sol Jo 430, 71 LGR 339, 25 P & CR 303, Digest Cont Vol D 915 412

Wood Mitchell & Co v Stoke-on-Trent City Council, [1977] JPL 315 360

Wormald v Cole, [1954] 1 QB 614, [1954] 1 All ER 683, 98 Sol Jo 232, CA, 2 Digest (Repl) 309 327

Wrotham Park Estate Co Ltd v Parkside Homes Ltd, [1974] 2 All ER 321, [1974] 1 WLR 798, 118 Sol Jo 420, 27 P & CR 296, Digest Cont Vol D 809 . . . . . . 286, 440

Z

Zarraga v Newcastle upon Tyne Corpn (1968), 19 P & CR 609, [1968] RVR 171 . 359, 360

Zetland Lodge of Freemasons Trustees v Tamar Bridge Joint Committee (1961), 12 P & CR 326 . . . . 249, 250

Zoar Independent Church Trustees v Rochester Corpn, [1975] QB 246, [1974] 3 All ER 5, [1974] 3 WLR 417, 118 Sol Jo 698, 72 LGR 641, 29 P & CR 145, [1974] RVR 282, CA, Digest Cont Vol D 103 . . . . 171, 240, 241, 242, 244, 247, 248, 249

Development of the Law of Compensation upon Compulsory Acquisition

1 INTRODUCTORY

Historical background to compulsory acquisition

The right to acquire an interest in land compulsorily has been recognised since very early times as inherent to the sovereign power. In modern times the right has assumed increasing importance as a result, first, of the Industrial Revolution and, secondly, of the acceptance by the State of growing responsibility for the provision of public services and amenities. Although prerogative powers still exist, the right is nowadays exclusively exercised, directly or indirectly, under statutory powers.

The first substantial growth in the application of powers of compulsory acquisition accompanied the expansion of the railways in the early part of the nineteenth century. With their need for relatively straight tracks and wide curves, railways were particularly susceptible to extortion by owners of land along proposed routes, and powers of compulsory acquisition soon became essential to economic development as a corollary both to their peculiar needs and to the obligations to the public which they were forced by Parliament to assume. Similar considerations apply equally to gas, electricity, water and sewerage undertakings; all require powers of compulsion, for all involve both the acquisition of land for exclusive use for the erection of main installations, and the acquisition of lesser interests, such as rights over other people's land, for the laying of pipes and cables.

Similarly, the duties laid by Parliament upon local authorities in respect of housing, health and education, on other statutory undertakings such as water companies, and on Government Departments in relation to defence, the police, postal services, etc. all necessitate the power to acquire the requisite land without laying the authorities concerned open to extortion.

As these needs have developed, there have been corresponding changes in the statutory methods by which the power of compulsory acquisition is conferred. Prior to 1845 compulsory powers of acquisition were embodied in the special Act empowering the particular acquisition. Such an Act might be a general Act or a private Act promoted by the undertakers; in either case it identified the land to be acquired and contained special provisions, which varied according to the type of operation covered by the Act, regulating such matters as the transfer of the land and the assessment and payment of compensation.

In 1845, however, the first Lands Clauses Consolidation Act laid down a more unified acquisition procedure and a unified code of compensation; authorisation procedure remained the province either of the special Act or, in the case of services to be provided throughout the country, rather than in a specific locality or for an isolated purpose, of public general Acts; in either case, the "parent" Act incorporated the procedure and compensation provisions of the Lands Clauses Consolidation Act in whole or in part and with or without amendment.

The wide scope of public general Acts, however, has made it virtually impossible to provide for the identification of specific land to be compulsorily acquired, and authorisation procedure has accordingly been further simplified by conferring on appropriate persons or corporations, such as the responsible Ministers, local authorities and boards of nationalised industries, a more general power of compulsory acquisition subject to confirmation as required by the particular statute. In the earlier Acts the confirming authority was usually Parliament. This procedure, known as the provisional order procedure, later gave way to the compulsory purchase order procedure, in which Parliamentary sanction has been dispensed with, and the powers of confirmation conferred upon an appropriate Minister.

This procedure has now become by far the most common, and its various forms to be found in different statutes have been unified as a standard procedure of almost universal application by the Acquisition of Land (Authorisation Procedure) Act 1946. This Act originally applied mainly to acquisition by local authorities, but later Acts have substantially widened its scope to include acquisition by Government Departments.[1]

Accordingly in these cases the "parent" public general Act, in so far as it may be concerned with acquisition of land, is normally confined to laying down the purposes for which land may be acquired, leaving its identification and the procedure of acquisition to be governed by the provisions of the Acquisition of Land (Authorisation Procedure) Act 1946,[2] and the payment and assessment of compensation by the Lands Clauses Consolidation Acts, and those other Acts which have amended them (see post).

There remain, however, a few public Acts which confer a general power to acquire limited acreages of land for specified purposes, and which neither identify the land nor require further authorisation or confirmation.[3] And there also remain a few private Acts of the same nature: the most notable, of which use is still not infrequently made, is

---

[1] E.g., the Ministry of Health under the National Health Service Act 1946, and the Board of Trade under the Distribution of Industry Act 1950, and by such bodies as statutory undertakers (Town and Country Planning Act 1947, s. 37) and the British Transport Commission (Transport Act 1947, s. 8).

[2] See pp. 30 *et seq, post*, and note the modifications of the procedure there laid down where acquisition is authorised by the Community Land Act 1975, pp. 74 *et seq, post*.

[3] E.g., Admiralty (Signal Stations) Act 1815; Defence Act 1842; Customs Consolidation Act 1853.

Michael Angelo Taylor's Metropolitan Paving Act of 1817, under which land may be taken as required for the widening and improving of streets in the Metropolis.

Similarly, a number of local Acts and a few public general Acts[1] subject to the provisional order procedure survive, but the Parliamentary procedure (formerly by confirming Act) has been modified by the Statutory Orders (Special Procedure) Act 1945,[2] and a confirming Act is now not normally required. In some circumstances, however, this procedure is also applied as an additional final stage in the process of confirming compulsory purchase orders.

Moreover, there are a few cases where the compulsory purchase order procedure is outside the standard procedure of the Acquisition of Land (Authorisation Procedure) Act 1946, the most important of which is probably that covering compulsory acquisition under Part III of the Housing Act 1957.[3]

2 THE LANDS CLAUSES ACTS

The Lands Clauses Consolidation Act 1845 set out, for the first time, to apply a uniform method of assessment of compensation in the case of acquisitions authorised by subsequent Acts[4] so that it and its amendment Acts,[5] collectively known as the Lands Clauses Acts,[6] gradually became of almost universal application except where specifically varied or excluded.[7] The general effect of the Act of 1845[8] as judicially interpreted was to provide:

(i) Compensation for the land taken on the basis of its value to the *owner* though including any potential use which might enhance its value[9] to a purchaser, plus a 10 % solatium[10] in recognition of the compulsory nature of the purchase and the vendor's consequent lack of option.

(ii) Compensation for damage caused to other land in the same ownership as a result of severance from the land taken or other injurious affection resulting from the compulsory acquisition.[11]

---

[1] E.g., Military Lands Act 1892; Light Railways Acts 1896 and 1912; Railways Act 1921.

[2] See pp. 51 *et seq, post*.

[3] See pp. 77 *et seq, post*.

[4] S.1, Lands Clauses Consolidation Act 1845.

[5] Lands Clauses Consolidation Act (Amendment Act) 1860; Lands Clauses Consolidation Act 1869; Lands Clauses (Umpire) Act 1883; Lands Clauses (Taxation of Costs) Act 1895.

[6] S.23, Interpretation Act 1889.

[7] See, e.g., Housing Act 1957, Part III, p. 257, *et seq, post*.

[8] Ss. 49–63; ss. 49–57 have now been repealed by, and in part incorporated in, the Compulsory Purchase Act 1965.

[9] See, e.g., Re *South Eastern Rly Co. and LCC's Contract, South Eastern Rly Co. v LCC*, [1915] 2 Ch. 252, CA; *R. v Brown* (1867), LR 2QB 630; and *Cedar Rapids Manufacturing and Power Co. v Lacorte*, [1914] AC 569.

[10] Apparently solely the result of customary practice, the only statutory reference being to its subsequent prohibition by the Acquisition of Land (Assessment of Compensation) Act 1919, *infra*. It is, however, a practice still adopted in the U.S.A. and frequently claimed so to reduce opposition that the savings in legal costs and the costs of delay more than offset the increased cost of the land.

[11] See p. 314, *post*.

(iii) Compensation for injurious affection to other neighbouring land provided that the damage affects the land itself and not merely some personal right; arises from the *construction* rather than the authorised use of the development of the land acquired; and would, apart from the statutory authorisation, be actionable as a tort.[1]

(iv) Compensation for disturbance.[2]

3 THE ACQUISITION OF LAND (ASSESSMENT OF COMPENSATION) ACT 1919

The modern statutory basis of compensation for land taken stems, however, from the Acquisition of Land (Assessment of Compensation) Act 1919, s. 2—commonly referred to as the "1919 Rules". Their principal effect was to prohibit any extra payment in recognition of the compulsory nature of the acquisition; to substitute open market value as between willing seller and willing buyer for value to the owner; to discount any special suitability of the land for any purpose for which there is no market apart from the special needs of a particular purchaser or a public authority or which is a purpose to which the land can only be put in pursuance of statutory powers; and to give statutory recognition to such Rules as to compensation for disturbance as had already been evolved in the Courts. Originally applicable only to bodies statutorily authorised to "carry on a railway, canal, dock, water or other public undertaking" and not trading for profit,[3] the Act of 1919 has, over the years, been extended to cover practically all bodies now exercising compulsory powers of acquisition so that the Rules of section 2 have gradually superseded the code of compensation evolved on the basis of the provisions of the Lands Clauses Consolidation Acts. Although successively modified in their application by the Town and Country Planning Acts of 1944, 1947, and 1954, these modifications were discarded in 1959 and the 1919 Rules incorporated in the Town and Country Planning Act of that year subject only to such provisions as were necessary to take into account the restrictions imposed upon the user of land by the operation of planning control. With the passing of the Community Land Act 1975 these latter provisions will themselves eventually become redundant.

4 BETTERMENT

The successive modifications of these Rules in the post-war years will, however, remain of something more than mere historical interest for

---

[1] This right, now substantially extended by the Land Compensation Act 1973 (see p. 328, *post*) arose only very indirectly from the Act as a result of such cases as *Imperial Gas Light & Coke Co.* v *Broadbent* (1859), 7 HL Cas. 600; and *Ricket* v *Metropolitan Railway* (1867), LR 2 HL 175.

[2] This right also arises solely from case law; see, for example, *Jubb* v *Hull Dock Co.* (1846), 9 QB 443, a case decided upon the similar wording of the Hull Docks Act 1844: see p. 344, *post*.

[3] By virtue of s. 1 of that Act; these Rules now appear as s. 5 of the Land Compensation Act 1961—itself a consolidation measure in this respect re-enacting s. 2, Act of 1919, together with Part I of the Town and Country Planning Act 1959. These rules are of fundamental importance and are reproduced in full at p. 164, *post*.

they stemmed in essence from the search for a satisfactory method by which the State might recover from the private landowner such increase in the value of his land (commonly referred to as "betterment") as is attributable to public expenditure on the development of neighbouring land. The political controversy which has recently been, and may well continue to be, at the root of frequent and sometimes drastic changes in the law governing compensation probably arises less from dispute as to the theoretical justice of the State's entitlement to recoupment than from the formidable practical difficulties in devising an acceptable means. In the first place, it is seldom possible in practice to define with any precision either what land has benefited by any particular public expenditure or to what extent—for betterment can clearly be a direct or indirect result of neighbouring development and can arise as much from private as from public development; so, indeed, can "worsenment", a problem which until recent years has received practically no attention at all.[1]

The search for a solution to this problem is, however, of very much older origin than any conflict between capitalism and socialism and it has long been accepted that when public works directly add to the value of identifiable property, owners should contribute to their cost in proportion to the benefit received. That is the principle underlying the large number of statutes, both general and local, which empower the imposition of sewerage and drainage rates and the levying of contributions by frontagers upon the public adoption of private streets. It is of very ancient origin[2] with a continuous history to modern times.

On the other hand, the history of the recoupment of indirect benefit arising from public expenditure, though also enjoying a respectable lineage has lacked both consistency and continuity. The principle seems to have been first adopted as long ago as 1662 in an Act[3] which levied a direct charge on owners of properties benefiting from the widening of certain London streets. Although similar provisions were included in the Acts providing for the rebuilding of London after the Great Fire[4] recoupment by direct levy does not reappear until the first quarter of the present century.[5]

The attempt to recover betterment was not, however, wholly abandoned, for a few Acts of the early 19th Century[6] provided that where land is compulsorily acquired any increase in the value of land in the same ownership resulting from the proposed development of the land

---

[1] I.e., the injurious affection to neighbouring property not in the same ownership as the land taken. See now, however, Land Compensation Act 1973, Parts I and II, p. 328, *post*. It is worth bearing in mind, however, that since both betterment and worsenment, whatever the cause, are reflected in rateable values, recoupment is in fact effected not all that inefficiently by the rating system.

[2] See, e.g., the Statutes of Sewers 1427 and 1531.

[3] 14 Cha. 2 c.2. The levy, which could be either a capital sum or an annual rent was in the event of disagreement to be determined by a specially empanelled jury.

[4] Act for the Rebuilding of London 1667; Rebuilding of London Act 1670.

[5] Housing, Town Planning, &c., Act 1909; Town Planning Act 1925; Town and Country Planning Act 1932.

[6] E.g., General Turnpike Act for Scotland 1831; Drainage (Ireland) Act 1842; Defence Act 1860.

taken is to be deducted from the compensation payable. Such is the principle of "set-off". It has been a feature of the Housing Acts since 1879,[1] and following widespread adoption in Private Acts and a few Public Acts, is now formally established by the Land Compensation Act 1961.[2]

The Uthwatt Report

Meanwhile the search for a more comprehensive method for recovering betterment continued, and in January 1941 the Uthwatt Committee was appointed with the following terms of reference:

> "To make an objective analysis of the subject of the payment of compensation and recovery of betterment in respect of public control and use of land:
> To advise, as a matter of urgency, what steps should be taken now or before the end of the war to prevent the work of reconstruction thereafter being prejudiced. In this connection the Committee are asked:
> to consider (a) possible means of stabilising the value of land required for development or redevelopment, and (b) any extension or modification of powers to enable such land to be acquired by the public on an equitable basis:
> to examine the merits and demerits of the methods considered: and to advise what alterations of the existing law would be necessary to enable them to be adopted."

The Committee reported in September 1942, and concluded that whereas in rural areas planning inevitably involved the sterilisation from building of considerable areas of land, in urban areas it tended to involve the demolition and replanning of already built-up areas. Having reviewed and found wanting the earlier attempts to recover betterment by set-off or the levying of a direct charge, the Committee concluded that in urban areas the only solution was to take for the community, by a system of site value rating, some fixed proportion of any increase in the value of land without attempting to analyse the causes to which it might be due. These recommendations were, however, never adopted, and the details are now of purely academic interest.

The Committee's recommendations in respect of rural areas, however, were to form the basis of the compensation provisions of the Town and Country Planning Act 1947. Their fundamental principle was the limitation of compensation to the value of the land in its existing use (i.e., ignoring any potential development value). Although the provisions of the 1947 Act relating to compensation for land compulsorily acquired were subsequently amended[3] and eventually repealed[4] it is to their underlying principle of "existing use" value as the basis of compensation for the compulsory acquisition of land to which the latest legislation will eventually return.[5] Despite the intervening amendments and repeals, certain aspects of the 1947 compensation provisions

---

[1] The Artisans and Labourers' Dwellings Act (1868) (Amendment) Act 1879.
[2] In this respect the Act of 1961 re-enacts the Town and Country Planning Act 1959, Part I, Sch. I; see the Act of 1961, s. 7 and Part I, Sch. I, pp. 219 *et seq*, *post*.
[3] Town and Country Planning Acts 1953 and 1954.
[4] Town and Country Planning Act 1959.
[5] Community Land Act 1975; but only after the as yet unforeseeable Second Appointed Day.

remained throughout as the basis of compensation for refusal of planning permission for "new" development.[1] At no period, therefore, have
they completely lost importance.

In the meantime, however, the Uthwatt Committee had submitted
an interim report on which was based the Town and Country Planning
Act of 1944, the compensation provisions[2] of which were, however,
enacted as a purely temporary measure and were repealed with effect
from 5 August 1947, by the Town and Country Planning Act 1947.

In their final report the Uthwatt Committee concluded that the main
obstacle to proper planning in undeveloped rural areas was the necessity of paying compensation for loss of development value, and the fact
that the cost was substantially increased by what are known as *floating
value* and *shifting value*.

FLOATING VALUE derives from the fact that the potential value of land for
development is by nature speculative; the expectation of future
development is spread over a much wider area than is in fact likely to be
developed. If, therefore, land is compulsorily acquired piecemeal,
compensation is claimed in respect of each plot on the assumption that
the "float" would in fact have settled on that particular plot, so that the
aggregate compensation, so it is argued, greatly exceeds the value of the
land taken as a whole.

SHIFTING VALUE expresses the effect of the artificial reduction in the total
supply of land for development as a result of planning controls. The
value of land designated for development is therefore increased at the
expense of land on which development is prohibited. The net result is
that values shift from one plot of land to the other, though they do not
alter in total. Nevertheless, compensation tends to be claimed on the
basis that but for the restrictions of planning control the value of the
land which is not to be developed would be the same as that of the land
designated for development. Once again, total compensation is likely
substantially to exceed the total value of the land considered as a whole.

It is obvious, however, that none of these difficulties affecting floating
and shifting values arises if the land is in a single ownership, and it was
this line of thought that the Committee pursued in framing their
recommendations. They accordingly proposed not land nationalisation
but the acquisition by the State of the full development rights in land, to
be achieved by absolute prohibition of development without consent
and payment of compensation for loss of existing development potential
out of a predetermined global fund in proportion to the development
value of individual plots.

[1] See p. 394, *post*.
[2] These provided for the assessment of compensation on the basis of prices ruling at 31 March
1939 on the assumption that the land was in the same state on that date as at the date of service of
the notice to treat and that the interest to be acquired subsisted on 31 March 1939 although
additional compensation might be payable in respect of improvements carried out between 31
March 1939 and the service of the notice to treat. Owner-occupiers were entitled to 130 % of the
March 1939 value in recognition of the need to rehouse themselves at the greatly enhanced prices
of the open market. Notice to treat is the notice required to be served by acquiring authorities
(after they have been authorised to acquire the land) requiring owners to state their estate or
interest therein and their claims in respect thereof. For details see pp. 66, *et seq*, *post*.

5 TOWN & COUNTRY PLANNING ACT 1947

These, then, were the principles underlying the compensation provisions of the Act of 1947 which, following the other recommendations of the Uthwatt Committee, established the basis of modern planning legislation which, subject to only relatively minor amendments, has since been extended and consolidated in the Town and Country Planning Act of 1971. With these planning provisions this book is not primarily concerned, but despite their somewhat chequered history, it is still necessary, in order to understand subsequent legislative changes and the basis of the Community Land Act 1975, to consider the compensation provisions of the 1947 Act in greater detail.

The total value of the then existing potential development value of land was fixed, perhaps somewhat arbitrarily, at £300 million, from which global fund compensation for loss of development value was to be paid.[1] Claims to compensation (which had to be submitted by 30 June 1949) were to be based upon the difference between the "unrestricted"[2] value of the land as at 1 July 1948 and the restricted value of the same land on the same date calculated upon the assumption that planning permission would be granted for any of the developments specified in the 3rd Schedule to the Act[3] but for no other. Both restricted and unrestricted values were to be calculated by reference to prices current at the beginning of January 1947 but on the basis of the "market value" provisions of Rules 1 to 4 of the Act of 1919.[4]

In the anticipated event of total claims exceeding the global sum of £300 million, accepted claims were to be reduced proportionately.[5] The Uthwatt Committee had proposed that land required for future development by private enterprise should be acquired by a central planning authority (established under the Act as the Central Land Board) and leased to developers on suitable terms. Although this is the concept to which the latest legislation returns[6] the Act of 1947 merely *empowered* the Central Land Board to acquire such land compulsorily, but if they did so they were required to dispose of it as directed by the Minister.[7] In practice, however, these powers were sparingly used, and

---

[1] Although there was a separate Act for Scotland, this global fund of £300 million was to cover claims from Scotland as well as from England and Wales and no claim was to be considered where the "development value" averaged less than £20 per acre or was less than one-tenth of the restricted value: Town and Country Planning Act 1947, ss. 58 and 63.

[2] I.e., the value of the land (at 1947 prices) including its potential for development.

[3] Now reproduced in an amended form as the 8th Schedule to the Town and Country Planning Act 1971, and reproduced in full in the Appendix, p. 456, *post*.

[4] See p. 164, *post*; rules 5 and 6, having no relevance in this connection, were omitted; Town and Country Planning Act 1947, s. 62.

[5] In fact, the White Paper, Cmnd. 8699, "The Town and Country Planning Act 1947 and the Town and Country Planning (Scotland) Act 1947—Amendment of Financial Provisions", presented in November 1952, estimated that agreed claims totalled about £350 million as compared with the Uthwatt Committee's estimate that due o the effect of *floating* and *shifting* values the total of individual claims might exceed the global figure by between 200 % and 300 %.

[6] See the White Paper "Land", Cmnd. 5730 of 1974 and p. 22, *post* and the Community Land Act 1975, pp. 23 and 296, *post*.

[7] Town and Country Planning Act 1947, s. 43.

for the most part private development was carried out on the basis of private purchase subject, in effect, to the repurchase by the developer of the nationalised development rights by the payment of a "development charge" assessed by the Central Land Board on the basis of the full increase in the value of the land resulting from the proposed development.[1]

The Central Land Board having acquired all the development rights in land, it follows that the residual value of the interest in land remaining to the owner would, in theory at any rate,[2] be confined to its value for its existing use[3] and this became the basis of compensation upon compulsory acquisition. At the same time compensation by reference to 1939 prices was abolished and once again the new code was enacted by modification of the 1919 Rules. The reinstatement provisions of Rule 5,[4] however, being in themselves an exception to the normal rule, remained unaffected by changes in the general basis of compensation.

Moreover, the planning provisions of Parts II and III of the Act[5] necessitated further provisions governing special cases where planning control affected the application of the general rule. The most important of these special provisions in the present context was that which recognised that the threat of future compulsory acquisition arising from the designation of land for some public purpose in development plans would itself depreciate the value of the land in the open market. Such property might well become difficult to sell and it might also become improvident even to effect minor improvements, however desirable they might be from the point of view of the economic use of the land in the meantime. The Act of 1947 accordingly provided that any depreciation in value directly attributable to such designation should be ignored when calculating the compensation payable upon eventual acquisition—a principle which has remained a feature of subsequent legislation.[6]

---

[1] I.e., 100 % of the "development value". The Uthwatt Committee, in considering their scheme for developed or urban land recommended that the proposed levy should not exceed 75 % of any increase in the value of the land on the ground that to charge 100 % of such increase would remove all incentive to private development. There is a considerable body of opinion that attributes the unsatisfactory working of the Act of 1947 in this respect to the rejection of this principle and the lack of incentive that a development charge of 100 % inevitably created. Unfortunately the unpopularity which the imposition of both planning control and development charge was bound to incur was exacerbated by the immediate post-war necessity of obtaining a building certificate—i.e. for the allocation of scarce building materials in accordance with the Government's view of national priorities. It was perhaps not surprising that after five and a half years of war such a combination of controls was felt to be excessive.

[2] In practice, "existing use value" offered no incentive to landowners to make their land available for development and prospective developers were compelled to offer more. Thus developed a "two-tier" price system (i.e., one price for land sold privately and a lower price paid by acquiring authorities by way of compensation)—a major cause of dissatisfaction with the working of the Act and one which may well apply when the Community Land Act 1975 is fully operative; see p. 25, *infra*.

[3] Subject, of course, to the permitted development of the 3rd Schedule to the Act (cf. 8th Schedule to the Act of 1971), Appendix p. 456, *post*.

[4] In certain cases involving specialised buildings compensation has long been based upon the cost of replacement: see pp. 165 and 238, *post*.

[5] The corresponding parts of the Town and Country Planning Act 1971 are Part II (Development Plans) and Parts III to V (Control of Development).

[6] Land Compensation Act 1961, s. 9, p. 176, *post*.

The Act of 1947 also recognised the hardship that in certain cases can arise from refusal of planning permission—e.g., for the development of land rendered valueless for agriculture or horticulture by the restrictions imposed by surrounding development; provision[1] was therefore made by which an owner, by serving a "purchase notice", could require the acquisition of the land on the grounds that it had been "rendered incapable of reasonably beneficial use".

Apart from further purely temporary or transitional provisions the Act of 1947 also contained special provisions in relation to compensation for the compulsory acquisition of requisitioned land and of war-damaged land. Although these latter provisions are still in force[2] such cases are now rare and will not be dealt with in this work.

In view of the continued housing shortage and the extension of security of tenure it is perhaps of more than passing interest, however, that the framers of the Act believed that the inflated values attributable to vacant possession would be confined to the immediate post-war period, and included temporary provisions designed to reduce their impact upon the compensation payable upon compulsory acquisition of such property.[3]

6 THE TOWN AND COUNTRY PLANNING ACTS 1953 AND 1954

In November 1952 the Government published, in a White Paper,[4] a summary of the practical difficulties which had arisen in the working of the Act of 1947, and of their proposals for amendment. The criticisms of the working of the 1947 provisions in practice may be summarised as follows:

(i) The obligation to satisfy all claims on the £300 million fund[5] by 1 July 1953[6] would be inflationary.

(ii) Some of these payments would be to people who in fact had suffered no loss at all as a result of the acquisition of development rights.[7]

(iii) Once the fund had been distributed, it would be extremely difficult to make subsequent financial changes, however desirable.

[1] Town and Country Planning Act 1947, s. 19: now re-enacted as the Town and Country Planning Act 1971, s. 180: see pp. 114 et seq, post.

[2] See the Land Compensation Act 1961, s. 13.

[3] Town and Country Planning Act 1947, s. 52. The effect of these provisions was to confine the vacant possession premium to its effect upon a notional lease under which the property was deemed to be held and which would expire on 1 January 1954.

[4] Cmd. 8699—Town and Country Planning Act 1947 and Town and Country Planning (Scotland) Act 1947: Amendment of Financial Provisions.

[5] The White Paper estimated that agreed claims would total about £350 million. Cf. the estimate of the Uthwatt Committee that the total of individual claims might exceed the global figures by between 200 % and 300 %.

[6] The date was to be fixed by a Treasury Scheme under the Town and Country Planning Act 1947, s. 58. By ss. 58 (3) and 65 (2) it was to be not later than 1 July 1953.

[7] E.g., those who, despite the incidence of development charge, had sold their property for a high price; or whose express purpose was to avoid, and as far as possible prevent, development on their land.

(iv) Development charges had removed all incentive to private landowners to make their land available for development, so that the "existing use value" price basis had either the effect of keeping land ripe for development off the market, or it broke down altogether, with the result that developers had to pay a higher price to which had to be added the development charge.[1] Private development was therefore inhibited, and only carried out at all at an inflated cost.[2]

(v) In practice, the public, unable to grasp the principle involved in separating development value from the value of the land itself, had come to regard the development charge not as the purchase price for an additional right, but as a particularly onerous tax, especially in the case of the owner wishing to develop his own land.[3]

In consequence of these defects, the Government in the first place resolved to abolish the development charge altogether[4] and, instead of paying out the £300 million fund, to pay compensation (subject to certain exceptions) as and when development of the land was prevented or severely restricted by refusal of planning permission. These two proposals were effected immediately by the Town and Country Planning Act 1953;[5] this Act also made necessary the approval of the Central Land Board to assignments of claims under Part VI of the Act of 1947[6] as a first step towards attaching such claims permanently to the land in respect of which they arose.[7] It was left to the following Parliamentary session to introduce the much more complicated Bill[8] to enact a new code of compensation, and to effect other amendments consequent upon the overall provisions of the Act of 1953.

The proposals with regard to compensation were summarised in the White Paper as designed "to use the once-for-all reckoning of the 1947 Act as setting the upper limit of compensation payable for loss of

[1] Note, however, the powers of the Central Land Board to acquire land compulsorily to prevent a sale at a price above existing use value: the Town and Country Planning Act 1947, s. 43. Cf. the somewhat similar situation arising under the Community Land Act 1975, p. 25, *post*.

[2] In practice, development, particularly on agricultural land, often results in a diminution of value to other land retained for agriculture (e.g., from the increased prevalence of damage by trespass) over and above what can be recovered by way of compensation for severance or injurious affection (see p. 314, *post*), a sale for development at the same price that can be obtained for agricultural purposes, therefore, in many cases results in a definite financial loss.

[3] This was particularly so in the period immediately following the passage of the Act of 1947 when the Central Land Board required payment of the development charge in full notwithstanding a developer's outstanding claim on the £300 million fund. Later, however, the Central Land Board agreed to set off, against claims on the fund, up to 80 % of the development charge.

[4] Amongst other alternatives considered was a substantial reduction in the rate of development charge (paras. 22–25 of the White Paper (Cmd. 8699)). It was rejected, however, on the ground that the amount of reduction would be arbitrary; it would have to be substantial with the result that there would be a considerable deficit to be borne by the Exchequer in meeting claims upon the £300 million fund; that it would still add to the cost of development, particularly where there was no claim on the £300 million fund against which it could be set off; and that it had proved "too unreliable an instrument to act as the lynch-pin of a permanent settlement".

[5] This Act abolished development charge in respect of all development commenced after 17 November 1952, the date of introduction of the Parliamentary Bill.

[6] I.e., claims on the £300 million fund and frequently referred to as "Part VI claims": under the Town and Country Planning Act 1947, s. 64, these claims were assignable as personal property.

[7] Subsequently achieved by the Town and Country Planning Act 1954, s. 60.

[8] Subsequently the Town and Country Planning Act 1954, which applied to compulsory acquisition in pursuance of notices to treat served on or after 1 January 1955.

development value"—i.e., compensation for planning restrictions[1] would not exceed the value of the claim ranking for payment from the fund, and compensation for compulsory acquisition would be based on the current value of the land for its existing use at the time of the acquisition plus any unexpended part of the claim.[2] Such in fact was the basis of compensation under Parts II and III of the Act of 1954. Part II dealt with compensation for refusal or modification of planning permission, and re-enacted in the Act of 1971,[3] it remains the current law.[4] Part III dealt with compensation for compulsory acquisition and has been successively amended.[5]

Between 1 July 1948 and 1 January 1955[6] there had inevitably been very many cases of compulsory acquisition, refusals and modifications of planning permission, development subject to development charge, dispositions of land at existing use value and the disposal of the value of the claims as personal property (thereby divorcing them from the land to which they related). In all these cases the parties concerned would inevitably have relied upon the promise that Part VI claims would be duly met.[7] Unless special provisions were made, those concerned would, therefore, be gravely prejudiced by the decision that these claims should not, after all, be paid out, and that, despite the fact that many development charges had already been paid, no such payments would be called for from other property owners in the future. Accordingly the Act of 1954 contained a number of provisions designed to place persons affected in a position comparable with that of other landowners involved in similar transactions after the enactment of the new proposals. In effect, the Act took the established Part VI claim as the starting point, made certain adjustments to rectify anomalies arising from the new proposals, amalgamated all claims subsisting in the same plot of land, and "credited" the result not to any particular person, but to the land to which the claims related. Further provision was made to "compensate", where appropriate, for any of the eventualities mentioned above which had already occurred, and any payment made was deducted from the amount credited to the land concerned. Finally, it might be necessary, when the land in respect of which

[1] This decision was based upon the proposition that it would be reasonable to pay compensation for loss of development value accruing prior to the coming into operation of the Act of 1947, but not in respect of that accruing thereafter; in the latter case the sums involved would cripple effective planning and in the future purchasers would be able to safeguard themselves by ensuring that planning permission would be forthcoming, or that a claim on the fund would be available before paying more than the existing use value of the land. Similarly, purchases between 1947 and 1 January 1955 would have taken place in the full knowledge of the limits of compensation under the £300 million fund. (See para. 31, Cmd. 8699.)
[2] The alternative compensation based upon current *market* value was rejected on the grounds of cost to local authorities, unfairness to owners the use of whose land was restricted to low-value development of a comparatively unprofitable nature, and the belief that since 1947 purchasers had been, and in the future would be, safeguarded as described in the previous note.
[3] Town and Country Planning Act 1971, Part VII.
[4] See p. 394, *post.*
[5] I. e., by the Town and Country Planning Act 1959, re-enacted in the Land Compensation Act 1961, p. 14, *infra*; and the Community Land Act 1975, p. 23, *infra.*
[6] I.e., between the appointed day of the Act of 1947 and the coming into force of the Act of 1954.
[7] Under the Town and Country Planning Act 1947 these payments would have been paid out by 1 July 1953, with interest from 1 July 1948.

the original claim was made had become subdivided or subject to additional interests, to apportion the resulting balance. What was left was the "unexpended balance of established development value", and that was the increment to be added, where it existed, to the "existing use value" of the land for the purpose of determining compensation for compulsory acquisition, and to which compensation for refusal of planning permission is still confined.

These claims on the £300 million fund were henceforth to be known as "established claims" and although the provisions governing the adjustments required in order to arrive at this "unexpended balance of established development value" were often complex and took up the greater part of the Act[1] at this distance in time detailed knowledge of their application is rarely likely to be required.[2] Such consideration of these provisions as seems likely to be necessary in the future is therefore confined to the section dealing with the only aspect of compensation to which the unexpended balance of established development value continues to be relevant, viz, compensation for planning decisions restricting "new" development.[3]

Criticisms of the Town and Country Planning Act 1954

As has been seen, the Town and Country Planning Act of 1954 deliberately preserved the "once-and-for-all" reckoning of the Act of 1947 as the basis of compensation for compulsory acquisition as well as for refusal of planning permission. By thus perpetuating a two-tier price system in which the gap between the price which land with development (or redevelopment) potential would fetch in the open market and the existing use value which remained the basis of compensation if it were compulsorily acquired, the Act perhaps inevitably became the target for a growing volume of criticism. Unfortunately that gap was not always appreciably narrowed by the addition to existing use value of the unexpended balance of established development value. In the first place, however adequate the agreed claim in 1947–8, it remained tied to 1947 money values which even the relatively modest inflation by contemporary standards had in the course of the ensuing decade significantly reduced. Moreover, planning being anything but an exact science it is hardly surprising that development has not in fact taken place precisely as then envisaged. Thus by 1959 the high potential development value of some areas of land might only have accrued fairly recently and could not therefore have been reflected in claims agreed in 1947.[4]

[1] The relevant sections are now re-enacted in the Town and Country Planning Act 1971, Part VII.

[2] For a detailed description see *Corfield on Compensation and the Town and Country Planning Act 1959*, pp. 38 *et seq*.

[3] See p. 394, *post*.

[4] N.B. Although the Town and Country Planning Act 1954, s. 35, made it possible, where no claim had been made under the Town and Country Planning Act 1947, Part VI to take into account what that claim would have been, had it in fact been made, it had still to be based upon the conditions ruling in 1947. It could in no way assist the person whose land had since acquired development value if, in the light of conditions ruling in 1947, such possibilities could not then have been reasonably foreseen.

Furthermore, with the passage of time the loss inflicted upon the owner of land compulsorily acquired ceases to be merely a comparative loss in the sense that existing use value truly represents the value of the use to which he is putting his land; it becomes an absolute loss where that owner has himself been a purchaser in the open market and has accordingly had to pay a price reflecting development value.

Similarly, if the person compulsorily deprived of his property at existing use value can only replace it by purchasing equivalent property possessing development potential which will inevitably be reflected in the price, he is bound to be out of pocket[1] and will almost certainly feel aggrieved, especially if his original property had at least equivalent development potential which had in effect been confiscated.

A further grievance arose from the fact that having imposed a depreciated value for the purposes of purchase, the "State" continued to insist upon full market valuation for the purposes of estate duty.[2]

These criticisms were further underlined by the report of the Franks Committee on Administrative Tribunals and Inquiries[3] and by the increasing reluctance of some local authorities to incur the odium which, in consequence of the basis of compensation, so often attached to compulsory purchase orders. They incurred even greater odium when, finding themselves with a surplus of land, they were compelled to sell at full market value even where the purchaser was the original owner.

To meet these criticisms the Government decided that the two-tier system must go and that the only practical means of achieving that end was the re-enactment of market value as the basis of compensation for compulsory acquisition. Part I of the Town and Country Planning Act of 1959 was the result: it established the current law[4] on this subject and despite the ultimate return to existing use value as the basis of compensation envisaged in the latest legislation[5] the 1959 provisions seem likely to continue in operation for some years to come.

7 THE TOWN AND COUNTRY PLANNING ACT 1959 AND THE LAND COMPENSATION ACT 1961

Although, as the source of the current code of compensation now consolidated in the Land Compensation Act 1961, the provisions of the

[1] Cf. "The General Rule", p. 161, *post*.

[2] In the event of compulsory acquisition within five years of inheritance the Inland Revenue did, however, allow a scaling down of probate valuation in accordance with the compensation received.

[3] The Committee's terms of reference particularly referred to the procedure for the compulsory purchase of land: they included no reference to the measure of compensation. Nevertheless, in making their recommendations and after emphasising that this aspect was beyond their remit, they felt impelled to add "But we cannot emphasise too strongly the extent to which these financial considerations (i.e., the extent to which compensation fell short of market value) affect the matters with which we have to deal. Whatever changes in procedure are made, dissatisfaction is, because of this, bound to remain".

[4] Re-enacted in The Land Compensation Act 1961.

[5] The Community Land Act 1975, the provisions of which are due to come into force in stages—on enactment, on the 1st Appointed Day, on the Relevant Date and, *in toto*, on the 2nd Appointed Day. It is only in the final stage that the basis of compensation is significantly altered: p. 305, *post*.

Act of 1959 are considered in detail in chapter 5 it is necessary, in order to trace the further developments effected by the Land Compensation Act of 1973 and the Community Land Act of 1975, to outline their effect here. In doing so, however, it will be convenient henceforth to refer to the consolidating Act of 1961 rather than to the original sections of the now-superseded compensation provisions of the Act of 1959.

The basic problem underlying these provisions was, of course, the reconciliation of the concept of market value as defined in the Act of 1919[1] with modern planning legislation and control. Market value depends, *inter alia*, upon development potential. Compulsory acquisition removes the prospects of any development other than that for which the land is actually acquired. A means of establishing the price at which the land would sell in the open market but for the acquisition was therefore an essential corollary to the restoration of market value as the basis of compensation. Much of the Act of 1961 is therefore devoted to prescribing the assumptions to be made in regard to the grant of planning permission when assessing the market value of land being compulsorily acquired.

PLANNING ASSUMPTIONS

The relevant provisions of the Land Compensation Act 1961[2] are considered in detail in chapter 5.[3] For the purposes of this chapter their effect may be broadly summarised by saying that the development for which planning permission is to be assumed is such development as might reasonably have been expected to be permitted had there been no question of the land being acquired by a body possessing powers of compulsory purchase. Planning permission is therefore to be assumed for:

(i) Any development for which planning permission has already been granted at the date of service of the notice to treat.

(ii) The development intended to be carried out on the land by the authority acquiring it.

(iii) The development specified in the Town and Country Planning Act 1971, Schedule 8.[4]

(iv) Development conforming with the current development plan.

If none of these heads provides an adequate guide, as, for instance, where no planning permission already attaches to land that is being acquired for a purpose for which there is little or no market demand (e.g., public open space) and for which it is allocated in the current development plan, the owner may apply to the local planning authority for a certificate stating what planning permission would have been granted if the land were not being acquired by a body possessing powers of compulsory purchase.[5]

[1] The Acquisition of Land (Assessment of Compensation) Act 1919, s. 2, now Land Compensation Act 1961, s. 5, p. 164, *post*.

[2] Land Compensation Act 1961, Part II, ss. 14–16 and Part III, ss. 17–22.

[3] For details see p. 185 *et seq, post*; and for a summary see pp. 216 *et seq, post*.

[4] This Schedule replaces the Town and Country Planning Act 1947, Sch. 3, and is reproduced in full in the Appendix, pp. 456, *et seq, post*.

[5] For these "certificates of appropriate alternative development" see the Land Compensation Act 1961, Part III, and pp. 204 *et seq, post*.

MODIFICATION OF THE 1919 RULES

Having dealt with the determination of what development might reasonably have been permitted had the land not been compulsorily acquired, the Act[1] proceeded to modify the application of the 1919 Rules, and in subsequent sections to amend certain provisions of other Acts which affect the assessment of compensation. These modifications may be summarised as under:

"BETTERMENT" AND SET-OFF

(a) In many cases involving compulsory acquisition, the value of the land being acquired will be enhanced by the development to be carried out around it. It would clearly be inequitable for local authorities to be called upon to pay for any such enhanced value that arises solely from their own proposals for the development of adjoining land. Obviously this problem does not arise where a plot of land is being acquired from a single owner for some "isolated" purpose, such as the erection of a school or a hospital, or even a housing estate, where no other development is contemplated in the immediate vicinity. If, on the other hand, the land is acquired from a number of different owners, or is acquired as part of a wider scheme involving acquisition at different dates, the value of any particular plot may be affected by the development to be carried out on the land of neighbouring owners being acquired contemporaneously or by the development, proposed or already carried out, as part of a scheme designed to be carried out in stages, whether such land is acquired from one or more landowners. The Act accordingly provides[2] that, where land is acquired in pursuance of a wider scheme,[3] assessment of compensation is to ignore the effect on the value of the land being acquired of the development, proposed or executed, on adjoining land. In other words, if land is acquired from, say, three adjoining landowners, A, B, and C, under a compulsory purchase order for a housing estate, A's land will be valued as land fit for housing, but that value will not be affected one way or the other by the fact that B's land may be scheduled to carry shops or C's sewage disposal works. Similarly, if the land is being acquired as part of a site for a new town, no account will be taken of the fact that adjoining land is intended to become the town centre, etc.

(b) It may equally be the case that, where an owner of land being compulsorily acquired owns other adjacent land, its value may also be enhanced either by the development being carried out on the land acquired from that person, or by the other development involved in the scheme as a whole. In such cases the Act[4] provides that such increase in value of adjacent land shall be set off against the compensation payable,

---

[1] Land Compensation Act 1961, ss. 6 and 7, and Sch. 1 (formerly the Town and Country Planning Act 1959, s. 9).

[2] Land Compensation Act 1961, Sch. 1, Part I.

[3] I.e., the scheme covered by the compulsory purchase order as a whole, schemes of redevelopment in relation to comprehensive development or action areas; town expansion schemes under the Town Development Act 1952, and the development of New Towns: Land Compensation Act 1961, s. 6 and Sch. I, and see pp. 220 *et seq, post.*

[4] Land Compensation Act 1961, s. 7: pp. 220 *et seq, post.*

thereby retaining the principle of set-off contained in many of the earlier enactments authorising compulsory acquisition.[1]

In the event of such adjacent land, in respect of which set-off provisions have operated, being itself compulsorily acquired at some later date, provision is made to ensure that neither the owner nor the acquiring authority is prejudiced by the set-off provisions of the relevant Act operating twice in respect of the same "betterment".[2]

(c) In probably the great majority of cases, the knowledge that a plot of land is likely to be compulsorily acquired has an immediately depressing effect on market value: to take such a factor into account in calculating compensation would, to a large extent, defeat the purpose of the return to market value as the basis of assessment. Accordingly, the Act provides that any depreciation in the value of the land so caused is to be ignored.[3]

A further problem that had become increasingly pressing since the passing of the Town and Country Planning Act 1947 for which the Act of 1959 provided was that which arises where long-term planning proposals virtually resulted in the land concerned becoming unmarketable. The most common example is that of highway proposals involving the demolition of sound houses which the owners are forced to vacate, e.g., on change of employment, before the land is actually required. In the meantime such land was said to suffer from "market blight". In the case of resident owner-occupiers[4] and the owners of small businesses[5] and land forming part of an agricultural unit, the Act accordingly conferred upon owner-occupiers the right to serve upon the authority which would ultimately be responsible for acquiring the land a "blight notice" requiring that authority to acquire forthwith and on the same market value basis as would have applied had the acquisition been initiated by them under the authority of a compulsory purchase order.[7]

Criticisms of the Town and Country Planning Act 1959 and the Land Compensation Act 1961

The basic criticism of the working of the code of compensation outlined above may be summarised by saying that whereas the previous code had resulted in financial hardship to landowners deprived of the full

[1] Land Compensation Act 1961, s. 7: if the acquisition is effected under a "corresponding" or local enactment (*ibid*, s. 8(5) and (7)) containing set-off provisions it is those provisions rather than those of the 1961 Act that govern the deductions to be made from the compensation payable for the interest acquired: see pp. 234–5, *post*.

[2] *Ibid*, s. 8(1) and (2).

[3] *Ibid*, s. 9, p. 176, *post*, and cf. the similar provisions of the Town and Country Planning Act 1947, p. 9, *supra*.

[4] The definition of resident owner-occupier includes a resident lessee provided at least three years of his term remains unexpired: Town and Country Planning Act 1959, s. 43, now the Town and Country Planning Act 1971, s. 203.

[5] Defined by reference to the rateable value of the property.

[6] For details of the blight notice procedure see pp. 120 *et seq, post*.

[7] These provisions, re-enacted in the Town and Country Planning Act 1971, ss. 192–207, have been further extended by later enactments, notably the Land Compensation Act 1973, Part V, ss. 68–76, and the Community Land Act 1975, s. 22(6): see pp. 137 *et seq*, and p. 142, *post*.

market value of their land, the new (and still current)[1] code resulted in excessive costs to local and other public authorities, and in some cases spectacular fortunes to landowners.

In the initial stages the most sensational prices causing public disquiet and political controversy arose in the more prosperous areas (particularly around London). In many cases, for example, local planning authorities had endeavoured to restrict further peripheral development by the creation of Green Belts, but were later forced by pressure of demand to review their proposals and consider releasing such pockets of land as could be developed without serious detriment to the function of the Green Belt. In such cases the supply of development land having been so severely restricted in areas where, by definition, demand was intense, the prices realised for these relatively small releases of land were inevitably high and in some cases almost astronomical. With market value as the basis of compensation such prices were also, of course, reflected in the compensation payable by local etc. authorities for land required for public purposes—including, of course, local authority housing. Similarly the planning permissions to be assumed, and particularly the effect of certificates of appropriate alternative development[2] resulted, in built-up areas, in very substantial compensation even for undeveloped land required for wholly unremunerative public purposes, e.g., for public open space, schools, hospitals, public conveniences, etc.

It is probably true to say, however, that public criticism was, at any rate initially, more particularly concerned with the alleged social evil of vast fortunes accruing to those who merely happened to own land ripe for development but who had done nothing to "earn" such enhanced values. Perhaps naturally, if somewhat illogically, public indignation was even greater in the case of fortunes accruing to those who had acquired their land relatively cheaply on a speculative basis in the hope that planning permission for profitable development would eventually be forthcoming. While such spectacular fortunes were no doubt offset to some extent by those who burnt their fingers and found planning permission unobtainable, few such deals received publicity, and in any case with land prices as a whole rising fairly consistently over the ensuing decade even the unlucky speculator probably suffered little serious financial loss.

In the meanwhile, however, the criticism that these high land prices imposed an unjustifiable burden on public authorities and indeed all those in the market for new houses, offices, factories, etc. gathered strength—the argument being, of course, that if development land could be purchased more cheaply then the price of the end product (criticism being particularly concentrated on the cost of houses) would inevitably fall.[3]

---

[1] Note that the 1959 provisions incorporated in the Land Compensation Act 1961 remain in force until the day to be appointed by the Secretary of State as the Second Appointed Day under the Community Land Act 1975, p. 23, *infra* and pp. 305 *et seq, post*.

[2] P. 15, *supra*.

[3] In the authors' view this argument is of doubtful validity. The price of houses is governed by the interaction of total demand and total supply in any particular area. If new houses are built on land

8 THE LAND COMMISSION ACT 1967

With these criticisms in mind the Labour Party fought the general election of 1964 on the basis of a proposal to set up a Land Commission somewhat on the lines of the Central Land Board of the Act of 1947.[1] It was to have two basic functions. First it was proposed to introduce a new form of land tenure to be known as Crownhold. The Land Commission were to be empowered to purchase land at a price "based on its value for its present use, together with an amount sufficient to cover any contingent losses by the owner, and to encourage the willing sale of land".[2] While the selling price of a Crownhold interest in houses built upon the land would reflect the original price paid for the land there was also to be provision for pre-emption in favour of the Land Commission to ensure that when the Crownholder came to sell his interest his, and all subsequent selling prices, would continue to reflect the relatively low original cost of the land.

The Land Commission Act of 1967 to which these proposals gave rise accordingly provided for the creation and disposal by the Commission of Crownhold interests. It did not, however, provide for the purchase of the land on anything like as favourable terms as those predicted and outlined above.[3] A major defect of this concept was, of course, that while the objective was to reduce the cost of owner-occupation it was not possible to incorporate one of its principal attractions, viz, its value as a hedge against inflation. In the conditions of rising house prices ruling throughout the ensuing years genuine owner-occupation provided an almost certain expectation that the price on resale would adequately cover the cost of replacement. A Crownholder, however, had no such expectation: even if he could feel confident if forced to move, for example, for employment reasons, that he could find another Crownhold property, prices of such property were as bound to rise as were the prices of freeholds or long leaseholds, for even the price of agricultural land was rising and so, too, were building costs. It was not perhaps surprising, therefore, that in practice the use of these provisions of the Act was never seriously contemplated by the Commission.

The second principal feature of this Act was another attempt to recoup "betterment" by the imposition of a betterment levy on all disposals of relevant interests in land. Although the provisions governing the calculation of the levy upon various categories of "disposal" were often extremely complicated and took up a large part of the

---

acquired free gratis the developer can, if disposed to do so, fix his selling price accordingly—but when the purchaser comes to resell at the highest price obtainable, that price will be no less than that of similar houses in the neighbourhood, whatever the original price of the land on which they were built. In other words, the market for houses determines the price of "housing" land, rather than the other way round. A buoyant market for houses enables developers to pay and landowners to demand high prices for land, but if there is a slump in the demand for houses etc., and therefore a slump in development generally, development land prices will fall, as indeed can be seen from the behaviour of land prices throughout 1974–5.

[1] P. 8, *supra*.
[2] The Labour Party pamphlet, "Signposts for the Sixties".
[3] See p. 20, *infra*.

lengthy schedules to the Act, their details need not now concern us.[1] It is sufficient to record only the basic principles which are fortunately relatively straightforward.

The levy was charged upon the "net development value", that is to say, the difference between "base value" on the one hand, and, on the other, the market value reduced by any expenditure incurred by the vendor which had had the effect of increasing the development value of the interest being assigned. The "base value" was the current existing use value plus 10 %,[2] plus any depreciation in value of any adjacent land held by the vendor (or in the case of a leasehold interest, the grantor) in the same capacity.[3]

The levy was initially fixed at 40 % of the net development value with a declared intention on the part of the Government to increase it—no doubt with the object of discouraging the withholding of land from the market in the hopes of better terms while keeping the door open for a more complete recovery of betterment. The only advantage afforded to the Commission in purchasing land themselves (e.g., for Crownhold development) was that they would purchase net of levy,[4] thereby reducing yet further the claimed advantages to purchasers of Crownholds as compared with freeholds.

While one of the main criticisms of these provisions was once again that the incentive to place land on the market was inadequate, it was also argued that the imposition of any tax on land, as on any other commodity, was bound to increase rather than decrease the market price, and that landowners, in conditions of buoyant demand, would inevitably try to hold out for a price sufficiently enhanced to cover their liability to levy.[5]

Finally, there remained the vexed problem of the owner-occupier selling a house with some development potential who particularly resented the taxation of a capital gain on what in many cases was his only significant investment, and remained unconvinced that the price less levy would cover the cost of replacement. Moreover, if he was a relatively recent purchaser he would himself have paid the full value, including development value, and might well actually be out of pocket on finding that element of his selling price reduced by 40 %. As more and more cases in which the levy hit the private householder came to be publicised it very soon became apparent that the public reaction to the taxation of such "windfall" profits was very different if the recipient was an identifiable private householder from that engendered by the much larger profits accruing to the more anonymous "developer" or "speculator". The levy thus became almost as unpopular in its even

---

[1] These provisions were, in effect, repealed with effect from 23 July 1970; Land Commission (Dissolution) Act 1971.

[2] I.e., the promised "incentive" to encourage the "willing sale" of land.

[3] I.e., the familiar concept of injurious affection. See p. 314, *post*.

[4] But the Commission remained accountable for the levy to the Exchequer.

[5] The original intention had been that the Land Commission should purchase *all* development land (cf. the provisions of the Community Land Act 1975, p. 22, *post*) but this proposal was abandoned, not least vociferous in opposition being local authorities anxious to retain their powers of direct acquisition.

shorter period of operation as had been the development charge of the Act of 1947.[1] The Conservative Opposition accordingly promised repeal, and from that moment, of course, such hopes as remained of encouraging a willing sale of land quickly evaporated. Following the general election of June 1970 the levy was abolished.

Ironically, however, because the policies of the new Government had the effect of restimulating economic demand, particularly in the housing field, and consequently increasing prices of land, it was not long before they themselves were faced with revived, and indeed intensified, public concern at the even greater profits accruing to landowners and speculators. It was not only that monetary policy increased economic demand for most types of development, but as inflation gathered speed even agricultural land prices soared as investors increasingly came to regard land as the safest hedge against falling money values.

9 THE DEVELOPMENT GAINS TAX

The Conservatives accordingly reacted, but this time purely fiscally, by the announcement[2] of proposals for a development gains tax: again ironically, it was left to their successors to introduce the requisite legislation in Part III of the Finance Act 1974. In doing so, however, the Chancellor made it clear that he adopted his predecessor's proposals only as an interim measure.

Basically the development gains tax was an extension of capital gains tax by which that part of the capital gain which was attributable to development was deducted from the total capital gain (the balance continuing to be chargeable to capital gains tax) and treated as income for tax purposes. In order to cover the case in which, on completion of the development the property is let, the tax was levied on a first letting as well as on a sale of the freehold. For this purpose a first letting—or occupation by the owner—was regarded as a simultaneous disposal and reacquisition of all the assets at market value.[3]

By the time that the development gains tax was introduced, however, the economic climate had already changed. Inflation was beginning to produce serious cash-flow problems in the construction and other industries, and to undermine the confidence in the future that is so necessary in stimulating investment; a number of large firms of developers and the financial institutions behind them began to experience financial difficulties; 1974–5 saw an exacerbation of such problems and a sharp decline in development with, for the first time since the 1939–45 war, a surplus of development land on the market and land prices actually falling. In such circumstances it is impossible to judge the effect upon development of the development gains tax taken by itself. Whether, in its absence, the fall off in activity would have been as severe as it has been therefore remains an open question.

[1] P. 9, *supra*.
[2] 17 December 1973.
[3] For a full exposition of this tax see *Development Gains Tax* by G. Dobry, QC, W. R. Stewart-Smith and M. Barnes, Butterworths, 1975.

10 THE COMMUNITY LAND SCHEME

The White Paper "Land" (Cmnd. 5730), 1974

However, on their return to power in 1974 the Labour Government decided to return to the basic principles underlying their earlier Land Commission Act (although very substantially modified in detail) in relation to taxation, and ultimately to those of the Town and Country Planning Act 1947 in relation to compensation. In September 1974 they published the White Paper "Land" setting out proposals later to be incorporated, with some modification, in the now current Community Land Act 1975 and the Development Land Tax Act 1976.

Broadly speaking, the basis of these proposals is that eventually all development land should be acquired, not by a central organisation such as the Central Land Board or Land Commission but by local authorities. It would then either be developed by the acquiring authorities themselves, or made available to developers upon terms designed to confine their profit to their development activities and leave future increases in land prices to accrue to the "community".[1]

Ultimately, land is to be acquired at existing use value but, recognising that it would take some time before local authorities can be in a position to deal with acquisition of land on such a scale and manage the proposed ten-year land-bank, the White Paper proposed an interim "development land tax"[2] to replace the development gains tax and to operate on somewhat similar lines to the betterment levy of the Land Commission Act.[3] The tax, however, not only operates on disposals of land but also on "any development value realised by the carrying out of development".[4] The basic concept is that "development value" on which the tax is charged is

"the difference between the disposal price (or market value where tax is chargeable on the carrying out of development) and a 'base' value which will be whichever is the highest of:
(a) the price paid for the land plus any increase in current use value since the date of acquisition;
(b) the current use value at the date of disposal plus 10 %; and
(c) the price paid for the land plus 10 %".

As the White Paper put it, "There will be allowance for expenditure (e.g., costs of sale) and for the cost of improvements, where appropriate".[5] Basically, the tax is 80 % of development value.[6] Pending such time as local authorities are in a position to handle all land required for development they will, like the Land Commission before them, purchase net of tax. During this interim period, therefore, compensation

---

[1] Thus it is specifically stated that disposal of land for commercial or industrial development will be on a leasehold basis: Cmnd. 5730, para. 55. But the White Paper was silent as to how increases in land values were to be preserved "for the community" in the case of land developed for residential accommodation for owner-occupation.

[2] See now the Development Land Tax Act 1976, p. 97, *post*.

[3] P. 19, *supra*.

[4] Cmnd. 5730, para. 40.

[5] *Ibid*, para. 41.

[6] There may, however, be an initial tranche taxed at a reduced rate: see p. 98, *post*.

will be assessed on the basis of the Land Compensation Act 1961[1] and the tax deducted.[2]

The Community Land Act 1975[3]

The principal objectives of the Community Land Act 1975 are therefore that prior to development all development land shall pass into public ownership and be acquired at current existing use values. In order to allow local authorities[4] time to prepare themselves for the acquisition and management of the ten-year reserve supplies of development land that they will ultimately be required to hold, the Act comes into force in five stages. Some of its provisions (for the most part administrative and procedural)[5] came into operation upon enactment or, in some cases, a month thereafter; others came into force on the First Appointed Day;[6] the remainder take effect upon a series of "relevant dates"[7] and the Second Appointed Day.

It is only after the Second Appointed Day that there is any fundamental change in the basis of compensation for compulsory acquisition, namely the return to compensation on the basis of market value of the land in its current existing use.[8]

In the meantime, since 6 April 1976 (the First Appointed Day) authorities have had the power, though not, as yet, any duty to acquire any "development land"—that is, land which, in accordance with the development plan and planning policies relevant to the consideration of planning applications, the authorities concerned[9] regard as suitable for "relevant development". Relevant development is, in effect, all development for which planning permission is required,[10] other than a very limited range of exempted developments.[11]

---

[1] To this there was to be one exception: the White Paper (para. 32) proposed the amendment of the Land Compensation Act 1961, ss. 17–19, viz the provisions relating to certificates of appropriate alternative development: p. 15, *supra*, and *ibid*, s. 17, pp. 204 *et seq*, *post*. The effect of the amendment ultimately enacted by the Community Land Act 1975 is considered on pp. 211–213, *post*.

[2] The White Paper also contained proposals (subsequently enacted in the Community Land Act 1975, for the acquisition, at a reduced rate of compensation, of new office blocks left unoccupied. Such provisions, designed to overcome a particular problem in a somewhat narrow field are not, however, part of the mainstream of historical development of the law and are not further considered in this chapter: see, however, pp. 286 *et seq*, *post*.

[3] For a detailed examination of the Community Land Act see *Corfield's Guide to the Community Land Act*, Butterworths, 1976.

[4] Although, following the White Paper, local authorities are the principal authorities for the implementation of the Act in England and Scotland, they also include New Town Development Corporations, and in England, the Peak Park Joint Planning Board, the Lake District Special Planning Board, and any joint board which the Secretary of State may decide to constitute for the purpose. In Wales, however, there is but a single Land Authority for Wales.

[5] For the procedural changes introduced by the Act see pp. 74 *et seq*, *post*.

[6] 6 April 1976; SI 1976, No. 330 (C. 10).

[7] See p. 24, *infra*.

[8] For details see pp. 305 *et seq*, *post*.

[9] I.e., any authority within whose area the land is situated: Community Land Act 1975, s. 1 (3); or in the case of a new town the development corporation in whose designated area the land is situated: *ibid*, s. 1 (2)(a).

[10] See the Town and Country Planning Act 1971, s. 22.

[11] Defined in the Community Land Act 1975, Sch. 1: see pp. 296 *et seq*, *post*; and note that although relevant development also excludes "excepted development" (p. 297, *post*) for which authorities will not have the *duty* to acquire land, they have *power* to acquire land for such development with effect from the First Appointed Day.

In due course the Secretary of State will make relevant date orders[1] applicable to such parts of the country as he deems appropriate.[2] The effect of any such order is to impose (with effect from the "relevant date" specified) upon the authorities concerned a duty to acquire all the land which they anticipate will be required in their areas within the ensuing ten years for the types of development designated in the order. When the entire country is subjected to relevant date orders covering all relevant development and preliminary steps have been taken to establish Financial Hardship Tribunals[3] the Secretary of State is free to appoint the Second Appointed Day.

Meanwhile planning permissions for any development (other than exempted or excepted development) that has not as yet been designated in a relevant date order for the area in which the land is situated, are suspended in order to give authorities time to decide whether they wish to acquire the land in question and to notify the applicant accordingly. Such a planning permission will revive in favour of the applicant if no authority notifies him within two months that it intends to acquire; otherwise it will normally remain suspended until an authority within whose area the land lies actually acquires it,[4] as will virtually all planning permissions for development which has been designated in a relevant date order operative in the area in which the land is situated.[5]

Once the land is acquired the authority may develop it themselves or make it available for development by others, although the Secretary of State's consent is required for disposals of land so acquired,[6] and in this context authorities are required to have regard, *inter alia*, to the land needs of local builders and developers.[7] As to the terms on which disposals may be made, the financing of acquisitions, the treatment of receipts, the interim management of reserve supplies of land, etc., the Act is silent. All these matters are left to administrative directions to be made by regulations and Departmental circulars.

Apart from the amendment of the provisions of the Land Compensation Act 1961 governing certificates of appropriate alternative development,[8] the suspension of planning permission is the only feature of the Community Land Act 1975 which, prior to the Second Appointed Day, can affect the assessment of compensation.[9] If development is carried out in pursuance of the planning permission while it is suspended and the land is subsequently compulsorily acquired, the value of the work done may have to be ignored in assessing compensation.[10]

[1] I.e., orders under the Community Land Act 1975, s. 18.

[2] Such orders may cover a number of local authority areas in whole or in part: *ibid.*

[3] As to the Financial Hardship Tribunals promised in the White Paper, see pp. 310 *et seq, post.*

[4] The provisions governing suspension of planning permission are, unfortunately, somewhat more complicated than the outline in the text suggests: they are considered in detail on pp. 300 *et seq, post.*

[5] There are, however, some exceptions to this general rule: see pp. 304 *et seq, post.*

[6] Community Land Act 1975, s. 42. Consent may be given in the form of a general consent, applicable to disposals fulfilling specified criteria, or specific. As to the current general consent see Department of the Environment Circular 26/76, Community Land and Circular 6, Land for Private Development: Acquisition, Management and Disposal.

[7] Community Land Act 1975, s. 17 and Sch. 6, para. 1(1)(ii).

[8] *Supra*: for details see pp. 211 *et seq, post.*

[9] For details see pp. 300 *et seq, post.*

[10] See p. 303, *post.*

Furthermore, a suspended planning permission is no defence in enforcement proceedings.[1]

Even following the Second Appointed Day, however, there will be cases to which the provisions of the Land Compensation Act 1961 will continue to apply, as in the case of the compulsory acquisition of land held by charities as an investment.[2] Moreover, since it is provided[3] that compensation is to continue to be assessed in accordance with the provisions of that Act where to do so would result in less compensation being payable than under the post-Second Appointed Day provisions of the Community Land Act 1975, it will in many cases be necessary to assess the compensation payable under both sets of provisions in order to establish which method of assessment is to be adopted.

The Development Land Tax Act 1976

As will already have been apparent, development land tax is intended as an impost on the "windfall" increase in the value of land attributable to planning permission that enables it to be developed. Since it applies to all disposals of land having a "development value" the fact that the purchaser is an authority possessing powers of compulsory acquisition paying compensation is purely incidental. It is only after the compensation has been assessed that the question arises whether tax is payable, and if so, how much. The only difference in this respect between a private sale and a compulsory acquisition is therefore that whereas in the former case the vendor remains accountable for tax to the Inland Revenue, in the latter case he is in effect accountable to the acquiring authority, the tax being deducted from the compensation payable. Consideration of development land tax does not, therefore, form any part of the law governing compensation upon compulsory acquisition. Nevertheless, a person threatened with the compulsory acquisition of his land will want to know how the net proceeds, after deduction of tax, are assessed and what they are likely to be. This will be especially important if he intends to try to replace the property acquired. Although the subject matter of this work is the law of compensation, it has been thought appropriate to include a short account of the effect of the Development Land Tax Act 1976.[4] For the purposes of the present chapter, however, enough has been said[5] to indicate the general nature of this tax and its relationship to the general and longstanding controversy surrounding the recovery of "betterment".[6]

Criticisms of the Community Land Scheme

In the light of experience of the working of the compensation provisions of the Town and Country Planning Act 1947[7] and the short-lived Land Commission Act 1967,[8] the first question that has to be asked in considering the Community Land Act 1975 must be whether an 80%

---

[1] Community Land Act 1975, s. 22.
[2] Pp. 309 et seq, post.
[3] Community Land Act 1975, s. 25(10).
[4] P. 97, post.
[5] Pp. 22 et seq, supra.
[6] Pp. 16 et seq, supra.
[7] Pp. 8 et seq, supra.
[8] Pp. 19 et seq, supra.

development land tax leading to current existing use value as the basis of compensation will provide sufficient incentive to induce landowners and developers to seek planning permission. Unfortunately, although the White Paper on which the Act was based received a considerable measure of support from professional bodies and the press, and even proved relatively non-controversial politically, the same cannot be said of the Act itself: indeed, so controversial did it prove to be that at a very early stage the Conservative Opposition were induced to promise repeal.[1] There is therefore bound to be a strong temptation on the part of landowners to resist the acquisition of their land in the hope of a change of Government and more favourable terms. Nevertheless, as will have been evident even from this very brief outline of the principles of the Act, the ability of authorities to counter such resistance is very formidable indeed. Moreover, since the interests of landowners and developers are likely to conflict, authorities will probably be able to continue to rely on developers bringing land forward by applying for planning permission without the consent of owners.[2] Perhaps therefore a more significant obstacle to the smooth working of the Act is likely to arise from clashes of principle between local authorities of different political persuasions within the same county.[3]

The most serious criticisms of the Community Land Act however are probably economic.

As relevant date orders are made and the duty to acquire a ten-year supply of land is imposed, many authorities will face considerable problems in economic use and management of such land until it is required for development. Furthermore, the costs of acquisition, the servicing of capital and the costs of management pending development or disposal are all to be met by borrowing.[4] There being no means of forecasting market conditions ten years ahead, there can be no guarantee that the ultimate return will show a profit notwithstanding initial acquisition net of development land tax. Moreover, in conditions of high unemployment authorities will inevitably be tempted to vie with one another in making land available to industrial and commercial undertakings on attractive terms, thereby flooding the market. On the other hand authorities which endeavour to increase profits by restricting the local supply of development land are likely to face almost as much criticism from their electorates as those who, by taking the opposite course, impose further burdens on tax and ratepayers. Nor, if they succeed in handling their land transactions profitably, can they expect to be permitted to devote any surplus to local purposes, for once

---

[1] For a critical analysis as to how far the provisions of the Act accord with the objectives defined in the White Paper (Cmnd. 5730) see the authors' article "The Community Land Bill: An Assessment", *Journal of Planning and Environment Law*, July 1975, pp. 385–91.

[2] Although before disposing of land the authority concerned are obliged to "have regard" to applications by owners to develop their own land (Community Land Act 1975, Sch. 6, para. 2) this is not a provision which in itself appears to afford much protection.

[3] Land Acquisition and Management Schemes are required to be prepared on a county basis, the County and District (and where applicable, New Town corporations or the Lakes and Peak planning authorities) acting jointly: *ibid*, s. 16.

[4] Department of the Environment Circular 5/76.

a land acquisition account is in credit they have to account therefor to the Secretary of State who may, with the approval of the Treasury, direct payment to him of such proportion of the surplus as he deems appropriate;[1] thereafter he may use such monies to support less successful authorities.[2]

Despite special arrangements to even out the rates of interest charged upon advances to local authorities from loan funds,[3] in order as far as possible to avoid land accounts appearing, even indirectly, to result in a charge on the rates, the risk remains. The truth is that land speculation, whether carried out by private individuals or local authorities, in practice results in loss as well as profit, and as in all other cases, borrowing for the purposes of the Community Land Act 1975 will be secured upon all the revenues of the authority concerned—i.e., upon the unrestricted powers to make good deficiencies from the rates.

In the light of the collapse of the market for development land in 1973–4, and the serious financial difficulties faced by developers and the losses incurred by local authorities embarking upon ambitious schemes of land acquisition under powers conferred by earlier enactments,[4] it is not surprising that authorities have been urged by the Secretary of State to confine their activities under the Community Land Act to schemes with prospects of showing an almost immediate return.[5] There cannot, in current economic circumstances, with restrictions upon public expenditure and borrowing, be much confidence that in the near future it is likely either that such projects will be numerous or that it will be economically prudent to permit borrowing on the scale required fully to implement the Community Land Scheme as envisaged in the White Paper and provided for in the Act.

The irony is that both the Chancellor of the Exchequer and the Secretary of State were already urging economy upon local authorities even before the Parliamentary Bill was published. As these exhortations increase in urgency, and more effective measures to control public spending are adopted, the Second Appointed Day, and indeed, the time when comprehensive relevant date orders covering any large parts of the country can be expected inevitably recedes further into the future.

Economic realism would seem, therefore, to require some compromise if the later stages of the Community Land Scheme are to have much relevance to what is economically practical, and if landowners and developers are to be relieved of the threat of yet further fundamental changes in the law under which they are required to operate.

A further difficulty likely to arise as relevant date orders are made is that in the areas to which they apply authorities will be monopoly buyers of all land with planning permission (or the prospects of obtaining planning permission) for the designated types of development. It

---

[1] Community Land Act 1975, s. 44(2).
[2] *Ibid*, s. 44(5).
[3] Department of the Environment Circular 5/76.
[4] E.g., the very wide powers of the Town and Country Planning Act 1971, s. 112.
[5] Department of the Environment Circular 121/75, para. 60.

will therefore become increasingly difficult to find comparable sales in the open market as a guide to valuation. Similarly, in disposing of the land acquired to developers, authorities will be monopoly sellers. Prices are bound to reflect the supply of land for the development concerned and that will be entirely in the hands of the local authority[1]—hardly an open market situation as hitherto understood.

It seems likely, therefore, that valuers and the Lands Tribunal[2] will be forced to resort to more indirect and less satisfactory methods of valuation than the more straightforward comparative method hitherto preferred.[3]

11 HISTORICAL SUMMARY

(i) ASSESSMENT OF COMPENSATION FOR COMPULSORY ACQUISITION

Prior to 8 May 1845. According to the terms of the statute authorising the acquisition.[4]

8 May 1845–31 August 1919. The value of the land *to the owner* plus a 10 % solatium in recognition of the compulsory nature of the transaction: The Lands Clauses Consolidation Act 1845.[5]

1 September 1919–16 November 1944. Market value; i.e., the amount which the land might be expected to fetch in the open market if sold by a willing seller: Acquisition of Land (Assessment of Compensation) Act 1919.[6]

17 November 1944–5 August 1947. Market value assessed on the prices current on 31 March 1939: Town and Country Planning Act 1944.

6 August 1947–30 June 1948. Existing use value as at 7 January 1947, subject to Third Schedule[7] tolerance: Town and Country Planning Act 1947.

1 July 1948–31 December 1954. Current existing use value, subject to Third Schedule tolerance: Town and Country Planning Act 1947.[8]

1 January 1954–28 October 1958. Current existing use value as above plus the unexpended balance of the established development value under the Town and Country Planning Act 1947, Part VI: Town and Country Planning Act 1954.[9]

29 October 1958–Second Appointed Day under the Community Land Act 1975. Market value, subject to the limitations imposed by planning control

---

[1] Of course there will always be at least two authorities operating the Community Land Scheme—the County and the County District Councils—and sometimes three (i.e., where a new town development corporation or either of the Lakes or Peak Planning Authorities is involved): see note 4, p. 223, *supra*, and note 4, p. 296, *post*. Competition between authorities is improbable and would, in any case, be contrary to the whole concept of the Act.

[2] For the functions and jurisdiction of the Lands Tribunal see p. 83 *et seq, post*.

[3] See pp. 184 *et seq, post*.

[4] Pp. 1 *et seq, supra*.

[5] Pp. 3 *et seq, supra*.

[6] Pp. 4 *et seq, supra*.

[7] Now Town and Country Planning Act 1971, Sch. 8, pp. 456 *et seq, post*.

[8] Pp. 8 *et seq, supra*.

[9] Pp. 13 *et seq, supra*.

and the ignoring of additional value attributable to development on neighbouring land acquired under the same authority or as part of the same scheme of development or the establishment of a new town, etc.: Town and Country Planning Act 1959, re-enacted as 'the Land Compensation Act 1961.[1]

From the Second Appointed Day under the Community Land Act 1975. Current existing use value subject to Eighth Schedule tolerance and such "hardship payments" as may be awarded by a Financial Hardship Tribunal.[2]

(ii) FISCAL, ETC. IMPOSITIONS UPON, OR DEDUCTIONS FROM, THE COMPENSATION

From 6 April 1965. Capital gains tax imposed at 30 % upon increases in existing use value between whichever is the later of 6 April 1965 or the date of acquisition by the vendor and the date of compulsory acquisition.[3]

From 6 April 1967–23 July 1970. Betterment Levy on "development value" at 40 %: Land Commission Act 1967 as amended by the Land Commission (Dissolution) Act 1971.[4]

From 6 April 1975. Development gains tax whereby the capital gain attributable to "development value" was taxed as income for the year in question.[5]

From 1 August 1977. Development land tax at 80 %.[6]

(iii) COMPENSATION FOR REFUSAL OF PLANNING PERMISSION[7]

6 August 1947–31 December 1954. Limited to refusal of planning permission for classes of development specified in the Town and Country Planning Act 1947, Schedule 3, Part II: the amount by which the land is depreciated in value by the refusal. Town and Country Planning Act 1947.

From 1 January 1955. As above plus, in the case of refusal of planning permission for "new" development (i.e., other than development within the Town and Country Planning Act 1947, Schedule 3)[8] the amount by which the value of the land is depreciated by the refusal, subject to a maximum equivalent to the unexpended balance of established development value. Town and Country Planning Act 1954.

---

[1] Pp. 14 *et seq, supra,* and Chaps. 5 and 6 *post.*
[2] Pp. 23 *et seq, supra* and Chap. 7, *post.*
[3] Finance Act 1965.
[4] Pp. 19 *et seq, supra.*
[5] Pp. 21.
[6] Pp. 22 *et seq, supra* and p. 97, *post.*
[7] See p. 393, *post.*
[8] Now the Town and Country Planning Act 1971, Sch. 8; Appendix, p. 456, *post.*

CHAPTER 2

Compulsory Purchase Procedure

1 INTRODUCTION

This chapter is concerned with the manner in which a compulsory purchase order is made and put into effect, and the next chapter with the procedure for assessment of compensation. In this, perhaps even more than in other areas of compulsory purchase law, it is dangerous to generalise.[1] In every case the only safe rule is to begin by consulting the Act which confers the compulsory purchase power. We shall call this the special Act. Examples of special Acts which confer compulsory purchase powers are the Town and Country Planning Act 1971, the Community Land Act 1975, the Housing Act 1957, the Highways Act 1959, etc. The section of the special Act which authorises the compulsory acquisition of land will indicate the procedure which is to be adopted. Generally this will be done by incorporation of the procedure contained in the Acquisition of Land (Authorisation Procedure) Act 1946, Schedule 1, but there are important exceptions, such as the Housing Act 1957, Part III, which apply their own procedure. Even when the 1946 Act procedure is incorporated, the special Act will often make some modification to the ordinary procedure to adapt it to the requirements of that particular Act. It is always essential, therefore, to refer to the special Act as a starting point.

It is, however, possible to outline a general pattern of procedure which is applicable, subject to modification in particular cases, to most compulsory purchase orders made under modern legislation and this is the purpose of this chapter. The process can be divided roughly into three stages.

(i) PROCEDURE UNDER THE ACQUISITION OF LAND (AUTHORISATION PROCEDURE) ACT 1946

The 1st Schedule of the 1946 Act provides a procedure for the making and confirmation of compulsory purchase orders. It deals with the process by which an order is made ready for implementation. Thus it makes provision for the publication of the order and for objections to it to be heard and considered. Special safeguards are provided for certain categories of land, and a procedure laid down for challenging the

---

[1] For general guidance see Department of Environment Circular 26/77.

validity of orders in the Courts. The procedure for objections has in most cases been supplemented by inquiries procedure rules[1] which regulate inquiries held for the purpose of considering objections to orders.

(ii) FROM CONFIRMATION TO ENTRY

The second stage is the process by which an order, once confirmed, is put into effect by the acquiring authority and by which the necessary interests in the land are conveyed to them. The order itself does not affect the interests in the land; it merely confers on the acquiring authority powers, which they may or may not decide to implement. The procedure in most cases is governed by the Compulsory Purchase Act 1965, which expressly applies to compulsory purchases made under the Acquisition of Land (Authorisation Procedure) Act 1946, Schedule 1,[2] and which has also been specifically applied to orders made under certain other Acts.[3] The Compulsory Purchase Act 1965 provides for the implementation of the order to be set in motion by the service of a notice to treat by the acquiring authority on the holders of the relevant interests. It also enables the authority to enter the land under certain conditions before compensation has been assessed and paid. This Act also contains provisions relating to the treatment of divided land, the overriding of lesser interests in the land and certain other matters relevant to the assessment and payment of compensation, which will be dealt with in later chapters of this book. An alternative procedure for implementing the compulsory purchase order, not involving service of a notice to treat, is the "General Vesting Declaration". This procedure is governed by the Town and Country Planning Act 1968, Schedule 3.[4]

(iii) ASSESSMENT OF COMPENSATION

The third stage which will be considered in the next chapter is the machinery for determination of compensation where the parties are unable to agree. This is the function of the Lands Tribunal, which is made responsible for assessment of compensation in respect of compulsory purchase orders by the Land Compensation Act 1961.[5] Although this Act is mainly concerned with the principles on which compensation is to be assessed, which will be considered in later chapters, it also makes provision for certain matters of procedure. Detailed procedure in the Lands Tribunal, however, is governed by rules made under the Lands Tribunal Act 1949.

The remaining sections of this chapter will deal with the first two of these procedural stages in turn, and with special provisions applicable to acquisitions under the Community Land Act 1975, the Housing Act 1957, Part III, and the New Towns Act 1965.

[1] Made under the Tribunals and Inquiries Act 1971.
[2] Compulsory Purchase Act 1965, s. 1(1).
[3] E.g. Housing Act 1957, Part III: see the Compulsory Purchase Act 1965, s. 35.
[4] This part of the 1968 Act remains in force, notwithstanding the re-enactment of most other parts of that Act in the Town and Country Planning Act 1971.
[5] Ss. 1–4.

2 A PROCEDURE UNDER THE ACQUISITION OF LAND (AUTHORISATION PROCEDURE) ACT 1946

1 Application of the Act

As explained in the previous chapter,[1] the Acquisition of Land (Authorisation Procedure) Act 1946, Schedule 1, provided a new procedure for the purchase of land by compulsory purchase order. The procedure was applied to any compulsory purchase by a local authority[2] under powers conferred by any public[3] general Act in force immediately before the commencement[4] of the 1946 Act.[5] The procedure has also been incorporated into most subsequent Acts conferring compulsory powers on Ministers, local authorities and others.[6] Thus the 1946 Act procedure now applies to the great majority of compulsory purchase powers of local authorities, Ministers, statutory undertakers, and analogous authorities. The most important exceptions for modern purposes are the powers of local authorities under the Housing Act 1957, Part III (slum clearance)[7] and the powers of acquisition under the New Towns Act 1965.[8] The Community Land Act 1975 incorporates the 1946 Act procedure but makes certain important modifications which are considered below.[9]

2 Purchases by Local Authorities

(i) THE MAKING OF AN ORDER

A compulsory purchase order is made by the authority requiring the relevant land, and submitted to the confirming authority[10] for confirmation.[11] The order must describe the land to which it applies by

---

[1] P. 2, *ante*.

[2] "Local authority" is defined as "the Council of a county, borough or county district, the Common Council of the City of London, the Receiver for the Metropolitan Police District or any other authority being a local authority within the meaning of the Local Loans Act 1875 and includes any drainage board and any joint board or joint committee if all the constituent authorities are such local authorities as aforesaid, and includes also the Honourable Society of the Inner Temple and the Honourable Society of the Middle Temple": Acquisition of Land (Authorisation Procedure) Act 1946, s. 8(1). This definition may be extended by other enactments which apply the 1946 Act: see, e.g., the Community Land Act 1975, s. 15(4). The reference to the Local Loans Act 1875 extends the definition to cover "the Justices of any county, liberty, riding parts or division of a county in general or quarter sessions assembled, the council of any municipal borough, also any authority whatsoever having power to levy a rate, as in this Act defined, also any prescribed authority": Local Loans Act 1875, s. 34.

[3] The procedure could be applied to local Acts by order made, by the Secretary of State, subject to special parliamentary procedure (as to which see p. 51, *infra*): Acquisition of Land (Authorisation Procedure) Act 1946, s. 7(1), (3).

[4] 18 April 1946.

[5] Acquisition of Land (Authorisation Procedure) Act 1946, s. 1(1)(a).

[6] See the list of enactments set out in 8 Halsbury's Laws (4th Edn.) para. 10, note 7.

[7] See pp. 77 *et seq*, *infra*.

[8] See pp. 80 *et seq*, *infra*.

[9] See pp. 74 *et seq*, *infra*.

[10] That is, the authority having power under the enactment in question to authorise the purchase: Acquisition of Land (Authorisation Procedure) Act 1946, Sch. 1, para. 1. This will normally be the Government Minister having responsibility for the functions with which the special Act is concerned. In this general description the confirming authority will be referred to as "the Secretary of State", since in most cases the confirming authority will be the Secretary of State for the Environment, or, in Wales, the Secretary of State for Wales.

[11] Acquisition of Land (Authorisation Procedure) 1946, Sch. 1, para. 1.

reference to a map.[1] The form of the order is prescribed by regulations[2] made under the Act.[3] Only "land" can be acquired under the 1946 Act. But the scope of this expression depends on its definition in the particular Act which authorises the compulsory purchase in question.[4] Thus, for instance, under the Town and Country Planning Acts "land" means "any corporeal hereditament, including a building, and, in relation to the acquisition of land under Part VI of this Act, includes any interest in or right over land".[5] Accordingly for the purpose of acquisitions under this Act the same definition will apply to the 1946 Act procedure.

Notices of the order must be published in one or more local newspapers circulating in the locality in two successive weeks.[6] Notices must also be served on every owner,[7] lessee or occupier[8] (other than a tenant for a month or less)[8] of any land comprised in the order.[9] The confirming authority may, however, direct in a particular case[10] that this latter requirement shall not apply.[11] If service on individuals is

[1] *Ibid*, Sch. 1, para. 2. For the contents of the map, see Department of the Environment Circular 26/77, Appendix IF.

[2] Compulsory Purchase of Land Regulations 1976, SI 1976 No. 300. See generally Department of the Environment Circular 26/77, Appendix IE. Appendix IA of that circular contains a check list of documents which should be sent with the order to the Secretary of State.

[3] Acquisition of Land (Authorisation Procedure) Act 1946, Sch. 1, para. 18. The power to make regulations is now exercisable by the Secretary of State: Secretary of State for the Environment Order 1970, SI 1970 No. 1681. These regulations apply to all acquisitions made under the Act.

[4] See definition of "land" in the Acquisition of Land (Authorisation Procedure) Act 1946, s. 8: "land in relation to any compulsory purchase under any enactment includes anything falling within the definition of the expression in that enactment".

[5] Town and Country Planning Act 1971, s. 290(1). For the meaning of "land" in relation to orders under the Housing Act 1957, see *Sovmots* v *Secretary of State*, [1977] 2 All ER 385, HL.

[6] Acquisition of Land (Authorisation Procedure) Act 1946, Sch. 1, para. 3(1)(a).

[7] "Owner" means a person other than a mortgagee not in possession who is for the time being entitled to dispose of the fee simple of the land, whether in possession or reversion, and includes also a person holding or entitled to the rents and profits of the land under a lease or agreement the unexpired term whereof exceeds three years: *ibid*, s. 8(1). Since the definition of "land" is governed by its definition in the special Act (see note 4, *supra*) the definition of "owner" must also be read in that context. Thus when the definition of "land" includes a "right over land" (e.g., Housing Act 1957, s. 189(1)), it seems that the owner, for example, of an easement for an interest equivalent to a fee simple (Law of Property Act 1925, s. 1(2)(b)) would be entitled to notice under these provisions if the easement were included in the compulsory purchase order (see *Grimley* v *Minister of Housing and Local Government*, [1971] 2 QB 96). However, an easement over the land which is to be acquired will not normally be included in the order, since such a right can be overridden on payment of compensation under the Compulsory Purchase Act 1965, s. 10 (see p. 321, *post*), and in such a case the owner of the right is not entitled to notice (*Grimley* v *Minister of Housing and Local Government*, *supra*). See also Department of the Environment Circular 26/77, para. 16.

[8] A statutory tenant under the Rent Acts is deemed to be a tenant for a period less than one month: Housing Repairs and Rent Act 1954, s. 50(1), reversing the effect of *Brown* v *Ministry of Housing and Local Government*, [1953] 2 All ER 1385.

[9] Acquisition of Land (Authorisation Procedure) Act 1946, Sch. 1, para. 3(1)(b). If the land is "ecclesiastical property" as defined in *ibid*, para. 3(3), a similar notice must also be served on the Ecclesiastical Commissioners: *ibid*, para. 3(2).

[10] No such direction can be made if the relevant owner, lessee or occupier is a local authority, or statutory undertaker, or the National Trust: *ibid*, Sch. 1, para. 3 proviso.

[11] *Ibid*, Sch. 1, para. 3(1)(b). The circumstances in which such a direction might be appropriate were described in Ministry of Health Circular 104/45, para. 11, as being:
"(i) where land is in multiple ownership and protracted inquiries would be necessary to obtain full particulars of all the owners, lessees and occupiers with a legal interest in the land;
(ii) where the land has been damaged by enemy action and the boundaries are obliterated."
However in practice the power is now rarely used and it is more usual to ask for a dispensation from personal service under para. 19(4): see Department of the Environment Circular 26/77, Appendix IH, and note 9 p. 34, *infra*.

dispensed with in this way an equivalent notice, addressed to the "owners and any occupiers" of the land, must be affixed to a conspicuous object on the land.[1] The contents of the notice in each case are prescribed by regulations.[2] The Act itself requires each notice to describe the land,[3] to state the purpose for which it is required, and to name a place within the locality where a copy of the order and map may be inspected. It must also specify the time[4] within which objections may be made and the manner of making them.[5]

Service of any notice under the schedule is effected by delivering it to the person to be served or by leaving it at his proper address[6] or by sending it by registered, or recorded delivery,[7] post.[8] If the Secretary of State is satisfied that reasonable inquiry has been made and that it is not practicable to ascertain the name or address of a person required to be served with notice, it may be served by addressing it to the "owner", "lessee" or "occupier" of the land in question, and delivering it to a person on the premises or, if there is no one there, by affixing it to some conspicuous part of the premises.[9]

(ii) CONFIRMATION

(a) Making of objections
There is no prescribed form for objections. As stated above, the notice of the order must indicate the manner in which objections are to be made. However the only requirements indicated in the prescribed forms[10] for such notices are that objections should be made in writing, should be addressed to the Secretary of State within the specified time limit,[11] and should state the grounds of objection. Where an objection is likely to raise complicated issues which cannot be fully explored within the specified time, it is normally sufficient in the first instance to

---

[1] Acquisition of Land (Authorisation Procedure) Act 1946, Sch. 1, para. 3(1)(c).

[2] Compulsory Purchase of Land Regulations 1976, SI 1976 No. 300, Forms 3 to 5. A newspaper notice must be "in such terms as are fairly and reasonably necessary to enable members of the public in the area of the land affected to appreciate that they are interested and to make representations or objections if they think fit": *Wilson* v *Secretary of State*, [1975] 1 All ER 428 at p. 436d, per Browne J. This was a case on para. 11(2) of the Schedule, as to which see p. 50, *infra*.

[3] "The heading . . . is of paramount importance": *Wilson* v *Secretary of State*, *supra*, at p. 437e. In that case a public notice which referred to the land by a name other than that which was normally used in the locality was held to be ineffective.

[4] Not less than 21 days—from the date of first publication in the case of notices in local newspapers, and from the date of service in the case of notices to individuals: Acquisition of Land (Authorisation Procedure) Act 1946, Sch. 1, para. 3(1).

[5] *Ibid*, Sch. 1, para. 3(1).

[6] The proper address of an incorporated company or body is its registered or principal office, and in other cases the last known address of the person to be served: *ibid*, Sch. 1, para. 19(3).

[7] Recorded Delivery Service Act 1962, s. 1 (1).

[8] Acquisition of Land (Authorisation Procedure) Act 1946, Sch. 1, para. 19(1). In the case of an incorporated company or body it should be served on the company secretary or the clerk: *ibid*, para. 19(2). Service by post in accordance with this provision is deemed "unless the contrary is proved to have been effected at the time at which the letter would be delivered in the ordinary course of post". (Interpretation Act 1889, s. 26); but this presumption can be rebutted by proof that the document was received at some other time or was not received at all (*Maltglade* v *St. Albans RDC*, [1972] 3 All ER 129).

[9] Acquisition of Land (Authorisation Procedure) Act 1946, Sch. 1, para. 19(4). The procedure for obtaining a dispensation from the Secretary of State is described in Department of the Environment Circular 26/77, Appendix IH.

[10] Compulsory Purchase of Land Regulations 1976, SI 1976 No. 300, Forms 3 to 5.

[11] See note 4, *supra*.

indicate the grounds in general and summary terms. However it is usually advisable to give as full as possible an indication of the grounds, if not in the initial objection, then in a subsequent amplification. This may enable the acquiring authority to make modifications to the order to meet specific objections and so avoid the need for the objection to be pursued.

(b) Confirmation of the order without an inquiry or hearing
The order may be confirmed without an inquiry, if no objection has been "duly made" by any owner, lessee or occupier or if all objections so made are withdrawn.[1] Thus an inquiry may be dispensed with, for instance, if the only objections are from persons who had no interest in the land at the times when their objections were made.[2] Even if there are objections by owners or occupiers an inquiry is not obligatory if the objections have not been "duly made", for example because they have been made out of time or do not contain a statement of the grounds of objection.[3] However in practice, if there are genuine objections from interested parties, the Secretary of State is unlikely to dispense with an inquiry merely because of a procedural defect. The Secretary of State may in any event require an objector to state in writing the grounds of his objection,[4] and may disregard any objection if satisfied that it relates exclusively to matters which can be dealt with by "the Tribunal by whom the compensation is to be assessed".[5]

If no inquiry or hearing is held the order may be confirmed with or without modifications.[6] The Secretary of State must first be satisfied that the proper notices have been published and served.[6] In any event he has a discretion to refuse to confirm the order, even if there are no objections, for instance if its purposes are in conflict with Government policy.[7] He may also refuse to confirm the order if the authority have

[1] Acquisition of Land (Authorisation Procedure) Act 1946, Sch. 1, para. 4(1).
[2] See *Middlesex County Council* v *Minister of Housing and Local Government*, [1953] 1 QB 12 CA. That case related to the then requirement of para. 9(1) of the schedule that an order should be subject to special parliamentary procedure if it included land which was the property of a local authority and if an objection was "duly made" by the authority. An objection was made by a local authority within the time limit, but it did not acquire any interest in the land until later. In these circumstances it was held that the Minister could confirm the order without special parliamentary procedure.
[3] *Ibid.*
[4] Assuming that the grounds were not stated in the original objection.
[5] Acquisition of Land (Authorisation Procedure) Act 1946, Sch. 1, para. 4(4). The Lands Tribunal can deal not only with the quantum of compensation and the apportionment of rent under a lease (Land Compensation Act 1961, s. 1(1)), but also with questions arising under the Compulsory Purchase Act 1965, s. 8 (e.g., whether part of a house can be taken without material detriment to the whole). The Secretary of State would be entitled to disregard an objection dealing exclusively with such matters. As to the extended grounds for disregarding objections under the Community Land Act 1975, see p. 74, *infra*.
[6] Acquisition of Land (Authorisation Procedure) Act 1946, Sch. 1, para. 4(1). He may not include additional land without the consent of all interested persons: *ibid*, Sch. 1, para. 5. He may correct errors in the form of the order: see *Re Bowman, South Shields (Thames Street) Clearance Order 1931* [1932] 2 KB 621.
[7] Thus the Secretary of State has refused to confirm unopposed orders under the Housing Acts made for the purpose of "municipalisation" of housing where the circumstances did not fall within the criteria set out in Department of the Environment Circular 64/75, para. 18. It is also the practice of the Secretary of State not to confirm orders unless the planning aspect has been covered, usually by the grant of planning permission: Department of the Environment Circular 26/77, Appendix IC.

entered into an agreement or formed an intention to use the land for purposes incompatible[1] with the authorising statute.[2] However, in such a case he is not apparently bound to refuse confirmation. He may instead "take that into account but still confirm the order, saying that the agreement was not to be operated or the intention implemented at all".[3]

His function at this stage is purely administrative. "The decision whether to confirm or not must be made in relation to questions of policy and the Minister, in deciding whether to confirm or not, will, like every Minister entrusted with administrative duties, weigh up the considerations which are to affect his mind, the preponderating factor in many, if not all, cases being that of public policy having regard to all the facts of the case".[4]

If the order is confirmed, the acquiring authority must "as soon as may be" publish a notice in one or more local newspapers, and serve a notice of confirmation on the persons[5] entitled to be served with notice of the original order.[6] The form of notice is prescribed by regulations.[7] The notice must include a description of the land, and must name the place at which a copy of the confirmed order may be inspected at reasonable hours.

(c) After an inquiry or hearing

If an objection is duly made by an owner, lessee or occupier and is not withdrawn, the Secretary of State must either cause a public local inquiry to be held or give the objector an opportunity of being heard by a person appointed for the purpose.[8] There is a general power to hold an inquiry in any event even where it is not specifically required by the Act.[9] After the inquiry or hearing the Secretary of State must consider the objections and the report of the person who held the inquiry or hearing, and may then confirm the order with or without modification.[10]

[1] See the discussion of this expression in *Sovmots Ltd.* v *Secretary of State*, [1976] 3 All ER 720 CA. at p. 735–736. The Secretary of State had found that an agreement by the acquiring authority not to serve a notice to treat in respect of the interest of another authority did not preclude the use of the land for the purpose for which it was acquired: it was therefore not "incompatible" and the agreement was *intra vires*.

[2] See *London and Westcliffe Properties Ltd.* v *Minister of Housing and Local Government*, [1961] 1 All ER 610. In that case an agreement was entered into by the acquiring authority before confirmation, involving use of the land in breach of the relevant statute. The resulting order was quashed because "he (the Minister) was in duty bound to reject this confirmation and refuse it because otherwise he would have been rendering himself a party to a proposal in direct conflict with the express provisions of the Act ..." (*ibid*, at p. 617, per Ashworth J.). However, it seems that this dictum may go too far in placing a *duty* on the Secretary of State to refuse confirmation in such a case: see *Wahiwala* v *Secretary of State*, *infra*.

[3] *Wahiwala* v *Secretary of State* (1977), *Times* 5 April 1977, per Lord Denning MR.

[4] *B. Johnson & Co. (Builders) Ltd.* v *Minister of Health*, [1947] 2 All ER 395 at p. 397H per Lord Greene MR

[5] See p. 33, *supra*.

[6] Acquisition of Land (Authorisation Procedure) Act 1946, Sch. 1, para. 6. The order will become operative on the date of publication of the notice, subject to the right of challenge in the Court within 6 weeks: *ibid*. para. 16.

[7] Compulsory Purchase of Land Regulations 1976, SI 1976 No. 300, Form 7.

[8] Acquisition of Land (Authorisation Procedure) Act 1946, Sch. 1, para. 4(2). For the procedure at an inquiry or hearing see p. 39, *infra*.

[9] Acquisition of Land (Authorisation Procedure) Act 1946, s. 5(1).

[10] *Ibid*, Sch. 1, para. 4(2). See notes 6–7, p. 35, *supra*.

Even where an inquiry is held, the Secretary of State's function in deciding whether or not to confirm the order is still an administrative one, although in relation to the inquiry he is required to act quasi-judicially, and in particular, to observe the rules of natural justice.[1] "The administrative character in which he acts reappears at a later stage because, after considering the objections, which may be regarded as the culminating point of his quasi-judicial functions, there follows something which again ... is purely administrative, viz, the decision whether or not to confirm the order".[2] Thus his duty in relation to the objections and the report of the inquiry is merely to consider them. He is not bound to base his decision on any conclusion that he comes to with regard to the objections.[3]

After an order is confirmed the Secretary of State must "as soon as may be" publish a notice in one or more local newspapers; and serve notices on the persons who were entitled to notice of the original order.[4] The form of notice is prescribed by regulations; it includes a description of the land and names the place where the confirmed order may be inspected at reasonable hours.[5]

(iii) INQUIRY PROCEDURE

Statutory requirements

Procedure is governed by the Compulsory Purchase by Public Authorities (Inquiries Procedure) Rules 1976.[6] These rules apply to all public local inquiries held under the Acquisition of Land (Authorisation Procedure) Act 1946, s. 5[7] or Schedule 1[8] for the purpose of inquiring into the authorisation of any compulsory purchase of land by a public authority.[9] The 1976 rules were principally designed to extend the previous rules to cover compulsory acquisitions under the Community Land Act 1975, and also to ensure that the rules would apply in cases where a discretionary inquiry is held under that Act.[10]

Notice of Inquiry

The Secretary of State first notifies the acquiring authority of the

---

[1] See pp. 61 *et seq, infra.*

[2] *B. Johnson & Co. (Builders) Ltd.* v *Minister of Health,* [1947] 2 All ER 395 at p. 399B.

[3] *Ibid,* at p. 397, and see the passage cited at note 4 on p. 36, *supra.* See also *Re City of Plymouth City Centre) Declaratory Order 1946, Robinson* v. *Minister of Town and Country Planning,* [1947] KB 702, but note that the extent to which the Secretary of State can have regard to material not discussed at the inquiry is now restricted by the inquiries procedure rules (SI 1976 No. 746, rule 9: see p. 43, *infra*).

[4] Acquisition of Land (Authorisation Procedure) Act 1946, Sch. 1, para. 6. This requirement is separate from the Secretary of State's duty to give notice of his decision on an inquiry into objections; see p. 44, *infra.*

[5] Compulsory Purchase of Land Regulations 1976 (SI 1976 No. 300) Form 7.

[6] SI 1976 No. 746, made under the Tribunal and Inquiries Act 1971, s. 11, by the Lord Chancellor.

[7] See note 8, p. 36, *supra.*

[8] See note 9, p. 36, *supra.*

[9] The expression "public authority" is used, rather than "local authority", in order to embrace those bodies, other than local authorities, which have powers of compulsory acquisition under the Community Land Act 1975, e.g., the Land Authority for Wales (see p. 74, *infra.*). "Public Authority" is defined in Rule 3(1) of the Rules (SI 1976 No. 746).

[10] See Department of the Environment Circular 59/76. As to procedure under the Community Land Act 1975, see p. 74, *post.*

substance of any objection by a statutory objector,[1] and so far as practicable, of other objections.[2] He then fixes a time and place for the inquiry, and must give at least 42 days' notice in writing to each statutory objector.[3] He may vary the time and place, and if he does so he must give such notice of the variation as appears to him reasonable in the circumstances.[4] Unless the Secretary of State otherwise directs, the authority must post a notice of the inquiry in a conspicuous place near to the land and in one or more places where public notices are usually posted in the locality. The Secretary of State may[5] also direct the authority to publish a notice of the inquiry in one or more newspapers circulating in the locality.[6]

Statement of reasons

"As soon as may be"[7] after being notified of the substance of the objections of statutory objectors and in any event not later than 28 days[8] before the inquiry, the authority must serve on each statutory objector a statement of their reasons for making the order, and must supply a copy to the Secretary of State.[9] If the authority propose to rely on a view expressed by a Government Department in support of the order they must include it in their statement of reasons and must send a copy of the statement to the Government Department concerned.[10] The statement must also be accompanied by a list of all documents including maps and plans to which the authority intend to refer, and must indicate the times and places at which they can be inspected by any statutory objector.[11] The authority must give not only statutory objectors but also "any other person interested"[12] a reasonable opportunity

---

[1] The expression "statutory objector" is used by the rules to denote any owner, lessee or occupier who was entitled to notice of the order (see p. 33, *supra*), and who has duly made an objection which has not been withdrawn or disregarded: SI 1976 No. 746, rule 3(1). In the case of an order made by the Land Authority for Wales, a county or district council which has objected and whose area includes any of the land to be acquired, is also a statutory objector: *ibid*, rule 3(2).

[2] *Ibid*, rule 4(1). This is to be done "as soon as may be" after receipt of the statutory objections: *ibid*.

[3] *Ibid*, rule 4(2). He may give lesser notice with the consent in writing of the statutory objectors and the acquiring authority: *ibid*, rule 4(2) proviso.

[4] *Ibid*, rule 4(2) proviso.

[5] Generally the Secretary of State asks authorities to inform the press of the arrangements for the inquiry, without making a formal direction—see Circular 49/62, Appendix, para. 24.

[6] SI 1976 No. 746, rule 4(3).

[7] Presumably this means "as soon as practicable". Normally, therefore, the statement of reasons should be served well before the 28 day period and, indeed, before the announcement of the inquiry. Authorities are in fact advised to serve the statement at the same time as the statutory notice of the order, and to furnish copies to anyone else who lodges a written objection: see Department of Environment Circular 26/77 para. 19.

[8] The Secretary of State may specify a lesser period if the normal 42 day period for notice of the inquiry has been reduced by consent under rule 4(2).

[9] *Ibid*, rule 4(4).

[10] *Ibid*, rule 4(5). The expression of view should either be quoted verbatim or be in a form agreed with the relevant Government Department: Ministry of Housing and Local Government Circular 9/58, para. 18.

[11] *Ibid*, rule 4(6). Apparently the Department does not regard proofs of evidence as "documents" for this purpose: see [1963] JPL 352.

[12] This expression is not defined. In the context it should be construed widely and should extend to anyone who has a genuine interest in the proceedings and who might be admitted to appear at the inquiry under rule 5(1): Cf. *Turner v Secretary of State* (1973), 72 LGR 380, as to which see p. 53, *infra*.

to inspect and where practicable to take copies of their statement and the listed documents.[1]

Although the rules require the statement to give the "reasons for making the order",[2] it is clearly intended that the authority should not limit its statement to the factors which were taken into account when the resolution to acquire was made, but should disclose fully the matters on which it intends to rely at the inquiry.[3]

It is important also from the authority's point of view that their statement of reasons and list of documents be as complete as possible. Although they may be allowed to alter or add to them at the inquiry, statutory objectors must then be given an adequate opportunity to consider any fresh reasons or documents, if necessary by adjourning the inquiry.[4] The costs of any such adjournment may have to be borne by the authority, and the inspector may make a recommendation to that effect in his report.[5]

Procedure at inquiry

At the inquiry the acquiring authority and the statutory objectors are entitled to appear as of right. Other parties may appear at the discretion of the inspector.[6] If a statutory objector does not appear, the inspector may nevertheless proceed with the inquiry.[7] He may in any event take into account any previous written representations received from a person who does not attend in so far as they are "proper[8] and relevant" to the matters in issue and subject to disclosing them at the inquiry.[9] The procedure is at the discretion of the inspector.[10]

Unless the inspector otherwise determines with the authority's consent, the authority begin and have the right of final reply. Other parties appear in the order determined by the inspector.[11] The authority and the statutory objectors have the right to call evidence and

---

[1] SI 1976 No. 746, rule 4(6), (7).

[2] *Ibid*, rule 4(4). Compare the Town and Country Planning (Inquiries Procedure) Rules, rule 6(2), which requires a written statement "of any submission which the local planning authority propose to put forward at the inquiry" to be served at least 28 days before an inquiry.

[3] For the information which should be included see Department of the Environment Circular 26/77, Appendix IB.

[4] SI 1976 No. 746, rule 7(5). The length of the adjournment will depend on the nature of the new material introduced: see *Performance Cars Ltd.* v *Secretary of State*, [1976] JPL 370, revsd. on appeal [1977] JPL 585

[5] *Ibid*, rule 7(5). "Where a postponement or adjournment of an inquiry is made necessary through the fault of any party ... the Minister will be prepared to consider applications by the other parties appearing at the inquiry for their extra costs, so far as occasioned by the postponement or adjournment, to be paid by the party at fault.": Ministry of Housing and Local Government Circular 73/65, para. 9.

[6] SI 1976 No. 746, rule 5(1). The authority may appear by their clerk or any other officer appointed for the purpose, or by counsel or solicitor, and any other person may appear on his own behalf or be represented by counsel, solicitor or any other person: *ibid*, rule 5(2). When two or more persons have a similar interest the inspector may allow one or more of them to appear for them all: *ibid*, rule 5(3).

[7] *Ibid*, rule 7(7).See *Ostreicher* v *Secretary of State* (1977), Times, 6th May where an objector sought unsuccessfully to quash an order on the grounds that the inquiry was held on a Jewish festival and that she had therefore been unable to attend for religious reasons.

[8] It follows that he can disregard representations which are relevant if they are "improper".

[9] *Ibid* rule 7(6).

[10] *Ibid*, rule 7(1).

[11] *Ibid*, rule 7(2).

to cross-examine other persons giving evidence. Other parties may do so only to the extent permitted by the inspector.[1]

In practice the procedure is operated very flexibly and it will vary depending on the complexity of the inquiry and the number of parties involved. Where the number of objectors is small or the main objectors are all represented by the same advocate, the inquiry will generally be conducted in a similar manner to a planning appeal inquiry. The authority will open its case and call its witnesses in the order chosen by it. Each witness will usually give evidence in chief by reading a written proof of evidence and will then be made available for cross-examination by the other parties in turn and for questioning by the inspector. When the authority has called all its witnesses, each objector in turn will make his submissions and call any witnesses in support, and they will be open to cross-examination by the authority.[2] When all the objectors have finished their presentations, the authority will have the final right of reply. Although the inquiry is primarily concerned with objections to the order, in practice representations from third parties in support of the authority's case are also heard. Normally they will be heard after the authority's case and before the objectors.

Where there is a large number of objectors (particularly in road inquiries) it is common for the procedure to be arranged so that each objection can be dealt with as far as possible as a separate case. When this happens the authority will open and call its witnesses, but they will not be made available for general cross-examination at that stage. Each objection will be taken in turn, and the objector will have the opportunity to present his own case and to recall any of the authority's witnesses for cross-examination. The authority may be allowed to call evidence in rebuttal related to the particular objection. In any event the authority will have the final right of reply, either at the end of the particular objection or at the end of the inquiry as a whole.

Representation of Government Departments

If the view of a Government Department has been relied on by the authority and set out in their statement of reasons, a representative of the Department concerned must attend the inquiry.[3] At the inquiry the representative must state the reasons for the view expressed by his Department and give evidence, and he is liable to cross-examination. However the inspector must disallow any questions which in his opin-

---

[1] SI 1976 No. 746, rule 7(3). In practice persons other than statutory objectors are allowed more latitude to cross-examine the authority's witnesses than to cross-examine the witnesses of other parties. As a general principle, any party to the inquiry, whether a statutory objector or not, who has a valid reason for wishing to challenge evidence which is given ought to be allowed to cross-examine: see *Wednesbury Corpn.* v *Ministry of Housing and Local Government* (No. 2), [1966] 2 QB 275. *Errington* v *Minister of Health*, [1935] 1 KB 249. However, the fact that hearsay evidence cannot be tested by cross-examination is not a valid reason for excluding it: *T. A. Miller Ltd.* v *Minister of Housing and Local Government*, [1968] 1 WLR 992.

[2] Statutory objectors also have a right to cross-examine persons giving evidence, including witnesses called by other objectors: *ibid*, rule 7(3).

[3] *Ibid*, rule 6(1). For the practice in relation to representations by the Ministry of Agriculture, see Ministry of Housing and Local Government Circular 43/58. Part II, Procedure under Circular 9/58.

ion are directed to the merits of Government policy.[1] There is no duty on the Secretary of State to make known in advance the policy considerations to which he will have regard in deciding whether or not to confirm the order.[2]

Evidence

The only other restriction on the evidence which may be admitted is that the inspector must exclude any evidence which "would be contrary to the public interest".[3] Otherwise he may admit any evidence at his discretion.[4] He may also direct that any documents tendered in evidence be made available for inspection and that facilities be given for taking copies.[5] He may also require evidence to be taken on oath.[6] The inspector has the power to require the attendance of any person either to give evidence or to produce any document in his custody or control, relating to matters in question at the inquiry.[7] He cannot, however, require the production of the title, or any instrument relating to the title, of land other than land owned by a local authority.[8] No person can be required to attend to give evidence or to produce any documents unless he is offered his necessary expenses.[9] It is an offence to disobey such summons or wilfully to suppress or destroy any document which might be required for production.[10]

[1] *Ibid*, rule 6(2). The inspector *must* disallow a question if in his opinion it is "directed to the merits of Government policy". Thus the determination whether it is so directed is left to him. His decision to disallow a question therefore could not be challenged unless the decision was wholly perverse or unreasonable. The representative may be questioned on "matters of fact and expert opinion" (see Ministry of Housing and Local Government Circular 9/58, para. 15). The line between these matters and matters of policy may be difficult to draw, particularly as the merits of the policy will usually depend on the merits of the expert opinion which underlies it (e.g., techniques of traffic forecasting in relation to Government road programmes). However, it may be noted that the rules do not preclude questions directed to clarification of the policy statement. Nor do they preclude other parties making representations or calling evidence as to the merits of Government policy.
[2] See *Lavender & Sons Ltd.* v *Minister of Housing and Local Government*, [1970] 1 WLR 1231 at p. 1241 per Willis J.
[3] *Ibid*, rule 7(4). In this case (unlike rule 6(2)—note 1, *supra*) the opinion of the inspector is not specifically made the test. Thus, although the decision not to allow the introduction of evidence contrary to the public interest will be for him in the first instance, it would be open to question in the Courts: see *Conway* v *Rimmer*, [1968] AC 910 HL, and compare *Wednesbury Corpn.* v *Ministry of Housing and Local Government* (No. 1), [1965] 1 All ER 186, in which an unsuccessful attempt was made to secure production of the inspector's terms of reference.
[4] *Ibid*, rule 7(4). Thus, for instance, he can admit hearsay evidence or any material which is "logically probative": *T. A. Miller* v *Ministry of Housing and Local Government*, [1968] 1 WLR 992. Although this provision gives the inspector a discretion, the purpose is to enable formal obstacles to be overcome rather than to give him a general power to restrict the evidence given at the inquiry. Thus the acquiring authority and the statutory objectors have a specific right to call evidence (rule 6(3)). This right cannot be restricted by the inspector unless their evidence is contrary to the public interest (provided, presumably, that the evidence is relevant).
[5] *Ibid*, rule 7(4).
[6] Acquisition of Land (Authorisation Procedure) Act 1946, s. 5(2), applying Local Government Act 1972, s. 250(2). As an alternative he may require the witness to subscribe to a declaration of the truth of any statement: *ibid*. The Local Government Act 1972, s. 250(2)–(5) re-enacts with modifications the procedural provisions formerly in the Local Government Act 1933, s. 290(2)–(5). References to the latter in other enactments are construed as references to the Local Government Act 1972: Interpretation Act 1889, s. 38(1).
[7] Local government Act 1972, s. 250(2).
[8] *Ibid*, s. 250(2)(b).
[9] *Ibid*, s. 250(2)(a). Formerly expenses could only be claimed for a journey of over ten miles from the place of residence: Local Government Act 1933, s. 290(2)(a).
[10] Local Government Act 1972, s. 250(3). The offender is liable on conviction to a fine of up to £100 or to imprisonment for up to six months, or both: *ibid*.

Site Inspection

The acquiring authority and the statutory objectors may require the inspector to inspect the relevant land after the close of the inquiry. The request must be made before or during the inquiry, and the inspector must announce the date and time of the inspection during the inquiry.[1] The authority and the statutory objectors are entitled to accompany him on such an inspection, but he is not bound to defer the inspection to enable such parties to be present.[2] He may in any event make an unaccompanied inspection at any time before or during the inquiry without giving notice.[3] If, at a site inspection after the close of the inquiry, the inspector observes a matter which he regards as material and which has not been raised at the inquiry, he should either reconvene the inquiry or invite the parties to express their views in writing.[4]

Procedure after the inquiry

After the close of the inquiry the inspector makes a report in writing to the Secretary of State. The report must include his findings of fact and his recommendations, if any, or his reasons for not making recommendations.[5] The report should be precise and unambiguous,[6] but the inspector is entitled to exercise his own judgment as to the matters which he considers material.[7] "... such an inspector is not merely trying an issue or issues between the local authority and the objector owner, and may from his professional experience supply deficiencies in the case as presented by the local authority ... he is not bound to accept as established a contention in evidence for the objector owner simply because it is not, or is not adequately, challenged or contested on the part of the acquiring authority at the hearing. Part of his function lies in his own knowledge of the subject".[8]

Secretary of State's decision

The Secretary of State must consider the inspector's report, and if he accepts his recommendations he may make a decision accordingly. If,

---

[1] Compulsory Purchase by Public Authorities (Inquiries Procedure) Rules 1976. SI 1976 No. 746, rule 8(2). In practice such an inspection is made as a matter of course.

[2] *Ibid.* rule 8(3).

[3] *Ibid,* rule 8. By implication, it seems that unless the parties, having been duly notified, fail to attend, he is not otherwise entitled to make an unaccompanied site inspection after the inquiry has closed.

[4] See *Fairmount Investments* v *Secretary of State,* [1976] 2 All ER 865, in which an order under the Housing Act 1957, Part III, was quashed because the decision had been influenced by the inspector's observation, at the site-view, of a broken tell-tale, which had not been mentioned at the inquiry. "What he should have done was either to reconvene the hearing or to invite the Secretary of State to do so: or, in a relatively straightforward case such as this, have, in writing, invited views on his provisional conclusions as to the foundations and financial feasibility": *ibid,* [1976] 2 All ER 865 at p. 874d per Lord Russell of Killowen. See also *Hibernian Property Co. Ltd.* v *Secretary of State* in (1973), 27 P & CR 197, in which a similar order was quashed because the inspector had on the site-view invited local residents to express their opinions, and there was a risk that this might have influenced the decision.

[5] SI 1976 No. 746, rule 9(1).

[6] *William Boyer & Sons Ltd.* v *Minister of Housing and Local Government* (1968), 20 P & CR 176. "Documents like inspectors' reports and letters of decision should no doubt be precise and unambiguous, intelligible and readily understood, but they cannot, I think, be expected always to be capable of satisfying the critical analysis of a schoolman": *ibid,* at p. 184 per Willis J.

[7] See *Continental Sprays Ltd.* v *Minister of Housing and Local Government* (1968), 19 P & CR 774.

[8] *Fairmount Investments Ltd.* v *Secretary of State,* [1976] 2 All ER 865 at p. 873j, per Lord Russell of Killowen.

however, he is disposed to disagree with any of the inspector's recommendations either:

    (i) because he differs from him on a finding of fact;[1]

    (ii) because of new evidence (including expert opinion on a matter of fact) received by him after the close of the inquiry;[2] or

    (iii) because he has taken into consideration a new issue of fact (not being a matter of Government policy)[3] which was not raised at the inquiry.

then he cannot make an immediate decision. He must first notify the acquiring authority and any statutory objector[4] who appeared at the inquiry of his disagreement and the reasons for it. They then have an opportunity to make written representations within 21 days. In cases (ii) and (iii) above, they also have the right to ask within 21 days for the inquiry to be reopened,[5] and if either the acquiring authority or a statutory objector asks for the inquiry to be reopened in such a case, the Secretary of State is required to do so.[6] The Secretary of State may in any event reopen the inquiry if he thinks fit even if he has not been required to do so.[6] If the inquiry is reopened the same notices must be given as for the original inquiry, save that the minimum notice is 28 days instead of 42.[6]

[1] The line between "issues of fact" and other matters may be difficult in practice to draw precisely. Although inspectors' reports usually contain a section headed "Findings of Fact" followed by a section headed "Conclusions", this division is not to be regarded as sacrosanct. "We must look into them and see which of his findings are truly findings of fact and which are expressions of opinion on planning merits": per Lord Denning MR in *Lord Luke of Pavenham* v *Minister of Housing and Local Government*, [1968] 1 QB 172 at p. 191. It seems that inferences of fact drawn by the inspector may also be issues of fact for this purpose: *ibid* at p. 194F per Russell LJ. But issues of fact are to be distinguished from "opinion on a planning matter" (*ibid* at p. 192) or "conjecture as to what is possible or feasible" (*Camden London Borough Council* v *Secretary of State*, [1975] JPL 661 per Lord Denning MR) or "aesthetic judgment" (*Vale Estates Acton Ltd.* v *Secretary of State* (1970) 69 LGR 543 at p. 557 per John Stephenson J). It seems that a question whether something is "reasonably necessary" is an issue of fact: see *Coleen Properties Ltd.* v *Minister of Housing and Local Government*, [1971] 1 All ER 1049 at p. 1055. See also *Pyford Properties* v *Secretary of State* [1977] JPL 724.

[2] Note that, although the statutory rules relate specifically only to new evidence or issues of fact which lead the Secretary of State to differ from the inspector's recommendation, the same principle will apply under the rules of natural justice to any new evidence relating to matters in issue at the inquiry, which is received by the inspector or the Secretary of State after the inquiry and which influences the result: see *Fairmount Investments Ltd.* v *Secretary of State*, note 8, p. 42 . It seems that the rules of natural justice may be invoked to supplement the statutory rules where necessary, since "it is to be implied, unless the contrary appears, that Parliament does not authorise by the Act the exercise of powers in breach of the principles of natural justice, and that Parliament does by the Act require, in the particular procedures, compliance with those principles"*ibid*, [1976] 2 All ER 865 at p. 872 per Lord Russell of Killowen. See also *Hamilton* v *Secretary of State for Scotland*, 1972 SLT 233, in which it was held that an allegation of a breach of the rules of natural justice was a relevant averment in relation to an inquiry governed by the inquiries procedure rules.

[3] See for example *Darlassis* v *Minister of Education* (1954), 4 P & CR 281, in which the Minister was held entitled to take into account, when confirming an order, views received after the inquiry from another Ministry as to the objections to a possible alternative site. Although this case did not relate to an inquiry under the inquiries procedure rules, it appears that such matters would be within the exclusion, in rule 9(2)(b), of matters of Government policy: see *Lavender & Son* v *Minister of Housing and Local Government*, [1970] 1 WLR 1231.

[4] Although parties other than the acquiring authority and statutory objectors are not entitled to ask for the inquiry to be reopened, the Secretary of State will in practice arrange for such other parties to be included in any consultations that take place as to the reopening of the inquiry: Ministry of Housing and Local Government Circular 49/62 para. 38.

[5] SI 1976 No. 746, rule 9(1).

[6] *Ibid*, rule 9(2).

Notice of decision

When the Secretary of State has finally made a decision he must notify his decision and his reasons[1] to the acquiring authority, the statutory objectors and any other person who appeared at the inquiry and asked to be notified.[2] If a copy of the inspector's report is not sent with the notice of decision the notice must include a summary of his conclusions and recommendations.[3] The parties may apply to the Secretary of State within one month of the notification of decision[4] for a copy of the inspector's report.[5] They may also apply to the Secretary of State within six weeks of the publication of the notice of confirmation of the order[6] for an opportunity to inspect the documents, photographs and plans[7] appended to the inspector's report.[8]

Costs

The Secretary of State may make orders as to payment of the costs of any parties at the inquiry.[9] Normally a successful objector to a compulsory purchase order affecting his property will be awarded his costs against the authority.[10] Otherwise costs are generally only awarded where a party has acted unreasonably,[11] or where extra costs have been occasioned by postponement or adjournment of the inquiry.[12] Although the power to award costs is not limited to awards in favour of or against the acquiring authority and statutory objectors, awards in favour of or against other parties will only be made in exceptional circumstances, even in cases of unreasonable behaviour.[13] Although

---

[1] The most commonly cited dictum as to the nature of the duty to give reasons is that of Megaw J. in *Re Poyser and Mills' Arbitration*, [1964] 2 QB 467 at 478: "Parliament provided that reasons shall be given, and in my view that must be read as meaning that proper, adequate reasons must be given. The reasons that are set out must be reasons which will not only be intelligible, but which deal with the substantial points that have been raised". This was cited with approval by the Court of Appeal in *Elliott v Southwark Borough Council*, [1976] 1 WLR 499 at p. 508 (see also *Earl of Iveagh v Minister of Housing and Local Government*, [1964] 1 QB 395 CA at p. 410). For an example of a case in which the Minister's reasons were held to be inadequate under the similar rules relating to planning inquiries (now SI 1974 No. 419 rule 13(1)) see *Givaudan & Co.* v *Minister of Housing and Local Government*, [1967] 1 WLR 250. An inspector's decision on a planning appeal transferred to him under the Town and Country Planning Act 1971, Sch. 9, was held to give inadequate reasons in *Hope* v *Secretary of State* (1975), 31 P & CR 120. Where the reason for the decision is simply that the Secretary of State does not feel justified in departing from his established policy, it may be enough for him simply to say "I find no reason for departing from the policy": *Vale Estates Ltd.* v *Secretary of State* (1970), 69 LGR 543 at p. 559, applying *Wheland* v *Minister of Housing and Local Government* (unreported).
[2] SI 1976 No. 746, rule 10(1).
[3] *Ibid.*
[4] Or the date of the first publication of notice of confirmation of the order, whichever is later: *ibid*, rule 10(2).
[5] *Ibid*, rule 10(2).
[6] If the decision is not to confirm the order it seems that there is no right to inspect the documents (presumably because the right to apply to the High Court within six weeks is conferred only in cases where the order is confirmed: Acquisition of Land (Authorisation Procedure) Act 1946, Sch. 1, para. 15, as to which see p. 52, *infra*).
[7] These documents, etc. will not be supplied as part of the "report": SI 1976 No. 746, rule 10(3).
[8] *Ibid*, rule 10(3).
[9] Acquisition of Land Authorisation Procedure) Act 1946, s. 5(2), applying the Local Government Act 1972, s. 250(5), as to which see note 6, p. 41, *supra*.
[10] Ministry of Housing and Local Government Circular 73/65, paras. 5–6.
[11] *Ibid*, paras. 9. Examples of "unreasonableness" are given in the Report of the Council on Tribunals on Award of Costs at Statutory Inquiries, Cmnd. 2471/1965, paras. 27–29 (set out in Encyclopaedia of Compulsory Purchase, paras. 4–107
[12] Circular 73/65, para. 10.
[13] See Report of Council on Tribunals, *supra*, para. 47.

submissions relating to costs can be made at the inquiry, the inspector does not normally[1] make a recommendation relating to costs and the award is a matter entirely for the Secretary of State.[2] Successful objectors are usually asked, when the decision is made, whether they wish to apply for costs.[3] The Secretary of State may limit his award to a proportion of the costs where an objector is only partly successful.[4] In default of agreement as to amount, the costs are taxed in the High Court.[5] The Secretary of State's order may be made a rule of the High Court on the application of any party named in the order,[6] and this will enable it to be enforced in the same way as an order for costs made in High Court proceedings.

The Secretary of State also has power to make directions requiring the authority or any other party to pay the costs incurred by the Secretary of State himself, including an amount not exceeding £30 per day for the services of any officer engaged in the inquiry. Any amount so certified by the Secretary of State is recoverable as a debt to the Crown or by the Secretary of State summarily as a civil debt.[7]

(iv) HEARINGS

Although we have hitherto been considering the procedure for the holding of an inquiry into objections, it should be noted that the Secretary of State has a discretion to hold either a "public local inquiry" or a "hearing".[8] The precise significance of the distinction between a "public local inquiry" and a "hearing" is not entirely clear. In the circular[9] explaining the 1946 Act the provision for a "hearing" was described as an "innovation". The Secretary of State was given the alternative of "having an informal hearing of an objector and of the representatives of the acquiring authority instead of holding a formal public local inquiry".[10] However the same rules of procedure now apply to a hearing as to a public local inquiry,[11] the only difference being that notice of a hearing is only given to the acquiring authority and the statutory objectors; there is no public notice or publication in a local newspaper.[12] This exception suggests that it is anticipated that a

---

[1] Except where he has allowed an adjournment because the acquiring authority have added to the matters referred to in their pre-inquiry statement: see note 5, p. 39, *supra*.

[2] Circular 73/65, para. 12. See also *R* v *Secretary of State ex parte Reinisch* (1971), 22 P & CR 1022, in which the Divisional Court refused to interfere with the Secretary of State's decision not to award costs to a successful appellant on an enforcement appeal, even though the decision might have been partly due to a mistake of law.

[3] Circular 73/65, para. 12.

[4] *Ibid*, paras. 14–15.

[5] *Ibid*, para. 13, as amended by Department of the Environment Circular 69/71, para. 3.

[6] Local Government Act 1972, s. 250(5). For a form and procedure (in relation to inquiries held into orders under the Housing Acts) see 20 Atkins Court Forms (2nd Edn.) 382, 425.

[7] Local Government Act 1972, s. 250(4). The use of this power appears to be rare.

[8] Acquisition of Land (Authorisation Procedure) Act 1946, Sch. 1, para. 4 (2), which provides that he may "either cause a public local inquiry to be held or afford to any person by whom any objection has been duly made as aforesaid and not withdrawn an *opportunity of appearing before and being heard by* a person appointed by the confirming authority for the purpose".

[9] Ministry of Health Circular 104/46.

[10] *Ibid*, enclosure para. 13. The requirement to hold a hearing is not fulfilled by "one of those interminable informal conferences so beloved of civil servants": per Upjohn J. in *Ealing Borough Council* v *Minister of Housing and Local Government*, [1952] 1 Ch. 856, 868.

[11] SI 1976 No. 746, rule 2. Thus the procedure is as outlined on pp. 37 *et seq, supra*.

[12] *Ibid*, rule 2 and rule 4(3).

hearing, unlike a public local inquiry, will not normally be open to the public.[1] However if a hearing is held for any objector, the acquiring authority have a right to be heard on the same occasion and the Secretary of State must afford the same opportunity to "any other persons to whom it appears to the Secretary of State expedient to afford it".[2] In addition the inspector may allow any other person to appear at his discretion.[3]

The main formal distinction appears to be that the general provisions of the Local Government Act 1972, s. 250[4] relating to public local inquiries do not apply to hearings.[5] Thus the inspector at a hearing cannot take evidence on oath and has no power to require the attendance of witnesses or production of documents. In addition the Minister has no power to make an order as to the costs of a hearing.[6] It seems unsatisfactory that a decision to hold a hearing instead of a public local inquiry, involving as it does a denial of these important procedural rights,[7] should be entirely at the discretion of the Minister. In practice, however, it is almost invariable for a public local inquiry rather than a hearing to be held where there are objections to a compulsory purchase order.

3 Compulsory Purchase by Government Departments

PROCEDURE

Where the compulsory purchase order is to be made by a Minister the procedure is substantially the same as when it is made by a local authority.[8] However instead of being first made by the authority and then confirmed by the Secretary of State the order is first prepared in draft by the Minister concerned, and then "made" by him after completion of the statutory formalities, and after the inquiry, if any.[9] The

---

[1] Neither the Acquisition of Land (Authorisation Procedure) Act 1946 nor the inquiries procedure rules (SI 1976 No. 746) impose any specific requirement for inquiries or hearings to be open to the public. However the expression "public local inquiry" (cf. Town and Country Planning Act 1971, s. 282, which refers simply to a "local inquiry") implies that the public will be allowed to attend. It appears that one of the purposes of a public local inquiry may be to "afford publicity in the local press which may in some way affect the decision of the Minister ...": see *Errington* v *Minister of Health*, [1935] 1 KB 249 at p. 271, per Maugham LJ "... a "local inquiry ... into the objections"—which may be contrasted with "an opportunity of appearing before and being heard by the Minister ..."—involves that the person appointed should listen not merely to representations by the objector but also to representations by other persons who have an interest in the subject matter of the objections whether in support of the objections or against them": *Wednesbury Corporation* v *Ministry of Housing and Local Government* No. 2, [1966] 2 QB 275 at p. 302 per Diplock LJ.
[2] Acquisition of Land (Authorisation Procedure) Act 1946, Sch. 1, para. 4(3).
[3] SI 1976 No. 746, rule 5(1).
[4] As to which, see pp. 41, 44, *supra*.
[5] By the Acquisition of Land (Authorisation Procedure) Act 1946, s. 5(2) the provisions of the Local Government Act 1972, s. 250(2)–(5) are applied only to "a public local inquiry held in pursuance of this Act". See [1953] JPL 644 for a decision of the Minister refusing, for this reason, to consider a claim for the costs of a "hearing".
[6] Local Government Act 1972, s. 250(2)–(5).
[7] The Report of the Council on Tribunals, Cmnd. 2471, recommended that the statutory provision for the award of costs should be extended to hearings, but this has yet to be implemented: see Ministry of Housing and Local Government Circular 73/65, para. 4.
[8] Acquisition of Land (Authorisation Procedure) Act 1946, Sch. 1, para. 7.
[9] *Ibid*, para. 7(1).

provisions of the 1946 Act relating to purchases by authorities[1] are applied with appropriate modifications to purchases by Ministers.[2] In particular, there is no prescribed form for the order, and apart from the requirement that the land shall be described by reference to a map,[3] the form of the order may be determined by the Minister.[4]

INQUIRY

Where an inquiry or hearing is held, procedure is governed by the Compulsory Purchase by Ministers (Inquiries Procedure) Rules 1967.[5] The procedure generally follows that contained in the rules for acquisition by local authorities.[6] The Minister has the same obligation to provide a statement of reasons at least 28 days before the inquiry, and to make available documents for inspection.[7] It may be noted that publicity requirements are slightly more stringent in that the Minister is bound both to post a notice of the inquiry in a conspicuous place near the land and in one or more places where public notices are usually posted in the locality, *and also* to publish notice in one or more newspapers circulating in the locality.[8]

The Minister is bound to make a representative available at the inquiry to answer questions in elucidation of the statement of reasons,[9] but not questions which, in the opinion of the inspector, are directed to the merits of Government policy.[10] The provisions of the Local Government Act 1972, s. 250(2)–(5), (powers of subpoena and to award costs) apply to such inquiries as to inquiries into acquisitions by local authorities.[11]

Following the inquiry, the Minister has the same duties in relation to

[1] See pp. 32 *et seq, supra.*
[2] Acquisition of Land (Authorisation Procedure) Act 1946, Sch, 1, para. 7(4).
[3] *Ibid.* para. 7(2).
[4] *Ibid,* para. 7(3).
[5] SI 1967 No. 720.
[6] Under the Compulsory Purchase by Public Authorities (Inquiries Procedure) Rules 1976, SI 1976 No. 746, as to which see pp. 37 *et seq, supra.*
[7] SI 1967 No. 720, rule 5(1). Compare SI 1976 No. 746, rule 4(1) (see p. 38, *supra*).
[8] SI 1967 No. 720 rule 4(2). Compare the Secretary of State's discretion under SI 1976 No. 746, rule 4(3) (see p. 38, *supra*).
[9] "It is plainly the duty of the Minister and his representatives to give to the public, as well as to those who may be directly affected by his proposals, the fullest information with regard to those proposals and to explain clearly the purposes he has in view and how such purposes will be achieved and also the statutory or other authority under which the proposals are made": *Re the Trunk Roads Act 1936,* [1939] 2 KB 515 at p. 522. It is thought that this statement of principle holds good even though the obligations of the Minister are now spelt out in the statutory rules which did not apply in that case.
[10] SI 1967 No. 720, rule 6(22), and see p. 41, *supra.* If the inspector decides that such a question is directed to the merits of Government policy the representative may refuse to answer, but he is not apparently bound to refuse. Cf. rule 7(3) which provides specifically, in relation to the supporting evidence of other Government Departments, that the inspector "*shall disallow* any questions which in his opinion are directed to the merits of Government policy" (see p. 41, *supra*). Where the evidence is that of the acquiring Minister the inspector may apparently allow the question if the representative is willing to answer it.
[11] Acquisition of Land (Authorisation Procedure) Act 1946, s. 5. See Ministry of Housing and Local Government Circular 73/65, para. 7: "The Minister will consider making an *ex gratia* payment of costs to successful objectors into similar orders or proposals initiated by him ...". It is not clear why objectors should be so dependent on the magnanimity of the Minister (cf. the policy in relation to acquisitions by authorities, p. 44, *supra*) but it is understood that in practice awards of costs are normally made to successful objectors.

the making and notification of his decision[1] as does the Secretary of State in relation to orders made by an authority.[2] He must consider the objections and the report of the inspector,[3] and he must give an opportunity for the inquiry to be reopened where he disagrees with the inspector on certain matters.[4] The notice of his decision must give clear and adequate reasons.[5]

4 Special categories of land[6]

In the cases of certain special categories of land the ordinary procedures outlined above are supplemented by certain additional requirements. The categories in question can be summarised as follows:

(i)   National Trust land;
(ii) Land of statutory undertakers;
(iii) Commons and open spaces;
(iv) Ancient monuments.

These categories will be defined and considered in turn.

(i) NATIONAL TRUST LAND

In so far as the order authorises the compulsory purchase of land belonging to the National Trust[7] which is held by the Trust inalienably[8] the order will be subject to special parliamentary procedure[9] in any case where objection to the order has been duly made by the Trust and has not been withdrawn.[10] A similar requirement formerly applied to land belonging to local authorities or statutory undertakers, but this has now been removed by the Community Land Act 1975.[11]

(ii) LAND OF STATUTORY UNDERTAKERS

A particular restriction applies if the order includes land which has

---

[1] SI 1967 No. 720, rules 11–12.

[2] SI 1976 No. 746, rules 9–10; see pp. 35 et seq, supra.

[3] Acquisition of Land (Authorisation of Procedure) Act 1946 Sch. 1, para. 7(4), applying ibid para 4(2), as to which see p. 36, supra.

[4] SI 1967 No. 720, rule 11, which lays down the same criteria as those contained in SI 1976 No. 720, rule 9, as to which see p. 43, supra.

[5] SI 1967 No. 720, rule 12(1): see p. 44, supra.

[6] See generally Department of the Environment Circular 26/77, Appendix IG.

[7] The "National Trust" is the "National Trust for places of Historic Interest or Natural Beauty" incorporated by the National Trust Act 1907: Acquisition of Land (Authorisation Procedure) Act 1946, s. 8(1).

[8] "Held inalienably" means that the land is inalienable under the National Trust Act 1907, s. 21, or the National Trust Act 1939, s. 8: Acquisition of Land (Authorisation Procedure) Act 1946, s. 8(1). The fact that land is made inalienable by any enactment does not exclude it from acquisition under the 1946 Act: ibid, s. 6(3).

[9] As to which, see pp. 51 et seq, infra.

[10] Acquisition of Land (Authorisation Procedure) Act 1946, Sch. 1, para. 9. This requirement will only apply if the land was owned by the National Trust at the time when objections had to be made, and objection was made by them in the capacity of owner: Middlesex County Council v Minister of Housing and Local Government, [1953] 1 QB 12.

[11] Community Land Act 1975, s. 41, which applies where notice of the making or preparation of an order was first published on or after 6 April 1976.

been acquired by statutory undertakers[1] for the purpose of their undertaking, and if the appropriate Minister[2] is satisfied, on a representation
made before the end of the time for objections to the order, that either:

(a) any of the land is used for the purposes of the carrying on of the
undertaking of the statutory undertakers in question; or

(b) an interest in any of the land is held for those purposes.

Such an order cannot be confirmed unless the appropriate Minister is
satisfied and certifies that the nature and situation of the land are such
that either:

(c) it can be purchased and not replaced without serious detriment to the carrying on of the undertaking; or

(d) if purchased it can be replaced by other land belonging to,
or available for acquisition by, the undertakers without serious
detriment to the carrying on of the undertaking.[3]

(iii) COMMONS AND OPEN SPACES

In so far as an order includes land forming part of a common,[4] open
space[5] or fuel or field garden allotment[6] it is subject to special parliamentary procedure[7] unless the Secretary of State certifies that there
has been or will be given in exchange other land not less in area and
equally advantageous to the public and to the persons if any entitled to
rights of common or other rights.[8] He must also be satisfied that the
exchange land will be vested in the same persons and subject to the

---

[1] "Statutory undertakers" means "any persons authorised by any Act (whether public general
or local), or by any order or scheme made under or confirmed by an Act, to construct, work or
carry on any railway, light railway, tramway, road transport, water transport, canal, inland
navigation, dock, harbour, pier or lighthouse undertaking or any undertaking for the supply of
electricity, gas, hydraulic power or water": Acquisition of Land (Authorisation Procedure) Act
1946, s. 8(1).

[2] Formerly the identity of the "appropriate Minister" varied with the nature of the undertaking
involved: Acquisition of Land (Authorisation Procedure) Act 1946, s. 8(1). However, the Secretary of State is now the appropriate Minister for all purposes except in relation to lighthouse
undertakings and the Post Office: Secretary of State for the Environment Order 1970 (SI 1970 No.
1681) Sch. 3, para. 15.

[3] Acquisition of Land (Authorisation Procedure) Act 1946, Sch. 1, para. 10.

[4] " 'Common' includes any land subject to be enclosed under the Inclosure Acts 1845 to 1882
and any town or village green": Acquisition of Land (Authorisation Procedure) Act 1946, s. 8(1).
Lands subject to enclosure under the Inclosure Acts are widely defined in the Inclosure Act 1845,
s. 11. The 1946 Act definition, which extends also to town and village greens and is no more than
an inclusive definition, is clearly intended to be very wide. It should be noted that the definition is
not identical with the definition of "common land" in the Commons Registration Act 1965, s.
22(1). Thus, for example, it is open to question whether "waste land of a manor not subject to
rights of common" (ibid, s. 22(1)(b)) would be a "common" for the purpose of the 1946 Act, since
such land would not be within the common law meaning of common land.

[5] " 'Open space' means any land laid out as a public garden, or used for the purposes of public
recreation, or land being a disused burial ground": Acquisition of Land (Authorisation Procedure) Act 1946, s. 8(1). It seems that the test is not satisfied if the land is only in the course of
being laid out as a public garden: see Wilcock v Secretary of State (1974), 232 Estates Gazette 1385,
[1975] JPL 150.

[6] A "fuel or field garden allotment" is "any allotment set out as a fuel allotment, or a field garden
allotment, under an Inclosure Act": Acquisition of Land (Authorisation Procedure) Act 1946, s.
8(1).

[7] See p. 51, infra.

[8] Acquisition of Land (Authorisation Procedure) Act 1946, Sch. 1, para. 11(1). The exchange
land may be less valuable to the owner, and if so, he can claim compensation notwithstanding the
certificate: see McKay v City of London (1966), 17 P & CR 564, LT.

same rights trusts and incidents as the land to be acquired.[1] There is an exception if the land falling within the special category does not exceed 250 square yards in extent, or if it is required for the widening or drainage of an existing highway. In that case the Secretary of State may, if satisfied that the giving of exchange land is unnecessary in the interests of the public or of the persons entitled to rights of common or other rights, certify accordingly. No exchange land will then be required, and the order can be put into effect without special parliamentary procedure.[2]

Before issuing a certificate relating to exchange land or a certificate that exchange land is not required, the Secretary of State must give public notice[3] of his intention to do so. He must then afford an opportunity to all persons interested to make representations and objections. He must also hold a public local inquiry[4] if it appears to him expedient having regard to any representations or objections made. Before giving the certificate he must consider the representations and objections, and, if there is an inquiry, the inspector's report.[5] The compulsory purchase order may itself include provisions for discharging the purchased land from the rights trusts and incidents to which it was previously subject, and for vesting the exchange land, if any, in the appropriate person and subject to the appropriate rights.[6]

(iv) ANCIENT MONUMENTS

In so far as the order includes land which is, or is the site of, an ancient monument[7] or other object of archaeological interest,[8] the order is subject to special parliamentary procedure[9] unless the Secretary of State certifies that the acquiring authority have entered into an undertaking with him to observe such conditions as to the use of land as in his opinion are requisite having regard to its nature.[10]

[1] Provision for the vesting of the land may be made in the order itself: see note 6, infra.

[2] Acquisition of Land (Authorisation Procedure) Act 1946, Sch. 1, para. 11(1).

[3] There is no prescribed form or procedure for giving notice, but the notice must be sufficiently clear and unambiguous to attract the attention of potential objectors: see Wilson v Secretary of State, [1974] 1 WLR 1083, where a notice, which described the land by a name other than that commonly used in the locality, was held to be ineffective. Prima facie, it will normally be sufficient to give notice in newspapers circulating in the area where the land is situated: McMeechan v Secretary of State, [1974] JPL 411 CA, citing Waitemata County v Local Government Commission, [1964] NZLR 689.

[4] Such inquiries are not subject to the Inquiries Procedure Rules, which are limited to inquiries "for the purpose of inquiring into the authorisation of any compulsory purchase of land ...": (SI 1976 No. 146, rule 2). However, they are subject to the Local Government Act 1972, s. 250(2)–(5) (as to which see pp. 41, 44 supra); Acquisition of Land (Authorisation Procedure) Act 1946, s. 5.

[5] Ibid, Sch. 1, para. 11(2).

[6] Ibid, Sch. 1, para. 11(3). The form of order in such cases is prescribed: Compulsory Purchase of Land Regulations 1976, SI 1976 No. 300, Form 2.

[7] "Ancient Monument" has the same meaning as in the Ancient Monuments Acts 1913 to 1931; Acquisition of Land (Authorisation Procedure) Act 1946, s. 8(1). For the provisions of the Ancient Monuments Acts see p. 427, post.

[8] This term is not defined. Local authorities are advised to ask the Chief Inspector of Ancient Monuments for an opinion as to whether land should be regarded as within this category: Department of the Environment Circular 26/77, Appendix IE, 6(1). A listed building, or any land or object within its curtilage, is not within the scope of these provisions: Town and Country Planning Act 1968, s. 59.

[9] As to which see p. 51, infra.

[10] Acquisition of Land (Authorisation Procedure) Act 1946, Sch. 1, para. 12. This provision does not apply where the Secretary of State is himself the acquiring authority: ibid.

CERTIFICATES GENERALLY

As soon as practicable after the giving of a certificate relating to special land the acquiring authority must publish a notice[1] in one or more newspapers circulating in the locality stating that the certificate has been given.[2] In appropriate circumstances the validity of a certificate may be challenged by appeal to the High Court within six weeks of the giving of the certificate on the grounds that the statutory requirements have not been complied with.[3]

5 Special Parliamentary Procedure

THE STATUTE

Where an order is subject to special parliamentary procedure,[4] the requirements of the Statutory Orders (Special Procedure) Act 1945 must be complied with before the order becomes effective. Special parliamentary procedure is in addition to the procedures already described, and does not come into play until the ordinary steps for confirmation of an order have been completed.[5]

PROCEDURE

At least three days' notice of the Secretary of State's intention to lay the order before Parliament must be given in the London Gazette.[6] The order must be accompanied by a certificate of compliance with the statutory requirements for confirmation of the order.[7] Petitions may be presented within 21 days. They are divided into "petitions of amendment" and "petitions of general objection".[8] The latter are ones which attack the order generally,[8] or "constitute a negative of the main purpose of the order";[9] the former are ones which ask for particular amendments.[8] The petitions are scrutinised by the Lord Chairman of Committees and the Chairman of Ways and Means, who certify them as "proper to be received",[10] and ensure that they have been properly categorised.[11] The Chairmen's report is then laid before both Houses of Parliament.[12] Unless either House resolves within 21 days to annul the order, the petitions are referred to a joint committee of both Houses.[13] If there are no petitions the order comes into operation at the end of the 21 days.[14]

The Joint Committee may report the order with or without amendments or, if there are petitions of general objection, they may report that

---

[1] The form of notice is prescribed: Compulsory Purchase of Land Regulations 1976, SI 1976 No. 300, Form 8.

[2] Acquisition of Land (Authorisation Procedure) Act 1946, Sch. 1, para. 13.

[3] *Ibid*, para. 15. The procedure is analogous to that for challenging a compulsory purchase order: see p. 52, *infra*, but note that a certificate cannot be challenged on the grounds that it is "not empowered" by the Act (the first ground on which the authorisation of a compulsory purchase order may be challenged: *ibid*, para. 15).

[4] See, e.g., pp. 48 *et seq*, *supra*.

[5] Statutory Orders (Special Procedure) Act 1945, s. 2(1). The Act also provides for the making of standing orders governing procedure generally: *ibid*, s. 9.

[6] *Ibid*, s. 2(1).   [7] *Ibid*, s. 2(2).

[8] *Ibid*, s. 3(2).   [9] *Ibid*, s. 3(4).

[10] *Ibid*, s. 3(3).   [11] *Ibid*, s. 3(4).

[12] *Ibid*, s. 3(5).   [13] *Ibid*, s. 4(2).

[14] *Ibid*, s. 4(3).

the order be not approved.[1] If the order is reported without amendments it comes into effect on the date when the report is laid before
Parliament unless a later date is specified in the order.[2] If there are
amendments and they are accepted by the Secretary of State, he may by
notice determine the date on which the order is to come into operation.[3]
If the Committee report that the order should not take effect, it will
require confirmation by Act of Parliament.[4] Similarly if the Secretary of
State does not accept the amendments reported by the Committee, he
may submit a Bill to Parliament to enable the order to be considered
further.[5] Provision is made for the costs of the proceedings in Parliament.[6]

6 Challenge in the Courts

SPECIAL PROCEDURE

A special procedure is provided by the Act to challenge the validity of a
compulsory purchase order.[7] This is the only means by which an order
can ordinarily be questioned in the Courts.[8] The statutory procedure,
however, is subject to significant limitations which will be considered in
this section.

(i) AGGRIEVED PERSON

An application to challenge the validity of a compulsory purchase order
can only be made by "a person aggrieved" by the order.[9] This expression is found in many statutory contexts unconnected with compulsory
purchase. In recent years, the Courts have leant in favour of a wider
interpretation. Until 1961 the most frequently adopted test was derived
from a 19th century case,[10] in which James LJ said:

> "But the words 'person aggrieved' do not really mean a man who is disappointed of a
> benefit which he might have received if some other order had been made. A 'person
> aggrieved' must be a man who has suffered a legal grievance, a man against whom a
> decision has been pronounced which has wrongfully deprived him of something, or
> wrongfully refused him something".[11]

This test was applied in the *Saffron Waldon Chalkpit* case[12] to exclude a
person whose only interest in a public inquiry was as a neighbouring
landowner. However in a Privy Council case in 1961[13] a much wider
test was formulated by Lord Denning:

[1] Statutory Orders (Special Procedure) Act 1945, s. 5.
[2] *Ibid*, s. 6(1).
[3] *Ibid*, s. 6(2).
[4] *Ibid*, s. 6(3). Where an order is so confirmed the statutory procedure for challenging the
validity of an order (see *infra*) does not apply: Acquisition of Land (Authorisation Procedure)
1946, Sch. 1, para. 17.
[5] *Ibid*, s. 6(4).
[6] *Ibid*, s. 7.
[7] Acquisition of Land (Authorisation Procedure) Act 1946, Sch. 1, para. 15.
[8] *Ibid*, para. 16. See *R* v *Secretary of State ex parte Ostler*, [1976] 3 All ER 90.
[9] Acquisition of Land (Authorisation Procedure) Act 1946, Sch. 1, *para.* 15(1).
[10] *Re Sidebotham ex parte Sidebotham* (1880), 14 Ch D 458.
[11] *Ibid*, at p. 465.
[12] *Buxton* v *Minister of Housing and Local Government*, [1961] 1 QB 278, which concerned an inquiry
relating to an appeal against refusal of an application for planning permission. At that time such
inquiries were not subject to inquiries procedure rules.
[13] *Attorney General of The Gambia* v *N'jie*, [1961] AC 617.

"The words 'person aggrieved' are of wide import and should not be subject to a restrictive interpretation. They do not include, of course, a mere busybody who is interfering in things which do not concern him; but they do include a person who has a genuine grievance because an order has been made which prejudicially affects his interests".[1]

Initially it was thought that this wider test was not applicable to "local authority cases".[2] However, it was cited in a "local authority case" by the Court of Appeal in 1964,[3] so as to include, within the expression "person aggrieved", a person whose legal rights had not been affected but who would suffer a loss of visual amenities as a result of the erection of a proposed building.[4]

The most recent examination of the question, in a context similar to the Acquisition of Land (Authorisation Procedure) Act 1946, was by Ackner J in *Turner v Secretary of State*.[5] In that case he decided that a person who had been permitted by the inspector to appear at an inquiry under the statutory rules[6] could be an aggrieved person, even though he had no legal interest in the land concerned. "Such persons have ... impliedly the right that the Secretary of State, in considering those representations, shall act within the powers conferred on him by the statute, and shall comply with the relevant requirements of the statute in just the same way (as is conceded to be the case) as has a person who makes representations at the inquiry being a person on whom the Secretary of State has required notice of the inquiry to be served."[7]

When a compulsory purchase order is confirmed by the Secretary of State following a public inquiry, it is clear that a person whose property is directly affected by the order would be "a person aggrieved".[8] However, in addition, when the inquiry is conducted under the inquiries procedure rules it seems that anyone who has been permitted to appear at the inquiry has a sufficient interest for these purposes and is entitled to be treated as a "person aggrieved".[9] Where there has been no inquiry it appears that the expression may not be limited to those who had statutory right to object.[10] However, it must be remembered that a compulsory purchase order is normally only concerned with the title to land, and not with the authorisation of any physical works on the land. It is unlikely, therefore, that a person whose only complaint is a potential loss of amenity would be a "person aggrieved" by the confirmation on a compulsory purchase order since his real concern

---

[1] *Ibid*, at p. 634.

[2] *R v Boldero ex parte Bognor Regis UDC* (1962), 60 LGR 292 at p. 296.

[3] *Maurice v LCC*, [1964] 2 QB 362 at p. 378, per Lord Denning MR (with whom Wilberforce J agreed: *ibid* at p. 384).

[4] *Ibid*.

[5] (1973), 28 P & CR 123. The applicants were members of a local preservation society.

[6] Town and Country Planning (Inquiries Procedure) Rules 1969, SI 1969 No. 1092, rule 7(2), which provided that "Any other person may appear at the inquiry at the discretion of the appointed person". The same words are used in the rule relating to compulsory purchase inquiries: SI 1976 No. 746, rule 5(1).

[7] (1973) 28 P & CR 123 at p. 139. But see *Bizony v Secretary of State*, [1975] JPL 306, where the point was thought still open to argument.

[8] *Burke v Minister of Housing and Local Government* (1956), 8 P & CR 25 at p. 28.

[9] *Turner v Secretary of State, supra*.

[10] *Attorney General of The Gambia v N'jie, supra*.

would be with the grant of planning permission, not with the transfer of title to the land.[1]

(ii) THE SIX WEEKS' PERIOD

The time limit laid down by the Act is absolute and cannot be extended even where there is an allegation of bad faith.[2] The time runs from the date on which notice of the confirmation[3] of the order is first published as required by the Act.[4]

(iii) GROUNDS FOR CHALLENGE

Introduction

The validity of the order or any provision in it may be challenged on the grounds either:

(a) that "the authorisation of a compulsory purchase thereby granted is not empowered to be granted under the relevant statutes";[5] or

(b) that any requirements of the relevant statutes or regulations[6] have not been complied with in relation to the order.[7]

These, or similar words, are found in a number of statutes which provide special procedures for challenging administrative decisions. In the past the Courts have found some difficulty in determining their scope, particularly in relation to the first ground.[8] However, the cir-

---

[1] This argument would not apply in cases where the confirmation of a compulsory purchase order confers a "deemed planning permission" (see Town and Country Planning Act 1971, s. 40(3)(b)). However, normally planning permission is granted before the order is submitted to the Secretary of State for confirmation: see Department of the Environment Circular 26/77, Appendix IC.

[2] *R* v *Secretary of State ex parte Ostler*, [1976] 3 All ER 90, in which the Court of Appeal held that the decision in *Smith* v *East Elloe RDC*, [1956] AC 736 should be followed notwithstanding the criticisms of that case expressed in *Anisminic Ltd.* v *Foreign Compensation Commission*, [1969] 2 AC 147.

[3] The Act refers to the "confirmation *or making* of the order". It is thought that the reference to the "making" of any order is intended to cover the case of a Ministerial order which is first prepared in draft and is only "made" after objections have been considered (see p. 46, *supra*). It does not enable the procedure to be used before confirmation of an order. In the case of an order to which Special Parliamentary Procedure applies (see p. 51 *supra*), the relevant date is the date on which it becomes operative: Acquisition of Land (Authorisation Procedure) Act 1946, Sch. 1, para. 17.

[4] *Ibid*, Sch. 1, para. 15(1). See p. 36, *supra* as to the requirement to publish notice of confirmation. This date may not be the same as the date on which notice of the Secretary of State's decision on the inquiry is given under the Inquiries Procedure Rules (see p. 44, *supra*) or the date on which notice of the order is given to individual owners or occupiers (see p. 36, *supra*).

[5] I.e., under the Acquisition of Land (Authorisation Procedure) Act 1946 itself, or under the Act conferring the compulsory purchase power.

[6] The requirements were originally limited to the requirement of the 1946 Act itself and regulations under it. They now include the requirements of the Tribunals and Inquiries Act 1971 and any rules made under that Act: (Land Compensation Act 1973, s. 64). This enables, *inter alia*, the requirements of the Inquiries Procedure Rules (SI 1976 No. 746) to be taken into account. Cf. *Hamilton* v *Secretary of State for Scotland*, 1972 SLT 233, in which it was decided (before this change in the law) that a breach of the Inquiries Procedure rules made under the Tribunals and Inquiries Act 1971 could not be relied on as a ground of challenge under these provisions.

[7] Acquisition of Land (Authorisation Procedure) Act 1946, Sch. 1, para. 15.

[8] Compare, for example, the opinions of Lord Radcliffe and Lord Reid (dissenting) in *Smith* v *East Elloe RDC*, [1956] AC 736 at pp. 767–9, and pp. 762–3 respectively. See also the discussion of that case in *Anisminic* v *Foreign Compensation Commission*, [1969] 2 AC 147 at p. 170 (Lord Reid) and p. 201 (Lord Pearce) and in the judgment of Browne J reported at [1969] 2 AC 223 at pp. 244–5.

cumstances in which the Courts will regard a case as coming within the statutory grounds are now relatively clearly settled, at any rate in the Court of Appeal. In *Ashbridge Investments Ltd. v Minister of Housing and Local Government*,[1] Lord Denning MR said (in relation to the corresponding provisions of the Housing Act 1957):[2]

> "The Court can only interfere on the ground that the Minister has gone outside the powers of the Act or that any requirement of the Act has not been complied with. Under this paragraph it seems to me that the Court can interfere with the Minister's decision if he has acted on no evidence, or if he has come to a conclusion to which on the evidence he could not reasonably come; or if he has taken into consideration matters which he ought not to have taken into account, or *vice versa*; or has otherwise gone wrong in law. It is identical with the position where the Court has power to interfere with the decision of a lower tribunal which has erred in point of law".

This statement has been cited on a number of occasions[3] and in at least one case can claim to have formed part of the *ratio* of a majority of the Court of Appeal.[4] If it is correct it clearly extends the grounds on which an order can be challenged considerably further than might appear from a strict reading of the statutory provision.[5] Indeed, the statement appears to cover all the grounds which are normally regarded[6] as justifying the interference of the Courts with the exercise of a discretion by an administrative body.[7] Thus in practice it seems that little, if any, effect is to be given to the actual words of the statutory provision, and one must look for guidance to the authorities on the power of the Courts to interfere with decisions of inferior tribunals or administrative bodies.

It seems also that no very clear distinction can be drawn between the first and second grounds of challenge set out in paragraph 15.[8] The practical importance of the distinction is that where the only ground of

---

[1] [1965] 3 All ER 371.

[2] *Ibid* at p. 374.

[3] See *Gordondale Investments Ltd. v Secretary of State* (1971), 23 P & CR 384, at p. 340; *Coleen Properties Ltd. v Minister of Housing and Local Government*, [1971] 1 All ER 1049 at p. 1052; *R v Secretary of State ex parte Ostler*, [1976] 3 All ER 90 at p. 94. See also *Re Lamplugh* (1967), 19 P & CR 125 at pp. 137–140 per Roskill J.

[4] See *Coleen Properties Ltd. v Minister of Housing and Local Government, supra*, at p. 1052 (per Lord Denning MR) and at p. 1054 (per Sachs LJ).

[5] In *R v Secretary of State, ex parte Ostler*, [1976] 3 All ER 90 Lord Denning MR accepted in effect that the words of the statute had been extended by the Courts (at p. 93h), but he went on to say (of the statement from the *Ashbridge* case, *supra*) that "... the Minister did not dispute it. It has been repeatedly followed in this Court ever since and never disputed by any Minister. So it is the accepted interpretation": (*ex parte Ostler, supra*, at p. 94a).

[6] See the classic statement of those grounds by Lord Greene MR in *Associated Provincial Picture Houses Ltd. v Wednesbury Corpn*, [1948] 1 KB 223 at pp. 228–234.

[7] This contrasts vividly with the approach of Lord Reid (dissenting) in *Smith v East Elloe RDC*, [1956] AC 736. Having quoted the material passages from Lord Greene's judgment in the *Wednesbury* case (*supra*), he said (at p. 763) "I can draw no other conclusion from the form in which paragraph 15 (of the Acquisition of Land (Authorisation Procedure) Act 1946, Sch. 1) is now enacted than that Parliament intended to exclude from the scope of this paragraph the whole class of cases referred to in the passages which I quoted". As a matter of pure construction Lord Reid's view is supported by a comparison with the corresponding provisions of the Local Government Act 1933, s. 162, which did not contain any express restriction on the grounds upon which an order might be challenged (see Lord Reid's opinion at p. 761). The introduction of specific grounds of challenge must have been intended to restrict in some way the grounds previously available.

[8] Acquisition of Land (Authorisation Procedure) Act, 1946, Sch. 1, para. 15(1): see p. 54, *supra*).

challenge is a failure to comply with the statutory requirements, the applicant must show in addition that his interests have been substantially prejudiced by the failure.[1] In most cases it is not necessary to distinguish between the two grounds "because there nearly always is substantial prejudice to the applicant".[2] Furthermore, in some cases a failure to comply with the statutory requirements will also mean that the authorisation contained in the confirmed order is "not empowered to be granted".[3] However, there have been cases in which the decision of the Court has turned specifically on the second ground of challenge, for example where it is alleged that the duty to give adequate reasons has not been complied with.[4]

It is probably not possible to achieve a precise classification of the principles upon which the Court will act. In any event, much will depend on the terms of the statutory provision which confers the power of compulsory purchase, since this will determine the scope of the power and the circumstances in which it can be exercised. A useful distinction can be drawn between cases where the Act requires the existence of a particular state of facts as a precondition to the exercise of the power, and those cases where a "general executive discretion" is conferred.[5] An example of the former is the Housing Act 1957, Part III, which enables land adjoining a clearance area to be acquired if it is "reasonably necessary for the satisfactory development or use of the cleared area".[6] This requires the Secretary of State, as a first step towards confirmation of the order, to decide whether as a matter of fact the adjoining land is reasonably necessary for that purpose.[7] The Court can then examine his conclusions to consider whether, as a matter of law, he applied the right test, and, if so, whether his conclusions on the questions of fact were ones which he could properly reach on the material before him.[8]

On the other hand, in many cases the exercise of the power conferred by the Act "is not preconditioned by the existence of any such substratum of fact".[9] For example, the Housing Act 1957, Part V, confers wide powers of acquisition of land for the provision of housing accommodation.[10] In such cases the Act itself does not require the estab-

---

[1] Acquisition of Land (Authorisation Procedure) Act 1946, Sch.1, para. 15(1)(b). As to what is required to show "substantial prejudice", see p. 61, infra.

[2] Gordondale Investments Ltd. v Secretary of State (1971), 23 P & CR 384 at p. 340, per Lord Denning MR.

[3] See Fairmount Investments Ltd. v Secretary of State, [1976] 2 All ER 865 at p. 871j, per Lord Russell of Killowen.

[4] See p. 62, infra.

[5] This distinction is taken from the discussion of the authorities in Re Lamplugh (1967), 19 P & CR 125 at pp. 135–141 (per Roskill J). Although this case related to a discontinuance order (made under what is now the Town and Country Planning Act 1971, s. 51) the provisions in question were similar to the Acquisition of Land (Authorisation Procedure) Act 1946, Sch. 1, para. 15, and the discussion is of general application.

[6] Housing Act 1957, s. 43(2). For a description of procedure under Part III of this Act see p. 77, infra.

[7] See Coleen Properties Ltd. v Minister of Housing and Local Government, [1971] 1 All ER 1049 (discussed at p. 58, infra).

[8] Ibid.

[9] Re Lamplugh, supra, at p. 138.

[10] Housing Act 1957, s. 96.

lishment of any particular state of facts. It will be a matter for the Secretary of State to decide, as a question of policy, the circumstances in which he will or will not confirm an order, the matters which he will require to be supported by evidence, and the party on whom the burden of proving or disproving a particular matter will lie.[1] In such cases the scope for judicial review will be much more restricted.

The cases can usefully be grouped under five headings; three derived from Lord Denning's summary,[2] which may be taken to cover the first limb of the Acquisition of Land (Authorisation Procedure) Act 1946, Schedule 1, para. 15; and the other two representing the second limb of that paragraph.[3] The groups are therefore:

(a) Conclusions not supported by evidence;
(b) Material and immaterial considerations;
(c) Other errors of law;
(d) Procedural defects; and
(e) Failure to give adequate reasons.

(a) Conclusions not supported by evidence

It is a normal function of appellate courts, even where the appeal is confined to questions of law, to consider whether there was material upon which the inferior tribunal could properly have reached the conclusion it did.[4] A distinction must be drawn between the primary facts and the inferences or conclusions drawn from those facts. The Minister "has to get from his inspector what the primary facts are and form an opinion on them. Thus far it is for the Minister. If he could not properly arrive at the opinion on his inspector's facts, that is law. . . . . We can interfere if the decision of the Minister was perverse and could not have been properly arrived at on the facts which his inspector gathered for him, but otherwise it seems to me that the legislature has entrusted that part of it to him, and not to us . . .".[5]

The test may be expressed in a number of different ways. "I do not think it much matters whether this state of affairs is described as one in which there is no evidence to support the determination or as one in which the evidence is inconsistent with and contradictory of the determination, or as one in which the true and only reasonable conclusion

---

[1] See, for example, *Vassily* v *Secretary of State*, [1976] JPL 364, where the Court upheld the confirmation of a compulsory purchase order made under the Housing Act 1957, Part V, with a view to securing the rehabilitation of the objector's house, notwithstanding the expressed willingness of the objector to do the work himself. It was "the Secretary of State's policy . . . to put the onus on the objector to satisfy him that he would reach the same standard of rehabilitation as that which it was assumed the Council would and could achieve" (*ibid*, per Phillips J). Contrast the more robust approach of Sachs LJ in *Coleen Properties Ltd.* v *Minister of Housing and Local Government*, [1971] 1 All ER 1049 at p. 1055: "When seeking to deprive the subject of his property and cause him to move himself, his belongings and perhaps his business to another area, the onus lies squarely on the local council to show by clear and unambiguous evidence that the order sought for should be granted". It is thought that this statement of principle is directed chiefly to the case where the Act in question requires the proof of a "substratum of fact" (see note 5, p. 56, *supra*).

[2] See p. 55, *supra*.

[3] See p. 54, *supra*.

[4] See *Edwards* v *Bairstow*, [1956] AC 14 at p. 35, and see the discussion of this case and other authorities in *Bowie* v *Reg Dunn (Builders) Ltd.*, [1974] STC, 234 (Brightman J).

[5] *Ashbridge Investments Ltd.* v *Minister of Housing and Local Government*, [1965] 3 All ER 371 at p. 375 per Harman LJ.

contradicts the determination. Rightly understood, each phrase pro-
pounds the same test."[1]

The circumstances in which it is possible to challenge a compulsory
purchase order under this head are unlikely to arise often in practice.
This is because the issues of fact which may arise in connection with the
confirmation of a compulsory purchase order are generally clear-cut.
Once the statutory provisions have been properly interpreted their
application to the evidence is, in most cases, relatively straightforward.

The clearest example of an order being successfully challenged under
this head is *Coleen Properties Ltd.* v *Minister of Housing and Local Government*.[2] In that case the Minister had confirmed a compulsory purchase order made under the Housing Act 1957, Part III, comprising a
clearance area and certain adjoining land.[3] Under the Act the adjoining
land could only be included if it was "land, the acquisition of which is
reasonably necessary for the satisfactory development or use of the
cleared area".[4] The inspector had concluded that its acquisition was
not reasonably necessary. The Minister disagreed because "by the very
nature of its position the property must inhibit the future development
of the rectangular block in which it stands".[5] The Court of Appeal held
that there was no evidence before the Minister to support this conclusion. No evidence had been given on this point at the inquiry by the
acquiring authority,[6] and the only evidence before the Minister was the
expert opinion of the architect inspector who had reached the opposite
conclusion.[7]

The *Coleen* case must, however, be regarded as exceptional.[8] There
will normally be *some* evidence before the Secretary of State on which he
can judge this issue, and it appears that it would be sufficient if there
were no more than the recommendation of a qualified inspector.[9] Since
the issue is one of planning or architectural judgment, the Court would
not normally interfere with his conclusion provided there is some
evidence to support it. Thus in another case,[10] relating to the same
provisions of the Housing Act 1957, it was held that the Secretary of
State was entitled to find that the acquisition of certain adjoining land
was "reasonably necessary", even though no plans or details of specific
redevelopment proposals had been provided at the inquiry. Evidence
had been given by a qualified planning officer, and had been accepted

---

[1] *Edwards* v *Bairstow, supra*, at p. 36 per Lord Reid. Lord Reid preferred the third formulation of
the test.

[2] [1971] 1 All ER 1049.

[3] For the procedure under the Housing Act 1957, Part III (slum clearance) see p. 77, *infra*.

[4] Housing Act 1957, s. 43(7).

[5] [1971] 3 All ER 1049 at p. 1052.

[6] "... the mere *ipse dixit* of the council is not sufficient. There must be some evidence to support
its assertion. And here there was none": *ibid*, at p. 1053, per Lord Denning MR.

[7] *Ibid*, at p. 1055, per Sachs LJ.

[8] Another example may be *Re Ripon (Highfield) Housing Order 1938*, [1939] 2 KB 838; see the
comments on that case by Harman LJ in *Ashbridge Investments Ltd.* v *Minister of Housing and Local
Government, supra*.

[9] The *Coleen* case would probably have been decided the other way if the inspector had reached
the same conclusion as the Minister, whether or not there was evidence at the inquiry; see *ibid*, at p.
1055 per Sachs LJ.

[10] *Migdal Investments Ltd.* v *Secretary of State*, [1976] JPL 365 (Bristow J).

by the inspector, and there was, therefore, evidence upon which the Secretary of State could reach a conclusion. The weight to be given to it was a matter for him.[1]

(b) Material and immaterial considerations

Perhaps the most frequently used grounds for attacking compulsory purchase orders and other similar administrative acts are that the Secretary of State has misdirected himself as to the matters which were in law relevant to his decision. ". . . a person entrusted with a discretion must, so to speak, direct himself properly in the law. He must call his own attention to the matters which he is bound to consider. He must exclude from his consideration matters which are irrelevant to what he has to consider".[2] An example of a material consideration being ignored was *Brinklow and Croft Bros. Ltd.* v *Secretary of State*,[3] which related to an order made under the Housing Act 1957, Part V, for the purpose of providing housing accommodation. Objections had been made to the order on the grounds, *inter alia*, that there would be no alternative accommodation for two businesses which would be displaced by the order. In confirming the order, the Secretary of State disregarded this question of relocation because he regarded it as irrelevant. The Court,[4] however, held that this was a relevant matter because objectors were entitled to have the Secretary of State consider the effect of the proposed order on themselves. The Secretary of State had therefore failed to consider a material issue, and the order was quashed.[5]

It seems right also to include under this heading cases in which the Secretary of State is held to have fettered the exercise of his discretion. *Lavender* v *Minister of Housing and Local Government*[6] is an example of a decision of the Minister which was quashed on these grounds, although the decision in question was a refusal of planning permission, rather than the confirmation of a compulsory purchase order.[7] The Minister had adopted a policy not to permit the working of minerals in certain areas unless the Minister of Agriculture was not opposed to the working, and he refused the application in question on the grounds that the "agricultural objection has not been waived".[8] The decision was quashed because he had "fettered himself in such a way that in this case it was not he who made the decision for which Parliament made him responsible".[9] He had applied "a policy which in reality eliminates all

---

[1] *Ibid.*

[2] *Associated Provincial Picture Houses Ltd.* v *Wednesbury Corpn*, [1948] 1 KB 223 at p. 229, per Lord Greene MR.

[3] [1976] JPL 299.

[4] Sir Douglas Frank QC, sitting as an additional Judge of The Queen's Bench Division.

[5] *Ibid*, citing the *Wednesbury Corpn* case, *(supra)* and *Hanks* v *Ministry of Housing and Local Government*, [1963] 1 QB 999.

[6] [1970] 3 All ER 871.

[7] The grounds upon which the Secretary of State's decision on a planning appeal may be challenged (see the Town and Country Planning Act 1971, s. 245) are substantially the same as under the Acquisition of Land (Authorisation Procedure) Act 1946, Sch. 1, para. 15. (See p. 54, *supra*.)

[8] [1970] 3 All ER 871 at p. 876.

[9] *Ibid*, at p. 880b.

the material considerations save only the consideration, when that is the case, that the Minister of Agriculture objects".[1]

An order may also be attacked on the grounds that the Secretary of State has taken into account considerations which were not material.[2] For example, in an Australian case,[3] an authority had power to acquire land for the purpose of extending streets, and it was found that they had in fact exercised that power not for the purpose of the extension, but solely for the purpose of appropriating the betterment arising from the extension. It was held by the Privy Council that this was not a valid exercise of their power. Although such cases are sometimes categorised as examples of power being exercised for an "ulterior" or "collateral" purpose,[4] it is simpler and clearer to treat them as cases where regard was had to immaterial considerations.[5]

The question of what considerations are capable in law of being material is a matter for the Courts, but the weight to be given to such considerations is a matter for the Secretary of State.[6] Whether the making or confirmation of an order has been influenced by taking into account immaterial considerations is a question of fact,[7] which is to be considered by reference to the time when the order is confirmed, rather than when it was originally made by the authority.[8]

(c) Other errors of law

Many of the cases already considered can probably also be categorised as being, to a certain extent, based upon alleged "errors of law" in the sense that the Secretary of State has misconstrued the scope of powers under the statute. However, it is possible to identify a more restricted class of cases which have turned on the construction of a specific word or phrase in the statute. If the Court disagrees with the view taken by the Secretary of State as to the construction of the word or phrase, the order may be quashed on these grounds. In many such cases the error of law will affect the jurisdiction to make the order in question. Thus, where an Act prohibited the inclusion in an order of land forming part

---

[1]*Ibid*, at p. 880c. There could have been no objection to the application of the policy if the Minister had shown himself willing to consider, in each case, whether an exception could be justified having regard to any other material factors. It would have been sufficient if the decision letter had gone on to say: "I find no reason for departing from the policy": see *Vale Estates (Acton) Ltd.* v *Secretary of State* (1970), 69 LGR 543, 559.

[2] See p. 55, *supra*.

[3] *Sydney Municipal Council* v *Campbell*, [1925] AC 338 PC. See also *Sadler* v *Sheffield Corporation*, [1924] 1 Ch. 483, in which notices of dismissal given under the Education Act 1921 were declared invalid because they were not based solely on educational grounds as the Act required. See also the dissenting judgment of Denning LJ in *Earl Fitzwilliam's Wentworth Estates Co. Ltd.* v *Minister of Town and Country Planning*, [1951] 2 KB 284, at pp. 306–308, cited by Lord Denning MR in *Webb* v *Minister of Housing and Local Government*, [1965] 2 All ER 193 at p. 201.

[4] See, e.g., *Loweth* v *Minister of Housing and Local Government* (1971), 22 P & CR 125 at p. 133 (Bridge J).

[5] *Hanks* v *Minister of Housing and Local Government*, [1963] 1 QB 999 at p. 1020 per Megaw J. In that case, which contains a valuable review of the authorities, it was held that in confirming an order made under the Housing Act 1957 the Minister was entitled to take into account "planning matters".

[6] See p. 57, *supra*.

[7] *Sydney Municipal Council* v *Campbell*, [1925] AC 338 PC.

[8] *Webb* v *Minister of Housing and Local Government*, [1965] 2 All ER 193; and *Wahiwala* v *Secretary of State* [1977] 75 LGR 651.

of a park, and the Minister had allowed such land to be included because he misdirected himself as to the meaning of the word "park" in that context, the order could be quashed because he had no jurisdiction to make it.[1] However the statement of Lord Denning in the *Ashbridge* case[2] is not confined to errors of law which affect the jurisdiction to make the order.[3]

(d) Procedural Defects

It is specifically provided that a challenge to the validity of an order may be made "on the ground that any requirement of this Act or of any regulation made thereunder[4] has not been complied with" so long as the interests of the applicant have been substantially prejudiced thereby.[5] However, there may be cases where a non-compliance with the requirements of the Act will take the authorisation outside the powers of the Act so that it can be attacked also under the first limb of the Acquisition of Land (Authorisation Procedure) Act 1946, Schedule 1, para. 15.[6] Thus if the Secretary of State purports to confirm an order which is required by the Act to be subject to special parliamentary procedure, not only has there been a failure to comply with the procedural requirements,[7] but his action may also be regarded as *ultra vires*.[8] Similarly there is to be implied into both the Act and the regulations made under it a requirement that its procedures should be conducted in accordance with the principles of natural justice. A failure to observe that requirement will result in the consequent authorisation being outside the powers of the Act.[9]

However, in most cases the defect of procedure will not affect the Secretary of State's power to authorise the order, and in such cases it will be necessary for the applicant to show that his interests have been substantially prejudiced by the defect. Thus, for example, a failure to serve notice of the making of the order on occupiers might result in them not having an opportunity to present their objections. In that case they could seek to have the order quashed.[10] But it would be otherwise if they had become aware of the order through other sources and had not been deprived of the opportunity to object.[11] The interests of an applicant

---

[1] *Re Ripon (Highfield) Housing Confirmation Order 1938* [1939] 2 KB 838; and see the comments of Harman LJ in *Ashbridge Investments Ltd.* v *Minister of Housing and Local Government* (note 5, p. 57, *supra*) at p. 375.

[2] See p. 55, *supra*.

[3] "A tribunal may often decide a point of law wrongly while keeping well within its jurisdiction": *R* v *Northumberland Compensation Tribunal, ex parte Shaw*, [1952] 1 KB 338, 346.

[4] See note 6, p. 54, *supra*.

[5] Acquisition of Land (Authorisation Procedure) Act 1946, Sch. 1, para. 15. The "requirements" include the requirement of the inquiries procedure rules made under the Tribunals and Inquiries Act 1971: see p. 54, *supra*.

[6] See p. 54, *supra*.

[7] *Richardson* v *Minister of Housing and Local Government* (1956) 8 P & CR 29.

[8] *Smith* v *East Elloe UDC*, [1956] AC 736, 770.

[9] *Fairmount Investments Ltd.* v *Secretary of State*, [1976] 2 All ER 865. See also *Hibernian Property Co. Ltd.* v *Secretary of State* (1973), 27 P & CR 197.

[10] See *Brown* v *Ministry of Housing*, [1953] 2 All ER 1385. (Note that the effect of this decision as to the interpretation of the word "occupiers" has been reversed by statute—see note 8, p. 33, *supra*.)

[11] *Grimley* v *Minister of Housing and Local Government*, [1971] 2 QB 96. See also *Performance Cars Ltd.* v *Secretary of State*, [1976] JPL 370, where a complaint that the inspector had not given sufficient time for consideration of letters put in by the authority at the inquiry (see SI 1976 No. 746, rule 7(5)) was rejected because the letters had not influenced the decision and so no prejudice had been caused. (revsd. on appeal [1977] JPL 585).

will be held to have been substantially prejudiced by a defect in procedure if he has lost "a chance of being better off in relation to the proposed order".[1]

(e) Failure to give adequate reasons

One of the most commonly alleged defects in procedure in cases under analogous statutory provisions is a failure to provide adequate reasons as required by the Tribunals and Inquiries Act 1971 or the rules made thereunder.[2] There is no reported case of a compulsory purchase order being attacked on these grounds, but this is no doubt explained by the fact that until 1973 failure to observe the requirements of the Tribunals and Inquiries Act 1971 was not a ground on which a compulsory purchase order could be challenged under the Act of 1946.[3] There is the further difficulty that the latter Act[4] confers the right to apply to the Court on a person who "desires to question the *validity*" of an order. In principle it is hard to see how a failure to give reasons should affect the validity of the order itself,[5] since the duty to give reasons only arises after the order has been confirmed.

It has been accepted in a line of authorities under the Town and Country Planning Acts, that a decision of the Secretary of State on a planning appeal may be quashed if inadequate reasons are given.[6] However the point has never been fully argued, since it was conceded on behalf of the Minister in the first relevant case that if the reasons were found to be inadequate, the appropriate remedy would be to quash the decision.[7] This has never been confirmed by the Court of Appeal and in the only case in which the question was referred to by that Court, Lord Denning MR seems to have assumed that the appropriate course would be to require the Secretary of State to provide further reasons rather than to quash the order.[8] The distinction is of much greater importance in relation to compulsory purchase orders than in relation to planning decisions. If the Secretary of State's decision on a planning appeal is quashed, the matter is simply remitted to him to make a fresh decision on the same appeal.[9] If, however, his confirmation of a compulsory purchase order is successfully chal-

---

[1] *Hibernian Property Co. Ltd.* v *Secretary of State* (1973), 27 P & CR 197 at p. 218 per Browne J. Thus in *Wilson* v *Secretary of State*, [1973] 1 WLR 1083 (approved in substance by the Court of Appeal in *McMeechan* v *Secretary of State*, [1974] JPL 411) it was held that the applicant had been prejudiced by a defective public notice, because it might have attracted other people to object and thereby have influenced the Secretary of State in his decision whether or not to hold an inquiry.

[2] P. 44, *supra*, and the cases there cited.

[3] I.e., under the Acquisition of Land (Authorisation Procedure) Act 1946, Sch. 1, para. 15. This anomaly was corrected by the Land Compensation Act 1973, s. 64: p. 54, *supra*.

[4] Sch. 1, para. 15.

[5] Cf. *Brayhead (Ascot) Ltd.* v *Berkshire County Council*, [1964] 2 QB 303 at p. 313, where it was said (per Winn J) in relation to a failure to give reasons for the imposition of conditions on a planning permission in the notice of planning permission, that "It does not necessarily follow that non-compliance ... will render the notice null in law, still less that the decision of which the notice purports to be given is itself of no legal effect".

[6] Beginning with *Givaudan* v *Minister of Housing and Local Government*, [1966] 3 All ER 696; see also *Hope* v *Secretary of State* (1975), 31 P & CR 120; *Kent Messenger Ltd.* v *Secretary of State*, [1976] JPL 372.

[7] *Givaudan's* case, *supra*.

[8] *Earl of Iveagh* v *Minister of Housing and Local Government*, [1964] 1 QB 395 at p. 410.

[9] *Givaudan's* case, *supra*. The Secretary of State may decide to reopen the inquiry, but this is a matter for him.

lenged, it seems that the whole order is quashed[1] so that, if the authority wish to proceed with compulsory purchase, they will have to make a completely fresh order and start the procedure again from the beginning.[2]

It is suggested that in deciding whether inadequacy of the reasons given is a sufficient ground for quashing an order under the Act of 1946[3] a distinction has to be drawn between cases where the complaint is simply that the reasons are not as full or clear as they should be, and cases where "from a failure to give reasons one may legitimately infer, on a balance of probabilities, that the tribunal's process of legal reasoning must have been defective".[4] In the former case, the right course is for the Court, not to quash the order, but to order the Secretary of State to supply adequate reasons. If, when the fuller reasons are eventually supplied, they reveal a ground for quashing the decision, the application can then be renewed and the order quashed.

Although neither the Act nor the rules[5] provide specifically for an order remitting the matter to the Secretary of State in the case of an application under provisions such as those of the Acquisition of Land (Authorisation Procedure) Act 1946, Schedule 1, para. 15, there seems to be adequate authority for the proposition that the Court has an inherent power to make such an order, and it is clearly the most convenient and appropriate remedy.[6]

(iv) PROCEDURE UNDER PARAGRAPH 15

The application is made to a single judge of the Queen's Bench Division by originating notice of motion.[7] The notice must state the grounds on

---

[1] See p. 65, *infra*.

[2] Cf, "Snakes and Ladders", square 99.

[3] I.e., Acquisition of Land (Authorisation Procedure) Act 1946, Sch. 1, para. 15.

[4] *Mountview Court Properties Ltd.* v *Devlin* (1970), 21 P & CR 689 at p. 696 per Bridge J. This was a case concerning the failure of a rent assessment committee to give reasons. It was held that such failure was not in itself a ground for quashing the decision, and the matter was remitted back to the committee with a direction to give adequate reasons.

[5] See RSC Order 94, rules 1–3. There is no equivalent to Order 55, rule 7, which gives the Court wide powers on an "appeal" (as opposed to an "application"), including the express power to remit the matter with the opinion of the Court.

[6] .*Earl of Iveagh* v *Minister of Housing and Local Government*, [1964] 1 QB 395 at p. 410 per Lord Denning MR. In *Grangewalk Properties Ltd.* v *Minister of Housing and Local Government* (1969) 31st October (unreported) a case relating to the validity of an order under the Housing Act 1957, Part III, Willis J said "If on a fair reading of the Minister's letter I had thought that it was impossible to tell whether he had applied his mind to the question of rehabilitation as an alternative to demolition, or that in considering it he had taken irrelevant matters into account, or that there appeared to be unresolved ambiguity in the essential reasoning for deciding that the most satisfactory method was demolition, I would in the circumstances of this case have sent the matter back for the Minister to state his reasons with greater clarity and precision. See *Earl of Iveagh* v *Minister of Housing and Local Government, supra: Pages Luxury Flats* v *Cockerill* (Divisional Court (1968), 11th December, unreported)". In *Parrish* v *Minister of Housing and Local Government* (1961), 59 LGR 411 at p. 418, Megaw J said that an application for *mandamus* could be made in such circumstances (cf. *Brayhead (Ascot) Ltd.* v *Berkshire County Council*, [1964] 2 QB 303. However, this is not really a practicable remedy, since the reasons would not be obtained in time for an application to be made to quash the decision; the six-week period would still run from the time of the notice of confirmation: see p. 54, *supra*.

[7] RSC Order 94, rule 1(1)(2). For a form of originating notice of motion see 20 Atkins' Court Forms (2nd Edn.) 414.

which the application is made.[1] The notice must be entered at the Crown Office and served on the Secretary of State and the acquiring authority[2] within six weeks of the publication of notice of the confirmation of the order.[3] Any affidavit in support must be filed and served within 14 days after the service of the notice of motion.[4] The respondent may file an affidavit in reply within a further twenty-one days.[5]

Normally the affidavit in support will be limited to setting out the background of the case and exhibiting the relevant documents, including copies of the order, the inspector's report on the inquiry, if any, and the decision letter. The Court will generally confine its consideration to the matters set out in the inspector's report.[6] It will not allow new matters to be raised which were not raised at the inquiry.[7] Nor will it review the evidence[8] or examine the inspector's notebooks to see whether he recorded all the material facts.[9] On the other hand the Court may exceptionally allow new evidence to be adduced if there has been a change of circumstances between the inquiry and the Secretary of State's decision which might have affected his jurisdiction.[10] Although the Court has power to order discovery,[11] an order is unlikely to be made in view of the restrictive approach of the Courts to the evidence which will be taken into account on an application.[12] An application for discovery against the Secretary of State is likely also to be resisted on the grounds of public interest,[13] although it will be for the Secretary of State in such circumstances to establish that the public interest requires non-disclosure.[14]

The Court has power to make an interim order suspending the

---

[1] In theory, the "grounds" of the application are those set out in the Acquisition of Land (Authorisation Procedure) Act 1946, Sch. 1, para. 15. It is common, therefore, for the detailed considerations which are alleged to bring the case within the statutory grounds to be set out as "particulars", or even in the affidavit in support. The Court may allow amendments to the notice (*Hanily* v *Minister of Local Government and Planning*, [1951] 2 KB 917), and it is unusual for any objection to be taken to amendments provided adequate notice is given.

[2] RSC Order 94, rule 2. Although the notice of motion must be filed within the time limit, the time for service on the other parties can be extended under RSC Order 3, rule 5. (See *Summers* v *Minister of Health*, [1947] 1 All ER 184).

[3] See p. 36, *supra*.

[4] RSC Order 94, rule 3(2).

[5] *Ibid*, rule 3(2).

[6] *Ashbridge Investments Ltd.* v *Minister of Housing and Local Government*, [1965] 3 All ER 371; *Green* v *Minister of Housing and Local Government*, [1967] 2 QB 606.

[7] *A. Crabtree* v *Minister of Housing and Local Government* (1965), 64 LGR 104.

[8] *Continental Sprays Ltd.* v *Minister of Housing and Local Government* (1968), 19 P & CR 774; *Deasy* v *Minister of Housing and Local Government* (1970), 214 Estates Gazette 415.

[9] *T. A. Miller* v *Minister of Housing and Local Government*, [1968] 1 WLR 992.

[10] See *Wilcock* v *Secretary of State*, [1975] JPL 150, where new evidence was admitted to show that the land in question had become "open space" within the statutory definition, between the time of the inquiry and the decision (see p. 49, *supra*). Cf. *Re Ripon (Highfield) Housing Confirmation Order 1938*, [1939] 2 KB 838, where evidence was admitted for a similar purpose, but not confined to matters which had occurred since the inquiry; however, this was before inspectors' reports were published (see the comments in *Ashbridge Investments Ltd.* v *Minister of Housing and Local Government*, [1965] 3 All ER 371 at pp. 374–375.

[11] RSC Order 24, rule 3.

[12] See *Wednesbury Corpn* v *Minister of Housing and Local Government*, [1965] 1 All ER 186, where an unsuccessful attempt was made to obtain disclosure of the Minister's briefing notes to the inspector, but the possibility of discovery being ordered in a proper case was not excluded.

[13] RSC Order 77, rule 12(2).

[14] See *Conway* v *Rimmer*, [1968] AC 910.

compulsory purchase order either generally or so far as it affects the applicant's property until the final determination of the proceedings.[1] If satisfied that the statutory grounds have been made out, the Court may make an order quashing the compulsory purchase order or any provision of it, either generally or so far as it affects the applicant's property.[2] Although neither the Act nor the rules make specific provision for any other remedy, it is thought that the Court has jurisdiction to make a different order if the interests of justice require it.[3] Even if the statutory grounds are made out, the Court still has a discretion whether or not to quash the order, although it will normally do so unless there is some special reason for refusing relief.[4] Costs normally follow the event.[5] However the applicant will not generally be ordered to pay two sets of costs[6] where both the acquiring authority and the Secretary of State appear, and, if the matter is in the nature of a test case of general public importance, the Court may decide to make no order as to costs.[7]

(v) OTHER PROCEEDINGS

Apart from the statutory procedure, a compulsory purchase order may not be questioned in any legal proceedings either before or after it has been confirmed or made.[8] This prohibition applies even where it is alleged that the order is a nullity or is vitiated by fraud or bad faith.[9] However, it is to be noted that the statutory procedure only applies to the validity of the order itself. Thus it does not provide a remedy where, for instance, an authority wishes to challenge the Secretary of State's refusal to confirm an order, or where a challenge is made to his decision on costs. In such cases the ordinary procedures, e.g., certiorari or action for a declaration, would still be available.[10] It is possible also that a

---

[1] Acquisition of Land (Authorisation Procedure) Act 1946, Sch. 15(1)(a).

[2] *Ibid*, para. 15(1)(b). It seems clear that the order to be quashed is the compulsory purchase order *ab initio*. Although in *Errington v Minister of Health*, [1935] 1 KB 249 it was said (per Greer LJ at p. 268) that the order to be quashed was the "confirming order" rather than the compulsory purchase order itself, this seems to overlook the fact that under the 1946 Act procedure (or indeed under the Housing Act 1930, Sch. 1, para. 4, which was then under consideration) there is no "confirming order". In practice the compulsory purchase order is quashed as a whole (see e.g., *Fairmount Investments Ltd.* v *Secretary of State*, [1976] 2 All ER 865).

[3] Cf. RSC 1965 Order 55, rule 7, which gives wide powers to make such order "as the case may require". Although this order deals with "appeals" and does not apparently extend to "applications" under Order 94, there is no statutory reason for the powers of the Court being less extensive in the case of applications. Cf. *Tiverton Estates v Wearwell*, [1975] Ch. 146 at 156C. As noted above, (p. 63, *supra*) it seems to be accepted that the Court has a power to order the Secretary of State to supply fuller reasons.

[4] *Gosling v Secretary of State*, [1975] JPL 406, following *Miller v Weymouth and Melcombe Regis Corpn* (1974), 27 P & CR 468.

[5] Note that, even if the respondents agree to the order being quashed, the applicant may expect his costs since an order of the Court is still required to give effect to the agreement: see *Granada Theatres Ltd.* v *Secretary of State*, [1976] JPL 96.

[6] *Re Mason* (1934), 50 TLR 392.

[7] See *Hanks v Minister of Housing and Local Government*, [1963] 1 QB 999 at p. 1040.

[8] Acquisition of Land (Authorisation Procedure) Act 1946, Sch. 1, para. 16. See also note 8, p. 52, *supra*.

[9] *R.* v *Secretary of State ex parte Ostler*, [1976] 3 WLR 288, applying *Smith v East Elloe RDC*, [1956] AC 736. See also *Routh v Reading Corpn* (1970), 217 Estates Gazette 1337.

[10] See, e.g., *R.* v *Secretary of State ex parte Reinisch* (1971), 22 P & CR 1022.

resolution to make a compulsory purchase order could be challenged without infringing the prohibition.[1]

3 FROM CONFIRMATION TO ENTRY

1 Introduction

When the compulsory purchase order has been confirmed and has become operative[2] the acquiring authority are in a position, if they are unable to reach agreement with the owners,[3] to compel the conveyance to them of the land comprised in the order. There are two methods by which they can do this, and these will be described in this section.

The most common method is that which is initiated by the service of a notice to treat. The notice to treat is in effect an invitation to owners of interests in the land to submit a claim for compensation. The notice to treat does not itself give the authority any interest in the land;[4] other than by agreement no interest will pass until compensation is assessed. However, the notice to treat gives both parties the right, subject to certain qualifications, to have compensation assessed, and it also gives the authority certain rights in relation to entry on the land before assessment of compensation. The notice to treat procedure is governed principally by the provisions of the Compulsory Purchase Act 1965.[5] The alternative procedure is the "General Vesting Declaration". This procedure was introduced by the Town and Country Planning Act 1968.[6] The effect of a general vesting declaration is to transfer the title in the interests comprised in the declaration to the acquiring authority at the end of a specified period, and in advance of the settlement of compensation.[7]

It will be seen that after confirmation of the order the initiative remains entirely with the acquiring authority. The owner of interests comprised in the order cannot compel the authority to serve a notice to treat and proceed with the acquisition unless his interest falls within one of the limited categories which are protected by the blight notice

---

[1] See *Swick* v *Chelsea Borough Council* (1964), 108 Sol Jo 376, an unsuccessful attempt to strike out such an action.

[2] See Acquisition of Land (Authorisation Procedure) Act 1946, Sch. 1, para. 16, and p. 36, *supra*.

[3] The Compulsory Purchase Act 1965, s. 3 empowers an acquiring authority to reach an agreement with owners of any of the land comprised in an order for the acquisition of their interest.

[4] It is not therefore registrable as an estate contract: see *Capital Investments Ltd.* v *Wednesfield UDC*, [1965] Ch. 774.

[5] The Compulsory Purchase Act 1965 applies to "any compulsory purchase to which the provisions of Sch. 1 of the Acquisition of Land (Authorisation Procedure) Act 1946 apply": Compulsory Purchase Act 1965, s. 1(1). Its provisions have also been applied, with modifications, to certain compulsory purchases not covered by the 1946 Act, including purchases under the Housing Act 1957, Part III: Compulsory Purchase Act 1965, Part II. They have also been specifically incorporated in certain later Acts: see, e.g., New Towns Act 1965, s. 12.

[6] Town and Country Planning Act 1968, s. 30. The provisions apply to "any Minister or local or other public authority authorised to acquire land by means of a compulsory purchase order": *ibid*, s. 30(2).

[7] For the possible advantages of this procedure see Department of the Environment Circular 26/77, Appendix IS.

procedure.[1] Otherwise he is left in a position of considerable uncer-
tainty. It is essential for him to maintain his property, since if the
condition of the property deteriorates before the acquiring authority
enter, this deterioration will normally be reflected in the level of compensation.[2] Similarly, it is difficult for him to make arrangements for
alternative accommodation (except with the co-operation of the
authority) since he does not know for certain whether his premises will
ultimately be required. His only protection is the fact that the notice to
treat must be served within three years of the order becoming operative.[3]

2 Notice to treat procedure

(i) WHEN A NOTICE TO TREAT MAY BE SERVED

If the notice to treat procedure is adopted the notice to treat[4] must be
served within three years of the date when the order becomes operative.[5] As we have seen, this will normally be the date when notice of the
confirmation of the order is first published.[6] Although the Act provides
that the compulsory purchase powers conferred by the order "shall not
be exercised"[7] after the three-year period, it has been held that provided the notice to treat is served within the period it does not matter
that the remaining steps are taken after the three years.[8] "Once that
notice was served, section 123[9] was out of the picture and no further
period is laid down by statute within which the next step to acquire the
property must be taken".[10] On the other hand, the authority's right
to proceed following service of notice to treat may be barred if the
acquiring authority delays unreasonably, or if it evinces an
intention to abandon its rights under the notice to treat, or if it seeks
to exercise its powers for a purpose other than that for which they were
conferred.[11]

---

[1] As to which see p. 129, post.

[2] See p. 167, post.

[3] See note 5, infra.

[4] The notice need not be in any special form, but it must (a) give particulars of the land to which
it relates; (b) demand particulars of the recipients' estate and interest in the land and of the claim
made by him in respect of it; and (c) state that the acquiring authority are willing to treat for the
purchase of the land and as to the compensation to be made for the damage which may be
sustained by reason of the execution of the works for which the authority propose to acquire the
land: Compulsory Purchase Act 1965, s. 5(2).

[5] Compulsory Purchase Act 1965, s. 4. It seems that, in calculating the three years, the date
upon which the order becomes operative should be excluded: see *Goldsmiths Co.* v *West Metropolitan
Rly, Co.* [1904] 1 KB 1.

[6] Acquisition of Land (Authorisation Procedure) Act 1946, Sch. 1, para. 16: see p. 36, supra.

[7] Compulsory Purchase Act 1965, s. 4.

[8] *Grice* v *Dudley Corpn*, [1958] 1 Ch. 329, following *Marquis of Salisbury* v *Great Northern Rly Co.*
(1852), 17 QB 840.

[9] I.e., Lands Clauses Consolidation Act 1845, s. 123, which was the same in effect as the
Compulsory Purchase Act 1965, s. 4.

[10] *Grice* v *Dudley Corpn (supra)* at p. 339, per Upjohn LJ.

[11] *Ibid*, at p. 339, approved in *Simpson's Motor Sales (London) Ltd.* v *Hendon Corpn*, [1964] AC 1088,
where it was held that the delay between a notice to treat served in 1952 and 1958 was not sufficient
to disentitle the authority from proceeding. See also *Capital Investments Ltd.* v *Wednesfield UDC*,
[1965] Ch. 774, where the validity of a notice to treat was unsuccessfully challenged on the grounds
that the purpose of the acquisition had changed.

(ii) WHO SHOULD BE SERVED

The notice must be served[1] on "all the persons interested in, or having power[2] to sell and convey or release, the land, so far as known to the acquiring authority after making diligent inquiry".[3] This includes mortgagees,[4] and persons with the benefit of a contract or option to purchase the land.[5] It also includes lessees other than tenants having no greater interest than a year or from year to year.[6] It does not include licensees[7] or persons entitled to an easement or to the benefit of a restrictive covenant over the land.[8]

(iii) EFFECT OF NOTICE TO TREAT

A notice to treat does not create a contract for the purchase of the land.[9] "A notice to treat does nothing more than establish conditions in which a contract might come into existence, either a voluntary contract or a statutory contract".[10] The significance of service of the notice to treat is threefold:

(1) It gives either party the right to have compensation determined and thereby to create a binding contract for the sale of the land.[11] Once the notice to treat is served the acquiring authority is committed to proceeding with the acquisition unless it withdraws the notice to treat in the limited circumstances allowed by the Land Compensation Act 1961, s. 31;[12]

(2) It gives the acquiring authority the right, subject to service of a notice of entry,[13] to take possession of the land;[14]

(3) After service of notice to treat the owner cannot increase the burden of compensation by creating any new interest in the land.[15]

---

[1] The method of service is that prescribed by the Acquisition of Land (Authorisation Procedure) Act 1946, Sch. 1, para. 19; (see p. 34, *supra*): Compulsory Purchase Act 1965, s. 30(3).

[2] Provision for enabling persons with some disability or incapacity to sell their land to the authority is made by the Acquisition of Land (Authorisation Procedure) Act 1946, Sch. 1.

[3] *Ibid*, s. 5(1). A special procedure is prescribed in the case where the owner is prevented from treating by absence abroad, or where the owner cannot be traced by diligent inquiry: s. 5(3), Sch. 2, see p. 88, *post*.

[4] *Cooke* v *LCC*, [1911] 1 Ch. 604, 609; *Martin* v *London, Chatham and Dover Rly. Co.* (1866) 1 Ch. App 501.

[5] *Oppenheimer* v *Minister of Transport*, [1942] KB 242; *Hillingdon Estates Co.* v *Stonefield Estates Ltd.*,[1952] Ch. 627.

[6] Compulsory Purchase Act 1965, s. 20; see p. 365, *post*.

[7] *Frank Warr & Co, Ltd.* v *LCC*, [1904] 1 KB 713.

[8] See, e.g., *Marten* v *Secretary of State* (1959), P & CR 390. No claim arises until the easement or the restrictive covenant is infringed, when compensation is payable under the Compulsory Purchase Act 1965, s. 10: see pp. 283, *et seq, post*.

[9] *Haynes* v *Haynes* (1861), 1 D & S 426.

[10] *Capital Investments Ltd.* v *Wednesfield UDC* [1965] Ch. 774 at p. 794 per Wilberforce J. A notice to treat, therefore, is not registrable as an estate contract: *ibid*.

[11] As to the procedure for securing the determination of compensation, see p. 83, *post*.

[12] See p. 84, *post*.

[13] Or, less commonly, on the making of a payment into Court under the procedure set out in the Compulsory Purchase Act 1965, Sch. 3; see p. 70, *infra*. However, in this case there is no express requirement that notice to treat should have been served first: *ibid*, s. 11(2).

[14] *Ibid*, s. 11(1): see p. 70, *infra*.

[15] See p. 69, *infra*. He may, however, continue to deal with the property, and a purchaser of his interest will take over his right to compensation; see e.g., *Cardiff Corporation* v *Cook*, [1932] 2 Ch. 115. The service of a notice to treat does not affect the enforceability of a contract for the sale of the land entered into previously: see *Hillingdon Estates Co. Ltd.* v *Stonefield Estates Ltd.*, [1952] 1 All ER 853.

(iv) CREATION OF NEW INTERESTS ETC.

Although an owner of land is free to deal with his interest not-withstanding the service of a notice to treat, he may not by altering the land or creating[1] new interests in it increase the burden of the acquiring authority as regards the compensation to be paid.[2] This principle also applies to interests created in adjoining land which could be the subject of a claim for injurious affection or severance.[3] It seems that the onus is on the acquiring authority to show that the burden of compensation has been increased in any particular case.[4]

This common law principle is extended by the Acquisition of Land (Authorisation Procedure) Act 1946 which provides:[5]

> "The Lands Tribunal shall not take into account any interest in land or any enhancement of the value of any interest in land by reason of any building erected, work done or improvement or alteration made, whether on the land purchased or on any other land with which the claimant is, or was at the time of the erection, doing or making of the building works, improvement or alteration, directly or indirectly concerned, if the Lands Tribunal is satisfied that the creation of the interest, the erection of the building, the doing of the work, the making of the improvement, as the case may be, was not reasonably necessary and was undertaken with a view to obtaining compensation or increased compensation".

It will be seen that this provision extends the common law rule in that it applies to transactions both before and after notice to treat.[6] On the other hand it is subject to the important limitation, which does not apply to the common law rule, that the Tribunal must be satisfied not only that the transaction was not "reasonably necessary"[7] but also that it was "undertaken with a view to obtaining compensation or increased compensation". Since an owner of land cannot assume definitely that the compulsory acquisition will be proceeded with until either compensation has been agreed or the authority have taken possession,[8] he has every justification for continuing to deal with the land as though it was going to continue in his ownership. Thus in practice it will be very difficult for the authority to establish that any works or other transactions were specifically directed to improving his compensation position, rather than being in the ordinary course of his management of the land.

---

[1] It seems that the principle will also apply where the burden of compensation is increased by the termination of an interest: see *Banham* v *London Borough of Hackney* (1970), 22 P & CR 922 L.T.

[2] *Birmingham City Corpn* v *West Midland Baptist Trust*, [1970] AC 874, 893, 904; following *Re: Marylebone (Stingo Lane) Improvement Act, ex p. Edwards* (1871), LR 12 Eq. 389 and *Mercer* v *Liverpool Etc., Rly. Co.*, [1904] AC 491.

[3] *Mercer* v *Liverpool etc. Rly. Co. supra*. In this case it was held that no additional compensation could be payable for injurious affection to the interest of a lessee of adjoining land, whose lease had been granted by the owner of the acquired land after the notice to treat, since any injurious affection to this land was to be taken as covered by the compensation payable to the owner.

[4] See *Banham* v *London Borough of Hackney*, *supra*.

[5] Sch. 2, para. 8.

[6] Cf. the similar provisions of Housing Act 1957, Sch. 3 para. 8(5) (p. 80, *infra*) which apply only to transactions after the date of publication of the compulsory purchase order.

[7] For a consideration of this expression in a different context, see *Coleen Properties Ltd.* v *Minister of Housing and Local Government*, [1971] 1 All ER 1049.

[8] See p. 66, *supra*.

3 Entry

ENTRY FOR THE PURPOSES OF SURVEY

At any time after the compulsory purchase order becomes operative,[1] on not less than three and not more than 14 days' notice, the acquiring authority may enter the land for the purpose of surveying or taking levels of the land or of probing or boring to ascertain the nature of the soil, or of setting out the line of the works.[2] Notice must be served on the "owners or occupiers"[3] of the land. Compensation must be paid for any damage caused.[4]

TAKING POSSESSION BEFORE CONVEYANCE

It is not necessary for the authority to wait for the land to be conveyed to them or for compensation to be assessed before taking possession of the land. If they have served a notice to treat they may, on giving not less than 14 days' notice[5] to the owner, lessee and occupier, enter[6] on and take possession of the land or any part specified in the notice.[7] It is common for the notice of entry to be served at the same time as the notice to treat, thus enabling the authority to carry out the works with the minimum delay and leaving compensation to be assessed subsequently. Interest on any compensation ultimately assessed runs from the date of entry,[8] and the owner will be entitled to claim an advance payment of compensation.[9]

ALTERNATIVE PROCEDURE FOR ENTRY

An alternative but less common procedure is provided by the Compulsory Purchase Act 1965, Schedule 3.[10] Under this procedure the authority must pay into Court by way of security either the amount claimed by the owner or a sum equal to the value of his interest[11] as determined by a specially appointed[12] surveyor.[13] They must also give

---

[1] See p. 36, *supra*.

[2] Compulsory Purchase Act 1965, s. 11(3).

[3] Presumably service on both is required, although it is to be noted that in s. 11(1) the expression "owner lessee *and* occupier" is used, rather than (as here) "owners *or* occupiers".

[4] Compulsory Purchase Act 1965, s. 11(3). In default of agreement it is settled by the Lands Tribunal.

[5] The notice should state specifically the date on which entry is proposed. A notice which merely refers to entry "on or after" a particular date gives the owner no adequate indication of when his land will be taken. There is, however, no way in which the authority can be compelled to take possession on the specified date.

[6] If the owner refuses to allow entry it may be enforced by the Sheriff: Compulsory Purchase Act 1965, s. 13.

[7] *Ibid*, s. 11(1).

[8] *Ibid*, s. 11(1). This means the *actual* taking of possession. Notice of entry has no significance unless it is followed by physical entry: see *Burson* v *Wantage Rural District Council* (1974), 27 P & CR 556. The rate of interest is prescribed: Land Compensation Act 1961, s. 32, and see the Acquisition of Land (Rate of Interest after Entry) Regulations for the time-being in force.

[9] Land Compensation Act 1973, s. 52: see p. 95, *post*.

[10] Compulsory Purchase Act 1965, s. 11(2).

[11] This includes any amount due for severance or injurious affection (see p. 314, *post*): *Field* v *Caernarvon and Llanberis Rly Co.* (1867), LR 5 Eq. 190.

[12] "An able practical surveyor" to be appointed by two parties acting together by an instrument in writing signed by them: Compulsory Purchase Act 1965, Sch. 3, para. 2(2).

[13] *Ibid*, para. 2(1).

to the owner a bond[1] for the same amount conditional on payment of all the compensation which may be agreed or awarded together with interest.[2] Once these requirements have been complied with they may enter on the land without further formalities.[3]

UNAUTHORISED ENTRY

Apart from the cases discussed above[4] the acquiring authority are not entitled, other than with the consent of the owner,[5] to enter the land until compensation has been settled and paid.[6] If the authority or its contractors wilfully[7] enter the land in contravention of this prohibition they must pay the amount of any damage done plus a forfeit of ten pounds.[8] This is recoverable summarily as a civil debt.[9] If they remain in possession after being adjudged so liable they will be liable to an additional forfeit of £25 per day.[10] It may be noted that the penalties under this provision have not been increased since 1845.[11] The section does not exclude the use of other remedies, e.g., an action for damages[12] or an injunction.[13]

4 General Vesting Declaration

INTRODUCTORY

The Town and Country Planning Act 1968 introduced an alternative procedure for vesting the land in the authority following confirmation of a compulsory purchase order.[14] This is the "general vesting declaration".[15] The effect of such a declaration is to vest the land in the authority at the end of a specified period without the need for any other formality,[16] and to bring into play the procedure for assessing compensation as though a notice to treat had been served on the date of the

---

[1] There must be two sufficient sureties to be approved, in default of agreement, by two justices acting together: *ibid*, para. 3(3).

[2] *Ibid*, para. 3(1). As to procedure for payment into Court see Compulsory Purchase Act 1965, s. 25.

[3] It is not clear whether they must also have served notice to treat under this subsection: see *Great Western Rly Co.* v *Swindon and Cheltenham Rly Co.* (1884), 9 App Cas 787, pp. 805–806, per Lord Watson. In principle one would expect a notice to treat to be necessary since this provides the basis for compensation to be assessed.

[4] There may be other exceptions contained in the special Act.

[5] The owner's consent to entry cannot be revoked once it has been acted on: *Knapp* v *London Chatham and Dover Rly Co.* (1863), 2 H & C 212.

[6] Compulsory Purchase Act 1965, s. 11(4).

[7] See *ibid*, s. 12(6), and *Steele* v *Midland Rly Co.* (1869), 21 LT 387.

[8] Compulsory Purchase Act 1965, s. 12(1).

[9] *Ibid*, s. 12(2). An appeal lies to the Crown Court: *ibid* s. 12(3), as amended by the Courts Act 1971, Sch. 10.

[10] *Ibid*, s. 12(4).

[11] See Lands Clauses Consolidation Act 1845, s. 89.

[12] *Ramsden* v *Manchester etc. Rly Co.* (1848), 1 Exch. 723.

[13] See *Cardwell* v *Midland Rly Co.* (1904), 21 TLR 22.

[14] Town and Country Planning Act 1968, Sch. 3. The procedure is not confined to acquisitions under the planning legislation.

[15] The form and contents of the declaration are prescribed: see Compulsory Purchase of Land Regulations 1976, SI 1976 No. 300, Forms 9–11.

[16] Town and Country Planning Act 1968, Sch. 3, para. 7. The period is specified in the declaration and must be at least 28 days: *ibid*, para. 1.

declaration.[1] Provision is made for dealing with severed land and for other special cases comparable to that contained in the Compulsory Purchase Act 1965.[2]

PROCEDURE

An authority which is intending to make a general vesting declaration must include in the published notice of the confirmation of the order,[3] or in a subsequent notice published and served in the same way before notice to treat, a statement of the effect of the general vesting declaration procedure and an invitation to any person with a claim to compensation to give information to the authority with respect to his name and address and the land in question.[4] The general vesting declaration must not be executed until two months after the notice,[5] unless every occupier of the land affected has consented in writing to a shorter period.[6]

The general vesting declaration is in a prescribed form,[7] and states that the land in question will vest in the authority at the end of a specified period from the date of the service of the notices of the declaration.[8] Notices,[9] specifying the land and stating the effect of the declaration, must be served on every occupier[10] of the land other than land in which there subsists a minor tenancy or a long tenancy which is about to expire,[11] and on any other person who has responded to the authority's invitation for information contained in the published statement.[12]

The effect of the declaration is that at the end of the specified period the land included in the declaration, together with the right to enter upon and take possession of it, vests in the authority in the same way as if they had duly executed a deed poll under the provisions of Part I of the Compulsory Purchase Act 1965.[13] The provisions for assessment and payment of compensation[14] are then applied as though a notice to

---

[1] Town and Country Planning Act 1968, Sch. 3, para. 6.

[2] *Ibid*, Sch. 3A (inserted by the Land Commission (Dissolution) Act 1971).

[3] See p. 36, *supra*.

[4] Town and Country Planning Act 1968, Sch. 3 para. 2. There is a prescribed form of statement for this purpose: see Compulsory Purchase of Land Regulations 1976 SI 1976 No. 300, Form 10.

[5] Or a longer period if so specified in the notice.

[6] Town and Country Planning Act 1968, Sch. 3, para. 3.

[7] SI 1976 No. 300, Form 9.

[8] Town and Country Planning Act 1968, Sch. 3, para. 1.

[9] The form of notice is prescribed: see SI 1976 No. 300, Form 11.

[10] Note that no notice of the making of the declaration is given to the owner or any other persons interested in the land unless they are also occupiers. Such persons will however have received notice of the authority's intention to proceed by general vesting declaration with the notice of confirmation of the compulsory purchase order: see note 3, *supra*.

[11] For the meaning of these terms and the procedure in relation thereto: see p. 73, *infra*.

[12] Town and Country Planning Act 1968 Sch. 3, para. 4. The authority's certificate of the date on which service of these notices was completed is conclusive: *ibid*, para. 5.

[13] *Ibid*. para. 7. For an example of the circumstances in which a deed poll could be executed under the Compulsory Purchase Act 1965 see p. 88, *post*.

[14] I.e. the provisions of the Land Compensation Act 1961 and the Compulsory Purchase Act 1965. Note that the provisions of the 1965 Act, s. 11(1) relating to entry before payment of compensation (see p. 70, *supra*) do not apply where a general vesting declaration is made: Town and Country Planning Act 1968, Sch. 3A, para. 1. Nor can the constructive notice to treat be withdrawn once the land has vested in the authority: *ibid*, Sch. 3A, para. 2.

treat had been served, on the date when the declaration was made, on every person upon whom a notice to treat could have been served, other than persons entitled to a minor tenancy or a long tenancy which is about to expire.[1] The declaration will not however have any effect on any interest in respect of which an actual notice to treat has been served.[2]

Where any land is subject to a minor tenancy[3] or a long tenancy which is about to expire,[4] the general vesting declaration does not entitle the authority to enter the land immediately. They must first serve a notice to treat in respect of that tenancy, and then serve on every occupier of the land in which the tenancy subsists a notice stating that at the end of a specified period, not less than 14 days, they intend to enter upon and take possession of the land specified in the notice.[5] The right to enter under the general vesting declaration does not arise until the specified period has expired, and, until that time the vesting of the land in the authority will be subject to the tenancy, unless it expires in the meantime.[6]

Procedure following the vesting of the land in the authority is generally the same as following a notice to treat.[7] There is a time limit for the submission to the Lands Tribunal of any question of disputed compensation. This must be done within six years from the date at which the person claiming the compensation, or a person under whom he derives title, first knew or could reasonably be expected to have known, of the vesting of the interest by virtue of those paragraphs.[8] There are also special provisions for the repayment of compensation if it is discovered, after payment of compensation by the authority, that the claimant's interest was subject to an incumbrance not disclosed in the particulars of his claim which would have reduced the compensation payable.[9] Similarly, if it is subsequently found that the claimant was not entitled to the interest in the land, or in part of the land, in respect of which the payment was made, the authority may recover the amount of the compensation, or the amount attributable to that part.[10] Any question of the amount to which the claimant was entitled or of the apportionment of the compensation between parts of the land is subject

[1] Ibid, Sch. 3, para. 6.
[2] Ibid, Sch. 3, para. 6(a).
[3] A "minor tenancy" means a "tenancy for a year or from year to year or any lesser interest": ibid. Sch. 3, para. 16(1).
[4] A "long tenancy which is about to expire" means a tenancy granted for an interest greater than a minor tenancy, but having at the date of the declaration a period still to run which is not more than a period specified for this purpose in the declaration (which must be longer than one year): ibid. Sch. 3, para. 16(1). It is assumed that the tenant will exercise any option to renew the tenancy, but not any option to terminate, but on the other hand that the landlord will exercise any option to terminate the tenancy: ibid. Sch. 3, para. 16(2).
[5] Ibid, Sch. 3, para. 8(a).
[6] Ibid, Sch. 3, para. 8(b).
[7] For the provisions relating to severed land see p. 109, post.
[8] This provision does not extinguish the claim after six years, but merely excludes the statutory right to refer it to the Lands Tribunal. Thus, if the authority consent, a voluntary reference may be made after the six years: see Smith and the Waverley Tailoring Co. v Edinburgh District Council (1976), 31 P & CR 484 (Scottish Lands Tribunal).
[9] Town and Country Planning Act 1968, Sch. 3, para. 11.
[10] Ibid. para. 12.

to determination by the Lands Tribunal,[1] but otherwise the authority may recover any amount which is repayable under these provisions in the same way as a simple contract debt.[2]

4 PROCEDURE UNDER THE COMMUNITY LAND ACT 1975[3]

1 Powers of Acquisition

The Community Land Act 1975 conferred a new power on local authorities to acquire "any land which in their opinion is suitable for development".[4] They were also empowered to acquire any adjoining land which is required for the purpose of executing works for facilitating the development or use of the development land,[5] and also any land required as "exchange land".[6] Although these powers are in addition to the various acquisition powers conferred by existing enactments, they are expressed in unusually wide terms. It is likely, therefore, that the new powers will be used increasingly, even in cases where the acquisition falls within the scope of some other more specific enactment.[7]

2 Modifications to the Acquisition of Land (Authorisation Procedure) Act 1946

The Community Land Act 1975 incorporates the procedure under the Acquisition of Land (Authorisation Procedure) Act 1946, but makes a number of important modifications to it.[8] These modifications only apply if the interests included in the order are all "outstanding material interests"[9] as defined by the Community Land Act.[10] In other cases the 1946 Act procedure applies in its ordinary form. Where the land to be acquired is suitable only for the building of a single house or for

[1] Town and Country Planning Act 1968, Sch. 3, para. 13.
[2] *Ibid.* para. 14.
[3] For the general purpose of this Act see pp. 23, *et seq, ante*; for its effects upon compensation see chapter 7, pp. 296, *et seq, post*, and for a detailed analysis see *Corfield's Guide to the Community Land Act*, Butterworths 1976. For policy guidance in relation to acquisitions under the Act: see Department of the Environment Circular 26/76 paras. 32–40 8, 26/77 para. 30 *et seq*.
[4] Community Land Act 1975, s. 15. Development has the same meaning as in s.22 of the Town and Country Planning Act 1971 save for the exclusion of what is termed "exempt development" (development permitted by the General Development Order and certain agricultural development): Community Land Act 1975, s. 6(1, 15(2), Sch. 1, and see p. 296, *post*.
[5] *Ibid*, s. 15(3)(a).
[6] I.e., land required to replace any common land, etc. included in the development land: *ibid*, s. 15(3)(b), and see p. 49, *supra*.
[7] See Department of the Environment Circular 26/77, para. 41, where it is suggested that the Community Land Act procedure would be less "administratively convenient" in relation to acquisitions for statutory functions for which the Secretary of State for the Environment is not responsible.
[8] Community Land Act 1975, s. 15(4)–(5). See generally Department of the Environment Circular 26/77, paras. 30 *et seq*.
[9] *Ibid*, s. 4. Generally an "outstanding material interest" is any interest which at the relevant time is not owned by a local authority or by a charity. The Secretary of State has a power to exclude also interests of other descriptions: s. 4(1)(c), and see Community Land (Outstanding Material Interests) Order 1976, SI 1976 No. 19; see p. 299, *post*.
[10] Community Land Act 1975, Sch. 1, para. 1(2). For the modifications to apply, the order must contain a certificate to the effect that there are no interests other than outstanding material interests.

"excepted development"[1] the modifications apply only in part; this position will be considered separately below.

The modifications

Schedule 4 of the Community Land Act 1975 enacts an amended version of Acquisition of Land (Authorisation Procedure) Act 1946, Schedule 1, para. 4.[2] There are two principal departures from the 1946 Act procedure:

(i) The Secretary of State may disregard objections on the ground that "the acquisition is unnecessary or inexpedient";

(ii) The Secretary of State is not required to hold an inquiry in certain cases.

UNNECESSARY OR INEXPEDIENT

In addition to disregarding objections which relate exclusively to compensation matters,[3] the Secretary of State is empowered[4] to disregard any objection "if satisfied that the objection is made on the ground that the acquisition is *unnecessary or inexpedient*".[5] This difficult expression[6] is understood by the Secretary of State as enabling him to disregard objections "to the principle of public acquisition of development land":[7] he will still feel bound to consider objections made on the ground that the development itself is unnecessary or inexpedient,[7] or objections based on prematurity of acquisition or personal hardship.[8] The provision will no doubt encourage objectors to state their objections in relatively wide terms and in practice it will be difficult for the Secretary of State to satisfy himself that an objection falls within the definition without holding an inquiry first.[9] The principal effect of this provision would therefore seem to be to exclude objections made solely on the ground that the development concerned could be satisfactorily

[1] "Excepted development" is a term applied to certain categories of development which the Secretary of State decides should be "outside the *normal* scope of the land scheme": see Department of the Environment Circular 26/76 para. 28. This is not to be confused with "exempt development" which is removed from the operation of the Act altogether by s. 3(2) and Sch. 1. The current categories of "excepted development" are prescribed by the Community Land (Excepted Development) Regulations 1976, SI 1976 No. 331, and see p. 297, *post*. For a full description see Department of the Environment Circular 26/76, Annex C.

[2] See p. 35, *supra*.

[3] See p. 35, *supra*.

[4] It would appear that before disregarding an objection on these grounds he must first "require" the objector to state the grounds of the objection in writing, even if some grounds have been given in the original objection.

[5] Acquisition of Land (Authorisation Procedure) Act 1946, Sch. 4, para. 4(b), as amended by the Community Land Act 1975, Sch. 1.

[6] The same expression is to be found in the New Towns Act 1965 (see p. 81, *infra*) but does not appear to have been considered by the Courts. It is clearly capable of a very wide interpretation, even though at present the Secretary of State takes a narrow view of his power to disregard objections under this provision.

[7] See Department of the Environment Circular 26/77, para. 31.

[8] These examples were given in a guidance note issued by the Department of the Environment in 1975.

[9] Note that the burden of establishing that an objection falls within the definition and can be disregarded is placed on the Secretary of State. He may disregard an objection if his requirement to state the grounds is not complied with (para. 4(7)): but if the grounds are stated in general or insufficiently precise terms, he has no power to require further and better particulars. In such a case his only means of "satisfying himself" that the objection can be disregarded would be to hold an inquiry.

carried out by the owner or by a developer prepared to purchase the land from him in the open market.

CONFIRMATION WITHOUT INQUIRY

As seen above,[1] under the ordinary procedure, if an objection has been duly made the Secretary of State is bound to hold an inquiry or give the objector an opportunity of being heard in person. However, under the modified procedure this requirement is excluded in certain cases, and in those cases the Secretary of State need only hold an inquiry or hearing if he considers it expedient to do so.[2]

The cases in which an inquiry may be dispensed with are[3] where either:

(1) the land is covered by a planning permission for relevant development granted by the Secretary of State after a public local inquiry; or

(2) the grant of planning permission for such development would be in accordance with an adopted or approved[4] local plan; or

(3) if no such local plan is in force, it would be in accordance with the old-style development plan and any approved structure plan.[5]

The intention evidently is that the Secretary of State should be able to dispense with an inquiry in cases where the future of the land has already been determined after some form of public consultation procedure, but not, for instance, where planning permission has been given without a public inquiry.[6]

EXCEPTED DEVELOPMENT

It is to be noted that the cases in which an inquiry may be dispensed with relate only to "relevant development". This expression excludes "excepted development"[7] and also development consisting of the building of a single dwelling-house only.[8] Thus the existence of a permission or allocation for excepted development does not confer power to dispense with an inquiry. However, the Secretary of State does not have to be satisfied that the acquisition itself is for relevant development. It is enough if the land in fact has permission or allocation for relevant development; the acquisition may be for some other purpose.

---

[1] See p. 36, *supra*.

[2] Acquisition of Land (Authorisation Procedure) Act 1946, Sch. 4, para. 4(2), as amended.

[3] *Ibid*, para. 4(3). This summary is based on Department of the Environment Circular 26/77, para. 35.

[4] See Town and Country Planning Act 1971, Part II. A local plan may be "adopted" by the local planning authority unless there is a direction by the Secretary of State requiring it to be "approved" by him: *ibid*, s. 14. The Secretary of State may, by order, extend this category to cover development according with local plans at an earlier stage of their preparation, or to other plans if he considers it necessary in the public interest, but the right to an inquiry will be preserved in the case of a dwelling-house: Community Land Act 1975, Sch. 1, para. 3. A draft of the order must be approved by both Houses of Parliament: *ibid*, para. 3(6).

[5] I.e., "the development plan" within the meaning of the Town and Country Planning Act 1971, s. 20 and Sch. 7.

[6] E.g., by the local planning authority, or by the Secretary of State after a written representations appeal.

[7] See note 1, p. 75, *supra*.

[8] Community Land Act 1975, s. 3(2).

The power to disregard objections based on the ground that the acquisition is unnecessary or inexpedient is not limited to acquisitions for relevant development.[1] Thus on an acquisition for excepted development the Secretary of State could apparently disregard objections made on these grounds, although he has said that as a matter of practice he will require special justification for the use of compulsory purchase powers in such cases.[2]

5 PROCEDURE UNDER THE HOUSING ACT 1957, PART III

POWERS OF THE HOUSING AUTHORITY

Part III of the Housing Act 1957 deals with treatment of "clearance areas". A housing authority is required to declare an area to be a "clearance area" if they are satisfied, first, that the houses in the area are unfit for human habitation, or that the houses and other buildings are dangerous or injurious to the health of the inhabitants by reason of bad arrangement; and, secondly, that the most satisfactory method of dealing with conditions in the area is the demolition of all the buildings in it.[3] Having declared a clearance area, the authority must[4] secure its clearance by purchasing the land comprised in the area and themselves carrying out the demolition of the buildings.[5] If they proceed in this way, the authority may also acquire any land which is surrounded by the clearance area and the acquisition of which is reasonably necessary for the satisfactory development or use of the cleared area.[6]

The land required under these provisions may be acquired compulsorily subject to the authorisation of the Secretary of State. However, the ordinary procedure under the Acquisition of Land (Authorisation Procedure) Act 1946 does not apply to acquisitions under this Part of the Housing Act 1957. A special procedure is laid down by the third and fourth Schedules of the Act.

PROCEDURE

The form of a compulsory purchase order under these provisions is prescribed by regulations.[7] The scope of the order must be described by reference to a map of the relevant land and must show which parts are outside the clearance area, and which parts are included only by reason of bad arrangement.[8] In the case of land within the clearance area the

---

[1] Acquisition of Land (Authorisation Procedure) Act 1946, Sch. 1, para. 4(6), as amended.

[2] See Department of the Environment Circular 26/76, paras. 34–37.

[3] Housing Act 1957, s. 42(1). For a general description of the procedure see Department of the Environment Circular 77/75. A clearance area may consist of a single house: *ibid*, para. 14.

[4] The alternative originally was the making of a clearance order requiring the owners to demolish the buildings. However this procedure is no longer available in relation to clearance areas declared since 31 August 1974. Housing Act 1974, s. 108.

[5] Housing Act 1957, s. 43(1).

[6] *Ibid*, s. 43(2).

[7] Housing (Prescribed Forms) Regulations 1972, SI 1972 No. 228, Form 24.

[8] Housing Act 1957, Sch. 3, para. 1. The prescribed form provides for the land within the clearance area to be coloured pink; the land included by reason of bad arrangement to be coloured pink hatched yellow; and the added lands to be coloured grey.

order must be made within six months of the date of the resolution declaring the clearance area. In the case of other land the order must be made within twelve months of the same date. In either case the period may be extended by the Secretary of State.[1]

Before submitting the order to the Secretary of State the local authority must publish a notice in the prescribed form[2] in one or more local newspapers, and serve a similar notice[3] on every owner, lessee and occupier other than tenants for a month or less,[4] and on any mortgagees so far as it is reasonably practicable to ascertain them.[5] In addition to other methods of effective service[6] a notice may be served by addressing it to the "owner", "lessee" or "occupier" and delivering it to some person on the premises or, if there is no person on the premises, fixing it to a conspicuous part of the premises.[7] The personal notice should normally be accompanied by a statement of the authority's reasons for having declared the clearance area and for making the order.[8] If any objection to the order is made on the grounds that a building included in the order is not unfit, the authority must serve upon the objector a notice stating the facts they allege as the principal grounds of unfitness. In such a case the Secretary of State cannot hold an inquiry or hearing into objections until 14 days after he has been satisfied that the notice has been served.[9]

If there are no outstanding objections from persons entitled to be served with notice of the order, the Secretary of State need not hold any inquiry and can confirm the order with or without modification.[10] If there are such objections duly made, he must arrange either for a public local inquiry or for a hearing[11] into the objections. He cannot then confirm the order until he has considered the report of the person appointed to hold the inquiry or hearing.[12] The Secretary of State may require any objector to state the grounds of his objection in writing, and, if it relates exclusively to questions of compensation or other matters which can be dealt with by the Lands Tribunal, he may disregard it.[13]

[1] Housing Act 1957, s. 43(4). For the Secretary of State's policy in relation to extensions of time see Department of the Environment Circular 77/75, Appendix B, paras. 8–9.

[2] Housing (Prescribed Forms) Regulations 1972, SI 1972 No. 228, Form 25.

[3] *Ibid*, Form 26.

[4] This expression includes statutory tenants under the Rent Acts: Housing Act 1957, Sch. 3, para. 2(3).

[5] Housing Act 1957, Sch. 3, para. 2. This differs from the ordinary procedure under the Acquisition of Land (Authorisation Procedure) Act 1946 in that notice in the press does not have to be given in two successive weeks, and there is no procedure for the Secretary of State to direct that personal notice shall not apply: see p. 33, *supra*.

[6] See Housing Act 1957, s. 169: Recorded Delivery Service Act 1962, s. 1.

[7] Housing Act 1957, Sch. 3, para. 2(2). This is a relaxation of the ordinary rule that allows this method of service only if it is not practicable after reasonable inquiry to ascertain the name and address of the relevant person: *ibid*, s. 169(1)(e).

[8] Department of the Environment Circular 77/75, paras. 31–32. Although this is not a statutory requirement, a failure to serve the statement could result in an adjournment of the inquiry into objections.

[9] Housing Act 1957, Sch. 3, para. 3(4).

[10] *Ibid*, Sch. 3, para. 3(2).

[11] For the distinction between inquiries and hearings, see p. 45, *supra*.

[12] Housing Act 1957, Sch. 3. para. 3(3).

[13] *Ibid*, Sch. 3, para. 3(6).

INQUIRIES OR HEARINGS

There are no inquiries procedure rules governing the conduct of inquiries under the Housing Act 1957, Part III. However, although the procedure is at the discretion of the person appointed to hold the inquiry, he must act judicially and conform to the rules of natural justice.[1] Thus, for instance, he may not take into account information which comes to his knowledge in the absence of either party.[2] Where an inquiry (as opposed to a hearing) is held, the Secretary of State has power to issue subpoenas and to make orders as to costs.[3] If an objection, made on the grounds that a building is not unfit, is pursued at the inquiry or hearing, but is not upheld by the Secretary of State, the objector is entitled, on making a request in writing, to be given a statement of the Secretary of State's reasons for deciding that it is unfit.[4] In any event the Secretary of State is bound, under the Tribunals and Inquiries Act 1971,[5] to give reasons for his decision on the order if so requested on or before the giving of the decision. It should be noted, however, that he is under no duty to do so unless requested, and a formal request should therefore be made at the inquiry.

CONFIRMATION

Although the Secretary of State has power to modify the order, he may not do so if the effect is to authorise the authority to acquire land not included in the order as originally made.[6] Nor may he include land within the clearance area which was outside the area as declared, or authorise the authority to purchase any building on less favourable terms as to compensation than would have applied to the order as made.[7] If he considers that land has been wrongly included in the clearance area, he may still confirm the order in respect of that land[8] by including it as added land under s. 43(2) of the Act.[9] The fact that the modifications made by the Secretary of State split the clearance area into two distinct areas does not affect its validity, and it is still treated for all purposes as a single clearance area.[10]

As soon as the order is confirmed the authority must publish in a local newspaper a notice in the prescribed form and a similar notice must be served on every person who appeared at the inquiry in support of an objection.[11] The procedure for challenging the validity of an order[12] is substantially the same as that for challenging an order under

---

[1] See *Fairmount Investments Ltd.* v *Secretary of State*, [1976] 2 All ER 865 *Hibernian Property Co. Ltd.* v *Secretary of State* (1973), 27 P & CR 197.

[2] *Steele* v *Minister of Housing and Local Government* (1956), 6 P & CR 386.

[3] Local Government Act 1972, s. 250: see p. 44, *supra*. The Secretary of State's policy in relation to costs is set out in Ministry of Housing and Local Government Circular 73/65.

[4] Housing Act 1957, Sch. 3, para. 3(5).

[5] S. 12.

[6] *Ibid*, Sch. 3, para. 4(1).For the meaning of "modification", see *Legg* v *Inner London Education Authority* [1972] 3 All ER 177.

[7] *Ibid*, Sch. 3, para. 4(2).

[8] *Ibid*, Sch. 3, para. 4(3).

[9] See p. 77, *supra*.

[10] Housing Act 1957, Sch. 3, para. 4(4).

[11] *Ibid*, Sch. 4, para. 1.

[12] *Ibid*, Sch. 4, para. 2.

the Acquisition of Land (Authorisation Procedure) Act 1946.[1] It should be noted, however, that in relation to orders under the Housing Act 1957, Part III, no appeal lies from a decision of the Court of Appeal except with the leave of the Court of Appeal itself.[2] If there is no application to the High Court the order takes effect six weeks after the publication of the notice of confirmation.[3] At that time the authority must serve a copy of the order on every person who was served with notice of the original making of the order.[4]

Procedure subsequent to the confirmation of the order follows generally the ordinary procedure under the Compulsory Purchase Act 1965.[5] The special provisions as to compensation are considered elsewhere.[6] Where the authority decide to retain unfit houses temporarily for housing purposes instead of demolishing them immediately,[7] they may effect a notional entry by serving a notice on the occupier authorising him to continue in occupation on the terms specified in the notice.[8] For certain purposes[9] the service of such a notice has the same effect as an actual taking of possession by the authority on the date of the notice.

6 PROCEDURE UNDER THE NEW TOWNS ACT 1965

DEVELOPMENT CORPORATIONS

"New towns" are areas which have been designated as such by the Secretary of State under the New Towns Act 1965, s. 1. He may designate an area as the site of a proposed new town if he is satisfied "that it is expedient in the national interest that any area should be developed as a new town by a corporation established under this Act".[10] The Act provides a procedure whereby the Secretary of State is required to consider objections to the designation order and to hold a public local inquiry for this purpose.[11] Once the designation is complete the Secretary of State is required to establish a corporation, known as a "development corporation",[12] charged with the duty of securing the laying out and development of the new town[13] in accordance with proposals which have to be approved by the Secretary of State.[14]

---

[1] See p. 52, *supra*.

[2] Housing Act 1957, Sch. 4, para. 4.

[3] *Ibid*, Sch. 4, para. 3. Compare Acquisition of Land (Authorisation Procedure) Act 1946 Sch. 1 para. 16, which provides that an order made under that Act becomes operative on the date of publication of the notice: see p. 36, *supra*.

[4] *Ibid*, Sch. 4, para. 5.

[5] Compulsory Purchase Act 1965, s. 34. See p. 66, *supra*. But note the more restricted provisions relating to interests created or works done with a view to enhancing compensation: p. 69, *supra*.

[6] See p. 257, *post*.

[7] Housing Act 1957, s. 48.

[8] *Ibid*, Sch. 3, para. 10.

[9] E.g., as to assessment of compensation and interest thereon: see pp. 95, 96, *post*.

[10] New Towns Act 1965, s. 1(1).

[11] *Ibid*, Sch. 1.

[12] *Ibid*, s. 2.

[13] *Ibid*, s. 3(1).

[14] *Ibid*, s. 6(1).

POWERS OF ACQUISITION

The development corporation within a new town area has the power to acquire land by agreement with the consent of the Secretary of State and to acquire land compulsorily by an order confirmed by him. The land which may be acquired is:

(i) any land within the area of the new town, whether or not it is proposed to develop that land;

(ii) any land adjacent to that area which they require for purposes connected with the development of the new town;

(iii) any land, whether adjacent to the new town area or not, which they require for the provision of services for the purposes of the new town.[1]

PROCEDURE

Like the Housing Act 1957, Part III, the New Towns Act 1965 provides its own procedure for the making and confirmation of compulsory purchase orders[2] and does not incorporate any part of the Acquisition of Land (Authorisation Procedure) Act 1946.[3] On the other hand, the procedure from confirmation to entry and for the assessment of compensation is governed by the Compulsory Purchase Act 1965 and the Land Compensation Act 1961,[4] although subject to certain modifications.[5] The chief difference from the Acquisition of Land (Authorisation Procedure) Act procedure[6] is that, within the designated new town area, the principle of public ownership is regarded as having been established by the designation order itself. Accordingly, where the compulsory purchase order relates to land within the designated area, the Secretary of State may disregard any objection which is made "on the ground that the order is unnecessary or inexpedient".[7] There are also other provisions designed to expedite the procedure. Thus the corporation is not required to serve notice of the making of the order on owners, occupiers and tenants.[8] Unless the Secretary of State directs notice to be served personally on owners,[9] it is sufficient that notice is published in the London Gazette and, in each of two consecutive weeks, in one or more newspapers circulating in the locality, and a copy of the notice addressed to "the owners and any occupiers" of the land is affixed to a conspicuous object on the land.[10] Furthermore the

---

[1] *Ibid*, s. 7(1). Highway authorities also have special powers to acquire land for road construction or improvement: *ibid*, s. 8(1). The development corporation may in addition be compelled by an owner to purchase any land within the designated area which has not been acquired within seven years of the date when the designation order became operative: *ibid*, s. 11.

[2] *Ibid*, s. 7(1) and Sch. 3. The form of orders and notices is prescribed by the New Towns (Compulsory Purchase of Land) Regulations 1977, SI 1977 No. 549.

[3] See p. 32, *supra*.

[4] New Towns Act 1965, s. 12.

[5] *Ibid*, Sch. 6.

[6] As to which see p. 32, *supra*.

[7] New Towns Act 1965, Sch. 3, para. 4(3)(b). Note that the same wording has been adopted by the Community Land Act 1975: see p. 75, *supra*.

[8] Cf. Acquisition of Land (Authorisation Procedure) Act 1946, Sch. 1, para. 9, p. 33, *supra*.

[9] New Towns Act 1965, Sch. 3, para. 2(1)(b).

[10] *Ibid*, Sch. 3, para. 2(1)(a), 2 (a).

Secretary of State is not required in every case to allow objectors an opportunity to be heard before making his decision.[1] If satisfied that he is sufficiently informed as to the matters to which the objection relates, he may make a final decision without further investigation.[2] If not, he must give the objector an opportunity of appearing before and being heard by a person appointed for the purpose.[3] In addition, if he considers that the matters to which the objection relates are such as to require investigation by public local inquiry, he shall cause an inquiry to be held before he makes his decision.[4] In other respects the procedure is similar to that laid down by the Acquisition of Land (Authorisation Procedure) Act 1946.[5]

[1] Cf. Acquisition of Land (Authorisation Procedure) Act 1946, Sch. 1, para. 4(2), p. 36, *supra*.
[2] New Towns Act 1965, Sch. 3, para. 4(4).
[3] *Ibid*, Sch. 3, para. 4(5).
[4] *Ibid*, Sch. 3, para. 4(6). There are no inquiries procedure rules governing such inquiries.
[5] See p. 33, *supra*. Note that special provisions apply to the acquisition of land of statutory undertakers: New Towns Act 1965, s. 10, Sch. 4.

CHAPTER 3

Determination and Payment of Compensation

1 DETERMINATION OF COMPENSATION

Lands Tribunal

(i) JURISDICTION

The Land Compensation Act 1961, s. 1, provides that any question of disputed compensation arising when land[1] is authorised to be acquired compulsorily under any statute, is to be referred to the Lands Tribunal.[2] The Lands Tribunal was set up by the Lands Tribunal Act 1949, and took over the jurisdiction of official arbitrators under the Acquisition of Land (Assessment of Compensation) Act 1919. The jurisdiction relates only to questions of compensation and does not extend, for instance, to questions of title.[3]

(ii) PROCEDURE

The procedure of the Lands Tribunal is regulated principally by rules made under the Lands Tribunal Act 1949 and by other provisions of that Act and the Land Compensation Act 1961. The current rules are the Lands Tribunal Rules 1975.[4] The Community Land Act 1975 now enables rules to be made for determination of compensation without an oral hearing if the claimant agrees.[5]

Notice of Claim

The notice to treat requires the recipient to give particulars of his interest in the land and the claim made by him.[6] Such a notice of claim is normally the first step towards settling compensation. The notice should state the exact nature of the claimant's interest, and give details

---

[1] "Land" is defined as including "any corporeal hereditament including a building as defined ... and ... any interest or right in or over land and any right to water.": Land Compensation Act 1961, s. 39.

[2] Land Compensation Act 1961, s. 1. This excludes any jurisdiction of the High Court to determine any question which is a step in the assessment of compensation: *Harrison* v *Croydon London Borough Council,* [1968] Ch. 479, in which the Court declined to consider a question relating to the assumptions as to planning permission to be taken into account in assessing compensation.

[3] See *Mountgarret* v *Claro Water Board* (1963), 15 P & CR 53, where it was conceded that under the similar words of the Acquisition of Land (Assessment of Compensation Act) 1919, s. 1, the Official Arbitrator did not have jurisdiction to decide questions of title, and it was held that the Lands Tribunal's jurisdiction under the Lands Tribunal Act 1949 was no wider.

[4] SI 1975 No. 299, made under the Lands Tribunals Act 1949, s. 3.

[5] Community Land Act 1975, Sch. 10, para. 3. No such rules have yet been made.

[6] Compulsory Purchase Act 1965, s. 5(2): see p. 67, *ante.*

of the compensation claimed, distinguishing the amounts under separate heads and showing how each is calculated.[1] It may be amended at any time until it has been accepted.[2] The service of a valid notice of claim is important since it gives the authority its last opportunity to withdraw the notice to treat.[3] If it does not do so within six weeks after the delivery of the notice it can be required to proceed with the purchase.[4] If no notice of claim is served the authority can withdraw its notice to treat after compensation has been assessed.[5] The notice of claim is also important in relation to the award of costs in the Lands Tribunal.[6]

Reference to Lands Tribunal

If no notice of claim is served by the owner within 21 days of the notice to treat or if the compensation is not agreed, the question is referred to the Lands Tribunal.[7] Either party may initiate proceedings in the Lands Tribunal by sending to the Registrar a notice of reference in the prescribed form,[8] together with copies of the notice to treat and any notice of claim.[9] The notice of reference cannot be given until at least 28 days after the service of the notice to treat.[10] Service of the notice on the other parties is effected by the Registrar.[11]

Interlocutory Matters

Provision is made for directions of an interlocutory nature to be made by the Registrar on application by either party.[12] But the Registrar may refer the application to the President of the Lands Tribunal, and must do so if either party wishes.[13] In any event there is a right of appeal to the President against a decision of the Registrar.[14] Such interlocutory matters include, for instance, an application to call more than one expert[15] or for the consolidation of two or more references relating to the same land,[16] or an order for evidence to be taken on affidavit, or an order for a preliminary hearing of a point of law.[17] In addition, the High Court has power to grant various forms of interlocutory relief, including orders for security for costs, and to issue subpoenas.[18]

Discovery

The Tribunal has the power to require either party to deliver to the Registrar any document or other information which it is in his power to

---

[1] Land Compensation Act 1961, s. 4(2).

[2] *Cardiff Corpn v Cook,* [1923] 2 Ch. 115.

[3] Land Compensation Act 1961, s. 31(1). The authority must pay compensation for any loss or expenses occasioned by the withdrawal: s. 31(3).

[4] *Ibid,* s. 31(5).

[5] *Ibid,* s. 31(2), but not if they have already taken possession: *ibid.*

[6] *Ibid,* s. 4(1): see p. 86, *infra.*

[7] Compulsory Purchase Act 1965, s. 6.

[8] Lands Tribunal Rules 1975, SI 1975 No. 299, rule 16(1), Form 4.

[9] *Ibid,* rule 16(2).

[10] *Ibid,* rule 16(3).

[11] *Ibid,* rule 17.

[12] *Ibid,* rule 45.

[13] *Ibid,* rule 45(7).

[14] *Ibid,* rule 45(8).

[15] *Ibid,* rule 42(3).

[16] *Ibid,* rule 36.

[17] *Ibid,* rule 39, 49. In these cases the application is made to the President in the first instance.

[18] Arbitration Act 1950, s. 12(4)–(6), applied by the Lands Tribunals Rules 1975, SI 1975 No. 299, rule 38.

deliver.[1] This power is not exercisable by the Registrar.[2] Any document so disclosed must be made available to the other parties for inspection and for copies to be taken.[3] Objection may be made to disclosure on the grounds that it is contrary to the public interest.[4]

Evidence

The parties may agree or the Tribunal may order that evidence should be by affidavit. Otherwise the evidence is given orally.[5] All the parties to a reference impliedly consent to be examined by the Tribunal on oath or affirmation, if required, and the Tribunal has the power to administer oaths or take affirmations.[6]

The Lands Tribunal is bound by the ordinary rules of evidence, including the rules against hearsay evidence.[7] This is a particularly important consideration when preparing valuation evidence, since the ordinary rule as to expert evidence in chief given by a valuer has been stated[8] as follows:

> "Putting matters shortly, and leaving on one side the matters that I have mentioned, such as the Civil Evidence Act 1968 and anything made admissible by questions in cross-examination, in my judgment a valuer giving expert evidence in chief (or in re-examination): (a) may express the opinions that he has formed as to values even though substantial contributions to the formation of those opinions have been made by matters of which he has no first-hand knowledge: (b) may give evidence as to the details of any transactions within his personal knowledge, in order to establish them as matters of fact; and (c) may express his opinion as to the significance of any transactions which are or will be proved by admissible evidence (whether or not given by him) in relation to the valuation with which he is concerned; but (d) may not give hearsay evidence stating the details of any transactions not within his personal knowledge in order to establish them as matters of fact. To those propositions I would add that for counsel to put in a list of comparables ought to amount to a warranty by him of his intention to tender admissible evidence of all that is shown on the list".

It is therefore desirable to ensure that facts relating to comparable transactions are agreed before the hearing, or that the appropriate notices are served under the Civil Evidence Acts[9] since otherwise it may be necessary to prove them by direct evidence.

---

[1] *Ibid*, rule 40. See also Arbitration Act 1950, s. 12(1) applied by *ibid*, rule 38.

[2] See definition of "Tribunal": *ibid*, rule 2(2); *Goldstyles Ltd.* v *LCC* (1964), 15 P & CR 317 LT.

[3] SI 1975 No. 299, rule 40.

[4] *Ibid*; presumably the Tribunal is entitled to decide whether the disclosure would be contrary to the public interest or not: see *Conway* v *Rimmer*, [1968] AC 910.

[5] SI 1975 No. 299, rule 39(1).

[6] Arbitration Act 1950, s. 12(1)–(3), applied by Lands Tribunal Rules 1975, SI 1975 No. 299, rule 38.

[7] This follows from the fact that the Tribunal took over the jurisdiction of the official arbitrators under Acquisition of Land (Assessment of Compensation) Act 1919 (Lands Tribunal Act 1949, s. 1 and see p. 83, *supra*). For the application of the rules of evidence to arbitrators, see *Re: Enoch and Zaretzky Bock & Co*, [1910] 1 KB 327.

[8] *English Exporters (London) Ltd.* v *Eldonwall Ltd.*, [1973] Ch. 415 at p. 423 per Megarry J.

[9] The Civil Evidence Acts 1968 and 1972 apply to proceedings in the Lands Tribunal (see the definition of "civil proceedings" in Civil Evidence Act 1968, s. 18(1)(a) and Civil Evidence Act 1972 s. 5(1)). Generally the 1968 Act enables indirect evidence of statements of fact to be admitted, subject to service of notices on other parties, and the 1970 Act extends this to certain statements of opinion. For a full treatment see 17 Halsbury's laws (4th Edn.). para. 53 *et seq*. The procedure for notices is governed by RSC Order 38 (applied by Civil Evidence Act 1968, s. 10(3)). For an example of the exercise of the Tribunal's discretion to admit indirect evidence under the 1968 Act, see *Gredley Co. Ltd.* v *London Borough of Newham* (1973), 26 P & CR 400, 414 LT.

Expert Witnesses

If either party wishes to call more than one expert witness leave must be obtained from the Tribunal or Registrar.[1] Where more than one party intends to call an expert, the Registrar may require copies of plans and valuations of the subject land and particulars of any comparables to be exchanged.[2]

Procedure generally

The Tribunal sits in public.[3] The parties may appear in person, or by Counsel, Solicitor or, with leave, any other person.[4] The Tribunal may view the subject land and also any land put forward as a comparable.[5] Rules may be made enabling the Tribunal to determine cases without an oral hearing, but in cases involving compulsory purchase, or depending directly or indirectly on the value of land, the consent of the claimant is required.[6]

(iii) DECISION

Award of the Tribunal

The decision of the Tribunal is normally given in writing and must include reasons.[7] The Tribunal has power to make an interim award.[8] It may be required by either party to specify the amount awarded in respect of any particular matter,[9] for instance, the split between compensation for the land and for disturbance. It may direct interest to run from the date of the award.[10] When the award depends on a decision on a point of law, the Tribunal should state the amount which would have been awarded on the alternative view.[11] The Tribunal is not bound by its own previous decisions on points of law.[12]

Costs

Although the Tribunal has a general discretion as to the award of costs,[13] this is subject to certain important restrictions contained in the Land Compensation Act 1961. Where the acquiring authority have made an unconditional offer equal to or exceeding the amount even-

---

[1] Land Compensation Act 1961, s. 2(3); Lands Tribunal Rules 1975, SI 1975 No. 299, rule 42. An additional expert witness is permitted where the claim includes a claim for compensation in respect of minerals or disturbance of business: *ibid*.

[2] *Ibid*, rule 42(4).

[3] Land Compensation Act 1961 s. 2(2): Lands Tribunal Rules 1975, SI 1975 No. 299, rule 33. This rule does not apply to a case which is determined without an oral hearing: see note 6, *infra*.

[4] *Ibid*, rule 44.

[5] *Ibid*, rule 34.

[6] Community Land Act 1975, Sch. 10, para. 3, amending the Lands Tribunal Act 1949, s. 3. No such rules have yet been made.

[7] SI 1975 No. 299, rule 54(1). It may be given orally if no injustice or inconvenience will be caused thereby: *ibid*.

[8] Arbitration Act 1950, s. 14, applied by Lands Tribunal Rules 1975, rule 38.

[9] Land Compensation Act 1961, s. 2(5).

[10] Arbitration Act 1950, s. 20, applied by SI 1975 No. 299, rule 38. A direction as to interest cannot be made subsequently: see *Merediths Ltd.* v *London County Council* (No. 2) (1957), 9 P & CR 258.

[11] SI 1975 No. 299, rule 54(3).

[12] See *West Midland Baptist Association* v *Birmingham Corpn*, [1968] 2 QB 188 at p. 210 per Salmon LJ.

[13] Lands Tribunal Act 1949, s. 3(5), which also gives the Tribunal the power to tax or settle the amount of costs. The general principle applied is that the claimant is awarded his costs whenever the award exceeds the authority's offer. The offer is normally lodged with the Tribunal as a "sealed offer" which is not opened until the decision.

tually awarded, the Tribunal must, unless there are special reasons,[1] make an order for payment by the claimant of the authority's costs from the date of the offer.[2] Similarly, if the claimant has failed to deliver a proper notice of claim[3] in time for the authority to make a proper offer, the authority is entitled, in the absence of special reasons, to its costs from the date when in the opinion of the Tribunal the notice should have been delivered.[4] On the other hand, if the claimant has submitted a proper notice of claim and has made an unconditional offer to accept a sum not more than that eventually awarded, he is entitled to his costs from the date of the offer, unless again there are special reasons.[5]

As a matter of practice the Tribunal will normally award the claimant his costs up to the date of the authority's offer, even if the sum ultimately awarded is less than the offer.[6] If, however, his claim fails altogether the ordinary rule that a successful party is entitled to his costs should normally be followed and an award made in favour of the acquiring authority.[7] The acquiring authority should not be asked to pay the costs of a wholly unsuccessful claimant except for very special reasons, which should be stated.[8] The Tribunal may direct that the costs awarded against a claimant shall be deducted from the compensation.[9] Otherwise they may be recovered summarily as a civil debt.[10]

(iv) APPEAL

Appeal is by way of case stated to the Court of Appeal.[11] The Tribunal may be required to state a case[12] within six weeks of the decision.[13] On receipt of the case signed by the Tribunal, the appellant must serve on every other party a copy of the case, and copies of a notice of motion setting out his contentions on the points of law must be served on the Registrar of the Tribunal.[14] Within two days of service the notice of motion and case stated must be lodged in the Court of Appeal.[15] The Court of Appeal has power to amend the case or to remit it to the Tribunal for amendment, and to draw inferences of fact from the facts

[1] If, for example, the offer was not made until immediately before the hearing, the acquiring authority may be made to pay the costs of the hearing: *Christodoulou* v *Islington London Borough Council* (1973), 230 Estates Gazette 233.

[2] Land Compensation Act 1961, s. 4(1)(a).

[3] The notice must contain all the required particulars: *ibid* s. 4(2) but see note 13, p. 86, *supra*.

[4] *Ibid*, s. 4(1)(b).

[5] *Ibid*, s. 4(3).

[6] *Pepys* v *London Transport*, [1975] 1 All ER 748 at p. 751g (per Lord Denning MR). The Tribunal may feel justified in departing from this principle if, for example, part of the claim was wholly fictitious or if the claim has been otherwise irresponsibly exaggerated: see *Hood Investment Co.* v *Marlow Urban District Council* (1963), 15 P & CR 229. However, in such a case reasons should be given: *Pepys* v *London Transport* (*supra*) at p. 751c.

[7] *Pepys* v *London Transport* (*supra*) at p. 753e Per Roskill LJ.

[8] *Ibid*, at p. 751, 753.

[9] Land Compensation Act 1961, s. 4(5). For taxation of costs, see Lands Tribunal Rules, SI 1975 No. 299, rule 56.

[10] *Ibid*, s. 4(6). See Magistrates' Courts Act 1952, s. 50.

[11] Lands Tribunal Act 1949, s. 3(4) and RSC 1965 Order 61. Appeal from the Court of Appeal to the House of Lords lies in the normal way with leave.

[12] For the form of case see *Routh's Trustee's* v *Central Land Board* (1957), 8 P & CR 290 CA: *Festiniog Railway Society Ltd.* v *Central Electricity Generating Board* (1962), 13 P & CR 248, CA.

[13] RSC Order 61, r. 1(1).

[14] *Ibid*, r. 3(1).

[15] *Ibid*, r. 3(2).

contained in the case.[1] If the Court of Appeal reverses the Tribunal's decision on a point of law it may either substitute the alternative award or it may remit the matter to the Tribunal for a revised assessment to be made.[2]

2 SPECIAL CASES

1 Absent and Untraced Owners

If a potential claimant is prevented from treating with the authority on account of absence from the United Kingdom, or if he cannot be found after diligent inquiry has been made,[3] the Compulsory Purchase Act 1965 provides a special procedure for assessment and payment of compensation.[4] The compensation to be paid for the relevant land or for any permanent injury to the relevant land, is to be determined by a valuation by a surveyor selected[5] from the members of the Lands Tribunal.[6] The valuation must be preserved by the authority and produced on demand to the owner of the land and to any other persons with an interest in it.[7]

After the valuation has been made, the authority may pay the appropriate compensation into court to be placed to the credit of the parties interested, giving their descriptions so far as possible.[8] Having done this, the authority may execute a deed poll containing a description of the land and declaring the circumstances under which the payment into court was made and the names of the parties credited with it.[9] The effect of the deed poll is to vest in the authority all the interests of the relevant parties, in respect of which the compensation has been paid into court, and to give the authority a right as against those persons to immediate possession of the land.[10] The High Court may make appropriate orders for the distribution of the money paid into court on the application of any person claiming any part of it.[11] However if a claimant is dissatisfied with the valuation he should, before applying to the Court, serve a notice in writing on the authority requiring the submission to the Lands Tribunal of the question whether any further sum should be paid into court.[12] If the Tribunal decides

---

[1] RSC Order 61, r. 3(4).

[2] See, e.g., *Myers* v *Milton Keynes Development Corpn*, [1974] 2 All ER 1096 at p. 1102.

[3] The mere fact that there is a doubt about the true ownership of the land does not enable these provisions to be invoked: see *Ex p. London and South-Western Rly. Co.* (1869), 38LJ Ch. 527.

[4] Compulsory Purchase Act 1965, s. 5(3) and Sch. 2. This does not apply where a general vesting declaration is made: Town and Country Planning Act 1968, Sch. 3A, para. 14.

[5] By the President of the Lands Tribunal: see Lands Tribunal Act 1949, s. 3(2).

[6] Compulsory Purchase Act 1965 Sch. 2, para. 1(1). The expenses of the valuation are borne by the authority: *ibid.* para. 1(4).

[7] *Ibid*, para. 1(3).

[8] *Ibid*, para. 2(1). Payment into court is governed by the Administration of Justice Act 1965, s. 4: see Compulsory Purchase Act 1965, s. 25.

[9] *Ibid*, para. 2(2).

[10] *Ibid*, para. 2(3). The deed poll must be under the official seal of the authority and stamped with the appropriate stamp duty: *ibid*. s. 28.

[11] *Ibid*, para. 3(1).

[12] *Ibid*, para. 4(1). The costs of the reference are borne by the authority if a further sum is found to be payable, but otherwise they are in the discretion of the Tribunal: *ibid*, para. 4(3).

that a further sum should be paid, the authority must pay it into court within 14 days of the award, and, if it fails to do so, the additional sum may be recovered by proceedings in the High Court.[1]

2 Omitted Interests

After the acquiring authority has entered on the land, it may subsequently be found that it has omitted duly to purchase or to pay compensation in respect of some "estate, right or interest in or charge affecting" the land.[2] In such a case, if the omission has occurred through "mistake or inadvertence",[3] it is entitled to remain in possession, provided that within a specified time limit it purchases, or pays compensation for, the relevant interest and pays full compensation for mesne profits.[4] This it may do even though the three year time limit for service of a notice to treat has expired.[5] The time limit for compliance with these requirements is six months from the time when the authority had notice of the estate, right, interest, or charge, or, if it is disputed by the authority, six months from the time when the claimant's right is finally established by law.[6] Compensation and mesne profits in such a case are assessed as at the date of entry and without regard to any works or improvements made by the authority thereafter.[7]

It is to be noted that this provision can only be relied on by the authority where it can show that the omission arose through "mistake or inadvertence".[8] It does not enable it to avoid the ordinary statutory requirements in a case where, for example, it has been unable to trace the owner of an interest of which it is aware,[9] or where it has entered knowing there was doubt as to the boundaries of the relevant interests.[10] In other cases the authority has no right to remain in possession, and the owner will be entitled in appropriate circumstances to an injunction and damages.[11]

3 Failure to convey

Special provision is made to deal with intransigent owners.[12] These

---

[1] *Ibid*, para. 4(2).
[2] Compulsory Purchase Act 1965, s. 22(1).
[3] See below.
[4] *Ibid*, s. 22(1). "Mesne profits" are defined as the mesne profits or interest which would have accrued to the persons concerned during the interval between the entry of the authority and the time when compensation is paid, so far as recoverable in any proceedings: *ibid*, s. 22(5).
[5] *Ibid*, s. 22(2).
[6] *Ibid*, s. 22(3).
[7] *Ibid*, s. 22(4).
[8] See *Cooke* v *LCC*, [1911] 1 Ch. 604 at p. 610.
[9] In such a case they should follow the procedure laid down by *ibid*, Sch. 22, *supra*. Cf. *Martin* v *London, Chatham and Dover Rly. Co.* (1866), 1 Ch. App 501, at p. 509.
[10] See *Stretton* v *Great Western and Brentford Rly. Co.* (1870), 5 Ch. App 751.
[11] *Ibid* and see p. 71, *ante*.
[12] Compulsory Purchase Act 1965, s. 9. These provisions are not applicable to cases where the defaulter has no title (see *Wells* v *Chelmsford Local Board of Health* (1880), 15 Ch D 108); or where the title is in dispute (see *Re Lowestoft Manor and Great Eastern Rly. Co.* (1833), 24 Ch D 253). Special provision is made for persons under a disability: Compulsory Purchase Act 1965, s. 2 and Sch. 1. If the failure to convey is due to failure to obtain necessary consents, the authority should proceed under the provisions of Schedule 1 (see p. 94, *infra*), rather than section 9, which is concerned with wilful default: see *Re Leeds Grammar School*, [1901] 1 Ch. 228.

provisions apply where an owner of any of the land purchased by the acquiring authority or of any interest in it, on tender of the compensation agreed or awarded,

  (i)   refuses to accept it, or
  (ii) neglects or fails to make out a title to the land or interest to the authority's satisfaction, or
  (iii) refuses to convey or release the land as directed by the acquiring authority.[1]

In any of these cases the authority may pay the compensation into Court and execute a deed poll containing a description of the land and the circumstances in which the payment was made.[2] The effect of the deed poll is to vest in the authority absolutely all the estate or interest in the relevant land of the parties for whose use the compensation has been paid into Court, and to give them as against those parties a right to immediate possession.[3] On application by a person claiming any of the money paid into Court or any interest in the relevant land, the High Court may make appropriate orders for its distribution.[4]

4 Mortgages

Where the land to be acquired is subject to a mortgage, the acquiring authority[5] may instead of serving a notice to treat[6] on the mortgagee, purchase or redeem his interest in one of two ways. It may pay or tender to him the principal and interest due on the mortgage, together with his costs and charges and six months' additional interest. The mortgagee must then immediately convey or release his interest to the authority, or as it directs.[7] As an alternative, it may give him notice in writing that it will pay all the principal and interest due on the mortgage at the end of six months from the day of giving notice.[8] At the end of the six months or at any intermediate period, on payment or tender by the acquiring authority of the principal due on the mortgage and the interest which would become due at the end of the six months, together with the mortgagee's costs and expenses, the mortgagee must convey or release his interest to the authority or as it directs.[9]

  If in either case the mortgagee fails to comply with the requirement,

[1] Compulsory Purchase Act 1965, s. 9(1).
[2] Ibid, s. 9(1), (3). The compensation must be placed to the credit of the parties interested; and the authority must, as far as it can, give their descriptions (ibid, s. 9(2)), and must declare their names in the deed poll (s. 9(3)). Detailed provision for payment into Court is made by ibid, ss. 25–26 and for the form of deed poll by ibid, s. 28.
[3] Ibid, s. 9(4).
[4] The Court has a wide discretion: see Re County of London (Devons Road, Poplar) Housing Confirmation Order 1945 (1956), 6 P & CR 133.
[5] The "acquiring authority" is defined as "the person authorised by the compulsory purchase order under the Acquisition of Land (Authorisation Procedure) Act 1946 to purchase the land": Compulsory Purchase Act 1965, s. 1(3). It follows that the power to redeem a mortgage under these provisions cannot be exercised until notice of confirmation of the order is published.
[6] Apart from these provisions, a mortgagee would have an interest entitling him to service of notice to treat (see p. 68, ante). For the obligations of the acquiring authority in respect of mortgaged land see generally Cooke v LCC, [1911] 1 Ch. 604.
[7] Compulsory Purchase Act 1965, s. 14(2).
[8] The person entitled to the equity of redemption may himself give six months' notice of intention to redeem, and in that case the same provisions will apply.
[9] Ibid, s. 14(3).

or fails to make out a good title to the interest to the satisfaction of the authority, it may pay into Court the sums which are payable in respect of the mortgagee's interest and execute a deed poll.[1] This will have the effect of vesting in the authority all the estate and interest of the mortgagee,[2] and, if he was entitled to possession, giving it the right to possession.[3] The authority's power to redeem under these provisions is exercisable whether or not it has purchased the interest of the person entitled to the equity of redemption,[4] and whether or not the mortgagee is in possession.[5] It may be exercised even though the mortgage includes other land not subject to compulsory purchase.[6]

Where the value of the mortgaged land is less than the principal interest and costs secured on the land, the authority will obviously not wish to redeem the mortgage. In such a case the value of the land, or the compensation to be paid in respect of it, are to be settled by agreement[7] between the mortgagee and the person entitled to the equity of redemption on the one part, and, on the other, the acquiring authority.[8] On payment or tender of the amount so determined the mortgagee must convey or release all his interest at the direction of the authority.[9] The making of payment to the mortgagor or into Court operates to discharge the land from all money due under the mortgage,[10] although the mortgagee's rights against the mortgagor in respect of the balance of the mortgage debt are preserved.[11]

Similar provisions apply where part only of the mortgaged land is required by the authority and the value of that part is of less value than the principal, interest and costs secured on the mortgaged land as a whole.[12] If the mortgagee does not consider that the remaining part of the land is sufficient security for the money charged thereon or is otherwise not willing to release the part required,[13] then the value of that part as well as any compensation to be paid for severance or otherwise, is to be settled[14] between both parties to the mortgage on the one hand and the acquiring authority on the other.[15] A memorandum of the amount paid must be endorsed on the mortgage deed and signed by

[1] *Ibid*, s. 14(4), (5). The procedure and the form of deed poll are the same as under *ibid*, s. 9 (p. 90, *supra*).
[2] As well as the interest of persons in trust for him, or for whom he is trustee.
[3] Compulsory Purchase Act 1965, s. 14(6).
[4] *Ibid*, s. 14(7)(a).
[5] *Ibid*, s. 14(7)(c).
[6] *Ibid*, s. 14(7)(d). However this does not enable the authority to redeem the mortgage in part. It merely enables it to exercise the power to redeem the mortgage as a whole, even though it only requires part of the land. If the value of the part acquired is less than the amount of the principal, interest and costs secured by the mortgage, the provisions of *ibid*, s. 16 apply: see below.
[7] Or, in default of agreement, by the Lands Tribunal.
[8] Compulsory Purchase Act 1965, s. 15(1).
[9] *Ibid*, s. 15(3). The remedies of the authority on default by the mortgagee (payment into Court and deed poll) are the same as under *ibid*, s. 14 (supra): *ibid*. s. 15(3)–(5).
[10] *Ibid*, s. 15(6).
[11] *Ibid*, s. 15(7).
[12] *Ibid*, s. 16(1).
[13] *Ibid*, s. 16(1)(b).
[14] By agreement, or in default by the Lands Tribunal.
[15] *Ibid*, s. 16(1). The provisions for securing the conveyance of the appropriate interest following the agreement or award are generally similar to those under ss. 14 and 15 (*supra*): *ibid*, s. 16(2)–(5).

the mortgagee, and if requested, the authority must at its own expense furnish a copy of the memorandum to the person entitled to the equity of redemption.[1] The rights of the mortgagee against the remainder of the land are preserved.[2]

In any of the cases considered above the mortgagee is entitled to be compensated if he is required to accept payment of the principal at a time earlier than the time limited for its payment by the mortgage deed.[3] In such a case the amounts payable by the authority must include an amount to cover the costs and expenses incurred by the mortgagee in respect of, or as incidental to, the reinvestment of the sum paid-off.[4] Furthermore if the rate of interest secured by the mortgage is higher than can reasonably be expected to be obtained on reinvestment at the time the mortgage is paid off,[5] the payment must include compensation in respect of that loss.[6]

5 Rent charges

Where land is subject to a rentcharge[7] the authority may require the person entitled to release the rentcharge on payment or tender to him of appropriate compensation.[8] If he fails to execute a release or if he fails to make out a good title to their satisfaction, it may pay the compensation into Court and execute a deed poll,[9] which will have the effect of extinguishing the rent charge, or the part of the rent charge in respect of which the compensation was paid.[10] If only part of the land is acquired, the apportionment must be settled between the person entitled to the rentcharge and the owner on the one hand, and the authority on the other.[11] If the land so released from the rentcharge was subject to it jointly with other land, the other land will thereafter be charged alone with the whole of the rentcharge, and the person entitled to the rentcharge will have the same rights and remedies over that land as he had previously over the whole.[12] The authority may be required to affix its common or official seal to a memorandum of the release endorsed on

---

[1] Compulsory Purchase Act 1965, s. 16(4).

[2] Ibid, s. 16(6).

[3] Ibid, s. 17(1).

[4] Ibid, s. 17(1)(a). In the case of dispute the costs are to be taxed and payment enforced in the same way as the costs of conveyances of the acquired land (under ibid, s. 23, see p. 93 infra), ibid, s. 17(2).

[5] Having regard to the current rate of interest.

[6] Ibid, s. 17(1)(b). In default of agreement the amount payable under this head is to be determined by the Lands Tribunal: ibid, s. 17(2).

[7] This includes any other payment or incumbrance charged on the land not otherwise covered by the provisions of the Act: ibid, s. 18(6).

[8] Ibid, s. 18(3). The compensation to be paid for the release is, in the case of dispute, referred to and determined by the Lands Tribunal: ibid, s. 18(2).

[9] As to payment into Court and the form of deed polls, see p. 88, supra.

[10] Compulsory Purchase Act 1965, s. 18(3).

[11] Ibid, s. 18(2). In default of agreement, the question is determined by the Lands Tribunal. If the remaining land is sufficient security for the rentcharge, the persons entitled may, with the consent of the owner, release the land required by the authority from the rentcharge on condition or in consideration of the remaining land remaining exclusively subject to the whole of the charge: ibid, s. 18(2).

[12] Ibid, s. 18(4).

the deed or instrument creating or transferring the charge.[1] The memorandum must show what part of the land originally subject to the rentcharge has been purchased, and what part (if any) of the rentcharge has been released and how much continues payable, or if the land has been released from the whole of the rentcharge, that the remaining land is to remain thereafter exclusively charged with the rentcharge.[1]

6 Apportionment of rent

Where the authority acquires only part of the land comprised in a lease, it is necessary for the rent payable under the lease to be apportioned, so that the rent payable by the lessee in respect of the part retained by him is reduced appropriately. In the case of the acquisition of a lease[2] for a term of years unexpired[3] special provision is made for the apportionment to be settled between the parties to the lease on the one hand, and the authority on the other, or, in default of agreement, by the Lands Tribunal.[4] After the apportionment the lessee will only be liable to pay the rent attributed to the part retained,[5] although in all other respects the rights and remedies of the lessor and lessee under the lease are preserved.[6] The authority must in addition pay to the lessee compensation for damage done to him in his tenancy by reason of the severance of the land or otherwise by reason of the execution of the works.[7]

7 Costs of conveyance

The authority is liable to pay the costs of all conveyances of land subject to compulsory purchase.[8] The costs must include all reasonable expenses incident to the investigation, deduction and verification of title and in particular all charges and expenses of all conveyances or assurances of any of the land and of any outstanding terms or interests; of deducing, evidencing and verifying the title to the lands, terms or interests; and of making out and furnishing any abstracts or attested copies required by the authority.[9] In default of agreement of the costs

---

[1] *Ibid*, s. 18(5). The expenses of the execution of the memorandum must be borne by the authority. The memorandum can be used as evidence of the facts there stated, but it does not exclude other evidence of those facts.

[2] "Lease" includes an agreement for a lease: *ibid*, s. 1(3).

[3] Tenancies from year to year, or tenancies of a year or less are not entitled to notice to treat and compensation is governed by *ibid*, s. 20: see p. 366, *post*.

[4] *Ibid*, s. 19(1), (2).

[5] *Ibid*, s. 19(3). This apparently applies even though the authority delays entry: see *Re War Secretary and Hurley's Contract*, [1904] 1 I.R 354.

[6] *Ibid*, s. 19(4).

[7] *Ibid*, s. 19(5). This provision appears unnecessary, since he would in any event be entitled to compensation for severance and injurious affection under *ibid*, s. 7 (as to which see pp. 314 *et seq*, *post*).

[8] *Ibid*, s. 23(1). Conveyances may be in the forms provided by *ibid*, Sch. 5, and if so will be effective to vest the land in the authority free of all interests compensated by the consideration mentioned in the conveyance: *ibid*, s. 23(6).

[9] *Ibid*, s. 23(2). The authority was held not to be liable for the costs of the widow of the vendor in taking out probate where the vendor had died after the contract, since her duty to take out probate was independent of the acquisition: *Re Elementary Education Acts*, [1909] 1 Ch 55. For the liability to conveyancing costs where compensation is paid into Court under *ibid*, s. 9 (p. 88, *supra*) see *ibid*, s. 26 and *Re Lloyd and North London Rly.*, [1896] 2 Ch. 397.

either party may obtain an order of the court for the costs to be taxed by a Master of the Supreme Court,[1] and the amount so determined may be recovered in the same way as any other costs payable under an order of the Court.[2] The costs of the taxation will be borne by the authority unless at least one-sixth of the costs claimed is disallowed, in which case the costs of taxation will be borne by the party whose costs have been taxed, and the amount will be deducted by the Master in his certificate of taxation.[3]

8 Ecclesiastical Property

Any compensation payable in respect of ecclesiastical property[4] is to be paid in any event to the Church Commissioners to be applied for purposes for which the proceeds of a sale by agreement of the land would be applicable under any enactment or measure authorising such a sale or disposing of the proceeds of such a sale.[5]

9 Persons under a disability

Schedule 1[6] of the Compulsory Purchase Act 1965 lays down the general rule that it shall be lawful for all persons seised or possessed of or entitled to any interest in land subject to compulsory purchase to convey or release it to the acquiring authority and to enter into the necessary agreements for that purpose.[7] This is specifically applied to corporations, tenants in tail or for life, trustees for charitable or for other purposes and to persons for the time being entitled to receipt of the rents and profits of the land.[8] Where the beneficial interest is vested in a person under some legal disability, it will normally be possible for the legal estate to be conveyed by trustees or personal representatives.[9] But in those cases where the land is owned by a person under a legal disability or incapability who otherwise has no power to sell or convey the land, the Schedule provides a special procedure[10] whereby the compensation can be determined, generally by the valuation of two surveyors nominated by the parties,[11] and the authority's liability discharged by payment into Court.[12] If the owner fails to execute a due

---

[1] Compulsory Purchase Act 1965, s. 23(3).

[2] *Ibid*, s. 23(4).

[3] *Ibid*, s. 23(5).

[4] "Ecclesiastical property" means land belonging to any ecclesiastical benefice or being or forming part of a church subject to the jurisdiction of the bishop of any diocese or the site of such a church, or being or forming part of a burial ground subject to such jurisdiction: Acquisition of Land (Authorisation Procedure) Act 1946, Sch. 1, para. 3(3), applied by Compulsory Purchase Act 1965, s. 31.

[5] *Ibid*, s. 31.

[6] Applied by Compulsory Purchase Act 1965, s. 2.

[7] *Ibid*, Sch. 1, para. 2(1).

[8] *Ibid*, Sch. 1, para. 2(2).

[9] See 8 Halsburys Laws (4th Edn.) paras. 117, 169.

[10] Compulsory Purchase Act 1965, Sch. 1, paras. 4 *et seq.*

[11] *Ibid*, para. 4(1).

[12] *Ibid, para.* 6(1). If the compensation is more than £20 but not more than £200, it may be paid instead to two trustees approved by the authority and nominated by the person entitled to the rents or profits: *ibid*, para. 7. If it is £20 or less, it must be paid to the person entitled to the rents or profits: *ibid*, para. 8.

conveyance, the authority may secure the vesting of the land by execut-ing a deed poll.[1] These special procedures are of rare application and are not considered in detail in this work.[2]

3 ADVANCE PAYMENT OF COMPENSATION

Since the acquiring authority has the power to take possession of the land before compensation has been assessed[3] there will often be a substantial delay between the time when the owner is dispossessed and the time when he receives compensation. Although he is entitled to interest in respect of this period he may have difficulty, for example, in financing the acquisition of a site for relocation of his business in the meantime. To meet this problem the Land Compensation Act 1973, for the first time, required an acquiring authority to make an advance payment of compensation if requested to do so after it has taken possession.[4]

An advance payment cannot be paid until the authority has taken possession of the land.[5] Where the acquisition relates to a right over land, the relevant time is when the authority first enters for the pur-poses of exercising the right.[6] However the request for payment may be made before it takes possession. It must be made by the person entitled to compensation, referred to in the section as "the claimant". His request must be in writing and must give particulars of his interest in the land (so far as not already given pursuant to the notice to treat[7]). He must also give any other particulars which the authority reasonably requires to enable it to estimate the amount of compensation.[8]

The amount of the advance payment is 90% of the compensation which the authority estimates will be payable, or, if the amount of compensation has already been agreed, the advance payment will be 90% of that agreed figure.[9] However, if the land is subject to a mortgage, the amount of the advance payment will be reduced by such sum as the authority considers it will require for securing the release of the mortgagee's interest.[10]

The advance payment must be made by the authority not later than three months from the date on which the request is made, provided it has taken possession by that time. If it has not, the payment is due on

[1] *Ibid*, para. 10. For the nature of a deed poll, see p. 88, *supra*.
[2] For a detailed description see 8 Halsbury's Laws (4th Edn.) paras. 169 *et seq*.
[3] See p. 70, *ante*.
[4] Land Compensation Act 1973, s. 52.
[5] For example, under the Compulsory Purchase Act 1965, s. 11(1): see p. 70, *ante*. For this purpose service of a notice under the Housing Act 1957, s. 98 or Sch. 3, para. 10 is equivalent to taking possession: Land Compensation Act 1973, s. 52(11). So also is the vesting of land in an authority pursuant to a general vesting declaration; Town and Country Planning Act 1968, Sch. 3A, para 13.
[6] Land Compensation Act 1973, s. 53(11).
[7] See p. 83, *supra* for the information which must be given in the owner's notice of claim following service of notice to treat.
[8] Land Compensation Act 1973, s. 52(2).
[9] *Ibid*, s. 52(4).
[10] *Ibid*, s. 52(6). If that sum exceeds the advance payment which would otherwise be payable, there is no right to any advance payment: *ibid*. For the power of the authority to pay off mortgages, see p. 90, *supra*.

the date on which it takes possession.[1] The acquiring authority must deposit with the district council for the area[2] particulars of the payment, the compensation and the interest in question, to be registered in the register of local land charges.[3] If the land is disposed of thereafter by the claimant, the amount of advance payment will be set off against any compensation which becomes payable to a subsequent owner.[4] If, when the compensation is ultimately agreed or determined, the amount of the advance payment is found to have exceeded the compensation due, the excess must be repaid. Similarly, if it is subsequently found that the claimant was not entitled to the payment at all, the amount of the payment may be recovered by the authority.[5] No interest is payable by the authority in respect of any period after the advance payment has been made except in so far as the total compensation exceeds the amount of the advance payment.[6]

4 INTEREST

Under the 1975 rules any sum directed to be paid by an award of the Lands Tribunal will, unless the award otherwise directs, carry interest from the date of the award at the same rate as a judgment debt.[7] Thus, in a case where compensation is determined by the Tribunal, interest will run automatically unless the contrary is directed by the Tribunal. The right to interest in respect of a period prior to the date of the award will depend on the statutory provisions under which the compensation is due. In the case of compulsory acquisition the acquiring authority is required to pay interest from the date on which they take possession until compensation is paid.[8] Similarly where compensation is payable for injurious affection under the Compulsory Purchase Act 1965, s. 10,[9] interest is made to run from the date of the claim until payment.[10]

However, where the statute itself makes no provision for interest it seems that the Lands Tribunal has no power[11] to make an award of interest in respect of a period antecedent to the date of the award.[12]

---

[1] Land Compensation Act 1973, s. 52(4). If the land is settled land under the Settled Land Act 1925 the payment is made to the persons entitled to give a discharge for capital money and is treated as capital money arising under that Act: *ibid*, s. 52(7).

[2] Or, in London, the borough council.

[3] Land Compensation Act 1973, s. 52(8).

[4] *Ibid*, s. 52(9).

[5] *Ibid*, s. 52(5).

[6] *Ibid*, s. 52(10)(b).

[7] Lands Tribunal Rules, SI 1975 No. 299, rule 38, applying the Arbitration Act 1950, s. 20. See *Burlin* v *Manchester City Council* (1976), 32 P & CR 115 at p. 132, for the change from the previous rules.

[8] Land Compensation Act 1961, s. 32. The rate of interest is prescribed by regulations made under s. 32, and is subject to frequent amendment. See the current Acquisition of Land (Rate of Interest after Entry) Regulations.

[9] Which applies where no land of the claimant is acquired: see p. 321, *post*.

[10] Land Compensation Act 1973, s. 63. The rate is that prescribed for the time being under the Land Compensation Act 1961, s. 32: see note 8, *supra*.

[11] Except perhaps where it is sitting as an arbitrator on a reference by consent: see *Burlin* v *Manchester City Council supra*, at p. 133.

[12] *Hobbs (Quarries) Ltd.* v *Somerset County Council* (1975), 30 P & CR 286, 292 LT. This must now be regarded as the settled, if reluctant, view of the Tribunal: see *Burlin*'s case (*supra*) at p. 131.

Thus, for example, where compensation is claimed pursuant to a revocation order,[1] there is no entitlement to interest between the date when the order becomes operative and the date of the award.[2] The same principle will apply to the other cases in which compensation is payable under the Town and Country Planning Act 1971.[3]

5 DEDUCTIONS FOR TAX

Where the compensation includes a sum calculated on the basis of loss of profits the question will arise as to whether the tax which would have been payable on those profits should be deducted in calculating compensation, or whether compensation should be assessed on the basis of gross profits, leaving the claimant to account to the Commissioners of Inland Revenue for whatever tax is appropriate. This problem has given rise to conflicting views in the past as a result of advice expressed by the Board of the Inland Revenue.[4] However the authorities have been reviewed in a recent case by the Lands Tribunal with the assistance of revenue counsel instructed as *amicus curiae* jointly by the parties.[5] This was a case in which compensation was awarded in respect of an order revoking permission for the working of a quarry, and compensation was assessed largely on the basis of loss of potential profits. The conclusions of the Tribunal were expressed as follows:

(i) Where the compensation is assessed by reference to loss of profits it must be reduced where tax would be paid on those profits in the lands of a recipient. The sum reduced should be grossed up by the amount of the extra tax payable.

(ii) No deduction for tax should be made where compensation is assessed by reference to the sale of the quarry.[6]

(iii) If interest is awarded it should be awarded gross and the tax deducted and accounted for by the acquiring authority.[7]

6 DEDUCTION OF DEVELOPMENT LAND TAX

Although a consideration of the general working of the Development Land Tax Act 1976[8] is not within the scope of this book,[9] that Act contains special provisions[10] applicable to the payment of development land tax on acquisitions by public authorities. Since these provisions have a major bearing on the amount actually received in respect of

---

[1] See p. 413, *post*.
[2] See cases cited in note 12, *supra*.
[3] See Chap. 10, *post*.
[4] See *Bostock Chater & Sons Ltd.* v *Chelmsford Corpn* (1973), 26 P & CR 321.
[5] *Hobbs (Quarries) Ltd.* v *Somerset County Council*, note 12, *supra*.
[6] This would apply equally to other types of land.
[7] *Hobbs* case, *supra*, at p. 294.
[8] 1976 c. 24.
[9] For a general treatment of the Development Land Tax Act 1976 see Land Development Encyclopaedia, Part II.
[10] Development Land Tax Act 1976, s. 39, Sch. 7.

compensation by an owner whose land is compulsorily acquired, a reference to them is desirable.

Development Land Tax—Summary

The Development Land Tax Act 1976 makes provision for a tax to be charged in respect of the realisation of development value of land.[1] Liability to development land tax ordinarily arises on the disposal of an interest in land.[2] However, liability arises also on the commencement of a project of material development, since the Act provides that immediately before such commencement every major interest in the land is "deemed to be disposed of for a consideration equal to its market value and to be immediately reacquired at that value".[3]

The tax is chargeable on "realised development value".[4] This value is arrived at by deducting "the relevant base value" from the net proceeds of the disposal.[5] There are three different methods of assessing "base value";[6] two[7] are based on the cost of the chargeable person's acquisition of the interest, the third[8] on the current use value of the interest. In each case appropriate allowance is made for improvements[9] to the property, although the formula varies depending upon which base is used. The "relevant base value"[10] is that one of the three methods of assessment[10] which gives the highest figure.[11] The tax is set generally by the Act at 80 % of the realised development value,[12] but in relation to disposals up to and including 31 March 1979 a rate of $66\frac{2}{3}$ % is applied to the first £150,000 of realised development value in any one financial year.[13]

Acquisitions by Public Authorities

It was a central feature of the "community land scheme"[14] that public authorities should be able to acquire land for development at a price which reflects the existing use value of the land rather than the inflated value conferred by planning permission or the prospect of planning permission.[15] As has been seen,[16] the intention is that eventually[17] the compensation code will be amended to exclude any value derived from the prospect of a planning permission for development other than

[1] Development Land Tax 1976, s. 1(1).
[2] Ibid, s. 1(2). For the meaning of "disposal" see ibid, ss. 3, 46(3).
[3] Ibid, s. 2.
[4] Ibid, s. 41(1).
[5] Ibid, s. 4.
[6] Ibid, s. 5.
[7] I.e., "Base A" and "Base C": ibid, s. 5(1)(a) and (c).
[8] I.e., "Base B", ibid, s. 5(1)(b).
[9] Ibid, s. 5(1)(a), (b), (c).
[10] See ibid, Sch. 3, Part I.
[11] Ibid, s. 5(1). See also p. 22, ante.
[12] Ibid, s. 1(3).
[13] Ibid, s. 13.
[14] This name is used to describe the scheme embodied in the Community Land Act 1975 and the Development Land Tax Act 1976.
[15] See p. 22, ante.
[16] See p. 23, ante.
[17] I.e., after the "second appointed day": Community Land Act 1975, s. 7.

permission for development within the 8th Schedule of the Town and Country Planning Act 1971.[1] Until that time the Development Land Tax Act 1976 enables authorities to buy development land at a price which excludes the major part of the value attributable to the prospect of development, by allowing them to pay compensation net of development land tax.[2] Instead of paying full compensation to the dispossessed owner and leaving him to account to the Commissioners of Inland Revenue for any development land tax which is payable, they are enabled first to deduct any development land tax and to pay only the balance to the owner.

Authorities within these provisions

The provisions for deduction of development land tax from compensation apply to disposals to:

(i) any local authority in England or Wales, including a new town authority and the Peak Park Joint Planning Board and the Lake District Special Planning Board, and the Land Authority for Wales.[3]

(ii) a joint board established by the Secretary of State for the purposes of the Community Land Act 1975,[4] or a body corporate established by the Secretary of State under s. 50 of that Act to take over the functions of an authority;[4]

(iii) any other "exempt body" which in relation to the relevant disposal is an authority possessing compulsory powers.[5] In this context, "exempt body" includes a Minister of the Crown or Government Department, and any other body which is exempt from development land tax by virtue of the Development Land Tax Act 1976, s. 11(1).[6]

However, these provisions do not apply to disposals by a body which is itself an exempt body.[7]

Procedure

(i) NOTICES TO THE COMMISSIONERS OF INLAND REVENUE

If it appears to an acquiring authority that the consideration for a disposal will exceed 110% of its estimate of the current use value[8] it must give "notice of acquisition" to the Commissioners of Inland Revenue.[9] Even if the consideration is less than 110% of current use

---

[1] *Ibid*, s. 25.

[2] Development Land Tax Act 1976, s. 39.

[3] *Ibid*, ss. 39(1)(a), 11(a)(d): Community Land Act 1975, s. 1(1)(a), (c).

[4] Development Land Tax Act 1976, ss. 39(1)(a), 11(a), (b): Community Land Act, ss. 2, 50.

[5] Development Land Tax Act 1976, s. 39(1)(b). An "authority possessing compulsory powers" means, in relation to a disposal, a person acquiring the interest compulsorily, or who has been or could be authorised to acquire it compulsorily for the purposes for which it is acquired, or for whom another person has been or could be authorised so to acquire it: *ibid*, s. 47(1).

[6] *Ibid*, s. 39(10).

[7] *Ibid*, s. 39(2). The provisions would in any event be otiose in the case of a disposal by an exempt body since no development land tax would be chargeable: *ibid*, s. 11.

[8] "Current use value" is assessed in accordance with the Development Land Tax Act 1976, s. 7(2)–(6).

[9] *Ibid*, Sch. 7, para. 1(1).

value, a notice of acquisition must be served if value attributable to development of the land is to be ignored[1] because it was carried out while permission was "suspended"[2] under the Community Land Act 1975, or if it was carried out without permission at all.[3] Where the disposal is by agreement the notice is given at the date of the contract, or if the contract is conditional at the date when the condition is fulfilled.[4] If the interest is acquired compulsorily, the notice is given at the time that compensation is agreed or determined, even if the authority has already acquired the relevant interest[5] or has made a general vesting declaration.[6] Where there is an interval between the agreement of the consideration and the actual disposal,[7] the authority may at any time during the interval give a "provisional notice of acquisition" to the Revenue[8] and it must do so if requested by the person from whom the interest is to be acquired.[9] Where the authority is required to make an advance payment of compensation[10] and the advance payment exceeds 110% of its estimate of the current use value of the interest, it must at the time that the advance payment is determined, give a "notice of advance payment" to the Commissioners.[11]

If the amount of compensation previously agreed or determined is varied so as to bring it above 110% of current use value, a notice of acquisition must be given at the time of variation.[12] If it comes to the authority's attention that a notice was incorrect or should not have been given it must immediately notify the Commissioners accordingly.[13]

The form of the notices under these provisions is as prescribed by the Commissioners,[14] and the notices must contain such information as the Commissioners may reasonably require.[15] A copy of the notice must be given by the authority to the person from whom the interest is being acquired.[16]

(ii) ACTION BY THE COMMISSIONERS OF INLAND REVENUE

(a) No liability to Development Land Tax

On receipt of a notice, the Commissioners may consider that the

---

[1] By virtue of the Community Land Act 1975, s. 22(2).

[2] Community Land Act 1975, ss. 19–22.

[3] Development Land Tax Act 1976, Sch. 7, para. 1(6).

[4] Ibid, Sch. 7, para. 1(2) and 45(2). As to what constitutes a "conditional contract" in this context see Eastham v Leigh London Provincial Properties Ltd., [1971] Ch. 871.

[5] Development Land Tax Act 1976, Sch. 7, para. 1(2).

[6] Ibid, para. 1(3). A General Vesting Declaration is made under the Town and Country Planning Act 1968, s. 30: see p. 71, ante.

[7] Development Land Tax 1976, Sch. 7, para. 1(2).

[8] Ibid, Sch. 7, para. 1(4)(a). The form is prescribed by the Revenue: ibid, Sch. 7, para. 1(1), (2).

[9] Ibid, Sch. 7, para. 1(4)(b).

[10] Under the Land Compensation Act 1973, s. 52, an authority which has entered on the land may be required to make an advance payment of 90% of its estimate of the compensation. See p. 95, supra.

[11] Development Land Tax Act 1976, Sch. 7, para. 1(5).

[12] Ibid, Sch. 7, para. 1(7).

[13] Ibid, Sch. 7, para. 1(8).

[14] Ibid, Sch. 7, para. 1(1)(b).

[15] Ibid, Sch. 7, para. 1(10).

[16] Ibid, Sch. 7, para. 1(9).

disposal will not give rise to any liability to development land tax. In this case they must notify the authority as soon as practicable that no deduction for development land tax should be made.[1] If the notice was a provisional notice of acquisition however, the Commissioners may only do this with the agreement of the person making the disposal.[2] Provided they remain of the view that no development land tax is payable, the Commissioners are not required to make any further notification even if they receive another notice from the authority relating to the same disposal.[3]

(b) Development Land Tax Liability

If the Commissioners of Inland Revenue take the view that a liability to development land tax arises, it becomes necessary to determine the deduction to be made in respect of development land tax. This may be either:

(i) A "specific deduction" based on an actual assessment to development land tax, or on an agreement between the Commissioners and the person making the disposal;

(ii) A "formula deduction" calculated according to a formula laid down in the Act.

Specific Deduction. If, before or after receipt by the Commissioners of a notice of acquisition, an assessment to development land tax is made, then they must give the acquiring authority particulars[4] of the assessment.[5] If either

(i) the assessment has become final either by agreement or because the time for appeal has expired; or

(ii) an appeal is pending but either an interim payment has become due,[6] or the amount charged by the assessment is less than the amount which would be arrived at by the formula method,[7]

the Commissioners must also notify the authority of the specific deduction to be made.[8] The particulars of the assessment and the notification of the specific deduction must be given within 21 days of receipt of the notice of acquisition, or if the notice of assessment is given later, the time of the notice of assessment.[9] In this case the specific deduction will be the tax charged by the assessment or the amount of the interim payment where that applies.[10]

Where the Commissioners are not required to give notice of a specific deduction under the above provisions—whether because the notice received by them was only a provisional notice of acquisition or a notice of advance payment,[11] or because the circumstances mentioned above

---

[1] *Ibid*, Sch. 7, para. 2(1). If a liability to development land tax is subsequently found to have arisen, the owner will be assessed directly: see p. 105, *infra*.

[2] *Ibid*, Sch. 7, para. 2(1)(c).

[3] *Ibid*, Sch. 7, para. 2(2).

[4] The particulars are those enumerated in the Development Land Tax Act 1976, Sch. 7, para. 3(2), (4).

[5] *Ibid*, Sch. 7, para. 3(1)(a).

[6] Under the Taxes Management Act 1970, s. 55.

[7] Development Land Tax Act 1976, Sch. 7, para. 4(2).

[8] *Ibid*, Sch. 7, para. 3(1)(b).

[9] *Ibid*, Sch. 7, para. 3(3).

[10] *Ibid*, Sch. 7, para. 4(3).

[11] *Ibid*, Sch. 7, para. 3(5)(a).

have not arisen,[1]—they may seek to agree with the person making the disposal a figure for a specific deduction.[2] This may be a figure representing either the amount of his prospective liability or so much of the tax as is not in dispute.[3] If an agreement is reached the Commissioners must notify the authority of the specific deduction so agreed.[4]

Where the authority is to make a payment of consideration following notification[5] of a specific deduction, it must deduct from the payment an amount equal to the specific deduction.[6] If, however, there have been previous payments of consideration for the same disposal, the specific deduction will be reduced by the amount of any previous deductions.[6] Furthermore, if there are to be further payments in respect of the same disposal, the residue of the specific deduction will be apportioned by taking a proportion equivalent to the proportion which the specific deduction itself (less any previous deductions) bears to the total consideration for the disposal.[7] If in any case the applicable deduction would exceed the amount of the payment, the deduction shall be taken as equal to the payment.[8] In all cases the amount of consideration is taken exclusive of any interest payable by the authority.[9]

Formula. Unless, by the time the authority comes to make a payment, it has either been notified that no deduction is to be made for development land tax, or has received notice of a specific deduction, then the deduction is assessed by means of a special formula and is referred to as a "formula deduction".[10] The formula is based on the assumption that no development land tax will be payable if the consideration is not more than £10,000[11] higher than 110 % of the authority's estimate of current use value. This amount (110 % of current use value plus £10,000) is referred to as "the exempt amount".[12] This assumption is, of course, an over-simplification. It takes no account of the possibility that the relevant base value may be governed, not by the current use value, but by the cost of acquisition.[13] Thus in some cases it may work to the disadvantage of the person making the disposal, and if so, it will normally be preferable for him to agree a specific deduction with the Commissioners.[14]

---

[1] Development Land Tax Act 1976. Sch. 7, para. 3(5)(b).

[2] *Ibid*, Sch. 7, para. 4(5).

[3] *Ibid*, Sch. 7, para. 4(5)(a), (b).

[4] *Ibid*, Sch. 7, para. 3(5).

[5] If more than one notification is received in respect of one disposal, the later one supersedes the earlier, but without prejudice to deductions already made: *ibid*, Sch. 7, para. 6(5).

[6] *Ibid*, Sch. 7, para. 6(1).

[7] *Ibid*, Sch. 7, para. 6(2).

[8] *Ibid*, Sch. 7, para. 6(3).

[9] *Ibid*, Sch. 7, para. 6(4).

[10] *Ibid*, Sch. 7, para. 5(1).

[11] The £10,000 figure is derived from the Development Land Tax Act 1976, s. 12, which exempts from liability to development land tax the first £10,000 of realised development value accruing to one person in any year. But note that the same formula applies even if the exemption could not in fact be claimed, because the relevant person has already exceeded the limit for the year in question.

[12] Development Land Tax Act 1976, Sch. 7, para. 5(3).

[13] See p. 98, *supra*.

[14] See p. 101, *supra*.

If the consideration for the disposal does not exceed the exempt amount the formula deduction will be nil. If it exceeds the exempt amount the formula deduction will depend on the date of the disposal and the amount by which the consideration exceeds the exempt amount. In the case of a disposal not later than 31 March 1979, provided the consideration does not exceed the exempt amount by more than £150,000,[1] the formula deduction[2] will be whichever is the less of the following two figures:

(i) 50 % of the "relevant payment", which is defined as the particular payment of consideration from which the deduction falls to be made, exclusive of any interest payable by the authority;[3] and

(ii) a figure derived from the excess of the total consideration for the disposal over the exempt amount, calculated by taking $66\frac{2}{3}$ % of the amount of the excess up to £150,000[4] and 80 % above that.[5]

In the case of disposals after 31 March 1979 the formula deduction will be whichever is the less of:

(iii) a specified[6] percentage of the relevant payment; and

(iv) 80 % of the excess of the total consideration over the exempt amount.[7]

When any previous payment of consideration has been made in respect of the same disposal, the amount calculated under the second part of the formula in either of the above cases is to be reduced by the amount of the deduction made from the previous payment or payments.[8]

ADVANCE PAYMENTS

Where the relevant payment is an advance payment of compensation under the Land Compensation Act 1973,[9] there are certain modifications to the rules stated above. If a specific deduction is applicable, the advance payment will be reduced by the whole amount of the specific deduction.[10] If there is no specific deduction, the formula deduction is calculated as though the total consideration for the disposal were equal to ten-ninths of the advance payment[11] and the relevant payment were equal to the amount of this assumed total consideration.[12] The actual deduction made from the advance payment will be the amount of the formula deduction calculated in this way less one-tenth of the assumed total consideration for the disposal.[13]

---

[1] This formula is designed to correspond to the reduced rate of development land tax applicable under s. 13 of the Act.

[2] Development Land Tax Act 1976, Sch. 7, para. 5(4).

[3] Ibid, Sch. 7, para. 5(2).

[4] Ibid, Sch. 7, para. 5(4).

[5] Ibid, Sch. 7, para. 5(5).

[6] The appropriate percentage is to be specified in regulations made by the Commissioners of Inland Revenue by Statutory Instrument, approved by resolution of the House of Commons: ibid, Sch. 7, para. 5(7).

[7] Ibid, Sch. 7, para. 5(6).

[8] Ibid, Sch. 7, para. 5(8).

[9] S. 52: see p. 95, supra.

[10] Development Land Tax Act 1976, Sch. 7, para. 7(5).

[11] Ibid, Sch. 7, para. 7(2).

[12] Ibid, Sch. 7, para. 7(3).

[13] Ibid, Sch. 7, para. 7(4). I.e., one-ninth of the amount of the advance payment: see note 11, supra.

MORTGAGES ENTERED INTO BEFORE 12 MAY 1976

When the land is subject to a mortgage or charge entered into before 12 May 1976[1] and the cost of redemption[2] exceeds the amount of consideration for the disposal which would remain after making the appropriate development land tax deduction, the deduction is limited to the amount by which the consideration exceeds the cost of redeeming the mortgage,[3] or, if the mortgage relates to a larger area, that proportion of the cost which is properly attributable to the relevant land.[4] No deduction at all will be made in cases where the compensation falls to be settled between the authority and the mortgagee,[5] because the cost of redemption exceeds the value of the land.[6] In this context, a mortgage or charge means "the interest of a creditor (other than a creditor in respect of a rent charge) whose debt is secured by way of a mortgage or charge of any kind over land or an agreement for any such mortgage or charge".[7] Even if the mortgage or charge was entered into after 11 May 1976, it will qualify provided it was entered into pursuant to an offer accepted before that date.[8]

PAYMENT OF COMPENSATION INTO COURT

In certain cases the authority may pay the purchase money into Court, for instance if the title is unclear or the owner fails to convey.[9] In these cases the development land tax deduction will be calculated as above and deducted from the payment into Court.[10]

PROCEDURE SUBSEQUENT TO MAKING OF DEDUCTION

Where an authority makes a payment from which it has made a deduction, it must provide the person to whom the payment is made with a statement[11] showing the amount of the payment without the deduction, the amount of the deduction, and the amount actually paid by way of consideration.[12] It must at the same time send a certificate to the same effect to the Commissioners of Inland Revenue.[13] On receipt of the statement the relevant person is treated for all purposes as having received, in addition to the consideration actually paid, the amount of the deduction, and as having paid development land tax equal to that

---

[1] The significance of this date is that it was the day on which the relevant provisions were considered in Committee.

[2] The "cost of redemption" is the amount required to discharge the mortgage at the date of disposal less the amount of any advance made after 11 May 1976.

[3] Development Land Tax Act 1976, Sch. 7, para. 8(1).

[4] *Ibid*, para. 8(2). Any dispute on the proper apportionment is to be settled by the Lands Tribunal: *ibid*, Sch. 7, para. 8(6).

[5] Under the Compulsory Purchase Act 1965, ss. 15(1), 16(1) see p. 91, *supra*.

[6] Development Land Tax Act 1976, Sch. 7, para. 8(3).

[7] *Ibid*, s. 47(2)(a), applied by Sch. 7, para. 8(5).

[8] *Ibid*, Sch. 7, para. 8(5)(a).

[9] See e.g. p. 88, *supra*.

[10] Development Land Tax Act 1976, Sch. 7, para. 9(1)–(2). No deduction is made from money paid into Court as security under the Compulsory Purchase Act 1965, s. 11(2), (as to which see p. 70, *ante*): Development Land Tax Act 1976, Sch. 7, para. 9(3)–(4).

[11] In a form prescribed by the Commissioners of Inland Revenue or authorised by them for use in substitution for the prescribed form: *ibid*, s. 39(4).

[12] *Ibid*, s. 39(4).

[13] *Ibid*, Sch. 7, para. 10(1), (4).

deduction.[1] If subsequently the development land tax payable is found by the Commissioners to exceed the amount of the development land tax deduction, the amount of the excess must be paid to the Commissioners in the ordinary way,[2] and the Commissioners will pay it to the relevant authority.[3] If the tax payable is found to be less than the deduction, the balance will be recovered by the Commissioners from the authority and credited to the person who made the disposal.[4] If the date on which the deduction is made is earlier than the date on which interest would ordinarily have become payable on development land tax in respect of the disposal, the person making the disposal is credited with interest on the amount of the development land tax deduction during that period.[5] On the other hand, no corresponding debit is made if the date on which the development land tax deduction is made is later than the date when interest would ordinarily have become payable.[6] Authorities making deductions under these provisions are required to make their records available for inspection by the Commissioners whenever called upon to do so.[7]

[1] *Ibid*, s. 39(5).
[2] *Ibid*, Sch. 7, para. 10(3).
[3] *Ibid*, s. 39(6).
[4] *Ibid*, Sch. 7, para. 10(2).
[5] *Ibid*, Sch. 7, para. 11.
[6] *Ibid*, Sch. 7, para. 12.
[7] *Ibid*, Sch. 7, para. 13.

CHAPTER 4

Purchase and Blight Notices

1 INTRODUCTORY

GENERAL

Although the purchase of land by public authorities possessing powers of compulsory acquisition is normally initiated by the public authority concerned, there are certain circumstances in which the process may be reversed and the landowner has the right to require the acquisition of his property by serving a *purchase notice* upon the appropriate authority. If the purchase notice is confirmed the acquiring authority is deemed to have served a notice to treat, and with certain relatively minor exceptions, compensation is payable and the transaction thereafter proceeds in the same way as in the case of an acquisition initiated by a compulsory purchase order.

The principle has long been established that an authority requiring only part of a building,[1] only part of a park or garden[2] or under the most recent legislation, only part of an agricultural unit,[3] may, in certain circumstances, be required by the owner[4] to purchase the whole.

Although no procedure was specifically laid down in any of the earlier statutes it became customary, under the Act of 1845, for an owner willing and able to take advantage of these provisions when served with a notice to treat for part only of his property, to serve a counter-notice requiring the acquiring authority to take the whole. The Land Compensation Act 1973, however, specifically provides for the service of such a counter-notice. Although the pre-1973 counter-notices are not commonly referred to.as purchase notices, and although the 1973 Act does not so refer to the statutory counter-notice for which it provides, these counter-notices are purchase notices in essence and may be regarded as the historical forbears of the statutory purchase and blight notices provided for and extended in successive Town and Country Planning Acts and in the Land Compensation Act 1973. They

---

[1] Lands Clauses Consolidation Act 1845, s. 92.

[2] Acquisition of Land (Authorisation Procedure) Act 1946, Sch. II, para. 4, since repealed by the Compulsory Purchase Act 1965, and re-enacted in s. 8 thereof.

[3] Land Compensation Act 1973, ss. 53–57; see p. 111, *infra*.

[4] Generally speaking the word "owner" is used in this introductory context to include freeholder and leaseholder but in the case of agricultural land *ibid*, s. 55, also confers analogous rights on a tenant from year to year where notice of entry is served in relation to part of his holding: p. 113, *infra*.

are therefore considered in detail under the next heading of this chapter[1] and referred to as "counter-notices of objection" to severance, a term derived from Schedules 3 and 3A to the Town & Country Planning Act 1968.

PURCHASE NOTICES UNDER THE TOWN AND COUNTRY PLANNING ACTS[2]

With the introduction of a comprehensive system of town and country planning in 1947 it was immediately apparent that in certain circumstances the effect of planning control could not merely deprive land of its potential development value, but by restricting existing user, actually reduce or even entirely eliminate the value of the land in its existing state. Where land suffers only a reduction in value, e.g., as a result of an order to discontinue a specified (but lawful) use or demolish a building, or an order revoking planning permission, the Acts provide for compensation.[3] But where, as a result of a planning decision in respect of the land, that land has become incapable of reasonably beneficial use, the Town and Country Planning Act 1947 conferred upon the owner the right to serve a notice[4] specifically described as a "purchase notice".

BLIGHT NOTICES[5]

With the passage of time and with greater experience of planning and planning control, it has become increasingly apparent that planning proposals incorporated in development plans or resulting from the longer term proposals incorporated in development plans or resulting from the longer term proposals of, for example, highway authorities, although not immediately depriving land of beneficial use, could nevertheless render it virtually unsaleable except at a considerable loss, at any rate in the short term. Since the re-establishment of market value as the basis of compensation in 1959[6] an owner or occupier who has had no particular reason to dispose of, or vacate, his property prior to it being required for the proposed development has been able to expect that he will ultimately be fully compensated. But if, for example, a householder, whether freeholder or lessee, is forced to move between the date on which his property is first designated and the date of ultimate compulsory acquisition (which may at the time be wholly indefinite) the market value of his property will be bound to reflect the anticipated expense and inconvenience facing prospective purchasers when the property is eventually acquired for public purposes. In other words, the market value of his property will be depreciated; his property is said to have become sterilised or subject to planning "blight".

A remedy for this state of affairs was initiated in 1959[7] by providing a

[1] Pp. 108, et seq, infra.
[2] Pp. 114, et seq, infra.
[3] See Chap. 10, p. 413, post.
[4] See now the Town and Country Planning Act 1971, Ss. 180–191.
[5] Pp. 129 et seq, infra.
[6] Town and Country Planning Act 1959, s. 5.
[7] Town and Country Planning Act 1959, Part IV.

right in certain limited circumstances to somewhat narrowly defined owner-occupiers of houses and agricultural land and the owners of small businesses[1] to serve a purchase notice requiring the appropriate authority to purchase forthwith and in advance of requirements. It is this type of purchase notice which in the course of consolidation of the law in the Town and Country Planning Act of 1971 first came to be described as a *blight notice*; the most recent legislation[2] which considerably extends the circumstances in which they can be served adopts the same nomenclature.

The various types of purchase and blight notices, the persons to whom and the circumstances in which they apply and the manner and effect of their confirmation are considered in succeeding sections of this chapter.

2 COUNTER NOTICES OF OBJECTION TO SEVERANCE OF LAND

1 Buildings, parks and gardens

The original provision of the Lands Clauses Consolidation Act 1845[3] that "no party should at any time be required to sell or convey . . . a part only of any house[4] or other building or manufactory,[5] if such party[6] be willing and able to sell and convey the whole thereof" was unconditional. The Acquisition of Land (Authorisation Procedure) Act 1946,[7] however, provided that the acquisition of only part of such a

---

[1] Defined by reference to the rateable value of the premises: pp. 131 *et seq. infra.*

[2] Land Compensation Act 1973 Part V.

[3] S. 92, which has not been repealed by later statutes: p. 3, *ante.*

[4] The word "house" has been very broadly defined to include not only the garden and curtilage of a dwelling (*Lord Grosvenor* v *Hampstead Junction Rly Co.* (1859), 26 LJ Ch. 731) and under the Compulsory Purchase Act, 1965 s. 8, *infra*, a "park or garden belonging to a house" but also a house "not used exclusively or even principally as a dwelling or residence". It may, for example, include or consist of a shop or inn and include other buildings used in conjunction therewith: *Richards* v *Swansea Improvement and Tramway Co.* (1879), 9 Ch. D. 425. It may also comprise a hospital (*St. Thomas' Hospital* (1861), 30 LJ Ch. 395) the test being single occupation or single purpose as long as some degree of physical occupation is involved: *ibid*: see also *Hills (Patents), Ltd* v *Board of Governors of University College Hospital*, [1955] 3 All ER 365, note 2, p. 132, *infra*. On the other hand, a garden used with, but separated from, the house will not be included: *Ferguson* v *London Brighton and South Coast Rly Co* (1864), 11 WR 1088, 33 LJ Ch. 29. See also *Harvie* v *South Devon Rly Co* (1874), 32 LT1 (semi-detached villas, not a single house).

[5] I.e., a building in which or land upon which goods are actually made: use in conjunction with a trade is not in itself enough to conform with the definition: *Reddin* v *Metropolitan Board of Works*, (1862) 31 LJ Ch. 660.

[6] The "party" on whom notice must be served is therefore the person "able and willing to sell the whole thereof": *Governors of St. Thomas' Hospital* v *Charing Cross Rly Co* (1861), 30 LJ Ch. 395.

[7] Sch. II, para. 4: now repealed and replaced by the Compulsory Purchase Act 1965, s. 8(1). By virtue of *ibid* s. 34(2), s. 8(1) does not apply to compulsory purchase orders under Part III of the Housing Act 1957 (clearance and redevelopment): the unconditional rights of the Lands Clauses Consolidation Act 1845, s. 92, are, however, specifically retained except in the case of clearance orders under the Housing Act 1957, s. 43, and compulsory purchase orders under *ibid* s. 51 (cleared land which the owner has failed to develop): in these cases reference can be made to the Lands Tribunal as outlined in the text. The savings of the Compulsory Purchase Act 1965, s. 8(1), in regard to *parks and gardens* do not, therefore, apply to compulsory purchase orders under the Housing Act 1957, Part III. See pp. 77 *et seq. ante.*

building can proceed if, in the opinion of the Tribunal responsible for the assessment of compensation (now the Lands Tribunal),[1] that part can be taken without material detriment to the building. The same Act contained a similar provision in relation to the acquisition of part of a park or garden with a corresponding jurisdiction in the Lands Tribunal to determine whether such part could be taken without "affecting the amenity or convenience of the house".

In reaching their decision the Lands Tribunal are now required to take into account not only the effect of the severance but the use to be made of the part that it is proposed to acquire; and where the acquiring authority's proposals for which the part of the property is required involve works upon, or change of use of, other land, the Lands Tribunal must also take into account the effect of the whole of the works and the use to be made of that other land.[2] The test, however, remains whether the taking of part of the property renders the remainder "less useful or valuable in some significant degree".[3] If it does the owner remains entitled to require acquisition of the whole irrespective of whether monetary compensation would make good the difference in value.[4] It is, of course, open to the acquiring authority either to agree or abandon the acquisition without reference to the Lands Tribunal, and even if the Lands Tribunal find in their favour it is still open to them to abandon.[5]

Where, as a result of the execution by an acquiring authority of a general vesting declaration[6] a notice to treat is deemed to have been served in relation to a part only of a building or part only of a park or garden, the effect of a counter-notice of objection to severance, if served within the prescribed period[7] is that the acquiring authority must either withdraw the deemed notice to treat, agree to purchase the whole[8] or refer the notice of objection to the Lands Tribunal.[9] In the latter event the Lands Tribunal's jurisdiction is somewhat wider than in the normal case described above, for it is also open to them to determine that the

---

[1] Lands Tribunal Act 1949.

[2] Land Compensation Act, 1973, s. 58. By virtue of *ibid*, sub-s. (2) except where specifically excluded, these provisions apply with any necessary modifications to any provision corresponding to, or substituted for Compulsory Purchase Act 1965, s. 8(1), whether passed before or after that Act and including in particular the Highways Act 1971, Sch. 6, para. 8, and the Gas Act 1972, Sch. 2, para. 14.

[3] *Ravenseft Properties* v *London Borough of Hillingdon* (1968), 20 P & CR 483, per JS David QC at p. 493.

[4] *Ravenseft Properties* v *London Borough of Hillingdon, supra.*

[5] *King* v *Wycombe Rly Co* (1860), 29 LJ Ch. 462: but contrast the position where a counter-notice is served in respect of part of an agricultural unit under the Land Compensation Act 1973, s. 53, where the acquiring authority have no such right to abandon: *ibid*, s. 54, p. 112, *infra.*

[6] Town and Country Planning Act 1968, Schs 3 and 3A: see pp. 71, *ante.*

[7] I.e., the period prescribed in the declaration: it must not be less than 28 days after the acquiring authority have served upon owners and occupiers individual notices specifying the land and explaining the effect of the declaration.

[8] The acquiring authority is thereby authorised to acquire the whole notwithstanding that part of the property concerned may not have been included in the compulsory purchase order.

[9] If no action is taken by the acquiring authority within three months of service of the notice of objection the deemed notice to treat is deemed to be withdrawn.

acquiring authority ought to acquire some larger proportion of the property than the compulsory purchase order authorises or the general vesting declaration covers, but which is nevertheless less than the whole.[1] Where the notice of objection is out of time because the objector did not receive the required notice specifying the land concerned and explaining the effect of the declaration, the deemed notice to treat can no longer be withdrawn and the acquiring authority can then only agree to take the whole of the property or refer the matter to the Lands Tribunal.[2]

2 Agricultural and other undeveloped land

(i) LANDS CLAUSES CONSOLIDATION ACT, 1845

Under the Lands Clauses Consolidation Act the right of an owner of "lands, not being situate in a town or built upon"[3] to respond to a notice to treat for part of his property by serving a counter-notice requiring acquisition of the whole, was confined to cases where, as a result of the proposed acquisition, the owner is left with isolated areas of land of less than half an acre. In such cases the acquiring authority has no option but to comply with the notice unless the owner has other land with which such isolated areas can be "conveniently occupied". In that event, however, the owner has the further right to require the acquiring authority to carry out at their expense such work as may be necessary (e.g., the resiting of fences, levelling, provision of access, etc.) to throw the two areas of land together.[4]

Somewhat similarly, where the special Act[5] requires an acquiring authority to provide a bridge or culvert across the land to be acquired[6] so as to retain communications between areas of land in the same ownership which will be severed one from the other as a result of the acquisition, the acquiring authority may insist upon acquiring the severed portion if it is either less than half an acre in area or of less value than the cost of providing the bridge, culvert, etc.[7]

---

[1] Town and Country Planning Act 1968, Sch. 3A, para. 11.

[2] In such a case inaction by the acquiring authority over a three-month period following service of the notice of objection results in the acquiring authority being deemed to have agreed to purchase the whole: *ibid*, Sch. 3A, para. 7.

[3] The word "town" is given its popular meaning: land is not "in a town" merely because it is administratively within the boundaries of a borough or predominantly urban district or parish: *London and South Western Rly Co v Blackmore* (1870), LR 4 HL 610. Similarly "built upon" has the popular meaning of "built up" and does *not* include land carrying buildings in the open country: *Carington v Wycombe Rly Co* (1868), 3 Ch App 377: and see *Falkner v Somerset and Dorset Rly Co.* (1873) LR 16 Eq 458.

[4] Lands Clauses Consolidation Act 1845, s. 93: now re-enacted as Compulsory Purchase Act 1965, s. 8(2).

[5] See p. 30, *ante*.

[6] Whether or not "in a town or built upon": see note 7, *infra*.

[7] The Lands Clauses Consolidation Act 1845, s. 94. Although s. 94 commences with the words "any such land" its operation is not confined to land "in a town or built upon" to which s. 93 refers: *Eastern Counties and London and Blackwell Rly Co's v Marriage* (1860), 9 HL C as 32. Cf. Compulsory Purchase Act 1965, s. 8(3) (which re-enacts s. 94 of the 1845 Act) in which the word "such" has been omitted. Any dispute as to the value of the land or the cost of providing appropriate communication between the severed portions is to be determined by the Lands Tribunal.

(ii) LAND COMPENSATION ACT, 1973: SEVERANCE OF AGRICULTURAL UNITS

The general principle underlying the above provisions (which are in themselves not affected, and indeed are specifically preserved) has been considerably extended by the Land Compensation Act 1973, ss. 53–57, whereby lessees having interests greater than that of a tenancy for a year or from year to year, as well as owners,[1] of land the subject of a notice to treat[2] may, by counter-notice, require the acquiring authority to purchase their interest in other land farmed therewith if the loss of the land subject to the notice to treat would render the farming of the remainder uneconomic.

The person on whom the notice to treat is served is referred to in the Act as the "claimant" and will be so referred to here. In order to serve a valid counter-notice he must show that the loss of the land the subject of the notice to treat not only renders the remainder of that particular agricultural unit[3] uneconomic, but also that it cannot be farmed economically together with any other land in his possession in which he also has an interest greater than a tenancy for a year or from year to year.

If this is so he can, within two months of the date of the notice to treat, serve a counter-notice requiring the acquiring authority to purchase his interest in the rest of the same agricultural unit. He cannot, of course, include any other land (referred to in the Act as "other relevant land"). Although a copy of the notice must be served on any other person having an interest[4] in the land covered by the notice, failure to do so does not invalidate the counter-notice.[5]

If it should happen that an acquiring authority has served other notices to treat in respect of other land in which the claimant has an interest greater than a tenancy for a year or from year to year, whether forming part of the same or of some other agricultural unit, such land is not to be regarded as available to him to make up an economic unit.[6] Similar provisions apply where an acquiring authority serves notice of entry[7] in respect of part only of an agricultural holding upon an occupier who has no greater interest than that of a tenant for a year or

---

[1] I.e., the person (other than a mortgagee not in possession) entitled to dispose of the fee simple or entitled to receive the rents and profits under a lease having more than three years unexpired: Acquisition of Land (Authorisation Procedure) Act 1946, s. 8(1) and Compulsory Purchase Act 1965, s. 11.

[2] Including notice to treat deemed to have been served either in response to a purchase notice under the Town and Country Planning Act 1971, ss. 180–189 (as to which see pp. 114 *et seq, infra*) or as a result of a General Vesting Declaration in accordance with the Town and Country Planning Act 1968, Sch. 3, para. 6: p. 71, *ante*.

[3] I.e., land and buildings (including a dwelling-house) occupied as a unit for agricultural purposes: Town and Country Planning Act 1971, s. 207(1) as applied by the Land Compensation Act 1973, s. 87. It need not, therefore, all be held under the same tenure and may comprise land owned by the occupier and/or land leased from several landlords.

[4] E.g., if the claimant is a lessee he must serve his immediate lessor and any superior lessors, rent charge owners, etc.; similarly if he is a freeholder he must serve any mortgagees. Note, however, that the claimant need not be in occupation (Land Compensation Act 1973, s. 53(1)) so that service of a counter-notice is open to lessors and freeholders as well as to the occupying lessee.

[5] *Ibid*, s. 58(2).

[6] *Ibid*, s. 53(4).

[7] Under the Compulsory Purchase Act 1965, s. 11(1).

from year to year, and the remainder of the holding is thereby rendered˙ uneconomic.[1]

(a) Procedure

The acquiring authority has two months from the date of service of the counter-notice to accept it as valid. If it fails to do so it, or the claimant, has a further two months in which either party may refer the notice to the Lands Tribunal to determine whether the claim is justified and to pronounce upon its validity or invalidity accordingly. Where the counter-notice is either accepted or declared valid by the Lands Tribunal, the acquiring authority is deemed to be authorised to acquire the claimant's interest in the land covered by the counter-notice and to have served a notice to treat in respect thereof on the date of service of the original notice to treat. In the meantime it remains open to the claimant to withdraw his counter-notice up to the time when compensation has been agreed or, in the case of a reference to the Lands Tribunal, up to six weeks after the Tribunal's determination. If he does withdraw his counter-notice then any notice to treat deemed to have been served in pursuance thereof is also deemed to have been withdrawn. On the other hand, and in contrast to the position under the Lands Clauses Consolidation Act, 1845[2], the acquiring authority has no right to respond to a counter-notice by withdrawing its notice to treat and it cannot exercise its normal statutory right to withdraw on receipt of the notice of claim.[3]

There being no prescribed forms of counter-notice it seems that the rules established by the Courts in regard to counter-notices served under the Act of 1845 are as applicable to notices served under the Act of 1973 as they are to those served under the former Act. All that appears to matter is that the notice should be clear:[4] it need not even be in writing[5] though it must be confined to such property as the acquiring authority may be compelled to purchase.[6] If it includes other property the notice is bad and cannot be upheld in part: a new and valid notice must be served in lieu.[7]

(b) Counter Notice by Lessee

Where, as a result of a valid counter-notice, the acquiring authority steps into the shoes of a lessee, it must offer to surrender the lease to the lessor and in default of agreement as to terms these must be settled by the Lands Tribunal, who are not bound by any terms of surrender contained in the lease.[8] If the lessor either refuses to accept the Lands Tribunal decision or fails to make title to the satisfaction of the acquiring authority, it may pay the sum decided upon by the Lands Tribunal into Court and exercise a Deed Poll in respect of the lessee's interest in

---

[1] Land Compensation Act 1973, s. 55, p. 113, *infra*.
[2] Page 108, *supra*.
[3] I.e., in accordance with the Land Compensation Act 1961, s. 31 and the 1973 Act, s. 54(4): see p. 109, *infra*.
[4] *Spackman* v *Great Western Rly Co* (1855), 1 Jur NS 790.
[5] *Binney* v *Hammersmith and City Railway* (1863), 8 LT 161.
[6] *Harvie* v *South Devon Rly Co* (1874), 32 LT 1; 23 WR 202 CA.
[7] *Harvie* v *South Devon Rly Co* (1874), 32 LT 1; 23 WR 202 CA.
[8] Land Compensation Act 1973, s. 54(6).

its own favour.[1] It is not, however, obliged so to do, and may elect to farm the land itself whether or not, in the case of a corporate body, its constitution includes powers to farm.[2]

(c) Counter Notice by Tenant for a year or less

In the case of a claimant whose interest does not exceed that of a tenancy for a year or from year to year[3] and on whom *notice of entry* is served,[4] there is no question, of course, of a notice to treat being deemed to be served upon him. Instead, provided the claimant has given up possession of the whole holding to the acquiring authority within twelve months of the date on which the counter-notice was accepted (or declared valid by the Lands Tribunal), the notice of entry is deemed to have extended to the whole holding and the acquiring authority is deemed to have taken possession on the expiration of the year of the tenancy current at that date.[5] Immediately thereafter the acquiring authority is required to give up possession of the land that is not being acquired, to the landlord (who is obliged to accept);[6] the tenancy is deemed to be terminated on the date on which the acquiring authority acquired possession of the whole holding,[7] and the acquiring authority takes the place of the tenant for the purposes of any claims between landlord and tenant arising from the termination of the tenancy.[8]

3 Rights of owners and others to require acquiring authorities to purchase additional land: Summary

(i) The basic principle is that if a body possessing compulsory powers seeks to acquire part only of a building[9] the owner may require acquisition of the whole unless the part can be taken without "material detriment" to the remainder.[10]

(ii) The same principle applies in the case of parks and gardens; here the test is whether the part can be taken without "affecting the amenity or convenience" of the houses to which they are attached.[10]

(iii) Disputes on the above matters are to be settled by the Lands

---

[1] Compulsory Purchase Act 1965, s. 9, applied by the Land Compensation Act 1973, s. 54(7).

[2] Land Compensation Act 1973, s. 54(8).

[3] The latter is the normal agricultural tenancy in England and Wales, subject, of course, to the security of tenure provisions of the Agricultural Holdings Act 1948.

[4] In addition to notices of entry served under the Compulsory Purchase Act 1965, s. 11(1) these provisions are extended by the Land Compensation Act 1973, s. 57 to cases in which possession is taken of part only of an agricultural holding under the Lands Clauses Consolidation Act 1845, s. 85 (which applies to entry by statutory undertakers prior to the determination of compensation); the Compulsory Purchase Act 1965, Sch. 3 (Procedure by payment into Court), for obtaining rights of entry alternative to that of *ibid*, s. 11; and under the Town and Country Planning Act 1968, Sch. 3 (General Vesting Declarations). They also apply, with such modifications as may be necessary, to notices of entry under the New Towns Act 1965 (Sch. 6, para. 4) and to notices under the Housing Act 1957, s. 101 (where the tenant is dispossessed as a result of acquisition by agreement of the freeholder or where the acquiring authority is itself the freeholder and appropriates the land for Part V purposes).

[5] Land Compensation Act 1973, s. 56(2).

[6] *Ibid*, s. 56(3)(b).

[7] *Ibid*, s. 56(3)(c).

[8] *Ibid*, s. 56(3)(d): In the event of failure to agree, reference is to be made to the Lands Tribunal.

[9] Which, in the case of a house, includes its curtilage.

[10] Pp. 108, *et seq, supra*.

Tribunal.[1] If the Tribunal finds in favour of the claimant he is under no obligation to accept compensation in lieu of purchase[2] although the acquiring authority may withdraw the notice to treat and abandon its proposals to acquire any of the land.[2]

(iv) In the case of undeveloped land similar rules apply where acquisition of the part would leave the owner with isolated plots of land of less than half an acre,[3] but where the acquiring authority is under an obligation to provide physical communication between areas of land that would be severed by its proposed acquisition, it may compulsorily acquire such severed portions if their value is less than the cost of providing the requisite bridge, culvert, etc.[3]

(v) Where the land to be acquired forms part of an agricultural unit the owner or occupier may require acquisition of his interest in the whole if the loss of this part renders the remainder non-viable, unless it can be farmed economically in conjunction with some other land in which the claimant has an appropriate interest.[4] Where the claimant is a tenant the acquiring authority steps into his shoes and must offer to surrender the tenancy to the landlord.[5]

3 PURCHASE NOTICES

1 Purchase Notices under the Town and Country Planning Acts

REQUIREMENTS

A purchase notice requiring the acquisition of land may be served by the owner[6] thereof upon the local authority[7] in whose area the land is situate where the land "has become incapable of reasonably beneficial use in its existing state" and has been the subject of a defined range of planning decisions (see below) which prevent it being put to beneficial use for some other purpose, limit its existing use, or deprive it of that use altogether.

(a) The Range of Planning Decisions
The original concept derives from the provisions of the Town and Country Planning Act 1947, s. 19, which were, however, confined to cases in which the inability to make reasonably beneficial use of the land followed either a refusal of planning permission (whether by the

---

[1] P. 109, *supra.*

[2] P. 109, *supra.*

[3] Pp. 110, *et seq, supra.*

[4] Pp. 111, *et seq.*

[5] Pp. 113, *et seq, supra.*

[6] I.e., "a person, other than a mortgagee not in possession, who, whether in his own right or as trustee for another person, is entitled to receive the rack rent of the land, or, where the land is not let at a rack rent, would be so entitled if it were so let": the Town and Country Planning Act 1971, s. 190(1). Thus in *London Corpn v Cussack-Smith*, [1955] AC 337, the Corporation, who were assignees of a lease at less than a rack rent, were held to be the "owners" entitled to serve a purchase notice, since had the property been let at a rack rent, they and not the freeholders would have been entitled to receive it. The rack rent falls to be assessed as at the date on which the lease is granted: *Borthwick-Norton v Collier,* [1950] 2 KB 594.

[7] I.e., the appropriate London Borough, Metropolitan District or County District: Town and Country Planning Act 1971, s. 181.

Local Planning Authority or the Minister on appeal or "call in"[1]) or the grant of planning permission subject to conditions so onerous as to have a like effect. These provisions have, however, since been considerably amended and extended to cover the analogous cases in which a similar result follows orders[2] revoking or modifying planning permission[3] by the imposition of conditions; orders[4] requiring discontinuance of use of land or the alteration or removal of buildings or works[5]; refusals or conditional grants of listed building consent[6] (referred to in the Act as a listed building purchase notice); tree preservation orders[7] and regulations controlling the display of advertisements.[8] For the compensation payable in respect of such orders see chapter 10.

It has to be emphasised that the requirement is that the land *has become* incapable of reasonably beneficial use in its *existing state* and *not* that it has been *rendered* incapable of reasonably beneficial use by the planning decision. The latter interpretation would, for example, render largely abortive the provisions of the Town and Country Planning Act 1971, s. 180, which entitle an owner to serve a purchase notice following refusal or conditional grant of planning permission. In the majority of such cases, of course, the land will already have become incapable of reasonably beneficial use in its existing state, the effect of the planning decision in most cases being to prevent its use in some other state.[9] Although in many cases involving revocation or modification of planning permission or discontinuance or limitation of existing use, the planning decision will in fact be the direct cause of the loss of beneficial use, this is not necessarily so (the existing use may itself have ceased to be beneficial or capable of continuing only under unreasonable conditions) and the same principle applies; indeed, the wording of this requirement is identical in each of the relevant sections of the Act.[10]

Where an application for planning permission is made for industrial development and requires an Industrial Development Certificate[11] but no Industrial Development Certificate is available, planning permission must be refused. Nevertheless, by virtue of s. 72 of the Act of 1971 the Local Planning Authority is required to decide whether, even

---

[1] The Department of the Environment insist upon an actual refusal of planning permission: a deemed refusal resulting from a local planning authority's failure to give a decision is not enough: Ministry of Housing and Local Government Circular 26/69, Appendix I, para. 1(a).

[2] I.e., "revocation" orders under the Town and Country Planning Act 1971, s. 45.

[3] *Ibid*, s. 188.

[4] I.e., "discontinuance" orders under *ibid*, s. 51.

[5] *Ibid*, s. 189.

[6] *Ibid*, s. 190: for provisions governing listed buildings see ss. 54 to 59, and Part II, Sch. 11, thereto.

[7] *Ibid*, s. 60, modified by s. 191.

[8] *Ibid*, s. 63, as modified by s. 191.

[9] See [1958] JPL 897 for a case in which the Minister expressly overruled his inspector's interpretation of the 1947 provisions as requiring that loss of reasonably beneficial use in the land's existing state must be the direct result of the refusal of planning permission. See also [1970] JPL 276 for a Ministerial decision to the effect that the words "has become" do not necessitate any comparison between the existing and some earlier state of the land.

[10] Town and Country Planning Act 1971, s. 180 (refusal or conditional grant of planning permission); s. 188 (revocation or modification of planning permission); s. 189 (discontinuance of use or alteration of buildings); s. 190 (refusal or conditional grant of listed building consent).

[11] In accordance with *ibid*, s. 67.

if an Industrial Development Certificate had been obtained, it would still have refused planning permission, and if so, to notify the applicant. In such circumstances the owner of the land may, if he claims that his land has no reasonably beneficial use, serve a purchase notice in exactly the same way as if he had had a formal refusal of planning permission.[1]

(b) Essential Prerequisites

The prerequisites to the service of a purchase notice are:

(i) That the land has become incapable of reasonably beneficial use in its existing state;[2] and

(ii) In a case where either planning permission or listed building consent was granted subject to conditions or modified by the imposition of conditions, that land cannot be rendered capable of reasonably beneficial use by the carrying out of the permitted development or works in accordance with those conditions;[3] and

(iii) In any case where the land cannot be rendered capable of reasonably beneficial use by the carrying out of any of the development or works for which planning permission or listed building consent has been granted or for which the Local Planning Authority or the Secretary of State has undertaken to grant planning permission or listed building consent.[4]

(iv) The person serving the purchase notice must be an owner.[5] If the purchase notice is challenged on the ground that he is not, the Secretary of State[6] must satisfy himself, by making the appropriate enquiries, that the matter is within his jurisdiction[7] as opposed to that of the Courts, as in the case of a disputed title.

Beneficial Use: Matters to be taken into account

The problem that immediately arises is, of course, to determine what, in any particular case, can be regarded as a reasonably beneficial use of the land. In doing so, no account is to be taken of any possibility of carrying out any *new*[8] development.

New development is any development outside the scope of Schedule 8[9] to the Act of 1971 which, in addition to including changes of use within the same use class[10] also covers, on the one hand, the rebuilding, enlargement, maintenance and internal alteration of existing buildings,

---

[1] Town and Country Planning Act 1971, s. 191(2).

[2] *Ibid*, ss. 180(1)(a); 188(1)(a); 189(1)(a); 190(1)(a). But note that in the case of a discontinuance order under s. 51, this state of affairs must be the result of the order: s. 189(1).

[3] This requirement is not, of course, applicable to a discontinuance order: *ibid*, s. 189, and see the previous note.

[4] *Ibid*, ss. 180(1)(c), 188(1)(c), 189(1)(b), 190(1)(c).

[5] I.e., "a person, other than a mortgagee not in possession, who, whether in his own right or as trustee for any other person, is entitled to receive the rack rent of the land, or where the land is not let at a rack rent, would be so entitled if it were so let": Town and Country Planning Act 1971, s. 290(1).

[6] For the Secretary of State's functions in regard to purchase notices see pp. 123, *et seq. infra.*

[7] *R* v *Minister of Housing and Local Government, ex parte Rank Organisation* (1958), 10 P & CR 9 (DC).

[8] *Ibid*, ss. 180(2), 188(2), 189(2) and 190(2). Note, however, that the Secretary of State may direct that planning permission for new development be granted, and may reject a purchase notice on the ground that implementation of such planning permission will render the land capable of beneficial use: see p. 123, *infra.*

[9] For further consideration of Sch. 8 as it affects the assessment of compensation see p. 195, *post*, and Appendix, p. 456, *post.*

[10] See the Town and Country Planning (Use Classes for Third Schedule Purposes) Order

and on the other hand, the carrying out on agricultural or forestry land of non-residential building or other operations for agricultural or forestry purposes. In the case of agriculture the working of minerals is included but the erection of horticultural buildings is not. In the case of the enlargement of a building there is a limit of 10 % over and above the original cubic capacity, or in the case of a dwelling house, 10 % or 1,750 cubic feet, whichever is the greater.[1]

The effect of these provisions is therefore that unless the planning refusal or a condition attached to planning consent itself prevents development of any of the types set out in Schedule 8, it is to be assumed that any such development would, if applicable, be permitted. Thus if, for example, such a planning decision has the effect of making it impossible to use premises for some particular light industry, but possible to use them for a different type of light industry, it cannot be said that the land has been rendered incapable of reasonably beneficial use in its existing state.[2]

In a case where deprivation of reasonably beneficial use is claimed following refusal of planning permission or the grant of planning permission subject to conditions (but *not* in other cases) the effect of the 8th Schedule is modified in two ways. In the first place, no account is to be taken of any 8th Schedule development which would contravene the conditions set out in Schedule 18 to the Act of 1971. The 18th Schedule to the Act is a re-enactment of the Town and Country Planning Act 1963 which, though applicable to all rebuilding and enlargement, was primarily aimed at preventing the replacement of the older office blocks in city centres, with their high ceilings, with modern buildings with very substantially increased floor space, albeit within a total cubic capacity increased only by the 10 % tolerance of the 8th Schedule.

The 18th Schedule therefore in effect limits such increase to 10 % of the *gross floor space* devoted to the same use in the original building, thereby at the same time preventing further extension of the area devoted to such uses by the application of the 10 % tolerance rule to successive replacements or enlargements.

The second modification of the 8th Schedule[3] as it applies to the refusal or conditional grant of planning permission relates to the provisions of paragraph 3 thereof; that paragraph expressly covers the

---

1948, (SI 1948 No. 995). Note that although the Town and Country Planning Act 1947, Sch. 3, is replaced with certain modifications by the Town and Country Planning Act 1971, Schs. 8 and 18 and although the current Use Classes Order for all other purposes is the Town and Country Planning (Use Classes) Order 1972 (SI 1972 No. 1385), the 1948 Order (SI 1948 No. 995, *supra*) remains the relevant order for these purposes and cannot be amended by a subsequent order: Town and Country Planning Act 1947, s. 111(4).

[1] As to the application of these "Schedule 8 tolerances" see the Town and Country Planning Act 1971, Sch. 18, *infra*. Note the Government's intention to increase these tolerances with effect from 1 January 1978 (announced 15 November 1977).

[2] Town and Country Planning (Use Classes for Third Schedule Purposes) Order 1948 (*supra*), Class III of the Schedule.

[3] Town and Country Planning Act 1971, s. 180(3)(a); there is a third modification of Sch. 8, effected by s. 180(3)(b) of less general importance, namely the omission for these purposes of para. 7 of the Schedule, which limits the application of the 10 % rule in the case of buildings used only in part for a particular use to a 10 % increase in cubic capacity of the part used for that purpose on the appointed day.

rebuilding, enlargement, etc., of buildings "as occasion may require", so that the 10 % tolerance rule may apply to successive enlargements or substituted buildings as well as to the "original" building, and for the purposes of determining what may be a "reasonably beneficial use" in these cases paragraph 3 is to be read as if the 10 % tolerance rule had no application to any increase in cubic content effected after the "appointed day" i.e., 1 July 1948. In other words, for the purpose of determining whether the site of a building has any reasonably beneficial use it is only permissible to assume planning permission to enlarge the building by 10 % of the 1948 cubic capacity. Thus, if the building was erected after 1 July 1948 the possibility of *any* increase in cubic capacity is to be discounted.

Again, in determining what is reasonably beneficial use in the case of a refusal or conditional grant of planning permission, section 180(4) provides that conditions imposed by sections 41 and 42 of the same Act and which provide for the lapse of planning permission if the development is not begun within the period laid down, are to be disregarded. In other words, it is not to be assumed for the purposes of determining whether land has been rendered incapable of reasonably beneficial use that any such planning permission will lapse.

It is also provided[1] that no account is to be taken of conditions attached to Industrial Development Certificates[2] and Office Development Permits[3] respectively. In the case of Industrial Development Certificates such conditions can include, for example, requirements for the removal of a building or the discontinuance of use of land after a specific period. It follows, therefore, that if the imposition of such conditions is the sole ground on which an owner claims that his land has been rendered incapable of reasonably beneficial use in its existing state, his claim will fail.

In determining what may be regarded as reasonably beneficial use in the case of a Listed Building Purchase Notice, precisely the same principles are applied as in the revocation or modification of planning permission or of discontinuance orders. The wording of the relevant provisions is, however, of necessity different, viz that no account is to be taken of the possibility of carrying out either new development or works for which listed building consent is required and is not forthcoming.[4] In effect, any work that would be likely to damage or affect the character of a building listed as of special architectural or historical interest, or a building currently subject to a building preservation notice, requires listed building consent.[5]

In contrast to the cases in which land is claimed to be incapable of reasonably beneficial use following a refusal or revocation of planning

---

[1] Town and Country Planning Act 1971, s. 180(4).
[2] *Ibid*, ss. 70 and 71.
[3] *Ibid*, ss. 77 and 82.
[4] *Ibid*, s. 190(2).
[5] For provisions governing listed buildings see *ibid*, ss. 54–58, and in particular, s. 55 (acts requiring listed building consent) and s. 58 (building preservation notices): for an explanation of these provisions in so far as they may give rise to a claim for compensation see pp. 274 *et seq*, *post*, and p. 424, *post*.

permission or refusal of listed building consent or conditional grant or modification of planning permission imposing conditions, Part IX[1] of the Act of 1971 contains no detailed provisions in relation to claims that land has been deprived of reasonably beneficial use following the making of a Tree Preservation Order[2] or of regulations controlling the display of advertisements.[3] Instead, the appropriate sections are applied[4] by reference to the relevant provisions of Part IV.[5] It should, however, be noted that in both cases such of the modifications of the 8th Schedule referred to above[6] as may be relevant are applicable.[7]

Where a tree preservation order[8] is designed to preserve trees purely for amenity purposes in circumstances which make their preservation wholly uneconomical, the land may well be deprived of any reasonably beneficial use. In such cases the order may itself make provision *inter alia* for applying "in relation to any consent under the order or to applications for such consent"[9] the appropriate provisions of the Town and Country Planning Act 1971, Part IX[10] (with which we are here concerned), governing the service of purchase notices. In that event the landowner may, if the other requirements for its service are fulfilled,[11] serve a purchase notice provided he has first applied for consent and has either been refused or has been granted consent subject to conditions.[11]

Corresponding provisions apply in the case of advertisement control[12] where the appropriate regulations[13] (which may make different provisions for different areas)[14] may make similar provision for the application of the purchase notice provisions mentioned above.[15]

What constitutes reasonably beneficial use

The fundamental difficulty in regard to purchase notices is of course to decide, in any particular case, whether or not such use as the land may have in its existing state can be regarded as 'reasonably beneficial'. Although this is a problem evoking much discussion since the expression first appeared in the Town and Country Planning Act 1947

[1] I.e., the Part entitled "Provisions Enabling Owner to Require Purchase of his Interest" with which this and the next section of this chapter are primarily concerned.

[2] For provisions governing Tree Preservation Orders see the Town and Country Planning Act 1971, ss. 59–62.

[3] For provisions governing advertisement control, see *ibid*, ss. 63–64.

[4] *Ibid*, s. 189(1): the sections of Part IX that are applied are ss. 180–183, 186 and 187.

[5] Part IV ("additional control in special cases") also includes the provisions relating to listed buildings: see note 5, p. 118, *supra*.

[6] Pp. 117, *et seq, supra*.

[7] Town and Country Planning Act 1971, s. 180. But in the case of advertisement control, modifications may be made by regulations under s. 63.

[8] I.e., orders under *ibid*, s. 60.

[9] *Ibid*, s. 60(1)(c) and (2)(b) as applied by s. 191(1).

[10] I.e., in this context *ibid*, s. 180.

[11] Pp. 116 *et seq, supra*. For compensation for refusal or revocation of consent see p. 433, *post*.

[12] Town and Country Planning Act 1971, s. 63(2)(c) as applied by s. 191(1).

[13] For the current regulations see the Town and Country Planning (Control of Advertisement) Regulations 1961 (SI 1969 No. 1532).

[14] Town and Country Planning Act 1971, s. 63(3) and note that areas of special control are designated by orders made or approved by the Secretary of State in accordance with Reg. 26 and Sch. 2 of the above regulations: *ibid*, s. 63(4) and (5).

[15] No such provision is, however, made in the current regulations (see note 13, *supra*).

there are but few points on which any degree of certainty emerges. In the first place, however, it can be said that the weight of judicial authority is very much against the adoption of any test based upon a comparison of the capital value of the land in its existing state and the value that it would have commanded had there been no refusal or conditional grant of planning permission; revocation or modification of planning permission; discontinuance order, etc. In short, the intention of these provisions is not to relieve an owner who is merely prevented from realising the full development value of his land.[1]

Thus in *R.* v *Minister of Housing & Local Government* ex parte *Chichester Rural District Council*[2] the Divisional Court granted an order of certiorari to quash the Minister's decision to confirm a purchase notice made on the sole ground that the land in question was of "substantially less use and value to the owner than it would have been if planning permission had been granted". As Lord Parker LCJ pointed out, the effect of a refusal of planning permission almost invariably has such an effect though he specifically left open the question whether the word 'reasonable' invokes *some* form of comparison. In the later case of *General Estates Co* v *Minister of Housing and Local Government*[3] Lawton J doubted the value and even the relevance of any "comparative" test except perhaps where the proposed development entailed only a change of use that would not change the existing state of the land. A similar view was taken by Fisher J in *Brookdene Investments Ltd* v *Minister of Housing and Local Government*[4] and like Lawton J he based his argument upon the necessity of looking at the land in its *existing* state. He nevertheless did not entirely dismiss the applicability of this comparative test which he thought might, "at the most" be one of the factors to be taken into account and that it was for the inspector or Minister to decide on the weight to be attached to it. Thus at the rehearing of the *Chichester RDC* case (*supra*) the inspector, while dismissing any comparison of capital value of the land in its existing state with that which it would have had if development within the terms of the 3rd Schedule to the Act of 1947[5] had been allowed, adopted a test based upon comparative annual values. He based his decision upon the proposition that since capital values took into account future development, their use was inappropriate in considering what the "existing state" of the land had "become". The test based upon annual values appears to have been accepted by the Minister as relevant "where appropriate";[6] but unless it is to be confined, as Lawton J suggested in the *General Estates Company* case (*supra*) to changes of use which both fall within the Schedule and require no change in the 'state' of the land, its adoption would seem to involve consideration of values based upon some inevitable change in the state

[1] See, for example, Ministry of Housing and Local Government Circular 26/69, Appendix I, para. 5.

[2] [1960] 1 WLR 587.

[3] (1965) reported in the Estates Gazette 17 April, 201 (QB).

[4] (1969) 21 P & CR 545.

[5] Now Town and Country Planning Act 1971, Sch. 8.

[6] Ministry of Housing and Local Government Circular 26/69, Appendix I, para. 5; there is, however, no indication of the Minister's views as to the circumstances in which such a test would be appropriate.

of the land, thereby departing from both the wording and the spirit of the statutory provisions.

However, despite the paucity of judicial authority, Ministerial decisions give some indication of the circumstances in which a purchase notice is likely to receive confirmation. Thus wholly undeveloped land can normally be expected to grow some sort of crop but it will not be held capable of reasonably beneficial use if the area is too small for reasonably economic cultivation and is divorced from other land with which it could be managed;[1] nor, of course, if it has been deprived of any reasonably convenient access.[2] Similarly, buildings will not be considered capable of reasonably beneficial use if the cost of adaptation or repair far outweighs any return which could reasonably be expected for any purpose to which they could be put.[3] Nor will it be considered reasonable to reject a purchase notice where 8th Schedule development, although achieving reasonably beneficial use, is likely to be indefinitely postponed,[4] overtaken by comprehensive redevelopment because of the obsolescence of the whole area,[5] or wholly out of character with the neighbourhood.[6] On the other hand the fact that there is no demand for premises as a whole will not make them incapable of reasonably beneficial use if they are capable of subdivision into parts which individually can be put to beneficial use.[7]

PROCEDURE[8]

(a) General

Although a purchase notice in some other form will not be invalid provided it contains all the relevant information,[9] Appendix III to Circular 26/69 provides a standard form for a purchase notice arising from a refusal or conditional grant of planning permission which may be suitably modified when the purchase notice arises from revocation or modification of planning permission or a discontinuance order. A suitable form of Listed Building Purchase Notice is provided in Appendix IV to the same circular. Normally the notice must be served upon the local authority in whose area the land is situate, within twelve months of the planning decision from which it arises.[10] If, however, a listed building is subject to a repairs notice[11] no Listed Building Purchase Notice can be served until after the expiration of three months from the date of service of the repairs notice; but if, following the service

[1] *Re Land at Broadleas, Devizes*, [1967] JPL 730.
[2] *Re Welton Station, Watford, Northants*, [1973] JPL 604.
[3] *Re H & C. Davis, Station Road, Godalming*, [1971] JPL 239.
[4] *Re Miles Lane, Tandridge, Surrey*, [1962] JPL 201.
[5] *Re 21/25 High Street, Chasetown, Lichfield*, [1971] JPL 535.
[6] *Re Land at Mason Street, Southwark*, [1968] JPL 180.
[7] *Re Land at Dorchester Road, Weymouth*. [1973] JPL 43.
[8] Practitioners may also find it helpful to refer to Ministry of Housing & Local Government Circular 26/69 and the Town and Country Planning General Regulations 1976, (SI 1976 No. 1419).
[9] The purchase notice must, however, be made in writing (cf. *Binney* v *Hammersmith City Rly Co*, p. 112, *supra*) and sent by pre-paid post to the Clerk to the local authority concerned: SI 1976 No. 1419, Reg. 14.
[10] Town and Country Planning General Regulations 1976 (SI 1976 No. 1419), Reg. 14.
[11] Under the Town and Country Planning Act 1971, s. 115.

of that repairs notice the local authority have started, and not discontinued, compulsory purchase proceedings,[1] the purchase notice should be served on the Council or the London Borough or County District of the area in which the land is situate within twelve months of the planning decision from which it arises.[2]

(b) Action by Local Authority on whom Purchase Notice Served

The Council concerned have then three months in which to decide how to deal with the purchase notice. If they decide to accept it or have found some other local authority or statutory undertakers willing to do so they must give written notice to that effect to the person who has served the purchase notice. Such notice then operates as a deemed notice to treat and that local authority, or such other local authority or statutory undertakers as mentioned above, is deemed to be authorised to acquire the land compulsorily.[3] If, however, the Council on whom the purchase notice is served is unwilling to accept it and has not found any other local authority or statutory undertakers willing to do so, it must similarly serve notice on the person who has served the purchase notice notifying him of its decision and of its reasons therefor and it must forward a copy of such notice to the Secretary of State.

(c) Action by Secretary of State where no local authority is willing to accept purchase notice

In such a case there is a number of courses of action available to the Secretary of State,[4] but except in the case of a Listed Building Purchase Notice,[5] before he finally adopts any of them he is required to notify the parties concerned[6] of his proposed decision, permit them to make representations and if required to do so by any of those parties, he must appoint a person to hold a hearing.[7]

But if none of the parties makes any objection or there is no demand for a hearing the Secretary of State cannot then change his mind without again notifying the parties and giving them a further opportunity to make representations and/or to require a hearing: otherwise his decision will be invalid.[8] Thereafter he is in no way bound by his

---

[1] Town and Country Planning Act 1971, s. 180(5): for what constitutes a start or discontinuance of compulsory purchase proceedings for this purpose see sub-s. (6).

[2] Town and Country Planning General Regulations 1976 (SI 1976 No 1419), Reg. 14.

[3] Town and Country Planning Act 1971, s. 181(1) and (2). A local authority is deemed to be authorised to acquire under the powers of *ibid*, Part VI, and in the case of statutory undertakers, under any statutory provision under which they have power or may be authorised to acquire land compulsorily: *ibid*, s. 181(4).

[4] If a purchase notice is challenged on any matter that raises a question of jurisdiction the Secretary of State must make such enquiries as may be necessary before deciding that question: *R. v Minister of Housing and Local Government*, ex parte *Rank Organisation* (1958), 10 P & CR 9 (DC).

[5] Town and Country Planning Act 1971, Sch. 19, para. 2.

[6] I.e., the person serving the purchase notice, the local authority upon whom it was served, the local planning authority for the area in question, and any other local authority or statutory undertaker involved by his proposal as a prospective acquiring authority; Town and Country Planning Act 1971, s. 182. Note, however, that despite the conferring of certain planning powers upon County District Councils by the Local Government Act 1972, the County Council still has to be notified as a local planning authority as well as the County District Council: Local Government Act 1972, s. 182.

[7] Town and Country Planning Act 1971, s. 182(3).

[8] *Ealing Corpn v Minister of Housing and Local Government*, [1952] Ch. 856.

original proposal and may take such other of the actions available to him as, in the light of that person's report, he may deem appropriate.[1]

The courses open to the Secretary of State are as follows:

(i) If he is satisfied that the relevant requirements (see paras. (a) to (c), page 114, *supra*) are fulfilled he may confirm the purchase notice or modify it by substituting, either in relation to the whole or to any part of the land, another local authority or statutory undertakers for the local authority on whom the purchase notice was served.[2] Confirmation of a purchase notice by the Secretary of State, with or without such modifications, has the same effect in relation to the powers under which the acquiring authority thereafter purport to acquire compulsorily as in the case of acceptance by a local authority.[3]

(ii) Alternatively, the Secretary of State may[4]:

   (a) In the case of a purchase notice arising from a refusal of planning permission or a revocation or discontinuance order, grant planning permission[5] or cancel the revocation or discontinuance order;[6] or

   (b) In the case of a purchase notice arising from the imposition of conditions,[7] or from a modification order imposing conditions,[8] revoke or amend those conditions[9] (or amend a discontinuance order[10]) so as to render the land capable of reasonably beneficial use by carrying out the development concerned.

(iii) As a third alternative he may direct that such planning permission be granted either as to the whole of the land or as to that part only of the land as he considers will enable the land to be rendered capable of reasonably beneficial use within a reasonable period and which in his view ought to be granted.[11]

(iv) If the purchase notice arises from a refusal or conditional grant of planning permission in respect of land that had previously been part of

[1] Town and Country Planning Act 1971, s. 182(4).
[2] *Ibid*, s. 183(4).
[3] See note 7, p. 122, *supra*.
[4] The Secretary of State's available courses of action in the case of a listed building purchase notice are separately set out in the Town and Country Planning Act 1971, Sch. 19; they follow almost exactly the same lines as those indicated in sub-paragraphs (a) and (b) in the text as applicable to other purchase notices except that he is also required to satisfy himself before confirming the notice, that the land comprises such land contiguous or adjacent to the building as is in his opinion required for preserving the building or its amenities, or for affording access to it, or for its proper control or management: *ibid*, para. 2(2). He may, however, confirm without notifying the parties and affording them an opportunity of being heard: para. 2(1). He may also confirm a listed building notice in respect of part only of the land if satisfied that the relevant requirements of the notice (see pp. 114 *et seq*, *supra*) are fulfilled only in respect of that part of the land. Note also that in this case the "land" includes land which the owner claims is substantially inseparable from the building and should be treated together with the building, as a single holding: s. 190(3).
[5] Town and Country Planning Act 1971, s. 183(2).
[6] *Ibid*, s. 188(3).
[7] *Ibid*, s. 183(2).
[8] I.e., an order under *ibid*, s. 45.
[9] *Ibid*, s. 188(3).
[10] I.e., an order under *ibid*, s. 51; see also s. 189(3).
[11] *Ibid*, s. 183(3).

a larger area in respect of which planning permission had been granted subject to a condition, express or implied,[1] that the land the subject of the purchase notice should be preserved as amenity land forming part of the overall development of the larger area, the Secretary of State may refuse to confirm the purchase notice if he is satisfied that the earlier requirement remains valid.[2] This provision overrules the decision in *Adams & Wade Ltd.* v *Minister of Housing and Local Government*.[3] It does not, however, prevent either the service or confirmation of a purchase notice and it seems that if only *part* of the land in respect of which the notice is served is "sterilised" by the previous planning permission the Secretary of State cannot, by virtue of these provisions, refuse confirmation even in part.[4]

It is, moreover, essential that the condition be enforceable, and an otherwise valid condition is not enforceable if the development covered by the planning permission to which it is attached is not carried out.[5] In *Sheppard* v *Secretary of State for the Environment*[6] planning permission had been granted for the reconditioning and change of use of a listed building and the erection of 13 houses on land adjoining. An adjoining paddock was shown uncoloured on the application plan but a condition was attached to the permission requiring the landscaping of the land within the curtilage of the site. Subsequently planning permission to develop the paddock was refused and the owner served a purchase notice, which the Secretary of State refused to confirm on the ground that he considered that the above condition required it to be laid out for the amenity of the development for which planning permission had been granted. On appeal it was held that the condition did relate to the paddock (having been shown as being within the overall site) but that as it referred only to the listed building, and not to the building of the 13 houses, it could not be enforced because the permitted change of use had not in fact taken place. The decision of the Secretary of State was accordingly quashed.

(v) The Secretary of State has a similar power of outright refusal to confirm any purchase notice where the land concerned is either within the metropolitan region[7] or for the time being within a controlled area for office development[8] in which planning permission already granted is thereby suspended,[9] or the land comprises a building which, at the

---

[1] Town and Country Planning Act 1971, s. 184(2)(b).

[2] *Ibid*, s. 184.

[3] (1965) 18 P & CR 60.

[4] *Plymouth City Corpn* v *Secretary of State for the Environment*, [1972] 3 All ER 225 [1972] 1 WLR 1347; (QBD).

[5] *F. Lucas & Sons Ltd.* v *Dorking and Horley RDC* (1964), 62 LGR 491.

[6] (1974) 233 Estates Gazette 1167.

[7] Town and Country Planning Act 1971, s. 185. As to what constitutes the metropolitan region see Sch. 13.

[8] Office development is controlled by providing that an application for planning permission for office development within the metropolitan region or in areas designated by order, is to be of no effect unless accompanied by a copy of an "office development permit" issued by the Secretary of State: Town and Country Planning Act 1971, s. 74(4). Such areas are "controlled areas": s. 81(2).

[9] I.e., certain planning permissions granted prior to 5 August 1965: see *ibid*, s. 83 and Sch. 12, para. 1(4).

date of the service of the purchase notice, contained offices or which was last used as such.[1] Such a refusal does not, however, prevent the service of a further purchase notice if and when these restrictions cease to apply[2] either because the land ceases to be within a controlled area or because of modifications or abolition of the restrictions either in the metropolitan region alone, or in the country as a whole.

(d) Deemed Confirmation of Purchase Notice in default of action by the Secretary of State.

If, nine months after the service of a purchase notice, or six months after the copy was submitted to the Secretary of State, whichever is the shorter period, he has neither confirmed the purchase notice nor taken any of the steps set out in paragraphs (ii) and (iii) above, and has not notified the person who served the purchase notice that he does not intend to confirm it, it is deemed to be confirmed and the local authority on whom it was served is deemed to be authorised to acquire the land compulsorily and to have served a notice to treat at the end of that period.

In this context, however, because of the ambiguous wording of the relevant statutory provisions[3] a distinction has to be drawn between the case in which the Secretary of State notifies the person serving the purchase notice that he proposes to confirm and the case in which the notification is to the effect that he does not propose to do so. In the former case the time limit still runs and if the Secretary of State reaches no final decision within the relevant period the purchase notice is deemed to be confirmed. In the converse case, however, it seems that the time limit is extended indefinitely and the Secretary of State can take as long as he likes to issue his final decision.[4]

In the event of any decision of the Secretary of State in relation to a purchase notice being quashed by the High Court upon an application

---

[1] Town and Country Planning Act 1971, s. 185(1). The logic of applying these provisions to buildings within these controlled areas with an existing use for office purposes irrespective of the nature of the planning decision giving rise to the purchase notice is not entirely clear, for the decision could, for example, be a refusal of planning permission for conversion to residential purposes. Presumably it is because once the restrictions are lifted the 10% tolerance rule of Sch. 8 comes into operation (see pp. 117 *et seq, supra*); but it does not necessarily follow that the application of Sch. 8 would restore a reasonably beneficial use.

[3] Town and Country Planning Act 1971, s. 185(3). Office development control was originally imposed for a seven-year period ending 4 August 1972, *ibid*, s. 86(1), and was subsequently extended to 4 August 1977 by the Town and Country Planning (Amendment) Act 1972, s. 5(1), subject to a power to end the control earlier by Order in Council. It has now been further extended to 5 August 1982, or to "such earlier date as may be provided by Order in Council": The Control of Office Development Act 1977, s. 1.

[4] Town and Country Planning Act 1971, s. 186(5), which provides that a notice will be deemed to be confirmed if, within the relevant period, "the Secretary of State has neither confirmed the purchase notice nor taken any such action in respect thereof as is mentioned in s. 183(2) or (3) of this Act and has not notified the owner by whom the notice was served that he does not propose to confirm the notice". Note, however, that the references to s. 183(2) and (3) include the references to ss. 188 and 189, *supra*. This is because the provisions of these sections (which deal with purchase notices pursuant to revocation or modification and discontinuance orders under ss. 45 and 51 respectively) are applied by modifying the operation of s. 183(2) and (3).

[5] *Sheppard* v *Secretary of State for the Environment* (1974), 233 Estates Gazette 1167.

in that behalf,[1] the purchase notice is treated as cancelled, but the owner may serve a further notice in lieu,[2] and for this purpose the twelve months' time limit runs from the date of the High Court decision.[3]

COMPENSATION

Subject to one exception, compensation upon acquisition in pursuance of a purchase notice is assessed in exactly the same way as if the acquiring authority had initiated the acquisition in the normal manner – i.e., by making a compulsory purchase order.[4] The exception relates to orders revoking or modifying planning permission[5] in respect of which compensation is payable in respect of abortive work carried out in pursuance of the planning permission or other loss directly attributable to the revocation or modification;[6] in such cases the compensation payable in respect of the acquisition is reduced by the value of the works in respect of which compensation has already become payable.[7]   Where, however, a purchase notice does not take effect or does not take effect in relation to a part of the land because the local authority refuse to purchase on the strength of a direction by the Secretary of State that planning permission be granted (if applied for) for some other development[8] it may so happen that the value of the claimant's interest is reduced to less than existing use value. This situation can arise, for example, where the purchase notice follows refusal of planning permission for some development within Schedule 8[9] and the Secretary of State directs that planning permission for a Schedule 8 development shall be granted subject to conditions. Since the local authority would have had to purchase at existing use value assessed on the assumption that Schedule 8 development would be permitted[10] the owner will be worse off than he would have been had the local authority acquired the land. It is accordingly provided that in

---

[1] In accordance with the Town and Country Planning Act 1971, s. 245 and s. 242(3)(i) and (j). N.B. Any such application to the Court must be made within six weeks of the Secretary of State's decision: s. 245. The decision of the Secretary of State may be quashed upon the application of either party directly concerned (i.e., the person serving the purchase notice or the local authority required to accept it) either on the ground that the action of the Secretary of State is not within the powers of the Act or that the applicant's interests have been prejudiced by the Secretary of State's failure to comply with some requirement of the Act: *ibid*.

[2] Town and Country Planning Act 1971, s. 186(4).

[3] *Ibid*, s. 186(5).

[4] See chaps. 5 to 8, *post*.

[5] I.e., orders under the Town and Country Planning Act 1971, s. 45. See p. 413, *post*.

[6] *Ibid*, s. 164. See pp. 416 *et seq*, *post*.

[7] *Ibid*, s. 187(1). Note, however, that these provisions do not necessarily result in a deduction equivalent to the compensation payable in respect of the revocation or modification under s. 164. The latter is based upon abortive costs, including architects fees, etc: s. 164(2) (see pp. 416 *et seq*, *post*): the *value* of such works to be deducted under s. 187(1) will not necessarily be the same.

[8] I.e. under the Town and Country Planning Act 1971, s. 183(3), p. 123, *supra*.

[9] *Ibid*, Sch. 8, p. 116, *supra*, and see Appendix p. 456, *post*. See, however, the next note.

[10] *Ibid*, s. 187(5), which decrees that for this purpose existing use value be assessed in accordance with the provisions of the Town and Country Planning Act 1947—i.e., by reference to Sch. 3 of that Act, which is not identical with its replacement by the Town and Country Planning Act 1971, Sch. 8: see note 7, p. 116, *supra* and note 2, p. 194 *post*.

such circumstances, if a claim is made[1] within six months of the Secretary of State's direction[2] the local authority shall pay compensation to the owner equivalent to the difference between the existing use value at which they would have had to acquire and the value of the land with the restricted planning permission directed by the Secretary of State.[3] Since compensation is payable for refusal of planning permission for development within Part II of Schedule 8[4] this concession will in most cases merely represent a substitute method of recoupment.

PURCHASE NOTICES UNDER THE TOWN AND COUNTRY PLANNING ACT 1971: SUMMARY

(i) The essential prerequisites for the service of a purchase notice are:
   (a) That the land has become incapable of reasonably beneficial[5] use in its existing state;[6] and
   (b) That this situation arises either:
      (a) because planning permission for some other use has been refused or granted subject to such onerous conditions that implementation of that planning permission would not enable reasonably beneficial use to be made of the land;[7] or
      (b) because of the service, upon the owners, of an order revoking or modifying existing planning permission[8] or requiring discontinuance of existing use or modification or removal of buildings or works;[9] or because of revocation or modification[10] or refusal or conditional grant of listed building consent.[11]

(ii) The purchase notice must be served within twelve months of the planning decision from which it arises.[12]

(iii) The local authority upon whom the purchase notice is served have three months in which to decide whether to accept the notice. If they do so they must notify the person who served the notice

---

[1] Town and Country Planning Act 1971, s. 187(2).

[2] *Ibid* and Town and Country Planning General Regulations 1974 (SI 1974 No. 596) Regulation 12.

[3] Town and Country Planning Act 1971, s. 187(2). But note that if the planning permission which the Secretary of State directs the local planning authority to grant is subject to conditions as to design, height or density of buildings the Secretary of State may direct that such conditions may, for this purpose, be disregarded either in whole or to such extent as he may direct: s. 187(3).

[4] There is a curious anomaly here in that although compensation is only payable in respect of refusal of planning permission for development within the Town and Country Planning Act 1971, Sch. 8, Part II (see s. 169) it is to be assumed, when assessing compensation at existing use value that planning permission would be granted for the classes of development listed in both Parts I and II of the Schedule: Land Compensation Act 1961, s. 15(3): see pp. 195 *et seq*, *post* and note 2, p. 194, *post*.

[5] See pp 116 *et seq, supra*.

[6] Town and Country Planning Act 1971, ss. 180, 188, 189 and 190.

[7] *Ibid*, s. 180, pp. 116 *et seq, supra*.

[8] I.e., an order under *ibid*, s. 45; see also s. 188.

[9] I.e., an order under *ibid*, s. 51; see also s. 189.

[10] In accordance with *ibid*, Sch. 11, Part II; see also s. 190.

[11] In accordance with *ibid*, s. 55; see also s. 190.

[12] Town and Country Planning General Regulations 1976 (SI 1976 No. 1419), p. 121, *supra*: note, however, the special provisions applicable to a listed building subject to a repairs notice: *ibid*.

accordingly and are thereby deemed to have served notice to treat for the compulsory acquisition of the land.[1] If they are unwilling to accept the purchase notice but have found another local authority or statutory undertakers willing to do so they again notify the person serving the notice and that other authority is deemed to have served a notice to treat.[1]

(iv) If the local authority is unwilling to accept the purchase notice (and unable to find another authority willing to do so) it must notify the person serving the notice, state its reasons and send a copy to the Secretary of State.[2]

(v) The Secretary of State[3] has nine months from the date of service of the purchase notice (or six months from its submission to him, whichever is the shorter period) in which to confirm the notice (with or without modifications); modify the planning decision giving rise to the purchase notice or grant a fresh planning permission so as to enable the land to be put to beneficial use; or reject the notice.[4] Before making his final decision, however, he is obliged to inform the parties concerned of his proposed decision, afford them an opportunity of being heard by one of his inspectors, and make his final decision in the light of the inspector's report on any such hearing.[5] Failure to take one or other of these decisions within the time prescribed results in a deemed acceptance of the purchase notice on behalf of the authority on whom it was initially served.[6]

(vi) The Secretary of State's decision may be challenged by either party by application to the High Court within six weeks of the decision. In the event of a decision of the Court to quash confirmation of a purchase notice a further notice may be served within twelve months of the Court's decision.[7]

2 Purchase Notices under the Housing Acts

The Housing Acts 1969 and 1974 make provision for the compulsory improvement of the older privately owned tenanted dwellings.[8] Initially the local authority must serve a provisional notice specifying the works it requires to be done and provide an opportunity for the "person having control of the dwelling"[9] to discuss them. Thereafter an improvement notice may be served requiring the works specified therein (which need not be the same as those specified in the provisional notice) to be executed.

Once a valid improvement notice has been served upon the person

---

[1] Pp. 122, *supra*.

[2] P. 122, *supra*.

[3] For details of the courses open to the Secretary of State and the grounds on which he may reject a purchase notice see pp. 123 *et seq, supra*.

[4] Para. (iv), pp. 123 *et seq, supra*.

[5] P. 122–123, *supra*.

[6] P. 125, *supra*.

[7] p. 125 and note 1, p. 126, *supra*.

[8] For details see Housing Act 1969, Part II and Housing Act 1974, Part VIII. In certain very limited circumstances these provisions can apply to owner-occupiers: see Housing Act 1974, s. 85(3).

[9] For definition see Housing Act 1974, s. 104(2).

having control of the dwelling he is entitled, within six months,[1] to serve upon the local authority a purchase notice requiring it to acquire his interest,[2] whereupon the authority is deemed to have served a notice to treat on the date of service of the purchase notice.[3] Thereafter the acquisition is carried out in exactly the same way as if notice to treat had been served in pursuance of a compulsory purchase order,[4] compensation being assessed in accordance with the ordinary rules.[5] These Housing Act purchase notices are therefore very different in character (and much simpler in operation) than those considered above and arising under the Town and Country Planning Act 1971.

4 BLIGHT NOTICES

1 Introduction

As explained in the introduction to this chapter, planning blight arises where land is known to be ultimately required for some public purpose, and in the meanwhile, therefore, becomes difficult to sell except at a substantial loss to the owner. The remedy provided by statute is the service of a "blight notice", which, like the purchase notices considered in the previous section of this chapter, requires the appropriate authority to purchase forthwith. That remedy does not, however, cover anything approaching the whole field. In the first place, rented or investment property[6] is excluded on the principle that the threat of ultimate compulsory acquisition need not necessarily affect revenue even though, of course, in the event of the property falling vacant it may well be virtually impossible to relet at an economic rent for the limited, although often wholly indefinite, period prior to compulsory acquisition, and even though tenants of such property are likely to feel impelled to find alternative accommodation before being forced to do so by the actual compulsory purchase.

In short, therefore, the remedy by way of the service of a blight notice is confined to a somewhat narrowly defined class of owner-occupier[7] who, as a result of the threat of compulsory acquisition, has been unable to sell except at a substantially reduced price.[8]

---

[1] Or in the event of appeal (in the first instance to the County Court) upon determination of the appeal. Housing Act 1974, s. 92.

[2] *Ibid*, s. 101(1).

[3] *Ibid*, s. 101(2).

[4] See pp. 67 *et seq, ante*, but note that no specific consent of the Secretary of State is required.

[5] Chap. 5, p. 158 *post*, and note the effect of the Land Compensation Act 1973, s. 45, see p. 165. *post*.

[6] Thus, although a lessee in occupation of a dwelling house, an agricultural unit, or small business premises may qualify, a lessor will not.

[7] Including an occupying lessee for a term of years certain and having three or more years unexpired: personal representatives and, in certain cases, a mortgagee.

[8] As originally enacted in the Town and Country Planning Act 1959 these provisions were primarily intended to meet the case of owner-occupiers *obliged* to vacate before the authority concerned required their property: since such people would normally expect to pay their own costs of removal, etc., compensation for disturbance was not payable: *ibid*, Sch. 5, para. 7: except in the case of an agricultural unit, compensation for severance (though not injurious affection) was also excluded on the grounds that the severance was voluntary: para. 6. Similar problems, however, faced those who could await acquisition (and obtain full compensation)

Secondly, the remedy is also confined to cases where the indications that the land will in fact ultimately be subject to compulsory acquisition are reasonably firm. Thus, although for example publication of possible alternative routes for a new highway will have the effect of blighting property affected by any of such routes, no remedy will be available until the final choice is made. Under the Act of 1971,[1] indeed, no blight notice could be served until the decision had been finalised by incorporation in a structure, local or development plan approved by the Secretary of State or by becoming subject to an appropriate order or scheme authorising acquisition. The effect of the Land Compensation Act 1973,[2] however, is to enable a blight notice to be served as soon as the appropriate authority[3] has made up its mind as to what it wants to do, even although the authority to acquire remains dependent upon the formal approval of its proposals or the confirmation of a compulsory purchase order by the Secretary of State, or where a Government Department is the appropriate authority, upon the making of the requisite order by the appropriate Minister.[4]

2 Requirements

Where a person finds that his land is threatened by compulsory acquisition at some future date, and wishes to take advantage of these provisions by unloading his property on to the appropriate authority there are four principal requirements that must be fulfilled:

(i) QUALIFYING PROPERTY

The owner must first ensure that his property is of such a nature that the service of a blight notice is an available remedy. Three categories of property are covered, namely:

(a) An hereditament[5] occupied wholly or as to a substantial part, as a dwelling by the person who serves the blight notice, who is referred to in the Act[6] as the claimant, and will be so referred to hereafter.

(b) Other hereditaments the net annual value of which does not

---

but only at the cost of missing a suitable alternative home or the opportunity to re-establish a business within a reasonable period before retirement age. These restrictions were therefore repealed with effect from 1 April 1969: Town and Country Planning Act 1968, s. 37(1) and Town and Country Planning Act (Commencement No. 4) Order 1969 (SI 1969 No. 275).

[1] Town and Country Planning Act 1971, s. 192(1), pp. 133, et seq, post.

[2] Ss. 68–76.

[3] I.e., in effect the authority which is liable ultimately to acquire the land: see p. 154, infra.

[4] See note 10, p. 32, ante. .

[5] I.e., the aggregate of the land which forms the subject of a single entry "(except entries relating solely to sporting rights or rights to exhibit advertisements)" in the current valuation list, provided that where the property straddles the boundaries of two or more rating areas it is to be considered as a single hereditament if, had it fallen wholly within one rating area, it would have formed the subject of a single entry: Town and Country Planning Act 1971, s. 207(1). Note that although valuation of an hereditament for rating purposes takes account of any rights appurtenant thereto and inseparable from the letting (Shell Mex and B.P. Ltd. v Langley (VO) (1962) 9 RRC 249) the blighting of other freehold land held with the hereditament does not give the owner-occupier thereof the right to serve a blight notice: such land is not part of the hereditament even though it enables the owner to exercise over it a private right of way: Ley and Ley v Kent County Council (1976) 31 P & CR 439: Lake v Cheshire County Council (LT Ref. 266, 1975) [1976] JPL 434.

[6] Town and Country Planning Act 1971, s. 193(4).

exceed the amount prescribed from time to time by Order. The purpose of this provision is to include small business premises the owners of which may face a similar degree of hardship (if, for example, they wish to retire or re-establish themselves well before the property is due for acquisition) to that faced by the ordinary householder who, for some reason, wishes, or is forced to move. The larger business is deemed to be capable of accepting the threat of compulsory acquisition as a normal commercial risk, and annual value has been selected as a convenient, if somewhat rough and ready, means of distinction. The current limit of annual value is £2,250.[1]

(c) An agricultural unit defined as "land occupied as a unit for agricultural purposes, including any dwelling-house or other building occupied by the same person for the purpose of farming the land".[2]

(ii) QUALIFYING INTERESTS
Occupation
A prospective claimant must further ensure that he has a *qualifying interest* in his property.[3] There are two requirements in this respect. The first relates to occupation. In all cases the claimant must have been in occupation for a continuous period of six months, either immediately prior to the date of the service of the blight notice or ending not more than twelve months previously. In the latter case, however, a distinction has to be drawn between either type of hereditament on the one hand, and an agricultural unit on the other, for in the case of an hereditament, but not in the case of an agricultural unit,[4] it must have been unoccupied in the meantime. Furthermore, in the case of an hereditament, occupation need only have been of part thereof provided it is a substantial part, whereas in the case of an agricultural unit it must be occupation of the whole even though the requisite legal interest extends only to part.

Occupation must, however, be such as to indicate "beneficial occupation": it is not therefore enough that the claimant should use a part of the premises for storage of articles unconnected with the running of his business but left there because "they were of no particular

---

[1] Town and Country Planning (Limit of Annual Value) Order 1973. Where the land in question is exempt from the payment of rates, the annual value is non-existent, cannot be regarded as nil, and cannot therefore be said to be less than the prescribed limit: consequently a blight notice cannot be upheld: *Essex County Council* v *Essex Incorporated Congregational Church Unit*, [1963] AC 808, [1963] 1 All ER 326. Since, however, the blight notice in this case was upheld because the County Council's objection was served too late to be considered, this decision, though carrying great weight, must be considered as *obiter*. For a suggested non-mandatory compromise see Ministry of Housing and Local Government Circular 4/59, para. 11.

[2] Town and Country Planning Act 1971, s. 207(1).

[3] Note that the qualifying interest need not extend to the whole hereditament or agricultural unit. The blight notice, however, must relate to the whole of the claimant's interest: *ibid*, s. 193(2).

[4] But to be qualified to serve a blight notice the claimant must, of course, retain his ownership throughout (see next paragraph of the text); Town and Country Planning Act 1971, s. 203(2). Although s. 203(1) and (3) contain no such specific requirement in regard to the owner of an hereditament who has given up occupation, he nevertheless has to have a qualifying interest at the date of the service of the blight notice; see s. 193(1), p. 132, *infra*.

importance".[1] Similarly, the Lands Tribunal has held that the mere
legal occupation such as that enjoyed by Governors of a hospital[2] does
not constitute a qualifying interest in the absence of actual physical
occupation.[3]

On the other hand, the fact that the owner of a business and of the
premises in which it is carried on, relies on someone else to manage it
does not affect the position of the owner as "owner-occupier". Thus in
Sparkes v *Secretary of State for Wales*[4] the fact that the husband of the owner
of a building enterprise largely managed the business (although the
wife kept the accounts as well as providing all the capital) was held to be
irrelevant. The husband was in the same position as an employee and it
was accepted on behalf of the Secretary of State that his objection that it
was the husband and not the wife who was in occupation would have
had no substance but for that relationship. The husband, however, was
an undischarged bankrupt, and it was contended that the wife's financial backing was but a device to keep him in business. As an undischarged bankrupt, however, he could not in any case have been in
business occupation on his own account, and the Lands Tribunal held
accordingly. Nor did the Tribunal pay any regard to the fact that
certain machinery on the premises (which the husband was no longer
able to use owing to an industrial accident) was operated on licence by a
wholly different firm.

Requisite Legal Interests
The second requirement in this regard relates to the necessary legal
interest which in all cases must be that of an "owner-
occupier"—i.e., a freeholder or a lessee under a lease for a term of
years certain of which not less than three years remain unexpired at
the date of the service of the blight notice[5]—or that of a mortgagee
entitled "by virtue of a power that has become exercisable" to sell an
interest in the hereditament or agricultural unit and to give immediate

---

[1] *Ministry of Transport* v *Holland* (1962), 61 LGR 134 following the decision in the rating case
of *LCC* v *Hackney Borough Council*, [1928], 2 KB 588. Although in the former case Denning LJ
thought that valuation cases should be followed in determining whether a claimant was an
occupier within what is now the Town and Country Planning Act 1971, s. 203, Pearson LJ was
prepared only to accept such cases as affording guidance.

[2] As in *Hill Patents Ltd* v *Board of Governors of University College Hospital*, [1955] 3 All ER 365,
a case under the Landlord and Tenant Act 1954.

[3] *Segal* v *Manchester Corporation* (1966), 18 P & CR 112. For an example of regular visits to
business premises constituting a sufficient degree of "physical" occupation see also *Sparkes* v
Secretary of State for Wales (1973), 27 P & CR 545.

[4] (1974) 27 P & CR 545.

[5] Town and Country Planning Act 1971, s. 203, which in the case of an owner-occupier of
residential property refers to the relevant interest as that of a "resident owner-occupier". In
Empire Motors (Swansea) Ltd v *Swansea County Council* (1972), 24 P & CR 377 the Lands Tribunal
held that a right to renew a lease having less than three years unexpired at the date of service
of the blight notice (2 years 9 months) did not constitute a qualifying interest because (a) the
right of renewal was not absolute but depended upon there being no breach of covenant; and
(b) because the effect of exercising the right would be the creation of a new lease which would
not therefore be an "extension" of the existing lease. In view of the special provisions of the
Land Compensation Act 1973, s. 12, whereby rights to an extension of a lease, or to purchase
the freehold under the Leasehold Reform Act 1967, are to be taken into account in deciding
whether a person holding a leasehold interest having at least three years unexpired is entitled
to compensation for injurious affection under Part I of the Act of 1973 (see p. 332, *post*) this
state of affairs appears somewhat anomalous.

vacant possession. However, since a mortgagee is not himself likely to have been in occupation, his qualifying interest is one in respect of which a blight notice could have been served by the then owner-occupier (or resident owner-occupier) either on the date of service of the blight notice or within six months prior to that date.[1] Furthermore, since the passing of the Land Compensation Act 1973 (on 23 May 1973) a blight notice may be served by a personal representative[2] of a person who would himself have been entitled to serve such a notice, but only, however, provided that one or more individuals (as opposed to any body corporate) are beneficially entitled to the deceased's interest. Although a corporate body may hold a qualifying interest[3] the death of a shareholder, or even of all the shareholders, does not, of course, prevent the company from serving a blight notice even though the company is controlled by the personal representatives of the deceased director(s).

Where an hereditament or agricultural unit is occupied by a partnership the rights and obligations of the claimant are those of the firm rather than of any individual partner: they are not, therefore, affected by any change in the partners subsequent to the service of the blight notice.[4]

(iii) WHAT CONSTITUTES BLIGHT

(A) Under the Town and Country Planning Act 1971

The third essential prerequisite to the service of a blight notice is that the property in question has become formally "blighted" as land falling within one or other of the categories set out in the Town and Country Planning Act 1971, s. 192(1)[1] as amended by the Land Compensation Act 1973, ss. 68–76. These categories are as follows:

    (a) *land indicated in a structure plan in force for the district in which it is situated either as land which may be required for the purposes of any functions of a government department, local authority or statutory undertakers, or of the National Coal Board, or as land which may be included in an action area.*[5]

For this purpose a structure plan includes any structure plan or proposals for the alteration of a structure plan which has been submitted to the Secretary of State,[6] and any modifications which the Secretary of State proposes to make thereto and of which he has given notice[7] but no blight notice can be served once the copies of

---

[1] Town and Country Planning Act 1971, s. 201.

[2] Land Compensation Act 1973, s. 78(1), reversing at least in part the Lands Tribunal decision in *Webb* v *Warwickshire County Council* (1971), 23 P & CR 63, in which it was held that since a "resident owner-occupier" has to be an individual it must be intended that the interest should be a strictly personal one which must therefore cease upon death, thus ruling out claims by personal representatives. The effect of extending the right to serve a blight notice to personal representatives presumably extends to trustees holding under a trust for sale created by will, provided one or more individuals are beneficially entitled to the proceeds.

[3] Town and Country Planning Act 1971, s. 204(4).

[4] *Ibid*, s. 204(1), (2) and (3).

[5] The provisions of s. 192(1) are printed in italic type.

[6] I.e., under the Town and Country Planning Act 1971, ss. 7 and 10, respectively; Land Compensation Act 1973, s. 68(1).

[7] In accordance with the Town & Country Planning (Structure & Local Plans) Regulations, 1974 (SI 1974, No. 1486), Regulation 15.

the plan or proposals for alteration or modification have been withdrawn or the Secretary of State has by advertisement notified his
decision to reject them. A blight notice already served, however, is
not invalidated by such subsequent withdrawal or rejection and this
applies even in a case where, under s. 10B of the Act of 1971,[1] a
withdrawn structure plan is to be treated as never having been submitted. Once such alterations etc., have come into force the ability to
serve a blight notice is governed by the original provisions of para.
(a) of s. 192 of the Act of 1971.[2] This paragraph does not, however,
apply where a local plan is in force which allocates any land in the
district either for the purpose of the functions mentioned or as the
site of any development for such a purpose.[3]

(b) *land allocated for the purposes of any such functions by a local plan in
force for the district or land defined in such a plan as the site of proposed
development for the purposes of any such functions.*[4]

Similarly, a local plan for this purpose includes a local plan, or
proposals for the alteration of a local plan where copies of such plan
or proposed alteration have been made available for inspection,[5] as
well as any modifications thereto of which notice has been given in
accordance with the relevant regulations.[6] Similar provisions as to
the position on withdrawal, rejection, and the coming into force of
such plans or alterations apply as in para. (a) above.[7]

However, once a local plan allocates land for the purposes of any
of the public authorities mentioned in para. (a) of s. 192(1), the
structure plan, in so far as it covers the area covered by the local
plan, is deemed to be superseded.[8] Thus, if land is indicated in the
structure plan as required for one of the public purposes mentioned
in para. (a) above, but such designation is omitted in the local plan,
no blight notice can be served in respect of the land.

---

[1] Inserted by the Town and Country Planning (Amendment) Act 1972, s. 2.

[2] Land Compensation Act 1973, s. 68(1), (4) and (5), but see para. (K) of the text, p. 138,
post, and notes thereto.

[3] Town and Country Planning Act 1971, s. 192(2): see, however, para. (b) of the text, below,
and see paras. (h), (i) and (j), pp. 137–8, *infra*.

[4] Town and Country Planning Act 1971, s. 192(1)(*b*). Land within an area designated for
redevelopment for residential purposes will not fall within this paragraph as, unless it is clearly
to be redeveloped by the local authority for council houses as opposed to private enterprise
development it is not allocated for any 'function' of a local authority to be carried out in the
exercise of its statutory powers: *Bolton Corpn* v *Owen*, [1962] 1 QB 470 overruling the Lands
Tribunal decision at (1961) 12 P & CR 97; the onus of proof is upon the claimant to show that
the land falls within the description and not upon the local authority to show the converse,
Bolton Corpn v *Owen*, *supra*, for the onus of proof generally see p. 153, *infra*. *Owen's* case was
followed in *Ellick* v *Sedgemoor District Council* (LT Ref. 243/1975), [1976] JPL 434, where the
subject land was shown in an informal town map as within an area "needing comprehensive
redevelopment". There were no detailed proposals as to which buildings might be demolished
or as to the extent to which redevelopment would be undertaken by the local authority and
private enterprise respectively. See also *Morris and Jacombs Ltd.* v *Birmingham District Council*
(1976), 31 P & CR 305 (p. 223, *post*) in which the absence of any indication that the land was
intended to be developed by any public authority would have made a blight, as opposed to a
purchase, notice inapplicable.

[5] Under the Town and Country Planning Act 1971, ss. 12(2) and 15(3) respectively.

[6] I.e., in accordance with the Town and Country Planning (Structure and Local Plans)
Regulations 1974 (SI 1974 No. 1486).

[7] Land Compensation Act 1973, s. 68(2), (4) and (5).

[8] Town and Country Planning Act 1971, s. 192(2).

Conversely, if no local plan of this nature exists and the pre-existing development plan allocates or defines land as provided under this para. in the case of a local plan, a blight notice may be served accordingly,[1] and for this purpose a development plan includes any proposals for its alteration submitted to the Secretary of State[2] or any modifications he proposes to make thereto and which have been advertised.[3]

   (c) *land indicated in a development plan*[4] *(otherwise than by being dealt with in a manner mentioned in the preceding paragraphs) as land on which a highway is proposed to be constructed or land to be included in a highway as proposed to be improved or altered;*[5]

This is a relatively wide category since the word "indicate" does not import any requirement of a resolution either as to adoption or programming of the highway or the allocation of money; a mere diagrammatic indication in a development plan is therefore sufficient.[6] Thus the fact that the construction of the highway is not proposed within the plan period is not material if the highway nevertheless forms "an integral part of the development plan".[7] Indeed, once the plan has been approved, the Lands Tribunal have consistently rejected arguments by the highway authority to the effect that the proposals are too vague or uncertain to constitute "blight"[8] and this is especially so where the claimant and/or would-be purchasers have been informed of the proposals upon inquiry of the authority.[9]

On the other hand, where there has been neither approval of the development plan by the Secretary of State nor adoption of the draft plan by resolution of the highway authority the Lands Tribunal has held that there is no sufficient 'indication' to support a blight notice.[10] Similarly, where planning permission was refused to safeguard the line of a proposed service road required in connection with town centre redevelopment proposals approved by the authority only in principle and in connection with which there was no resolution or other act by the Council which could be construed as a resolution for a highway 'to be constructed, improved or altered' or any resolution approving plans therefor, the authority's objection was upheld.[11]

---

[1] Town and Country Planning Act 1962, s. 138(1)(b), as incorporated by the transitional provisions of the Town and Country Planning Act 1971, Sch. 24, Part X, para. 58.

[2] Under Town and Country Planning Act 1971, Sch. 5, paras. 3 or 9.

[3] Land Compensation Act 1973, s. 68(3).

[4] For the definition of development plan in this context see para. (K), pp. 138 *et seq, infra*.

[5] Town and Country Planning Act 1971, s. 192(1)(c).

[6] *Bowling* v *Leeds County Borough Council* (1974), 27 P & CR 531 (Lands Tribunal).

[7] *Mercer* v *Manchester Corpn* (1964), 15 P & CR 321 (Lands Tribunal) in which the written statement stated that the proposals for the area in question had been included in the plan "to give proper guidance to prospective developers".

[8] *Williams* v *Cheadle and Gatley UDC* (1966) 17 P & CR 153.

[9] *Smith* v *Somerset County Council* (1966), 17 P & CR 162.

[10] *Link* v *Worcestershire County Council* (1965), 16 P & CR 255.

[11] *Bone* v *Staines UDC* (1964), 15 P & CR 450: it was further held that even if the proposal had been firm it could not be regarded as sufficiently definite until the Minister had approved the necessary amendments to the development plan; but note now the effect of the Land Compensation Act 1973, s. 71 (see para. (K), p. 138, *infra*). See also *Page* v *Gillingham Borough*

(d) *land on or adjacent to the line of a highway proposed to be constructed,
improved or altered, as indicated in an order or scheme which has come
into operation under the provisions of Part II of the Highways Act 1959
relating to trunk roads or special roads or as indicated in an order which
has come into operation under section 1 of the Highways Act 1971, being
land in relation to which a power of compulsory acquisition conferred by
any of the provisions of Part X of the said Act of 1959 or Part III of
the said Act of 1971 (including a power compulsorily to acquire any
right by virtue of section 47 of the said Act of 1971) may become exercisable, as being land required for purposes of construction, improvement
or alteration as indicated in the order or scheme.*[1]

As with paras. (a) and (b) above, these provisions of the Town and
Country Planning Act 1971, s. 192 have been extended by the Land
Compensation Act of 1973[2] so that the relevant "order or
scheme" includes an order or scheme submitted for confirmation to,
or prepared in draft by, the Secretary of State[3] and in respect of
which a notice has been published.[4] Again, there is the proviso that
such *extension* ceases to operate as a ground for the service of a blight
notice once the scheme has come into operation (with or without
modification) or the Secretary of State has decided not to confirm or
make the order or scheme.[5]

An even more important extension of this paragraph arises from
those sections of the Land Compensation Act 1973, which provide
for the amelioration of injurious affection of property resulting from
the use of neighbouring land for some public purpose likely to give
rise to various forms of nuisance.[6] In the case of nuisance arising
either from the construction or use of a highway, s. 22 of that Act
empowers the highway authority to acquire such land for the purpose of mitigating adverse effects on the immediate surroundings. By
virtue of s. 74, this new power conferred upon a highway authority is
to be included in the powers mentioned in para. (d) above, and a
blight notice may be served in relation to the land concerned if it is
shown either on plans approved by a resolution of a local highway
authority as land proposed to be acquired by it for these purposes[7] or
in a written notice given by the Secretary of State to the local planning authority as land proposed to be acquired by him for such
purposes in connection with a proposed trunk or special road.

It should, however, be noted that the powers conferred upon a

---

Council (1970), 21 P & CR 973, in which a draft plan, still in the 'consultation' stage was
regarded as too fluid to constitute blight: see now, however, paras. (a) and (b), pp. 133 and
134, *supra*.
[1] Town and Country Planning Act 1971, s. 192(1)(*d*).
[2] S. 69(1).
[3] Under Part II, Highways Act 1959 or submitted for confirmation under the Highways Act
1971, s. 1, and notified in accordance with the Highways Act 1959, Sch. 1, para. 2.
[4] Under *ibid*, Sch. 1, paras. 1, 2 or 7.
[5] Land Compensation Act 1973, s. 69(1)(a).
[6] *Ibid*, Part II. For these provisions see note 1, p. 341, *post*.
[7] I.e., the purposes of *ibid*, s. 22.

local highway authority by s. 22 of the Act of 1973 to acquire compulsorily are exercisable only with the approval of the Secretary of
State. Nevertheless, it is not for the owner of the land concerned to
question whether the local highway authority has secured that
approval before serving a blight notice, and it seems that if the blight
notice is "accepted"[1] the appropriate authority may acquire even
though the Secretary of State's approval has not been obtained, for
in such circumstances it is deemed to be authorised to acquire compulsorily under any enactment by which a highway authority *could*
by so authorised.[2]

(e) *land shown on plans approved by a resolution of a local highway
authority*[3] *as land comprised in the site of a highway as proposed to be
constructed, improved or altered by that authority;*[4]

(f) *land on which the Secretary of State proposes to provide a trunk road or
a special road and has given to the local planning authority written
notice of his intention to provide the road, together with maps or plans
sufficient to identify the proposed route of the road;*[5]

(g) *land in the case of which*—(i) *there is in force a compulsory purchase
order providing for the acquisition of a right or rights over that land;*[6]
and

(ii) the appropriate authority *have power to serve but have not
served, notice to treat in respect of a right or rights.*[6]

This paragraph now[7] includes land in respect of which a compulsory purchase order has been submitted for confirmation to, or
prepared in draft by, a Minister and in respect of which the appropriate notice[8] has been published but on which, at the date on which
it is proposed to serve a blight notice, no decision has been reached;
thereafter a blight notice can, of course, only be served if the order is
confirmed, in which case it is to be served by virtue of the provisions
of para. g(i) above, as opposed to the extending provisions of the
Land Compensation Act 1973.[9]

(h) *land indicated by information published in pursuance of section 31 of the
Housing Act 1969 as land which a local authority propose to acquire in the*

[1] I.e., becomes operative; see pp. 144 *et seq, infra.*
[2] Town and Country Planning Act 1971, s. 206(3).
[3] Land shown on a plan recommended by resolution of a joint planning committee is not within
s. 192(e) above since such a committee is not a local highway authority: *Oxley* v *Keighley Corporation*
(1960), 11 P & CR 465. A resolution by a planning committee of a local planning authority having
delegated powers would now, however, bring such land within the prescribed categories: see para.
(K), p. 138, *infra.* There must, however, be a resolution of formal approval and not merely
approval "in principle": *Fogg* v *Birkenhead County Borough Council* (1971), 22 P & CR 208.
[4] Town and Country Planning Act 1971, s. 192(1)(e)
[5] *Ibid,* s. 192(1)(f).
[6] *Ibid,* s. 192(1)(g). The words not in italics were substituted for the original wording (which
confined this paragraph to land affected by compulsory purchase orders made by highway
authorities) by the Land Compensation Act 1973, s. 75.
[7] Land Compensation Act 1973, s. 70.
[8] I.e., under the Acquisition of Land (Authorisation Procedure) Act 1949, Sch. 1, para.
3(1)(a), or any other corresponding statutory provisions applicable to the compulsory purchase
order in question: Land Compensation Act 1973, s. 70(1).
[9] S. 70(2), and see the next paragraph in the text and the note thereto.

> *exercise of their powers under Part II of that Act (general improvement areas);*[1]

(i) *land authorised by a special enactment to be compulsorily acquired, or land falling within the limits of deviation within which powers of compulsory acquisition conferred by a special enactment are exercisable;*[2]

(j) *land in respect of which a compulsory purchase order is in force, where the appropriate authority have power to serve, but have not served, notice to treat in respect of the land.*[3]

By virtue of the Land Compensation Act 1973, s. 70, these paragraphs are extended in precisely the same manner as in para. (g) above.[4]

(B) Blight under the Land Compensation Act 1973

In addition to extending the effect of paras. (a), (b), (d), (g) and (j) of s. 192(1) of the Town and Country Planning Act 1971, the Land Compensation Act 1973 adds four further categories of land by providing that they be included in the categories there specified. Although it does not do so by adding further paragraphs to s. 192(1), it will nevertheless be convenient to indicate these new categories by adding further sub-paragraphs to this section of this chapter, but to distinguish them from paragraphs taken direct from s. 192(1) by using capital reference letters.[5] These additional categories are:

(K) *land affected by resolution of planning authority or by directions of the Secretary of State,*[6] viz:

(a) *land indicated in a plan (not being a development plan) approved by a resolution passed by a local planning authority for the purpose of the exercise of their powers under Part III of that Act*[7] *as land which may be required for the purposes of any functions of a government department, local authority or statutory undertakers;*[8] *or*

(b) *land in respect of which a local planning authority have resolved to take action to safeguard it for development for the purposes of any such functions or been directed by the Secretary of State to restrict the grant of planning permission in order to safeguard it for such development.*[9]

Because the Land Compensation Act 1973, s. 71(2), specifically states that para. (a) of s. 192(1) of the Act of 1971[10] is *not* to apply to

---

[1] Town and Country Planning Act 1971, s. 192(1)(*h*). Where a local authority declares an area to be a general improvement area under the Housing Act 1969, s. 28 (Part II), it is obliged to notify owners and occupiers of property therein of the action it proposes to take to effect the requisite improvement: s. 31. In so far as it proposes to exercise its powers of acquisition (whether by agreement or by means of a compulsory purchase order) conferred by *ibid*, s. 32, a blight notice may be founded upon para. (h) above. Note, however, that general improvement areas must be predominantly residential: s. 28; and that they and clearance areas are mutually exclusive: s. 29.

[2] Town and Country Planning Act 1971, s. 192(1)(*i*).

[3] *Ibid*, s. 192(1)(*j*).

[4] Note the distinction between paragraph (j), above, which applies to the acquisition of an *interest* in land and para. (g) above, which applies to the acquisition of a *right* in or over land, e.g., an easement, right of common, etc.

[5] The relevant paragraphs taken directly from the Land Compensation Act 1973 are printed in italic type.

[6] Land Compensation Act 1973, s. 71.

[7] I.e., Town and Country Planning Act 1971.

[8] Land Compensation Act 1973, s. 71(1)(*a*): cf. *Comley and Comley* v *Kent County Council*, [1977] JPL 666 (Town map not part of development plan).

[9] *Ibid*, s. 71(1)(*b*).

[10] P. 133, *supra*.

land within para. (K)(a), above, it becomes important to distinguish these two paragraphs. The distinction lies in the definition of "development plan" which, for any district outside Greater London, comprises any approved plan and the relevant structure and local plans for the time being in force, together with any alterations thereto approved by the Secretary of State or adopted by resolution of the local planning authority as the case may be.[1] In Greater London the development plan comprises the Greater London Development Plan together with the relevant structure and local plans and alterations thereto similarly approved or adopted.[2] Pending the repeal of Schedule 5 to the Act of 1971 and pending the introduction of structure and local plans in those areas in respect of which Part II of the Act of 1968 has been brought into force by Order,[3] references to a development plan are references to the development plan prepared under the pre-1968 legislation, subject to such amendments as may have been approved either before or after the passing of the Act of 1968.[4]

(L) *Land affected by orders relating to New Towns*[5]
viz:

(a) *land within an area described as the site of a proposed new town in the draft of an order in respect of which a notice has been published under paragraph 2 of Schedule 1 to the New Towns Act 1965;*[6] or

(b) *land within an area designated as the site of a proposed new town by an order which has come into operation under section 1 of the said Act of 1965.*[7]

These provisions are in substitution for, and considerable extension of, those of the New Towns Act 1965 s. 11, under which an owner could require a development corporation to acquire land within an area designated as the site of a new town only after the expiration of seven years from the date of designation. Since these new provisions enable a blight notice to be served even before formal designation, the situation could arise in which no development corporation on whom to serve it has been appointed; in that event the Secretary of State is the appropriate authority and has the requisite

---

[1] Town and Country Planning Act 1971, s. 20(1).

[2] *Ibid*, s. 20(2).

[3] Town and Country Planning Act 1968, Part II (the provisions of which are incorporated in Part II of the Act of 1971 and amended by the Town and Country Planning (Amendment) Act 1972, ss. 1–4) introduced the concept of structure and local plans: these provisions are being applied to different parts of the country by a series of orders. Up to November 1977 Orders made affect only Greater London and parts of the counties of Cleveland, Gwynedd, Hampshire, Hereford and Worcester, Leicestershire, West Midlands and Warwickshire (House of Commons Official Report 14th and 16th November 1977). The effect of such orders is to repeal the interim provisions of the Town and Country Planning Act 1971, Schs. 5 and 6 in respect of the areas covered by the orders. Meanwhile Sch. 5 keeps alive the older form of development plan and the arrangements for its periodic amendment, and Sch. 6 applies the requisite interim modifications to the provisions of the Act dealing with development plans.

[4] The Town and Country Planning Act 1971, Sch. 7, para. 1, provides that pending the repeal of Sch. 5, proposals for alterations of or additions to the older form of development plan are not to be submitted to the Secretary of State without his prior approval.

[5] Land Compensation Act 1973, s. 72.

[6] *Ibid*, s. 72(1)(a).

[7] *Ibid*, s. 72(1)(b).

powers of acquisition.[1] Once the Secretary of State has decided whether or not to confirm the draft order of paragraph (a) above, a blight notice can only be served if the land in question is in fact within a designated area and in accordance with paragraph (b).[2]

(M) *Land affected by a slum clearance resolution*[3]
viz:
(a) *land within an area declared to be a clearance area by a resolution under section 42 of the Housing Act 1957;*[4] *or*
(b) *land surrounded by or adjoining an area declared as aforesaid to be a clearance area, being land which a local authority have determined to purchase under section 43 of that Act.*[5]

Where a local authority declare a clearance area they must either ensure that clearance is effected by the owners by making clearance orders[6] or by purchasing[7] the land (and thereafter effecting clearance themselves) by making compulsory purchase orders. Since both types of order require the confirmation of the Secretary of State, these provisions follow the general principles of these extensions effected by the Land Compensation Act 1973, by recognising the blighting effects of the earlier stages of the procedures leading up to the final designation of the land as subject to compulsory acquisition. In this case, however, the Land Compensation Act 1973, s. 73, unlike the other sections of that Act which extend the effect of the Town and Country Planning Act 1971, s. 192(1), contains *no* express prohibition against the service of a blight notice after the Secretary of State has decided not to confirm the orders or to confirm subject to the exclusion of the property concerned. Should such a decision be made by the Secretary of State it would seem that a blight notice can still be served, presumably because the passing of the resolution itself confers upon the local authority power to purchase by agreement, and can be taken as evidence of their willingness to do so; hence, presumably, the original provision,[8] since repealed,[9] preventing them from objecting to a blight notice[10] on the ground that they do not, after all, propose to acquire the land either in whole or in part.

(N) *Land affected by new street orders,*[1] *viz land which is*
(a) *either——*

---

[1] Land Compensation Act 1973, s. 72(3).   [2] *Ibid*, s. 72(2).
[3] *Ibid*, s. 73.
[4] *Ibid*, s. 73(1)(a). The listing of property for consideration of slum clearance is not sufficient to support a blight notice: *Boderick* v *Erewash Borough Council*, [1977] JPL 666.
[5] *Ibid*, s. 73(1)(b).
[6] The Housing Act 1969, s. 108, provides for the abolition of clearance orders, but that section is not, as yet, in force: see pp. 259 *et seq, post*.
[7] The local authority may also purchase, or be authorised to purchase compulsorily, land surrounded by a clearance area in order to provide a cleared area of convenient shape and size and also adjoining land the acquisition of which is reasonably necessary for the satisfactory development or use of the cleared area: Housing Act 1957, s. 43(2). For compensation in respect of houses declared unfit for human habitation see p. 258 *post*.
[8] Land Compensation Act 1973, s. 73(2).
[9] By the Housing Act 1974, s. 130 and Sch. 15.
[10] For grounds on which the appropriate authority may object to a blight notice see "Notices of Objection", pp. 145 *et seq, post*.
[11] Land Compensation Act 1973, s. 76.

(i) *within the outer lines prescribed by an order under section 159 of the Highways Act 1959 (orders prescribing minimum width of new streets); or*
(ii) *has a frontage to a highway declared to be a new street by an order under section 30 of the Public Health Act 1925 and lies within the minimum width of the street prescribed by any bye-laws or local Act applicable by virtue of the Order:*[1]

(b) *or is part of—*
(i) *a dwelling erected before, or under construction on, the date on which the order is made; or*
(ii) *the curtilage of any such dwelling.*[2]

The purpose of a new street order is to ensure that future development along the frontage of the new street shall not encroach upon the land required for the ultimate widening or extension of an existing highway. Although it has no immediate effect upon the curtilages of existing buildings, the implication, of course, is that ultimately the highway will be widened or constructed throughout its length to the full prescribed width and this, of course, may well have a blighting effect upon properties which were in existence or under construction when the order was made. Despite the fact that the Highways Act 1959 was a consolidation Act in which the provisions of section 159 superseded those of the Public Health Act 1925, s. 30, there are still in force many new street orders made under the latter provisions (which differ significantly from those of the 1959 Act); hence the inclusion of both enactments in this paragraph. It is to be noted, however, that it applies only to dwelling-houses and their curtilages. There is no blighting effect in the case of houses built after the making of the order because, as soon as such development takes place, such land as fronts the existing highway but lies within the prescribed width of the new street immediately becomes part of the highway (without compensation) under the 1959 Act.[3] Under the 1925 Act the owner is deemed to be laying out a new street along that frontage though he may remain in ownership of the land concerned until such time as it is required by the highway authority.[4] The eventual decision of the highway authority to widen, etc., may be made many years after the making of the new street order so that its blighting effect on pre-existing property may be of long and wholly indefinite duration.

Because of these very long periods between the making of a new street order and the responsible highway authority's[5] need to acquire, it may well not wish to retain a freehold or leasehold interest which it has been forced to acquire under these provisions until such time as it decides to widen the road. It is presumably to protect the authority from further blight notices served by a purchaser from

---

[1] *Ibid*, s. 76(1)(*a*).
[2] *Ibid*, s. 76(1)(*b*).
[3] Highways Act 1959, s. 159(6).
[4] Public Health Act 1925, s. 30(4).
[5] The highway authority for the road in question is the "appropriate authority" in these cases: Land Compensation Act 1973, s. 76(3).

it, or his assigns, that the Act provides[1] that no blight notice can be served under these provisions in respect of any land in which the appropriate authority has already acquired "an interest" (i.e., *any* interest) in pursuance of a blight notice or by agreement in circumstances in which it could have been forced to acquire in response to such a notice. The wording of this limitation is, however, such that it equally prevents service of a blight notice by a freeholder or superior lessee who goes into occupation (and thereby acquires what would otherwise be a qualifying interest) on the termination of a lease or sub-lease acquired in these circumstances by a highway authority. This seems unfair and was probably not intended, for in the case of land falling within any of the other categories of this paragraph there is nothing to prevent service of successive blight notices in these circumstances even though it is likely to be relatively uncommon for a qualifying leasehold interest acquired by an appropriate authority to expire before the land is actually required.

(C) Blight under the Community Land Act 1975
A further ground on which a blight notice may be served arises where planning permission is suspended under the relevant provisions[2] of the Community Land Act 1975.[3] Under that Act planning permission for relevant development[4] granted in pursuance of an application made after 6th April 1976 is automatically suspended, but if granted before the relevant date[5] it may revive in favour of the applicant if no authority wishes to exercise its powers of compulsory acquisition.[6] Planning permission granted after the relevant date normally only revives after acquisition by such an authority.[7]

(iv) INABILITY TO SELL

The final prerequisite to the service of a blight notice is that the claimant must have made reasonable endeavours to sell[8] his interest but has been unable to do so except at a price substantially lower than he might reasonably have expected to obtain were it not for the fact that the property concerned, whether in whole or in part was, or was likely to be, comprised in one or other of the categories of land mentioned in para. (iii) above.

Prior to the passing of the Land Compensation Act 1973 (23 May

[1] Land Compensation Act 1973, s. 76(4).
[2] Community Land Act. ss. 19–22. For details of these provisions see pp. 300, *et seq, post*.
[3] Community Land Act 1975, s. 22(6).
[4] For definition see p. 296, *post*.
[5] For definition see pp. 297, *et seq, post*.
[6] By virtue of Community Land Act 1975, s. 15, authorities under the Act (see note 4 on p. 296, *post*) have power compulsorily to acquire any "development land" (for definition see p. 296, *post*): following the relevant date they will have a duty to acquire all land required for relevant development within the ensuing ten years. See pp. 296, *et seq, post*.
[7] See pp. 304 *et seq, post*.
[8] The payment of a premium to an assignee of a lease, depreciated in value by, for example, a proposed road improvement scheme, is almost certainly not a sale for this purpose: see *Bowling* v *Leeds County Borough Council*; *E and H Kitchin* v *Leeds County Borough Council*, *Hicks* v *Leeds County Borough Council* (1974), 27 P & CR 531. In those cases, however, the parties having agreed to accept such transactions as conforming with this requirement, the blight notices were upheld.

_1973) this attempt to sell had to be made since the "relevant date",[1] i.e., the date on which the land became formally blighted by the coming into force of the various provisions of paragraphs (a) to (j) of section 192(1) of the Act of 1971[2] by which the land was brought into one or other of the relevant categories. This, however, is no longer necessary.[3]

Thus, if, for example, a claimant has already put his property on the market and accepted an offer subject to contract and that offer is subsequently withdrawn or reduced as a result of the purchaser discovering that some public body is considering proposals that would affect the property, the vendor need not again go through the motions of endeavouring to obtain the full market price if these proposals are later adopted in a manner that has the effect of bringing the land into one of the categories of para. (iii) above.

Two problems, however, arise in this regard, viz, what constitutes a reasonable endeavour to sell and what will be regarded as a substantially lower price[4] than that which could reasonably have been expected but for the effect of blight? These two matters are, of course, inter-related, since the 'reasonableness' of attempts to sell will depend upon the reasonableness of the price demanded. In this connection the Lands Tribunal has held that the receipt of only two offers approximating to the asking price, which were subsequently withdrawn, may just as well indicate the effect of blight as the possibility that the asking price was too high.[5] The Tribunal will also take account of the amount of any mortgage.[6] It has also held that provided a substantial loss in value can be attributed to the authority's proposals they need not be the sole cause of diminution therein.[7] Normally the claimant will be expected to have adequately advertised the property and employed estate agents but this will depend upon the nature of the property. Thus owners of a shop in a poor trading area were held to have made reasonable endeavours to sell by placing a notice in the shop window and notifying persons in the same trade who visited the shop, the Lands Tribunal recognising that in the circumstances of the case the cost of further advertisement or the employment of agents would not have been justified.[8] Similarly, where the vendor's agent made direct approaches to a large number of firms but did not advertise, that has been held to amount to a reasonable endeavour to sell.[9] On the other hand, this requirement will not be fulfilled merely by relying upon professional advice to the effect that a purchaser at a reasonable price is unlikely to be found.[10]

---

[1] More particularly defined in the Town and Country Planning Act 1971 s. 193(3).
[2] Para. (iii)A, pp. 133 *et seq, supra*.   [3] Land Compensation Act 1973, s. 77.
[4] *Stubbs* v *West Hartlepool Corpn* (1961), 12 P & CR 365.
[5] As to what constitutes a substantial reduction in price, see e.g., *Preece and Preece* v *Worcester City Corpn* (1967), 18 P & CR 103, in which a reduction of $16\frac{2}{3}$% was held to be "substantial".
[6] *Stubbs* v *West Hartlepool Corpn, supra*: the mortgage constituted no less than 88% of the asking price.
[7] *Bowling* v *Leeds County Borough Council* (1974), 27 P & CR 531.
[8] *Lade and Lade* v *Brighton Corpn* (1971), 22 P & CR 737.
[9] *Louisville Investments Ltd.* v *Basingstoke District Council* (1976), 31 P & CR 419.
[10] *Perkins* v *West Wiltshire District Council* (1976), 31 P & CR 427.

As to what is a substantially lower price, some assistance may perhaps be derived from *Palser* v *Grinling*[1] in which the meaning of "a substantial portion" for the purposes of the Rent Acts was in issue. Viscount Simon thought that the phrase "requires a comparison with the whole rent" and that "substantial", in this connection, is not the same as "not insubstantial", i.e., just enough to avoid the *de minimis* principle. One of the primary meanings of the word is "considerable, solid or big ..."[2]

3 Procedure

(i) ACCEPTANCE OF BLIGHT NOTICES

When a blight notice is served,[3] the authority[4] on whom it is served may, within two months from the date of service, serve upon the claimant a notice of objection. If it does not do so it is deemed to be authorised to acquire and to have served a notice to treat at the expiration of that period.[5] In contrast to the provisions governing the service of purchase notices[6] there are no other provisions for formal "acceptance" of the notice.

However, whereas the authority is thus deemed to be authorised to acquire the whole of the claimant's interest in any hereditament, it can only be authorised to acquire his interest in the affected area[7] of an agricultural unit—i.e., in such parts of the unit as actually fall within one or other of the categories of para. (iii), above,[8] unless (in the case of a blight notice served after 23 May 1973[9]) the claimant includes in his blight notice a claim that what will be left to him if the affected area is acquired will be incapable of being farmed either as it stands or in conjunction with other land in which he has an "owner's interest".[10] In such a case he must also include in the blight notice a claim that the appropriate authority shall purchase his entire interest whether it be in the whole or only part of the unit.[11]

It is to be noted that these latter provisions of the Land Compensation Act 1973 s. 79, are in substitution of those of s. 53 of the same Act[12] which do not apply when the notice to treat is deemed to be served

---

[1] [1948] AC 291: in *Stubbs* v *West Hartlepool Corpn* (*supra*) for example, £750 was held to be substantially lower than £850, i.e., approaching 12 %.

[2] [1948] AC 291 at pp. 316–317.

[3] For the appropriate prescribed forms of blight notice see the Town and Country Planning (General) Regulations 1976 (SI 1976 No. 1419) Reg. 18 and Sch. 1.

[4] As to the "appropriate authority" on whom the notice should be served, see p. 154, *infra*.

[5] Town and Country Planning Act 1971, s. 196(1) and (2)(b). Acceptance does not, however, prevent a reference to the Lands Tribunal to value the property so long as the price has not been unconditionally agreed: *Margery* v *Brighton Corpn* (1962), 13 P & CR 438, in which the authority unsuccessfully argued that agreement of price subject to the solicitors agreeing the contract precluded reference to the Lands Tribunal.

[6] Pp. 121, *et seq*, *supra*.

[7] Town and Country Planning Act 1971, ss. 196(1) and 207(1).

[8] Pp. 133, *et seq*, *supra*.

[9] Land Compensation Act 1973 s. 79.

[10] Town & Country Planning Act 1971, s. 203(4), p. 132, *supra*.

[11] See Town and Country Planning (General) Regulations, *supra*,, Sch. 1, para. 5.

[12] Pp. 111 *et seq*, *supra*.

in response to a blight notice;[1] nor apparently do those of the Lands Clauses Consolidation Act, 1845, s. 93.[2]

(ii) COUNTER-NOTICES OF OBJECTION

If, on the other hand, the appropriate authority does not wish to accept the blight notice it must serve a counter-notice stating its grounds of objection (hereinafter alternatively referred to as an objection notice) which must be one or more of those set out in the Town and Country Planning Act 1971, s. 194(2) as amended by the Land Compensation Act 1973.[3] The claimant may then, within a further period of two months from the date of the counter-notice, require the objection to be referred to the Lands Tribunal.[4]

Since the courses open to the Lands Tribunal are to some extent dependent upon the grounds of objection set out in the counter-notice, it will be convenient, in considering the grounds upon which an objection may be based to note at the same time any restrictions etc., upon the Lands Tribunal that objection on any particular ground may impose. The grounds of objection are:[5]

(a) *that no part of the hereditament or agricultural unit to which the blight notice relates is comprised in land of any of the specified descriptions.*[6]

Note that although in the case of some of the extensions to the categories of blight of the Town and Country Planning Act 1971, s. 192(1), effected by the Land Compensation Act 1973,[7] the latter Act specifically forbids the service of a blight notice under these extensions once the proposals concerned have become finalised,[8] it is not enough for the appropriate authority to object only on the ground that the land does not fall within the specific category mentioned in the blight notice. They must claim that it does not fall within *any* of the categories of s. 192(1) of the Act of 1971 as amended by the Act of 1973.

(b) *that the appropriate authority (unless compelled to do so by virtue of*

---

[1] Land Compensation Act 1973, s. 53(5).

[2] Town and Country Planning Act 1971, s. 202(1) which specifically preserves a claimant's rights under Lands Clauses Consolidation Act 1845, s. 92, but only where an objection to the purchase of the whole is upheld (see the next subsection of this chapter). By implication (and logic) the provisions of s. 93 are therefore not available: see p. 110, *supra*.

[3] An authority which fails to serve a counter-notice cannot thereafter object on the ground that the blight notice is invalid—or indeed on any other ground: *Church of Scotland Trustees* v *Helensburgh Council* (1972), 25 P & CR 105. Nor can further grounds of objection be added once the matter is before the Lands Tribunal nor, by implication, after the expiry of the two months' period: *Essex County Council* v *Essex Incorporated Congregational Church Unit*, [1963] AC 808: [1963] 1 All ER 326: in short, an acquiring authority cannot change its ground: see *Lockers Estates Ltd.* v *Oadby UDC* (1970), 21 P & CR 448.

[4] Town and Country Planning Act 1971, s. 195(1).

[5] The relevant paragraphs of *ibid*, s. 194(2) are printed in italic type. Paragraphs summarising the effect of amendments resulting from the Land Compensation Act 1973, are shown with capital letters.

[6] Town and Country Planning Act 1971, s. 194(2)(a). I.e., is land within any of the categories of para. (iii), of section 4 of this chapter, pp. 133 *et seq*, *supra*. See, for example, *Bolton Corpn* v *Owen*, [1962] 1 QB 470, note 4, p. 134, *supra*.

[7] Pp. 133 *et seq*, *supra*.

[8] See Land Compensation Act 1973, ss. 68(4) & (5); 69(2); 70(2) and 72(2): Note also s. 71(2) which forbids the service of a blight notice under category (a) if the land also falls within category (K): see pp. 133 and 138 respectively, *supra*.

these provisions[1]*) do not propose to acquire* or to acquire any rights over *any part of the hereditament or (in the case of an agricultural unit) any part of the affected area, in the exercise of any relevant powers.*[2]

Where an objection on this ground is upheld by the Lands Tribunal or has not been referred to it within two months of the service of the objection notice and a compulsory purchase order has been made in respect of any of the land in question or if, in the case of land falling within category (i),[3] the special Act confers powers for the compulsory acquisition of the claimant's interest, the powers so conferred by either the compulsory purchase order or the special Act cease to have effect in relation to that interest.[4] In other words, the appropriate authority cannot have it both ways by avoiding the blight notice on the ground that it does not propose to acquire while maintaining the power to do so compulsorily. It is not, however, prevented from making another compulsory purchase order covering the claimant's interest at some future date in which case the claimant also preserves a right to serve a further blight notice.

In *Perkins* v *West Wiltshire District Council*[5] planning permission for residential development had been refused as contrary to the approved town map and draft review (on which the local planning authority based its planning decisions) in both of which the subject land was shown as public open space. The Lands Tribunal dismissed the local authority's objection under this paragraph on the ground that the designation clearly implied ultimate public ownership.[6]

In the *Louisville Investments*[7] case a compulsory purchase order[8] had

---

[1] I.e., by a decision of the Lands Tribunal. In *The Duke of Wellington Social Club* v *Blyth Borough Council* (1964), 15 P & CR 212, the Lands Tribunal refused to uphold an objection based on these provisions because it was held to be unreasonable to refuse planning permission in May 1962 on the grounds that the land was designated as subject to compulsory acquisition in pursuit of dock development, then in May 1963 to object to the purchase notice because the local authority (which was not the local planning authority responsible for the designation of the land) no longer wished to acquire but relied upon "the stranglehold of the Docks Company to preserve the land for the planning purposes". In *Rawson* v *Minister of Health* (1965), 17 P & CR 239, in which the Lands Tribunal accepted the statement of the Minister that he did not intend to acquire land allocated for a hospital extension in the Manchester Development Plan, it was explained that although normally the issue is simply the accuracy of the relevant authority's statement of intention, this would not be so if the result would "nullify the intention of the Act to give protection to certain specified interests affected by what is conveniently termed 'planning blight'": in such cases the question of reasonableness and hardship, as in *The Duke of Wellington Social Club* case, *supra*, therefore falls to be applied. In *Rawson*'s case, however, the claimant knew of the designation when he purchased the property and was accordingly assumed to have paid a price reflecting the "blight".

[2] The words not in italics are to be inserted where the appropriate enactment confers powers to acquire *rights* over land: Town and Country Planning Act 1971, s. 194(4), as amended by the Land Compensation Act 1973, s. 75(3)(a).

[3] Page 138, *supra*.

[4] Town and Country Planning Act 1971, s. 199(2).

[5] (1976) 31 P & CR 427.

[6] Indeed there was an admission to this effect by the authority's planning witness.

[7] *Louisville Investments Ltd.* v *Basingstoke District Council, Planned Properties Ltd.* v *Basingstoke District Council* (1976), 31 P & CR 419.

[8] I.e., the blight notice was served in pursuance of the Town and Country Planning Act 1971, s. 192(1)(j), as extended by the Land Compensation Act 1973, s. 70: para. (iii) A (j), p. 138, *supra*.

been made in 1972 in respect of some 34½ acres required as part of a local authority industrial estate. Planning permission for industrial development had been refused on the grounds that the authority itself intended to develop the land and, subsequent to the making of the compulsory purchase order, agreement had been reached as to price. Since the sale could not proceed for lack of funds, and the owners' further offer to develop the land themselves was again refused they served a blight notice. The authority (on the advice of Counsel) then withdrew the compulsory purchase order: it also withdrew its own application for planning permission to develop the land and contended that the blight had been removed. It stated, moreover, that there was adequate undeveloped industrial land in the area, that it regarded the claimants' land as a useful long-term reserve, and would continue to oppose the grant of planning permission for development by private enterprise. The Lands Tribunal, however, regarded the withdrawal of the compulsory purchase order as a matter of expediency rather than a change of policy, and confirmed the blight notice. It also expressed the view that in determining the validity of a counter-notice the circumstances to be considered were those ruling at the date on which the counter-notice was served.[1]

A blight notice was also confirmed in somewhat similar circumstances in *McKinnon Campbell* v *Greater Manchester Council*.[2] In that case the claimant had found two successive potential purchasers for her house, both of whom withdrew on learning that as soon as money was available, the Council intended to embark upon a road widening scheme which would involve the demolition of the house. An official certificate of search issued subsequently (in February 1975) stated that there were no existing or known road proposals that would affect the house prior to 1984, and little probability of any thereafter. The claimant nevertheless served a blight notice on the Council, who objected on the grounds of this paragraph, it being shown that the original road proposals had first been modified in 1967 by resolution of the Local Planning Committee, so as not to affect the house, but an improvement line affecting the house remained until 1969. A further plan compiled in 1971, however, showed neither road widening proposals nor any improvement line that affected the property. There was, however, no evidence to suggest that these latter plans had been approved by any resolution until 1976. The blight notice was upheld on the ground that the property remained blighted by the improvement line up to 1976 (i.e., long after the service of the counter-notice of objection) for it was only possible to regard the 1971 plan as an officer's working plan.

Neither this nor the next following ground of objection is available in response to a blight notice served in respect either of land affected by a slum clearance resolution or of land affected by new street orders.[3]

---

[1] See the "relevant date", p. 153, *infra*.
[2] (Lands Tribunal Ref. 149/1975) [1976] JPL 700.
[3] Paragraphs (iii) *B* (M) and (N) of the previous section of this chapter, pp. 140–141 *supra*.

(c) *that the appropriate authority propose in the exercise of relevant powers to acquire a part of the hereditament or (in the case of an agricultural unit) a part of the affected area specified in the counter-notice, but (unless compelled to do so by these provisions)* propose neither to acquire nor to acquire any right over[1] *any other part of that hereditament or area in the exercise of any such powers.*

Where such an objection is relied upon in respect of part of a garden it is, however, open to the claimant to counter that the part required cannot be taken without seriously affecting the amenity or convenience of the house.[2] In such cases the onus is probably upon the authority to satisfy the Tribunal that the claimant's contention is unfounded.[3]

The same principles no doubt apply where part of a "house or other building or manufactory"[4] is to be taken or where the claimant would be left with small isolated pockets of agricultural land.[5]

[(C)[6] In the case of a blight notice claiming that the appropriate authority should acquire the whole of an agricultural unit on the grounds that acquisition of the affected area will leave the claimant with an uneconomic holding[7] the authority may object to the blight notice on the ground that this latter claim is not justified. If it objects on ground (c) above then it is obliged also to object on ground (C).]

If such a "double" objection is made the Lands Tribunal, in determining whether or not to uphold the objection, is required to treat any part of the affected area which the appropriate authority states that it does not propose to acquire as available to the claimant for the purpose of assessing whether the land he retains is reasonably capable of being farmed.[8] If it upholds the objection on both these grounds (but on no other) it must declare the blight notice valid but only in respect of that part of the affected area which the authority proposes to acquire.[9] The same requirement applies to any other case in which an objection is upheld, but only on ground of objection (c).[10] If, however, in the case of a blight notice claiming the acquisition of the whole of an agricultural unit, the Lands Tribunal upholds an objection only on ground (C), it must declare the blight notice valid, but only in respect of the affected area.[11]

---

[1] Town and Country Planning Act 1971, s. 194(2)(c). Where the appropriate enactment confers no powers to acquire *rights* over land the words "do not propose to acquire" should be substituted for the words not in italics: Town and Country Planning Act 1971, s. 194(4).

[2] *Hurley* v *Cheshire County Council* (1976), 31 P & CR 433.

[3] Note 2, p. 153, *infra*.

[4] See pp. 108 *et seq*, *supra*.

[5] See pp. 110 *supra*.

[6] This ground of objection was added by the Land Compensation Act 1973, s. 80, as a corollary to s. 79: p. 144, *supra*.

[7] P. 144, *supra*.

[8] Land Compensation Act 1973, s. 80(3).

[9] *Ibid*, s. 80(5).

[10] Town & Country Planning Act 1971, s. 195(5).

[11] Land Compensation Act, 1973, s. 80(4).

In all these cases it is for the Lands Tribunal to give directions as to the date on which the notice to treat is deemed to have been served.[1]

Where the appropriate authority objects to a blight notice served in respect of the whole of an agricultural unit and accompanied by the appropriate claim as to non-viability of the land remaining to the claimant, only on ground (C) above, it is open to the claimant to accept the position by withdrawing his claim in regard to the unaffected area and giving notice to that effect to the appropriate authority before the time for referring the matter to the Lands Tribunal has expired, whereupon the authority is deemed to be authorised to acquire the claimant's interest in so far as it subsists in the affected area only and to have served a notice to treat on the date on which the claimant notified the authority of the withdrawal of his claim in respect of the unaffected area.[2]

A similar situation arises where the Lands Tribunal upholds the objection *only* on ground (C), subject to the date of the deemed notice to treat being a matter for the Lands Tribunal.[2]

Parallel provisions govern the situation in which objection is made on both grounds (C) and (c), but only on those grounds, in which case a withdrawal by the claimant of his claim in regard to any part of the unit which the appropriate authority does not propose to acquire—or a decision of the Lands Tribunal upholding the objection notice on both counts—has the effect of a deemed authorisation to acquire (with a notice to treat deemed to be served by reference to the date of the claimant's withdrawal or the directions of the Lands Tribunal, as the case may be) in respect of the claimant's interest in so far as it subsists in the part of the unit specified in the objection notice but not otherwise.[3]

As in the case where an objection on ground (b) is either upheld by the Lands Tribunal or is 'accepted' by the claimant (i.e., by failing to refer the matter to the Lands Tribunal within the two-month period) any compulsory purchase order already made or, in the case of land falling within category (i), any compulsory powers derived from the relevant order or special Act cease to have effect in regard to any part of the hereditament or affected area not required.[4]

In such cases, however, the claimant's rights under the Lands Clauses Consolidation Act 1845, s. 92, or under the Compulsory Purchase Act 1965, s. 8, to require the appropriate authority to acquire the whole hereditament or the whole of the affected area of an agricultural unit[5] are specifically preserved.[6]

Accordingly, in the case of the acquisition of part only of a

---

[1] Land Compensation Act, 1973, s. 80(6).
[2] *Ibid*, s. 81(1), (2) and (3).
[3] *Ibid*, s. 81(4) and (5).
[4] Town and Country Planning Act 1971, s. 199(3) and (4).
[5] See note 5, p. 108, *supra*.
[6] Town and Country Planning Act 1971, s. 202. Note, however, that in the case of an agricultural unit this right is restricted to the *affected area*. As to a claim that the whole of the remainder of the *unit* should be acquired, see p. 144, *supra*.

hereditament the Lands Tribunal is required to consider whether, in the case of a house, building or manufactory the part to be acquired can be taken without material detriment to the building etc., or whether, in the case of a park or garden the acquisition will seriously affect the amenity or convenience of the house.[1]

    (d) *that (in the case of land falling within paragraph (a) or (c) but not (d), (e) or (f) of section 192(1) of this Act)[2] the appropriate authority (unless compelled to do so by virtue of these provisions) do not propose to acquire in the exercise of any relevant powers any part of the hereditament or (in the case of an agricultural unit) any part of the affected area or to acquire any right over any part thereof during[3] the period of fifteen years from the date of the counter-notice or such longer period from that date as may be specified in the counter-notice.*

This ground of objection recognises the very long-term and therefore somewhat speculative nature of many proposals included in development plans (and/or structure plans) particularly in the case of plans or modifications thereto awaiting the Secretary of State's approval that have been added by section 68(1) of the Act of 1973[4] and particularly in the case of many road programmes—hence the specific inclusion of the Town and Country Planning Act 1971, s. 192(1) paragraph (c); paragraphs (d), (e) and (f)[4] of that sub-section are specifically excluded because, in many cases, they represent a more advanced and more definite stage in the programming of highways which are included in development and structure plans. Similarly, the fact that this ground of objection is not extended to paragraph (b) reflects the more definitive stage in the planning process that allocation of land for specific purposes in a local plan implies.

It should, however, be noted that this ground of objection cannot be used as a second string to ground (b) above;[5] if the acquiring authority has no present intention to acquire, it must rely exclusively on ground (b).[6] On the other hand, despite the fact that on a reference to the Lands Tribunal the onus of substantiating its contention that it will not acquire within the 15-year or longer period rests with the appropriate authority, there is nothing to prevent it from changing its mind within that period and seeking to obtain the necessary authorisation. In the debate on the Committee Stage of the Bill[7] in the House of Commons, however, the then Secretary of State undertook to ensure that the fact that an objection on ground (d) had been accepted by the claimant, or upheld by the Lands Tribunal, would

---

[1] Town and Country Planning Act 1971, s. 202(2).

[2] I.e., the Town and Country Planning Act 1971: See the corresponding sub-paragraphs of para. (iii) *A* of the previous section of this chapter, pp. 133 *et seq, supra.*

[3] See note 1, p. 148, *ante.* Note that this objection would not have been available to the respondent authorities in either the *Louisville Investment* or *McKinnon Campbell* cases, pp. 146 and 147, *supra.* In the former case the blight notice was served pursuant to para. (j) of s. 192(1) and in the latter pursuant to para. (e).

[4] See paragraph (iii) *A*, pp. 133, *et seq, supra.*

[5] Pp. 145, *et seq, supra.*

[6] Town and Country Planning Act 1971, s. 194(3).

[7] Subsequently the Town and Country Planning Act 1968.

not be lightly disregarded in considering whether to confirm any subsequent compulsory purchase order made within that period.[1] Conversely, the claimant remains equally free to serve a series of blight notices in order to ascertain the appropriate authority's intentions from time to time and thereby, if it still does not wish to acquire within 15 years or longer, to extend the period over which he can expect to continue in the enjoyment of his property. Moreover, if he wishes to sell his interest the local authority may, subject to such conditions as may be approved by the Secretary of State, advance money to the purchaser,[2] such advance presumably being repayable upon ultimate acquisition, if not before.

Where the land concerned is subject to a compulsory purchase order or is land falling within category (i)[3] and the provisions of the relevant order or special enactment empower its acquisition, such powers of acquisition cease to have effect in relation to any part of the hereditament or agricultural unit in respect of which an objection under this head is upheld by the Lands Tribunal or is "accepted" by the claimant.[4]

(e) *That, on the date of service of the notice under section 193 of this Act[5] the claimant was not entitled to an interest in any part of the hereditament or agricultural unit to which the notice relates.*

If the claimant is either a mortgagee entitled to give vacant possession or a personal representative, this and the two remaining grounds of objection must be appropriately modified. In the case of a mortgagee the appropriate authority may contend that at the date of service of the blight notice the claimant had no interest as mortgagee in any part of the hereditament or agricultural unit.[6]

In the case of a personal representative the corresponding ground of objection is that the claimant is not the representative of a deceased person who, at the date of his death, was entitled to an interest in the property the subject of a blight notice.[7]

However, neither a mortgagee nor a personal representative is entitled to serve a blight notice if some other blight notice already served by some other claimant with an owner's interest (who may or may not be the mortgagor or the deceased) is outstanding. On the other hand, if a blight notice has been served by the deceased and has not been disposed of, his personal representatives stand in his shoes.[8]

(f) *That (for reasons specified in the counter-notice) the interest of the claimant is not an interest qualifying for protection under these provisions.[9]*

---

[1] Official Report, Standing Committee G, 28 March 1968, Column 729.
[2] Town & Country Planning Act 1971, s. 256.
[3] See paragraph (iii) A, p. 133, *et seq, supra*.
[4] Town and Country Planning Act 1971, s. 199(1) and (2).
[5] I.e., a blight notice served under the Town and Country Planning Act 1971, s. 193.
[6] Town and Country Planning Act 1971, s. 201(6)(a).
[7] Land Compensation Act 1973, s. 78(3)(a).
[8] Town & Country Planning Act 1971, s. 200.
[9] *Ibid*, s. 194(2)(*f*).

In the case of a mortgagee the corresponding ground of objection is that the mortgagee has no power exercisable at the date of service of the blight notice to give immediate possession[1] and/or that his interest is not one that would have qualified any person to serve a blight notice either on the date on which it was in fact served or within a period of six months prior thereto.[2]

Where the claimant is a personal representative this objection, if relevant, must be to the effect that the deceased's interest was not a qualifying one.[3]

(g) *That the conditions specified in paragraphs (c) and (d) of section 193(1) of this Act are not fulfilled;*[4]

i.e., that there has been no genuine effort to sell which has proved abortive except at a price substantially lower than could be expected but for the blighting effect resulting from the inclusion of the land in one or other of the categories of paragraph (iii) of the previous section of this chapter.

This ground of objection may apply to a blight notice served by a mortgagee or a personal representative in the same way as to any other claimant except that in the case of a personal representative there may be an additional ground of objection, namely that a corporate body as opposed to one or more private individuals is beneficially entitled to the interest in respect of which the notice has been served.[5]

While it is open to the appropriate authority to withdraw any objection at any time before the Lands Tribunal has made its determination[6] the authority can only *substitute* a second objection notice where the blight notice has been served in respect of the blighting effect of a proposed structure, development or local plan, or alterations or modifications to such plans or proposals which have not been finally approved; that is to say, where the land falls within paragraph (a) or (b) of section 192(1) of the Act of 1971 by virtue of the extensions of those categories effected by section 68 of the Act of 1973.[7] If, in such circumstances, the relevant plan or alterations come into force before the Lands Tribunal has made its determination and the original objection notice has not been withdrawn the appropriate authority may substitute a second objection notice on grounds appropriate to the new situation provided it does so within two months from the date on which the plan or alteration

---

[1] Town and Country Planning Act 1971, *Ibid*, s. 201(6)(b).
[2] *Ibid*, s. 201(3), and see pp. 132–3, *supra*.
[3] Land Compensation Act 1973, s. 78(3)(b).
[4] Town and Country Planning Act 1971, s. 194(2)(*g*).
[5] Land Compensation Act 1973), s. 78(1) and (3).
[6] While it is specifically laid down that no substituted notice may be served after determination by the Lands Tribunal (Land Compensation Act 1973, s. 68(6)) no such specific provision applies to withdrawal of notice; it must, however, be implied because if the Lands Tribunal has upheld the objection the acquiring authority will have no authority to acquire; if the Lands Tribunal has rejected the objection, withdrawal becomes pointless. Since, however, there is nothing to prevent the claimant serving a second blight notice, there is equally nothing to prevent an authority wishing to change its mind inviting him to do so.
[7] See para. (iii) *A*, pp. 133, *et seq*, *supra*.

etc., takes effect. If it does so the claimant has a further two months in which to refer the matter to the Lands Tribunal.[1]

(iii) ONUS OF PROOF

In proceedings before the Lands Tribunal the onus of proof rests upon the party having the relevant knowledge. Thus, if objection is made on the grounds that the land does not fall within any of the requisite categories or that the claimant has no interest or no qualifying interest, has made no genuine effort to sell, or having done so, was able to obtain a reasonable price, it is for the claimant to substantiate the converse. On the other hand, where the appropriate authority objects on the grounds that it does not propose to acquire any part of the land in question or does not propose to do so within 15 years, it is for the authority to satisfy the Lands Tribunal that such is its genuine intention.[2]

If the Lands Tribunal does not uphold any of the appropriate authority's objections it must declare the blight notice to be valid[3] and specify the date on which notice to treat is to be deemed to have been served.[4]

(iv) THE RELEVANT DATE

Although there is neither express statutory provision nor, as yet, any decision of the Courts, logic would seem to demand that in determining the validity of a counter-notice of objection the circumstances to be considered are those ruling at the date on which the notice is served. That is the view that has been expressed by the Lands Tribunal[5] which has refused to accept that withdrawal of the blight between that date and the date of the hearing constitutes sufficient ground for refusing to uphold a blight notice.[6]

(v) WITHDRAWAL OF BLIGHT NOTICE

While there are thenceforth no means by which the appropriate authority can withdraw a deemed notice to treat it remains open to the claimant to withdraw his blight notice at any time before the expiration of six weeks from the determination of compensation by

[1] Land Compensation Act 1973, s. 68(6).
[2] Town and Country Planning Act 1971, s. 195(2) and (3): *Bolton Corpn v Owen*, [1962], 1 QB 470, note 4, p. 134 *supra*. It has also been held, though somewhat tentatively, that where part of a garden is shown on plans approved by resolution of a local highway authority as required for highway purposes and the owner serves a blight notice in respect of the whole hereditament, and the authority responds with a counter-notice in accordance with para. (ii)(c) (p. 148, *supra*), the onus is on the authority to satisfy the Lands Tribunal that the land it requires can be taken without seriously affecting the amenity or convenience of the house (see p. 109, *supra*): *Hurley v Cheshire County Council* (1976), 31 P & CR 433. In that case, however, the Lands Tribunal stated that it would have come to the same decision (i.e., to uphold the blight notice) even if it was wrong in regard to the onus of proof.
[3] If the Lands Tribunal upholds an objection under para. (c), (p. 148, *supra*), it must declare the blight notice valid in so far as it affects that part of the land which the appropriate authority does not propose to acquire.
[4] Town and Country Planning Act 1971, s. 195.
[5] *Louisville Investments Ltd. v Basingstoke District Council*: p. 146, *supra*: *McKinnon Campbell v Greater Manchester Council*: p. 147, *supra*.
[6] See *McKinnon Campbell*'s case, *supra*.

the Lands Tribunal or before the appropriate authority has exercised any right to enter and take possession—whichever is the earlier.[1] Should he do so, then and then only is the deemed notice to treat deemed to have been withdrawn.

It should, however, be noted that if compensation is agreed and not therefore referred to the Lands Tribunal, the period within which the claimant may withdraw his blight notice is not governed by statute and is therefore only terminated by the completion of a valid contract of sale or entry by the appropriate authority, whichever is the earlier.

(vi) THE APPROPRIATE AUTHORITY

As already indicated, the appropriate authority is the public author-ity which in any particular case would, but for the service of the blight notice, ultimately be liable to acquire the land when even-tually required.[2]

In cases of doubt as to whether the appropriate authority is the Secretary of State or a local Highway authority, or as to which of two or more local highway authorities or local authorities is the appropriate authority the matter may be referred to the Secretary of State for final determination.[3]

Special provision[4] is, however, made to ensure that neither the claimant nor the authority on whom he serves the blight notice is prejudiced by any delay resulting from such a reference. Thus, if the authority makes the reference, the two-month period allowed for the service of any objection notice is extended to run from the date of the Secretary of State's determination instead of from the date of the service of the blight notice. Conversely, if the claimant is in doubt as to the appropriate authority, refers the matter to the Secretary of State, and delays service of the blight notice accordingly, he will not be prejudiced by the fact that, as a result, the period of his occu-pation of the hereditament or agricultural unit concerned ended more than twelve months[5] prior to the date on which the Secretary of State reaches his decision and he is enabled to serve his notice. In such cases the twelve-month period is extended by the time taken by the Secretary of State to determine the matter. Similar protection is afforded to a mortgagee who finds that by the time the Secretary of State's decision is made it is more than six months[6] since the interest which he has power to sell could have been the subject of a blight notice by an owner-occupier or resident owner-occupier as the case may be.[7]

---

[1] Town and Country Planning Act 1971, s. 198.

[2] Town and Country Planning Act 1971, s. 205(1): see also para. (N), pp. 140–141, *supra*.

[3] *Ibid*, s. 205(2), but note that there is no right of reference to the Secretary of State in other cases: in the case of blight notices served under the Community Land Act 1975, s. 22(6)—see para. (C), p. 142, *supra*—the appropriate authority is the authority nominated for this purpose in the County Land Acquisition and Management Scheme: note 1, p. 303, *post*.

[4] Town and Country Planning Act 1971, s. 205(3).

[5] *Ibid*, s. 205(3) and see p. 131, *supra*.

[6] See *ibid*, s. 201(3)(b), and pp. 132–133, *supra*.

[7] *Ibid*, s. 205(3)(b): see p. 133, *supra*.

(vii) THE APPROPRIATE ENACTMENT

When a blight notice is either "accepted" as valid (i.e. by failure of the appropriate authority to serve an objection notice within the prescribed two-month period) or is declared to be valid by the Lands Tribunal on its rejection of the appropriate authority's grounds of objection, the question arises as to the statutory provisions under which the authority is deemed to be authorised to acquire.[1]

The general rule is that the *appropriate enactment* is the enactment that provides for the compulsory acquisition of land within the particular category or description. Where land is "blighted" as a result of the making of a compulsory purchase order or by proposals to make such an order (whether in respect of the land itself or of rights thereover) the answer to this question is quite straightforward: the appropriate enactment is the enactment under which the compulsory purchase order has been or is to be made.[2]

Where the blight notice is served in respect of land allocated in a local plan[3] or pre-1968 type development plan,[4] or is similarly affected by proposals for the alteration or modification of such plans, or is the subject of an appropriate resolution of a local planning authority,[5] the appropriate enactment will be the enactment which provides for the compulsory acquisition of land for the particular function of the appropriate authority for which the land is allocated or proposed to be allocated. In some cases, however, the plan may merely allocate land for the purposes of a public body without specifying the *particular* purpose or function for which it is required; in that event the appropriate enactment may be any enactment that provides for the compulsory acquisition of land for the purpose of any of its functions.[6]

In the case of land indicated as required for highway purposes the appropriate enactment is any enactment under which a highway authority can be authorised to acquire land compulsorily upon the coming into operation of the appropriate order or scheme[7] or upon the making or approval of plans. If there is more than one such enactment the appropriate enactment is that under which it is most likely that the land in question would ultimately be acquired if there were no question of advance acquisition in response to the blight notice.[8]

In cases of doubt as to the appropriate enactment, however, the matter is to be referred for final determination to the Minister in charge of the Department where a Government Department is the

[1] Town and Country Planning Act 1971, s. 206(1).
[2] *Ibid*, and see also the Land Compensation Act 1973, ss. 70(3) and 73(3).
[3] Town and Country Planning Act 1971, s. 206(2).
[4] Land Compensation Act 1973, s. 68(10): see para. (b), p. 135 and note 2, p. 139, *supra*.
[5] Under *ibid*, s. 71: para. (K), p. 138, *supra*.
[6] In such cases it would now seem that the Community Land Act 1975 will almost always be an "appropriate enactment": see p. 296, *post*.
[7] I.e., an order or scheme under the Highways Act 1959, Part II, relating to trunk or special roads as the case may be; an order under *ibid*, s. 1; or a scheme under the Highways (Miscellaneous Provisions) Act 1961, s. 3; or the Town and Country Planning Act 1971, s. 206(3).
[8] Town and Country Planning Act 1971, s. 206(5).

appropriate authority, to the responsible Minister where the latter are statutory undertakers, and in all other cases to the Secretary of State.[1]

BLIGHT NOTICES: SUMMARY

(i) Land will suffer from planning blight in any case in which market demand is depressed as a result of the land being earmarked for some public purpose in respect of which powers of compulsory purchase are conferred upon a public body to acquire the requisite land.[2]

(ii) The provisions whereby an owner of an interest in such land may serve a blight notice requiring the acquisition of his interest forthwith are *not*, however, comprehensive. They apply only to:

(a) Certain categories of property (qualifying property);

(b) Specific interests in the land (qualifying interests);

(c) Planning blight occasioned by intentions of acquiring authorities that have been promulgated in the appropriate specified manner; and

(d) Owners who have found it impossible to sell their interests except at a substantially reduced price.[3]

(iii) *Qualifying property* is confined to:

(a) Hereditaments occupied wholly, or as to a substantial part as a dwelling;[4]

(b) Other hereditaments, the net annual value of which does not exceed the amount prescribed in the current Town and Country Planning (Limit of Annual Value) Order;[5] and

(c) Agricultural units.[6]

(iv) *Qualifying interests.* First, there must in all cases be occupation by the person serving the blight notice (the claimant) for a continuous period of six months either immediately prior to the date of service of the blight notice or ending not more than twelve months previously.[7] Secondly, the claimant's interest must be that of an owner-occupier in right of the freehold interest or of a lease for a term of years certain having at least three years unexpired at the date of service of the notice.[8] Special provisions apply to mortgagees,[8] personal representatives[9] and partnerships.[9]

(v) *Blight.* The blight must be the result of the land falling within one or other of the specified categories.[10]

---

[1] Town and Country Planning Act 1971, *Ibid*, s. 206(6).

[2] Pp. 107 and 129, *supra*.

[3] See pp. 130 *et seq*, *supra*.

[4] P. 130, *supra*.

[5] Pp. 130–1, *supra*.

[6] For definition see p. 131, *supra*.

[7] Pp. 131–132, *supra*, and note the distinction in this regard as between hereditaments and agricultural units.

[8] Pp. 132–133 *supra*.

[9] Pp. 132–133, *supra*.

[10] I.e., as specified in (i) the Town and Country Planning Act 1971, s. 192, as amended by the Land Compensation Act 1973, ss. 68–76 (see paras. (iii) *A*, pp. 133–138, *supra*); (ii) the Land Compensation Act 1973, ss. 71–73 and 76 (see para. (iii) *B*, pp. 138–142, *supra*); (iii) Community Land Act 1975, s. 22(6) (see para. (iii) *C*, p. 142, *supra*).

(vi) If the authority on whom a blight notice is served[1] does not serve upon the claimant a counter-notice of objection within two months from the date of service of the blight notice, that authority is deemed to be authorised[2] to acquire the interest in question and to have served a notice to treat at the expiration of that period.[3]

(vii) If the authority is unwilling to acquire the interest in question it may, within the same period, serve a counter-notice of objection. Objection can only be made on one or more of the specified grounds of objection[4] which must be set out in the notice.[5] If no action is taken by the claimant within two months of the date of the counter-notice he is deemed to have accepted the validity of the objection. There is nothing, however, to prevent the service of a further blight notice, provided his interest still qualifies him to do so.[6]

(viii) If the claimant does not accept the validity of the counter-notice he may, within the above two months' period, require the objection to be referred to the Lands Tribunal.[5]

(ix) It is for the Lands Tribunal to decide whether or not to uphold the objection.[7] If they do so the blight notice is invalidated:[8] if they do not they must declare the blight notice valid[8] and give directions as to the date on which the blight notice is to be deemed to have been served.

---

[1] As to the "appropriate authority" on whom the blight notice should be served, see p. 154, *supra*.

[2] Note the limitations of this authorisation where the blight notice is served in respect of an agricultural unit: p. 144, *supra*.

[3] P. 144, *supra*.

[4] I.e., those specified in the Town and Country Planning Act 1971, s. 194(2) as amended by the Land Compensation Act 1973: see paras. (a) to (g), pp. 145, *et seq, supra*.

[5] P. 145, *supra*.

[6] See particularly in this context para. (d), pp. 150–151 *supra*.

[7] As to the onus of proof see p. 153, *supra*.: see also in this connection "The Relevant Date", p. 153 *supra*.

[8] Note, however, the case in which a blight notice may be held valid as to part of the land to which it refers and invalid as to the remainder: see para. (c), pp. 148 *et seq, supra*.

CHAPTER 5

Compensation for Land Taken

1 GENERAL INTRODUCTION TO THE LAW OF COMPENSATION: CHAPTERS 5–10

1 The heads of compensation

The law of compensation for land compulsorily acquired falls to be considered under four main heads as under:

(i) COMPENSATION FOR THE LAND TAKEN

The current law governing the compensation payable for the interests in land actually acquired is based upon the proposition that the owner is entitled to the full market value of his interest, less any increase in the value of his interest in other land retained by him which results from the development proposed for the land acquired.

The detailed rules applicable are considered in the succeeding sections of this chapter.

In addition there is a number of special cases to which special rules apply. These are considered in chapter 6. In some of these cases it has been found more convenient to deal at the same time with such special acquisition procedure as may be applicable rather than to divide consideration of these special cases between chapter 2 and chapter 6. This approach, it is hoped, will avoid burdening the reader with excessive cross-referencing. Conversely, and for the same reason, the one special, and not very commonly encountered, rule relating to the assessment of compensation for property acquired in pursuance of a purchase notice has been outlined in chapter 4.[1]

It is worth noting under this head that prior to 14 February 1977,[2] unless the special Act specifically empowered an authority possessing compulsory powers to create easements or other rights in or over land,[3] such an authority requiring an easement had no alternative, in the absence of agreement, but to acquire the land over or under which the easement was required. The compensation payable in respect of the

---

[1] P. 126, *ante*.

[2] The date on which the Local Government (Miscellaneous Provisions) Act 1976, s. 13, came into effect by virtue of the Local Government (Miscellaneous Provisions) Act 1976 (Commencement) Order 1977 (SI 1977 No. 68 (C3)).

[3] Normally by including easements or such other rights within the definition of the word "land".

acquisition of easements, etc. is considered as a special case in chapter 6.[1]

Finally, under this head, it will be recalled[2] that the rules as to the assessment of compensation will ultimately be radically altered by the operation of the Community Land Act 1975, by virtue of which the basic measure of compensation will revert to existing use value. The effect of this Act is considered in chapter 7.

(ii) COMPENSATION FOR SEVERANCE AND INJURIOUS AFFECTION

This is the head under which compensation is payable for the loss in value of other land retained by the vendor, where such depreciation results either from the severance therefrom of the land taken, or the damage thereto resulting from the development proposed for the land acquired.

Thus acquisition of an easement or the contravention of a restrictive covenant will normally give rise to a claim for compensation for injurious affection to the land over or under which the easement is acquired or to the land having the benefit of the restrictive covenant. Similarly, if an existing easement is acquired compensation will normally be payable in respect of the resultant damage to the dominant tenement.

Compensation for injurious affection may also be claimed by other owners of land adjoining the land acquired where their land is depreciated in value as a result of the execution (though not of the use[3]) of the works authorised upon the land acquired. The rules governing such claims are, however, very much narrower than those governing claims made by the vendor of the land being acquired in respect of other land held therewith and retained by him. These matters, together with the analogous provisions of the Land Compensation Act 1973, are considered in chapter 8.

(iii) COMPENSATION FOR DISTURBANCE

Under this head compensation is payable for the cost of vacating the land acquired and, where relevant, of reinstatement in alternative premises. It includes, for example, removal expenses and legal and surveying fees incurred in finding alternative accommodation. Where the subject land comprises business premises it may also include loss of profits or goodwill resulting from the enforced vacation of the land acquired. To this there is one exception, perhaps more apparent than

---

[1] Pp. 283 et seq, post. Two other categories of land to which special statutory provisions apply are war-damaged land and requisitioned land: both arise from the exigencies of the 1939–1945 war and the relevant statutory provisions governing the compensation payable are to be found in the Land Compensation Act 1961, s. 13 and the War Damage Act 1943, in the case of war-damaged land, and in the Requisitioned Land and War Works Act 1945 in the case of requisitioned land. Under neither head are cases now likely to arise. They are not therefore further considered in this book.

[2] Pp. 22 et seq, ante.

[3] Note, however, the limited exception to this rule created by the Land Compensation Act 1973. Pp. 328 et seq, post.

real, in the case of licensed premises. A justices' licence is not, of course, an interest in land and will not automatically be taken over by the acquiring authority. However, if it is taken over, the interest of the owner or lessee will normally be assessed on the assumption that the premises would have continued to be licensed so that the value of the licence will in effect be included in the purchase price.[1] Similarly, the value of a tying covenant must be taken into account in assessing compensation for the land taken since such a covenant runs with the land.[2] If, on the other hand, the licensee has no interest in the land,[3] compensation for the loss of the licence may be claimed under the head of disturbance.[4] Where the licence is retained, however, compensation must be adjusted accordingly[4] for it is a basic principle of the law of compensation that compensation must be limited to the real loss sustained.[5]

It is also worth noting, in this connection, that in the case of residential and agricultural property an occupier having no legal interest in the land (e.g., upon termination of a tenancy, the acquiring authority having acquired the freehold or head lease) may nevertheless be entitled to a home or farm loss payment. Although such payments arise from specific statutory provisions differing significantly from the rules governing compensation for disturbance, they are clearly analogous thereto and are accordingly described under that head in chapter 9.[6]

(iv) COMPENSATION IN RESPECT OF CERTAIN PLANNING DECISIONS

Broadly speaking, compensation payable under this head is confined to cases in which the planning decision results in preventing the full use of the land concerned either in accordance with an existing planning permission or in its existing use, which for this purpose includes a presumption that planning permission will be forthcoming for the limited classes of development set out in the Town and Country Planning Act 1971, Schedule 8, Part II.[7] Compensation is similarly payable in respect of restrictions imposed upon the alteration, etc. of listed buildings of historical and architectural merit.

To this general proposition there is, however, an exception now relatively rarely encountered, viz compensation for refusal of planning permission to develop land in respect of which there is an "unexpended balance of established development value".[8]

These matters are considered in chapter 10.

[1] *Tull's Personal Representatives* v *Secretary of State for Air*, [1957] 1 QB 523.
[2] *Re Chandler's Wiltshire Brewery Co and the LCC*, [1903] 1 KB 569.
[3] E.g., where he is a manager, or where the acquiring authority, having acquired the freehold, allow a lessee to remain in occupation until the termination of the lease.
[4] As to which see p. 356 *post*.
[5] *Tull's case, supra*, and *Horn* v *Sunderland Corpn*, [1941] 2 KB 26.
[6] Section 4, pp. 372 *et seq*, *post*.
[7] Town and Country Planning Act 1971, Sch. 8; see Appendix *post*, and note that for certain other purposes existing use includes a presumption that planning permission will be forthcoming for the developments in Part I as well as Part II: Land Compensation Act 1961, s. 15, pp. 195 *et seq*, *post*.
[8] Pp. 394 *et seq*, *post*. For an explanation of the origin of this phrase see pp. 116 *et seq*, *ante*.

2 Principles of compensation

The basic principle of the law of compensation is that the sum awarded should as far as practicable place the claimant in the same financial position as he would have been in had there been no question of his land being compulsorily acquired.[1] Indeed, it is fair to say that the failure of the compensation provisions of the Town and Country Planning Act of 1947 to accord with this basic principle constituted the principal reason for their repeal and the ultimate return, in 1959, to full market value[2] as the basis of compensation.[3] No doubt, moreover, it was realisation of the fundamental difficulty of reconciling any code of compensation that departs from full market value with the basic principle that induced the framers of the Community Land Act 1975 to include provision for the establishment of Financial Hardship Tribunals[4] where, following the 2nd Appointed Day under that Act, the basis of compensation will once more revert to current existing use value.

In the meantime, however, as explained in chapter 1,[5] compensation will fall to be assessed on the basis of full open market value subject to the relevant assumptions as to the availability of planning permission,[6] in accordance with the Land Compensation Act 1961.[7] The provisions of this latter Act are of general application[8] and it is with these provisions that this chapter is principally concerned. It must be borne in mind, moreover, that since the Community Land Act 1975[9] brings about the return of current existing use value as the basis of compensation (after the 2nd Appointed Day) by modifying the provisions of the Land Compensation Act 1961 rather than by repeal and replacement, an understanding of the latter Act and many of the judicial decisions to which it has given rise will continue to be necessary.[10]

3 Chapters 5–10: guidance note

In the following chapters each main heading and, where appropriate, sub-heading, is introduced by a short introduction explaining the general principles. The subject matter is then considered in detail and finally summarised with the requisite cross-references to the preceding detailed consideration. While it is hoped that the introductory paragraphs will be of assistance to those coming to this branch of the law afresh, it is recognised that others more familiar with its principles will be more concerned quickly to find the details of some particular rule of

[1] See, for example, *Horn*'s case, note 5, p. 160, *supra*.
[2] I.e., taking into account development potential and not merely the value of the land as it stands in its existing use.
[3] Pp. 10 *et seq, ante*.
[4] See p. 310, *post*.
[5] Pp. 23 *et seq, ante*.
[6] For the general principles see p. 15 *ante*. For details see pp. 185 *et seq, infra*.
[7] Re-enacting the compensation provisions of the Town and Country Planning Act 1959—as to which, see pp. 14 *et seq, ante*.
[8] Subject, of course, to any modification imposed by the Special Act under which the acquisition is authorised.
[9] S. 25.
[10] Note that certain land acquired from charities will continue to be assessed in accordance with the provisions of the Land Compensation Act 1961 for some years after the 2nd Appointed Day under the Community Land Act 1975: pp. 308, *et seq, post*.

law applicable to a particular case: hence the inclusion of summaries where it is hoped that sufficient information will be found to direct the inquirer to the relevant detailed exposition. For those less familiar with this branch of the law a check list is provided below.

4 Basic questions: check list

(i) COMPENSATION WHERE NO LAND TAKEN

(a) *Compensation in respect of certain planning permissions*
Where compensation is claimable in respect of some planning decision reference should immediately be made to the introduction to chapter 10, and thence, if the particular planning permission appears to be one in respect of which compensation may be claimable, to the appropriate section of that chapter.

(b) *Compensation for injurious affection where no land acquired from the claimant*
Similarly, if the claim is based upon the injurious affection to land as a result of construction of works upon or the use of neighbouring land by a public body, reference will have to be made to chapter 8.[1]

(ii) COMPENSATION WHERE LAND ACQUIRED

In all other cases claims to compensation will arise from a compulsory acquisition of land. The following is a suggested check list of the appropriate considerations:

(a) *Claimant with no legal interest*
The first question that arises is "Has the claimant a legal interest in the land?" If not, he may, if an occupier, nevertheless be entitled to compensation for disturbance[2] or for a home or farm loss or disturbance payment.[3] If the subject land comprises his sole or principal residence there may also be an obligation upon the local authority to rehouse.[4]

(b) *Claimant with legal interest*
A. *Special case.* Where the claimant has a legal interest in the land acquired the next question to be asked is whether the nature of the land or interest being acquired is such that it is a special case falling under any of the heads of chapter 6. If so, reference should immediately be made to the relevant section of that chapter.

B. *The "ordinary" case of chapter 5.* Here the questions to be asked are as follows:

(i) What planning permission is to be assumed in assessing market value?[5]

(ii) If no planning permission that enhances the value of the land can be assumed on any other basis, is a certificate of appropriate alternative development relevant?[6]

(iii) Does the development proposed for the land acquired form

---

[1] See Injurious Affection to Land of Third Parties, pp. 321 *et seq, post*, and Compensation under the Land Compensation Act 1973, pp. 328 *et seq, post.*

[2] See Chap. 9, p. 344, *post.*

[3] See pp. 372 *et seq, post.*

[4] See pp. 389, *post.*

[5] See pp. 185 *et seq, infra.*

[6] See pp. 204 *et seq, infra.*

part of a scheme of development[1] and if so, how does it affect assessment of compensation?

(iv) Is the land being acquired land previously held with other land already acquired by a body possessing compulsory powers, and in respect of which an increase in its value resulting from the first acquisition, was deducted from the compensation payable on that occasion? If so, account must be taken of this deduction in assessing the compensation payable on the subsequent acquisition.[2]

(v) Has the claimant an interest in other land contiguous to or adjoining the land being acquired? If so, is it affected in value by the acquisition and/or the development proposed for the land acquired? If any such land is increased in value a corresponding deduction will have to be made from the compensation payable.[3] If such land is decreased in value there will normally be a claim in respect thereof under the head of compensation for severance and injurious affection.[4]

(vi Is the claimant an occupier either of residential or business premises? If so, there will be a claim for disturbance.[5] If it has been necessary to find alternative accommodation this can include legal and surveyors' costs and costs incurred in looking for such alternative accommodation, and necessary costs of adapting new business premises to meet the needs of the business displaced.

(vii) In the event of a business occupier with a localised clientele successfully rehabilitating his business in other premises, has he nevertheless suffered a loss of goodwill? If so, compensation may be claimable under the head of disturbance;[6] so too in the case of loss of profits—whether temporary, as a result of the interruption of business occasioned by the move, or permanent, resulting from the comparative unsuitability of the new premises as compared with the old.[7]

2 COMPENSATION FOR LAND TAKEN: PARTS II AND III, LAND COMPENSATION ACT 1961[8]

The basic rules governing compensation for land taken are derived from the Acquisition of Land (Assessment of Compensation) Act 1919, s. 2,[9] and are frequently referred to as the "1919 Rules". They have

---

[1] See pp. 217 et seq, infra.   [2] See pp. 231 et seq, infra.
[3] Pp. 217 et seq, infra.   [4] Chap. 8 p. 314, post.
[5] Chap. 9, p. 344 post.   [6] Pp. 357 et seq, post.
[7] Pp. 358 et seq, post.

[8] Note that references in this Act to provisions of the then current Town and Country Planning Act 1947 are to be construed as references to the corresponding provisions of the Town and Country Planning Act 1971: Sch. 24, para. 2.

[9] The Act of 1919 at first applied only to acquisitions by bodies authorised by Act of Parliament "to carry on a railway, canal, dock, water or other public undertaking" and not trading for profit (s. 12(2)). Gradually, however, its application was extended to cover practically all bodies now exercising compulsory powers.

been re-enacted as the Land Compensation Act 1961, s. 5[1] which, because of its fundamental importance is reproduced below in full.

The 1919 rules

"5. Compensation in respect of any compulsory acquisition shall be assessed in accordance with the following rules:

(1) No allowance shall be made on account of the acquisition being compulsory:

(2) The value of land shall, subject as hereinafter provided, be taken to be the amount which the land if sold in the open market by a willing seller might be expected to realise:

(3) The special suitability or adaptability of the land for any purpose shall not be taken into account if that purpose is a purpose to which it could be applied only in pursuance of statutory powers, or for which there is no market apart from the special needs of a particular purchaser or the requirements of any authority possessing compulsory purchase powers:

(4) Where the value of the land is increased by reason of the use thereof or of any premises thereon in a manner which could be restrained by any court, or is contrary to law, or is detrimental to the health of the occupants of the premises or to the public health, the amount of that increase shall not be taken into account:

(5) Where land is, and but for the compulsory acquisition would continue to be, devoted to a purpose of such a nature that there is no general demand or market for land for that purpose, the compensation may, if the Lands Tribunal is satisfied that reinstatement in some other place is bona fide intended, be assessed on the basis of the reasonable cost of equivalent reinstatement:

(6) The provisions of rule (2) shall not affect the assessment of compensation for disturbance or any other matter not directly based on the value of land:

and the following provisions of this Part of this Act shall have effect with respect to the assessment".

It will be observed that the basic principle on which an interest in land is to be valued, namely the "amount which the land if sold on the open market by a willing seller might be expected to realise" is laid down in Rule 2. That general proposition is amplified not only by Rules 1, 3 and 4 but by subsequent sections of the Act designed, as explained in Chapter 1, to take account of the effect upon value of the planning provisions of the Town and Country Planning Acts and to produce in effect the "full" open market value as opposed to one restricted to the value of the land in its current existing use. In other words, these later sections of the Land Compensation Act 1961 set out to give effect to such expectations in regard to planning permissions as would influence a purchaser in the open market in assessing price. In doing so, by providing for certain assumptions as to the planning permission with the benefit of which the land is to be valued, these sections inevitably introduce a considerable degree of artificiality since in practice once an authority possessing compulsory powers[2] is authorised to acquire any particular land for a specified purpose, assuming planning permission for any other purpose can only be a somewhat hypothetical exercise.

It will be observed that Rule 6 in effect specifically preserves the rules

---

[1] Despite the various changes in the law of compensation outlined in chapter 1 these rules have never been abandoned. They were re-enacted in toto as a separate section in the Town and Country Planning Acts of 1944, 1947 and 1959, the modifications effecting the changes in the assessment of compensation under those Acts being contained in subsequent sections, as in the current Land Compensation Act 1961.

[2] This may include a parish council for whom the County Council is acting as acquiring authority: Land Compensation Act 1961, s. 39(1).

governing compensation for disturbance which are considered in Chapter 9: it is not relevant to the subject matter of this chapter.

Before considering the assessment of market value under these provisions of this Act attention must also be drawn to Rule 5. Rule 5 deals with the problem that arises where there is no general market for the land in question for the particular purpose for which it is used, and for which there cannot therefore be a market value, but the loss of which would result in replacement costs exceeding the market value for any other purpose for which the land might be suitable. The most common and perhaps most typical example of property to which, provided there is a genuine intention to rebuild elsewhere, Rule 5 applies is a church,[1] although there are, of course, many other special-purpose buildings and installations subject to similar considerations and to which Rule 5 applies; they now specifically include, at the option of the claimant, a dwelling specially adapted for a disabled person.[2]

Thus compensation under Rule 5 cannot, by definition, be related to market values—only to current costs of replacement, i.e., costs of land, labour and materials and in some cases, of specialist equipment that cannot be moved. Its application and the assessment of compensation is therefore considered in detail separately in Chapter 6.[3]

THE RELEVANT DATE

A prerequisite to the assessment of compensation for land taken (and indeed, for severance and injurious affection) is to determine the date at which the interest falls to be valued.

Prior to 1968 it had been regarded as settled law that compensation fell to be assessed on the basis of current values as at the date of the notice to treat. In that year, however, the West Midland Baptist (Trust) Association (Inc.) appealed from a decision of the Lands Tribunal upholding that rule, in a case falling under Rule 5 above. In that case[4] the acquiring authority was deemed to have served notice to treat in 1947[5] upon the mutual understanding that the Baptist Association would be permitted to continue in possession until the property (a chapel) was actually required which, as things turned out, was not until 1961.

The gravamen of the appellants' argument was that it would have been unreasonable for them to acquire an alternative site and build a new chapel before it was necessary to vacate their existing chapel which might not be required by the respondents for a very long time indeed. In

---

[1] It does not, of course, necessarily follow, even in the case of such a highly specialised building as a church that if the site is suitable for development for which there is buoyant demand, market value will fall short of the cost of "equivalent reinstatement": note in this connection the special provisions of the Community Land Act 1975 in relation to charities; p. 308, *post*.

[2] Land Compensation Act 1973, s. 45.

[3] P. 238, *post*.

[4] *West Midland Baptist (Trust) Incorporated* v *Birmingham Corpn*, [1968] 2 QB 188.

[5] It will be recalled that powers of compulsory acquisition conferred by a compulsory purchase order must be exercised within three years of the date on which the compulsory purchase order comes into force: Compulsory Purchase Act 1965, s. 4. Service of a notice to treat within the three-year period has, however, the effect of keeping the compulsory purchase order alive: p. 67, *ante*.

such circumstances, the respondent Corporation being at all times fully in agreement with the appellants continuing in occupation, it would be patently unfair and a contradiction in terms to base compensation for equivalent reinstatement on the wholly outdated costs ruling at the much earlier date of the notice to treat. The Court of Appeal, after reviewing the cases and comparing the stable money conditions of the 19th Century (in which the old rule had been formulated) with those of the post 1939–45 war period, upheld this argument and decided that the relevant date for the assessment of compensation is whichever is the earlier of the date of entry or the date at which compensation falls to be determined. Although this decision referred specifically to the case of equivalent reinstatement under Rule 5, the House of Lords,[1] in affirming the decision of the Court of Appeal, went somewhat further and decided that the earlier of these two dates should also be the relevant date for the assessment of compensation under Rule 2.[2]

WHAT CONSTITUTES ENTRY

In determining the date of entry there must, with one exception, be some overt physical act on the part of the acquiring authority. Thus where farm land was acquired and notice of entry served expiring on 4 February, but the first physical entry did not take place until 30 June, the latter date was held to be the date of entry;[3] the fact that the overt act is of a minor nature such as the erection by contractors of a small office-hut in one of the fields[4] is, however, immaterial. Similarly, where the subject land was a tenanted house, a 14-day notice of entry was served and the tenant was rehoused by the acquiring authority. The authority then contended that it had displaced the tenant, that the date of entry was therefore the date on which he was rehoused, and that compensation therefore fell to be assessed on the basis that the house was tenanted. But it was not until some days later that the authority had taken any overt steps—however small—to "enter upon and take possession" of the premises by sending officials to padlock the doors.[5] By that time, of course, the house was empty and compensation was awarded on the basis of vacant possession.

The exception arises from the statutory provisions designed to overrule this latter case and the many others covering similar facts.[6] It is now provided[7] that where an acquiring authority rehouses a tenant in pursuance of duties conferred upon it in that regard[8] it is to be deemed to have entered coincidentally with the vacation of the premises by the tenant.[6]

---

[1] *Birmingham Corpn* v *West Midland Baptist (Trust) Association (Inc.)*, [1970] AC 874.

[2] It is, however, to be noted that the statutory provisions relating to the planning permissions to be assumed for the purposes of valuation (which, of course, pre-date the *West Midland Baptist* case *supra*) for the most part relate to the conditions ruling as at the date of notice to treat: see the Land Compensation Act 1961, ss. 14–16, pp. 185 *et seq, infra*.

[3] *Burson* v *Wantage RDC* (1973), 27 P & CR 556.

[4] *Burson* v *Wantage RDC, supra*.

[5] *Buckingham Street Investments Ltd.* v *Greater London Council* (1975), 31 P & CR 453.

[6] See p. 170, *infra*, and the cases sited in note 3.

[7] Land Compensation Act 1973, s. 50(2).

[8] *Ibid*, s. 39.

It is worth noting in this connection that a prior agreement as to price, expressed throughout as subject to contract, is not binding and affords no bar to the claimant reopening negotiations on the basis of prices ruling at the later date of entry;[1] *aliter*, however, where, following notice to treat there is an unconditional agreement as to price, for that will create a binding contract[2] even though there is no written memorandum sufficient to satisfy the Law of Property Act 1925, s. 40.[1] This is because the notice to treat itself binds the acquiring authority to purchase and the owner to sell at a price to be ascertained.[3] The converse follows, so that an agreement reached before notice to treat can be challenged for want of a written memorandum of its terms and the claim for compensation can be reopened and determined by the Lands Tribunal on the basis of prices ruling at the date of entry.

Where the expedited procedure of the Town and Country Planning Act 1968, Schedule 3,[4] is employed the date of entry is the date of vesting.[5] In almost all such cases it will also be the relevant date for, by definition, there will have been insufficient time between the confirmation of the compulsory purchase order and the date of vesting to determine the price.

THE DATE ON WHICH COMPENSATION FALLS TO BE ASSESSED

Where entry precedes determination of the compensation payable no difficulty arises in determining the relevant date: nor will there be any difficulty in the converse case, where compensation has been the subject of agreement. Where, however, no agreement can be reached and the matter is referred to the Lands Tribunal there are three possible dates on which it may be said that the compensation "falls to be determined" viz:

    (i)   The date of the notice of reference to the Lands Tribunal;
    (ii) The date of the hearing;
    (iii) The date of the decision.

Although it is only after the final decision of the Lands Tribunal that there is a completed contract upon which the claimant can sue for specific performance it would only in practice be possible for the decision to reflect values at that date in cases in which the decision is given at the conclusion of the hearing or within a few days thereafter. Even then, in the case of a protracted hearing, particularly when there have been long adjournments, it might well be necessary to extend the hearing further in order to consider more recent sales of comparative properties and arrive at up-to-date values. The date of hearing, of course, introduces similar practical difficulties: not only may values change in the course of a prolonged hearing, but in times of fluctuating

---

[1] *Munton* v *Newham Borough Council*, (1976) 32 P & CR 269 (CA): *Munton* v *Greater London Council* [1976] 2 All ER 815.

[2] *Munton* v *Newham Borough Council*, (1976) *per* Lord Denning MR at 32 P & CR p. 271; and see *per* Lord Hatherley LC in *Harding* v *Metropolitan Rly Co* (1872), 7 Ch. App. 154.

[3] *Mercer* v *Liverpool, St. Helens and South Lancashire Rly Co*, [1903] 1 KB 652, 664 CA.

[4] As to which see p. 71, *ante*.

[5] *Ware* v *City of Edinburgh District Council* (1976), 31 P & CR 488 (Lands Tribunal for Scotland).

land values they are more likely than not to change between the lodgement of documents[1] and commencement of the hearing.

Thus it has been held by the Lands Tribunal that in conditions of market instability compensation is to be based upon values ruling on the last day of the hearing. If, however, values change materially between that date and the promulgation of the award further evidence may be heard and arrangements made for the final awards to follow immediately after the further hearing.[2] In such cases it is open to the acquiring authority to make a further sealed offer to protect themselves in respect of costs where market values are rising.[3]

On the other hand, however, in the case of *Hull Trinity House Corpn* v *Humberside County Council*[4] a preference for the date of reference of the dispute to the Lands Tribunal was expressed although, because of agreement between the parties to that effect, they in fact adopted the date of the hearing. They were careful to do so, however, without prejudice to the possibility that in some later case the date of notice of reference might be put forward and adopted.

The basis of the Lands Tribunal argument in that case was that the latter date has the advantage that no adjustments of valuation are required during the hearing and there is the further advantage that this is the one date within the control of the parties. In effect it is the date on which one or other of the parties formally concludes that agreement is beyond reach. In most cases the acquiring authority is able to fix the relevant date by taking possession. Only, therefore, if, in the absence of either agreement or entry, the relevant date is the date of reference, does the claimant have any corresponding control over that date.[5] Nevertheless, since the objective is to put the vendor in the same position financially as he would have been but for the acquisition, the later the relevant date for valuation purposes the more likely is it that the compensation payable will reflect the cost of acquiring an alternative property in the market. Except, therefore, in circumstances of market stability the reasoning in the *W. & S. (Long Eaton)*[2] case is to be preferred to that in the *Hull Trinity House* case.

In the former case it was emphasised that no distinction is to be drawn in this regard between acquisitions pursuant to purchase notices (and by analogy, blight notices) and acquisitions pursuant to notices to treat served by the acquiring authority; in the case of acquisition pursuant to a purchase notice it is not, in any event, until compensation is agreed or determined that the acquiring authority has an enforceable right to complete the transaction.[6]

---

[1] Under the Lands Tribunal Rules 1975 (SI 1975 No. 299), Rule 42. For the relevant procedure see Chap. 3, p. 83, *ante*.

[2] *W & S (Long Eaton) Ltd.* v *Derbyshire County Council* (1976), 31 P & CR 99(CA)—a case of acquisition in pursuance of a purchase notice in conditions of falling land values between the date of deemed notice to treat and determination of compensation.

[3] As to costs, see p. 86, *ante*.

[4] (1975), 234 Estates Gazette 915.

[5] In this case the reference to the Lands Tribunal followed two agreements as to value between the claimants' valuer and the County Land Agent which the acquiring authority refused to accept, thus emphasising the value of the claimants' right to determine a relevant date.

[6] See note 2, *supra*.

The date on which compensation is deemed to be assessed will affect any claim there may be for the payment of interest.[1]

INSURANCE

An important side effect of the decision in the *West Midland Baptist* case relates to the risk of damage to, or destruction of, the property pending entry or determination of the compensation. In *Phoenix Assurance Co.* v *Spooner*,[2] for example, it was held that destruction of premises by fire subsequent to the notice to treat but before completion did not affect the owner's right to full compensation based on the value of the property as at the notice to treat and prior to the fire. In the *West Midland Baptist* case *Spooner*'s case was specifically held to have been wrongly decided:[3] in other words, responsibility for insurance remains with the owner until entry or determination of the compensation—whichever is the earlier.

Logically it would seem to follow that the same principle applies where, prior to entry or determination of compensation, the property being acquired is damaged by vandals. Nevertheless in one such case[4] the contrary approach, adopted by the agreement of the parties, was specifically approved by the Lands Tribunal on the ground that but for the scheme[5] underlying the acquisition the vandalism would not have occurred. It seems difficult, however, to accept that vandalism can be *directly* attributable to the scheme, except perhaps where the acquiring authority take possession of surrounding property, leave it vacant, and thereby increase the incidence of vandalism in the vicinity. But even in that situation it is arguable that the question of liability is more a matter of nuisance[6] than of compensation since the liability of the authority would not depend upon whether or not they proceeded[7] to acquire the affected property.[8]

DETERMINATION OF INTERESTS TO BE VALUED

As already indicated, prior to the *West Midland Baptist* case it had been regarded as settled law that valuation of land compulsorily acquired must be based upon values ruling, interests subsisting and circumstances prevailing as at the date of the notice to treat. The crucial factor in the *West Midland Baptist* case was the inflation in land values and building costs between the date of notice to treat and the date of entry (or date of determination of the compensation). No other changes were in issue and the question arises whether, when there have been changes in interests or other relevant circumstances since service of the

---

[1] See pp. 96–97 *ante*.

[2] [1905] 2 KB 753.

[3] *Birmingham Corpn* v *West Midland Baptist (Trust) Association Inc.* [1970] AC 874, [1969] 3 All ER 172 HL per Lord Reid at p. 180.

[4] *Kirby and Shaw* v *Bury County Borough Council* (1973), 228 Estates Gazette 537.

[5] It is a fundamental principle that the effect on value of the scheme in pursuance of which land is acquired is to be ignored: see pp. 217 *et seq, infra*.

[6] See, e.g., *A-G* v *Corke*, [1933] Ch. 89.

[7] Note that even if notice to treat has been served it is open to the authority to withdraw within six weeks of receipt of the notice of claim: Land Compensation Act 1961, s. 31.

[8] See R. Carnwath's article "Compulsory Purchase—Vandalism and 'The Scheme'," R & VR (1974) 562.

notice to treat, the old rule prevails. In other words, is the effect of the *West Midland Baptist* case merely that date of entry values are to be applied to the interests subsisting in, and the other circumstances affecting the value of the land as at the date of notice to treat, or is it the interests subsisting and circumstances prevailing at the date of entry that are to be those governing the valuation?

For example, between date of notice to treat and date of entry the owner of the land inherits[1] adjoining land that will be injuriously affected by the acquisition: is he entitled to compensation for such injurious affection? Again, if, in the interval, planning permission for the development of adjoining land has affected market value either of the land retained[2] or of land taken, is that to be taken into acount? Interests may also change as when, between these dates, a lease expires or following the death of a protected tenant the landlord becomes entitled to possession.

There is a number of cases in which the Lands Tribunal has assumed that the date of entry is the relevant date for all purposes.[3] Thus in both *Metcalfe*'s case and the *Midland Bank* case[3] the issue was whether houses occupied by statutory or controlled tenants, rehoused by the acquiring authority, should be valued on a vacant possession or a "tenanted" basis, the authority being, by definition, unable to take possession until the tenants had vacated. It was held that the interests to be valued were those existing at the date of entry, by which time the houses were, of course, vacant. In the *Midland Bank* case the Tribunal went so far as to express the view that valuation at the time of entry could only be a sensible exercise or principle if the interests were to be taken as those existing on that date.

Similarly, in *Banham*'s case the President of the Lands Tribunal[4] said

> "It seems to me impossible to say that the interests in land compulsorily acquired are immutably fixed by the service of a notice to treat. The correct rule would seem to be that interests as well as values must be taken as at the date of valuation or entry unless the owner has done something which so altered the interests as to increase the burden of compensation to the acquiring authority".

The Land Compensation Act 1973[5] now provides, however, that where property is subject to a tenancy at the date of notice to treat and the tenant is rehoused in accordance with the obligations imposed by that Act upon local and other authorities,[6] the acquiring authority is to be deemed to have taken possession on the date on which the tenant gives it up and no account is to be taken of any increase in value

---

[1] If such land is purchased for value it is, of course, to be expected that the price will reflect the injurious affection.

[2] For the effect upon compensation of enhancement or diminution in value of land retained by a vendor of land compulsorily acquired see pp. 217 *et seq, infra,* and Chap. 8, p. 314 *post.*

[3] *Banham* v *London Borough of Hackney* (1970), 22 P & CR 922; *Bradford Property Trust Ltd.* v *Hertfordshire County Council* (1973), 27 P & CR 228; *Metcalfe* v *Basildon Development Corpn* (1974) 28 P & CR 307; *Midland Bank Trust Co. Ltd. (Executors)* v *London Borough of Lewisham* (1975), 30 P & CR 480: see also *David* v *London Borough of Lewisham* [1977] JPL 528 (occupancy not amounting to a tenancy).

[4] Sir Michael Rowe, QC.

[5] Land Compensation Act 1973, s. 50(2).

[6] By *ibid,* s. 39(1)(a): see p. 389, *post.*

attributable to the tenant giving up possession. In short, compensation is to be based upon tenanted[1] as opposed to vacant possession value.[2] This is not, of course, to say that the date of service of the notice to treat therefore becomes the relevant date, for if the tenant himself finds alternative accommodation or is rehoused by the landlord or otherwise than by or on behalf of the acquiring authority, the relevant date remains that of the date of entry.

Nevertheless, there are also important cases in which it has been held, or assumed, that the appropriate rule is that the interests to be valued and the relevant surrounding circumstances are to be considered as they existed immediately before or immediately after the service of notice to treat.[3] In the *Shaw-Fox* case for example, Lord Pearson suggested[4] that the latter rule was confirmed by the statutory requirement to serve a notice to treat, *inter alia*, demanding "particulars of the recipient's estate and interest in the land and of the claim made by him in respect of the land".[5] However, since the implication of the *West Midland Baptist*[6] case is that a claim (i.e., for compensation) made in response to a notice to treat is subject to revision if values change between service of the notice and determination of the compensation (or date of entry), this would not appear to take the matter very much further. It cannot *follow* that the interests in the land then held by the recipient are not similarly subject to change with the passage of time.

Moreover, in the *Shaw-Fox* case the alternative of considering the interests as at the date of entry was not in issue; indeed, the case turned upon the wholly different problem of the effect of the scheme of acquisition.

It is a principle of the law of compensation that no account shall be taken of the effect on value of the scheme of acquisition and development in pursuance of which the land is acquired.[7] Thus if land including a quarry is acquired for a development requiring large quantities of stone the reflection of that increased demand on the value of the quarry is to be ignored if no such demand would have arisen but for the scheme.[8] Schemes of acquisition may, however, affect the *interests* to be valued. For example, under the Agricultural Holdings Act 1948 an effective notice to quit may be served upon a tenant of agricultural land where the land is required for some non-agricultural purpose for which

---

[1] Note that these rehousing obligations are not confined to cases involving statutory etc. tenancies: p. 389, *post*.

[2] See, e.g., *Bailey* v *Reading Borough Council* (1977), 33 P & CR 124, and *Babij* v *Metropolitan Borough of Rochdale* [1976] JPL 701 in which the Land Compensation Act 1973, s. 50(2) was applied even though there was no obligation to rehouse.

[3] See, e.g., *Rugby Joint Water Board* v *Shaw-Fox*, [1972] 2 WLR 757, per Lord Pearson at p. 764: *Zoar Independent Church Trustees* v *Rochester Corpn*, [1974] 3 WLR 417 CA, a case under Rule 5, *supra*, following service of a purchase notice (as to which see pp. 114 *et seq, ante*): *Toogood* v *Bristol Corpn* (1973), 26 P & CR 132, and (1974) 28 P & CR 473 (LT), also a "purchase notice" case.

[4] At p. 764.

[5] Compulsory Purchase Act 1965, s. 5(2).

[6] And see the *W & S (Long Eaton)* case, p. 168, *supra*.

[7] Commonly referred to as the *Pointe Gourde* principle; see the following note and pp. 218 *et seq, infra*.

[8] *Pointe Gourde Quarrying and Transport Co. Ltd.* v *Sub-Intendent of Crown Lands*, [1947] AC 565: and see pp. 218 *et seq, infra*.

planning permission has been granted.[1] In other words, the planning permission deprives the tenant of the protection afforded by the Act by the restrictions it imposes upon the landlord's freedom to obtain possession upon the expiration of the tenancy. Thus, where, as in the *Shaw-Fox* case[2] agricultural land was required for a reservoir it was argued on behalf of the acquiring authority that since the loss of protection arose only from the scheme it fell to be ignored. It was held, however, by the House of Lords, that it was the planning permission rather than the scheme which had activated this provision of the Act so that planning permission having preceded the notice to treat, the landlord's interest for compensation purposes was a freehold interest subject to an unprotected tenancy rather than the much less valuable interest subject to a protected tenancy. In other words, although the effect of "schemes of acquisition" may affect the compensation payable, they do not affect the interests falling to be valued.

Although the Land Compensation Act 1961[3] specifically overrules this decision by enacting, in effect, that the right of the landlord to serve an effective notice to quit in these circumstances is to be ignored, it does not affect the *ratio decidendi* of the decision in the Shaw-Fox case. That decision specifically depended upon the planning permission having been granted before service of notice to treat. The implication is, therefore, that it would have been different if the relevant date had been in issue and the planning permission had been granted between the date of notice to treat and entry (or, if earlier, the determination of the compensation).

Nevertheless, since it was held that it was the planning permission that activated the relevant provision of the Agricultural Holdings Act 1948 it is difficult to see what difference it would have made if the relevant date had been the date of entry and the permission had been granted at any time before that date. It is doubtful, therefore, whether the *Shaw-Fox* case can be accepted as a reliable authority for adhering to the date of notice to treat as the relevant date for the purpose of determining the interests to be valued.[4]

Different considerations arise, however, where between service of notice to treat and entry (or, if earlier, the date of determination of the compensation) an interest has ceased to exist, e.g., where a lease has expired.[5] Thus in *Holloway* v *Dover Corporation*[6] a lease, having more than five years to run at the date when the notice to treat was deemed to have been served, had expired before the date of entry. It was held that by that date there was no proprietary right capable of acquisition and

---

[1] Agricultural Holdings Act 1948, s. 24(2)(b): see also *ibid*, s. 23(1)(b), which makes similar provision where notice to quit is given in pursuance of a provision in the tenancy agreement authorising resumption of possession for some specified non-agricultural use.

[2] *Rugby Joint Water Board* v *Shaw-Fox*, [1972] 2 WLR 757, HL.

[3] S. 48(1).

[4] In the other cases cited in note 3, p. 171, *supra*, the relevant date was also not in issue but appears to have been either assumed or agreed by the parties to be the date of notice to treat.

[5] As to the effect of agreements reached prior to the date of entry see *Munton* v *Newham Borough Council*, p. 167, *supra*.

[6] [1960] 1 WLR 604 CA, i.e., prior to the *West Midland Baptist* case.

therefore no subject matter for which a claim for compensation could be made.

Similarly, in a very much older case, where a lease, having some thirty years to run at the date of service of the notice to treat, reserved to the lessor the right to regain possession upon giving three months' notice at stated intervals, and the landlord exercised that right after notice to treat but before the acquiring authority exercised their right of entry, it was held that the lessee could only claim compensation in respect of the outstanding balance of the three months period of notice.[1]

In *Soper & Soper v Doncaster Corporation*[2] on the other hand the claimants' lease was due to expire on 31 January 1963. In July 1962 agreement had been reached for a new lease for five years from 1 February 1963. Notice to treat was served in August 1962 and notice of entry on 25 September 1963. It was held that the agreement for a new lease gave them a compensatable interest on the ground that "every man's interest shall be valued *rebus sic stantibus*, just as it occurs at the very moment when the notice to treat is given".[3] This case was distinguished from *Holloway*'s case on the ground that whereas in that case neither party had taken any action in pursuance of the notice to treat so that the lease had simply expired with effluxion of time, in the *Sopers'* case the claimants had responded to the notice to treat by lodging their claim in the proper form and within the prescribed period. The inference, of course, is that the claimant in *Holloway*'s case could have had a price based upon his interest as it had been at the date of notice to treat had he taken the necessary steps.[4] It must, however, be borne in mind that both these cases preceded the *West Midland Baptist* case and that the only reason why, in *Holloway*'s case, the date on which proceedings were instituted in the Lands Tribunal was the relevant date was the fact that no other action had been taken following notice to treat.

The difficulty in accepting a rule that in the absence of prior agreement or determination of the compensation payable, the date of entry is universally applicable as the date as at which the interests to be valued are to be determined, arises from the fact that in certain circumstances such a rule can cut right across two fundamental principles—though in practice probably only when there is a substantial interval between the dates of notice to treat and entry. In the first place if interests are acquired by purchase between notice to treat and entry the financial burden upon the acquiring authority may, contrary to the basic rule,[5]

---

[1] *R. v Kennedy*, [1893] 1 QB 533.

[2] (1964) 16 P & CR 53.

[3] Per Wood V-C in *Penny v Penny* (1868), LR 5 Eq. 227, cited at 16 P & CR p. 60.

[4] *Per* Lord Evershed MR in *Holloway v Dover Corpn*, [1960] 1 WLR 604, at p. 609.

[5] Acquisition of Land (Authorisation Procedure) Act 1946, Sch. 2, para. 8: p. 69, *supra*. In such cases there seems little doubt that the general rule will prevail: *Cardiff Corpn v Cook*, [1923] 2 Ch. 115: *Dawson v Great Northern and City Rly Co.*, [1905] 1 KB 260 CA, and see the views of Sellers and Salmon LJJ in the *West Midland Baptist* case, [1968] 2 QB at pp. 206 and 215 respectively. In such cases as *Holloway*'s and the *Sopers'* the question whether the relevant date is that of notice to treat or entry does not affect the total compensation payable by the acquiring authority; it merely affects its distribution as between lessor and lessee, for the decline in the value of the lease with effluxion of time is reflected in the increasing value of the reversion: see *Banham v London Borough of Hackney* (1970), 22 P & CR 922, and see the views of the President of the Lands Tribunal in that case, p. 170, *supra*.

be increased:[1] similarly if the vendor is impelled to dispose of interests in adjoining land,[2] or his position is prejudiced by the action of the acquiring authority[2] and compensation fails to represent his true loss.[3]

On the other hand, as has been seen,[4] even before the *West Midland Baptist* case exceptions had to be made to the universal adoption of the date of notice to treat to ensure that no compensation was payable where the claimant suffered no loss. There seems no logical reason, therefore, why exceptions should not be made to the rule, now evidently generally accepted, that the crucial date is the date of entry, in order to meet cases where acquisitions or dispositions between that date and the date of notice to treat have either increased the burden upon the acquiring authority or faced the claimant with financial loss. That, even *post* the *West Midland Baptist* case, this rule has not been rigidly applied at least obtains some support from the *Shaw-Fox* case[5] while it may not be entirely without significance that for the purpose of deciding whether compensation for a house should be based upon vacant possession or tenanted value, the Land Compensation Act 1973 has reverted to the date of notice to treat as the crucial date—provided, of course, subsequent vacation by the tenant is attributable to his rehousing by or on behalf of the acquiring authority.[6]

In certain circumstances the notice to treat can itself change the interests to be valued. Thus where an underlease was subject to a proviso for re-entry if the land should be required or taken by a railway or other public company under compulsory powers conferred by statute, the service of notice to treat by the railway company activated the proviso and the owners of the headlease were held to be entitled to compensation based on the value of the lease, freed from the underlease.[7]

THE RELEVANT DATE: SUMMARY

(a) The general rule is that the interests to be valued for compensation purposes and any surrounding circumstances that affect their value are those existing at the date of entry or the date on which compensation falls to be determined, whichever is the earlier.[8]

(b) To this general rule there may be the following exceptions:

    (i) Where the land being acquired comprises a dwelling house, tenanted at the date of notice to treat but vacated by the

---

[1] E.g., where adjoining land so acquired is depreciated in value by severance from the land taken or suffers injurious affection from the proposed development thereon.

[2] E.g., by a change in the development plan, and note that in assessing what planning permissions are to be assumed for the purposes of valuation it is the date of notice to treat that is normally crucial: see pp. 185 *et seq*, *infra*.

[3] See p. 161, *supra*.

[4] *Holloway*'s case and *Kennedy*'s case, *supra*.

[5] But see p. 172, *supra*. See, however, *Walters, Brett and Pack* v *South Glamorgan County Council* (1976), 238 Estates Gazette 733 (LT), a case in which acquisition was in pursuance of a blight notice and the date of the deemed notice to treat was held to be the crucial date in determining when the claimants vacated: see p. 352, *post*.

[6] P. 170, *supra*.

[7] In re *Morgan and London and North Western Rly Co.*, [1896] 2 QB 469. Note the similarity in principle with the decision in the *Shaw-Fox* case, p. 171–172, *supra*.

[8] Pp. 169 *et seq*, *supra*.

tenant upon being rehoused by or on behalf of the acquiring authority,[1] the authority is deemed to have taken possession upon the date of vacation and compensation falls to be assessed at "tenanted" as opposed to vacant possession value.[2]

(ii) Where subsequent to the date of notice to treat the vendor of the subject land has taken actions that increase the burden upon the acquiring authority the effect of such actions upon value are to be ignored.[3]

(iii) Where the vendor is prejudiced by events beyond his control occurring between the date of notice to treat and the date of entry (or determination of the compensation) the date of notice to treat *may* be substituted for whichever of the later dates is applicable, particularly where the claimant has initiated the acquisition by service of a purchase or blight notice.[4]

(iv) It is open to the parties to agree an alternative date.

(c) The assessment of the value of the relevant interests falls to be made in the light of the relevant circumstances and values ruling at the date of entry or the date on which the compensation falls to be determined, whichever is the earlier.[5]

(d) Where there has been no entry the relevant date for the purposes of valuation is the date on which the compensation is agreed.

(e) In the absence of agreement it is the date of the Lands Tribunal's award,[6] although in conditions of market stability it is open to the Lands Tribunal to opt for, or the parties to agree upon, the date of the notice of reference.[7]

(f) If the service of the notice to treat itself affects the pre-existing interests in the land, that effect is to be taken into account in determining the relevant interests.[8]

(g) Interest[9] is normally payable at the rate prescribed from whichever of the following dates is applicable:

(i) If entry precedes determination of compensation, the date of entry;

(ii) If compensation is determined prior to entry and a good title has by then been shown, the date of determination;

(iii) If compensation is determined prior to entry but title has not been made, the date on which title is made—provided that entry does not intervene. If it does, (i) above applies.

---

[1] I.e., under Land Compensation Act 1973, s. 39, p. 170, *supra*.
[2] *Ibid*, s. 50(2).
[3] P. 173, *supra*, and note 5, thereon.
[4] P. 174, *supra*, and note particularly the case cited in note 5 thereon.
[5] But see p. 171, *supra*.
[6] *W & S (Long Eaton) Ltd* v *Derbyshire County Council*, p. 168, *supra*.
[7] *Hull Trinity House Corpn* v *Humberside County Council*, p. 169, *supra*.
[8] *In re Morgan and the London and North Western Rly Co.*, p. 174, *supra*.
[9] See p. 96, *ante*.

EFFECT ON VALUE OF PROSPECT OF COMPULSORY ACQUISITION

Once it is known that land is likely to become the subject of compulsory acquisition market interest inevitably wanes: indeed, where the plans of the prospective acquiring authority are reasonably definite, market demand will probably be entirely eliminated. Such land may therefore have had little or no genuine market value for some years before it is actually required by the authority concerned—let alone at the date of entry or the date on which compensation falls to be determined. It is fundamental to the principle that the purpose of compensation is to put the vendor in the same financial position as he would have been in but for the acquisition that this blighting effect of the prospect of compulsory acquisition should be disregarded. It is accordingly provided that:

> "No account shall be taken of any depreciation of the value of the relevant interest which is attributable to the fact that (whether by way of designation, allocation or other particulars contained in the current development plan, or by any other means) an indication has been given that the relevant land is, or is likely to be acquired by an authority possessing compulsory purchase powers".[1]

It is to be noted, however, that this provision is solely applicable to the valuation of the interest being acquired and has no application to the determination of that interest. Thus in *Tranter* v *City of Birmingham District Council*[2] the owner of a building with an established use as a warehouse was unable to find a tenant for the building for that purpose, allegedly because of an indication that the property was likely to be compulsorily acquired. He accordingly let the property as a residence, for which purpose it was occupied by a protected tenant both at the date of notice to treat and the date of entry. It was held that the premises must be valued in accordance with the circumstances ruling at the date of notice to treat[3] (i.e., as a residence subject to a protected tenancy)[4] and that their value as a warehouse was irrelevant.[5]

It is also to be emphasised that there must be an indication that the land is likely to be compulsorily acquired. Accordingly, if land is intended to be laid out as a road by developers and there is no indication of any intention that it is ultimately to be acquired by the local highway authority the owner cannot rely on this provision simply

---

[1] Land Compensation Act 1961, s. 9.

[2] (1976) 31 P & CR 327.

[3] Note that although the Tribunal referred throughout to the situation as at the date of notice to treat, the relevant date for the purpose of determining the interest to be valued was not in issue, the position being precisely the same at the date of entry: see p. 169, *supra*.

[4] The residential use in fact contravened planning control. Had that aspect been in issue rule 4 (pp. 164, *supra* and 179, *infra*) would seem to preclude the assessment of compensation on the basis of that use. Presumably, therefore, there would have been no alternative but to value the premises on a warehouse basis but subject to a protected tenancy, with all the difficulties of obtaining possession imposed by the Rent Acts.

[5] The Lands Tribunal also took the view that the letting for residential purposes was an independent act on the part of the claimant: cf. *Walters, Brett and Park* v *South Glamorgan County Council*, [1976] 238 Estates Gazette 733, LT, p. 352, *post*. For a case in which the threat of compulsory acquisition was held not to have affected the value of an outstanding planning permission because there were other reasons for failing to implement it, see *J. Davy Ltd.* v *London Borough of Hammersmith* (1975), 30 P & CR 469.

because the land is subsequently acquired in pursuance of a purchase notice.[1]

MARKET VALUE

The basic Rule: Rule 2

Except where the land (and/or the buildings thereon) has been adapted for a specialised use to suit the special needs of the owner for which there is no general market demand[2] compensation for land taken is based upon Rule 2,[3] i.e., "the amount which the land, if sold in the open market[4] by a willing seller might be expected to realise." The rule thus reverses the principle previously applied under the Lands Clauses Consolidation Act 1845, s. 63, that compensation should be based upon the value to the owner[5]— in the sense that special attributes of the land of personal value to the owner but which do not increase market value are to be ignored in the assessment of compensation.[6] Instead, the basis of compensation becomes the value to the owner in the stricter financial sense of the value realisable in the open market.[7]

Rules 1, 3 and 4[8] may in a sense be said to be merely corollaries of the requirement in Rule 2 that the compensation be assessed in relation to sales in the open market.

Rule 1

Thus Rule 1 abolished the pre-1919 practice of awarding, in addition to the value of the land to the owner, a solatium by way of compensation for the compulsory nature of the acquisition and the fact that, in such circumstances, few vendors can be assumed in fact to be willing sellers. It is to be noted, however, that it is specifically enacted that any depreciation in the value of the land attributable to the prospect of threat of compulsory acquisition is also to be disregarded.[9] Obviously, once it is known that there is a likelihood of compulsory acquisition the actual market will be much reduced if not eliminated altogether so that without this provision compensation would be reduced far below any sum that the land would be likely to fetch if, in the absence of any requirement by a public body, the vendor was in fact free to sell in the open market.

---

[1] *Morris and Jacombs Ltd.* v *City of Birmingham District Council* (1976), 31 P & CR 305.

[2] I.e., under Rule 5 (p. 164, *supra*), for a general explanation of which see p. 165, *supra*: for detailed application of the rule see Chap. 6, pp. 239, *et seq, post*.

[3] Land Compensation Act 1961, s. 5(2), p. 164, *supra*.

[4] I.e., the market in which vendor and purchaser could have legitimately operated at the date concerned, and *not* a purely hypothetical free market: *Priestman Collieries Ltd.* v *Northern District Valuation Board*, [1950] 2 KB 398—a case under the similar provisions of the Coal Industry Nationalisation Act 1946, in which post-war price restrictions operative at the date at which valuation of the property fell to be made were held to be those to be taken into account although sale in a completely free market would have produced significantly higher figures.

[5] See, e.g., *Glover* v *Edmonton Corpn* (1953), 3 P & CR 451.

[6] The old rule is, however, preserved under Rule 5; see p. 239 *et seq, post*; it is also specifically restored in the case of dwellings specially adapted for a handicapped person: Land Compensation Act 1973, s. 45, p. 165, *supra*.

[7] See pp. 217 *et seq, infra*.

[8] Land Compensation Act 1961, s. 5(1), (3) and (4), p. 164, *supra*.

[9] *Ibid*, s. 9.

It may therefore be more helpful—and equally accurate—to re-define the basis of compensation for land taken as the amount which the land would realise if, *there being no question of the land being required by an authority possessing compulsory powers*, it is sold in the open market by a willing seller.

Rule 3

Similarly Rule 3 in effect requires the land to be valued on the basis of a potential use for which there is likely to be more than one probable bidder—in other words, there must be a genuine *general* market demand and not merely a special demand from someone with a special need for a particular purpose to which the land is suited but for which it commands no general market demand.

It must, however, be emphasised that the rule goes somewhat further than to eliminate special values to a particular purchaser. For example, the first part of the rule eliminates value attributable to any special suitability or adaptability of the land for a purpose for which it can only be used in pursuance of statutory powers, even though there may be more than one authority with the requisite powers in the market for land suitable for that purpose. In other words, the rule eliminates the effect of competition from two or more such authorities which, under the Lands Clauses Acts could be taken into account.

It must also be noted that it is the special suitability or adaptability conferred by the quality and location of the land that is crucial and not the special suitability or adaptability of the *products* of the land for a particular purpose. Thus the additional value conferred upon a quarry because of the special suitability of the stone obtainable from it for some special purpose is *not* a factor that falls to be deducted under the rule. But if that additional element of value arises solely from the additional demand created by the proposed development it will fall to be ignored as additional value arising from the "scheme of acquisition".[1]

Similarly the special value of the land to a neighbouring owner anxious to extend his own property falls to be ignored.[2] On the other hand, if, for example, the subject matter of the acquisition is the reversion to a lease, its "special" value to a sitting tenant (as opposed to an investor) has nothing whatever to do with the quality or location of the land, and the desire of the sitting tenant to merge these interests is not a "special purpose" within the rule.[3]

Similarly, if there is a general market demand for the land for some

---

[1] *Pointe Gourde Quarrying and Transport Co. Ltd.* v *Sub-Intendent of Crown Lands*, [1947] AC 565; and see pp. 217 *et seq*, *infra*.

[2] In *IRC* v *Clay*, [1914] 3 KB 466 CA, a case on provisions in the Finance (1909–10) Act 1910 similar to those of Rule 2, it was held that the fact that purchasers would know that the neighbour would be willing to pay a high price would therefore increase the market value. Cf. *Barstow* v *Rothwell UDC infra*.

[3] *Lambe* v *Secretary of State for War*, [1955] 2 QB 612. In that case the acquiring authority (The War Department) was the sitting tenant. It does not follow that, had the War Department been acquiring the freehold with the intention of entering and developing the land only after the expiration of a lease held by a third party, the value of the reversion would have been the value to the sitting tenant. In such a case any prospect of the tenant paying a price above investment value would seem to represent a special value to the owner rather than a reflection of market demand as in *Glover* v *Edmonton Corpn* (1953), 3 P & CR 451.

purpose, that purpose is not excluded simply because there is a particular purchaser willing to pay more than others for the land for that purpose, whether taken by itself or in conjunction with other land owned by him. Thus in *Barstow* v *Rothwell UDC*[1] the land the subject of the acquisition was a narrow strip of backland of only about one-fifth of an acre in area. It was bordered on the one side by allotments and on the other by a strip of frontage land owned by the acquiring authority. The authority required the subject land in order satisfactorily to develop it along with their own frontage land, which on its own was of insufficient depth for the residential development proposed. The acquiring authority accordingly argued that this was a classic Rule 3 case since the subject land had no market for residential purposes apart from the needs of the owner of the adjoining frontage land, namely the authority themselves. The evidence, however, clearly showed that in the light of a falling demand for allotments and increasing pressure for more residential development the probability was that planning permission for residential development of the allotment land would ultimately be granted and that there would therefore be a demand for the subject land for development in conjunction therewith. It was accordingly held that Rule 3 did *not* apply. In these circumstances the Tribunal had no doubt "that under Rule 2 there would be a lively higgling period to arrive at the market value of the subject land" and awarded compensation on the basis of its value as a potential addition to the adjoining allotment land.[2]

Similarly in *Corrie* v *Central Land Board*[3] the subject land had considerable value, for tipping, to the prospective purchaser, the National Coal Board. But it also had *some* value for the same purpose to certain other persons. Although the demand from such other persons appeared somewhat problematical, it was nevertheless held that, since there could be said to be a market for the land, Rule 3 did not apply and the compensation was asssessed as the price that the Coal Board would have paid in free negotiations with a willing seller.

Rule 4

As a general proposition one would not in any case expect a purchaser to pay a price reflecting the value of a use of the land that "can be restrained by any Court or is contrary to law". It is therefore somewhat difficult to see what this Rule adds to or detracts from Rule 2. Nevertheless, there can of course be cases where land is perfectly legitimately being used for a purpose which under certain circumstances could give rise to an injunction in respect, for example, of noise. It is not, for example, unusual for the owners of dance halls, gambling clubs and the like to be restrained from operating outside certain hours—a "restraint" that would presumably affect profits and hence the market value of the premises for that purpose.

[1] (1970) 22 P & CR 942.
[2] See also *Vyricherla Narayana Gajapatiraju* v *Revenue Divisional Officer, Vizagapatam*, [1939] AC 302 (PC), in which what was envisaged was a "friendly negotiation" between a willing seller who expects a reasonable price for his land with its potentialities, and a willing purchaser, who may be the acquiring authority.
[3] (1954) 4 P & CR 276.

Although there appears to be no judicial authority on this matter it would seem that where such premises are situated in a residential area and are known to be the source of nuisance, it could be argued by an acquiring authority that the likelihood of "restraint" should be taken into account where the market value is assessed on the basis of sales of otherwise comparable property situated where nuisance is unlikely to be caused to occupiers of neighbouring property.

It must, however, be emphasised that Rule 4 only applies where the value is increased by actual as opposed to potential use for some purpose that can be restrained or is contrary to law. In other words, Rule 4 has no application to "hope value"—that is, a value reflecting the market's estimate of the chances of some use, currently restrainable[1] or contrary to law, ultimately becoming authorised.[2] That is a matter for the market, however mistaken such an estimate may appear to be to those who would be responsible for authorisation.

An increasingly common example of land values being inflated by mistaken beliefs as to their *potential* use arises where undeveloped land is sold in small plots as "leisure units". Although in most cases the "small print" indicates that no planning permission is currently available, purchasers are frequently led to believe that planning permission for residential development is ultimately likely to be forthcoming (even where the land is in the Green Belt). In such cases, of course, it being only this mistakenly assumed development potential and not any existing use that can be restrained, Rule 4 has no application. On the contrary, the basis of valuation for such plots compulsorily acquired will be the prices at which similar plots are currently changing hands in the open market.[3]

ASSESSMENT OF MARKET VALUE

The concept of market value as the basis of compensation for the compulsory acquisition of land of necessity involves consideration not merely of the price that a purchaser can be expected to pay for the land in its existing use, but the price that the land will command when full account is taken of its potential for some more valuable development.[4] That in turn involves an assessment of the types of development that would be permissible within the confines of planning control. As explained in chapter 1,[5] Part I of the Town and Country Planning Act 1959[6] accordingly made provision whereby in appropriate cir-

---

[1] E.g., by enforcement proceedings under the Town and Country Planning Act 1971, Part V (ss. 87–111).

[2] E.g., by the grant of planning permission or of some appropriate licence.

[3] Recent examples of sales of agricultural land in plots of one-quarter and one-half acre have produced prices equivalent to over £6,000 per acre as against local agricultural values of £600 to £700 per acre!

[4] See *Vyricherla Narayana Gajapatiraju* v *The Revenue Divisional Officer, Vizagapatam*, [1939] AC 302 at p. 313. Conversely, the effect of any restrictions subject to which the vendor holds the land must similarly be taken into account (*Corrie* v *MacDermott*, [1914] AC 1056), though since the passing of the Acquisition of Land (Assessment of Compensation) Act 1919 the question to be considered is the extent to which such restrictions affect the value to the purchaser.

[5] Pp. 14 *et seq, ante.*

[6] Now the Land Compensation Act 1961, Parts I and II.

cumstances planning permission for certain classes of development is to be assumed when assessing market value for the purposes of compensation.

In considering these assumptions, however, it must be borne in mind that they apply *only* to the land in which the interest being acquired subsists.[1] They do not extend to other land retained by the vendor and are not therefore specifically applicable to such land for the purposes of assessing compensation for severance or injurious affection.[2] Nevertheless the basis of compensation under that head is the depreciation in the value of such retained land resulting from the compulsory acquisition—i.e., the difference in market value before and after the severance. Such depreciation can in many cases in practice only be assessed on the basis of a purchaser's reasonable expectation as to development likely to be permitted in the absence of severance, and of the extent to which those expectations are reduced by the acquisition of, and the development proposed on, the land acquired. There will be many cases, therefore, in which the planning permission to be assumed in relation to the land acquired will be highly relevant.

It has also to be borne in mind that the assumptions for which the Land Compensation Act 1961 provides are not exclusive, for it is also specifically provided that "nothing in those provisions shall be construed as requiring it to be assumed that planning permission would necessarily be refused for any development which is not development for which, in accordance with those provisions, the granting of planning permission is to be assumed".[3]

It will no doubt be obvious to practitioners that the planning permissions to be taken into account in the assessment of compensation are only of relevance in so far as they affect market value.[4] Unfortunately, however, the development boom of the early 1960s and early 1970s, and the accompanying very high prices obtained for land carrying the appropriate planning permission, have in many circles led to the belief that it is the grant of planning permission in itself that almost automatically confers a substantial increase in the value of the land. This is of course not so, the effect on value depending purely upon the market demand for the land with the planning permission in question. This in turn broadly depends upon two sets of factors: on the one hand there are local factors such as the location of the land, proposals for the development of the neighbourhood as a whole and their effect upon the local environment, the existence of services, prospects of employment, and so on. On the other hand are national factors relating to the economy, such as the general level of prosperity and the expectations to which that gives rise, the availability of loan finance etc. Thus in areas of high unemployment where Government has responded by the provision of "advance factories" in the hope of attracting industry there may be

[1] Land Compensation Act 1961, s. 14(1).
[2] See Chap. 8, p. 314 *post*.
[3] Land Compensation Act 1961, s. 14(3).
[4] *J. Davy Ltd.* v *Hammersmith London Borough Council* (1975), 30 P & CR 469. See also *Bromilow* v *Greater Manchester Council* (1974), 29 P & CR 517 (LT) and 31 P & CR 398 (CA), and *Viscount Camrose* v *Basingstoke Corpn* [1966] 3 All ER 161, *per* Lord Denning MR at p. 164.

very little demand for other land carrying planning permission for industrial development. Similarly, despite acute housing shortages in some of our larger cities, census returns have over the past decades shown a national excess of dwellings compared with the total number of households—in other words, in some areas supply already exceeds demand—a situation which is sometimes disguised by the demand for holiday cottages and second homes—a demand which in the current economic climate may not be maintained.

Before considering the planning permissions to be assumed in the assessment of compensation there are certain more general matters relevant to the assessment of market value which need to be noted. In the first place, where business premises are acquired, they are to be valued as part of a going concern.[1]

Secondly, in valuing business premises held on a lease or agricultural land held either on a lease or from year to year, account has to be taken of the tenant's right to the renewal of his lease under the Landlord and Tenant Act 1954[2] in the case of business tenancies and of the security of tenure provisions of the Agricultural Holdings Act 1948 in the case of agricultural tenancies.[3] Since these considerations are of perhaps even more importance in relation to the assessment of compensation for disturbance they are considered in greater detail in chapter 9.[4]

Where, however, the value of a leasehold interest in business premises (and the same principle applies to other categories of land) is mainly attributable to the potential of the land for redevelopment—in which case the landlord is likely to be able to resist renewal of the lease under the Act of 1954[5]—it may nevertheless be reasonable to assume renewal if the prospect of the redevelopment is of mutual advantage to both lessor and lessee. Thus in the *Trocette Property Company*'s case[6] a disused cinema was held on a lease having some eleven and a half years unexpired from the Greater London Council. It was intimated to the lessees that the lessors would probably renew the lease and conditional planning permission was granted for the erection of shops etc. Subsequently the Greater London Council produced plans for a new road crossing the site, and the lessees were told that a new lease could no longer be contemplated. The lessees applied to the Southwark London Borough Council for permission to build shops on the site and upon that application being refused, served a purchase notice.[7] The Lands Tribunal held that it was to be assumed that apart from the road scheme the planning permission to be expected would be such as to attract the interest of the landlord so that the grant of a new long lease could also be assumed. Although they were overruled on this point by the Court of Appeal, it was only because the evidence clearly showed

---

[1] *Park Automobile Co.* v *City of Glasgow District Council* (1975), 30 P & CR 491: see p. 356, *post.*
[2] Land Compensation Act 1973, s. 47.
[3] *Ibid*, s. 48.
[4] See pp. 370 *et seq, post.*
[5] Landlord and Tenant Act 1954, s. 30(1)(f), p. 370, *post.*
[6] *Trocette Property Co. Ltd.* v *Greater London Council and Southwark London Borough Council* (1973), 27 P & CR 256 (LT); (1974) 28 P & CR 408 (CA).
[7] See pp. 114 *et seq, ante.*

that after the formulation of the road proposals the landlords (the Greater London Council) were not in fact prepared to consider a further lease.[1]

Although it was emphasised in the *Trocette* case that the fact that the landlord happened to be the local planning authority was immaterial, that is not to say that the relationship between lessor and lessee is necessarily irrelevant in valuing a lease. Thus, where the lessor was a wholly owned subsidiary of the lessees it was held that the chances of the parent company, as lessees, allowing anyone else to acquire the freehold and enforce the lessee's covenants against them were nil; the repairing covenant in the lease did not, therefore, add to the value of the reversion.[2]

Thirdly, in valuing *any* land with development potential, allowance has to be made for the 'market' cost of remedying any restrictions upon the carrying out of the development for which planning permission is to be assumed. Thus in the case of the compulsory acquisition of backland a deduction will have to be made equivalent to the amount that the owner would be likely to have to pay to his neighbour in order to secure access. In *Stokes* v *Cambridge Corpn*,[3] which has become a leading case in this regard, the Lands Tribunal considered that in such circumstances the owner of the access land would demand a share of the development value of the backland, which the sale of his land would enable its owner to realise; the proportion considered appropriate by the Lands Tribunal was one-third of the realisable development value[4] of the backland.

A similar principle applies where difficulties of access or other problems cast doubt upon the likelihood of a planning permission (which it would otherwise be reasonable to anticipate) being granted.[5] So also where the development of the subject land depends upon its release from the burden of a restrictive covenant prohibiting or limiting its development. Thus in *SJC Construction Co. Ltd.* v *Sutton London Borough Council*[6] the reasonable cost of buying out the rights of the owner of the dominant tenement was assessed at 50 % of the realisable development value of the servient land.

It is also to be noted as a matter of practice that, valuation being a

[1] The appeal by the two local authorities was nevertheless dismissed because, for other reasons, the Court of Appeal's decision on this point made no difference to the compensation awarded. For further cases illustrating the valuation of a leasehold interest see *Hibernian Property Company* v *Liverpool Corpn* (1973), 25 P & CR 417; *Mountview Estates Ltd.* v *London Borough of Enfield* (1968), 20 P & CR 729; *Wilrow Engineering Ltd. and Stapleton* v *Letchworth UDC* [1973] RVR 221; see also *Alexandre* v *Cambridge City Council* (1976), 31 P & CR 444, p. 369, note 7, *post*.

[2] *Odeon Associated Theatres Ltd.* v *Glasgow Corpn* (1973), 27 P & CR 271 (Lands Tribunal for Scotland).

[3] (1961) 13 P & CR 77; and see pp. 284 *et seq, post*: *Stokes'* case was followed in *Challinor* v *Stone RDC* (1974), 27 P & CR 244, where the proportion was reduced to 25 % in recognition of the fact that a possible alternative access deprived the owner of the access land of a complete 'key' to the development of the backland.

[4] I.e., the difference between the existing use value of the land and its value after making the appropriate assumption as to planning permission (see pp. 185 *et seq, infra*).

[5] *Hoveringham Gravel Co.* v *Chiltern District Council* (1975), 31 P & CR 466, where a 50 % deduction was made: see pp. 213 *et seq, infra*.

[6] (1975) 29 P & CR 322 CA, and see pp. 285 *et seq, post*.

specialised art, claimants appearing before the Lands Tribunal in person are apt to find themselves at a considerable disadvantage when faced with the expertise of the district or other professional valuer called by the acquiring authority on whom, in the absence of an equally experienced witness appearing for the claimant, the Lands Tribunal almost inevitably place more reliance.[1] Wherever possible, moreover, a straightforward valuation based upon sales of comparable property in similar surroundings or, in the absence of such sales, upon the capitalisation of rents obtainable on leasing similar property, is to be preferred.[2] Values derived from settlements reached between local authorities and prospective tenants constitute very much less reliable evidence since such transactions do not constitute an open market[3]—especially where the local authority exercises a quasi-monopolistic position in regard to the type of accommodation in question.[4] The same applies to valuations determined by the Lands Tribunal itself in "absent owner" cases, for where an owner of land being compulsorily acquired cannot be found and the Lands Tribunal is required to determine the compensation payable,[5] the Tribunal acts professionally rather than judicially.[6]

However, where the value of prospective development is in issue and sales or leases of closely similar property in comparable surroundings are not available, the outline residual method of valuation may be employed.[7] In essence the method involves an estimate of the future revenue from the development for which planning permission is to be assumed, multiplied by an appropriate number of "years purchase". From this is deducted the estimated cost of the development (including developer's profit) to give the value of the cleared site in possession. In the case of a leasehold interest a further deduction falls to be made comprising the value of the site subject to the lease (i.e., ground rent multiplied by the number of years unexpired and subjected to an appropriate discount rate), plus the value of the reversionary interest in the cleared site (i.e., its deferred value, arrived at by multiplying its present value by the discounted value of the pound as at the end of the lease). This will give the surrender value of the lease from which a further deduction must be made, if a merger of the freehold and leasehold interest is contemplated, to allow a reasonable profit to the freeholder and to cover the costs of the merger.

---

[1] See the cases cited in note 7, p. 328, post.

[2] *Fairbairn Lawson Ltd.* v *Leeds County Borough Council* (1970), 222 Estates Gazette 561.

[3] *Shaw* v *London Borough of Hackney* (1974), 28 P & CR 477.

[4] *Trustees of the Manchester Homeopathic Clinic* v *Manchester Corpn* (1970), 22 P & CR 241, where the terms upon which local doctors held purpose-built clinics provided by the acquiring authority were rejected as providing evidence of the market for similar premises being compulsorily acquired: see p. 241, post.

[5] Under the Compulsory Purchase Act 1965, s. 5 and Sch. 2, compensation being assessed by "a surveyor selected from the members of the Lands Tribunal": *ibid*. Sch. 2, para. 1(1)(b).

[6] *Bousefield* v *Chatham Corpn* (1973), 27 P & CR 241.

[7] For an example see *Trocette Property Co. Ltd.* v *Greater London Council* (1973), 27 P & CR 256 (LT), p. 182, supra.

Planning permissions to be assumed

The planning permissions to be taken into account in the assessment of compensation are laid down in the Land Compensation Act 1961, ss. 15–16. They fall into three broad categories, viz planning permissions in force at the date of notice to treat; planning permissions to be assumed, though not directly derived from development plans; and assumptions as to planning permission which depend directly upon development plans.

(I) PLANNING PERMISSIONS IN FORCE AT THE DATE OF NOTICE TO TREAT

It is specifically provided that any planning permission to be assumed in accordance with these provisions of the Land Compensation Act 1961 are to be in *addition* to any planning permission in force at the date of service of the notice to treat[1] whether such planning permission be unconditional or subject to conditions;[2] whether it be full or outline planning permission;[3] whether granted by a general development order;[4] whether it covers other land as well as the land being acquired;[5] or whether it is deemed to have been granted by virtue of some enactment.[6]

In this context it is to be borne in mind that the value of a planning permission or established use may be lost if, in pursuance of a subsequent grant of planning permission, the land is developed in a manner inconsistent with the first planning permission or the existing use. Thus in *Thomas Langley Group Ltd.* v *Royal Borough of Leamington Spa*[7] planning permission had been granted for residential development of land subject to a condition that two acres of filled land was not to be developed until ten years after completion of tipping. A subsequent planning permission enabled the developers to increase the density of houses on the rest of the site and part of the two acres but was subject to a condition that the remainder of the two acres of filled land should be preserved as a public open space. The developers later served a

---

[1] Land Compensation Act 1961, s. 14(2).

[2] *Ibid*, s. 14(4)(a).

[3] *Ibid*, s. 14(4)(c).

[4] *Ibid*, and see currently the Town and Country Planning General Development Order 1977 (SI 1977 No. 289). But note the effect of Article 4 of the order, under which directions may be given limiting the planning permissions granted by the order in areas to which the direction applies. In such areas planning permission for the developments specified will be required in the normal way—i.e., upon application to the local planning authority.

[5] *Ibid*, s. 14(4)(b).

[6] *Ibid*, s. 14(4). An example of an enactment under which planning permission may be deemed to have been granted is the Town and Country Planning Act 1971, s. 40, which provides that where authorisation of development by a Government Department is required, the Minister may include a direction that planning permission be deemed to be granted. Provisions to a similar effect are to be found in the Opencast Coal Act 1958, s. 2; the Electric Lighting Act 1909, s. 2; the Electric Lighting (Clauses) Act 1899, para. 10 of the Schedule; The Electricity Act 1957, ss. 32 and 34. Note also that in all these cases the Ministers may direct that conditions be attached to the deemed permissions; similarly conditions attached to Industrial Development Certificates and Office Development Permits are deemed to attach to the planning permissions: Town and Country Planning Act 1971, ss. 70 and 77. By s. 64 planning permission is also deemed to be granted for advertisement displays conforming to regulations made under s. 63.

[7] (1974) 29 P & CR 358 CA.

purchase notice in respect of the filled land, claiming compensation on the basis of the original planning permission—i.e., that there was an existing planning permission, at the date of the deemed notice to treat, for its eventual development. It was held by the Lands Tribunal, and confirmed by the Court of Appeal, that the second planning permission was clearly intended to replace the first, with which it was inconsistent, the quid pro quo for the public open space allocation being the higher density and advancement of the date on which part of the two acre site could be developed.

Although under the Community Land Act 1975 planning permissions may be suspended, they are only suspended until the land is acquired by an authority[1] under that Act;[2] suspension does not, therefore, affect the position in so far as the assessment of compensation is concerned.[3]

In this connection it is to be noted that planning permission once granted normally runs with the land in perpetuity.[4] Planning permission may, however, be granted subject to both conditions and time limits[5] and the conditions imposed may restrict the planning permission to a particular person (generally the applicant); such a planning permission is therefore purely a "personal" permission which is not transferable.

In this context it may be of interest to note the means by which local planning authorities may obtain a deemed planning permission either to develop land in the ownership of others within their area or for the development of their own land by others. In the former case the essence[6] of the procedure is the passing of resolutions declaring their intention to carry out the proposed development; the service of notice upon all persons with a material interest[7] in the land; the provision of a minimum period of 21 days in which such persons may submit objections; the consideration of any such objections and the passing of a second resolution to carry out the development. The procedure where the local planning authority[8] seeks a deemed planning permission for the development of its own land by others follows similar lines.[9] There

---

[1] I.e., in England for the most part local authorities and New Town Corporations. See, however, Note 4, p. 296, *post*.

[2] The circumstances in which suspended planning permissions may revive earlier are not relevant in this context.

[3] Unless development proceeds during suspension. See pp. 303 *et seq*, *post*.

[4] Town and Country Planning Act 1971, s. 33.

[5] *Ibid*, s. 30.

[6] For full details see Town and Country Planning General Regulations 1976 (SI 1976 No. 1419), reg. 4, and Department of the Environment Circular 89/76.

[7] I.e., "a freehold or a lease the unexpired term of which, at the relevant time, is not less than seven years": Community Land Act 1975, s. 6(1).

[8] Note that although in the English and Welsh counties there will always be two local planning authorities able to exercise these powers, they may do so entirely independently one from the other. Thus a County District Council need not consult the County Council even although an application for planning permission in respect of the same development and the same land would have been for the County Council to decide—and vice versa. This does not, however, apply in London or the Metropolitan Counties: see the Town and Country Planning Regulations 1976, (*supra*) regs. 2 and 3.

[9] *Ibid*, reg. 5.

is no corresponding procedure by which a local planning authority can acquire a deemed planning permission to develop its own land itself: it has, however, very wide powers to appropriate[1] land held by it for any purpose.

There is, however, an important difference between these two types of deemed planning permissions for only the deemed planning permission for the development of the authority's own land runs with the land in the normal way and therefore falls to be taken into account in the assessment of compensation under this head.[2] A deemed planning permission for the local planning authority to develop another person's land is personal to that authority.[3]

Thus, where an existing planning permission has been made personal to the vendor by the imposition of appropriate conditions its effect upon value will depend upon the likelihood of either a similar personal permission or an unconditional planning permission being granted to a purchaser. This in turn may depend upon the reasons for confining the original planning permission to a named person. If a planning application is for a change of use involving possible nuisance to neighbours, e.g., say, the establishment of a restaurant in or near a residential area, the local planning authority may be influenced in deciding whether to grant permission by the responsible character and reputation of the applicant or personal undertakings given by him. In such cases an equally responsible purchaser willing to give similar undertakings might expect to obtain a similar personal permission. Conversely, if the planning permission was granted against all normal planning policy and criteria in order to alleviate hardship that would otherwise fall on the then owner or occupier, extension of the planning permission to a purchaser would probably not be contemplated.

Similarly, a personal planning permission may be granted, contrary to normal land use criteria, in order to enable the applicant to meet some particular local need, and to ensure that in the event of disposal of the land the local planning authority have an opportunity to reconsider the position and assess the suitability of the purchaser or lessee to continue to provide the services in question. An obvious example is the grant of a personal planning permission to a charity meeting a social need in the area. In such cases, particularly where the premises have been purpose-built or specially adapted, compensation may be payable on an equivalent reinstatement basis under Rule 5.[4]

The deemed planning permission personal to a local authority

---

[1] See Community Land Act 1975, s. 15(5) and Sch. 4, para. 23(1): and see pp. 191 *et seq, infra*.

[2] It must not, of course, be assumed that because this land, by definition, is owned by a local authority it cannot become the subject of a compulsory purchase order. (Special Parliamentary Procedure for the acquisition of such land is now abolished: Community Land Act 1975, s. 41(2).) Particulars of these deemed planning permissions may therefore be of importance; they will be obtainable from the register of planning applications maintained by local planning authorities under the Town and Country Planning Act 1971, s. 34; see Town and Country Planning General Regulations 1976 (*supra*) reg. 5(5)(b).

[3] *Ibid*, reg. 4(7).

[4] Pp. 165, *supra*, and pp. 239 *et seq, post*.

described above does, however, appear to be in a very different category. Basically planning is about land use—i.e., the suitability of the proposed development to the land in question, as judged in relation to the public or community interest as opposed to the narrower personal interest of the applicant. The occupation of permanent buildings cannot be controlled indefinitely so that consideration of the personality of the applicant or initial occupier is normally wholly irrelevant; hence the general rule that planning permission runs with the land irrespective of who, for the time being, is either owner or occupier. The personal planning permission has therefore hitherto always been regarded as very much the exception to the rule and it is difficult to see any logical justification for *all* planning permissions deemed to have been granted by local planning authorities to themselves under the procedure outlined above being automatically "personal" to that authority. Indeed, there seem likely to be relatively few cases in which there can genuinely be said to be grounds for maintaining that the proposed local authority development would not be just as suitable to the land in question if carried out by some other public body or by private enterprise.

In any event this provision seems likely to have little effect upon compensation since a local planning authority obtaining for itself a deemed personal planning permission in this manner must be presumed to intend to acquire the land for the development covered by such planning permission. In that event planning permission for the same development, but running with the land will be assumed for the purpose of the assessment of compensation as explained in para. 2(i) below.[1]

Under the Community Land Act 1975, ordinary planning permissions (i.e., those granted in pursuance of an application) are in any event suspended until either the land is acquired by an authority under the Act or all authorities within whose area the land is situated[2] have indicated that they do not intend to acquire.[3] Suspension, moreover, may form a ground for the service of a blight notice.[4] There is no corresponding suspension or right to serve a blight notice in the case of deemed permissions. Cases could nevertheless occur in which

---

[1] Land Compensation Act 1961, s. 15(1), p. 191 *infra*.

[2] In England there will always be at least two local planning authorities in whose area the land is situated—the County and District Councils or, in London, the GLC and the London Borough. Exceptionally there may be three, as where the land falls within the designated area of a New Town or within the Peak Park Joint Planning Board or the Lake District Special Planning Board, since all these bodies are authorities for the purpose of the Community Land Act 1975. Although in Wales there is but a single authority for the purposes of that Act (the Land Authority for Wales) County and District Councils remain local planning authorities able to grant themselves deemed planning permission under the Town and Country Planning General Regulations 1976 and to acquire land under the wide powers of the Town and Country Planning Act 1971, s. 112 or other more specialised enactments such as the Housing, Highways, Education, etc., Acts. In addition, the Welsh Development Agency and the Welsh Rural Development Board also have wide powers of compulsory acquisition, so that there could be up to five authorities with power to acquire the land in question. Furthermore, none of these provisions affects the power of acquisition of Government Departments on behalf of the Crown.

[3] For the time within which notification must be given and other details see pp. 300 *et seq, post.*

[4] I.e., provided the owner's interest qualifies: see the Town and Country Planning Act 1971, . 193, (pp. 131 *et seq, ante*) the Community Land Act 1975, s. 22(6), pp. 302–303, *post.*

another authority seeks to acquire for a different and less valuable purpose. In such an event the question will arise whether the more valuable personal permissions in favour of the first authority can be taken into account in assessing the compensation payable. Since, by definition, that authority is a local planning authority it would, it is submitted, be very difficult for the acquiring authority convincingly to argue that the development covered by the deemed planning permission is inappropriate on planning grounds and ought not to be considered in assessing market value for the purpose of compensation,[1] despite the personal nature of the planning permission concerned.

The purpose of making these deemed planning permissions personal to the local planning authority concerned is presumably to prevent the land changing hands in the open market at a price enhanced by the planning permission. Here again, however, in the majority of cases it would seem to be stretching the logic of planning for a local planning authority which, by granting itself planning permission, has accepted the proposed development of the land as conforming to their planning policies, to refuse an application for an ordinary planning permission (i.e., running with the land) for the same development and in respect of the same land.[2]

To this general proposition it is, however, necessary to enter a caveat. The Community Land Act 1975 has, of course, two ultimate objectives: first, that virtually all development shall either be carried out by local authorities or on land owned by them and leased or licensed to developers; secondly, to ensure that all land changes hands at current existing use value. It may be, therefore, that these provisions for deemed planning permissions personal to local planning authorities are intended to accelerate these objectives and, in particular, to ensure that such planning permissions do not affect prices in the open market, or, save where the assumptions as to planning permissions of the Land Compensation Act 1961[3] apply, the compensation payable. But if this is so, it represents a basic change in the whole concept of land use planning by giving precedence to the personality of the developer over the suitability of the proposed development—judged by planning criteria—to the subject land. It seems very questionable whether such a fundamental change is appropriate to a Statutory Instrument which was presented to Parliament and came into operation while Parliament was in recess. It remains to be seen, therefore, how these deemed personal planning permissions will operate in practice, and what view will be taken of their effect upon compensation by the Lands Tribunal and the courts.

Apart from conditions imposed upon ordinary planning permissions making them personal to the applicant or other named person, the

---

[1] In this context attention is directed to the overriding provisions of the Land Compensation Act 1961, s. 14(3): see p. 181, *supra*.

[2] See also in this context the assumptions described under sub-heading (iii) of this chapter, pp. 196 *et seq, infra*.

[3] Ss. 14–16, pp. 185 *et seq, supra*.

other conditions which may be imposed and which are of importance in this context are, first, those by which, unless the development permitted is commenced within a stated period, the planning permission lapses.[1] If no such condition is imposed the statutory period is five years in the case of a "full" planning permission[2] and in the case of an outline planning permission, whichever is the later of five years from the grant of the outline planning permission or two years from the final approval of the reserved matters.[3]

Secondly, applications for planning permission may be refused purely on the grounds that to carry out the development proposed would be premature[4]—e.g., because access depends upon completion of a new road or because services will not be available until some date in the future. In such cases it is not uncommon for such a refusal to be specifically "without prejudice" to a more favourable consideration of a subsequent application when services, etc. are available. Such refusals accordingly strengthen the presumption that planning permission for the proposed development will ultimately be forthcoming, and the market will react accordingly.

Thus where an existing planning permission is personal to the vendor or is subject to a time limit[5] its effect upon value will in the first instance depend upon the likelihood of a similar "personal" permission being granted to a purchaser or the time limit being extended, as the case may be. Subject to the *caveat* entered above, the same general principle would appear to apply to deemed planning permissions personal to local planning authorities. Similarly, where a planning permission is on the point of lapsing through failure to commence implementation within the above periods, the prospect of its renewal becomes a vital factor in assessing its effect upon value.[6]

In the case of a condition postponing the carrying out of the development concerned the effect on value will, of course, be to 'discount' the value of the permission over the period of postponement.

---

[1] Town and Country Planning Act 1971, s. 41(1)(b).

[2] *Ibid*, s. 41(1)(a).

[3] *Ibid*, s. 42(2)(b); note that application for approval of the reserved matters must be made within three years from the grant of outline planning permission: s. 42(2)(a).

[4] Although it is doubtful whether a condition deferring commencement of development can be imposed in such circumstances, it is specifically provided that where the development plan indicates future development there is to be an assumption that planning permission therefor would be granted "at the time when, in accordance with the indications in the plan, that permission might reasonably be expected to be granted": Land Compensation Act 1961, s. 16(6)(b). Similarly, a certificate of appropriate alternative development (as to which see pp. 204 *et seq, infra*) may indicate that planning permission would, but for the compulsory acquisition, be granted at a stated future date: s. 17(5).

[5] Note the contrast between the Land Compensation Act 1961, s. 14(4)(a), whereby such existing conditional planning permissions may be taken into account (for what they are worth) and s. 15(2), whereby "personal" planning permissions are to be ignored in determining whether there is an extant planning permission for the development of the land acquired as proposed by the acquiring authority: see p. 186 *et seq, infra*.

[6] These latter limitations do not, however, apply to local authorities since the Town and Country Planning Act 1971, ss. 41–44, are not included in the sections applied to local authorities by s. 270 and Sch. 21, Part V.

(ii) PLANNING ASSUMPTIONS NOT DERIVED FROM DEVELOP-MENT PLANS[1]

(a) Planning permission for the development for which the land is being acquired[2]
The principle is straightforward and perhaps most readily illustrated by an example. If the land is being acquired for residential development at, say, a net density of twelve dwellings to the acre and there is no extant planning permission enuring to the permanent benefit of the land for that development,[3] planning permission therefor is to be assumed. Simple as this proposition appears, it may nevertheless give rise to some anomaly, if not indeed some difficulty,[4] particularly in relation to the Community Land Act 1975. In the first place the "authorities" for the purpose of that Act[5] will eventually be under a duty to acquire and hold a ten-year supply of land required for "relevant development".[6] Although acquiring authorities are still required, in making a compulsory purchase order, to state the purpose for which the land concerned is required,[7] it seems inconceivable that in practice all such land will in fact be developed for the purpose originally proposed; indeed, the Act confers upon authorities virtually unfettered powers of appropriation of land acquired for one purpose for use for some other purpose—even though it may still be required for the original purpose.[8] There are, however, no provisions whereby such change of purpose can be reflected in the compensation payable.[9] Consequently, as far as the assumption under consideration is concerned, planning permission can only be assumed for the development proposed at the time of acquisition. In this connection the precise wording of the relevant provision of the Land Compensation Act 1961 may be of particular importance; the relevant subsection[10] reads as follows:

---

[1] Land Compensation Act 1961, s. 15.

[2] *Ibid*, s. 15(1). In most cases of acquisition in pursuance of a compulsory purchase order and notice to treat planning permission for the proposed development will already have been granted. The importance of this provision is therefore likely to be confined to acquisitions by agreement or in pursuance of purchase or blight notices (Chap. 4, *ante*) where the land is acquired in advance of actual requirements; see in this connection *Myers* v *Milton Keynes Development Corpn* (1974), 27 P & CR 518, p. 226, *infra*.

[3] *Ibid*, s. 15(2); an extant "personal" planning permission for such development is therefore to be ignored in this context; cf. note 5 p. 190, *supra*.

[4] Note, however, that there is no conflict between this provision and the requirement that the effect of the scheme of acquisition upon the value of the subject land is to be discounted (see p. 217 *et seq, infra*). Thus if the plans of a New Town Development Corporation show the subject land as required for residential development some time in the future, deferred planning permission for such development is to be assumed under *ibid*, s. 15(1). That assumption is not to be defeated by the argument that but for the overall scheme (i.e., in this case, the proposal to develop a new town) there would be no prospect of development being permitted: *Myers* v *Milton Keynes Development Corpn*, [1974] 1 WLR 696, 27 P & CR 518, CA, and see note 2, *supra*.

[5] For the authorities concerned see the Community Land Act 1975, s. 1, and note 4, p. 296, *post*.

[6] For definition see *ibid*, s. 3(2): see also pp. 296, *post*, and Corfield's *A Guide to the Community Land Act 1975*, Butterworths, 1976. At the time of going to press, however, it seems likely that the restrictions upon public expenditure will make these provisions of the Community Land Act of little more than academic interest for some years to come.

[7] Pp. 32, *et seq, ante*.

[8] Community Land Act 1975, s. 15(5), and Schedule 4, para. 23(1).

[9] Cf. the repealed provisions of the Town and Country Planning Act 1959 (ss. 18–21) which made such provision.

[10] Land Compensation Act 1961, s. 15(1).

"In a case where—

(a) the relevant interest is to be acquired for purposes which involve the carrying out of proposals of the acquiring authority for development of the relevant land or part thereof, and

(b) on the date of the notice to treat there is not in force planning permission for that development it shall be assumed that planning permission would be granted, in respect of the relevant land or that part thereof, as the case may be, such as would permit development thereof in accordance with the proposals of the acquiring authority".

In the first place it is to be noted that this provision only applies where there is no planning permission actually in force[1] at the date of service of the notice to treat. In the second place the words "where the relevant interest *is to be* acquired" imply a reference to immediate future intentions rather than any earlier intentions that may have been superseded. It follows, therefore, that if, subsequent to the confirmation of the compulsory purchase order, but before the date of entry or the date on which the compensation falls to be determined (whichever is the earlier)[2] there is a change of purpose, it is the later purpose for which planning permission is to be assumed. Admittedly an acquiring authority cannot appropriate land until it has acquired it. But it can pass a resolution between confirmation of a compulsory purchase order and acquisition of the land expressing or implying[3] an intention to do so. In such cases it is submitted that it is for the then proposed purpose that planning permission is to be assumed—and it would not appear to make any difference whether the change in purpose is revealed before or after service of notice to treat.

In other words, as with other circumstances affecting value the planning considerations, it seems, will be those applicable as on the relevant date. A difficulty may still arise, however, if land carrying planning permission for such development commands a lower price in the market than land with planning permission for the development originally intended. In that event, it is suggested, planning permission for such development—provided that the development conformed to the current development plan—will be a planning permission to be assumed under the later provisions of the Act dealing with assumptions derived from development plans.[4]

If the development is not in conformity with the current development plan resort will, it is suggested, have to be had to a "certificate of appropriate alternative development".[5]

It should further be noted that it is the proposals of the acquiring authority that are relevant: it matters not whether they are to be carried out *by* that authority or on its behalf. Under the Community Land Act, however, authorities may not only acquire land in order to develop it themselves or arrange for it to be developed on their behalf; they may also acquire land in order to make it available for development by

---

[1] I.e., for the development in question, see pp. 185 *et seq*, *supra*.
[2] See the "relevant date", pp. 165, *et seq*, *supra*.
[3] E.g., highway proposals affecting the land, proposals for changes of density, etc.
[4] Land Compensation Act 1961, s. 16, pp. 196 *et seq*, *infra*.
[5] *Ibid*, s. 17, pp. 204, *infra*.

private enterprise[1] in which case the question may arise whether the development is in accordance with the proposals of the acquiring authority or with those of the developer. Here again there may be difficulties. Authorities are statutorily required to consider "the needs of builders and developers engaged in or wishing to engage in, the carrying out of development in the area"[2] and it is clearly envisaged that having acquired land to be made available to such private developers the details of the development shall be subject to negotiation. Nevertheless since, in England, the authorities under the Community Land Act are also local planning authorities the final proposals must, it is submitted, be regarded as those of the acquiring authority.

In Wales the position is, prima facie, somewhat different for although the Land Authority for Wales may use local authorities as their agents, it is the former authority that will normally be the acquiring authority and it is not a planning authority. The functions of local planning authorities remain with the County and District Councils whom the Land Authority for Wales are required to consult.[3] It is not, however, bound by the views of local planning authorities so that although the Land Authority for Wales is *not* formally a planning authority it seems that the situation in this regard is the same in Wales as in England.

These final details may not, however, be determined at the time of acquisition. Once again, the planning permission to be assumed under this provision of the Land Compensation Act 1961 will, it is submitted, depend solely upon the proposals of the acquiring authority as at the date of acquisition. No doubt in the vast majority of cases where land is acquired with a view to it being made available to private developers there will be no change of general purpose, e.g., between residential, industrial or commercial development. Nevertheless, restrictions on density, requirements as to layout, landscaping, etc. can have significant effects upon value.

In the immediate future the current restrictions upon public expenditure, and upon local authority expenditure in particular, will result in confirming authorities[4] insisting upon a fairly strong case being made by acquiring authorities before they are prepared to confirm compulsory purchase orders; that in turn no doubt will necessitate the purpose of the acquisition being stated with some precision. There should therefore be little difficulty in identifying the planning permission to be assumed under this head. But if and when economic and political conditions permit the full implementation of the Community Land Act 1975, this seems likely to become more difficult. Moreover, since important details affecting market value thus seem likely to remain open to argument, the use of this assumption as a guide to market value may well prove less helpful than it has been in the past.

[1] They have indeed been urged to do so; see Department of the Environment Circular 121/75.
[2] Community Land Act 1975, Sch. 6, para. 1(b)(ii).
[3] *Ibid*, s. 17(3).
[4] I.e., the Secretaries of State for the Environment and Wales (and in Scotland the Secretary of State for Scotland).

(b) Planning permissions for development included or deemed to be included in existing use

By virtue of the Town and Country Planning Act 1971, s. 22(2), there are certain operations that may be carried out upon land and certain uses to which land may be put without obtaining planning permission. In other words, these operations and uses do not constitute "development". It follows, therefore, that in assessing the market value of land for the purpose of compensation account can *always* be taken of the somewhat limited potential that these exceptions to the general rule[1] confer.

These operations and uses are set out in paragraphs (a) to (f) of section 22(2) as under:

"(a)   the carrying out of works for the maintenance, improvement or other alteration of any building, being works which affect only the interior of the building or which do not materially affect the external appearance of the building and (in either case) are not works for making good war damage or works begun after 5th December 1968 for the alteration of a building by providing additional space therein below ground;

(b)   the carrying out by a local highway authority of any works required for the maintenance or improvement of a road, being works carried out on land within the boundaries of the road;

(c)   the carrying out by a local authority or statutory undertakers of any works for the purpose of inspecting repairing or renewing any sewers, mains, pipes, cables or other apparatus, including the breaking open of any street or other land for that purpose;

(d)   the use of any buildings or other land within the curtilage of a dwelling-house for any purpose incidental to the enjoyment of the dwelling-house as such;

(e)   the use of any land for the purposes of agriculture or forestry (including afforestation) and the use for any of those purposes of any building occupied together with land so used;

(f)   in the case of buildings or other land which are used for a purpose of any class specified in an order[2] made by the Secretary of State under this section, the use thereof for any other purpose of the same class."

"For the avoidance of doubt" subsection (3) of this section goes on to declare that:

---

[1] I.e., that "the carrying out of building, engineering, mining or other operations in, over or under land, or the making of any material change in the use of any building or other land" constitutes development (Town and Country Planning Act 1971, s. 22(1)) and therefore, subject to very minor exceptions (*infra*) requires planning permission (*Ibid*, s. 23).

[2] Currently the Town and Country Planning (Use Classes) Order 1972, (SI 1972 No. 1385). This order is to be distinguished from the Town and Country Planning (Use Classes for Third Schedule Purposes) Order 1948 (SI 1948 No. 955), as to which see note 7, p. 116, *ante*. The 1972 Order replaces an order made in 1948 under the Town and Country Planning Act 1947 in which the use classes specified were identical to those of SI 1948 No. 955. The Act of 1947, s. 111(4), however, provided that the latter order should not be revoked or amended after the appointed day (1 July 1948); it is now specifically incorporated in the Town and Country Planning Act 1971 (Sch. 8, para. 6). Thus there is no longer a complete identity of use classes specified in the two orders and reference must accordingly be made to the current order made under this subsection in order to check what other uses of the land fall within the same class so that a change to any of such uses does not constitute development and can therefore be effected by a purchaser without planning permission. It should, however, be noted that planning permission for a change of use may be subject to conditions limiting a further change of use within the same use class without obtaining a further planning permission; see e.g., *City of London Corpn* v *Secretary of State for the Environment* (1971), 23 P & CR 169. In such a case compensation must be based upon the assumption that a purchaser will be similarly restricted, any change infringing the condition being restrainable by law: see Land Compensation Act 1961, s. 5(4), p. 179, *supra*. See also *Williams and Stevens* v *Cambridgeshire County Council*, [1977] JPL 529 (land acquired as caravan site for gypsies: compensation cannot be assessed on the basis of value as a site for other caravans).

(a) The use as two or more separate dwelling-houses of any building previously used as a single dwelling-house involves a material change in the use of the building and of each part thereof which is so used;

(b) the deposit of refuse or waste materials on land involves a material change in the use thereof, notwithstanding that the land is comprised in a site already used for that purpose, if either the superficial area of the deposit is thereby extended, or the height of the deposit is thereby extended and exceeds the level of the land adjoining the site."

In addition to the above operations and uses of land that do not constitute development and can therefore be carried out or effected by a purchaser without planning permission, the Town and Country Planning Act 1971, s. 22(5) introduces the term "new development"[1] defined as "any development other than development of a class specified in Part I or Part II of Schedule 8" to the Act of 1971.

These latter classes of development are referred to in the Land Compensation Act 1961 not, as might have been expected, as "old development" but as "development included in the existing use of land".[2] They are perhaps more conveniently referred to as "Schedule 8 Developments". They are important in this context because although planning permission is required for such development and can therefore be refused or granted only subject to conditions, refusals or conditional grants of planning permission in respect of the development set out in Part II of Schedule 8 have, ever since the Town and Country Planning Act 1947, been the subject of compensation based upon the amount by which the value of the claimant's interest in the land would have been increased if permission had been granted unconditionally.[3] Schedule 8 is accordingly reproduced in full in the Appendix.[4]

Accordingly, the Land Compensation Act 1961[5] provides that planning permission for Schedule 8 developments shall be assumed in assessing market value for the purposes of compensation unless compensation has already become payable in respect of a refusal of planning permission, the imposition of conditions,[6] or in respect of an order[7] requiring the removal of any building or the discontinuance of any use.[8]

[1] An expression first used in the Town and Country Planning Act 1954. The Town and Country Planning Act 1947 provided for compensation to be paid in the event of refusal or conditional grant of planning permission for those classes of development set out in Part II of Sch. 3 to that Act (now the Town and Country Planning Act 1971, Sch. 8, Part II). The 1954 Act provided certain limited rights to compensation in respect of refusals or conditional grants of planning permission for other classes of development. Because of the wholly different principles upon which these rights were based it was necessary to distinguish the two types of development to which they applied—"non-Schedule 3 development" presumably being regarded as unnecessarily clumsy. For the basis of compensation for refusal or conditional grant of planning permission for such classes of development see pp. 394, *et seq, post.*

[2] S. 15(3). These developments are not, however, so described in the Town and Country Planning Act 1971 itself which uses the expression "development other than new development" (s. 169) or "development not constituting new development" (Sch. 8).

[3] See Town and Country Planning Act 1971, s. 169, formerly Town and Country Planning Act 1947, s. 20.

[4] P. 456, *post.*   [5] S. 15(3) and (4).

[6] Land Compensation Act 1961, s. 15(3)(a) and (b), compensation being payable under Town and Country Planning Act 1971, s. 169, on the basis described in the text and amplified on pp. 405, *et seq. post.*

[7] I.e., an order under *ibid,* s. 51, as to which see pp. 415, *et seq, post.*

[8] Land Compensation Act 1961, s. 15(4)(c); compensation is payable under Town and Country Planning Act 1971, s. 170, as to which see pp. 421, *et seq, post.*

There is, however, a curious anomaly in these provisions for they cover the developments enumerated in Part I of Schedule 8 as well as those of Part II, despite the fact that a refusal or conditional grant of planning permission for the former does not give rise to a claim for compensation.[1] It follows, therefore, that even if planning permission for any development specified in Part I of the Schedule has been refused, planning permission for that development is nevertheless to be assumed for the purposes of assessing compensation because these Schedule 8 assumptions are only excluded where as a result of refusal or conditional grant of planning permission compensation has become payable. Since Part I developments do not rank for compensation there are no means by which compensation in respect of refusal or conditional grant of planning permission for such development *can* become payable.

In short, it may be said under this heading that for the purpose of assessing compensation planning permission is to be assumed for the continuation of the use persisting at the date of acquisition[2] including:

(a) The right to carry out such works or effect such limited changes of use as do not constitute development within the meaning of the Town and Country Planning Act 1971, s. 22(2), provided that no compensation has become payable in respect of any order for the removal of any building or the discontinuance of any use;

(b) The right to carry out any change of use within the same "Use Class" of the current Town and Country Planning (Use Classes) Order, provided no condition has been imposed restricting that right;

(c) The right to carry out any of the developments listed in Parts I and II, Schedule 8 to the same Act, except in so far as that right has been restricted in respect of any of these developments by the refusal of planning permission or the imposition of conditions as a result of which compensation has become payable.

(iii) PLANNING PERMISSION FOR DEVELOPMENT IN ACCORDANCE WITH THE CURRENT DEVELOPMENT PLAN[3]
(a) General
Broadly speaking, when assessing compensation, planning permission may be assumed for such development of the land in question as would, if there were no question of any of that land being compulsorily acquired,[4] accord with the provisions of the current development

---

[1] See the heading to Part I, Sch. 8, p. 456, *post*, and Town and Country Planning Act 1971, s. 169(1).

[2] Note that grant of planning permission for a change of use does not remove the right to continue the existing use; *aliter* if the development for which permission was granted has been carried out and is inconsistent with the former existing use; see, e.g., *Thomas Langley Group Ltd.* v *Royal Borough of Leamington Spa*, p. 185, *supra*. Thus in appropriate cases the planning permission to be assumed under this head may include planning permission for a former existing or "established" use (see the Town and Country Planning Act 1971, ss. 23 and 94). But if the land is not available for any such use at the relevant date, e.g., where a building with an established warehouse use was occupied by a statutory residential tenant, it cannot affect the assessment of market value: see *Tranter* v *Birmingham District Council* (1976), 31 P & CR 327: p. 176, *supra*.

[3] Land Compensation Act 1961, s. 16.

[4] *Ibid*, s. 16(7).

plan,[1] and for which planning permission could therefore reasonably have been expected. The "current development plan" in this context is the development plan for the area in which the land is situated that is in force at the date of the notice to treat.[2] It will, however, be recalled that it is *not* to be presumed that planning permission would necessarily be refused for classes of development other than those for which planning permission is to be assumed under specific provisions of the Act.[3] It follows, therefore, that where, for example, at the date of notice to treat an amendment to the development plan is imminent and involves changing the proposed use of the subject land, it remains open to an owner of an interest in the land to argue—if it is to his advantage to do so—that compensation should be assessed on the assumption that but for the acquisition planning permission would be available to a purchaser for the development proposed in the amendment to the development plan. The significant difference is, of course, that whereas he has a right to the value of any development potential conferred by an assumed planning permission in accordance with the development plan current at the date of notice to treat (subject to the limitations explained below), the value of any planning permission for the development proposed by the amendment will depend upon the extent to which a prospective purchaser is likely to rely upon the amendment being made. If, however, the amendment were to be effected between

[1] The new concept of structure and local plans introduced by the Town and Country Planning Act 1968 and incorporated as the Town and Country Planning Act 1971, Part II (ss. 6-21) are to be applied by a series of orders under *ibid*, s. 21 to the areas specified in the particular order. At the time of going to press such orders have only been made in respect of Greater London, Coventry and parts of the West Midlands (see note 3, p. 199, *infra*). In the meantime the current development plan for areas in respect of which no order has been made remains the "old style" development plan of the Town and Country Planning Act 1947. Details are incorporated in the Town and Country Planning Act 1971, Schs. 5 and 6. Once the provisions of Part II are brought into effect by orders covering the whole of England and Wales these Schedules will be totally repealed (as opposed to being repealed only as they affect the areas to which particular orders apply). As individual orders are made, the development plan for the areas concerned will comprise, for areas outside Greater London:
    (a) the provisions of the structure plan for the time being in force for that area or the relevant part of that area, together with the Secretary of State's notice of approval of the plan;
    (b) any alteration to that plan, together with the Secretary of State's notices of approval thereof;
    (c) any provisions of a local plan for the time being applicable to the district, together with a copy of the authority's resolution of adoption or, as the case may be, the Secretary of State's notice of approval of the local plan; and
    (d) any alterations to that local plan, together with a copy of the authority's resolutions of adoption or, as the case may be, the Secretary of State's notices of approval thereof: Town and Country Planning Act 1971, s. 20(1).
The development plan for Greater London (SIs 1976 Nos. 1162 and 1163) comprises:
    (a) the provisions of the Greater London development plan and of the structure plan prepared by the council of that borough and for the time being in force in that area or the relevant part of that area together with the Secretary of State's notices of approval of the plans;
    (b) any alterations to those plans, together with the Secretary of State's notices of approval thereof;
    (c) any provisions of a local plan for the time being applicable to the district, together with a copy of the resolution of adoption of the relevant council or, as the case may be, the Secretary of State's notice of approval of the local plan; and
    (d) any alterations to that local plan, together with a copy of the resolutions of adoption of the relevant council or, as the case may be, the Secretary of State's notices of approval thereof: Town and Country Planning Act, 1971, s. 20(2).
[2] Land Compensation Act 1961, s. 39(1).
[3] *Ibid*, s. 14(3), p. 181, *ante*.

the date of notice to treat and date of entry[1] it is submitted that planning permission for either or both developments is to be assumed for the purpose of assessing compensation. In practice, of course, any amendment pending at the date of notice to treat is likely to reflect the purpose for which the land is being acquired.[2] Nevertheless there are circumstances in which such an amendment can significantly affect value. For example—land is being acquired for highway purposes; the adjoining agricultural land is shown on the development plan current at the date of notice to treat as Green Belt; an amendment to the development plan is under consideration showing a substantial area of former Green Belt on either side of the highway as an industrial estate. The primary use of the whole area is therefore to become industrial as opposed to agricultural; the value of the land being acquired will be increased accordingly.[3] Conversely, however, if the amendment proposes to change the plan so that the proposed use of the area in which the subject land is situated is to cease to be, for example, residential and to become open space, the compensation must still be based upon the assumption that planning permission will be available for residential development no matter how soon after the date of notice to treat or how long before the date of entry the amendment comes into force. That is, of course, provided such planning permission could reasonably have been expected in accordance with the plan.[4]

The Land Compensation Act 1961[5] makes detailed provision for the application of this general principle to four specific categories of information directly derived from development plans. They are considered in the following sub-paragraphs.

(b) Land allocated for a particular purpose

In the older type of development plan it was specifically provided that the plan might particularly define the sites of proposed roads, public and other buildings (e.g., schools, hospitals, etc.) and works, airfields, parks, pleasure grounds, nature reserves and other open spaces.[6] The Act of 1961[7] accordingly provided that where land the subject of compulsory acquisition (referred to in the Act as "the relevant land") or any part of it forms part of such a specifically designated site, planning permission for the development specified is to be assumed. To this there is, however, one overriding exception, viz where the relevant land falls within an area allocated in the plan as an area of comprehensive development.[8]

---

[1] Or the date on which compensation falls to be assessed: pp. 167, *et seq. supra.*

[2] See pp. 191, *et seq, supra.*

[3] See below.

[4] See e.g., *Provincial Properties (London) Ltd.* v *Caterham and Warlingham UDC* [1972] 1 QB 453, p. 199, *infra.*

[5] S. 16.

[6] See now the Town and Country Planning Act 1971, Sch. 5, para. 1(3).

[7] Land Compensation Act 1961, s. 16(1).

[8] I.e., "land which consists or forms part of an area defined in the current development plan as an area of comprehensive development": s. 16(8). Such an area is generally referred to as a Comprehensive Development Area (or CDA); for definition see Town and Country Planning Act 1962, s. 4(4), and for the powers of local planning authorities to acquire such areas see Town and Country Planning Act 1971, s. 112. In relation to the newer type of development plan (see note 1,

It is, moreover, to be noted that where only a part of the relevant land is included in the designated site there is no qualification whereby the planning permission to be assumed is to be confined to that part; it may be assumed as applicable to the whole.[1]

In the great majority of cases this provision is, however, unlikely to produce an assumed planning permission that will add significantly to the market value of the land in its existing use. In the first place, as will be observed from the above list of purposes for which such specific allocations of land might be made, few, if any, are likely to stimulate much demand in the open market. In the second place, as the newer forms of development plan comprising structure and local plans[2] gradually supersede the older development plans[3] such precise definitions of sites for specific public or quasi-public purposes will, with the exception of the sites of proposed roads, become something of a rarity.

(c) Land falling within an area allocated for a specified use

Where the relevant land or any part of it falls within an area allocated primarily for some specified use, planning permission is to be assumed for any development "for the purposes of that use".[4] Once again there is the overriding exception of land shown as subject to comprehensive development,[5] but there are two important differences to the application of this assumption from that considered in the previous paragraph. First, if only a part of the relevant land falls within such an area, the assumed planning permission applies to that part only. Secondly, the development for which planning permission is to be assumed must be development for which planning permission "might reasonably be expected to be granted in respect of the relevant land"[6] "if no part of the relevant land were proposed to be acquired by an authority possessing compulsory purchase powers".[7] Thus in *Provincial Properties (London) Ltd.* v *Caterham and Warlingham UDC*,[8] although the subject land fell within an area allocated for residential use in the current development

---

p. 197, *supra*) CDAs are now superseded by "action areas"—*ibid*, s. 7(5)—but the assumptions as to planning permission for the purpose of assessing compensation for land falling within CDAs as laid down in the Land Compensation Act 1961, s. 16, also apply to land falling within action areas for which a local plan is in force: Town and Country Planning Act 1971, Sch. 23. As to these assumptions, see para. (*e*) of the text, p. 202, *infra*.

[1] Cf. the converse rule applicable to the remaining assumptions derived from development plans—paras. (*c*) to (*e*) of the text, *infra*.

[2] First introduced in the Town and Country Planning Act 1968 and now defined in the Town and Country Planning Act 1971, ss. 6–21.

[3] I.e., those deriving from the Town and Country Planning Act 1947 and continuing in force until the relevant provisions of the Act of 1971 that incorporate the 1947 development plan provisions are repealed by order of the Secretary of State designating the area to which the repeal applies. As at 19 October 1976 Orders had been made only for Greater London and Leicestershire (excluding Rutland District) and the pre-1974 counties of Herefordshire, Worcestershire and Warwickshire and the County Boroughs of Coventry and Solihull. No Orders had been made for Wales. *Official Report*, 19 October 1976.

[4] Land Compensation Act 1961, s. 16(2).

[5] See note 8, p. 198, *supra*.

[6] Land Compensation Act 1961, s. 16(2)(b).

[7] *Ibid*, s. 16(7).

[8] [1972] 1 QB 453.

plan, the owners had on no less than six occasions been refused planning permission (both by the local planning authority and on appeal to
the Minister) on the grounds that the land formed part of a prominent
ridge, the development of which would damage the amenities of the
adjoining green belt. A purchase notice[1] having been served and
accepted, the vendors claimed compensation based upon the assumption that residential development would be permitted; it was agreed
that the land would accommodate three houses, and that, on that basis,
the compensation payable would be £10,500, but only £500 if no such
permission could be assumed. Overruling the Lands Tribunal, the
Court of Appeal held that since the evidence showed that planning
permission could not, in the circumstances, reasonably have been
expected to be granted if the land was not being compulsorily acquired,
the fact that the land was allocated in the development plan for residential development was not in itself enough to justify the assumption
of planning permission for that development for the purpose of assessing compensation. In order to do so, in other words, it is essential
that there should be *both* the requisite development plan allocation
and a reasonable expectation that but for the compulsory acquisition
planning permission for such development would be forthcoming.

The effect of the proviso that the assumption of planning permission
under this head must be related to the situation which would have
prevailed if there had been no question of compulsory acquisition was
considered in *Margate Corporation* v *Devotwill Investments Ltd.*[2] In that case
the land was again allocated for residential development in the current
development plan but planning permission had been refused on the
grounds that part of the land was required for a by-pass and that the
application was premature pending final resolution of the local traffic
problems. The Lands Tribunal (upheld by the Court of Appeal) held
that since construction of the by-pass presupposed compulsory acquisition the proposals relating thereto fell to be ignored so that compensation fell to be assessed upon the basis that planning permission
had to be assumed for immediate residential development, it being also
assumed that since no by-pass could be constructed on the claimant's
land if there was to be no compulsory acquisition, the traffic difficulties
would be resolved by some other method not affecting the subject land.

The House of Lords, however, held that this latter assumption was
unjustified and remitted the case to the Lands Tribunal on the grounds
that the likelihood of some alternative to the proposed by-pass being
found was a matter of fact to be determined on the evidence and so also,
therefore, was the planning permission that might reasonably have
been expected to be granted if there were no proposals for compulsory
acquisition.

It must also be borne in mind that where, in the absence of any

---

[1] See pp. 114, *et seq, ante*; and note particularly in this context that once a purchase notice has
been confirmed by the Secretary of State a notice to treat is deemed to have been served and
compensation falls to be assessed in precisely the same way as if the acquisition had been initiated
by the acquiring authority exercising compulsory powers.

[2] (1970) 22 P & CR 328 HL.

proposals for compulsory acquisition, planning permission could only reasonably be expected to be granted subject to conditions—e.g., as to density, provision of access, etc.—the planning permission to be assumed will be one subject to those conditions.[1] Similarly, where the current development plan includes programme maps or other indications that the development concerned will not be carried out until a future date, the planning permission to be assumed will be subject to a condition that development be deferred until that date.[2] Prior to the passing of the Community Land Act 1975 local authorities would not normally acquire land outside Comprehensive Development Areas substantially in advance of requirements, so that the assumption of a planning permission limited in this manner was largely confined to the acquisition of land within a comprehensive development area which is to be developed over a period of time; or to acquisitions in response to purchase or blight notices.[3] Acquisitions of land under the Community Land Act will, however, make such assumed conditions more common.[4]

Finally, it must be stressed that planning permission can only be assumed under these provisions for development within the "primary" use shown in the development plan. Thus if the primary use is residential there can be no assumption of planning permission for a range of shops, even although the size of the area so allocated in the development plan would clearly justify the provision of local shopping facilities. Conversely, the fact that the relevant land lies upon the route of a proposed road or forms part of a proposed public open space within the residential allocation will not in itself inhibit the assumption of a planning permission for residential development—provided there are no other grounds to indicate that such a planning permission could not have been reasonably expected if the land was not being compulsorily acquired.[5]

(d) Land falling within an area allocated for a range of specific uses[6]
The current development plan may also allocate land primarily for a mixture or range of uses, e.g., residential and commercial, industrial and commercial, commercial and administrative, etc. If the relevant land, or any part of it, falls within such an area (not being an area subject to comprehensive development)[7] planning permission may be assumed for any development of the land (or the appropriate part thereof) for which in all the circumstances planning permission could reasonably have been expected to be granted[8] in the absence of any proposals for compulsory acquisition.[9]

[1] Land Compensation Act 1961, s. 16(6)(a).
[2] *Ibid*, s. 16(6)(b).
[3] See pp. 144 and 129, *et seq, ante*, respectively.
[4] Under the Community Land Act 1975 local, etc., authorities will ultimately be under a duty to acquire a ten-year supply of "development land"; see Corfield's *A Guide to the Community Land Act*, Butterworths 1976.
[5] Cf. the *Devotwill Investment* case 200, *supra*, and see further, para. (iv), p. 204, *infra*.
[6] Land Compensation Act 1961, s. 16(3).
[7] See note 8, p. 198, *supra*.
[8] Land Compensation Act 1961, s. 16(3)(b).
[9] *Ibid*, s. 16(7).

Apart from the fact that in these circumstances there may be a choice of uses for which planning permission may be assumed, the conditions that have to be fulfilled are precisely the same as under the previous head,[1] viz the planning permission must be such as could reasonably be expected to be granted but for the compulsory acquisition (with or without conditions) and it applies only to that part of the land falling within the relevant area shown on the current development plan.

(e) Land falling within Comprehensive Development or action areas[2]

Where the relevant land, or any part of it, falls within a Comprehensive Development or Action Area the rules governing the planning permissions to be assumed are, subject to two very important qualifications, substantially the same as those set out in the previous paragraph, where the area in question is allocated primarily for a range of uses. In other words, planning permission is to be assumed for such of the range of uses shown for the comprehensive development of the area as may be appropriate—i.e., a use for which, but for the compulsory acquisition, planning permission could reasonably have been anticipated.

The more important of these two qualifications is that it also has to be assumed that none of the adjoining land is to be developed in accordance with the comprehensive development proposals of the development plan[3] and that no such development of adjoining land has at the date of the notice to treat already taken place.[4]

In other words, the relevant land has to be considered in isolation, i.e., as if it were subject to none of the benefits and suffered none of the disadvantages of the development proposed, or already carried out, on other parts of the land in pursuance of the comprehensive development proposals of the plan. Account can therefore only be taken of such development of the neighbouring land within the Comprehensive Development Area that might reasonably be expected to be, or to have been, carried out if there had been no comprehensive development proposals.

This is perhaps best illustrated by a hypothetical example. Suppose the Comprehensive Development Area comprises a virtually undeveloped area of agricultural land to be developed comprehensively to provide an industrial estate, offices, residential accommodation for industrial and office workers, etc., together with the requisite shops, doctors' clinics, etc. The land in respect of which compensation is being assessed—the relevant land—itself comprises undeveloped farm land. The planning permission to be assumed will first have to be for a class of development within these uses and secondly for a development for

[1] Para. (c), p. 199, supra, and see the cases there mentioned.

[2] Land Compensation Act 1961, s. 16(4), (5) and (8), and note that the rules relating to assumptions of planning permission here described apply equally to land falling within action areas for which a local plan is in force: Town and Country Planning Act 1971, Sch. 23: see note 8, p. 198, supra. Note also that by virtue of the Land Compensation Act 1961, s. 6 and Sch. 1, somewhat similar rules apply to land within the designated area of a New Town or New Town extension; an area defined as an area of town development under the Town Development Act 1952; and to all land comprised in the same compulsory purchase order: see, however, para. 2(ii), pp. 224, et seq, infra.

[3] Land Compensation Act 1961, s. 16(5)(a).

[4] Ibid, s. 16(5)(b).

which it would be reasonable to expect planning permission to be granted if the neighbouring land within the Comprehensive Development Area were to remain in agricultural use. Quite clearly in such circumstances it would not be reasonable to expect planning permission for a block of shops or offices standing isolated in such a "rural" setting. Residential development might, on the other hand, be appropriate, but only if the grant of planning permission therefor might, in the absence of any comprehensive development proposals, be a reasonable expectation, e.g., as extending an adjoining village. Similarly, if the relevant land immediately adjoined an established industrial area it might well be reasonable to assume planning permission for further industrial development on the relevant land, although not necessarily immediately. If, however, that adjoining industrial area had itself been developed as part of the same Comprehensive Development Area its existence would have to be ignored unless its development in turn would, in any case, most probably have been carried out, for example, as itself an extension of an adjoining but established industrial area. It will also have to be borne in mind, of course, that in so far as the suitability of the relevant land to any particular class of development within the range of uses of the Comprehensive Development Area may depend upon communications or services, the matter must be looked at in relation to the communications or services that exist or would exist if there were no comprehensive development proposals. Thus if access depends solely upon roads constructed or to be constructed only as part of the comprehensive development proposals it must be assumed that the relevant land lacks access, in which event the prospects of obtaining planning permission for *any* development in the absence of compulsory acquisition and/or the comprehensive development proposals will probably be remote.[1]

The second qualification to be kept in mind when considering what planning permission can be assumed is that it is *not* confined to planning permission for any specific use for which the relevant land may be allocated within the Comprehensive Development Area or for which it is actually being acquired. Thus a development plan that defines land as a Comprehensive Development Area will normally also indicate, at least broadly, the areas within the Comprehensive Development Area primarily reserved for specific uses, e.g., residential, commercial, industrial, open space, roads, etc. But if the relevant land happens to form part of the route of a main road, a public open space, etc., it is still open to the claimant to consider whether in the absence of these proposals planning permission could reasonably have been expected for development within any of the range of uses to which the Comprehensive Development Area as a whole is to be devoted.

This does not, of course, affect the position under the Land Compensation Act 1961, s. 15.[2] Thus if the relevant land is being acquired

---

[1] See in this connection *Myers* v *Milton Keynes Development Corpn*, [1974] 1 WLR 696: 27 P & CR 518, a case involving the very similar provisions in relation to land falling within an area designated as the site of a new town; pp. 226, *et seq, infra*.
[2] Para. (ii)(a) pp. 191, *et seq, supra*.

for residential development planning permission for such development, subject to such conditions as to density, lay-out, etc., as may be relevant, will be assumed in any event. But it will also be open to the vendor to consider whether, under this head, planning permission might also have been reasonably anticipated, if there had been no compulsory acquisition, for any other development within the Comprehensive Development Area range, such as planning permission for commercial or industrial development which is likely to be more valuable. Thus if, for example, the relevant land adjoins an existing industrial estate outside the Comprehensive Development Area but is earmarked as part of an open space and is being acquired for that purpose, it may well be reasonable to suppose that but for the designation of the area as a Comprehensive Development Area planning permission could have been granted for industrial development. This will depend, of course, upon there being a need to extend the industrial estate and the likelihood of the relevant land being chosen as the site for such an extension—both matters for consideration in the light of the evidence. That is, provided industry is a use included within the Comprehensive Development Area range of uses. The fact that the development proposed for neighbouring land has to be ignored in assessing what planning permission could reasonably be expected in the absence of compulsory acquisition may, moreover, operate both ways. For example, a proposal to site a sewage disposal plant on immediately adjoining land would also have to be ignored as an inhibiting factor in assuming a planning permission for residential development on the relevant land.

It will no doubt have been observed that the rule that land within a Comprehensive Development or Action Area must be looked at in isolation when considering what planning permission is to be assumed when valuing the land for the purpose of compensation is in essence but an extension of the general rule that a landowner whose land is compulsorily acquired is entitled to be placed in the same financial position as he would have been but for the acquisition.[1] In other words, he cannot make a profit by including elements of value that arise solely from the intentions of the local planning authority (which in most cases will also be the acquiring authority) in regard to land in someone else's ownership. It will be seen that this same principle is followed in relation to benefits or disadvantages (i.e., injurious affection) that affect the value of land retained by the vendor as a result of development proposed to be carried out by or on behalf of the acquiring authority on neighbouring land.[2]

(iv) CERTIFICATE OF APPROPRIATE ALTERNATIVE DEVELOPMENT[3]
(A) General
It will also have been appreciated that the application of the above assumptions[4] can, under certain circumstances, result in the assump-

---

[1] P. 161. *supra.*
[2] See para. 3. 1. pp. 217. *et seq. infra.*
[3] Land Compensation Act 1961, Part III (ss. 17–22).
[4] Paras. (*a*) to (*d*), *supra*, and the Land Compensation Act 1961, Part III, ss. 14–16.

tion of planning permission only for some form of public building or works for which there cannot be any general market demand. For example, where the relevant land is being acquired for the construction of a school, a highway, a cemetery, a public open space, public conveniences, etc., assumption of planning permission for such development,[1] which ex hypothesis involves acquisition by a body possessing compulsory powers, still leaves open the question as to what planning permission might reasonably be expected to be granted "if no part of the land were proposed to be acquired" by such a body.[2] The same situation may arise where any part of the relevant land is defined in the current development plan as the site for such development[3] or falls within an area defined for a specified use[4] or range of specified uses[5] which include only such uses.

Where, however, the area within which the relevant land falls is defined in the current development plan as an area of comprehensive development[6] or is allocated primarily for residential, commercial or industrial use or a range of uses which includes one or more such uses, this problem does not arise.[7]

To meet this difficulty the Act[8] makes special provision whereby either the vendor or the acquiring authority may apply to the local planning authority[9] for a "certificate of appropriate alternative development". Upon such an application being made the local planning authority is required to consider what planning permission *would*[10] have been granted but for the compulsory acquisition and to issue a certificate accordingly. Provision is made for appeal to the Secretary of State[11] who in effect considers the application *de novo*.[12]

(B) Requirements prerequisite to an application for a certificate of appropriate alternative development

(a) There must be a proposal by an authority possessing compulsory purchase powers to acquire the interest in the land in respect of which it

[1] Para. (*b*), *supra*, and Land Compensation Act 1961, s. 15.
[2] See e.g. *Scunthorpe Borough Council* v *Secretary of State*, [1977] JPL 653.
[3] Para. (*c*), *supra*, and *ibid*, s. 16(1).
[4] Para. (*c*) *supra* and *ibid*, s. 16(2;.
[5] Para. (*d*) *supra*, and *ibid*, s. 16(3).
[6] Para. (*e*) *supra*, and *ibid*, s. 16(4) and (5).
[7] This is not quite true in the case of areas of comprehensive development, for the older type of development plan may define an area as a CDA solely for "the replacement of open space in the course of the development or redevelopment of any other area": Town and Country Planning Act 1971, Sch. 5, para. 1(4)(b). In practice such an allocation has seldom, if ever, been made and it does not appear to be applicable to "action areas" which, where a local plan is in force, supersede Comprehensive Development Areas in the modern development plan; *ibid*, Sch. 23; see note 2, p. 202, *supra*. See also note 4, p. 206, *infra*.
[8] Land Compensation Act 1961, s. 17, now amended by the Community Land Act 1975, s. 47 and Sch. 9, Part I; see p. 208, *infra*.
[9] As to the appropriate local planning authority see the Local Government Act 1972, Sch. 16, para. 55.
[10] By the Land Compensation Act 1961, s. 17, the local planning authority was required to state for what class or classes of development, if any, planning permission "might reasonably be expected to be granted"; this has now been amended by the Community Land Act 1975, s. 47: as to the effect of the amendment see p. 211, *infra*.
[11] Land Compensation Act 1961, s. 18.
[12] *Ibid*, s. 18(2).

is desired to apply for a certificate of appropriate alternative development.

Such a proposal only exists where:[1]

(aa) The notice of the making of a compulsory purchase order covering the relevant land has been published or served;[2] or in the case of land authorised to be acquired by Private Act, the notices provided for by Parliamentary Standing Orders on promotion of the Parliamentary Bill, have been served or published;

(bb) A notice to treat has been deemed to have been served upon acceptance of a purchase or blight notice;[3] or

(cc) An offer in writing has been made by or on behalf of the acquiring authority to negotiate for the purchase of the interest.

(b) No part[4] of the relevant land must fall within any area defined in the current development plan as an area of comprehensive development or, under the modern development plan provisions, where a local plan for the area is in force, as an action area;[5] and no part[4] must fall within an area "allocated primarily for a use which is of a residential, commercial or industrial character, or for a range of two or more uses any of which is of such a character".[6]

Where there have been recent amendments to the development plan which create new areas of the type described above, or which delete or amend such areas, difficulties may arise in determining what precisely is the *current* development plan for these purposes.

Where the acquisition arises either in response to a purchase or blight notice or the acquiring authority has served a notice to treat the current development plan is the plan in force[7] at the date of the deemed notice to treat or actual notice to treat, as the case may be.[8]

Where the acquiring authority has entered into a contract for the purchase of the interest in the relevant land the current development plan is that which is in force at the date of the contract.[9] Unless it proves impossible for the vendor and the acquiring authority to agree a price—in which case the matter will be referred to the Lands Tribunal[10]—such a contract will normally follow the notice to treat as a matter of course. In that event the current development plan will depend upon the date of application for the certificate. If it is before a

---

[1] Land Compensation Act 1961, *Ibid*, s. 22(2).

[2] As required by the Acquisition of Land (Authorisation Procedure) Act 1946, Sch. 1, para. 3; p. 32, *ante*.

[3] As to which see pp. 114, *et seq, ante*.

[4] This requirement may produce difficulties, for if only part of the land falls within such an area the planning permissions to be assumed under paras. (c), (d) and (e) of the text (Land Compensation Act 1961, s. 16(2)–(5)) *supra*. apply only to that part, as explained on pp. 199 *et seq, supra*. Although those provisions will not, therefore, give any guide to the planning permission to be assumed in relation to the other part, no application can be made in respect thereof for a certificate of appropriate alternative development: see *ibid*, s. 17(1), which applies only where the "land *or part* thereof" does not fall within the proscribed areas.

[5] Land Compensation Act 1961, s. 17(1)(a).

[6] *Ibid*, s. 17(1)(b).

[7] Whether such plan be the development plan as originally approved or made by the Secretary of State or as for the time being amended by him: Land Compensation Act 1961, s. 22(3).

[8] *Ibid*, s. 22(3)(a).

[9] *Ibid*, s. 22(3)(b).

[10] *Ibid*, ss. 1 and 2.

contract has been entered into it will be the plan in force at the date of notice to treat; if afterwards, it will be the plan in force at the date of contract.[1]

It sometimes happens, however, that an acquiring authority will purchase by agreement without recourse to compulsory powers, or having made a compulsory purchase order, will anticipate its confirmation by entering into a contract to purchase. In the former case there can be no notice to treat, and in the latter, such a notice being unnecessary, it is unlikely to be served.[2] Thus, although the Act provides[1] that where there is both a contract and a notice to treat the current development plan shall be the plan in force at whichever is the later of the date of the notice to treat or the date of the contract, a contract preceding a notice to treat is likely to be a rarity.

In all other cases the current development plan is the development plan in force at the date of the application for the certificate.[1]

(c) Only the parties directly concerned may apply for a certificate, i.e., the owner of the interest, the subject of the proposed acquisition, and the acquiring authority, who in most cases will no doubt itself be the local planning authority.[3] Since the purpose of this procedure is to obtain a certificate indicating that a planning permission which will enhance the value of the land would be obtainable in the absence of proposals for acquisition, there is little or no incentive for acquiring authorities to apply for a certificate. In practice they seldom, if ever, do so; it may, of course, be in their interest to appeal against the grant of a particular certificate (if they themselves are not the local planning authority responsible for issuing it) but that of course is a very different matter.

(d) Finally, an application for a certificate of appropriate alternative development can only be made with the consent of the other party "directly concerned" or of the Lands Tribunal if, following notice to treat or the conclusion of an agreement to sell (i.e., without determining price) a reference has been made to the Lands Tribunal to determine the amount of the compensation payable in respect of the interest in question.[4]

There may, of course, be more than one interest being acquired in the same land. In that event, if a reference has been made to the Lands Tribunal in respect of one of those interests it may be convenient for the acquiring authority to refer the determination of compensation payable in respect of the other interests to the Lands Tribunal so that the respective claims can be heard together.[5]

---

[1] Land Compensation Act 1961, s. 22(3); and see *Jelson* v *Minister of Housing and Local Government* (1969), 20 P & CR 663 (CA).
[2] Such a notice cannot, of course, be served prior to confirmation of the order.
[3] See note 1, p. 208, *infra.*
[4] Land Compensation Act 1961, s. 17(2).
[5] Note that although either party may refer the determination of compensation to the Lands Tribunal, only the acquiring authority is entitled to ask that all the claims be heard by the same member or members of the Tribunal and heard together. *Ibid*, s. 3. The value of the several interests must, of course, still be separately assessed: *Ibid*. For the procedure see Lands Tribunal Rules 1975 (SI 1975 No. 299) Rule 36.

(C) Procedure
The Application. Provided the above requirements have been fulfilled the party concerned may apply to the local planning authority[1] for a certificate of appropriate alternative development. In his application he must first state "whether or not there are, in the applicant's opinion, any classes of development which, either immediately or at a future time, would be appropriate for the land in question if it were not proposed to be acquired by any authority possessing compulsory purchase powers and, if so, shall specify the classes of development and the times at which they would be so appropriate".[2]

The applicant must then state the grounds for his views in this matter[3] and attach "a statement specifying the date on which a copy of the application has been or will be served[4] on the other party directly concerned".[5] He must also attach a "map or plan sufficient to identify the land to which the application relates".[6]

Upon receipt of the application the local planning authority must, not earlier than 21 days after the date on which the copy thereof was served on the other party or, subject to this latter requirement, not later than two months from the date on which they received the application,[7] issue a certificate.

The Certificate. That certificate must state that if the land in question were not proposed to be compulsorily acquired the local planning authority are of the opinion either:

"(a)[8] that planning permission for development of one or more classes specified in

---

[1] As to the appropriate local planning authority see the Local Government Act 1972, Sch. 16, para. 55. This is not, however, a matter that should give rise to difficulty for if the application is inadvertently sent to a County District Council or London Borough Council instead of the County Council or Greater London Council (or vice versa) it will normally be transferred without undue delay.

[2] Land Compensation Act 1961, s. 17(3)(a) as amended by the Community Land Act 1975, s. 47 and Sch. 9, Part I. There is, of course, little point in the vendor applying for a certificate if he does not consider that there is any alternative class of development appropriate to the land, and hitherto applicants have in practice been confined to owners of interests being acquired—i.e., vendors (see para. (C), p. 207, *supra*). The original wording of this subsection accordingly merely required the applicant to state what class or classes of development appeared to him as "appropriate to the land in question if it was not proposed to be acquired by an authority possessing compulsory purchase powers". In substituting the new wording Parliament presumably had in mind the great increase in compulsory acquisition inherent in the Community Land Act concept of the ultimate public ownership of all development land (see pp. 22, *et seq*, *ante*) and envisaged that acquiring authorities will in future not always wish to wait for the vendor to make an application but will themselves seek 'nil' certificates; i.e., certificates indicating that, but for the proposals to acquire, planning permission would not be granted for any development other than that for which the land is being acquired.

[3] Land Compensation Act 1961, s. 17(3)(b).   [4] As to the methods of service see *ibid*, s. 38.

[5] Land Compensation Act 1961, s. 17(3)(c). For the parties directly concerned see para. (c), p. 207, *supra*.

[6] Land Compensation Development Order 1974 (SI No. 539) Art. 3(1).

[7] Land Compensation Act 1961, s. 17(4); Land Compensation Development Order 1974, SI 1974 No. 539, Art. 3(2). Note that although this period is the same as that formerly allowed to local planning authorities in which to issue decisions upon applications for planning permission, the latter period is now eight weeks: Town and Country Planning General Development (Amendment) Order 1976 (SI 1976 No. 301) Art. 7(3).

[8] Land Compensation Act 1961, s. 17(4)(a). Note that the words "would have been granted" were substituted by the Community Land Act 1975, s. 47(3), for the words "might reasonably have been expected to be granted".

the certificate (whether specified in the application or not) would have been granted; or

(b) that planning permission would not have been granted for any development other than the development (if any) which is proposed to be carried out by the authority by whom the interest is proposed to be acquired".[1]

A certificate to the latter effect is commonly referred to as a "nil" certificate. In the case of a "positive" certificate it is open to the local planning authority, if it considers it appropriate to do so, to state in the certificate that the planning permission which would be granted would be subject to such conditions as it thinks would be imposed if there were no acquisition backed by compulsory powers, or that the planning permission would only be available at some future time; indeed it may do both.[2]

In considering whether planning permission would be granted for any particular class of development the local planning authority is not, however, to assume that planning permission therefor would necessarily be refused solely because such development (either of the land in question or of that land together with other land) would not accord with the development plan.[3]   It need only give reasons for its opinion if it indicates in the certificate that planning permission would be granted for some class of development which was not specified in the application or if planning permission for such development is contrary to representations made by the other party.[4] This latter is a somewhat curious provision since neither the Act nor the Development Order confers upon that other party any right to make representations; nor is there anything to require the local planning authority to consider such representations.[5] It is also only in these circumstances that the local planning authority is required to give particulars as to the manner in which and the time within which an appeal may be made to the Secretary of State.[4] Since an appeal lies to the Secretary of State in *all* cases[6] this again seems a curious limitation upon the duties of local planning authorities in this respect, although no doubt in practice most local planning authorities will include this information as a matter of course.

In all cases the local planning authority must serve a copy of the certificate on the other party directly concerned.[7]

Finally in this context, a County Council is required to copy all certificates issued by them to the relevant District Council or Councils

[1] Land Compensation Act 1961, s. 17(4)(b). Here again the words "planning permission would not have been granted" replace "planning permission could not reasonably have been expected to be granted": Community Land Act 1975, s. 47(3). For the effect of these amendments see p. 211, *infra*.

[2] Land Compensation Act 1961, s. 17(5). The local planning authority may also formulate general requirements in respect of specified cases and may, instead of spelling such requirements out in the certificate in the form of conditions, incorporate them therein by reference, with or without modifications: *Ibid*, s. 17(6).

[3] *Ibid*, s. 17(7).

[4] Land Compensation Development Order 1974 (SI 1974 No. 539) Art. 3(3).

[5] Cf, for example, Town and Country Planning Act 1971, s. 29(3), by which a local planning authority is required to take account of the representations of owners and agricultural tenants.

[6] Under the Land Compensation Act 1961, s. 18, *infra*.

[7] *Ibid*, s. 17(9).

(i.e., where the land in question lies across a County District boundary) and County District Councils must send copies of any certificate that specifies any class of development that relates to a county matter to the County Council. Similar arrangements are made for London Borough Councils and the Common Council of the City to copy certificates to the Greater London Council.[1]

(D) Appeals

Where a local planning authority has issued a certificate in respect of an interest in land the Land Compensation Act 1961 provides a right of appeal to "the person for the time being entitled to that interest"[2] and to "any authority possessing compulsory purchase powers by whom the interest is proposed to be acquired".[3]

The right of appeal is not therefore confined to the original "parties directly concerned"; thus, if the owner at the date of the application has parted with his interest or died, the right of appeal lies with his successor in title; similarly if the public authority originally intending to acquire gives place to another authority possessing compulsory purchase powers.

Notice of appeal must be given in writing to the Secretary of State[4] within one month of the date of receipt of the certificate by the party lodging the appeal.[5]

Where the local planning authority fails to issue a certificate within the prescribed period[6] (or such extended period as has been agreed in writing between the parties and the local planning authority)[7] such failure has the same effect for the purpose of an appeal as if the local planning authority had issued a nil certificate. In such circumstances notice of appeal must be given within one month of the expiry of the prescribed period or of such extended period as may have been agreed.[8]

[1] Land Compensation Development Order 1974 (SI 1974, No. 539) Art. 3(4).
[2] Land Compensation Act 1961, s. 18(1)(a).
[3] *Ibid*, s. 18(1)(b).
[4] Land Compensation Development Order 1974 (*supra*) Art. 4(1)(a).
[5] Note that if the certificate when issued is sent by post it must either be registered (Land Compensation Act 1961, s. 38(1)(c)) or sent by recorded delivery service (Recorded Delivery Service Act 1962, s. 1(1)). The same applies to the copy served upon the other party: *ibid*. In such cases the date of receipt is readily ascertainable. Difficulties may, however, arise where these documents are served by leaving them "at the usual or last known place of abode" of the person concerned (Land Compensation Act 1961, s. 38(1)(b)) and he has moved or is temporarily absent. Since the Secretary of State has no power to extend the period for lodging an appeal (*aliter* in the case of appeals under the Town and Country Planning Act 1971) it is essential that private vendors likely to be away from home make effective arrangements for dealing with the local planning authority or appoint agents. Such difficulties are not, of course, likely to arise in the case of a company or the acquiring authority.
[6] I.e., two months from receipt of the application provided at least 21 days have elapsed since a copy thereof was served upon the other party. Land Compensation Development Order 1974 (SI 1974 No. 539) Art. 3(2), *supra*.
[7] Land Compensation Act 1961, s. 18(4). Curiously, this, the only mention of the right to agree an extended period for the issue of a certificate, appears in the section dealing solely with appeals (i.e., s. 18) rather than in that dealing with the content and issue of certificates (*ibid*, s. 17, *supra*).
[8] Land Compensation Development Order 1974 (*supra*) Art. 4(1)(b). Note that this article in fact refers to the expiry of the "time or extended time" mentioned in the Land Compensation Act 1961, s. 17(4). The only reference to time in that subsection is, however, the minimum period of 21 days that must elapse following service of the copy application that must be sent to the other party directly concerned, before the local planning authority can issue a certificate. The power to prescribe a time limit within which a certificate must be issued (by order) arises from *ibid*, s. 20.

Before deciding the appeal, which he must do as if the application had been made direct to him at the outset,[1] the Secretary of State must, if either of the parties or the local planning authority so desire, provide an opportunity for them to be heard by a person appointed by him for that purpose.[2] He may then confirm or modify the certificate or issue an entirely new one in its place.[3]

As has been noted,[4] the Community Land Act 1975[5] introduced important amendments to these provisions. It is therefore necessary to consider their effect, and in particular the extent to which decided cases under the original provisions are likely to be applicable. The practical effect of these amendments can best be illustrated by recalling the reasons for the original provisions. Local planning authorities must obviously provide, *inter alia*, for a number of public services involving development that, in the sense that it yields no financial return, may be regarded as uneconomic development and comprising such things as schools, hospitals, public buildings, public open space, cemeteries, public conveniences, etc. The selection of sites for such development can be regarded, however, from the landowner's point of view as the luck of the draw. It was accordingly felt that the owners of land required for such purposes should not be placed at a financial disadvantage *vis-à-vis* neighbouring owners, upon whose land residential or other "profitable" development takes place.

The certificate procedure was accordingly designed and hitherto operated[6] so that owners of land that has become entirely or mainly surrounded by urban development could expect to obtain a certificate indicating that development of a similar nature would be appropriate on their land, thus enabling them to value their land on that basis for the purposes of compensation. The principle was that where the public development for which such land was being acquired could equally well have been sited on neighbouring developed land it would be unfair to expect landowners to accept a lower value. This, of course, resulted in acquiring authorities being required to pay development land prices for land which they had no intention of developing in accordance with the development certified as appropriate. Moreover, in many cases there

---

Strictly speaking, therefore, if no certificate is issued the time for appeal runs from one month from the date of application extended only to the extent that may be necessary to allow 21 days to elapse from the date of service of the copy of the application on the other party directly concerned. If, however, an extended period has been agreed and a "nil" certificate is assumed upon its expiry, the time within which an appeal has to be lodged may already have expired. This is clearly not intended, and in practice the rule operates as stated in the text.

[1] Land Compensation Act 1961, s. 18(2).
[2] *Ibid*, s. 18(3).
[3] *Ibid*, s. 18(2).
[4] See notes 1 and 2, p. 209, *supra*.
[5] The amendments came into effect on 12 December 1975: Community Land Act 1975, s. 47(6). It is worthy of note that following the 2nd Appointed Day under that Act (when compensation reverts to existing use value: s. 25; see pp. 305, *et seq, post*) regulations relating to Financial Hardship Tribunals may provide for the continued use of this procedure for obtaining certificates of appropriate alternative development under the Land Compensation Act 1961, Part III: Community Land Act 1975, s. 27(8)(a); pp. 310, *et seq, post*.
[6] See, for example, Ministry of Housing and Local Government Circular 48/59, paras. 2–6, particularly para. 4.

was no prospect whatever of planning permission ever actually being granted for any of the classes of development specified even if the land remained indefinitely in private ownership—the most obvious example being that given in the White Paper,[1] viz land surrounded by urban development which has remained undeveloped whether fortuitously or deliberately (e.g., to preserve the private amenities of a large house) and which for good planning reasons must remain undeveloped (or confined to low density development such as schools with adequate playing fields) indefinitely. It is in cases such as this that the amended provisions will bite. They will no doubt result in "nil certificates" in the case of much open land (or land developed at exceptionally low densities) in and adjoining urban areas (and its consequent acquisition at current use values) where in the past a more valuable certificate might have been expected.

Although, therefore, these amendments seem likely in some cases to result in somewhat more realistic certificates, the decision as to what planning permission would be granted remains a purely hypothetical exercise, for it will still be necessary to envisage the situation in which there can be no question of the land being compulsorily acquired. That in turn, of course, makes it necessary to ignore any change of use of the land that can only in practice be effected by a public authority. If, therefore, land is being acquired for a school to serve an existing or proposed residential area, for example, it obviously cannot be assumed that if there is to be no school (because such development clearly presupposes acquisition by the local education authority) the land would be left in its existing use. On the face of it, therefore, except in the cases noted above these amendments appear unlikely to have any very significant effect upon the compensation payable by acquiring authorities.

Thus in *Bennett and Another* v *Minister of Housing and Local Government*,[2] the subject land was shown in the current development plan as part of a larger area allocated for acquisition as public open space. The northern boundary of the subject land was a brook and it was part of the acquiring authority's proposals that the brook should be diverted (so that it would then traverse the subject land) and thereafter form the basis of a public riverside walk. The certificate issued by the Minister on appeal certified residential development for that part of the subject land lying between the existing course of the brook and its proposed straightened course, and amounted to a "nil" certificate in relation to the remainder of the land. The certificate was quashed[3] on the ground that the proposed straightening of the brook was the essential foundation upon which the Minister had considered this matter and that since that was something which could only be effected by the acquisition of the land by the acquiring authority it could not properly be

---

[1] Cmnd. 5730, 1974, paras. 31 and 32.

[2] An unreported case in the Queen's Bench Division, dated 30 July 1970, before Bridge J.

[3] For the relevant procedure and the grounds on which such a decision may be challenged in the Courts, see Land Compensation Act 1961, s. 21, and note the similarity of the procedure and grounds applicable to compulsory purchase orders: pp. 52 *et seq, ante.*

taken into account. Going on to consider (*obiter*) whether it was open to the Minister to base his decision on the proposition that the desirability of ultimately acquiring the land for public open space itself provided a planning reason for refusing planning permission, Bridge J. said:

> "In my judgment that is not a legitimate approach under s. 17. The primary purpose, as it seems to me, of the provision of subsection (7)[1] of s. 17 . . . is precisely to exclude that kind of consideration.
>
> "In the last analysis, as it seems to me, it would wholly defeat the purpose of s. 17 if it were open to the planning authority or to the Minister to say: "Although we must disregard the present proposal to acquire the land in question, nevertheless this land ought to be acquired for public purposes at some time in the future; the need for that is apparent, and that in itself affords a sufficient reason why no planning permission for other development *might have been*, apart from the proposed acquisition, *expected to be granted*".[2] Presumably, whenever land is proposed to be acquired for public purposes there is a good reason for the acquisition and accordingly if the mere fact that the land ought to be acquired is a reason for refusing notional planning permission under s. 17, there could hardly ever be a case in which s. 17 could lead to the issue of an affirmative certificate."

The substitution of the words "would have been granted"[3] for those in italics[4] would in no way appear to affect the logic of this reasoning.

(E) The effect of a certificate

When a certificate is issued indicating that planning permission for any particular class of development would have been granted if the land were not proposed to be acquired by any authority possessing compulsory purchase powers, planning permission for such development is to be assumed in exactly the same way as if that assumption arose directly from the provisions of the Act[5] outlined in paras. (*a*) to (*e*) above.[6]

As in the case of other planning permissions whether actual or to be assumed, a "positive" certificate is, of course, only of value if there is a market for land with the planning permission indicated in the certificate. In *Bromilow* v *Greater Manchester Council*[7] for example, a certificate was issued indicating commercial development as the appropriate alternative development, but the land adjoined an industrial estate and, in particular, a bone factory emitting obnoxious smells. It was held by the Lands Tribunal (and upheld on appeal[8]) that there would be no demand for commercial development on land so situated; the certificate was therefore valueless.

A more debatable case is that of *Hoveringham Gravels Ltd*. v *Chiltern District Council and Buckingham County Council*[9] in which a purchase notice was served in respect of land required for the construction of a road. A

---

[1] For Land Compensation Act 1961, s. 17(7) see p. 209, *supra*.

[2] Author's italics.

[3] I.e., the relevant words of the Land Compensation Act 1961, s. 17(4)(a) and (b), as amended by the Community Land Act 1975, s. 47 and Sch. 9.

[4] I.e., the relevant words of the Land Compensation Act 1961, s. 17(4)(a) and (b) as originally enacted and on which *Bennett* v *Ministry of Housing and Local Government* fell to be decided.

[5] Land Compensation Act 1961, s. 15(5).

[6] *Ibid*, Part II, ss. 14–16; pp. 191–204, *supra*. These provisions and those of ss. 17–22 reproduce the Town and Country Planning Act 1959, Part I, ss. 2–8. It is not at all clear why the Land Compensation Act 1961 (a consolidation Act) separated ss. 17–22 into a separate Part III.

[7] (1974) 29 P & CR 517.

[8] (1975) 31 P & CR 398.   [9] (1976) 31 P & CR 466.

s. 17 certificate was obtained indicating that planning permission for residential development might reasonably have been expected. In confirming the purchase notice, however, the Secretary of State introduced a modification by which the County Council, as local highway authority, was to acquire the land actually required for the roadworks and the District Council the remainder. It was held that, although the certificate was valid, it could not add to the compensation since a local planning authority, confronted with separate planning applications in respect of the two portions of the land in different ownership, would be bound to say that development in separate plots was not the development contemplated; in other words, planning permission for the comprehensive development of an area of land does not permit piecemeal development not forming part of a scheme for the whole. The Lands Tribunal consequently reduced the compensation claimed by 50 % of the development value to take account of the risk that planning permission for the separate development of the two plots might not be granted.

This seems a curious decision because a s. 17 certificate is not a planning permission; it is merely an indication of what planning permission might reasonably be expected[1] if the land in question "were not proposed to be acquired by an authority possessing compulsory purchase powers". The purpose of the certificate is to show the development for which the land is suited in planning terms; ownership would not therefore appear to be relevant. But even if it is, it was only because of the acquisition by these two local authorities that ownership became divided.[2]

Somewhat paradoxically, however, a "nil" certificate does not (at least in theory) conclusively rebut an argument based upon general planning criteria that planning permission for some development ought to be assumed. This is because the Act provides only that "in determining whether planning permission for any development could in any particular circumstances reasonably have been expected to be granted in respect of any land, *regard shall be had* to any contrary opinion expressed in relation to that land" in any such certificate.[3] In practice, however, the issue of such a nil certificate, especially in the light of the amendments effected by the Community Land Act 1975 and considered above, is likely to make any such argument difficult to sustain.

A difficulty can arise where a change in the development plan,

---

[1] This case fell to be decided upon the Land Compensation Act 1961, s. 17, unamended by the Community Land Act 1975, s. 47 and Sch. 9. It does not, however, seem that that amendment would have made any difference: see pp. 211 *et seq, supra*, and *Bennett*'s case in particular, p. 212, *et seq, supra*.

[2] On appeal in respect of the back-land acquired by the District Council it was held that although no account should be taken of the *acquisition* of the rest of the land by the County Council, account should be taken of the depreciation in the value of that land (as "land retained") resulting from its severance from the District Council's back-land. The inference would seem to be that had the back-land acquired by the District Council been similarly regarded as retained land when assessing the compensation payable in respect of the front-land, total compensation would have been no less than if there had been a single acquisition of the whole: *Hoveringham Gravels Ltd.* v *Chiltern District Council* [1977] RVR 243. Note that both parties obtained leave to appeal to the House of Lords.

[3] Land Compensation Act 1961, s. 14(3).

advantageous to the applicant, takes effect after the issue of a nil certificate. Since the relevant date for valuation purposes is whichever is the earlier—the date of entry or the date on which compensation falls to be determined[1]—the relevant planning situation should logically be related to the situation ruling at the same date. This should be so even if the relevant date for the purpose of determining the interests to be valued is taken as the date of notice to treat,[2] because the grant of planning permission does not normally[3] affect the nature of the interests being acquired. Although the matter has yet to be considered by either the Lands Tribunal or the courts, there seems no logical reason to differentiate in this matter between cases in which a certificate has been issued[4] and others. It would seem anomalous if the fact that the certificate has to be based upon the planning conditions ruling at the date of notice to treat (or, in the case of acquisition by agreement, the date of the contract)[1] should override the position ruling at the date of actual acquisition.

The question is, of course, only of importance where the planning position as at the latter date is more advantageous to the vendor than that certified, because he is entitled to assume that planning permission would be granted in accordance with the certificate, come what may.[6]

Thus in one case[7] in which the local planning authority had offered to negotiate for the purchase of land[8] for development as a public open space the owner applied for a certificate for commercial development on the grounds that the local planning authority had already passed a resolution to amend the development plan by including the land in a comprehensive development area. A nil certificate was issued, by which time both the comprehensive development area and the subsequent compulsory purchase order had been confirmed. The applicant then maintained that he was entitled to assume planning permission for commercial development as one of the classes of development included in the comprehensive development area, and which would have been appropriate had there been no question of compulsory acquisition, although his land remained earmarked as part of a public open space within the Comprehensive Development Area.[9] The problem, therefore, was that despite the more favourable assumption arising from the Comprehensive Development Area, regard had to be had to the nil certificate in assessing compensation. Planning permission for commercial development had, some years previously, been refused, but

[1] See pp. 165, et seq, ante.
[2] See pp. 169, et seq, ante.
[3] For examples to the contrary see *Rugby Water Board* v *Shaw-Fox*, [1972] 2 WLR 757 HL, p. 172, supra, and *In re Morgan and London and North Western Rly Co.*, [1896] 2 QB 469, pp. 172 and 174, supra.
[4] Indeed, the same considerations logically apply to the case where the current development plan at the relevant date differs from that in force at the date of notice to treat, which is the plan from which assumptions as to the planning permissions that can reasonably be expected are to be derived: Land Compensation Act 1961, s. 16, pp. 196, et seq. supra.
[5] P. 207, supra.
[6] P. 213, supra.
[7] Not yet before the Lands Tribunal.
[8] See para. cc, p. 206, supra and Land Compensation Act 1961, s. 22(2)(c).
[9] See p. 202, supra.

only on the ground that such development would at the time have been premature; the applicant wished to rely upon that fact in arguing before the Lands Tribunal that planning permission for such development might in these new circumstances reasonably be expected.[1]

He was accordingly anxious to get rid of the nil certificate and appealed to the Secretary of State. By agreement with the local planning authority, at the opening of the hearing the Secretary of State was asked to issue a certificate to the effect that planning permission could reasonably be expected for such of the Comprehensive Development Area range of uses as would have been appropriate under the Land Compensation Act 1961, s. 16(4) and (5).[2] The Secretary of State, however, maintained (no doubt correctly) that he was only empowered to issue a certificate for some specific class or classes of development. The appellant being unwilling to risk confirmation of the nil certificate by the Secretary of State thus faced a dilemma, for there were no means of reverting to the position in which he would have been had he never applied for a certificate. By this time, however, the local planning authority had decided that it could not afford to follow up its compulsory purchase order by acquisition and withdrew its offer to negotiate. Moreover, since three years had elapsed since the confirmation of the compulsory purchase order and no notice to treat had been served its authorisation for the compulsory acquisition had lapsed.[3] There was therefore no point, in any case, of proceeding with the appeal. But since the Comprehensive Development Area remained part of the development plan and the owner's interest in the land was not such as to qualify him to serve a blight notice,[4] the land, which was undeveloped and of little or no agricultural value, remained virtually unsaleable to anyone other than the local planning authority.

Unusual as the circumstances of this case may be, it does, it is suggested, illustrate the necessity of very careful consideration before applying for a certificate when details of changes known to be contemplated by the local planning authority are available.

SUMMARY OF PLANNING ASSUMPTIONS

In assessing market value it is to be assumed that planning permission for the following types of development will be available in the circumstances described:

(a) Planning permission for any development for which planning permission is in force at the date of service of the notice to treat.[5]
(b) Planning permission for the development for which the land is being acquired.[6]
(c) Planning permission for developments deemed (by virtue of the

---

[1] The case fell to be decided upon the provisions of Land Compensation Act 1961, s. 17, prior to the coming into force of the Community Land Act 1975.
[2] Para. (e), p. 202, supra.
[3] Compulsory Purchase Act 1965, s. 4.
[4] See Town and Country Planning Act 1971, s. 193, pp. 133 et seq, ante.
[5] Pp. 185 et seq, supra.
[6] Pp. 191 et seq, supra.

Town and Country Planning Act 1971, s. 22 and Schedule 8) to be included in existing use.[1]

(d) Subject to the special provisions relating to land falling within an area of comprehensive development (or under the more modern Structure and Local plans, within an action area), planning permission for developments that accord with the current development plan, provided such planning permission could have been reasonably expected[2] if there had been no question of compulsory acquisition.

In the case of land falling within an area of comprehensive development or an action area, planning permission may be assumed for any of the uses comprised in that area provided such planning permission could have been reasonably expected if there had been no question of compulsory acquisition and subject to the further proviso that in assessing market value the effect on the value of the subject land of development on neighbouring land (other than development that would be likely to have been or to be carried out if there were no comprehensive development or action area) is to be discounted.[3]

(e) Planning permission certified in a certificate of appropriate alternative development as planning permission that would have been granted but for the compulsory acquisition.[4]

(f) Where the planning situation changes in favour of the vendor between the date with reference to which the planning assumptions under the Act are related (normally the date of notice to treat) and the relevant date,[5] the effect of such changes upon market demand may, it is submitted, be taken into account in the assessment of compensation.[6]

3 ADJUSTMENTS TO COMPENSATION WHEN THE VALUE OF AN OWNER'S INTEREST IS AFFECTED BY DEVELOPMENT OF NEIGHBOURING LAND: THE "SCHEME"

1 The general rule

As has already been indicated, a basic principle of the law of compensation for compulsory acquisition is that the vendor should be left neither better nor worse off financially as a result of the acquisition. Where, however, land is acquired in pursuance of a scheme of acquisition and development going wider than the isolated development of the land taken, development of adjoining land, as part of the same scheme, may either enhance or depreciate the value of the land being acquired. It follows that if compensation were to be based upon such enhanced values the vendor would be better off than he would have been if there

---

[1] Pp. 194 *et seq, supra.*
[2] Pp. 196, *et seq, supra.*
[3] Pp. 202, *et seq, supra.*
[4] Pp. 204 *et seq, supra.*
[5] I.e., the date of entry or the date on which compensation falls to be determined, whichever is the earlier.
[6] Pp. 197–8 and 215 *supra.*

were no such scheme and he had been left to sell his land in the open market. Conversely he would, of course, be worse off if the effect of the scheme were to depreciate the market value of the land to be taken.

Similarly, where the development proposed for the land being acquired itself affects the potential of some physical attribute of the land, the value to the acquiring authority may be greater (or less) than its value to the owner if he were to realise his capital by sale in the open market.

The scheme of acquisition and development may also, of course, affect the value of other land in the neighbourhood that is retained by the owner of the land being acquired, so that when he comes to sell that land he may be better off than he would have been but for the scheme, to which, of course, he has made no direct financial contribution. If his retained land is depreciated by the scheme he will be entitled to compensation for injurious affection.[1]

In recognition of these effects upon value of the overall scheme, in pursuance of which land is acquired, it has long been established that such effects are to be ignored in the assessment of compensation. Although generally referred to as the *Pointe Gourde* principle, derived from the decision in *Pointe Gourde Quarrying and Transport Co.* v *Sub-Intendent of Crown Lands*, decided in 1947,[2] its origin is considerably older.[3]

Thus where an electricity generating authority acquired land including a waterfall for hydroelectric generation, and also acquired other land farther upstream for the construction of a reservoir in order to increase the generating capacity of the waterfall, it was held that the basis of compensation must be the financial value to the owner, i.e., the value of the waterfall based upon its existing capacity and not upon its ultimate capacity, attributable to the construction of the reservoir which constituted part of the same scheme.[4]

Similarly, to take a more modern example, where property within a clearance area was being acquired it was held that, since the clearance of the area was wholly attributable to the scheme, compensation fell to be based upon the value of the cleared sites[5] surrounded by unfit houses, and not on the basis that the surrounding area had been cleared and made ready for redevelopment.[6]

In the *Pointe Gourde* case itself, the Crown, pursuant to the provisions of the Land Acquisition Ordinance 1941,[7] compulsorily acquired

---

[1] See Chap. 8, p. 314, *post.*

[2] [1947] AC 565 (PC).

[3] See e.g., *Re Gough and Aspatria, Silloth and District Joint Water Board* [1904] 1 KB 417 and *South Eastern Rly Co and LCC's Contract South Eastern Rly Co* v *LCC* [1915] 2 Ch. 252.

[4] *Fraser* v *City of Fraserville*, [1917] AC 187 (PC), in which the Privy Council overruled the arbitrator's assessment of compensation based on the ultimate hydroelectric capacity of the land: cf. the similar case of *Cedar Rapids Manufacturing and Power Co.* v *Lacoste*, [1914] AC 569 (PC), in which the arbitrators were overruled because they had gone to the other extreme of basing compensation on the existing use (i.e., agricultural) value and made no allowance for the natural potential of the land for other purposes.

[5] See pp. 255, *et seq, post.*

[6] *Davy* v *Leeds Corpn*, [1965] 1 WLR 445 (HL).

[7] Those provisions were identical to those of Land Compensation Act 1961, s. 5(3), as to which see p. 164, *supra.*

certain of the appellants' land which included a limestone quarry of considerable potential and which the appellants operated commercially. Some $15,000 of the compensation awarded reflected the special value of this limestone for construction of the naval base for which the land was being acquired. It was held, however, that that part of the award could not stand because compensation for the compulsory acquisition of land cannot include an increase in value which is entirely due to the scheme underlying the acquisition.[1]

It will have been observed that the *Pointe Gourde* case was confined to the effect of the scheme underlying the acquisition upon the commercial potential of a physical attribute of the land being taken, i.e., its quarrying potential. It is therefore somewhat unfortunate that it is this case that is almost universally referred to as embodying the basic principle with which we are here concerned, for, as has been seen, that principle goes considerably wider and includes the effect upon value of development proposed for other land subject to the same scheme.

Statutory recognition of this general principle is now conferred by the Land Compensation Act 1961.[2] The efforts of the framers of that Act in this regard have not, however, proved nearly as comprehensive as the "common law" principle under consideration. In the initial period after the passing of the Act in which these provisions first appeared[3] there was inevitably, therefore, some doubt as to whether the statutory provisions overruled the wider concept of the *Pointe Gourde* principle and were exclusive,[4] or whether the somewhat narrower provisions of the Act were merely a statutory expression of a principle that remained good law. The latter view has now been accepted.[5]

The practical problem in this context is, of course, to decide precisely what the scheme is, and in some cases to decide whether there is a scheme at all.[6]

This is basically a matter of fact rather than law, and "it is for the Tribunal in fact to consider just what activities—past, present or future—are properly to be regarded as the scheme".[7] "A scheme is a progressive thing. It starts vague and known to few. It becomes precise and better known as time goes on. Eventually it becomes precise and definite and known to all. Correspondingly, its impact has a progressive effect on values. At first, it has little effect because it is so vague and

---

[1] As to the effect of the decision in this case on the Land Compensation Act 1961, s. 5(3), see p. 178, *supra*.

[2] Ss. 6–8 and Sch. 1.

[3] Town and Country Planning Act 1959, s. 9.

[4] *Kaye* v *Basingstoke Development Corpn* (1968), 20 P & CR 417.

[5] *Davy* v *Leeds Corpn*, [1964] 1 WLR 1218 (CA) and [1965] 1 WLR 445 (HL); see also *Viscount Camrose* v *Basingstoke Corpn*, [1966] 1 WLR 1100 (see note 7, p. 226, *infra*); *Wilson and Wilson* v *Liverpool County Borough Council*, [1970] 22 P & CR 282; *Minister of Transport* v *Pettitt* (1969), 20 P & CR 344; *Rugby Joint Water Board* v *Shaw-Fox*, [1973] AC 202; and *Myers* v *Milton Keynes Development Corpn*, [1974] 1 WLR 696. It is, however, to be remembered that although the scheme is relevant in valuing the interests to be acquired, it is of no relevance in determining the interests to be valued: *Rugby Joint Water Board* v *Shaw-Fox*, *supra*, pp. 172 *et seq*, *supra*.

[6] For an example of a case in which the Lands Tribunal and the Court of Appeal differed as to whether there was a scheme at all see *Morris and Jacombs Ltd.* v *Birmingham District Council* (1975), 31 P & CR 305, LT; [1976] JPL 694, CA; p. 223, *infra*.

[7] *Wilson* v *Liverpool Corpn*, [1971] 1 WLR 302 (CA) *per* Widgery LJ at p. 310.

uncertain. As it becomes more precise and better known, so its impact increases until it has an important effect. It is this increase, whether big or small, which is to be disregarded as at the time when the value is to be ascertained."[1]

In *N. E. Housing Association* v *Newcastle upon Tyne Corporation*[2] a less usual effect of the scheme upon values was in issue. A side effect of the scheme, involving acquisition and demolition of offices, was substantially to increase demand for, and therefore market value of, those that remained. It was held that such increases in demand represented the "scheme in action" so that the inflated value of the remaining offices could not be used as reliable comparables for the purpose of assessing the value of the subject premises.[3]

2 The provisions of the Land Compensation Act 1961[4]

It is now necessary to consider the scheme underlying the acquisition as defined in the Land Compensation Act 1961 and its relationship with the older and in several respects wider *Pointe Gourde* principle. The Act sets out five situations that constitute a scheme in this context. For convenience, however, the last four are grouped together.

(i) ANY ACQUISITION OF LAND IN SEVERAL OWNERSHIPS[5]

What is provided for is the case in which an area of land being acquired includes the property of a number of landowners so that there is a number of different parcels of land and therefore a number of different interests falling to be acquired as part of a single scheme of acquisition and development. The Act describes such an area as "the land authorised to be acquired";[6] the land the subject of a particular acquisition[7] as "the relevant land"; and the individual interests being acquired as "the relevant interests".[7]

Under this head the land authorised to be acquired will normally be the whole area comprised in a single compulsory purchase order or if the acquisition is authorised by a special Act, the aggregate of the land

---

[1] *Wilson* v *Liverpool City Council*, [1971] 1 All ER 628 *per* Lord Denning MR at p. 309. For an example of a scheme "progressing" after this manner see *Bird* v *Wakefield Metropolitan District Council*, [1977] JPL 179, p. 223, *infra*. See also *Myers* v *Milton Keynes Development Corpn* (1974), 27 P & CR 518, in which, although the area in question was not designated as the site of a new town until 1966, it was held by the Lands Tribunal that the scheme originated with a County Council planning report in 1962.

For a case in which a number of comprehensive development areas in a city centre were held to constitute a single scheme, see *Bell* v *Newcastle upon Tyne Corpn* [1971], RVR 209. For other cases involving comprehensive development areas see *Laitner* v *Sheffield County Borough Council* (1964), 192 Estates Gazette 245; *Clayton* v *Sheffield County Borough Council* (1964), 192 Estates Gazette 309; *Hunter* v *Cardiff City*, [1971], RVR 186 (LT). For cases involving new towns and town development see *Domestic Hire* v *Basildon Development Corpn* (1969), 21 P & CR 299; *Collins* v *Basildon Development Corpn* (1969), 21 P & CR 318.

[2] (1972) 25 P & CR 178.

[3] It follows that had the vendor wished to re-establish himself by purchasing strictly comparable accommodation in the same neighbourhood the compensation payable would not have covered the purchase price of the replacement property—a departure from the basic principle that compensation is intended to inflict no loss as well as to provide no gain.

[4] Ss. 6–8.

[5] Land Compensation Act 1961, Sch. 1, para. 1.

[6] *Ibid*, s. 6(3).

[7] *Ibid*, Sch. 1, Part 1.

comprised in that authorisation.[1] In the case of land being acquired under powers exercisable by virtue of any enactment for defence purposes,[2] however, the land authorised to be acquired is "the aggregate of the land comprised in the notice to treat and of any land contiguous or adjacent thereto which is comprised in any other notice to treat served under like powers not more than one month before and not more than one month after the date of service of that notice".[3]

In the case of a compulsory purchase order each self-contained parcel of land in the same ownership and in which the vendor has the same interest will, of course, be covered by a single notice to treat. Accordingly, whether the acquisition is authorised by compulsory purchase order or by defence powers, the notice to treat[4] determines what is "the relevant land" for the purpose of any particular claim for compensation.

The effect of these provisions is that in assessing the market value of the relevant land any element of value attributable to any development[5] or prospective development of any other part of the land authorised to be acquired is to be ignored, unless it be an increase in value attributable to development that would have been likely to be carried out even if the acquiring authority had had no proposals for the acquisition of any of the land authorised to be acquired.[6]

Furthermore, if at the date of service of the notice to treat the vendor, in the same capacity,[7] has an interest[8] in other land contiguous or

---

[1] *Ibid*, s. 6(3)(a).

[2] As to the meaning of "defence purposes" see the Land Powers (Defence) Act 1958; Land Compensation Act 1961, s. 6(3).

[3] *Ibid*, s. 6(3)(b).

[4] *Ibid*, s. 39(2). In *King* v *Birmingham Corpn* (1970), 21 P & CR 979 the freehold owner of certain adjoining properties within a clearance area (see note 5, *infra*) had agreed to sell, but had not conveyed, three of the properties (adjoining one another) to the tenant of one of them. The acquiring authority sought to treat the land as two separate holdings and accordingly served one notice to treat on the tenant in respect of the three properties the subject of the agreement, and another on the freeholder in respect of the balance. The Lands Tribunal, however, held that the whole property was a single unit, the freeholder being a trustee for the tenant in respect of the latter's equitable interest in the three properties which he had contracted to buy. Because of the very special facts of this case, however, it is doubtful whether any general principle of wider application can be derived from it.

[5] In this context "development" includes the clearing of land: Land Compensation Act 1961, s. 6(3). Thus if the land to be valued (the relevant land) falls within a clearance area under Part III of the Housing Act 1957, no account may be taken of the prospect of the neighbouring land being cleared unless such clearance would be likely to be effected even if there had been no question of acquisition by the acquiring authority: *Davy* v *Leeds Corpn*, [1964] 1 WLR 1218 CA and [1965] 1 WLR 445 HL. On the other hand, account may of course be taken of clearance resulting from demolition orders (under Part II of the Act) since such orders do not involve acquisition by the housing authority concerned.

[6] Land Compensation Act 1961, s. 6(1)(a).

[7] A person is entitled to two interests in land in the same capacity if, but only if, he is entitled to both of them beneficially, as trustee of one particular trust or as personal representative of one particular person. *Ibid*, s. 39(6). These provisions do not, therefore, affect the compensation payable where the vendor holds the relevant land as a trustee, but adjoining land as an individual, or trustee under a different trust. The same, of course, applies where the two parcels of land are held by different companies even although the ownership of the two companies is precisely the same.

[8] Note that the interest in the relevant land need not be the *same* interest as that held in the adjoining land. Thus if the relevant land is held under a lease and the lessor is the freeholder of adjoining land the provisions of the Act will operate.

adjacent to the relevant land, any increase in the value of that other land attributable to the proposed development of any of the land authorised to be acquired (including the development, if any, proposed for the relevant land) is to be deducted from the compensation payable in respect of the land being acquired (i.e., the relevant land).[1]

It will have been observed from the above that the operation of these provisions may well result in the enhancement of the value of retained land contiguous or adjacent to the relevant land exceeding the compensation payable in respect thereof.[2] This is particularly likely to be the case where the vendor's interest in the relevant land is a leasehold with but a short time to run and he has a freehold (or longer leasehold) interest in the contiguous or adjacent land retained. In such cases there will be no compensation payable;[3] there are, however, no provisions by which the acquiring authority can recoup any enhancement in the value of the retained land in excess of the compensation payable in respect of the land taken.

It will no doubt have been observed that in an important respect the effect of these provisions may in certain circumstances be somewhat narrower than the *Pointe Gourde* principle for in that case the quarry, to the increased potential profitability of which the increased value of the land was attributable, was included in the land taken, i.e., in this context the relevant land.

The Land Compensation Act of 1961, on the other hand, does not provide for any deduction in respect of any enhancement to the value of the relevant land resulting from development or proposed development of any part of *that* land. Conversely, since the *Pointe Gourde* case was not concerned with the effect of the scheme upon any neighbouring land retained by the vendor, the *Pointe Gourde* principle may, in that respect, be said to be somewhat narrower[4] than the provision of the Act[5] now under discussion.

As already indicated, however, the effect of these provisions in no way affects the application of the basic underlying principle of the *Pointe Gourde* case. It follows, therefore, that in certain circumstances that principle and the provisions of the Act may both be applicable, and the

---

[1] Land Compensation Act 1961, s. 7. Note, however, the saving provisions in respect of certain local, etc. Acts, p. 234, *infra*.

[2] Since the operation of these provisions depends upon the interest in the contiguous or adjoining land being held by the vendor of the relevant land at the date of the notice to treat, *ibid*, s. 7(1), a transfer of ownership of the land retained before that date will avoid this result; if, however, such a transfer takes place at a time when the prospects of compulsory acquisition for the development in question are known, the land transferred will be valued accordingly for the purpose of capital gains tax; in the case of capital transfer no tax is payable as between husband and wife: Finance Act 1975, s. 29 and Sch. 6.

[3] See, e.g., *Cotswold Trailer Parks Ltd.* v *Secretary of State for the Environment* (1974), 27 P & CR 219, where a part of some land carrying planning permission for a motel was acquired for highway purposes. But for the roadworks the owners would have had to improve the access to the motel at a cost exceeding the value of the land taken; i.e., the benefit to the land retained outweighed the value of the land taken and no compensation was payable. But the benefit must be directly attributable to the scheme: see *Cooke* v *Secretary of State for the Environment* (1973), 27 P & CR 234, note 6, p. 346, *post*, and *Bowling* v *Leeds County Borough Council* (1974), 27 P & CR 531, p. 142, *ante*.

[4] But cf. *Davy* v *Leeds Corpn*, [1965] 1 WLR 445 (HL) note 5, p. 221, *supra*.

[5] I.e., Land Compensation Act 1961, s. 6.

Lands Tribunal has expressed the view that in such cases both the relevant section of the Act[1] and the principle must be applied where they are capable of application independently of each other.[2] Thus the fact that the Courts have for convenience referred only to these provisions of the Act where the Act and the principle cover the same ground should not be taken as either excluding or modifying the principle.

There would therefore appear to be two sets of circumstances in which the *Pointe Gourde* principle applies and in which section 6 of the Act of 1961 does not. The first has already been mentioned, viz the case in which the development of the relevant land itself affects the value of some attribute of that land or of some existing development thereon. The second is the case in which a defined scheme is nevertheless carried out in phases and the requisite land is acquired not under the authority of a single compulsory purchase order but by a series of such orders.[3]

It must be borne in mind, however, that the application of the *Pointe Gourde* principle is not confined to cases in which the scheme has the effect of increasing the value of the land acquired; it is equally applicable where the effect is to depreciate values. Thus in *Morris & Jacombs Ltd.* v *Birmingham District Council*[4] planning permission had been granted for residential development conditional upon the allocation of three-quarters of an acre to provide rear access to an existing row of houses fronting upon a main road. No access road was provided and the claimants later unsuccessfully sought planning permission for the inclusion of this strip in their residential development. They thereupon served a purchase notice, and obtained a certificate of appropriate alternative development[5] for "private service road purposes". It was held by the Lands Tribunal that the scheme underlying the acquisition was the provision of an access road at the rear of, and to serve, the houses in question and that since the difference between the value of the land if available for residential development (£15,000) and its value for a private road (£4,000) entirely resulted from the scheme, the decrease in value (£11,000) could not be taken into account in assessing compensation,[6] which was therefore £15,000. The Court of Appeal,[7]

---

[1] I.e., Land Compensation Act 1961, s. 6.

[2] *Sprinz* v *Kingston upon Hull City Council* (1975), 30 P & CR 273 at p. 282. In *Kaye* v *Basingstoke Corpn* (1968), 20 P & CR 417 it had been held that the only function of the *Pointe Gourde* principle was the "plugging of gaps" in the scope of the Land Compensation Act 1961, s. 6. The currently more accepted view is that this is too narrow a concept.

[3] See for example *Bird and Bird* v *Wakefield Metropolitan District Council* [1977] JPL 179 in which the acquiring authority successfully contended that the acquisition in 1969 of some 30 acres of land for industrial use was in pursuance of a scheme formulated in 1968 to include the development of the subject land as an extension of 37½ acres allocated for industry prior to 1966. On the other hand it was held that development of part of the latter land carried out prior to 1968 could not be regarded as part of a scheme not then in existence.

[4] (1975) 31 P & CR 305: see also *Jelson* v *Blaby District Council* (1974), 28 P & CR 450.

[5] Pp. 204 *et seq, supra*.

[6] It was also held in this case that since the acquiring authority had clearly intended that the access road be provided at the expense of the developers and had in no way indicated any intention of acquiring the land itself, the provisions of the Land Compensation Act 1961, s. 9 (that in assessing compensation no account be taken of any "blighting" effect of any such indication) had no application: see p. 176, *supra*.

[7] [1976] JPL 694, CA.

however, held that the strip of land in question had been worth £4,000 as an access way, rather than £15,000 for residential development, not by reason of any scheme but by reason of the condition imposed on the planning permission granted to the owners and accepted by them. The *Pointe Gourde* principle was therefore inapplicable to adjust the compensation upwards; accordingly £4,000 was the amount payable.[1]

(ii) ACQUISITION OF LAND WITHIN:

   (a)   A comprehensive development or action area;[2]
   (b)   an area designated as the site of a new town[3] or extension of a new town;[4]
   (c)   an area defined in the current development plan as an area of town development.[5]

In these cases the principle is precisely the same as that already discussed, the difference in its application being twofold. First, the criterion by which the scheme is defined for the purposes of the Act (as opposed to the *Pointe Gourde* principle) is whether or not any of the relevant land forms part of any of these categories of land; whether or not the other land comprising the relevant land is being acquired under the same authorisation is irrelevant.[6]

Secondly, in deciding the extent to which the effect on the value of the relevant land of development on neighbouring land is to be discounted, the test is whether or not that development (whether already carried out or to be carried out) would have been likely to have been carried out if there had been no definition of the area in the current development plan as a comprehensive development area, action area, or town development area, or no designation thereof as the site of a new town or new town extension, as the case may be.[7]

The same criterion applies in assessing the effect on the value of any land retained by the vendor. If that value is enhanced by development, proposed or executed, in pursuance of the scheme for the comprehensive development or action area, for the new town or extended new town, then that enhancement is to be deducted from the compensation payable for the land being acquired.[8] In many cases where part of an estate is acquired and the neighbouring land retained, the retained land, or part of it, will itself be within the area defined in the

---

[1] For a case in which a series of acquisitions of land within the protective radius of sensitive electronic equipment operated by the Defence Department could not be regarded as falling within any formulated scheme see *Packwood Poultry Products Ltd*. v *Metropolitan Borough of Solihull* (1975), 31 P & CR 315.

[2] Land Compensation Act 1961, Sch. 1, para. 2; action areas were added by the Town and Country Planning Act 1971, Sch. 23.

[3] Land Compensation Act 1961, Sch. 1, para. 3; i.e., an area designated by order under the New Towns Act 1946.

[4] Land Compensation Act 1961, Sch. 1, para. 3A. This paragraph was added by the New Towns Act 1966, and applies to land designated by an order under the New Towns Act 1965 coming into operation after 13 December 1966, i.e., the date of commencement of the New Towns Act 1966.

[5] Land Compensation Act 1961, Sch. 1, para. 4, i.e., an area defined in the current development plan as an area of town development under the Town Development Act 1952.

[6] Land Compensation Act 1961, Sch. 1, paras. 2–4.

[7] *Ibid*, s. 6(1)(b).

[8] *Ibid*, s. 7.

current development plan as that of a comprehensive development or action area or designated as part of a new town. Since, by the nature of the definition or designation, it is to be expected that such land will itself be later acquired, the landowner is unlikely to benefit from any enhancement in its value, for in assessing compensation in respect of such later acquisition such enhancement will again have to be discounted. The Act does, however, allow for this contingency by providing, in effect, that these "discounting" provisions do not operate twice over.[1] These special provisions are considered below.[2]

For the purposes of valuation, the relevant land therefore has to be considered, so to speak, in isolation from the rest of the comprehensive development area, new town, etc. In short, as far as the valuation of the relevant land is concerned, the principle in each case is similar to that already discussed when considering the planning permissions to be assumed in respect of land falling within a comprehensive development or action area.[3]

There is, however, one important distinction in that whereas in the case of land falling within a comprehensive development or action area it is specifically provided that planning permission is to be assumed for such of the range of uses shown for the comprehensive development of the area as may be appropriate[4] no such provision is applicable to land within the designated site of a new town or new town extension or defined as an area of town development. In such cases it therefore follows that unless there is some planning permission that enhances the value of the land over and above its existing use value[5] already attached to the land, or that can be derived from the current development plan,[6] the owner will have to rely upon planning permission for the development for which the land is being acquired. Although, if he is unfortunate enough to have his land acquired for some purpose for which there is no market value, he may apply for a certificate of appropriate alternative development,[7] he may be faced with a "nil" certificate unless the land is close enough to some existing town or village which, even without the new town or town development proposals, might be expected to expand.[8] To take a hypothetical example, let us suppose that the relevant land is a relatively small area within a much larger area designated as the site of a new town, and is acquired for residential development. Compensation for the relevant land will be its value for residential development upon the assumption that no new town is being developed in the area and that none of the services—roads, water, electricity, shopping facilities, etc.—required for the new town will be available.

[1] Land Compensation Act 1961, s. 8.
[2] Pp. 231 *et seq, infra.*
[3] Pp. 202 *et seq, supra.*
[4] Land Compensation Act 1961, s. 16(4) and (5), p. 202, *supra.*
[5] *Ibid,* s. 15(3), p. 194, *supra.*
[6] *Ibid,* s. 15(1) to (3), pp. 196 *et seq, supra.*
[7] *Ibid,* s. 17, pp. 204 *et seq, supra.*
[8] Where a new town is intended to accommodate natural increase in the local population as opposed to immigrants from elsewhere, the probability is that in the absence of the new town some of the requisite expansion would have taken place within the designated area.

Thus in *Myers* v *Milton Keynes Development Corporation*[1] the land being acquired fell within the area designated as the site of the new town, and was shown on the Corporation's plans as being ultimately required (in some ten years' time) for residential development. The Corporation contended[2] that, but for the new town, the land, which had formerly been included in a Green Belt, would have had no development potential at all. In other words, such potential as it had was solely attributable to the scheme, i.e., the creation of a new town. The Court of Appeal, dismissing this contention on the ground that there was no conflict between the *Pointe Gourde* principle and the relevant provisions of the Land Compensation Act 1961,[3] held that the proper measure of compensation was the value of the land with a "deferred" planning permission for residential development, ignoring the development that, in pursuance of the scheme, was planned for the surrounding land and the provision of any services which would not have been available but for the overall objective of creating a new town.

It is, however, to be noted that a crucial element of this decision was that planning permissions for residential development fell to be assumed in accordance with the Land Compensation Act 1961, s. 15(1)[4] which, unlike the planning permissions to be assumed under s. 16[5] do not depend upon whether the grant of the planning permission in question might reasonably have been expected in the absence of any proposal compulsorily to acquire. The result is therefore somewhat anomalous, for the compensation payable for land falling within the designated area of a new town will depend entirely upon the particular purpose for which the land is proposed to be developed. The owners of land shown on the relevant plans as public open space, for example, will obtain no benefit from s. 15(1) and seem unlikely to obtain a certificate of appropriate alternative development certifying that but for the acquisition, planning permission would be granted for any purpose other than development as public open space.[6]

It does not, of course, follow that even where planning permission for residential, commercial, industrial, etc., development is to be assumed in accordance with s. 15(1), the value of the land will necessarily exceed existing use value. It may be that the cost of providing the requisite infrastructure will be such that there is no open market demand for such land at a price exceeding, say, the price of agricultural land, or that the situation or acreage of the land is such that it cannot economically be developed on its own.[7]

---

[1] (1974) 27 P & CR 518 (CA).
[2] In which contention they had been upheld by the Lands Tribunal (1972), 25 P & CR 475.
[3] S. 15(1)(a).
[4] See p. 191, *supra*.
[5] See p. 196, *supra*.
[6] Cf. the somewhat more equitable provisions applicable to land falling within a comprehensive development or action area: pp. 202 *et seq*, *supra*.
[7] As in *Halliwell and Halliwell* v *Skelmersdale Development Corpn* (1965), 16 P & CR 305, and *Viscount Camrose* v *Basingstoke Corpn*, [1966] 3 All ER 161. In the latter case the Court of Appeal, affirming the decision of the Lands Tribunal, explained the provisions of the Land Compensation Act 1961, s. 6(1) in these terms: "The explanation of s. 6(1) is, I think, this. The legislature was aware of the general principle that, in assessing compensation for compulsory acquisition of a defined parcel of

Similar considerations apply to land within an area of town development. Where land situated outside an area defined as an area of town development, or designated as the site of a new town, is compulsorily acquired solely to meet the requirements of the town development or new town, the question arises whether such an acquisition can be said to be in pursuance of the overall scheme of town development or the creation of a new town, as the case may be. In such cases values can clearly be affected by the scheme either way. For example, by concentrating development within the designated or defined areas there may be less demand than would otherwise be the case for development land on the outskirts of neighbouring towns and villages. Conversely, the influx of population may create demand for certain types of property not available within the new town or town development area. On principle it would seem that if such land is acquired for new town or town development purposes the *Pointe Gourde* principle applies.[1]

The case of land within an extension of a new town is, however, somewhat different, for by definition the initial site of the new town will have been designated some years previously and the new town will almost certainly have been commenced, if not substantially completed, to its original population target. Again, by definition, land within an area designated as an extension of the site of a new town will have been without the original designated area. No deduction, therefore, falls to be made in respect of an enhancement in value that reflects the development of the new town within its previous boundaries.[2] The effect of the designation of land as the site of a new town or of an extension of an existing new town may, moreover, be widened by an

---

land, you do not take into account an increase in value of *that* parcel of land if the increase is entirely due to the scheme involving the acquisition. That was settled by *Pointe Gourde Quarrying and Transport Co. Ltd.* v *Sub-Intendent of Crown Lands* .... It is left untouched by s. 6(1), but there might be some doubt as to its scope. So the legislature passed s. 6(1) and Schedule 1 in order to make it clear that you were not to take into account any increase due to the development of the *other* land, i.e., land other than the claimed parcel. I think that the decision in the *Pointe Gourde* case covers one aspect, and s. 6(1) covers the other, with the result that the tribunal is to ignore any increase in value due to the Town Development Act 1952, both on the relevant land and on the other land. That is the way the tribunal did value it here. The tribunal said:

   'Not only is the development already carried out and the development in prospect, in so far as both are consequent on town development, to be ignored on land other than the relevant land, but it must also be ignored in relation to the relevant land itself'.

I think that was right": *per* Lord Denning MR at p. 164.

[1] In *Kaye and Sharp* v *Basingstoke Development Corpn* (1968), 20 P & CR 417 (LT), it was held that the *Pointe Gourde* principle could not be invoked to exclude additional value accruing to land outside the defined area as a result of the development of land within that area, even though the acquisition was for town development purposes. This decision, however, rested upon the somewhat doubtful assumption that since the Land Compensation Act 1961, s. 6 and Sch. 1, precisely defined the effect to be given to a town development scheme, and that the Court of Appeal decision in *Viscount Camrose* v *Basingstoke Corpn (supra)* and the House of Lords' decision in *Davy* v *Leeds Corpn*, [1965] 1 All ER 753 (note 5, p. 219, *supra*) limited the application of the *Pointe Gourde* rule to cases in which there would otherwise be a gap in the legislative code. Cf. *North Eastern Housing Association* v *Newcastle upon Tyne Corpn* (1972), 25 P & CR 178, p. 220, *supra*.

[2] It is submitted that the relevant provisions of the Land Compensation Act 1961 (s. 6 and Sch. 1) have the effect of making the original new town and its extension two different schemes. Cf. *Bell* v *Newcastle upon Tyne Corpn* [1971] RVR 209, 221, 228, 234 (LT), in which a number of comprehensive development areas within the city centre were held to form a single scheme.

order under the Land Compensation Act 1973, s. 51. That section empowers the Secretary of State to direct by order that in valuing the land taken, the diminution or increase in value to be left out of account shall include the effect upon value attributable to certain specified public development,[1] even if carried out on land outside the designated area.

Similarly, if that public development has the effect of increasing the value of other land retained by the vendor that increase falls to be deducted from the compensation payable for the land taken.[2]

The order must be made after the Secretary of State has prepared the draft designation order and published the requisite notice[3] but before he finally makes the designation order.[4] It is therefore submitted that the power to revoke or modify the direction by subsequent order, which is conferred by the Act without qualification,[5] can only be exercised up to the time when the designation order is made. Subsequent revocation or modification would not only leave the compensation provisions indeterminate, thereby presumably defeating the object of requiring the direction to be given prior to the making of the designation order,[6] but could have the effect of different landowners being accorded different treatment depending upon whether their land was acquired before or after revocation or modification.

The power to give such a direction applies in the case of orders either designating the site of a new town or extending an area already so designated.[7] Although this power is very wide it is limited by the requirement that "the main purpose or one of the main purposes", for which the designation order is proposed is "the provision of housing or other facilities required in connection with or in consequence of the carrying out of any public development".[8]

This requirement can, unfortunately, be read in two ways. First, it can be read as on the one hand applying where a main purpose of the designation order is the provision of housing, and on the other to cases where a main purpose is the provision of "other facilities required in connection with or in consequence of the carrying out of any public development". Alternatively it can be read as applying only to cases where housing and/or other facilities are both required in connection with or in consequence of the carrying out of any public development. Since the provision of housing is invariably a main purpose of a new

---

[1] For definition see *infra*. These provisions were introduced in anticipation of the then proposed designation of a site for a new town at Maplin, to take account of the effect of the proposed air and sea port complex.

[2] If the effect is to reduce the value of other land retained by the vendor he will be entitled to compensation under the head of injurious affection: see Chap. 8, p. 314 *et seq, post*.

[3] For these requirements see the New Towns Act 1965 Sch. 1. The notice must, *inter alia*, describe the proposed area, announce the Secretary of State's intention of making the order, and specify the date by which, and the manner in which, objections may be lodged.

[4] Land Compensation Act 1973, s. 51(1).

[5] *Ibid*, s. 51(4).

[6] Since the direction order affects compensation it seems a defect that it does not have to be made before the time allowed for objections to the designation order to be lodged.

[7] Land Compensation Act 1973, s. 51(1).

[8] *Ibid*.

town and almost invariably of a new town extension, the latter interpretation is, it is submitted, to be preferred, for unless it is adopted there will in most cases be practically no limit to the public development that may be made the subject of a direction. This is because public development in this context is very widely defined as *any* development in the exercise of statutory powers carried out by any Government Department, any statutory undertakers[1] or any other body having power to borrow money with the consent of a Minister.[2] The latter category of public authorities therefore clearly includes, besides local authorities, such bodies as a new town corporation, the Housing Corporation and such nationalised industries as are not also statutory undertakers, e.g., the National Coal Board. Moreover, the definition of public development for these purposes specifically includes "such development which has already been carried out when the direction in respect of it is given as well as such development which is then proposed".[3]

On the face of it, therefore, it would appear that the public development in question need have no direct association with the new town and could include a long-established reservoir or sewage works serving areas without the designated area, a rail or motorway link required and planned independently of any new town proposals, and so on. Such developments will have already affected land values and the compensation payable for injurious affection of land retained by the former owner of the land acquired.

It is therefore submitted that what was intended and what is likely to be the practice is the use of this power of direction only in the case of designation orders, one of the main purposes of which is to establish or extend a new town in order to take in the requirements of some sort of public establishment, existing or proposed, static or expanding, such as the housing requirements of an airport, a Government Research Establishment, a hospital, a university, a newly opened coal mine, etc.

Nevertheless, the fact remains that a local authority housing estate is clearly a public development within the definition and could presumably, therefore, be made the subject of a direction order provided a main purpose of the designation order is the provision of "facilities required in connection with or in consequence of the carrying out of any public development". Depending upon the size of the estate, "facilities" would probably include the provision of shops, places of entertainment, schools, etc. on the principle that such facilities are normally associated with residential areas. Whether the provision of a trading estate in order to stimulate employment could be so regarded seems rather more doubtful. But the position is highly anomalous since if these facilities can be said to be required in connection with housing they are as much required in connection with private enterprise as with local authority estates.

[1] As defined in the Town and Country Planning Act 1971, s. 290.
[2] Land Compensation Act 1973, s. 51(6).
[3] *Ibid*, s. 51(6).

The relevant date for determining whether these provisions apply

It will have been noted that as far as land within a comprehensive development or action area or an area of town development is concerned, the crucial factor is definition in the current development plan; for this purpose the current development plan is the development plan comprising the relevant land, "in the form in which (whether as originally approved or made by the Minister or as for the time being amended) that plan is in force on the date of service of the notice to treat".[1]

In this case of land falling within the designated site of a new town or new town extension this aspect is rather more complicated.

Although in the first place there must, of course, be a designation order made prior to the date of service of the notice to treat, any amendment to a designation order made after 29 October 1958 is to be ignored. In other words, in the case of orders made before that date, amendments made prior thereto are to be taken into account, but in the case of orders made after that date they are to be considered only in their original form.[2]

Secondly, new towns may, when substantially completed be transferred to the New Towns Commission: judging by current Ministerial pronouncements they may in future be transferred to local authorities. It is accordingly provided that land is not to be treated as forming part of the designated site of a new town if the notice to treat is served after the "transfer date".[3] The transfer date is defined as "the date on which by virtue of any enactment contained in any Act relating to new towns, whether passed before or after this Act[4] the development corporation established for the purposes of that new town ceases to act, except for purposes of or incidental to the winding up of its affairs".[5]

Nevertheless, provided the notice to treat is served before the transfer date, the effect on value of development likely to be carried out in pursuance of the development of the new town is to be discounted (or in the case of the effect upon land retained, set off) even though there is no prospect of that development being carried out before the transfer date,[6] for transfer of responsibility for the development of a new town does not imply that that further development will be abandoned.

Furthermore, in the case either of the designation of a site for a new town or of an extension of a new town the Secretary of State may, where the order is required in connection with some public development, give a direction, prior to the making of the requisite order, to the effect that in any compulsory acquisition of land in the designated area the effect on its value of both the new town and the public development shall not be taken into account.[7]

---

[1] Land Compensation Act 1961, s. 39(1).
[2] *Ibid*, Sch. 1, para. 7.
[3] *Ibid*, Sch. 1, para. 6.
[4] I.e., Land Compensation Act 1961.
[5] *Ibid*, Sch. 1, para. 5.
[6] *Ibid*, Sch. 1, para. 8.
[7] Land Compensation Act 1973, s. 51.

SUBSEQUENT ACQUISITION OF ADJOINING LAND: AVOIDANCE OF
DOUBLE RECOUPEMENT OF BETTERMENT OR INJURIOUS
AFFECTION

As towns and villages expand an owner of a substantial area of land on
the outskirts may well find that, having had part of his land compulsorily acquired, other parts of his estate are later also required by,
for example, the local authority, so that he is faced with a second
compulsory acquisition. In assessing compensation in respect of the
initial acquisition any enhancement in the value of adjoining or contiguous land in his ownership resulting from the scheme of development
in pursuance of which that initial acquisition was undertaken will have
been deducted. If the second acquisition is in pursuance of the same
scheme, compensation in respect thereof would, in the absence of
special statutory provisions, once again be subject to deduction equivalent to any enhancement in the market value of this second parcel of
land resulting from development in pursuance of the scheme on
neighbouring land. In other words, the effect of the scheme on value
would be deducted twice over.

In short, it is clearly only equitable to deduct any enhancement in the
value of retained land on the occasion of the first acquisition on the
assumption that the owner is able to obtain the full enhanced value of
the retained land if he should either decide to sell or be faced with
compulsory acquisition.

It would be equally inequitable, of course, if a vendor had been
compensated for diminution in the value of retained land (injurious
affection)[1] caused by the scheme and was able to leave such injurious
affection out of account when that land itself came to be acquired, for he
would in effect be doubly compensated for the same loss.

To meet this problem the Act[2] accordingly provides that in so far as
any enhancement or diminution in the value of retained adjoining land
has already been taken into account in assessing the compensation
payable in respect of an earlier acquisition[3] it shall not be taken into
account upon a later acquisition of any of that adjoining land initially
retained.

It is to be observed, however, that these provisions apply only to the
extent to which the enhancement in value has already been taken into
account; thus if that enhancement exceeded the value of the land
acquired so that no compensation was payable in respect of the initial
acquisition, it is open to the acquiring authority to make a proportionate[4] deduction in respect of the excess when assessing the
compensation payable in relation to the second acquisition.

---

[1] For compensation for injurious affection see Chap. 8, p. 314, *post*.

[2] Land Compensation Act 1961, s. 8.

[3] But only where such adjustment to the compensation has been taken into account in accordance with the provisions of the Land Compensation Act 1961 (ss. 6 and 7) considered in the
previous section of this chapter or in accordance with "any corresponding enactment", *infra*. As to
"corresponding enactments" see pp. 234 *infra*, and note 1, p. 235, *infra*.

[4] Note, however, that compensation payable in respect of the second acquisition remains to be
assessed in relation to then current market values. Thus if the value of the land was increased by
100 % as a result of the scheme but the compensation payable in respect of the land taken only

If only part of the land in respect of which an enhancement or diminution in value was taken into account in assessing compensation in respect of the initial acquisition is subsequently acquired that increase or diminution will have to be apportioned when assessing its effect upon the compensation payable in respect of the second acquisition. On the other hand if the latter acquisition covers other land the value of which is affected by the same scheme, compensation will have to be assessed as if the land being acquired comprised two separate parcels, the compensation in respect of that "other land" being subject to the same rules as if it were an "initial" acquisition. This situation will, of course, only arise where this other land has been acquired by the vendor subsequently to the initial acquisition, and from a person who owned no land previously acquired in pursuance of the same scheme, so that the acquiring authority has had no occasion to take account of any enhancement or depreciation to his land resulting from the scheme.

In this connection it is important to note that these provisions only apply where the interest acquired by the second acquisition is the same as the interest previously taken into account;[1] or the person entitled to the interest acquired is or derives title from, the person who at the time of the previous acquisition was entitled to the interest previously taken into account.[2]

Thus if the freeholder of the land first acquired held the adjoining land the subject of the second acquisition only as a leaseholder his compensation will have reflected the effect of the scheme on his leasehold interest. If, by the date of the second acquisition, the lease has expired the vendor's compensation will be assessed in the ordinary way, i.e., the effect of development of other land (in accordance with the scheme) on the value of his land must be discounted,[3] for there is no question of him having been penalised by a reduction in the compensation paid to his former lessee. Were it not for this provision, moreover, he would be penalised if the effect of the neighbouring development were to depreciate the value of his land for he derives no benefit from any additional compensation paid to that lessee. If, on the other hand, he himself, or a predecessor in title had been a lessee who had subsequently purchased the freehold the price paid would almost certainly have reflected the enhancement or diminution in value for which he had already been penalised or compensated. Hence the second leg of this proviso.

It is important to note, however, that although the Act of 1961 requires that both enhancement and diminution in the value of the land being acquired (the relevant land) that results from development of other land covered by the same scheme,[4] shall be taken into account, in

---

offset 50 %, 50 % of the current enhanced value falls to be deducted in assessing the net compensation payable in respect of the second acquisition. Conversely, however, a fall in land values in the interim may reduce, or even eliminate, the amount to be deducted.
[1] Land Compensation Act 1961, s. 8(3)(a).
[2] *Ibid*, s. 8(3)(b).
[3] Under *ibid*, s. 6.
[4] *Ibid*, s. 6.

itself it provides only for offsetting enhancement in the value of *adjoining or contiguous land* against the compensation payable for the land taken.[1] Compensation for diminution in the value of such land falls to be claimed under the head of compensation for injurious affection.[2] Injurious affection, of course, often arises from the schemes of development covered by the Act and considered in the previous section of this chapter, i.e., the development on other land authorised to be acquired;[3] in the remainder of a comprehensive development or action area;[4] within the same area designated as the site of a new town or extension of a new town;[4] or within the same town development area.[4]

In these cases the Land Compensation Act 1961 makes similar provision to ensure that such compensation shall not be claimed twice in respect of the same land as it does to ensure that the vendor is not prejudiced by a double deduction in respect of enhancement.[5]

Injurious affection to land retained may, however, arise from other causes, in which case these provisions have no relevance. For example, if a parcel of land is compulsorily acquired for, say, a sewage works, adjoining land will probably be reduced in value and, if in the same ownership as the land acquired, compensation for the loss in value will be added to the market value of the land acquired when assessing the compensation payable.[6] But if at some later date that adjoining land is acquired, for industrial development for instance, its market value for the purposes of compensation (i.e., its value with an assumed planning permission for such development)[7] may well exceed its original value; but there having been no scheme of development[8] at the time of the original acquisition of the sewage farm land, no account is taken of the fact that compensation has been paid for injurious affection of the industrial land when assessing compensation for its acquisition.

The case of an enhancement in the value of adjoining land is slightly different because whereas there is a well-developed code[9] establishing a right to compensation for injurious affection to adjacent land retained by a vendor from whom land is compulsorily acquired, the right of an acquiring authority to offset enhancement in the value of such adjacent land (betterment) is mainly dependent upon the Act of 1961.[10] Thus if the land acquired forms no part of a larger area of land authorised to be acquired, or is not part of a comprehensive development, action or town development area, or within the designated site of a new town or new town extension, there can be no set-off. Consequently, if the adjoining

[1] Land Compensation Act 1961, s. 7.
[2] Under the Compulsory Purchase Act 1965, s. 7; see Chap. 8, p. 314, *post*.
[3] See p. 220 *et seq*, *supra*.
[4] See p. 224 *et seq*, *supra*.
[5] Land Compensation Act 1961, s. 8(2).
[6] See Chap. 8, p. 314 *post*.
[7] See pp. 191 *et seq*, *supra*.
[8] I.e., no scheme covered by the Land Compensation Act 1961, s. 6 and Sch. 1, Part I: see pp. 220 and 224 *supra*.
[9] Derived from the Lands Clauses Consolidation Act 1845, s. 63 (now the Compulsory Purchase Act 1965, s. 7); see Chap. 8, p. 314, *post*.
[10] I.e., the Land Compensation Act 1961, s. 7 (p. 220, *supra*) and similar provisions in other statutes—see the next following section of this chapter, pp. 234–235.

land is subsequently compulsorily acquired these special provisions designed to prevent a double set-off have no relevance.

It is also important to note that these provisions are expressly applied where the first acquisition was by agreement in circumstances in which, had it been compulsory, an increase or diminution in the value of adjoining land would have fallen to be taken into account.[1] The assumption is that an authority possessing compulsory powers will not have acquired by agreement at a price significantly higher than the compensation which they would be liable to pay upon a compulsory acquisition. In short, the price is likely to have taken account of any significant enhancement or diminution in the value of land retained by the vendor in so far as any such enhancement or diminution was attributable to the scheme[2] in pursuance of which the land was acquired. To the extent to which the price did reflect such enhancement or diminution in the value of the land now being acquired compulsorily (the second acquisition) the resultant reduction or increase in the compensation payable on the first acquisition is to be taken into account in assessing the compensation in respect of the second acquisition. In other words, if the price paid in respect of the first acquisition was reduced by the full amount by which the value of the land the subject of the second acquisition was enhanced by the scheme, compensation will reflect its full market value without further deductions. But if the price paid in respect of the first acquisition only partially reflected the enhancement or diminution in the value of the land the subject of the second acquisition the compensation therefor will be decreased or increased proportionately.

SAVINGS IN RESPECT OF LOCAL ACTS AND CERTAIN "CORRESPONDING ENACTMENTS"

Acquisitions may, of course, be authorised by enactments which themselves specifically provide for account being taken of any enhancement in the value of contiguous or adjacent land. In the case of most general public enactments the above provisions of the Land Compensation Act 1961 prevail. On the other hand, in the case of local enactments which provide (in whatever terms) that account is to be taken of any increase in the value of an interest in contiguous or adjacent land attributable to the works authorised by that enactment, the terms of the local enactment prevail.[3]

However, in the case of four specified general public enactments, described as "corresponding enactments", which make such provision for taking enhancement of contiguous or adjacent land into account, and only in these cases, the same rules apply upon a subsequent acquisition of any such contiguous etc., land as if the deduction from

---

[1] Land Compensation Act 1961, s. 8(4).

[2] There can, of course, only be a relevant scheme in these cases if the land forms part of one of the areas set out on p. 220, *supra*, for land acquired by agreement cannot by definition be part of a larger "area authorised to be acquired"; see pp. 224 *et seq*, *supra*.

[3] Land Compensation Act 1961, s. 8(5).

the compensation payable in respect of the initial acquisition had been made under the Act of 1961.[1]

In the case of local enactments there is, however, a further proviso that any provision to the effect that compensation is to be restricted to existing use[2] is to be ignored.[3]

Thus, where the authorising enactment, whether public general, or private or local, provides for enhancement in the value of adjacent land, in the same ownership as the land taken, to be offset against the compensation payable, those provisions are to be followed in preference to the corresponding provisions of the Land Compensation Act 1961[4] considered above. But if any of that adjacent land is itself subsequently acquired the relevant provisions of the Act of 1961,[5] whereby the compensation payable is to include that enhanced value (in so far as it has already been offset), remain operative, *except* where the offset was effected in accordance with an enactment other than those public general enactments which are specifically designated "corresponding enactments". For the most part, such enactments will be local or private; it will depend on their terms whether or not the result is doubly to set off enhancement. These savings have no effect upon the treatment of compensation for injurious affection of contiguous or adjacent land.

Summary of Adjustments to Compensation to take account of the effect of the Scheme of Development upon Neighbouring Land retained by the Vendor

1. In this context the scheme of development may be:

(i) A scheme to be carried out in phases, the requisite land being acquired by a series of separate compulsory purchase orders;[6] or

(ii) One of the schemes set out in the Land Compensation Act 1961, Schedule 1, Part I, viz:

(a) Development for which the whole of the "land authorised to

---

[1] *Ibid*, s. 8(1): these corresponding enactments are listed in s. 8(7); they are: The Light Railways Act 1896, s. 13; The Development and Road Improvement Funds Act 1909, Schedule, para. (2)(c); The Highways Act 1959, s. 222(6); The Housing Act 1957, Sch. 3, Part III para. 4. Note that although the Land Compensation Act 1973 was not constituted a "corresponding enactment" it contains similar provisions to those of the Act of 1961 for offsetting compensation paid under the 1973 Act for injurious affection where the land in respect of which such compensation was paid is subsequently acquired: Land Compensation Act 1973, s. 6(3); pp. 340 *et seq, post*.

[2] I.e., a provision restricting the planning permission to be assumed in the assessment of compensation to planning permission for those classes of development specified in the Town and Country Planning Act 1971, Sch. 8 (Appendix, p. 456, *post*); Land Compensation Act 1961, s. 8(6) and see note 2, p. 196, *supra*, which applies as much to *ibid* s. 8(6) as to *ibid*, s. 15.

[3] Land Compensation Act 1961, s. 8(6); this provision, designed to bring local Acts into line with the Town and Country Planning Act 1959 (which abandoned existing use value as the basis of compensation), will, however, cease to apply in respect of acquisitions on or after the 2nd Appointed Day under the Community Land Act 1975, s. 25 of which provides for the general return of existing use value as the basis of compensation, notwithstanding "anything in any other enactment": *ibid*, s. 25(8): see pp. 305 *et seq, infra*.

[4] Land Compensation Act 1961, s. 7.

[5] *Ibid*, s. 8(1).

[6] I.e., a scheme within the *Pointe Gourde* principle but outwith the Land Compensation Act 1961: p. 217, *et seq, supra*.

be acquired", i.e., normally[1] the land covered by a single compulsory purchase order[2] is to be used.

(b) Development of land defined in the current development plan as a comprehensive development or action area.[3]

(c) The development of land designated as the site of a new town by order under the New Towns Act 1946.[4]

(d) The development of land designated as the site of an extension of a new town by order under the New Towns Act 1965.[5]

(e) The development of land defined in the current development plan as an area of town development.[6]

2. Where the market value of land being acquired (the relevant land) is increased solely as a result of this scheme of development then, subject to the operation of the Land Compensation Act 1961, s. 15(1)[7] such enhancement in value is to be ignored whether that enhancement arises from the development proposed for the relevant land itself[8] or from development proposed or carried out in pursuance of the scheme on neighbouring land.[9]

3. Similarly, any decrease in the value of the land attributable to any of the schemes in para. 1(ii) above is to be ignored in assessing its market value.[10]

4. Where, in the same capacity, the vendor has interest in other contiguous or adjoining land and that land is enhanced in value as a result of a scheme falling within para. 1(ii) above, then in assessing the net compensation payable that enhanced value is to be deducted from the value of the land being acquired.

5. Where, however, the acquisition is authorised by one of the corresponding enactments[11] or a local Act providing for any enhanced value of retained contiguous or adjacent land to be taken into account in assessing compensation for the land taken, the provisions of those Acts operate to the exclusion of the corresponding provisions of the Act of 1961.[12]

6. Where contiguous or adjacent land in the same ownership is depreciated in value as a result of the acquisition, compensation for such injurious affection is claimable by virtue of the Compulsory Purchase Act 1965, s. 7.[13]

---

[1] See, however, the special provisions relating to acquisitions for defence purposes, p. 221, *supra*.

[2] Land Compensation Act 1961, s. 6 and Sch. 1, Part I, para. 1.

[3] *Ibid*, para. 2, as amended by the Town and Country Planning Act 1971, Sch. 23; p. 224 *et seq, supra*.

[4] Land Compensation Act 1961, s. 6, and Sch. 1, Part I, para. 3, p. 224 *et seq, supra*.

[5] *Ibid*, para. 3A, p. 224 *et seq, supra*.

[6] *Ibid*, para. 4, p. 224 *et seq, supra*.

[7] See *Myers* v *Milton Keynes Development Corpn* (1974), 27 P & CR 578, p. 226, *supra*.

[8] I.e., the *Pointe Gourde* principle, pp. 217 and 220 *et seq, supra*.

[9] Land Compensation Act 1961, s. 6 and Sch. 1, Part I, p. 220 *et seq, supra*.

[10] *Ibid*, s. 6 and Sch. 1, Part I, para. 1, p. 224, *supra*.

[11] For these enactments see note 1, p. 235, *supra*.

[12] Land Compensation Act 1961, s. 8(5), p. 234, *supra*.

[13] As to which see Chap. 8, p. 314, *post*, but note that such compensation is normally claimable only in respect of the depreciation resulting from the development for which the land acquired from the same owner is required, and not in respect of development on other land affected by the scheme. For the limited circumstances in which compensation is payable where there is no such common ownership see pp. 321 *et seq, post*.

7. Where an interest in any of such contiguous or adjacent land is subsequently compulsorily acquired any enhancement or depreciation in its value due to the scheme[1] which has been accounted for in the assessment of compensation in respect of the initial acquisition is to be taken into account provided:

    (i) that in assessing compensation in respect of the initial acquisition that increase fell to be deducted from the value of the land taken under the Act of 1961[2] or a corresponding enactment[3] but not otherwise;[4] and

    (ii) that the interest is either the same as that in respect of which the enhancement was taken into account or the claimant is the person who was entitled to the interest previously taken into account, or derives title from him.[5]

8. Similarly, depreciation in the value of contiguous or adjacent land which resulted from the scheme,[1] in respect of which compensation for injurious affection was added to the value of the land initially acquired, is to be taken into account in assessing compensation in respect of a subsequent acquisition of the land concerned.[6]

---

[1] I.e., one of the schemes of para. 1(ii) above; a *"Pointe Gourde* scheme" has no relevance in this connection: pp. 235–236, *supra.*

[2] I.e., under the Land Compensation Act 1961, s. 7, p. 231, *supra.*

[3] See note 1, on p. 235, *supra.*

[4] I.e., if the increase in value fell to be taken into account under some private enactment or a public general enactment other than the Land Compensation Act 1961 and its "corresponding enactments": *Ibid*, s. 8(1).

[5] *Ibid*, s. 8(3).

[6] *Ibid*, s. 8(2): note that no deduction falls to be made in respect of any compensation for injurious affection not dependent upon the scheme; nor does any deduction fall to be made in respect of compensation for injurious affection paid to persons from whom no land has been taken, except where such compensation was payable by virtue of the Land Compensation Act 1973, Part I: *ibid*, s. 6(3); see note 1, p. 235, *supra*, and pp. 328 *et seq, post*. Broadly speaking, such compensation arises only in respect of development on neighbouring land which gives rise to nuisance. While such development may be part of a scheme (except in the cases to which the Act of 1973 (above) applies) it is not the scheme as such that gives rise to these very limited claims: they arise (somewhat indirectly) under the Compulsory Purchase Act 1965, s. 10: see pp. 328 *et seq, post*.

CHAPTER 6

Compensation for Land Taken: Special Cases

1 INTRODUCTORY

As previously explained, the basic principle of the modern code of compensation is that owners of interests in land should, as far as possible, be neither worse nor better off financially as a result of the compulsory acquisition of their property.[1] Compensation based upon full market value (subject to the adjustments summarised at the end of the previous chapter) normally achieves this objective.[2] Such a basis of compensation clearly breaks down, however, where the property being acquired commands no market but is nevertheless of substantial value to the owner and possibly others.[3]

Similar considerations may arise in relation to the compulsory acquisition of installations belonging to statutory undertakers. Conversely market value may result in unjustifiably high compensation in the case of houses declared unfit for human habitation under the Housing Acts. If a house is unfit as a house and for planning or other reasons cannot be used for any other purpose it follows that the house, as opposed to the land on which it stands, has, as such, no value. Such houses do tend, however, particularly in areas of housing shortage, to sell in the open market for sums considerably in excess of the value of the land and special provision for the assessment of compensation is accordingly provided. These cases, along with the special rules applicable to minerals, which are related more to the exigencies of planning control than to defects in market value as the basis of compensation, are considered in the next following sections of this chapter: so also are the special rules applicable to the acquisition of common land and the acquisition or extinguishment of rights over land.

[1] Cf. the pre-1919 code, whereby under the Lands Clauses Consolidation Act 1845 owners of such property became entitled to compensation based upon its value *to them* plus a 10 % solatium: p. 3, *ante*.

[2] But *only*, of course, in financial terms, for although the total assets of a man whose compensation is offset by the enhanced value of other adjoining property remain the same (and may even be increased if that enhancement in value exceeds the compensation payable: p. 222, *ante*) he is not actually provided with funds with which to replace the acquired property unless he disposes of an interest in that other property. The existing use value basis of compensation operating under the Town and Country Planning Act 1947 (pp. 8 *et seq, ante*) was not a conscious departure from this principle because it was assumed that land would change hands in the open market on the same basis. For the reasons why the market did not respond see note 2, p. 9 *ante*. As to the similar provisions of the Community Land Act 1975, see pp. 22 *et seq, ante*, and pp. 306 *et seq, infra*.

[3] E.g., a church, village hall, school, hospital, specialised business premises, etc.

Market value as a basis of compensation is only partially effective in restoring the vendor's financial position, moreover, where the property has been specially adapted to the vendor's convenience in a manner that does not add significantly to market value. Although compensation for specialised equipment installed in commercial or industrial premises may, in appropriate circumstances, be included in a claim for compensation for disturbance[1] it is only recently that it has been recognised that the householder is likely to be out of pocket where the cost of amenities provided for his own convenience have no proportional effect upon market value.[2] This defect has, however, now been met, albeit in a somewhat rough and ready fashion, by the "Home Loss Payments" available under the Land Compensation Act 1973 and considered under the heading of "Compensation for Disturbance" in chapter 9.[3]

This general principle that compensation should leave the vendor of compulsorily acquired property in substantially the same financial position as hitherto, applies, of course, only to the code of compensation with which this work is primarily concerned. It can only apply to the net amount receivable (which will normally be the principal concern of the vendor) where the compensation payable is subject to either development land tax or capital gains tax, if the vendor desirous of replacing his property is fortunate enough to find a similar property with little or no development potential.

2 PROPERTY FOR WHICH THERE IS NO MARKET DEMAND: COMPENSATION ON THE BASIS OF THE COST OF EQUIVALENT REINSTATEMENT

(i) THE REQUIREMENTS

It will be recalled that Rule 5 of the "1919 Rules"[4] makes special provision for the assessment of compensation on the basis of the cost of equivalent reinstatement where the land being compulsorily acquired is devoted to some special purpose for which there is no general demand or market.

In deciding whether cost of equivalent reinstatement is the appropriate basis of compensation in any particular case three essentials have to be fulfilled:
  (a) The land must be "devoted to a purpose of such a nature that there is no general demand or market for land for that purpose".[5]
  (b) The circumstances must be such that, but for the acquisition, the land would continue to be devoted to that purpose.[5]

---

[1] P. 354, post.

[2] For example, although the fact that a house is wired for electricity will no doubt affect market value, particular electrical installations may not.

[3] Pp. 372 et seq, post.

[4] I.e., now the Land Compensation Act 1961, s. 5(5), for which see the previous chapter: see also p. 165 ante. N.B. the application of Rule 5 is not affected by the Community Land Act 1975: pp. 22 et seq, ante, and pp. 306 et seq, infra.

[5] Land Compensation Act 1961, s. 5(5).

(c) The Lands Tribunal must be satisfied that there is a bona fide intention to reinstate in some other place.[1]

(ii) THE RELEVANT DATE

It will also be recalled that until the decision in the *West Midland Baptist Trust* case[2] it had always been assumed that the date at which compensation fell to be assessed was the date of notice to treat.

That case—itself a case to which it was agreed that Rule 5 applied—decided that for the purpose of assessing compensation under Rule 5 the cost of equivalent reinstatement falls to be estimated by reference to prices and wages ruling on the date on which the work of reinstatement could reasonably have been commenced. That is not, of course, to imply that the owner is expected to seek an alternative site and prepare plans and estimates immediately upon receipt of notice to treat, for service of notice to treat does not necessarily imply an immediate requirement by the acquiring authority: it may be served merely to prevent a compulsory purchase order from lapsing.[3] Furthermore, the owner may well be in no financial position to consider reinstatement until he knows whether or not Rule 5 will apply. If the acquiring authority is in no hurry to acquire there may well be a mutual interest in postponing taking further steps until it does; in such a case the appropriate date will probably be the subject of agreement. In other cases the owner's first concern will be to discover whether compensation will be assessed under Rule 5: if this can be agreed and there are no further preliminary matters in issue he will be wise to take steps to find an alternative site and prepare plans and estimates. If, however, these cannot be agreed and a reference to the Lands Tribunal becomes necessary, estimates may have to be revised to take account of changes in costs in the interim, since he can hardly be expected to proceed until the compensation payable has been finally determined. In other words, it is submitted, the same general rule applies in this respect as under Rule 2.[4]

On the other hand the date of notice to treat (or deemed notice to treat where the acquisition arises from service of a purchase or blight notice) remains the critical date on which the subject land must be devoted to a purpose of such a nature that there is no general demand or market for land for that purpose; at which it must be evident that but for the acquisition the land would continue to be devoted to that purpose; and at which there must be an intention to reinstate elsewhere.[5]

---

[1] Land Compensation Act 1961, s. 5(5).
[2] *Birmingham Corpn v West Midland Baptist (Trust) Association (Inc.)*, [1969] 3 All ER 172 HL [1968] 1 All ER 205 CA; (1966) 18 P & CR 125 LT. See pp. 165 *et seq, ante.*
[3] By virtue of the Compulsory Purchase Act 1965, s. 4, if no notice to treat is served within three years from the date on which the compulsory purchase order became operative (i.e., the date of publication of confirmation) the powers thereunder lapse.
[4] See the heading "The Relevant Date", pp. 297 *et seq, ante.*
[5] *West Midland Baptist* case, *supra*, and see *Zoar Independent Church Trustees v Rochester Corpn*, [1974] 3 WLR 417 CA, p. 171, *ante*, per Buckley LJ, where he says that the date of notice to treat (in that case a deemed notice to treat) "is the material date at which to consider the rules governing the assessment of compensation" at p. 422.

(iii) THE DISCRETION

If the prerequisites of paras. (a) to (c) above (they are considered in greater detail below) are fulfilled, compensation *may* be assessed "on the basis of the reasonable cost of reinstatement".[1] In other words, the decision is in terms discretionary—that is to say, that it is on the one hand open to the claimant to opt for compensation on the ordinary basis (i.e., market value of the land for development) or on the other, to the Lands Tribunal to refuse to sanction the payment of compensation equivalent to the reasonable cost of reinstatement if, for example, they are not satisfied of the genuineness of the intention to reinstate. That does not, however, mean that the Lands Tribunal decision in this regard is necessarily final for their decision is challengeable in the courts as a point of law.[2] The Lands Tribunal's discretion is not, however, confined to the question of intent—thus a refusal to exercise their discretion on the ground that where the cost of reinstatement exceeded the total value of the undertaking it could not afford a reasonable basis of compensation has been upheld by the Court of Appeal on the ground that the Lands Tribunal had not exercised their discretion unreasonably.[3]

(iv) THE PURPOSE AND THE INTENTION

It is not enough that the purpose to which the land is devoted should be of so specialised a nature that there is no general demand or market for that purpose if the land is equally suitable for some other purpose for which there is a market demand. Thus in *Trustees of the Manchester Homeopathic Clinic* v *Manchester Corporation*[4] it was accepted that although the subject premises had been specifically designed for consultancy and treatment in homeopathy (to be provided on a charitable basis) they could, with but slight structural alteration, be equally well used for medical consultation generally and that it was therefore for this wider purpose that the market demand had to be considered.[5] Similarly, the charitable nature of the institution was irrelevant.[6] It follows, therefore,

---

[1] Land Compensation Act 1961, s. 5(5).

[2] And this includes their deductions from the evidence: see *Edwards (Inspector of Taxes)* v *Bairstow*, [1955] 3 All ER 48 per Lord Radcliffe, pp. 57–58. For an example of decisions of the Court of Appeal overruling the Lands Tribunal's refusal to exercise their discretion see *Zoar Independent Church Trustees* v *Rochester Corpn*, [1974] 3 WLR 417 CA 3 All ER 5, p. 242, *infra*.

[3] *Festiniog Rly Co* v *Central Electricity Generating Board* (1962) 13 P & CR 248: for the Lands Tribunal decision see 11 P & CR 448. See also *A. and B. Taxis, Ltd.* v *Secretary of State for Air*, [1922] 2 KB 328, in which it was stated that it would be "unreasonable to incur great expense in reinstating a business that could only be carried on at a loss" or in reinstating only for a short period—per Banks LJ at p. 337.

[4] (1970) 22 P & CR 241.

[5] Note, however, that it is structural adaptability for a purpose for which there may be a market (provided, of course, there are no planning objections that would prevent use for such an alternative purpose) that is relevant, and the fact that no planning permission is required for some other purpose is irrelevant if use for such other purpose would involve anything other than minor structural modification. In other words, the Town and Country Planning (Use Classes) Order 1972 (SI 1972 No. 1385) in itself provides no guide: *ibid.*, and see also *Rowley* v *Southampton Corpn* (1959) 10 P & CR 172, p. 248, *infra*.

[6] As put (and accepted) in the *Manchester Homeopathic* case, *supra*, (at p. 251) in order to see whether Rule 5 applied "the tests to be used were to look at the process which had been carried on and the physical characteristics of the structure ... a shop which sold 16th Century Russian ikons

that Rule 5 will very rarely, if ever, be applicable to land devoid of buildings or other structures, no matter how specialised the purpose to which it is put or how limited the market for land for that purpose.[1] It is not, therefore, surprising that the cases are confined to the acquisition of buildings or other structures of a specialised character. The most common examples are churches. Indeed, in *Trustees of Zoar Independent Church* v *Rochester Corpn*[2] a church was said to be "the *locus classicus* for assessment under Rule 5 requiring very strong positive evidence to show there was a general demand or market for it".[3] Nevertheless, the Lands Tribunal[4] reluctantly refused to exercise their discretion in favour of assessment under Rule 5. In that case the church had been built in 1796 but environmental changes had resulted in many members of the congregation moving to new housing estates and in access becoming difficult. In order to finance the building of a new church elsewhere the trustees sought planning permission to develop the site for shops and offices: their application being refused (on grounds of access) they served a purchase notice in 1964 on the grounds that the church had become incapable of reasonably beneficial use, the congregation having by then been reduced to four or five. By 1966 the building had fallen into disrepair but the trustees had been advised not to repair because it was subject to compulsory acquisition. Services were held in another building (known as Waterford House) although with a different congregation and under a somewhat different trust; but planning permission had been obtained in 1970 for the demolition of Waterford House and the erection of a new church on the site. The *ratio decidendi* of the Lands Tribunal decision was that there was no likelihood of the land the subject of the purchase notice[5] (i.e., the original church) continuing to be devoted to worship but for the acquisition, since there was virtually no congregation in 1964 and there could be no bona fide intention to rebuild elsewhere for the same purpose since

---

was still a shop and that was its purpose; it could make no difference whether the purpose was charitable or not; if a charity, e.g., St. Dunstan's, occupied a factory, then the purpose to which the building was devoted was that of a factory".

[1] Moreover, in the case of the specialised use of bare land market value is likely fully to meet the cost of purchasing an alternative site—*aliter*, however, where special handling equipment or security fencing, etc., of a permanent nature has been installed, or where a licence is required under the Control of Pollution Act 1974 for, e.g., the dumping of radioactive or dangerous chemical waste: but see *Rowley* v *Southampton Corpn* (1959) 10 P & CR 172, p. 248, *infra*.

[2] (1973) 25 P & CR 198.

[3] Per J. Stuart Daniel, QC, at p. 209–210.

[4] They were, however, overruled on appeal: *infra*.

[5] It was held that the fact that the claimants had initiated the acquisition on the ground that the land was incapable of reasonably beneficial use in its existing state did *not* automatically exclude Rule 5: see *ibid*, p. 209, and see also the similar decision in this regard in *Incorporated Society of the Crusade of Rescue and Homes for Destitute Catholic Children* v *Feltham UDC* (1960) 11 P & CR 158. In that case the suitability of the claimants' premises (two houses) for the purposes of a children's home had been much reduced and possibly rendered dangerous because of the flight-path of aircraft using extended runways at Heathrow Airport. Planning permission had been refused for industrial development. There was little doubt that, having regard to their financial position the claimants intended to continue this use, despite the inconvenience and danger, until funds permitted them to move to new premises. Note that the question whether these houses could have been used with or without adaptation as ordinary residences was not discussed: cf. the *Manchester Homeopathic* case, *supra*.

Waterford House had, in effect, attracted a wholly different congregation. The Court of Appeal,[1] however, held that the word
"devoted" in Rule 5 was employed to cover cases in which, at the date
of the notice to treat, the land was temporarily out of use, e.g., when a
building was under repair, or was in use temporarily or occasionally, or
in part for some purpose or purposes other than the primary or principal purpose for which it was used or intended to be used. The word
did not signify that the land had to be committed to that use for any
particular length of time, definite or indefinite. The date at which to
enquire whether, but for the compulsory acquisition, the land would
have continued to be devoted to its existing purpose within Rule 5 was
the date of the notice to treat, i.e., 22 July 1964. The only reasonable
conclusion from the evidence was that at that date the chapel would,
but for its acquisition by the corporation, have continued to be devoted
to public worship, for it was then in regular use and there was no
evidence to support a finding that the trustees would have discontinued
the use of the chapel in 1964; in fact the course of subsequent events
proved the contrary.

It was further held that the question whether reinstatement in some
other place was bona fide intended by the trustees depended not on
whether the former congregation or any part of it was to be reinstated,
or a chapel associated with a particular name, but on whether the
purpose which the former chapel had served was to be reinstated. It
followed that "reinstatement in some other place" was "bona fide
intended", within Rule 5, since (a) the place of worship existing at the
new church, and the proposed place of worship which the trustees
intended to establish there, both answered the description of a meeting
house having the characteristics specified in the trust deed, (b) the bona
fides of the trustees' intention was not in question, and (c) (per Russell
LJ) the fact that the realisation of that intention was dependent on the
receipt of compensation assessed under Rule 5 did not deprive the
intention of any necessary quality.

It followed that the tribunal had power under Rule 5 to assess
compensation on a reinstatement basis and, having regard to the
circumstances and to the views expressed by the tribunal, the discretion
should be exercised in favour of awarding compensation on that basis.

The decision to the effect that Rule 5 is not necessarily ruled out
because of a temporary use of the buildings for some other purpose
followed the principle of the earlier decision in *Aston Charities Trust,
Ltd.* v *Stepney Corpn*,[2] in which the issue was whether the premises were
devoted to the particular purpose at the relevant date—i.e., the date of
notice to treat. In that case the charitable and religious activities of the
claimant trust carried on in the subject premises having been severely
curtailed by war damage and the exodus of much of the local population, the premises were let for other purposes, although the trustees
retained two rooms. Despite the acquiring authority's contention that
since nearly the whole of the premises were let, they could not as such

[1] [1974] 3 All ER 5.
[2] (1952) 3 P & CR 82; upheld by the Court of Appeal, [1952] 2 QB 642; [1952] 2 All ER
228.

any longer be said to be "devoted" to their original purpose it was held that the words "devoted to a purpose" introduced the concept of intention, and indicated a different test from that of *de facto* use at the date of the notice to treat.[1]

Thus, although the Lands Tribunal appear to have relied upon the retention of the two rooms as constituting a *de facto* use for the purposes of the charity at the date of notice to treat, the Court of Appeal does not appear to have been particularly concerned whether that was the case or not (except in so far as it was evidence of intention to resume such use). In upholding the Lands Tribunal decision it took the view that temporary interruption in the use of land for the original purpose being in so many cases the inevitable result of bombing, such interruption should be disregarded, there being, at the date of notice to treat, no change of intention.[2] It was also held that reinstatement being a question of degree and of fact, the proposal to reinstate four miles away, in the circumstances of the particular case, fulfilled the requirements of Rule 5.[3]

Somewhat similar considerations arose in the *Kidderminster Theatre* case[4] where, before the acquisition, the finances of the local theatre had been reduced to the state at which it was threatened with closure. The threat of closure, however, produced a revival of local support and an agreement with the local authority whereby in return for a substantial annual subvention it would take over the theatre and establish a new trust. Shortly thereafter it was found necessary to acquire the site of the theatre in connection with certain highway proposals: an alternative theatre site was available but the local authority challenged the application of Rule 5 on the ground that, since the balance of the trust funds, including the compensation payable, were to be handed over to the new trust, it could not be said that the owners at the date of the notice to treat (i.e., the original trustees) had a genuine intention to reinstate. Indeed, they had no money with which to do so. It was held, however, that the threat to close the theatre constituted shock tactics designed to stimulate financial support (in which they had clearly proved remarkably successful) rather than an expression of intention, that the heads of agreement and other correspondence with the local authority demonstrated both a clear intention to continue the use of the building as a theatre but for the acquisition, and an equally clear intention, when the threat of acquisition emerged, to reinstate. The new theatre being clearly designed to fulfil the same purpose as the old, the proposed change in ownership was irrelevant. It being agreed that there was no general demand or market for the theatre, compensation fell to be assessed on the basis of the cost of the alternative site plus the cost of erecting thereon a similar building.[4]

---

[1] [1952] 2 All ER per Somerville LJ at p. 231: (1952) 3 P & CR at p. 86.

[2] See also *Cunningham* v *Sunderland CBC* (1963), 14 P & CR 208, where Rule 5 was applied despite the fact that, at the date of notice to treat, the use of the premises (a former chapel and vestry) for various parochial purposes and functions had fallen off, and the premises had fallen into disrepair, owing to the redevelopment of the area and the consequent threat of compulsory acquisition.

[3] But see *Roberts* v *Dover Corpn* (1962), 14 P & CR 47; pp. 245 *et seq, infra*.

[4] *Trustees of the Nonentities Society* v *Kidderminster Borough Council* (1970) 22 P & CR 224; *Zoar, etc.* v *Rochester Corpn*, p. 242, *supra*.

On the other hand, where, for example, a church hall has become redundant due to a movement of population, the intention to provide a new hall in a new centre of population will not necessarily amount to an intention to reinstate the original hall. The crucial issue is to determine when that intention was formed. Thus application of Rule 5 was refused where a church hall was bombed and the intention to build a new hall arose only some time after the notice to treat and when the expansion of the new parish, which had absorbed the former parish, had created an entirely fresh need for a new hall in another area.[1]

Moreover, since the evidence showed that the new estates for which the new hall was required would have been built even if the original hall and the surrounding houses had not been destroyed by enemy action, it followed that the new hall was an independent project not linked with the original hall and not affected by its compulsory acquisition.[2] Nevertheless it is not at first sight easy to reconcile this part of the Lands Tribunal's decision with that in the *Aston Charities* case[3] in which the provision of a new church four miles from the church acquired (and therefore inevitably serving a somewhat different community) was held to be a reinstatement of the latter, so that Rule 5 applied. It seems questionable, therefore, whether, in *Roberts'* case the Lands Tribunal would have considered this absence of a "link" between the proposed new hall (in another part of what had become the same parish) and the original hall fatal to the application of Rule 5 had they not already found that there had been no intention to reinstate at the date of notice to treat. As Somerville LJ put it in the *Aston Charities* case,[4] "reinstatement might take place a long way off but, having regard to the purpose, could still be described as 'reinstatement'. On the other hand, one can imagine a purpose confined locally to a narrow area, and, if the same sort of activity was started somewhere else it might be said not to be 'reinstatement'. It must, in my opinion, be a question of degree . . .". It is by no means clear why the functions of a church hall should be regarded as any more localised than that of a church. It is submitted, therefore, that in *Roberts'* case this argument must be regarded more as confirming a lack of intention to reinstate than as defining what would have constituted reinstatement had there been such an intention.

Furthermore, in order to qualify for compensation under Rule 5, the purpose must be one to which the premises had been voluntarily and deliberately devoted by the claimants. Thus, where surplus church premises were leased to a local authority who used them in connection with the provision of school meals, and subsequently acquired the freehold, it was held that Rule 5 was inapplicable.[5]

It is not, however, essential that the building be purpose-built: thus

---

[1] *Roberts and Others (Trustees of the St. James' Parish Hall Charity, Dover) v Dover Corpn* (1962) 14 P & CR 47.
[2] For a similar rejection of Rule 5 on the grounds that there was no intention to reinstate at the date of notice to treat (and indeed, no firm and unconditional intention much later) see *Edge Hill Light Rly Co v Secretary of State for War* (1956), 6 P & CR 211.
[3] P. 243, *supra*, note 2.
[4] [1952] 2 All ER at p. 231.
[5] *Trustees of the Central Methodist Church, Todmorden v Todmorden Corpn* (1959) 11 P & CR 32.

in *London Diocesan Fund* v *Stepney Corporation*[1] Rule 5 was applied to a mission hall and two buildings, originally dwelling-houses, to which there was intercommunication with the hall; one of these houses had been used in connection with the hall, the other as a dwelling for the caretaker. It was held that Rule 5 should be applied to these buildings as well as to the hall, on the ground that account had to be taken of the situation at the date of service of the notice to treat. At that date the Lands Tribunal were satisfied that the whole of the premises were owned and occupied by the claimants for the purposes of a mission hall since the accommodation of a caretaker was, in the circumstances, virtually essential for administrative and security purposes. It was held, first, that it was immaterial whether that accommodation was structurally integral with the premises as a whole, or capable of being separated therefrom and occupied independently; and secondly, that it was not permissible to "consider whether part of the premises might be used for some other purpose or whether any of the purposes for which it was used by the claimants as part of the general purpose might, if used for that purpose by some other person have taken it outside the provisions of Rule 5".[2]

The case of *Viscount Vaughan* v *The Cardiganshire Water Board*[3] is sometimes said to be authority for the proposition that in order to come within Rule 5 the purpose to which the land is devoted must be a "general purpose . . . not merely a localised purpose".[4] It seems doubtful, however, whether any such general conclusion can justifiably be drawn from this case, or if it can, where the distinction is to be drawn between a general and a localised purpose. In that case part of the subject land comprised a cottage occupied by a keeper and his wife only between April and October. In the course of two short annual visits the estate owner found it convenient to combine estate business with pleasure (fishing) by taking the opportunity to meet his tenants and discuss estate matters of mutual interest. The owner claimed that the purpose to which the land was devoted was estate management, and that there being no demand from anyone else in the neighbourhood for a cottage devoted to such a purpose, Rule 5 should be applied. The Lands Tribunal understandably rejected the basic proposition that the cottage was "devoted" to estate management:[5] having done so, however, it went on to suggest that if it was wrong in so doing, Rule 5 would

---

[1] (1953) 4 P & CR 9: for a case in which Rule 5 was applied to a building no part of which was purpose-built see *St. John's Wood Working Men's Club* v *LCC* (1947) 150 Estates Gazette 213, a case decided by an official arbitrator, in which it seems (no reasons for the decision being given) that the arbitrator upheld the claimant's contention that the purpose was more important than the structure, and that its adaptability was but a partial pointer to the true purpose. In the light of the *Manchester Homeopathic* case, p. 241, *supra*, however, it seems necessary to add the rider that where the premises are suitable for other purposes (with or without some adaptations) for which there is a general demand or market, Rule 5 will not be applied: see also *Viscount Vaughan* v *Cardiganshire Water Board*, *infra*.

[2] Per Erskine Simes, QC (1953), 4 P & CR 9 at p. 11.

[3] (1963) 14 P & CR 193.

[4] *Ibid*, per Erskine Simes, QC at p. 200.

[5] A parallel suggested by the Lands Tribunal being the use of his house by a secretary of a cricket club to transact the business of the club, a function that clearly does not involve "devoting" the house to that purpose in this context.

still not be applicable because the purpose was localised rather than general. It is, however, submitted that it would be wrong to conclude from this case that "estate management" as such is necessarily a purpose excluded from Rule 5. If the owner of a remote rural estate provides himself or his agent with an estate office in an area where there is no conceivable demand for office accommodation for any other purpose or for the same purpose from neighbouring landowners, there seems no reason why Rule 5 should not apply, unusual as such a state of affairs is likely to be. In short, the management of such estates would seem no more localised than ministering to the religious or medical needs of a specific community.[1] In *Vaughan*'s case of course, the sole estate management function of the cottage seems to have been as a meeting place: as such it could no doubt be said to be highly "localised" but it seems very doubtful whether this case can safely be relied upon as establishing any general principle in this regard—the purpose of a small chapel built to serve a remote and thinly populated section of a larger parish (and to which Rule 5 would almost certainly apply) would seem to be equally "localised". The distinction, of course, is that a chapel, *qua* chapel, commands no general market demand and an office or house used as a meeting place normally does. Perhaps the importance of this case is in providing a further example of a case in which there was no question of Rule 5 being inapplicable solely on the ground that the cottage had clearly not been specifically designed for the purpose to which it was alleged to be devoted.

It should also be noted that although the position is not entirely clear, there may be cases in which Rule 5 may apply where the claimant is but a tenant from year to year. Thus, where purpose-built club premises (for which it was accepted that there was no market demand) were rented by a club on an annual tenancy and were compulsorily acquired, it was held that the Rule applied.[2] However, although the tenants' claim was in part based upon their right to take into account their expectation that their tenancy would be renewed,[3] the actual decision appears to have turned on the particular relationship between the landlord and the tenant. The former were a limited company whose objects included the letting of club premises; the tenant was the club, which was also a major shareholder in the limited company.[4]

In deciding whether the purpose to which land is devoted is such that there is no general demand or market for land for that purpose, it is important to bear in mind that since, by definition, we are concerned with outright acquisition of the relevant interest in the land, the question to be asked is whether a purchaser (at a reasonable price) is likely

---

[1] As, for example, in the *Zoar* and *Manchester Homeopathic Clinic* cases, *supra*.

[2] *Harpurhey Conservative & Unionist Club and Harpurhey Constitutional Club Ltd.* v *Manchester City Council* (1975), 31 P & CR 300.

[3] Land Compensation Act 1973, s. 47: as to which see p. 367, *post*.

[4] Furthermore the issue being upon a preliminary point of law it was not necessary to decide whether the landlord company (who intended to carry out the reinstatement) or the tenant club would be entitled to the compensation. In this connection see *Smith, Stone, Knight Ltd.* v *The Lord Mayor, Alderman and Citizens of Birmingham*, [1939] 4 All ER 116, and *DHN Food Distributors Ltd.* v *Tower Hamlets London Borough Council* (1976), 32 P & CR 240; p. 347, *post*.

to be found for land for that purpose or such "allied" purpose for which it is equally suitable. Thus, in the case of the acquisition of a freehold, and in the absence of likely purchasers, evidence that the premises could be leased, although a matter for consideration, will not of itself be sufficient to refute a contention that there is no general demand or market.[1] And this is particularly the case where the evidence relates to transactions that cannot be said to have been negotiated in the open market, for example, where a local authority provide premises for a restricted purpose such as group medical practice (the numbers of which in relation to the local population are restricted by the local Health Executive) and the rent is negotiated between the tenants and the District Valuer.[1]

On the other hand, the fact that certain uses of land are restricted—e.g., offensive trades (under planning control)[2]—may, by restricting supply, actually increase market demand, in which case the application of Rule 5 will be inappropriate. Thus, where premises with planning permission (or existing use rights) for the melting of tallow and tripe dressing were acquired it was held that although specially equipped for these trades the local shortage of premises in which such trades could be carried on must be assumed so to enhance the market value of the premises that market value provided adequate compensation, and therefore the appropriate basis for its assessment.[3]

(v) EQUIVALENT REINSTATEMENT

It has already been noted that the question whether the proposed site of the replacement building is such that it can be said to "reinstate" the purpose of the building acquired is a matter of degree and of fact.[4] The same considerations apply when considering the structure and design of the proposed replacement. Thus where the cost of replacement is increased solely by the need to conform with building bye-laws or regulations or planning requirements such as provision of minimum car parking space, such extra costs may be included as part of the cost of equivalent reinstatement for the purpose of assessing the compensation payable. On the other hand, where the proposed replacement building includes substantial elements of improvement or replacement of outworn facilities which are not necessitated by the compulsory acquisition, the extra expense must be borne by the claimant.[5]

As a general rule, however, the claimants are entitled to decide the size of the rooms they require in the new building provided they do not claim compensation for larger accommodation than they had in the old building. Thus, where a chapel which had been converted for use as a

[1] *Trustees of the Manchester Homeopathic Clinic* v *Manchester Corpn*, p. 241, *supra*.
[2] See, for example, Town and Country Planning (Use Classes) Order 1972, (SI 1972 No. 1385), Classes I(ii) and IX.
[3] *Rowley* v *Southampton* (1959), 10 P & CR 172.
[4] *Aston Charities Trust Ltd.* v *Stepney Corpn*, p. 243, *supra*. See also *Zoar etc. Trustees* v *Rochester Corpn*, p. 242, *supra*, and *Roberts* v *Dover Corpn*, p. 245, *supra*.
[5] *Lane* v *Dagenham Corpn* (1961), 12 P & CR 374. In that case only part of the claimants' premises were being acquired; as that part did not include somewhat outdated lavatories it was held that, however desirable their replacement, since such replacement did not arise from the acquisition, the additional cost could not be included in the cost of equivalent reinstatement.

masonic hall was acquired, arguments on behalf of the acquiring authority that a new purpose-built hall with an equivalent number of smaller rooms (and therefore a reduction in total cubic capacity) would provide adequate accommodation, were rejected,[1] although the Tribunal added that had the acquiring authority shown that advances in architectural design could reduce cubic capacity solely by eliminating unnecessary height and waste space in passages, that would have been a matter to be taken into account in assessing the compensation payable.[2]

Application of Rule 5: summary

1. The land must be devoted to a purpose of such nature that there is no general demand or market for land for that purpose.

The test is whether the activities or processes which have been carried on or the physical characteristics of the structure of the property render it improbable that a purchaser willing to offer a reasonable price can be found.[3] The premises need not be purpose built.[4]

2. The purpose must be one to which the land is voluntarily and deliberately devoted by or on behalf of the claimant.[5]

3. The land must either be devoted to such a purpose at the date of the notice to treat[6] or previous devotion thereto must imply an intention to resume the use of the land for that purpose;[7] a purely temporary interruption spanning the date of notice to treat is to be disregarded.[7]

4. The circumstances as at the date of notice to treat must be such that it is clear that, but for the acquisition, the land would continue to be devoted to the purpose[7] although not necessarily either indefinitely or for any fixed or stated minimum period.[8] Evidence that continuance over only a short period is likely is a factor of which the Lands Tribunal are entitled to take account in exercising their discretion.[9]

5. The fact that compulsory acquisition is initiated by the claimant by service of a purchase notice on the grounds that the land has been rendered incapable of reasonably beneficial use is not necessarily a bar to the application of Rule 5 or evidence that the use of the premises for the purpose concerned would not have continued but for the acquisition.[10]

---

[1] *Trustees of the Zetland Lodge of Freemasons* v *Tamar Bridge Joint Committee* (1961), 12 P & CR 326.
[2] Per The President, Sir William Fitzgerald QC, at p. 328.
[3] *Trustees of the Manchester Homeopathic Clinic* v *Manchester Corpn* (1970), 22 P & CR 241, p. 241, *supra*.
[4] *London Diocesan Fund* v *Stepney Corpn* (1953), 4 P & CR 9; *St. John's Wood Working Men's Club* v *London County Council* (1947), 150 Estates Gazette 213; note 1, p. 246, *supra*. See also *Viscount Vaughan* v *Cardiganshire Water Board* (1963), 14 P & CR 193; p. 246, *supra*.
[5] *Trustees of the Central Methodist Church, Todmorden* v *Todmorden Corpn* (1959), 11 P & CR 32; p. 245, *supra*.
[6] *Zoar Independent Church Trustees* v *Rochester Corpn*, [1974] 3 WLR 417; p. 242, *supra*.
[7] *Aston Charities Trust Ltd.* v *Stepney Corpn* (1952), 3 P & CR 32; 243, *supra*.
[8] *Zoar Independent Church Trustees* v *Rochester Corpn* (*supra*), p. 242, *supra*.
[9] *A & B Taxis Ltd.* v *Secretary of State for Air*, [1922] 2 KB 328; note 3, p. 241, *supra*.
[12] *Zoar Independent Church Trustees* v *Rochester Corpn* (*supra*); *Incorporated Society of the Crusade of Rescue and Homes for Destitute Catholic Children* v *Feltham U.D.C.* (1960), 11 P & CR 158; note 5, p. 242, *supra*.

6. There must be a genuine intention to reinstate elsewhere at the date of notice to treat.[1] It is submitted that a subsequent inability to do so due to unforeseen circumstances will not, therefore, affect the compensation although a probability of such inability arising before the compensation is determined would seem a legitimate ground on which the Lands Tribunal may refuse to exercise their discretion.

7. Whether or not location or design of the building proposed as a replacement of the building compulsorily acquired constitutes equivalent reinstatement is a question of degree and of fact. The location must be such as to retain some link between the new building and the old.[2] The more localised the purpose the more local must be the reinstatement.[3] The cost of improvements or additional facilities, the need for which does not arise from the compulsory acquisition, will be disallowed.[4]

8. While there is no limit to the amount of compensation payable provided it represents the reasonable cost of equivalent reinstatement, the Lands Tribunal are entitled to refuse to exercise their discretion in the case of commercial premises if the cost is wholly disproportionate to the value of the undertaking of which the land acquired formed part;[5] if the business is running at a loss;[6] or in any case where the continuance of the enterprise is, apart from the acquisition, likely to be short-lived.[6]

3 LAND AND/OR APPARATUS OF STATUTORY UNDERTAKERS[7]

Acquisition of land

(i) INTRODUCTORY

The measure of the compensation claimable by statutory undertakers in respect of land compulsorily acquired from them depends upon whether the compulsory purchase order is accompanied by a certificate from the appropriate Minister.[8]

Under the Acquisition of Land (Authorisation Procedure) Act 1946,[9] if a compulsory purchase order covering land belonging to statutory

---

[1] *Roberts* v *Dover Corpn* (1962), 14 P & CR 47; p. 245, *supra*.

[2] *Ibid*; see also *Aston Charities* v *Stepney Corpn* (1902) 3 P & CR 82, p. 243, *supra*.

[3] *Ibid*.

[4] *Lane* v *Dagenham Corpn* (1961), 12 P & CR 374; note 5, p. 248, *supra*; *Trustees of the Zetland Lodge of Freemasons* v *Tamar Bridge Joint Committee* (1961), 12 P & CR 326; p, 249, *supra*.

[5] *Edge Hill Light Railway Co.* v *Secretary of State for War* (1956) 6 P & CR 211; note 2, p. 245, *supra*.

[6] *A & B Taxis* v *Secretary of State for Air*, note 3, p. 241, *supra*.

[7] "Statutory undertakers" are defined as "persons authorised by any enactment, to carry on any railway, light railway, tramway, road transport, water transport, canal, inland navigation, dock, harbour, pier or lighthouse undertaking, or any undertaking for the supply of electricity, gas, hydraulic power or water": Town and Country Planning Act 1971, s. 290(1).

[8] Defined in the Acquisition of Land (Authorisation Procedure) Act 1946, s. 8, and the Town and Country Planning Act 1971, s. 224, as the Minister in charge of the sponsoring Department. The various reorganisations of Government Departments under the Machinery of Government Acts have, however, effected a number of changes since 1971. Any doubt as to which is the appropriate Minister in any particular case is to be settled by the Treasury: *ibid*, s. 290(2).

[9] Sch. 1, para. 10.

undertakers is made, and representations[1] are made to the appropriate Minister, the compulsory purchase order can only be confirmed so as to include land that is certified by that Minister as held and used for the purposes of the undertaking to the extent that he certifies that it can be acquired without serious detriment to the carrying on of the undertaking on the land, or such part thereof as is specified in the certificate, or that it can be replaced by other land owned or available for acquisition by the undertakers.

It follows that if no representations are made the compulsory purchase order can be confirmed without the appropriate Minister's certificate.[2]

Furthermore if the compulsory purchase order is made under the Town and Country Planning Act 1971[3] in respect of land acquired by statutory undertakers for the purpose of their undertaking, the appropriate Minister's certificate may be dispensed with provided the compulsory purchase order is confirmed jointly by the appropriate Minister and the Minister who, in accordance with the enactment under which the compulsory purchase order is made, is the confirming authority.[4]

(ii) MEASURE OF COMPENSATION WHERE NO CERTIFICATE IS ISSUED

In cases in which there is no certificate the statutory undertakers may, at their option,[5] claim compensation on the ordinary basis of market value;[6] they cannot, however, claim compensation on the basis of the cost of equivalent reinstatement[7] since, as is explained below, this is in effect provided for if they do *not* exercise their option.

If they do not exercise their option and the acquisition necessitates adjustment to the manner in which they have to carry on their undertaking, the measure of compensation is the amount of any expenditure reasonably incurred in acquiring other land, providing apparatus, erecting buildings or doing works for the purpose of making that adjustment.[8]

To this expenditure is to be added the estimated amount of any decrease in net receipts directly attributable to the acquisition (whether in respect of the period during which the adjustment is being carried out or after its completion[9]).

[1] Representations must be made within the time allowed for the making of objections to the order: Sch. 1, para. 10.

[2] Since the Minister's Certificate is only required in relation to land used by statutory undertakers for the purpose of their undertaking and in which they hold an interest for that purpose, representations in respect of non-operational land will not result in the issue of any certificate (Acquisition of Land (Authorisation Procedure) Act 1946, Sch. 1, para. 10) and compensation will then be assessed in the normal way: *infra*.

[3] S. 229(2).

[4] Although the compulsory purchase order may be confirmed by the confirming authority alone, it is of no effect; to be effective, therefore, it either has to be jointly confirmed or accompanied by a certificate: Town and Country Planning Act 1971, s. 229(3).

[5] The option may be exercised in respect of all or part of the land being acquired, and must be exercised within two months following the date of notice to treat: *ibid*, s. 239.

[6] I.e., under the Land Compensation Act 1961, s. 5: pp. 177 *et seq, ante*.

[7] I.e., under *ibid*, s. 5(5), pp. 239 *et seq, supra*; Town and Country Planning Act 1971, s. 239(1).

[8] *Ibid*, s. 238(2)(a).

[9] *Ibid*, s. 238(2)(b)(i).

From the total compensation thus assessed there falls to be deducted, however, the estimated value of any property (whether moveable or immoveable) belonging to the statutory undertakers which ceases to be used in connection with their undertaking and the estimated amount of any net increase in net receipts following, and consequent upon, the completion of the adjustment.[1]

Where no adjustment is necessitated the compensation is to be "such amount as appears reasonable compensation for any estimated decrease in net receipts from the carrying on of the undertaking which is directly attributable" to the acquisition.[2]

(iii) MEASURE OF COMPENSATION WHERE THE APPROPRIATE MINISTER ISSUES A CERTIFICATE

In all other cases compensation is to be assessed in the normal way[3] it being open to the statutory undertakers in cases in which the land carries purpose-designed apparatus to claim compensation on the basis of the cost of equivalent reinstatement,[4] account being taken of the value of any part of such apparatus that can be moved and re-used elsewhere and the cost of dismantling and re-erecting it.

(iv) EXTINGUISHMENT OF RIGHTS OR INTERFERENCE WITH APPARATUS

(a) Introductory

Where any land has been acquired by an authority under either the Town and Country Planning Act 1971, Part VI, or the Community Land Act 1975, Part III, and there subsists over the land any right of way or right of laying down, erecting or maintaining apparatus vested in or belonging to statutory undertakers, or where such apparatus actually exists under or on the land, powers are conferred on the authority to extinguish such rights or to have the apparatus removed.[5] The authority must, however, be satisfied that such extinguishment or removal is necessary in order to enable it to develop the land and it must give the statutory undertakers at least 28 days' notice.[6] The latter then have 28 days from the date of service of such notice in which to serve a counter-notice objecting to all or any provisions of the notice

---

[1] Town and Country Planning Act 1971, s. 238(3). The arbiter as to what deduction is to be made is the Lands Tribunal: *ibid*. Note the inclusion of land by the use of the word "property"—the market value of land no longer used for the purposes of the undertaking will normally be enhanced. Apparatus (i.e., "moveable property") no longer used will presumably have some salvage value.

[2] *Ibid*, s. 238(2)(b)(ii).

[3] I.e., under the Land Compensation Act 1961, pp. 164 *et seq, ante*. But these cases include, of course, acquisition of land owned by statutory undertakers but not acquired by them for the purpose of their undertaking, e.g., land which they have been obliged to acquire when acquiring operational land under the Lands Clauses Consolidation Act 1845 or the Land Compensation Act 1973 (pp. 108 *et seq, post*) or in response to a blight notice (pp. 129 *et seq, ante*). Similarly, it includes land acquired for operational purposes but not as yet used therefor, for in such cases the appropriate Minister's certificate is inapplicable. See the Acquisition of Land (Authorisation Procedure) Act 1946, Sch. 1, para. 10 and note 2, p. 251, *supra*.

[4] P. 248, *supra*.

[5] Town and Country Planning Act 1971, s. 230; Community Land Act 1975, Sch. 4, para. 17.

[6] Community Land Act 1975, Sch. 4. para. 17(1).

and stating the grounds of their objection.[1] On receipt of such a counter-notice the authority may withdraw the original notice.[2] Withdrawal is, however, without prejudice to the service of a further notice;[2] if, therefore, the statutory undertakers object only in part, a further notice designed to meet their objections may be substituted. Equally, however, the authority may leave the matter in abeyance to be reopened when its plans for the development of the land are further advanced. Alternatively the authority may apply to the Secretary of State and the appropriate Minister[3] for an order embodying the provisions of the notice with or without modification.[4] If that course is adopted the Secretary of State and the Minister must afford to the statutory undertakers a *further* opportunity to object to the application for the order and, if objection is made, afford to them an opportunity of being heard by a person appointed for that purpose.[5] The application may be made in the form applied for, modified in such manner as the Ministers deem appropriate, or refused. Statutory undertakers affected by these provisions and anxious to resist the authority's requirements must therefore register their objections twice, once to the authority's notice and again to its application for an order.

If no objection is made to the authority's initial notice or an order is made, the rights are extinguished or the apparatus must be removed, as the case may be, in accordance with the terms of the notice or order.[6] But if, in the latter case, the apparatus has not been removed by the date specified in the order (or in the original notice if no objection was made thereto) the authority may make such arrangements for its removal and disposal as it deems fit.[7]

Similar provisions[8] enable statutory undertakers who claim that proposed development of land acquired by an authority requires resiting of apparatus, to serve notice on the authority (not later than 21 days after the development has begun)[9] claiming the right to enter upon the land and carry out the necessary work.[10] If the authority objects it may serve a counter-notice within 28 days specifying the grounds of objection[11] and the statutory undertakers may then either withdraw their original notice or apply to the Secretary of State and the

---

[1] Community Land Act 1975, Sch. 4, para. 17(2).

[2] *Ibid*, para. 17(4).

[3] In the case of those bodies which are statutory undertakers for the purposes of the Town and Country Planning Act 1971 the appropriate Minister is the Minister defined as such in s. 224 of that Act: Community Land Act 1975, s. 5(4). In other cases the expression is to have the meaning ascribed thereto by any order made under that subsection: see currently the Community Land (Statutory Undertakers) Order 1976, (SI 1976 No. 18). In cases of doubt the appropriate Minister is to be determined by the Treasury: Community Land Act 1975, s. 5(5).

[4] *Ibid*, Sch. 4, para. 17(4).

[5] *Ibid*, Sch. 4, para. 18(1); cf. Town and Country Planning Act 1971, s. 231, but note that the requirement of sub-s. (1) of that section that a draft order be prepared by the Minister is *not* applied by the Community Land Act 1975, Sch. 4, para. 18.

[6] Community Land Act 1975, Sch. 4, para. 18(2).

[7] *Ibid*, paras 17(1) and 18(2)(b).

[8] *Ibid*, para. 19—a reproduction of the Town and Country Planning Act 1971, s. 232.

[9] Community Land Act 1975, Sch. 4, para. 19.

[10] The work required to be done must be specified in the notice: Community Land Act 1975, Sch. 4, para. 19(1).

[11] *Ibid*, Sch. 4, para. 19(3).

appropriate Minister for an order conferring upon them the rights claimed or such modified rights for which the order may provide.[1] Thereafter—or if the authority has raised no objection upon the expiration of 28 days from the date of service of the original notice—the statutory undertakers may either enter upon the land and execute the requisite works (or such work as may be authorised by the order, as the case may be) or arrange for the authority to do so on their behalf and under their supervision.[2]

(b) Measure of compensation

Subject to the undermentioned qualifications, the measure of compensation for such extinguishment of rights or removal of apparatus is on the same basis as that described above where land is compulsorily acquired from statutory undertakers and no certificate has been issued by the appropriate Minister,[3] except that:

(i) Compensation for the acquisition of interests in land being inapplicable, the statutory undertakers have no right to elect for the assessment of compensation under the Land Compensation Act 1961, s. 5.[4] It follows, therefore, that they are equally debarred from opting for assessment of compensation on the basis of the effect of the extinguishment of their rights or the removal of their apparatus on the market value of the land.

(ii) Where removal of apparatus is necessitated, compensation is payable in respect of the cost of removal, reduced by the value of the apparatus removed.[5]

(iii) Such compensation is additional to the compensation payable in respect of the expenditure of acquiring land, providing new apparatus, erecting buildings, or doing any work for the purpose of any necessary adjustment to their undertaking, but the value of any property[6] which as a consequence of the adjustment is unused remains to be deducted in so far as, in the case of apparatus, it has not already been accounted for under para. (ii) above.

(iv) The compensation claimable under para. (ii) above is additional to any compensation in respect of any resultant decrease in net receipts.[7]

(v) Where the statutory undertakers fail to remove apparatus which by the terms of the notice or order they are required so to do, the acquiring or appropriating authority may itself carry out the requisite work and dispose of the apparatus removed as it deems fit.[8]

(vi) Where, however, "the Secretary of State and the appropriate Minister are satisfied, having regard to the nature, situation

[1] Community Land Act 1975, Sch. 4, para. 19(5).
[2] *Ibid*, Sch. 4, para. 19(6).
[3] P. 251, *supra*, and note 2.
[4] Town and Country Planning Act 1971, ss. 238(1)(c) and 239(1).
[5] *Ibid*, s. 238(2)(c).
[6] See p. 252, *supra*, and note 1 thereon.
[7] As in the case of land compulsorily acquired: p. 251, *supra*.
[8] Community Land Act 1975, Sch. 4, paras. 17(1) and 18(2)(b).

and existing development of the land or of any neighbouring land, and to any other material considerations, that it is unreasonable that compensation should be recovered" they may direct accordingly.[1]

Compensation payable to statutory undertakers where land is compulsorily acquired, rights over land extinguished or apparatus required to be removed: summary

1. If the land has been acquired by statutory undertakers for the purpose of their undertaking and the appropriate Minister has issued no certificate, then unless the statutory undertakers elect for the assessment of compensation on the basis of market value[2] the compensation will be the cost of any works etc. necessary for the adjustment of their undertaking. To this is to be added an allowance in respect of any consequential temporary or permanent decrease in net receipts reduced by any enhancement in the value of the land resulting from removal of apparatus and by any salvage value of the apparatus removed.[3]

2. If no such adjustment is necessitated, compensation will be the estimated consequential decrease in net receipts less the above deductions as applicable.[4]

3. In all other cases compensation will be in accordance with the normal code.[5]

4. Subject to para. 5 below, where the rights of statutory undertakers over land are extinguished, compensation will be on the same basis as in paras. 1 and 2 above—depending upon whether or not any adjustment to their undertaking is necessitated.[6] In addition, the statutory undertakers are entitled to the cost of removal of apparatus less the value of such part thereof as is re-usable, reduced by the salvage value of those parts that are not re-usable.[6]

5. Where satisfied that in the circumstances the payment of compensation is unreasonable, the Secretary of State and the appropriate Minister may direct accordingly.[7]

4 HOUSES UNFIT FOR HUMAN HABITATION: COMPENSATION BASED ON SITE VALUES

1 Introductory

As has already been indicated,[8] where the property being acquired is a house declared by the local housing authority to be unfit for human

---

[1] Town and Country Planning Act 1971, s. 237(4).
[2] Pp. 251 *et seq*, *supra*.
[3] *Ibid*.
[4] P. 252, *supra*.
[5] I.e., in accordance with the code of compensation described in Chap. 5, and section 2 of this chapter, p. 239, *et seq. supra*.
[6] Pp. 251, *et seq*, *supra*.
[7] P. 254, para. (iv), *supra*.
[8] P. 238, *supra*.

habitation the basic assumption is that the house, *qua* house, is of no value. The measure of compensation is, therefore, the value of the cleared site.[1] In practice, however, there is a market demand for much of this type of property for residential purposes as it stands, and at a price that in most cases is likely to exceed that value.

While this demand reflects a local housing shortage it is also no doubt partly due to the fact that unfitness for human habitation is inevitably both a matter of degree and a matter of opinion, and partly because there is always a certain number of people who are relatively indifferent to housing standards.

The fact that there is such a market demand, however, has resulted in the general application of site value as the measure of compensation, producing anomalies and injustice, particularly where the owner has been at pains to maintain his property in a good state of repair or has comparatively recently purchased at full market value without grounds for anticipating early condemnation of his property as unfit for human habitation.

This hardship is exacerbated, moreover, where, as is very often the case with a house declared unfit for human habitation, the site by itself may be too small for any profitable form of redevelopment. Indeed, perhaps in the majority of cases the most valuable planning permission which can be assumed in assessing market value is likely to be that based upon existing use,[2] namely redevelopment for residential purposes. But if the site of the particular house is too small for the erection of another house to modern standards it will have but a nominal value (often as little as a pound or so) even though it adjoins other unfit houses the sites of which, when amalgamated in the single ownership of the acquiring authority constitute an area of substantial value for redevelopment.

Attempts to meet these difficulties without infringing the fundamental principle of site valuation[3] have resulted in special payments, over and above the value of the site, being made available in appropriate cases. Thus, in so far as compensation may be based upon site value, with or without the addition of some additional allowance, compensation under the Housing Acts requires special treatment. Nevertheless, once it has been established that site value is applicable, the ordinary rules governing the assessment of compensation in general apply.[4] Any "allowance" that may be applicable in any particular case is additional.[5] Despite the fact that these special provisions stem

---

[1] Housing Act 1957, ss. 29 and 59. Apart from the logic of so valuing an unfit house, the adoption of site value compensation was intended to discourage the old-type slum landlord: see p. 262, *infra.*

[2] See pp. 194, *et seq, ante.*

[3] Apart from the logic of confining compensation to the value of the site in such cases, there is also, of course, a social argument for its retention; see p. 262, *infra.*

[4] I.e., the market value of the site subject to such modification as may be necessary to reflect the effect of the overall scheme of proposed redevelopment: pp. 217, *et seq, ante,* and see particularly *King* v *Birmingham Corpn* (1970), 21 P & CR 979 and *Davy* v *Leeds Corpn,* [1964] 1 WLR 1218 CA and [1965] 1 WLR 445 HL (Note 4, p. 221, *ante*).

[5] Subject, however, to the total compensation payable (i.e., including such allowances) being limited to the market value of the property as it stands, and discounting any effect thereon of any clearance area within which the property may be situated: Land Compensation Act 1961, Sch. 2,

from, and specifically apply to, compulsory acquisitions under the Housing Acts[1] it must be emphasised that they may equally apply where unfit houses are acquired under a number of other enactments[2] provided an order declaring the house to be unfit for human habitation and incapable of being rendered so fit at reasonable expense has been made by the local authority and confirmed by the Secretary of State either before or concurrently with the confirmation of a compulsory purchase order covering the land in question.[3]

It is of particular importance to note that the above specifically applies to acquisitions under the very wide powers of Part III of the Community Land Act 1975.[4]

2 The Housing Act 1957

Part II of the Housing Act 1957 contains the provisions of that Act for securing the maintenance and sanitary standards of houses: it commences by setting out the matters to be taken into account in determining, for any of the purposes of the Act, whether a house is unfit for human habitation.[5] Part III deals with clearance and redevelopment and Part V with the provision of housing accommodation. Each of these functions involves the acquisition of land and buildings.

---

para. 1(2). Moreover, where the house is in fact of no value, market value will reflect the value of the site less the cost of demolition and clearance. But for this limitation, therefore, site value compensation could actually exceed what the vendor could obtain in the market.

[1] The powers of acquisition under those Acts with which we are here concerned are (subject to relatively minor amendments) contained in the Housing Act 1957, Parts II and III.

[2] Set out in the Land Compensation Act 1961, Sch. 2, para. 2(1). They comprise compulsory acquisitions under the Town and Country Planning Act 1971, Parts VI and IX; the Town Development Act 1952, s. 6; the Housing Act 1969, Part II; the Community Land Act 1975 III; and acquisitions by the Greater London Council under the Housing Act 1957, Part V; or by a Development Corporation, local highway authority, or Minister of Transport under the New Towns Act 1946, or under any enactment as applied by any provision of that Act; and any acquisition of land within the site of a new town as designated by order under the New Towns Act 1946, s. 1.

[3] Land Compensation Act 1961, Sch. 2, para. 2(2): where the acquisition is in response to a purchase or blight notice (pp. 114, et seq, ante) the order must be made *before* the notice to treat is deemed to have been served. The order must be in the prescribed form: see Housing (Prescribed Forms) Regulations 1957 (SI 1957 No. 1842) as amended by the Housing (Prescribed Forms) (Amendment) Regulations 1959 (SI 1959 No. 1400) and 1962 (SI 1962 No. 1021).

[4] Land Compensation Act 1961, Sch. 2, para. 2(1)(i) as amended by the Community Land Act 1975, Sch. 10, para. 4(4). For an outline of these powers see pp. 22, et seq, ante and Chap. 7, post; for a more complete explanation see Corfield's *A Guide to the Community Land Act 1975* and for procedural modifications applicable to the exercise of these powers see pp. 74, et seq, ante.

[5] Housing Act 1957, s. 4 (as amended by the Housing Act 1969). The relevant considerations are: repair; stability; freedom from damp; natural lighting; ventilation; water supply; drainage and sanitary conveniences; facilities for storage, preparation and cooking of food and the disposal of waste water; internal bad arrangement. A house is to be deemed "unfit for human habitation if and only if it is so far defective in one or more of the said matters that it is not reasonably suitable for occupation in that condition". "Internal bad arrangement is any feature which prohibits the safe or unhampered passage of the occupants in the dwelling, e.g., narrow, steep or winding staircases, absence of hand rails, inadequate landings outside bedrooms, ill-defined changes of floor levels, a bedroom entered through another bedroom and also includes a WC opening directly from a living-room or kitchen": *Report of the Central Housing Advisory Committee*: Ministry of Housing and Local Government Circular 68/69, para. 24.

3 Acquisition of unfit houses under Part II of the Housing Act 1957

Under this Part of the Act compulsory powers of acquisition are confined to houses[1] which are both unfit for human habitation and incapable of being rendered so fit at reasonable expense. But compulsory acquisition is not available where the estimated cost of the work necessary to render a house fit for human habitation is not unreasonable in relation to the value of the house when the work has been completed, nor is it the only remedy where the cost is prohibitive.[2] Inevitably, however, there will be differences of opinion between local authorities and owners both as to estimated cost of rehabilitation and as to whether that cost is or is not reasonable. If the initial opinion of the local authority is that the defects can be remedied at reasonable cost they must serve upon the "person having control of the house"[3] a notice requiring him to carry out such work, which must be specified in the notice, as in the opinion of the authority will render the house fit for human habitation.[4] The owner may, within 21 days, appeal against such a notice to the county court[5] and if the appeal is upheld, the judge, if requested to do so by the local authority, must include in his judgment a finding as to whether or not the house can or cannot be rendered fit for human habitation at reasonable expense.[6] If that finding is in the negative the local authority may purchase the house by agreement or be authorised by the Secretary of State to acquire it compulsorily.[7] Similarly, where the local authority takes the view that the house cannot be rendered habitable at reasonable expense, the "owner" may give an undertaking to carry out such work as may be necessary. Where there is no such undertaking, or the undertaking is not accepted by the local authority or is not fulfilled, the local authority may again acquire by agreement or seek authority to acquire compulsorily.[8]

---

[1] "House" includes any building constructed or adapted wholly or partly as, or for the purposes of, a dwelling: Housing Act 1957, s. 189.

[2] E.g., the local authority may accept an undertaking that the requisite works will be carried out despite the cost (Housing Act 1957, s. 16); they may also make a demolition or closing order either in the first instance or upon failure of the person concerned (usually the owner) to fulfil his undertaking (*ibid*, s. 17).

[3] This expression "person having control of the house" broadly corresponds with the normal conception of the word "owner", which is used in that Act and the enactments it replaces in a somewhat different sense. For the purposes of the Act, the "owner" of land or buildings is defined as "a person other than a mortgagee not in possession, who is for the time being entitled to dispose of the fee simple, whether in possession or in reversion, and includes also a person holding or entitled to the rents and profits . . . under a lease or agreement, the unexpired term whereof exceeds three years": Housing Act 1957 s. 189(1). The "person having control of the house" is he "who receives the rack-rent of a house, whether on his own account or as agent or trustee of another person or who would so receive it if the house were let at a rack-rent": *ibid*, s. 39(2).

[4] *Ibid*, s. 9(1).

[5] If there is no appeal, or if, on appeal, the notice is confirmed and the works are not carried out within the time specified in the notice (which must not be less than 21 days), or within 21 days from the determination of the appeal, as the case may be, the local authority may enter, carry out the works themselves and recover the cost as a civil debt: *ibid*, s. 10.

[6] Housing Act 1957, s. 11.

[7] *Ibid*, s. 12. Before confirming a compulsory purchase order under this section the Minister must afford to owners and mortgagees the opportunity to carry out the works specified in the original notice: s. 12(2).

[8] See note 2, *supra*.

In that event, compensation is to be the value, at the time when the valuation is made,[1] "of the site as a cleared site available for development in accordance with the requirements of the building bye-laws[2] for the time being in force in the district", but such compensation is without prejudice to the payment in addition of any "well-maintained" or "owner-occupier's" allowance.[3]

As has already been noted, the site of an individual unfit house may, of itself, be of but very nominal value.[4] This is particularly the case with older houses in urban areas built, as they so often are, to very high densities. It follows, therefore, that the compensation payable in respect of the site of a block of say 10 or 20 unfit houses in single ownership is likely to be worth a good deal more than 10 or 20 times the compensation payable in respect of a single house, provided, of course, that the cleared site of the block is of a suitable shape for some form of redevelopment for residential purposes without amalgamation with land in other ownership. Thus if ownership of tenanted houses can be consolidated before any action in regard to unfitness is taken by the local housing authority, total compensation receivable may be considerably enhanced, particularly when few, if any, well-maintained allowances are likely to be payable.[5] In the case of persons qualifying for an owner-occupier's allowance, however, there may be no advantage to be gained by such consolidation since the owner-occupier's allowance brings the compensation up to the maximum payable, i.e., the full market value of the property as it stands.[6]

4 Acquisition of land and buildings under Part III of the Housing Act 1957

Clearance areas
Clearance areas arise where a local authority is satisfied, with regard to any particular area, that the houses therein are unfit for human habitation or that they or any other buildings in that area are, by reason of their bad arrangement or the narrowness or bad arrangement of the streets, dangerous or injurious to the health of the inhabitants. In such circumstances, the local authority must, if satisfied that the most satisfactory method of dealing with such conditions is demolition of all buildings in the area and that it has the resources to carry out the project, including the rehousing of persons displaced, declare the area a "clearance area".[7] In doing so, however, it must ensure that the delineation of the area is such that it is confined to property within one or other of the above categories; "sound" property must be excluded however awkward the resultant shape of the area.[7] Thereafter it must

---

[1] Note that by departing from the date of notice to treat as the date at which value is to be assessed the Housing Act 1957 in a sense anticipated the decision in the *Birmingham Corpn* v *West Midland Baptist Trust* [1969] 3 All ER 172 HL: see pp. 165, *et seq, ante.*
[2] Now replaced by the Building Regulations.
[3] As to these allowances see pp. 262, *et seq*, and 265, *et seq* respectively, *infra.*
[4] P. 256, *supra.*
[5] Pp. 262, *et seq, infra.*
[6] Pp. 265, *et seq, infra.*
[7] Housing Act 1957, s. 42.

deal with the area in one of two ways, or partly in one way and partly in the other; either it must make one or more "clearance orders" requiring owners to demolish their property[1] and conferring powers on the local authority to do so in cases of default and to recover the cost;[2] or it may purchase the various properties comprised in the area and make itself responsible for demolition.[1]   In the latter event it may either acquire by agreement or be authorised by the Secretary of State to acquire compulsorily and these powers of acquisition are not confined solely to property within the strict confines of the clearance area. They extend to any land surrounded by or adjacent to it that is reasonably required for the satisfactory redevelopment of the area when cleared.[3] The local authority may also acquire cleared land where, within 18 months of the clearance order becoming operative, redevelopment in accordance with plans approved by the authority was not commenced.[4]

5 Obstructive buildings

Under the Housing Act 1957, ss. 72–74, a local authority may require demolition of an "obstructive building", i.e., one which by reason of its contact with, or proximity to, other buildings is dangerous or injurious to health.[5] Section 72 provides for the prior notification of, and discussions with, the owner, the service of a demolition order and the owner's right of appeal to the county court. Although these provisions confer no power compulsorily to acquire such a building, the owner may, at any time within the period within which it is required by the demolition order to be vacated, offer the building to the local authority at a price to be assessed as if it were compensation for compulsory acquisition. Provided such offer involves the sale of a sufficient interest to enable the local authority to demolish, it must be accepted,[6] and the "compensation" assessed accordingly.[7]

6 Compensation

The general rule is that the compensation payable in respect of any land, including buildings thereon, comprised in a clearance area is the value, at the time the valuation is made of the land, as a site cleared of buildings and available for development in accordance with the requirements of the building regulations for the time being in force.[8] To this general rule there is, however, an important exception; site value is

---

[1] Housing Act 1957, s. 43. The power to make clearance orders is abolished by the Housing Act 1974, s. 108(1). At the time of going to press, however, no order had been made bringing s. 108 into effect.

[2] Housing Act 1957, s. 44. Any amount by which the value of materials salvaged exceeds the cost of demolition must be held on behalf of the owners: *ibid*, s. 23.

[3] *Ibid*, s. 43(2).

[4] *Ibid*, s. 51. This section has also been repealed by the Housing Act 1974, s. 130(4) and Sch. 15. The repeal had not, however, been brought into force at the time of going to press: power to acquire such cleared land would, however, appear now to fall within the Community Land Act 1975, Part III.

[5] Housing Act 1957, s. 72(4).

[6] *Ibid*, s. 74(1).

[7] Note that no question of site value arises in these cases; see under "Compensation", *infra*.

[8] Housing Act 1957, s. 56; and see note 4, *supra*.

not applicable as the basis of compensation where the building concerned has been included in the clearance area solely because of its bad arrangement in relation to other buildings, or because of the narrowness or bad arrangement of the streets resulting in its being dangerous or injurious to the health of the inhabitants, provided that if any part of it is a dwelling-house, that part is not unfit for human habitation.[1]

As far as houses are concerned, therefore, site value compensation under this part of the Act of 1957, as under Part II, above, is only applicable where the house is unfit for human habitation; under this provision, however, it may also be applicable to other buildings but only where they are both included in a clearance area and are either themselves dangerous or injurious to health or comprise a part which is used as a dwelling and that part is unfit for human habitation.

These site value provisions are, however, extended to cover the acquisition of unfit houses under other enactments by the Land Compensation Act 1961, Schedule 2.[2]

7 Compensation for compulsory acquisition where site value does not apply

Apart from the special cases already referred to where compensation is confined to the value of the site (plus one or other of the additional allowances where appropriate[3]) compensation for other land or buildings acquired under the Housing Act 1957, Parts III[4] or V[5] is assessed according to the general code of compensation in operation at the date of service of the notice to treat[6] or, in the case of an obstructive building,[7] the date of the offer. However, in so far as compensation is based upon rent[8] and the actual rent reflects an enhancement due to the use of the premises for illegal[9] purposes or to overcrowding,[10] compensation is to be based upon the rent which would have been

---

[1] Housing Act 1957, s. 56; and see note 4, p. 260, *supra*.

[2] An adaptation of the Town and Country Planning Act 1959, Sch. 2, which in turn replaced the Town and Country Planning Act 1944, Sch. 5. See note 2, p. 257, *supra*.

[3] See pp. 262, *et seq*, *infra*.

[4] E.g., land and buildings outside a clearance area required for the satisfactory redevelopment of the area; land and buildings within a redevelopment area other than unfit houses; obstructive buildings, etc.; see pp. 261, *et seq*, *infra*, and the next note.

[5] I.e., land required for the provision of new houses, other than that acquired under Part III for the rehousing of persons displaced from a redevelopment area: Housing Act 1957, s. 57(1).

[6] Note that, although the date of notice to treat is no longer the crucial date for the assessment of compensation (p. 165 *et seq*, *ante*, and see note 1, p. 259, *supra*), legislative changes in the code of compensation have invariably been enacted to take effect in respect of compulsory acquisitions in pursuance of which notice to treat is served on or after either the coming into force of the enactment or some other date therein specified, e.g., in the case of the Community Land Act 1975, the Second Appointed Day: *ibid*, s. 25(1)(a), p. 305, *et seq*, *post*.

[7] P. 260, *supra*.

[8] Since the market value of investment property reflects the return obtainable it will normally equate with a capitalisation of rent (if let at a rack-rent). As the long-term provisions of the Community Land Act 1975 take effect and local authorities become monopoly buyers in the greater part of the property market, capitalisation of market rent is likely, of necessity, to become an increasingly common basis of valuation. See pp. 27 *et seq*, *ante*.

[9] Cf. the Land Compensation Act 1961, s. 5(4) (Rule 4 of the "1919 Rules"), p. 164 and 179, *ante*.

[10] For definition of "overcrowding" see the Housing Act 1957, (Part IV), s. 77.

obtained had the use been legal or had the premises not been over-crowded.[1]

8 Allowance[2] for well-maintained houses

Although, as has already been suggested, the site value basis of compensation referred to in earlier sections of this chapter may be justified on the assumption that, as a house, one that is unfit for human habitation can theoretically have no value, there is also a social aspect. Before the war of 1939–45 "slum" conditions were largely attributed, in some cases no doubt unjustly, to the avarice of landlords intent upon maintaining the highest possible rent from the maximum number of tenants in return for the minimum outlay in repairs and improvements. Consequently Parliament displayed small inclination to be generous in the matter of compensation where such property was acquired as unfit for human habitation solely for the purpose of demolition in the interests of sanitation, the tenants being left to be rehoused at public expense.

It was probably these considerations which first led to the idea that the landlord who, despite the unsatisfactory layout and amenities of his property, at least tried to maintain it in a decent state of repair, deserved more generous treatment. Special provision has accordingly been made for extra compensation to be paid in respect of houses acquired as unfit for human habitation, but well maintained. The relevant provisions are contained in the Housing Act 1957, s. 30, as regards houses acquired under Part II of the Act and in s. 60 as regards houses acquired under Part III. The former, however, has now been extended, first to include the owner of unfit houses acquired for the provision of temporary accommodation,[3] and secondly to dispel the previously existing doubt as to whether a well-maintained allowance was claimable in respect of a house listed, or considered for listing, as a building of special architectural or historic interest.[4] A third extension provides for the allowance to be paid where houses have only been partially well maintained.[5]

The amount of the well-maintained allowance is now to be assessed in accordance with the provisions of the Housing Act 1969.[6] Under the Housing Act 1957, s. 30, any person may, within three months of the service of the demolition order or notice of intention to purchase under

---

[1] Housing Act 1957, Sch. 3, Part III, para. 1. Note that *ibid*, para. 2, contained provisions whereby compensation for premises in a defective state of sanitation or repair was to be the value of the premises with the defects remedied less the cost of doing so. Since the value in the market is likely to reflect such costs the return to market value as the basis of compensation rendered this provision unnecessary, and by virtue of the Town and Country Planning Act 1959, Sch. 2, para. 4 it ceased to have effect in relation to acquisitions pursuant to notices to treat served after 30 October 1958. Similarly, the provisions of the Housing Act 1957, Sch. 3, Part III, para. 4, providing for any increase in the value of other property in the same ownership being offset against the compensation payable for the land acquired has been overtaken by the Land Compensation Act 1961, s. 7: see pp. 217, *et seq*, *ante*.

[2] These "allowances" are referred to throughout the Housing Act as well-maintained *payments*: the word allowance however avoids constant reference to payment of payments, payments payable, etc., and seems equally apposite.

[3] I.e., acquisition under the Housing Act 1957, s. 12.

[4] Housing Act 1969, s. 65.

[5] *Ibid*, s. 67, p. 264, *infra*.

[6] *Ibid*, Sch. 4, replacing the Housing Act 1957, Sch. 2, Part I.

Part II of that Act, represent to the local authority that the house has been well maintained; and that its good maintenance is attributable wholly or partly to work carried out at his expense. In the event of disagreement by the local authority "any person aggrieved" may appeal to the county court, or the parties, by mutual agreement in writing, may submit the matter to arbitration.

Under s. 60 the procedure is somewhat different. Pending the abolition of clearance orders[1] it is the Secretary of State who, upon a report submitted to him by one of his inspectors, decides whether or not the house is well maintained, the local authority being responsible for any payment authorised. Once clearance orders are abolished this procedure will be somewhat modified so as to place the initiative in the hands of the local housing authority,[2] who will be required to notify all those with an interest in the house—i.e., owners, lessees, mortgagees and occupiers—whether it considers the house (or individual dwelling within a house in multi-occupation or partly used for other purposes, etc.[3]) to have been well maintained.[4] Where, however, the local authority is not satisfied that a well-maintained allowance is justified it must state its reasons[5] and an appeal continues to lie to the Secretary of State, who continues to decide upon the report of a person required by him to carry out an inspection.[6]

The basis of the well-maintained allowance is rateable value.[7] Originally based upon net annual value,[8] a higher multiplier was employed where the claimant was the owner-occupier.[9] This special weighting in the latter's favour is now abolished.[10]

There remains, however, a limit: total compensation, i.e., site value plus well-maintained allowance, cannot exceed the "full" value of the house—i.e., the compensation that would have been payable if the house had not been declared unfit for human habitation.[11]

---

[1] Housing Act 1974, s. 108(1): see note 1, p. 260, *supra*.

[2] Housing Act 1957, s. 60, as amended by the Housing Act 1974, s. 108(2), and Sch. 9.

[3] See the heading "Allowances for partially well-maintained houses", *infra*.

[4] Or well-maintained externally but not internally, or vice versa: see p. 264 *et seq, infra*.

[5] Housing Act 1957 (as amended, see note 2, *supra*) s. 60 (1B.).

[6] *Ibid*, sub-s. 1D.

[7] Originally fixed at four times the rateable value or such other multiplier as the Secretary of State may by order prescribe: Housing Act 1969, Sch.4, para. 1(1). The current multiplier takes account of the subsequent revaluation and is 3⅛: Housing (Payments for Well-Maintained Houses) Order 1973, (SI 1973 No. 753).

[8] Housing Act 1957, Sch. 2, para. 3(2).

[9] Housing Act 1957, Sch. 2, para. 3(1); the concept of special treatment of the owner-occupier stemmed from provisions of the Slum Clearance (Compensation) Act 1956, designed to remedy some of the hardships resulting from the high price commanded for vacant possession of even the most indifferent houses as a consequence of the post-war housing shortage. If and when such houses were eventually compulsorily acquired at site value, people who had purchased with vacant possession since the outbreak of war, for their own occupation or that of their families, stood to lose very considerable sums. The Rent Acts, drastically extended by the Rent and Mortgage Interest Restrictions Act of 1939, at least ensured that no one was likely to pay inflated prices simply for letting as an investment. The Act of 1956 was accordingly aimed solely at relieving the position of the owner-occupier who had purchased since 1939. It did so in part by weighting the well-maintained allowance in favour of the owner-occupier.

[10] Housing Act 1969, Sch. 4, which inserts in the Housing Act 1957 a new Sch. 2 in place of the original: also abolished by this amendment is the provision of *ibid*, Sch. 2, para. 2, whereby if expenditure on maintenance during the previous five years exceeded annual value multiplied by the appropriate multiplier the well-maintained allowance was to be increased accordingly.

[11] Housing Act 1969, Sch. 4, para. 1(2).

9 Allowances for partially well-maintained houses

Under the Housing Act 1957 the criterion for determining whether a claimant qualified for a well-maintained allowance was the condition of the whole house. In the case of rented property where the landlord retained responsibility for external decoration as well as structural repairs and had done everything he reasonably could to fulfil his obligations, no well-maintained allowance was payable if his tenant had neglected the interior: similarly where the tenant's efforts to maintain the interior were frustrated by neglect by the landlord in maintaining the exterior. In such cases the party who has fulfilled his obligations in this regard may now[1] claim an amount equal to half the full well-maintained allowance.[2] Although the different responsibilities of landlord and tenant and the frequent cases in which the one fulfils his obligations while the other does not no doubt constitute the *raison d'être* of these provisions,[3] it is not a prerequisite that the responsibility for exterior and interior maintenance be divided; in other words, the reduced allowance is payable if either the exterior or interior (though not both) is well maintained, even though the responsibility rests with the same person, e.g., the owner-occupier.

Although the application of these provisions is straightforward enough in the case of a house in single occupation, difficulties clearly arise where an unfit house comprises more than one dwelling (e.g., separate flats) or is occupied partly as a dwelling or dwellings and partly for other purposes (e.g., a business). To meet these difficulties each dwelling is deemed to be a house[4] and the expression "exterior" is defined so as to include any part of the house not included in the interior of a dwelling. Thus for this purpose, communal staircases, lobbies, passages, etc. will be part of the exterior; so also will any part of the building occupied for non-residential purposes. Accordingly, if part of the building is used as a shop it will be necessary for the shop premises as well as the communal parts of the building and its exterior, as normally understood, all to be well maintained if a partial well-maintained allowance in respect of the exterior is to be payable,[5] a provision which may still leave a landlord's claim dependent upon the standard of maintenance achieved by his tenants (if any) of the non-residential parts of the building.

On the other hand, of course, if a flat within the building is occupied by the owner thereof and is well maintained, his neglect of other parts of the building will not prevent him receiving a partial well-maintained allowance in respect of his flat even though that neglect has been greatly to the detriment of tenants occupying other dwellings within the same building.

Where, in the case of several claims in respect of buildings in multi-occupation or multi-purpose occupation, the whole building or several

---

[1] By virtue of the Housing Act 1969, s. 67.
[2] I.e., currently $1\frac{9}{16}$ times the rateable value: *ibid*, Sch. 4, para. 1(1), and note 7, p. 263, *supra*.
[3] See Ministry of Housing and Local Government Circular 68/69, para. 8.
[4] Housing Act 1969, s. 67(1).
[5] *Ibid*, s. 67(2).

parts thereof appear as a single hereditament in the current valuation list it will, of course, be necessary to apportion the rateable value. Provision for such apportionment—or where necessary aggregation—of rateable values is accordingly made,[1] any dispute being referred for determination to the Valuation Officer.[2]

10 Owner-Occupier's allowances: qualifications

These allowances stem originally from the Slum Clearance (Compensation) Act 1956.[3] They applied to both private dwellings and business premises in owner-occupation. Designed to meet what were regarded as temporary problems arising from the post-war housing shortage, the allowances in respect of private dwellings were confined to purchases or demolitions on or before 13 December 1965.[4]

In a modified form they have, however, become a permanent feature of the code of compensation applicable to the compulsory acquisition of unfit houses.[5]

(i) PRIVATE DWELLINGS

The current code[6] is applicable to houses[7] purchased at site value as a result of action taken by the acquiring authority after 23 April 1968.[8] The acquisition must be authorised by a compulsory purchase order under the Housing Act 1957, Part II or III, and in the cases to which the Land Compensation Act 1961[9] applies the local authority must make an unfitness order;[9] or the house must have been vacated in pursuance of a demolition[10] or a closing[11] order. Finally, there must have been owner-occupation,[12] although not necessarily by the same person or family, for a period of not less than two years prior to the local authority's action.

Thus the only owner-occupier who will not be able to claim this

---

[1] Housing Act 1969, Sch. 4, para. 3(1).

[2] As defined by reference to the General Rate Act 1967: *ibid*, para. 3(2).

[3] See note 9, p. 263, *supra*.

[4] I.e., 10 years after the date on which the Parliamentary Bill was presented to Parliament. In the case of houses purchased by owner-occupiers between 13 December 1950 and 13 December 1955 this period was subsequently extended to 15 years from the date of such purchase—i.e., to expire in all cases by 13 December 1970: Housing (Slum Clearance Compensation) Act 1965, s. 1.

[5] Housing Act 1969, s. 68 and Sch. 5.

[6] *Ibid*, Sch. 5, paras. 1–3.

[7] "House" includes any building constructed or adapted wholly or partly as, or for the purpose of, a dwelling: Housing Act 1969, Sch. 5, para. 5(2).

[8] *Ibid*, para. 5.

[9] I.e., under the Land Compensation Act 1961, Sch. 2, para. 2, as to which see note 2, p. 257, *supra*.

[10] Under the Housing Act 1957, Part II: a payment will also be payable under these provisions in respect of a house vacated and demolished in pursuance of an undertaking for its demolition given to the local authority, notwithstanding that no demolition order has in fact been made: Housing Act 1969, Sch. 5, para. 5(3).

[11] Under the Housing Act 1957, s. 17.

[12] An owner-occupier for this purpose is one who by right of an interest in the house (other than one of a year or less or one by which a right to possession depends solely upon the Rent Acts) is either in occupation thereof himself as a private dwelling or permits a member of his family to occupy it as a private dwelling: Housing Act 1969, Sch. 5, para. 1(1). His family includes a wife or husband, a son or daughter, a son or daughter-in-law, a stepson or daughter and parents and parents-in-law: *ibid*, s. 86(2) and Sch. 6, para. 2.

special owner-occupier's allowance in respect of the compulsory acquisition of a house condemned as unfit for human habitation will be an owner-occupier who has not been in occupation for a full two years prior to the local authority's action, and whose immediate predecessor in title was not an owner-occupier whose period of occupancy aggregated with his own totalled a minimum of two years at the relevant date.[1]

Subject to the above, there must be continuous occupation. Thus in *Reeve* v *Hartlepool Borough Council*[2] six houses had been sold by owner-occupiers. The purchasers all intended to go into occupation but did not do so immediately. In each case a void period had been allowed by the rating authority although some of the purchasers had gone into possession to redecorate and renovate. It was held that since the Act required occupation as a private dwelling *throughout* the qualifying period, breaks of this nature were fatal to the claims for owner-occupiers' allowances.

On the other hand it is not necessary that successive occupiers hold the same proprietary interests.[3] Nor is it necessary for the owner to have occupied the whole house throughout the period, provided the rest of the house is occupied as a private dwelling. Thus in *Hunter* v *Manchester City Council*[4] an owner-occupier, on learning of the proposal to include his house in a clearance area, bought another house, moved his family into it, continued to sleep in one of the upstairs rooms and let the ground floor to a tenant. It was held that since the whole house was still used "as a private dwelling"[5] there was no ground for the Lands Tribunal decision to reduce the owner-occupation allowance, i.e., the full value of the house less the site value.[6]

It was also held[7] that "the over-riding intent of the Act is not that an owner-occupier should only be compensated in respect of his own personal occupation of the house and not for parts which he lets off to tenants, but to mitigate hardship to those persons who have been

[1] In relation to any house purchased or vacated, "the relevant date" and "the authority concerned" mean respectively:
   (a) if the house was vacated in pursuance of a demolition order or closing order, the date when, and the authority by whom, the order was made;
   (b) if the house was declared unfit for human habitation by an order under the Land Compensation Act 1961, Sch. 2, para. 2, the date when the order was made and the acquiring authority within the meaning of the Act;
   (c) if the house was purchased compulsorily under the Act of 1957, s. 12, the date when and the authority by whom, the notice mentioned in that section was served;
   (d) if the house was purchased compulsorily in pursuance of a notice served under the Act of 1957, s. 19, the date when and the authority by whom the notice was served;
   (e) if the house was comprised in an area declared to be a clearance area, the date when and the authority by whom the area was so declared;
and "the qualifying period" means the period of two years ending with the relevant date, except that where that date is earlier than 22 April 1970, it means the period beginning with 23 April 1968 and ending with the relevant date: Housing Act 1969, Sch. 5, para. 5.
[2] (1975) 30 P & CR 517. Note that in this case none of the claimants was able to rely on the Housing Act 1969, Sch. 5, para. 1(2): p. 268, *infra*.
[3] *Robson & Wood* v *Teesside County Borough Council*, [1974] JPL 365.
[4] (1975) 30 P & CR 58.
[5] See Housing Act 1969, Sch. 5, para. 3(1).
[6] See p. 268–269, *infra*.
[7] Per Curiam, 30 P & CR 517.

driven by the shortage of housing to buy unsound and substandard dwellings to live in themselves".

Scarman LJ appears to have gone somewhat further when he said[1] that "from the moment when a house is declared as being within a clearance area it appears reasonable that an owner-occupier—almost certainly a family man—should be looking around for accommodation and should have a reasonable expectation that part of the capital needed for his alternative accommodation will come from the compensation for the loss of the house which sooner or later he is going to be compelled by law to vacate. Paragraph 3 of Schedule 5 does no more than ensure that someone who has qualified for compensation is not going to be permitted to make a profit out of his situation".

The implication appears to be that Mr. Hunter would have been held entitled to the full allowance even if he himself had not remained in occupation. He would clearly have retained an owner-occupier's interest[2] in the part of the house he retained, but if the tenant occupied the greater part of the house it is a little difficult to see how it could have been said to be occupied by Mr. Hunter in the right of an owner's interest at the relevant date[3] (i.e., the date on which the area was declared to be a clearance area).[2]

It seems, moreover, that in assessing the full owner-occupier's supplement awarded, the house was valued on a vacant possession basis. The issue before the court, however, was solely the effect on the owner-occupier's allowance of partial occupation, and not whether the tenancy affected the valuation of the house. There is ample authority for the proposition that in such cases (assuming, as appears to have been the case, that Mr. Hunter's tenant was in occupation at the relevant date or had been rehoused by the acquiring authority) the proper basis of valuation is "tenanted" value.[4]

Furthermore, the implication of the Court of Appeal's interpretation of the over-riding intent of the Act would seem to be that their decision would have been the same even if Mr. Hunter had let part of his house throughout the qualifying period. That a permanent letting[5] of part of a house would not deprive the owner, in occupation of another part, of his owner-occupier's allowance certainly appears to conform with a literal interpretation of the statutory provisions. The intention may well have been to confine the payment of the allowance to cases in which the house was occupied "as a private dwelling" in the singular: but since, in

---

[1] [1975] 2 All ER at p. 969.

[2] *Supra.*

[3] See *Babij*'s case, note 4, *infra.*

[4] See p. 170, *ante*, and the cases cited in note 3 thereon. See also *Babij v Metropolitan Borough of Rochdale*, [1976] JPL 701, in which it was held that compensation fell to be assessed on the basis of "tenanted value" even though the tenant had only been let in by the former owner-occupiers (who had, as in Hunter's case, *supra*, moved to a new house in anticipation of the compulsory acquisition) solely to prevent vandalism. The owner-occupier's supplement was reduced accordingly. This case can, of course, be distinguished from *Hunter*'s case in that no part of the house was retained in the owner's occupation.

[5] A series of short lettings of several different parts of a house would almost certainly constitute a business and deprive the house of its status as a "private dwelling": such a business does not, however, enable the owner to qualify for the owner-occupier's allowance payable in respect of business premises: see note 7, p. 269, *infra.*

the interpretation of statutes,[1] the singular includes the plural, the division of the house by letting, into several "dwellings" would not appear to affect the position.[2] Nevertheless payment of the allowance to a person occupying but a single room in a large house and letting the remainder would certainly contravene the basic purpose of these allowances. Some distinction therefore needs to be made. But unless it is to be assumed that only lettings in anticipation of compulsory acquisition, as in *Hunter*'s case, are to be ignored, as Scarman LJ seemed to suggest, it is difficult to see where else the line can be drawn.

Cases can obviously arise in which, at the date of the local authority's action, the house is vacant pending sale, the owner having died or having had to give up occupation and move elsewhere owing, for example, to a change of employment. In such cases, since he or his personal representatives retain an owner-occupier's interest at the relevant date the allowance is claimable. Similarly, special provision is made where the two-year period has been broken because the owner has had to move elsewhere purely temporarily (e.g., a member of H.M. Forces posted abroad) and has every intention of resuming occupation even although he has let the house in the meantime and a tenant is in occupation at the relevant date.[3]   On the other hand, if the last occupant of a vacant house was a tenant, the landlord's right to possession cannot, of course, qualify him for an owner-occupier's allowance.

The reason for this two-year minimum qualifying period is said to be to prevent last-minute collusive sales by slum landlords to sitting tenants in order to obtain the extra compensation. Nevertheless, cases inevitably occur where a sale to a sitting tenant takes place in good faith with neither landlord nor tenant having any reason to anticipate action by the local authority within the two-year or any other period. In such cases, provided he qualifies in all other respects, the purchaser will be entitled to the owner-occupier's allowance, notwithstanding action by the local authority within two years of his purchase provided the latter are satisfied that, prior to his purchase, he made all reasonable enquiries as to the possibility of local authority action within the two-year period, and had no reason to believe such action was likely; and this applies to any purchaser whether or not he was the previous tenant.[4]

Amount of owner-occupier's allowance

The amount of the owner-occupier's allowance is a sum equivalent to

---

[1] Interpretation Act 1889, s. 1.

[2] Note, however, that "The use as two or more separate dwelling-houses of any building previously used as a single dwelling-house involves a material change in the use of the building, and of each part thereof": Town and Country Planning Act 1971, s. 22(3)(b). Since such use, if embarked upon without planning permission, is therefore restrainable by law, it would be open to acquiring authorities in such cases to pray in aid Rule 4 (p. 179, *ante*). It is doubtful, however, whether the "restrainable" use would in practice have added to the market value of the property (and therefore to the amount of the owner-occupier's allowance: *infra*) in the particular circumstances of Hunter's case; it may also be open to doubt whether his occupation of a single room constitutes "use as a separate dwelling-house" if, as seems likely, he was in occupation of his new house for all purposes other than sleeping.

[3] Provided the total period of absence within the two-year qualifying period does not exceed one year: Housing Act 1969, Sch. 5, para. 1(3).

[4] *Ibid*, para. 1(2).

the difference between the site value and the full compulsory purchase value,[1] i.e., total compensation will be the same as if the site value provisions of the Housing Act 1957 did not apply.

Since total compensation cannot exceed the "full" market value[2] it follows, of course, that where an owner-occupier's allowance is payable there can be no entitlement to a full well-maintained allowance unless the former allowance is payable in respect of only part of the house.[3] In that case a well-maintained allowance may be payable in respect of other parts of the house.[3] Similarly, a person who has already received either allowance following a closing order cannot obtain any second payment if the house is subsequently made the subject of a demolition order.[4]

Where any part of the house is not used as a private dwelling a deduction is to be made, in respect of such non-residential part, from the "additional compensation" payable.[5] In case of disagreement as to the amount payable, the question is to be determined by the Lands Tribunal in the same way as other matters of compensation under the Act of 1957.[6]

(ii) BUSINESS PREMISES

As in the case of private dwellings, the owner-occupier's allowance available in respect of houses which are occupied wholly or in part for the purpose of a business[7] stems from the Slum Clearance (Compensation) Act 1956. However, in the case of such houses the "occupancy" qualification was that the person entitled to the receipts of the business must have held an interest[8] in the premises either on 13 December 1955 or continuously during the ten years preceding the making of the order.[9] There being therefore no final time limit[10] and no indefinite reference to the state of affairs on 13 December 1955 there was no change of principle in perpetuating these allowances, and only one significant change in the Housing Act 1969 was required to bring these allowances wholly into line with those now applicable to houses occupied as such, i.e., as private dwellings. The ten-year qualifying period is accordingly reduced to two years[11] and "owner occupiers" of

---

[1] Housing Act 1957, Sch. 2, Part II, para. 4(4).
[2] Housing Act 1969, Sch. 4, para. 1(2).
[3] *Ibid*, Sch. 4, para. 1(3), and see particularly pp. 264, *et seq, supra*.
[4] *Ibid*, Sch. 5, para. 5(4).
[5] Housing Act 1957, Sch. 2, Part II, para. 4(4).
[6] *Ibid*, para. 4(5), and Lands Tribunal Act 1949.
[7] "Business" does not include the letting of accommodation whether with or without service: Housing Act 1957, Sch. 2, Part II, para. 6(5).
[8] See note 9, p. 263, *supra*.
[9] Housing Act 1957, Sch. 2, Part II, para. 6(2).
[10] In so far as the "occupier" of a house used for business purposes was permanently provided for he was treated rather more generously than the owner-occupier of a private dwelling. It should, however, be borne in mind that neither the argument that condemnation of a house as unfit for human habitation eliminates its value, nor the social considerations which arise from the use of such premises as a private dwelling are particularly apposite, where the house is in fact used for some other purpose.
[11] Housing Act 1969, s. 68(2), Sch. 6, Para. 3.

unfit houses used for business premises are now treated in exactly the same way as owner-occupiers of dwellings.

Since, however, the requisite qualification is that "the person entitled to the receipts of the business holds an interest in the house"[1] difficulties may arise where the business is carried on as a private limited company. Thus in *Marzell* v *Greater London Council*[2] a business was transferred (some time before the compulsory purchase order was made) to such a company jointly owned by a husband and wife. But as the wife had no interest in the house it was held that no "owner-occupier's" allowance was payable.

The amount of the allowance is assessed on the same basis, viz the difference between site value and "full value" and is subject to a proportionate reduction in respect of any part of the house not used for the purpose of the business.[3]

11 Repayment of allowances

Where a house is vacated in response to a demolition order[4] the local authority does not necessarily acquire any interest therein. Nevertheless, a well-maintained or owner-occupier's allowance may be payable. Similarly, if a leasehold interest in a house the subject of a closing order is acquired, a well-maintained allowance may be payable to the freeholder. Under various provisions of the Housing Acts of 1957 and 1969, however, local authorities have power to renovate such houses, make them fit for human habitation (in whole or in part) and revoke the demolition order[5] or determine (or modify) the closing order.[6] In such circumstances allowances paid to persons still retaining an interest[7] in the house may be recovered, as to the whole where the whole house (or dwelling) in respect of which the allowance was paid is rendered fit for human habitation[8] or as to an appropriate proportion where a part of the house, e.g., a basement, remains unfit and subject to a closing order.[9]

12 Discretionary payments to persons displaced under the Housing Act 1957

In addition to the mandatory payments already considered, the Housing Act 1957 contained, in each Part which embodies powers of acquisition, sections which conferred upon local authorities wide powers to make purely discretionary payments to persons affected.[10] With one exception these provisions are repealed[11] and are replaced by the

---

[1] Housing Act 1957, Sch. 2, Part II, para. 6.
[2] (1975) 30 P & CR 259.
[3] Housing Act 1957, Sch. 2, Part II, para. 6(3).
[4] Or, prior to 1969, a clearance order: see note 1, p. 260, *supra*.
[5] Under the Housing Act 1957, s. 24.
[6] Under *ibid*, s. 27(2).
[7] Allowances paid to persons having an interest of less than a year or to statutory tenants are not recoverable.
[8] Housing Act 1969, s. 69.
[9] Local Government (Miscellaneous Provisions) Act 1976, s. 10.
[10] Housing Act 1957, ss. 32, 63 and 100.
[11] By the Land Compensation Act 1973, Sch. 3.

mandatory provisions of Part III of the Land Compensation Act 1973[1] covering much the same ground. The exception[2] relates to the damage that may be inflicted upon retail traders where the clearance of residential property results in a "material" decrease in the population of the locality. In such circumstances local authorities are empowered to pay to any person carrying on a retail shop in a locality affected by any action taken in connection with clearance areas "such reasonable allowance as they think fit towards any loss involving personal hardship which in their opinion he will thereby sustain, but in estimating any such loss they shall have regard to the probable future development of the locality".[3]

13 Summary of provisions governing compensation for unfit houses

1. The responsibility for declaring houses as unfit for human habitation rests with the local housing authority.[4] Under Part II of the Housing Act 1957[5] it may (subject to the owner's right of appeal to the county court or to undertake to make good the defects[6]) acquire the house compulsorily. If it takes action under Part III of that Act[7] the final decision as to fitness rests with the Secretary of State,[8] as it does where the acquisition is one to which the Land Compensation Act 1961, Schedule 11, para. 2(1) applies,[9] in which case the local housing authority's order requires the Secretary of State's confirmation.[10]

2. Once it has been determined that the house is unfit for human habitation compensation is to be the market value of the cleared site assessed in the normal way.[11]

3. Subject to the total compensation payable not exceeding the full market value of the house as it stands,[12] the following additional payments or allowances may be payable:

(i) In the case of a house subject to a demolition order and demolished by the local authority in default of action by the owner, the value of any salvaged materials in so far as it exceeds the cost of demolition;[13]

---

[1] As to which see Compensation for Disturbance, Chap. 9, pp. 372, et seq.

[2] Housing Act 1957, s. 63(2).

[3] Note, however, that in assessing compensation for business premises *acquired* as part of the scheme of clearance and redevelopment, changes in population consequent upon the scheme will be ignored: *aliter* if the premises merely adjoin the clearance area and are acquired for some other reason: see *Bowling v Leeds County Borough Council* (1974), 27 P & CR 531.

[4] Referred to in the Land Compensation Act 1961, Sch. 2, as the "appropriate local authority" and defined as "the local authority who, in relation to the area in which the land is situate, are a local authority for the purposes of the provisions of Part III of the Act of 1957 relating to clearance areas".

[5] P. 258, *supra*.

[6] Housing Act 1957, s. 10, p. 258, *supra*.

[7] P. 259, *supra*.

[8] P. 79, *ante* and 257, *supra*.

[9] P. 257 *supra*, and N.B. note 2 thereon.

[10] Land Compensation Act 1961, Sch. 2, para. 2(2).

[11] P. 256, note 4 *supra*, and Chap. 5, p. 158, *ante*.

[12] Housing Act 1969, Sch. 5, para. 1(2), p. 263, note 2, *supra*.

[13] Housing Act 1957, s. 23 (p. 260, *supra*) but note that in so far as the cost of demolition is not covered by the value of materials salvaged the owner is liable therefor: *ibid*.

(ii)   A well-maintained allowance equivalent to $3\frac{1}{8}$ times the rateable value.[1] Except in the case of an acquisition under the Housing Act 1957, Part III, if there is disagreement between the local authority and the owner the latter may appeal to the county court or the parties may agree to arbitration.[2] In the case of an acquisition under the Housing Act 1957, Part III, as in acquisitions to which the Land Compensation Act 1961 applies, the final arbiter is the Secretary of State.[3]

(iii)   A partially well-maintained allowance where either the exterior[4] or the interior of the house, but not both,[5] has been well maintained. This allowance is half the full well-maintained allowance.[4]

(iv)   An owner-occupier's allowance payable both in respect of houses occupied as such[6] and houses occupied wholly or in part for business purposes.[7] In either case there must have been owner-occupation[8] (though not necessarily by the same owner or family) for the whole of the two years immediately preceding the relevant date.[9] The allowance is equivalent to the difference between site value and full market value;[10] i.e., compensation will be assessed on the normal basis of the market value of the property as it stands and as if the house were fit for human habitation and the site value basis was therefore inapplicable.

4. Both owner-occupier and tenant may also be entitled to compensation for disturbance.[11]

5. It follows that where the claimant is an owner-occupier he obtains the maximum compensation payable: he cannot also claim either a full or a partial well-maintained allowance; nor is he entitled to any payment in respect of salvaged materials.

6. Where the owner-occupier is a lessee, compensation will be the full market value of his interest (i.e., of the unexpired portion of his lease). The freeholder may therefore, if responsible for the maintenance of the exterior of the house under the terms of the lease, be entitled to a partial well-maintained allowance as well as any excess of the value of salvaged materials over the cost of demolition—subject to his total compensation not exceeding the value of his interest in the reversion.

---

[1] See note 7, p. 263, *supra*.

[2] Housing Act 1957, p. 258, *supra*.

[3] In the former case only if there is an appeal. In the latter in his capacity as confirming authority: pp. 257, *et seq*, *supra*.

[4] Housing Act 1969, s. 67, p. 264, *supra*.

[5] See, however, para. 6 of the text, *infra*, and p. 264, *supra*.

[6] Housing Act 1969, s. 68, and Sch. 5, p. 265, *et seq*, *supra*.

[7] *Ibid*, p. 269, *supra*.

[8] *Ibid*, pp. 265, *et seq*, and 269, *et seq*, *supra*.

[9] See note 1, *p*. 268, *supra*.

[10] Housing Act 1969, Sch. 5, para. 2. But if any other part of the house is occupied for purposes other than that of the private dwelling (*ibid*, para. 3(1)) or the business which gave rise to the claim (Housing Act 1957, Sch. 2, para. 6(3)) as the case may be, at the date of the making of the compulsory purchase, demolition or closing order or order under the Land Compensation Act 1961, the allowance must be reduced by the amount, if any, attributable to that other part of the house.

[11] See generally Chap. 9, p. 344, *post*, and particularly the Land Compensation Act 1973, Part III, pp. 372, *et seq*, *post*.

Similarly, where the occupier is a tenant responsible for internal maintenance both he and his landlord may be entitled to a partially well-maintained allowance.[1]

5 MINERALS

The general rule is that since "development" for the purposes of the Town and Country Planning Acts includes mining operations in, on or under land,[2] the compensation payable upon the acquisition of mineral-bearing land will depend upon whether there is planning permission for working the minerals and the conditions, if any, attached thereto or, in the absence of any planning permission, whether any such permission is to be assumed.[3]

The Coal Act 1938 provided for the acquisition by the Coal Commission of the fee simple in coal and mines of coal—now vested in the National Coal Board.[4] Since 1938, therefore, with few exceptions, coal or coal mines cannot be the subject of acquisition unless specifically authorised by Parliament.[5]

A compulsory purchase order made in accordance with the Acquisition of Land (Authorisation Procedure) Act[6] may however provide for the incorporation of the Railways Clauses Consolidation Act 1845, s. 77 and ss. 78–85.[6] The incorporation of the former section allows the acquisition of the surface[7] of mineral-bearing land only, so that unless the "ironstone, slate or other minerals"[8] are expressly purchased,[9] the acquiring authority can only work the minerals in so far as it is necessary for it to do so in the course of constructing the works for which the land is acquired.

Where ss. 77–85 of the Railways Act 1845 are incorporated the owner or lessee is entitled to work[10] the minerals lying under the land acquired, or within 40 yards therefrom, or to receive compensation if the acquiring authority is of the opinion that such workings would be detrimental to the works or buildings for which the land is required. In

[1] Pp. 264, et seq, supra.
[2] Town and Country Planning Act 1971, s. 22(1).
[3] Pp. 185, et seq, ante.
[4] Coal Industry Nationalisation Act 1946, which vested in the National Coal Board the interests of the Coal Commission and of "colliery concerns"; the latter does not include the interests of the "free miners" of the Forest of Dean.
[5] Coal Act 1938, s. 17.
[6] Acquisition of Land (Authorisation Procedure) Act 1946, s. 1(3) and Sch. 2, para. 7.
[7] I.e., contrary to the general rule that the surface cannot be acquired as a separate entity.
[8] The meaning of "other minerals" in this context is not the same as the definition of minerals for the purposes of the Town and Country Planning Acts: see the Act of 1971, s. 290(1). On the contrary, it is for the Courts to determine in the light of current usage in the mining and commercial world; thus in particular cases limestone has been held to be a mineral but not sandstone; brick clay and china clay but not the ordinary clay commonly found in the soil or subsoil.
[9] The incorporation of this section does not prevent compulsory acquisition of the minerals and they may be the subject of a subsequent purchase: Errington v Metropolitan District Rly Co (1882), 19 Ch.D 559.
[10] Subject to liability for any damage caused by improper working.

such cases it seems that compensation is to be assessed in the same manner as compensation for injurious affection where no land is taken.[1]

6 BUILDINGS OF SPECIAL ARCHITECTURAL OR HISTORICAL INTEREST

The fact that a building is listed as of special architectural or historical interest does not in itself affect the code of compensation applicable upon a compulsory acquisition: the market value basis of assessment is affected only in so far as the restrictions upon exterior alterations reduce, or the prospects of obtaining planning permission for such alterations or even demolition increase, market value. In this connection, however, it is important to appreciate that external alterations to, or extension or demolition of a listed building normally requires "listed building consent"[2] as well as planning permission for the work involved. Only where planning permission expressly authorises and describes the works for the alteration or extension of the building does it operate as listed building consent.[3] Nevertheless, in assessing compensation upon the compulsory acquisition of a listed building it is to be assumed that listed building consent would be granted for its alteration or extension,[4] except in so far as a refusal or conditional grant of listed building consent has already given rise to a claim for compensation.[5] This is the case where listed building consent for work which would not constitute development or in respect of which planning permission is granted by a development order is refused or granted conditionally by the Secretary of State.[6] In other cases where a listed building is compulsorily acquired it is treated for compensation purposes as if it had not been listed, subject to the proviso that it cannot be demolished without consent.

Compensation where a listed building is deliberately neglected

To the general rule outlined above there is, however, an important exception. This occurs where local authorities exercise their special powers of acquisition available as a safeguard against an owner's neglect of an important building. The significance of listing a building is, of course, that it is regarded as prima facie worthy of preservation: the objective is to ensure (by requiring the owner to apply for listed

[1] I.e., under the Lands Clauses Consolidation Act 1845, s. 68 or the Compulsory Purchase Act 1965, s. 10, pp. 321, *et seq, post.*

[2] I.e., the consent of either the local planning authority or the Secretary of State upon the application of the owner under the Town and Country Planning Act 1971, s. 55.

[3] Town and Country Planning Act 1971, s. 56(2).

[4] But not for its demolition other than demolition with a view to rebuilding etc. included in the developments of *ibid*, Sch. 8: *ibid*, s. 116 as amended by the Town and Country Amenities Act 1974, s. 6: for the assumption of planning permission for such "existing use" developments see pp. 194, *et seq, ante,* and Appendix p. 456, *post.*

[5] Town and Country Planning Act 1971, s. 116. For compensation for refusal or conditional grant of consent see pp. 424, *et seq, post.*

[6] I.e., either upon appeal or upon reference of the application to him: *ibid.* Note, therefore, that a refusal or conditional grant of listed building consent by the local planning authority unconfirmed by the Secretary of State does not give rise to any claim to compensation.

building consent for any alteration to, or extension or demolition of the building) that full consideration is given to the merits and importance of the building, on the one hand, and the practicability of preservation, on the other, before demolition or any change in character is permitted.

Where, however, preservation of such a building is threatened by sheer neglect and there is therefore no question of the future of the building being considered by the local planning authority in pursuance of an application for listed building consent, special provisions are required to ensure that the local planning authority retains some control.

Thus, where the Secretary of State is of the opinion that proper steps are not being taken for the preservation of a listed building[1] he may authorise the appropriate local authority to acquire it, together with such land as in his opinion is necessary for its management and the preservation of its amenities, or for affording access thereto.[2]

A necessary prerequisite to such authorisation, however, is that the owner should have been given the opportunity to put the building into a reasonable state of repair. For this purpose the local authority or Secretary of State, as the case may be, is required to serve upon the owner a "repairs notice" specifying the works which they (or he) regard as reasonably required for the preservation of the building. This notice must have been served at least two months before publication of the notice of the making of any compulsory purchase order[3] in respect of the building; and it must indicate the nature and effect upon compensation[4] of the powers of acquisition available.[5]

Although there is no express statutory provision to the effect that compliance with the repairs notice negates the power of compulsory acquisition under this head, if the works required by the notice are in fact carried out, or reasonable steps are being taken in that regard, the authority claiming that such works are necessary for the proper preservation of the building can hardly thereafter maintain that proper steps to that end are not being taken, at least until the owner has had a reasonable chance to fulfil the requirements of the repairs notice.

If, however, there is no response to the repairs notice a compulsory purchase order may be made and, subject to a right of appeal,[6] confirmed.

In such cases, where the acquiring local authority or the Secretary of

---

[1] Other than an ecclesiastical building for the time being used for ecclesiastical purposes (which for this purpose does not include a building used wholly or mainly as a residence for a minister of religion for the performance of the duties of his office); a building included in a scheme or order under enactments for the time being in force with respect to ancient monuments; or a building included by the Secretary of State in a published list of ancient buildings under any of the latter enactments: Town and Country Planning Act 1971, ss. 58(2) and 114(3).

[2] Ibid, s. 114.

[3] I.e., the notice required under the Acquisition of Land (Authorisation Procedure) Act 1946, Sch. 1, para. 3(1)(b): p. 32, ante.

[4] As to which see below.

[5] Town and Country Planning Act 1971, s. 115.

[6] Appeal by any person having an interest in the building lies by way of application to the magistrates court (with an appeal to the Crown Court) for an order staying further proceedings on the compulsory purchase order if the court is satisfied that reasonable steps have been taken to preserve the building: ibid, s. 114(6) and (7).

State, as the case may be, are satisfied that the neglect of the building has been deliberate *and* with a view to justifying demolition and the development or redevelopment of the site or of any adjoining land, a "direction for minimum compensation" may be included in the compulsory purchase order, the effect of which— in the absence of a successful appeal[1]—is to limit the compensation payable to the market value of the property upon the assumption that neither planning permission nor listed building consent will be available for any works other than those required to restore the building to a proper state of repair and maintain it in such state.[2]

It must, however, be emphasised that this power to give a minimum compensation direction is not available merely because the property is being neglected—even if that neglect is clearly deliberate: it has to be deliberately allowed to fall into disrepair *for the purpose of justifying demolition and redevelopment.* Consequently, if the owner can show, upon application to the magistrates court that that was not his purpose, the court may order the direction for minimum compensation to be excluded from the compulsory purchase order.[3]

Finally, it is to be noted that if the acquisition is in pursuance of a blight notice and a compulsory purchase order containing a direction for minimum compensation is in force, the acquisition is deemed to be in pursuance of that compulsory purchase order, and compensation is assessed accordingly.[4]

Compensation for listed buildings: summary

1. The general rule is that the compensation payable upon the compulsory acquisition of a listed building is assessed in the normal way but on the assumption that it cannot be demolished and the site redeveloped.[5]

2. If listed building consent for works that do not require planning permission or for which planning permission is granted by a development order is refused or granted conditionally, compensation is payable to the extent to which such refusal or imposition of conditions reduces the market value of the property.[6]

3. Where a claim to compensation under para. 2, above, has been established at the date of the making of the compulsory purchase order (i.e., where such refusal or conditional grant is in pursuance of an application made prior to the date of order)[7] compensation for the acquisition of the building is on the basis that no listed building consent would be available for such works.[7]

---

[1] *Infra.*

[2] Town and Country Planning Act 1971, s. 117(4).

[3] *Ibid*, s. 117(5): appeal (by either party) lies from the magistrates court to the county court: *ibid*, s. 117(6). The owner may, however, still appeal for a stay of further proceedings on the compulsory purchase order on the grounds that reasonable steps have been taken to maintain the building in a proper state: *ibid*, ss. 117(7) and 114(6) and (7).

[4] *Ibid*, s. 197.

[5] *Ibid*, s. 116, p. 274, *supra.*

[6] *Ibid*, s. 171, pp. 424, *et seq, post.*

[7] *Ibid*, s. 116, p. 274, *supra.*

4. Where the Secretary of State or a local authority compulsorily acquire a listed building on the grounds that it is being deliberately allowed to become derelict in order to justify demolition and redevelopment, a minimum compensation direction may be included in the compulsory purchase order.[1]

5. Subject to the outcome of any appeal,[2] the effect of a minimum compensation direction is to limit the assumptions as to planning permission and listed building consent to such as would be required to restore the building to, and maintain it in, a proper state of repair.[3]

6. If an acquisition is in pursuance of a blight notice and a compulsory purchase order containing a direction for minimum compensation is in force, compensation is assessed as if the deemed notice to treat had been served under that compulsory purchase order,[4] i.e., as under para. 5, above.

7 COMMONS, etc.

The compulsory acquisition of any land forming part of a common,[5] open space,[6] or fuel or field garden allotment[7] is subject to the special parliamentary procedure of the Statutory Orders (Special Procedure) Act 1945[8] unless the Minister of Agriculture, Fisheries and Food[9] certifies that he is satisfied:

(a) that land of at least equivalent area and equally advantageous to the public and to persons having rights over the land to be acquired is available, and will be vested in the vendor subject to the same rights as attach to that land; or

(b) that the land to be acquired does not exceed 250 square yards in extent, is required for the widening and/or drainage of a public highway, and that, having regard to the interests of the public and of the persons entitled to rights over the land, the giving of land in exchange is unnecessary.[10]

Unfortunately the modern statutory provisions affecting the assessment of compensation for the compulsory acquisition of this category of

---

[1] Town and Country Planning Act 1971, s. 117(1) and (2), p. 275–276, et seq, supra.

[2] Ibid, ss. 117(5), (6) and (7), and s. 114(6 and (7); see note 6, p. 275, supra, and note 3, p. 276, supra.

[3] Ibid, s. 117(4), p. 276, supra.

[4] Ibid, s. 197, p. 276, supra.

[5] A common includes any land subject to be enclosed under the Inclosure Acts and any town or village green: Acquisition of Land (Authorisation Procedure) Act 1946, s. 8(1).

[6] An open space in this context is any land set out as a public garden, land used for public recreation or a disused burial ground: ibid.

[7] A fuel or field garden allotment is any allotment set out as a fuel allotment or field garden allotment by an award under the Inclosure Acts: ibid.

[8] As to this procedure, see pp. 49, et seq, ante; note that it does not apply where the acquisition is under the Defence Acts, nor will it apply where the acquisition is under a Private Act which does not so provide.

[9] Or in the case of an open space not being a common, the Secretary of State.

[10] Acquisition of Land (Authorisation Procedure) Act 1946, Sch. 1, para. 11. Before giving such a certificate the Minister must publicise his proposals, consider objections and if necessary, convene a public inquiry or hearing: ibid. See also the corresponding provisions of the Housing Act 1957 Part III, the New Towns Act 1946, and the Light Railways Acts 1896 and 1912.

land[1] are little more than a consolidation of the relevant provisions of the Lands Clauses Consolidation Act 1845.[2] They are concerned with the method of settling compensation rather than with its measure and they are founded on concepts that precede the "1919 Rules".[3] Indeed, their principal concern is to ensure that the acquisition of the freehold from the owner of the soil is an entirely separate transaction from the acquisition of the rights of common or other rights over it:[4] these are acquired from the commoners[5] collectively.

Technically, the acquisition of the freehold in the soil presents little difficulty: compensation is assessed in the normal way[6] as the market value of the land subject to the rights of the commoners. In the past a principal difficulty has often been to establish ownership and, more particularly, to identify the holders of rights and to quantify the rights themselves.

To meet this latter difficulty the Commons Registration Act 1965 required registration of ownership of common land and of all rights of common, the latest date for registration being 2 January 1970.[7] Maintenance of the Register, which comprises separate "ownership" and "rights" sections, is the responsibility of the council of the county[8] in which the land is situate. There are, however, two limitations upon the reliability of the Register. In the first place, initial registrations were subject to challenge, and although the time for registering objections is long past,[9] many of them still remain to be resolved.[10] In such cases an assessment will have to be made as to the likelihood of such objections being upheld before estimating market value.[11] Secondly, the quantification of rights in the rights section of the Register is not necessarily final. The Commons Registration Act 1965 was intended to be but a first step in clarification of rights and ownership; the second

[1] Compulsory Purchase Act 1965, s. 21, and Sch. 4.
[2] Ss. 99–107.
[3] Pp. 164, et seq, ante.
[4] The owner of the freehold of common land in private hands is normally the lord of the manor who usually himself has rights thereover, often extensive; these rights are rights of ownership and not strictly rights of common at all. For the purposes of compensation they are nevertheless treated as rights of common and are acquired from the commoners collectively and not directly from the lord as part of the freehold: Lands Clauses Consolidation Act 1845, s. 99: Compulsory Purchase Act 1965, Sch. 4, para. 1(2).
[5] Which for this purpose includes holders of all rights over the land whether or not they are strictly rights of common, e.g., owners of other profits à prendre, easements and purely contractual rights: ibid. Also included in this "collective" procedure are the owners of rights of sole vesture, i.e., rights held to the exclusion of the owner of the soil; at common law land over which the latter has no rights, is not common land, so that such rights are not strictly rights of common at all: see now, however, the definition of common land and rights of common in the Commons Registration Act 1965, s. 22(1).
[6] See pp. 163, et seq, ante.
[7] The Commons Registration (General) Regulations 1966, (SI 1966, No. 1471), Reg. 5.
[8] Commons Registration Act 1965, ss. 1 and 2.
[9] The Commons Registration (Time Limits) Regulations, 1966, (SI 1966 No. 1470).
[10] Resolution of these objections is by reference to a Commons Commissioner (who decides after hearing the parties involved) with an appeal on matters of law by way of a case stated to a Judge of the Chancery Division: Commons Registration Act 1965, ss. 17 and 18.
[11] In some cases where owners of common land have acquiesced in the use of the land by the public at large (which cannot be a right of common: see Hammerton v Honey (1876), 24 WR 603) extravagant and sometimes almost wholly unfounded claims to rights of common have been registered in an endeavour to secure continued public access and enjoyment.

step providing for the proper management of the commons—which will involve precise "stinting"—awaits further legislation. In some cases, therefore, it will be found that the aggregate of registered rights patently exceeds the capacity of the common to support them. In that event, no doubt, an estimate of the capacity of the common will have to be made and the claims reduced accordingly.

In assessing the market value of the freehold it is also to be noted that apart from limitations imposed by the rights of commoners on the use to which the freeholder may put the land, there are also statutory limitations. In the first place all metropolitan commons[1] and manorial waste or commons wholly or partly situated in areas which, prior to the Local Government Act 1972, were within boroughs or urban districts, are subject to a statutory right of public access[2]—a provision which will in most cases result in a purely nominal market value.[3] Secondly, the right to fence or build upon any other land which was subject to common rights on 1 January 1926[4] requires the consent of the Minister of Agriculture, Fisheries and Food,[5] who, before giving his consent, is required to take into account the same considerations as are applicable in the case of an application to enclose a common under the Inclosure Acts and if necessary to hold similar public enquiries.[6] Briefly the Minister must be satisfied that the fencing or building is in the interests both of the local community and of those with rights in or over the land.[6]

Where land is given in exchange[7] the principle is similar to that of compensation based upon the cost of equivalent reinstatement,[8] although payable in kind rather than money.[9] The cost of that land to the acquiring authority will, in most cases where the land acquired is to

---

[1] I.e., commons within the Metropolitan Police District as defined in the Metropolitan Commons Act 1866.

[2] Law of Property Act 1925, s. 193.

[3] The owner may, of course, have special rights over the land in his capacity as owner but these, together with the rights of commoners will be assessed for compensation separately: see note 5, p. 278, *supra*.

[4] I.e., the date of commencement of the Law of Property Act 1925: *ibid*, s. 209(2).

[5] *Ibid*, s. 194.

[6] See the Commons Act 1876.

[7] In which case the compulsory purchase order may provide for vesting the land (subject to the rights, trusts and incidents to which the land acquired was subject) in the owner of the land acquired: Acquisition of Land (Authorisation Procedure) Act 1946, Sch. 1, para. 11(3). Note that this Act does not itself confer power compulsorily to acquire land to be given in exchange. Such powers need to be found in the special Act: see now the very wide powers in this regard under the Community Land Act 1975, s. 15(3), and note the powers conferred on local authorities to acquire land to replace common land appropriated by them: Town and Country Planning Act 1971, ss. 120 and 121.

[8] Pp. 239, *et seq*, *supra*.

[9] Where the Minister, or in the case of an acquisition of open space not subject to common rights, the Secretary of State, certifies that exchange land is available, and will be vested in the vendor subject to the same rights as attached to the land taken, the vendor cannot insist upon monetary compensation in lieu: *Freeman v Middlesex County Council* (1965), 16 P & CR 253. But the fact that the exchange land is certified as of at least equivalent area and as advantageous to commoners, etc. (see p. 277, *supra*) does not preclude the vendor from contending that there has not been equality of exchange and claiming further compensation equivalent to the difference between the value of the exchange land and the value of the land taken: *McKay v City of London Corpn* (1966), 17 P & CR 264; see also *Eton College v Eton RDC* (1959), 11 P & CR 66.

be developed, be substantially less than the value to it of the common land acquired. This will not, however, give rise to any claim by the owner of the land acquired in respect of the difference, for it is the essence of common land and common rights[1] that the latter are exercisable over the whole common, and that would prevent the lord of the manor from taking advantage of any planning permission to be assumed for the purposes of valuing the land taken.[2] To this there may be an apparent exception, for the lord of the manor may be entitled to "approve", i.e., enclose parts of the common lands provided he leaves a sufficiency of common to satisfy the rights of the commoners. Any such enclosures will, however, cease to be common land, will be valued for compensation in the ordinary way and will not be taken into account in assessing the area required to be given in exchange.

Thus, where the value of the land being acquired is likely to be enhanced by permissible assumptions of planning permission and the lord of the manor has sufficient notice of the intentions of the acquiring authority before any compulsory purchase order is made it may well be to his advantage to attempt to buy out the rights of the commoners on a reasonably generous basis.

The provisions relating to the assessment and payment of compensation in relation to common and other rights are somewhat more complicated. The normal procedure is for the commoners to appoint a committee to negotiate on their behalf, but if the compensation cannot be agreed, or no committee is appointed, the matter is to be referred for determination to the Lands Tribunal.[3] Where there is a committee, however, their agreement binds all those entitled to rights[4] and even where the compensation is determined by the Lands Tribunal it is for the committee to apportion it. Payment by the acquiring authority to the committee or any three members thereof (or if there is no committee, payment into Court) discharges the acquiring authority's obligations and entitles it to execute a deed poll vesting the rights in itself.[5]

In view of the different categories of common rights, however, attempts to negotiate collectively would appear to introduce unnecessary difficulties, especially where there are both rights appurtenant[6] and rights in gross.[7] The true value of a right appurtenant must, it is submitted, be related to its contribution to the economic viability of the holding to which it is attached—the "dominant tenement". That value may be quite different from the value of the same right in gross or even

[1] Note that although there may be other rights in respect of which compensation may be claimable, unless there are also genuine common rights (or rights closely analogous thereto such as rights of sole vesture: see note 5, p. 278, *supra*) the land will not be common land for the purposes of these provisions.

[2] See pp. 185, *et seq, ante*.

[3] Lands Clauses Consolidation Act 1845, ss. 105 and 106: Compulsory Purchase Act 1965, Sch. 4, paras. 5(4) and 6.

[4] Lands Clauses Consolidation Act 1845, s. 104: Compulsory Purchase Act 1965, Sch. 4, para. 5(1).

[5] Lands Clauses Consolidation Act 1845, s. 107: Compulsory Purchase Act 1965, Sch. 4, para. 6.

[6] Since by virtue of the Statute Quia Emptores 1289–90 rights appendant cannot be created after that date, such rights are rare and unlikely to be encountered.

[7] I.e., personal rights not attached to land; and see note 2, p. 281, *infra*.

the same right attached to dominant tenements of different sizes and types.

In many districts, particularly where the common land comprises extensive moorland, grazing rights of pasture appurtenant constitute a considerable part of the value of the farm to which they are appurtenant. In such cases the only feasible and equitable method of assessing compensation would seem to be on the basis of the difference between the market value of the dominant holding with its rights appurtenant and its market value without them: in other words, an assessment of the compensation payable for their severance from, and the resultant injurious affection to, the dominant tenement.[1]

To attempt to value such rights as a whole without reference to the individual holdings to which they are attached—in other words, treating them as a collection of rights in gross—would seem bound to produce injustice, for grazing rights, for example, attached to a small farm may be much more vital to its economic viability than the same rights appurtenant to a larger holding. Similarly, common rights in the soil, e.g., to dig and take sand and gravel, may be of somewhat limited value if appurtenant since such rights are confined to the requirements of the dominant tenement: rights in gross may not be nearly so limited, and if they are not, will be of substantially greater value.[2] Rights in gross are, of course, the personal property of the owner, who may or may not exercise them in connection with other land. If he does not, then it is clearly both possible and equitable to value them as separate marketable entities. But if in practice such rights are exercised in conjunction with a distinct holding or series of holdings in the same ownership or occupation and form part of the economy of such holding or holdings, the same considerations would seem to apply as those suggested as appropriate in the case of rights appurtenant.

In short, it is submitted that despite the convenience of negotiating with a committee and leaving it to them to apportion the total compensation amongst the commoners, the only fair method of valuation will be to value, and then aggregate, individual claims and apportion accordingly. In other words, members of such committees will be wise to ensure that they have fully documented detailed claims from each person whom they represent and are then in a position to negotiate, and if necessary argue their case before the Lands Tribunal, on that basis.

If there is no committee and the compensation is paid into court it will, of course, be for the court to direct how the money is to be distributed; in most cases, however, it will be preferable to appoint a committee lest there be no proper representation of the commoners' case before the Lands Tribunal.

There is, however, an alternative procedure for apportionment in

---

[1] As to compensation for severance and injurious affection see Chap. 8, pp. 314, *et seq, post.*

[2] Rights in gross frequently derive from a deliberate separation of rights appurtenant from the holding to which they were formerly appurtenant, but not necessarily so: they may have been created by grant (or acquired by prescription or the doctrine of the lost modern grant) in which case the limits imposed may be relatively insignificant. In any event the lord's rights are limited only by the need to ensure that there is a sufficiency of common land undisturbed to meet the commoners' rights.

that the Committee may apply to the Minister of Agriculture, Fisheries and Food to call a meeting of the persons interested for the appointment of trustees of the compensation money, the investment of the money and the application of the income to such purposes for the benefit of the persons interested, as the Minister may approve. Payment of the compensation money to the trustees discharges the committee from all liability.[1]

A second alternative is for a majority of the committee to apply to the Minister to call a meeting of those interested and if a majority resolve upon apportionment, the compensation money is paid into the Bank of England; the committee is discharged and the Minister is then empowered to apportion the compensation to the persons concerned according to their respective interests in the land taken.[2]

A third alternative is for the committee, any three members thereof or, upon the expiration of twelve months from the payment of the compensation to the committee, any three of the persons interested, to apply to the Minister to call a meeting of the persons interested at which resolutions may be passed by a majority in number and in value[3] for the application of the money in one or more of the following ways:

(i)   in the improvement of the remainder of the common;
(ii) in defraying the expenses of a scheme under the Metropolitan Commons Acts, or a provisional order for regulation of the common under the Inclosure Acts, or an application to Parliament for a Private Bill for the preservation of the common as a public open space;
(iii) in defraying legal expenses incurred in protecting the common or the commoners' rights;
(iv) in purchasing additional land to be used as common land;
(v)   in purchasing additional land to be used as a recreational ground for the neighbourhood.[4]

Clearly the use of these alternatives will depend upon the nature of the common and whether the commoners regard their rights primarily as economic or primarily as providing amenities. In the former case, if the committee is unwilling or unable to apportion to their satisfaction the second alternative would seem appropriate, unless a high priority is given to reimbursement of legal expenses or the replacement of the lost common land, in which case the third alternative (paras. iii and iv above) would seem appropriate as it would if the commoners are primarily interested in the amenities of their neighbourhood. There seems little advantage in the first alternative, a view reflected by the introduction of the second alternative only two years after enactment of the first.

[1] Inclosure Act 1852, s. 22.
[2] Inclosure Act 1854.
[3] A requirement which appears to make some assessment of the value of individual rights as suggested in the text, a necessary prerequisite.
[4] Commonable Rights Compensation Act 1882.

8 EXTINGUISHMENT OR ACQUISITION OF EASEMENTS, PROFITS A PRENDRE AND BREACHES OF RESTRICTIVE COVENANTS

Extinguishment

The Special Act normally empowers the acquiring authority to override such easements or other rights over the land that may be inimical to the development for which the land is required. In the case of acquisitions under the very wide powers of the Community Land Act 1975[1] such interference with interests in or rights[2] over the land which results from its development in accordance with planning permission, becomes "authorised",[3] although the authority remains liable to pay compensation in accordance with the provisions of the Compulsory Purchase Act 1965.[4] This provision does not, however, apply to certain rights[5] vested in statutory undertakers for the purpose of their undertaking.

Acquisition

Normally[6] compulsory acquisition involves the acquisition of the whole of any interest in the land required, and does not extend to the acquisition of particular levels.[7] Whether easements or other rights in or over land may be acquired depends upon whether they are included in the definition of land in the authorising statute. There is, moreover, a number of special Acts, almost exclusively confined to those dealing with public utilities, which specifically empower statutory undertakers to acquire easements.[8] A general power to acquire easements has now been conferred by the Local Government (Miscellaneous Provisions) Act 1976, s. 13.

Where land is compulsorily acquired, easements, profits, etc.,

---

[1] As to which see pp. 23, et seq, ante.

[2] The interests and rights in question comprise "any easement, liberty, privilege, right or advantage annexed to land and adversely affecting other land, including any natural right of support": Community Land Act 1975, Sch. 4, para. 10(3). Breach of restrictive covenants falls into the same category: Sch. 4, para. 10(1). Cf. the corresponding provisions of the Town and Country Planning Act 1971, s. 118, and New Towns Act 1965, s. 19.

[3] Community Land Act 1975, Sch. 4, para. 10.

[4] I.e., under the head of compensation for severance and injurious affection: Compulsory Purchase Act 1965, ss. 7 and 10, pp. 314, et seq, and 321, et seq, respectively, post.

[5] See pp. 252 et seq, supra.

[6] The question whether acquisition powers extend to the acquisition of easements and other rights in or over land normally depends on whether "land" or "interests in land" are defined to include such rights.

[7] In Knott Hotels Co. of London Ltd. v London Transport Executive (1975), 31 P & CR 294, where the special Act (The British Transport Commission Act 1965) not only conferred no special powers in this regard but specifically provided that the Commission should "not acquire any part of the scheduled lands". The Lands Tribunal understandably expressed considerable doubt whether the compulsory acquisition of an underground easement for the construction of the Victoria Line could have been intra vires. See, however, the heading "Minerals", pp. 273, et seq, supra.

[8] E.g., for the laying of water and gas mains, erection of overhead electricity and telephone cables, etc.

appurtenant thereto will, of course, be included, and need not be specifically mentioned in the compulsory purchase order.[1]

Compensation

Profits à prendre appurtenant to land may, in many cases, be severed therefrom and become rights in gross.[2] As such they may well have a recognised market value as in the case of shooting and fishing rights.[3] If such rights are extinguished by the acquisition of the land over which they are exercisable, compensation will, as in the case of acquisition of a freehold or leasehold interest in land, be based on market value. If such rights are acquired as appurtenant to land compulsorily acquired, compensation will, of course, be based on the market value of the vendor's total interest; he may, however, base his valuations on the most profitable method of sale: i.e., he may if he thinks it to his advantage, base his valuation on the assumption that but for the compulsory acquisition he could have sold his property, including rights of common or of other profits à prendre, in separate lots.[4]

EASEMENTS

In *Stokes* v *Cambridge Corporation*[5] the subject land was "back-land" and the acquiring authority happened to own the only land through which satisfactory access could be obtained. It was held that compensation must be assessed on the assumption that the owner of access land would be expected to demand a price reflecting the fact that he held the key to the development of the back-land. Compensation was accordingly based on the full development value of the land on the assumption that it was accessible, less the "key money" likely to be demanded by the owner of the access land, assessed as one-third of development value of the land acquired. The principle would seem equally applicable to the acquisition of a mere right of way.

---

[1] *Sovmots Investments Ltd.* v *Secretary of State for the Environment* (1975), 31 P & CR 59, in which the Court of Appeal overruled the Court of first instance where it was held that this only applied to true easements in existence when the compulsory purchase order was made, and that in the case of quasi-easements of convenience or those necessary for enjoyment, words adequate to cover them must be included in the compulsory purchase order. In that case the Camden London Borough Council sought to acquire six upper floors of maisonettes within the Centre Point complex. At the date on which the compulsory purchase order was made the whole building was unoccupied and in single ownership. The maisonettes therefore had no separate rights of support, access by lift, etc., although such rights would have arisen upon the separation of ownership or occupation if they were then either granted or enjoyed. Although such separation and enjoyment had taken place subsequently, the House of Lords, overruling the Court of Appeal and upholding the Court of first instance, held that such separation and enjoyment could not be related back to the making of the compulsory purchase order, and that no such rights, albeit rights of necessity, would pass upon a compulsory acquisition since in such cases it could not be inferred that the vendor so intended: see *Wheeldon* v *Burrows* (1879) 12 Ch. D 31. It seems, however, that although under the Local Government (Miscellaneous Provisions) Act 1976, s. 13, such rights can now be acquired, they will need to be specified in the compulsory purchase order.

[2] That is to say, if they remain exercisable over the servient land either permanently or for a term of years, as in the case of common rights.

[3] Shooting and fishing rights unattached to land may, however, merely amount to licences.

[4] *Colman* v *Basingstoke RDC* (1966) 17 P & CR 270 (LT): see also p. 183, *ante*.

[5] (1961) 13 P & CR 77.

Nevertheless, there appears to be no authority for applying the principle of the *Stokes* case in reverse, i.e., where the authority own the back-land and seek to acquire access thereto. The reason no doubt is that the compulsory acquisition of access land will, almost by definition, be in pursuance of a scheme to develop the back-land. The enhanced value of the access land resulting from any such scheme consequently falls to be discounted under the *Pointe Gourde* rule:[1] compensation for the compulsory acquisition of the right of way will, therefore, fall to be assessed under the head of injurious affection to the interest in the land retained, i.e., on the basis of the depreciation in the value of the land over which the right of way or other easement is created. Similarly, where a right of way or other easement is extinguished by the compulsory acquisition of the servient land, compensation will be payable to the owner of the dominant tenement on the basis of the consequent depreciation in its market value.

INTERFERENCE WITH RESTRICTIVE COVENANTS

Since ample planning powers exist to restrict development of privately owned land,[2] it is difficult to envisage circumstances in which a public body possessing compulsory purchase powers will require to create a restrictive covenant over privately owned land for the benefit of land held by themselves. Consequently liability to compensation in respect of restrictive covenants is only likely to arise where the burden of a restrictive covenant over land compulsorily acquired is thereby extinguished. The compensation payable will again be the amount by which the dominant land is depreciated in value, i.e., the difference between its value with and without the benefits of the covenant. In valuing such benefits under the Law of Property Act 1925,[3] the Lands Tribunal, with the approval of the Court of Appeal, has, in effect, asked itself the question "what, in an ordinary friendly negotiation, would the owner of the dominant tenement expect to receive for abrogating his rights, and what would a purchaser be willing to give in order to enable him to carry out the development proposed for the servient land?".

In a leading case under these provisions of the Law of Property Act 1925,[4] the Lands Tribunal followed the principle adopted in *Stokes'* case,[5] and assessed the compensation as 50 % of the increase in the value of the servient tenement resulting from the removal of the restrictions upon its development imposed by the covenant. The Court of

---

[1] See pp. 217, *et seq, ante*.

[2] Under the Community Land Act 1975, when that Act is fully operative no development, other than exempted and excepted development (p. 296, *post*) and development permitted by a General Development Order, will be permitted on privately owned land other than land acquired from an authority within the meaning of the Act. Such an authority will, of course, be at liberty to impose such restrictive conditions on the sale or lease of the land as it deems fit.

[3] S. 84, under which the owner of land subject to a restrictive covenant may apply to the Lands Tribunal for the discharge of the covenant, and the Tribunal may award such compensation as it deems appropriate.

[4] *SJC Construction Ltd.* v *Sutton London Borough Council* (1974), 28 P & CR 200.

[5] P. 284 *supra*.

Appeal[1] upheld the Lands Tribunal's approach[2] as being a perfectly lawful method of assessment. Lord Denning MR indeed likened the assessment of damages for the loss of amenity, view, etc. suffered by the dominant tenement to the assessment of damages for pain and suffering, as something incapable of any logical translation into money terms. Both were intangible and the method adopted by the Lands Tribunal was a fair and sensible way of assessing the compensation—but not necessarily the only way.

On the principle that, for the purpose of assessing compensation, interests in land are to be valued on the basis of a friendly negotiation as between a willing seller who expects a reasonable price for his interest, with its potentialities, and a willing purchaser,[3] this method of valuation would seem to be as appropriate for the purpose of assessing the compensation payable for the compulsory extinguishment of a restrictive covenant as in assessing compensation for its discharge under the Law of Property Act 1925. Such a method obviously cannot be universally applicable however, for its adoption presupposes that planning permission for the development to be carried out on the land being acquired (the servient land) will so enhance its value that a private developer will be prepared to pay a sum representing a substantial proportion of that enhancement for the discharge of the covenant. This will clearly not always be the case where the developer is a public body. Indeed, developments that may be particularly damaging to the amenities of the dominant land which the covenant was designed to protect, may well have no commercial value at all. Obvious examples are sewage works, motorways, power stations, etc.

9 UNOCCUPIED OFFICE PREMISES

As has already been explained[4] the special provisions of Community Land Act 1975, Part IV,[5] for the acquisition by the Secretary of State of new office premises which are kept unoccupied following completion are wholly outside the Community Land Scheme. They could equally well—and indeed, more appropriately—have formed a separate Act. Their purpose is to provide a sanction in the hands of the Secretary of State where planning permission is granted for the erection or use of buildings as offices and the owner or developer, by failing to ensure their use as offices, not only wastes resources but in effect defeats the purpose of the planning permission and therefore the assessment of the

---

[1] (1975) 29 P & CR 322. It is worth noting that although the owners of the dominant tenement happened to be a local authority they were in no way involved in the exercise of any compulsory powers.

[2] In doing so the Court of Appeal followed *Wrotham Park Estate Co. Ltd.* v *Parkside Homes Ltd.* (1973), 27 P & CR 296, in which the same principle was applied in assessing damages for breach of a restrictive covenant in lieu of an injunction. In that case, however, only 5% of the realisable development value was awarded.

[3] See *Vyricherla Narayana Gajapatiraju* v *Revenue Divisional Officer, Vizagapatam,* [1939] AC 302, PC.

[4] P. 23, note 2, *ante.*

[5] Community Land Act 1975, ss. 28–36.

supply of office accommodation in relation to demand on which planning policy, and indeed the formulation of up-to-date development plans, depends.

These provisions are therefore more properly an addition to the weapons of planning control—in short, a form of enforcement. They do, however, introduce special powers of acquisition and modify the law of compensation.

Powers of Acquisition: Scope of Powers

The Secretary of State's powers of acquisition arise only in the case of land on which office buildings consisting of, or containing a minimum of, 5,000 square metres of floor space[1] have been erected whether before or after the passing of the Act[2] and to any other land used or intended to be used for the purpose[3] of the building,[4] provided at least 75 % of the office accommodation[5] is unoccupied and has been unoccupied throughout a minimum period of two years commencing with the completion date.[6]

The Secretary of State may not, however, use compulsory powers to acquire "the interest of any person who in right of that interest is occupying any part of the office building and is effectively using it for the purpose for which planning permission was given".[7] It follows, therefore, that the interest of such a person cannot be compulsorily acquired even if he is occupying only a part of the building which his interest entitles him to occupy—a provision which may, it seems, enable an owner to keep the larger part of an office building empty without fear of compulsory acquisition.

Secondly, the Secretary of State cannot compulsorily acquire an interest "if he is satisfied that the person entitled to possession of the unoccupied office accommodation has tried his best to let it.[8] In determining whether he has done so the Secretary of State is particularly required to consider:

"(a) the rent sought, compared with rents of similar accommodation in the area,

(b) the other covenants and conditions required by that person to be contained in any proposed lease,

---

[1] I.e., gross floor space to be measured by external measurement: Community Land Act 1975, s. 28(6).

[2] *Ibid*, s. 28(1).

[3] E.g., car parking, etc.

[4] Community Land Act 1975, s. 28(1).

[5] Calculated by reference to the proportion of floor space unoccupied: *ibid*, s. 28(2)(a).

[6] *Ibid*, s. 28(3)(a). The period ends on the date on which the Secretary of State either enters into a binding contract to purchase, in the case of acquisition by agreement, or in the case of a compulsory acquisition, first publishes a notice that a draft compulsory purchase order has been prepared: *ibid*, s. 28(3)(b). Provided, therefore, that the offices are occupied before the end of the period, the Secretary of State has no power to acquire (*ibid*, s. 28(2)(a)), but his power to do so may revive if the offices are again unoccupied within a period of six months: *ibid*, s. 32(2), and see p. 288, *infra*.

[7] *Ibid*, s. 28(4)(a).

[8] *Ibid*, s. 28(4)(b), and note that in neither of these cases is the power to acquire by agreement affected.

(c) whether or not that person indicated to prospective lessees that he was prepared to let the accommodation in parts,

(d) the number and resources of firms of estate agents retained for the purpose of letting the accommodation, and

(e) the nature and extent of advertising of the accommodation by that person or those agents."[1]

It will be noted that attempts to sell the freehold interest is not particularly mentioned, although the Secretary of State is required also to "have regard" to "other relevant factors".[2] It may, however, be an oversight, for these considerations appeared at a late stage in the parliamentary proceedings: or it may be that if the freehold is for sale no hardship is involved in selling by agreement to the Secretary of State (the "penal" compensation provisions apply only to compulsory acquisitions).[3]

Powers to acquire other land

In view of these limitations upon the use of compulsory powers in relation to the acquisition of office premises it is somewhat surprising to find that once such premises have been acquired (either by agreement or compulsorily) the Secretary of State may acquire *any* other land compulsorily as well as by agreement and without restriction if he is satisfied that it is "necessary" to do so "in order to facilitate the disposal" of any office premises he has acquired under these provisions.[4]

Two other questions arise. First, in what circumstances is office accommodation to be regarded as unoccupied for the purposes of the Act; secondly, what are the criteria for determining the completion date. These matters are dealt with in the succeeding paragraphs.

Occupation

The Secretary of State is entitled to assume that any office building or part of such building which is rated as unoccupied[5] for any period remained unoccupied throughout that period unless a notice has been given to the rating authority to the effect that the premises have become occupied—in which case it is to be assumed that they ceased to be unoccupied with effect from the date of the notice.[6] However, if an unoccupied[7] office building becomes occupied for a period of less than six months the Secretary of State may, for the purposes of this enactment, assume that it has been unoccupied throughout.[8] In other words, occupation for less than six months at a time (provided the premises are unoccupied between such periods of temporary occupation) does not

---

[1] Community Land Act 1975, s. 28(5).
[2] *Ibid.*
[3] *Ibid*, s. 29, and p. 239, *infra.*
[4] *Ibid*, s. 30(1).
[5] I.e., under the General Rate Act 1967, Sch. 1.
[6] Community Land Act 1975, s. 32(1).
[7] I.e., the building must have been unoccupied for some period immediately following completion.
[8] Community Land Act 1975, s. 32(2).

constitute a break in the required minimum two-year period of non-occupation beginning with the date of completion. But the Secretary of State cannot acquire (even by agreement) during a period of temporary occupation even if he knows that the occupiers intend to vacate within six months of the date on which they went into possession. His powers do not revive until the premises are again unoccupied. A series of short tenancies in total exceeding six months will therefore result in the Secretary of State permanently losing his powers of acquisition provided there are no intervening periods during which the premises are unoccupied.

The Secretary of State also has powers to demand of persons having an interest[1] in the building any "information which may reasonably be demanded for the purposes of this Part" of the Act[2]—which would no doubt include information as to occupation. He also has powers to authorise entry for the purpose of "examining and surveying" the building:[3] presumably "examining" covers inspection designed to establish whether or not the premises as a whole or any parts thereof are occupied in fact.

The Completion Date

For this purpose this is defined, in the case of a building consisting solely of office accommodation, as the date on which erection[4] of the building was completed;[5] and in the case of a building which also comprises other accommodation, the date of the completion of such part as consists of office accommodation.[6]

Two alternative methods of determining the completion date within the above definitions are provided. First, if the building (or any part thereof) has been assessed for rates as unoccupied property and treated for that purpose as completed on any specified date that date is the completion date unless the Secretary of State serves a "completion notice"[7] specifying an earlier date.[8] A completion notice must be served on every person entitled to possession of any part of the office building.[9] Thereafter it is open to recipients of such a notice each to agree a completion date with the Secretary of State (in which case the completion notice is deemed to have been withdrawn)[10] and/or appeal

---

[1] "Interest" is used here in its wide, non-legal, sense: as to the persons of whom information may be demanded see Community Land Act 1975, s. 34(1), and p. 291, *infra*.

[1] Community Land Act 1975, s. 34(2)(c).

[3] *Ibid*, s. 35: p. 292, *infra*.

[4] "Erection" in this context includes conversion of a building for office use by extension, alteration or re-erection: Community Land Act 1975, s. 28(7).

[5] *Ibid*, s. 28(8)(a).

[6] *Ibid*, s. 28(8)(b). This latter part of the definition will normally only be applicable to conversions: in practice office accommodation in new buildings will rarely be habitable until erection of the building as a whole is completed.

[7] Community Land Act 1975, s. 33(1).

[8] *Ibid*, s. 33(3). Note: The requirement that the date be earlier is mandatory.

[9] Community Land Act 1975, s. 33(2). "Office building" is "any building which consists of or comprises office accommodation occupying more than 5,000 square metres of floor space", *ibid*, s. 28(1). Completion notices must therefore be served on persons entitled to possession of any non-office accommodation in the building as well as those entitled to possession of the office accommodation.

[10] *Ibid*, s. 33(4).

to the county court within 21 days of the date of service of the completion notice[1] on the ground that the building had not been completed by the specified date.[2]

It should be noted, however, that the requirement is that each person on whom the completion notice has been served shall agree in writing with the Secretary of State that the completion date shall be the date specified in the agreement.[3] If there is a number of such persons (some of whom may well be temporarily unavailable), agreement within 21 days may be a somewhat optimistic target, particularly since account has to be taken of a further provision regarding "work of a kind which was customarily done to a building of the type in question after its erection had been substantially completed".[4] This presumably includes interior decoration, installation of electric fittings and appliances, etc. Such work is not, however, further defined but it is provided in the Act[4] that where at any time[5] only such work remains to be done it is to be assumed "that the erection of the building was completed at the expiration of such period beginning with the date of its completion, apart from the work, as was reasonably required for carrying out the work".[6] While the purpose of this provision is presumably to ensure that the completion date is not unreasonably delayed by dilatoriness in completing such post-erection work, the difficulties in agreeing how long completion of such work might reasonably be expected to have taken may be considerable—and very important to owners threatened with acquisition. Owners who maintain that the true completion date is significantly later than the date specified in the completion notice will therefore be wise, if anxious to protect themselves against the acquisition of their property, to initiate proceedings in the county court rather than rely upon ultimate agreement between *all* parties and the Secretary of State. Obviously the problem of reaching agreement on these matters will be very much easier if there is only one person entitled to possession of the whole building (and therefore entitled to receive any completion notice served by the Secretary of State) but experience shows that 21 days is not an over-generous allowance of time within which to finalise such matters with a Government Department (it is, after all, only 15 working days and could be less).

The Secretary of State may, however, withdraw a completion notice by serving a "subsequent notice" on all the persons on whom the completion notice was served at any time before an appeal against that notice has been brought[7] or, if all those persons agree, at any time before the appeal is heard.[8]

---

[1] As to service of notices see Community Land Act 1975, s. 36: p. 293, *infra*.
[2] *Ibid*, s. 33(6).
[3] *Ibid*, s. 33(4).
[4] *Ibid*, s. 33(8).
[5] Not necessarily, therefore, at the date specified in the completion notice; indeed, it seems that such work could still be outstanding at the date of service of that notice if the Secretary of State considers it could "reasonably" have been completed two years earlier.
[6] Community Land Act 1975, s. 33(8). The commas have been inserted by the author.
[7] *Ibid*, s. 33(5)(a).
[8] *Ibid*, s. 33(5)(b).

What may not, however, be immediately clear is whether the "sub-sequent notice" is confined to withdrawing the original completion notice or may take the form of a new completion notice (specifying a different completion date) in substitution of the old. It is to be noted that in so far as this "subsequent notice" is further defined it is as a "notice under this subsection": the sole purpose of such a notice mentioned is to "withdraw a completion notice" and not, for example, "an earlier" or "original completion notice". There is therefore nothing to suggest that this subsequent notice can take the form of an alternative completion notice and nothing elsewhere in the Act to indicate that a completion notice can be varied or revoked by a subsequent completion notice.

It follows, therefore, that if a completion notice is withdrawn the deemed completion will revert to the date on which the building was treated as having been completed for rating purposes if the building has been rated as unoccupied.[1] But the right of appeal is confined to persons on whom a completion notice has been served who appeal on the ground that the erection of the building was not completed by the date specified in the notice. It also follows, therefore, that if the completion notice is withdrawn before appeal there can be nothing against which to appeal. The principle, of course, is that if a person has committed himself to a completion date for rating purposes he cannot later argue that the building was not in fact completed until afterwards.

If a completion notice is not withdrawn and there is no appeal (or all appeals are abandoned or dismissed) the erection of the building is deemed to have been completed on the date specified in the notice. If an appeal is pursued and not dismissed the completion date is "such as the court shall determine".[2]

POWERS TO OBTAIN INFORMATION

In order to implement this Part of the Act the Secretary of State will clearly require to know the names and addresses of persons having an interest in an unoccupied office building, the nature of such interest, etc. He is accordingly empowered to require certain specified classes of persons to provide him with such information. He is required to do so by notice, and the persons on whom he may serve such a notice are "any person appearing to him to have an interest in the whole or any part of any[3] office building,[4] any person claiming possession of the whole or part of any such building; any person who receives rent in respect of the

---

[1] P. 289, *supra*.

[2] Community Land Act 1975, s. 33(7). Note that the court's discretion is unfettered: it is not required to have regard to the date on which the building is treated as completed for rating purposes, although in the absence of special circumstances (e.g. notification to the rating authorities in anticipation of a completion date not actually achieved) there can be little doubt that the court would be reluctant to determine a later date.

[3] Note that although these persons are not in terms confined to those with interests etc. in unoccupied office buildings the Secretary of State can only use these powers for the purposes of this Part of the Act.

[4] For definition see p. 289, note 9, *supra*.

whole or part of such building; or any person who manages the whole or part of any such building as agent or otherwise".[1]

The information required must be specified in the notice and must be confined to the nature of the interest (if any) of the person to whom the notice is addressed, the name and address of any other person known to him to have an interest in the building and any other information that may "reasonably be demanded from him for the purposes of this Part"[2] of the Act. Such person may also, however, be required to state whether he has in his possession any document that is evidence of any lease or other disposition of an interest in the building and, if he has, to produce it to a person appointed for that purpose by the Secretary of State and permit copies or extracts to be taken.[3] The notice must specify the time within which[4] the information (and/or any document) is to be supplied and may specify the manner in which it is to be furnished.[5] Refusal to comply with such a notice or the deliberate or reckless making of any statement that is false in any material particular constitutes an offence: so also does the production "with intent to deceive" of a document which is false in any material particular. The penalty on summary conviction is a fine limited to £400; upon conviction on indictment it is a fine or imprisonment for a maximum term of two years, or both.[6]

POWERS OF ENTRY

A person duly authorised in writing by the Secretary of State may "at any reasonable time enter any office building, or any building which he reasonably believes to be an office building, for the purpose of examining and surveying it".[7] He must, however, produce evidence of his authority if required to do so, and may not demand entry as of right unless seven days' notice has been given to the occupier.[8] Wilful obstruction of any duly authorised person "acting in exercise of his powers under this section"[9] is an offence punishable, on summary conviction, by a fine not exceeding £100.[9]

It is to be noted that this right of entry is very wide: it is not confined to office buildings reasonably believed to be unoccupied even in part; it is, however, limited by the fact that the right extends only to entry "for the purposes of this Part of the Act";[7] but it must be borne in mind that the purpose of this Part of the Act is only to enable the Secretary of State to acquire unoccupied office buildings in the sense that at least 75 % of the office floor space is unoccupied and then only if they have been unoccupied since completion. These powers therefore cannot properly extend

---

[1] Community Land Act 1975, s. 34(1). Note that a solicitor acting for any of these persons cannot be required to divulge any privileged communication made to him by his client: *Ibid*, s. 34(5).
[2] *Ibid, s.* 34(2).
[3] *Ibid*, s. 34(4).
[4] It must not be less than 14 days: *Ibid*, s. 34(3).
[5] *Ibid*, s. 34(3).
[6] *Ibid*, s. 34(6).
[7] *Ibid*, s. 35(1).
[8] *Ibid*, s. 35(2).
[9] *Ibid*, s. 35(3).

to an examination of buildings the greater part of which are obviously occupied, or to old established office buildings that are known to have been occupied for prolonged periods. If, however, entry were to be demanded in such circumstances in purported exercise of these powers there is unfortunately no appropriate method provided by which the Secretary of State's authority can be challenged other than wilful obstruction on the ground that the person concerned is not acting under the powers conferred—a not very satisfactory procedure.

SERVICE OF NOTICES

Where the address of the person on whom the notice is to be served is known, no difficulty in serving a notice under these provisions arises: it may be delivered to him personally, left at his usual or last known address or sent thereto by prepaid registered letter (or recorded delivery). Similarly in the case of a company or other incorporated body, notices may be delivered or sent by registered post (or recorded delivery) to the registered or principal office addressed to the secretary or clerk, as may be appropriate.[1] By the nature of these provisions, however, there may be cases where it is difficult, if not impossible, to identify persons having interests in or being entitled to possession of the building in question, or the various parts thereof, let alone to ascertain their addresses. In such cases the notice will be taken to have been duly served if it is addressed to "the owner" or "the person entitled to possession" (as the case may be) of the building (or part thereof) and delivered to the building or sent thereto by registered post or recorded delivery[2] and in either case is not returned.

If, however, the notice, having been sent by registered post or recorded delivery, is returned to the Secretary of State it will be taken as duly served if delivered to some person in the building or affixed conspicuously to some part of the building.[3]

Compensation

The sanction against retaining new office buildings unoccupied will not always be confined to the threat of compulsory acquisition in accordance with the powers described above, for in some cases the owners of interests compulsorily acquired may be entitled only to a reduced level of compensation. In cases of acquisition by agreement, however, no such penalty arises and compensation is assessed on the ordinary basis.[4] The penalty that may be incurred in cases of compulsory acquisition arises from the fact that compensation is to be assessed as at the date on which the erection of the building was completed[5] unless to do so would result in a higher value than assessment as at

[1] Community Land Act 1975, s. 36(1).
[2] Ibid, s. 36(2)(a).
[3] Ibid, s. 36(2)(b).
[4] Note, too, that Pt. I (other than s. 31) of the Compulsory Purchase Act 1965 (as far as applicable) applies to acquisitions by agreement in England and Wales (Community Land Act 1975, s. 31(3)) and s. 31(4), and cf. Sch. 4, para. 7.
[5] Community Land Act 1975, s. 29(1) and (2); and pp. 289, et seq. supra.

the date of notice to treat.[1] Part IV of the Community Land Act 1975 was devised in conditions of very rapidly rising land values in which this provision would in most cases have resulted in a very substantial reduction in the compensation payable. In the conditions of stable or falling land prices experienced since the introduction of these proposals it is unlikely that the exercise of this option to assess compensation as at the date of completion of the building will in fact have any very substantial effect: indeed, since it would seem quite likely, in many cases, to result in more generous compensation than assessment as at the date of notice to treat, it may in practice be very seldom invoked. Moreover, in circumstances in which there is no expectation of the value of land (and of office development in particular) rising in real terms it is improbable that many owners will in the immediate future deliberately retain office property unoccupied in the hope of securing an appreciation in vacant possession value that will more than offset the loss of rent.

In short, the probability is that the compulsory powers of acquisition of this Part of the Act may well turn out to be a classic example of shutting the stable door after the horse has bolted, and be very little used.

However that may be, where it is required to assess compensation as at the completion date (even if merely to determine whether it does result in a lower value than if assessed at the date of notice to treat) it is first necessary to assess the value of the unencumbered freehold[2] interest in the whole of the land comprised in the compulsory purchase order as at the completion date. Where such an interest is acquired that value will be the basis of the compensation payable.[3] In the case of all other interests, however, the value of the unencumbered freehold must be multiplied by the value of the interest in question and divided by the aggregate value of all the interests subsisting in the land at the date of service of the notice to treat—in both cases valuation being made on the basis of current values on the date on which the Secretary of State takes possession of the interest concerned or the date on which the compensation is determined, whichever is the earlier.[4]

In other words, for determining the proportion that the value of any particular interest bears to the total value of all the interests, current values (as above defined) are to be used; they are then reduced to completion date values by multiplying by the value of the unencumbered freehold at values ruling on the latter date.

Compulsory Purchase Procedure

With one exception the procedure to be adopted is perfectly nor-

---

[1] Community Land Act 1975, s. 29(5).

[2] I.e. free from all encumbrances other than easements or restrictive covenants: *ibid*, s. 29(4).

[3] I.e. together with any compensation payable for disturbance, severance, inrurious affection or other matters not directly based on the value of the interest acquired; assessment of compensation under these heads is not affected by the Act: *ibid*, s. 29(6).

[4] *Ibid*, s. 29(2) and (4).

mal—that is to say, it is that laid down in Acquisition of Land (Author-isation Procedure) Act 1946, Schedule 1.[1]

The exception is that it is not necessary either in notices relating to the compulsory purchase order or the compulsory purchase order itself to specify the purpose for which the land is required[2]—but this does not apply to the subsequent acquisition of extra land considered necessary to facilitate the disposal of any "office land" already acquired under this Part of the Act.[3]

---

[1] *Ibid*, s. 31(1). Note that the reference is to these Schedules without the alternative para. 4 inserted by *ibid*, Sch. 4, Pt. I, for the purposes of the Community Land Scheme (Pt. III of the Act).

[2] This provision applies only to acquisitions under Community Land Act 1975, s. 28: *ibid*, s. 31(2).

[3] Such additional land can only be acquired under *ibid*, s. 30: p. 288, *supra*.

CHAPTER 7

Compensation Under the Community Land Act 1975[1]

INTRODUCTORY

Although, with one relatively minor exception,[2] the Community Land Act 1975 has no effect upon the code of compensation until the Second Appointed Day, the new code to come into effect thereafter cannot be fully understood without an appreciation of the provisions for the suspension of planning permission that operate following the First Appointed Day,[3] on the one hand, and the making of Relevant Date Orders on the other. This in turn requires some understanding of the purpose of the Act and of certain fundamental definitions.

The ultimate purpose of the Act is to place a duty upon all local authorities[4] to acquire and hold a ten-year reserve supply of "development land", i.e., land required for "relevant development"[5] within that period. "Relevant development" is in effect any development for which planning permission is required[6] except "exempt development"[7] and "excepted development".[8]

EXEMPT DEVELOPMENT

Exempt development is wholly outside the scheme of the Act and comprises:[9]

[1] For an outline of the purport and provisions of this Act see pp. 22 *et seq, ante*. For a detailed exposition of the Act see Corfield's *A Guide to the Community Land Act*, Butterworths, 1976.

[2] I.e., the amendment of the Land Compensation Act 1961, s. 17 p. 205, *ante*. And note the effect on compensation where development is carried out while planning permission is suspended: Community Land Act 1975, s. 22, p. 303, *infra*.

[3] 6 April 1976: Community Land Act 1975 (First Appointed Day) (England and Wales) Order 1976 (SI 1976 No. 330 (C. 10)).

[4] Although in England the "authorities" on whom this duty is imposed are for the most part local authorities, they also include New Town Corporations, the Peak Park Joint Planning Board and the Lake District Special Planning Board (Community Land Act 1975, s. 1) plus any joint board established (with the consent of the constituent authorities concerned) by the Secretary of State by order under s. 2. The Secretary of State may also set up, by order, corporate bodies to exercise the functions of recalcitrant authorities: s. 50. In Wales the relevant authority is the Land Authority for Wales, s. 1, as to whose powers and duties see Part II, ss. 8—14. Local authorities in England are the County and County District Councils, the Greater London Council and London Borough Councils, and the Council of the Isles of Scilly—for the purpose of the Act regarded as a County Council: s. 6(1).

[5] Community Land Act 1975, s. 3(1).

[6] Defined as any development within the meaning of the Town and Country Planning Act 1971, s. 22: Community Land Act 1975, s. 6(1).

[7] I.e., the development described in the Community Land Act 1975, Sch. 1: *ibid*, s. 3(2).

[8] See pp. 297 *et seq, infra*.

[9] Community Land Act 1975, Sch. 1.

(a) Development for which planning permission is granted by a general development order for the time being in force;[1] or would have been granted but for a direction given under the order.[2]

(b) Buildings or other operations erected or carried out on agricultural or forestry land for agricultural or forestry purposes[3] other than the erection of dwelling-houses.[4]

EXCEPTED DEVELOPMENT

Excepted development is development in respect of which authorities have the power but will not have the duty to acquire the land.[5] It comprises:

(a) Development consisting exclusively of the building of a single dwelling-house. This reference to the building of a single dwelling-house, however, "includes a reference to the construction or laying-out of any garage, outhouse, garden, yard, court, forecourt or other appurtenance for the occupation with, and for the purposes of, a single dwelling-house",[6] i.e., *any* dwelling house, and not merely single dwelling-houses built in the future in accordance with these provisions. Moreover, this definition appears to include a single dwelling-house on agricultural or forestry land, e.g., for a farm worker, despite the exclusion of dwelling-houses from the exempted developments (*supra*).

(b) Development of such class or classes as may be prescribed by the Secretary of State by regulations.[7]

The relevant date

In introducing the Community Land Act 1975 the Government recognised that it would be some years before authorities would have the administrative and financial capacity to acquire, hold and manage anything approaching a ten-year rolling supply of land required for all types of relevant development. They also recognised that both capacity and urgency would be likely to vary considerably from one authority to another, and even within different parts of an authority's area.

---

[1] It follows that these classes of development may be altered from time to time. It is essential, therefore, to ensure that reference is made to the most recent order; at the time of going to press the current order is the Town and Country Planning (General Development) Order 1973 (SI 1973 No. 31), as amended by SI 1976 No. 301.

[2] I.e., a direction under Article 4 of the above order.

[3] Including the working of minerals on agricultural land for agricultural purposes, e.g., lime for fertilisation or stone for repairs, etc., to agricultural buildings; Community Land Act 1975, Sch. 1, para. 3.

[4] But see the definition of excepted development in the text below.

[5] No new duty to acquire any land for any type of development arises until a "relevant date order" is made covering the types of development therein designated and prescribing the areas in which such a duty is imposed: see "The relevant date", below..

[6] Community Land Act 1975, s. 3(3). As the only development excepted by the Act (as opposed to regulations that may be amended from time to time) this is the only class of development which may be said to be permanently excepted.

[7] As in the case of development exempted by virtue of a general development order (note 1, *supra*) it will be necessary to make sure that reference is made to the regulations in force at the time that any such development is to be carried out. For development currently excepted see the Community Land (Excepted Development) Regulations 1976 (SI 1976 No. 331).

Provision was accordingly made for the Secretary of State to make a series of orders designating the descriptions of "relevant development" in the areas to which a particular order applies. The date on which any such order comes into force is the "relevant date" for the relevant development designated in the order ("designated relevant development") and the area to which the order applies. An order may cover the whole or any part of the area of a county authority. It follows that there may be different relevant dates in the same area for different descriptions of relevant development and different relevant dates for the same descriptions of relevant development in different areas, even within the same county. It also follows that there will eventually be not less than one order per county[1] and probably many more.

As soon as a relevant date order[2] comes into force it is the first duty of all authorities whose areas include any of the land to which the order applies to decide between themselves as to which of them shall acquire the outstanding material interests[3] in the various parcels of land needed for the designated relevant development.[4] Where no authority wishes to acquire any particular piece of such land then the duty to acquire it devolves upon the authority designated in the order. Where two or more[5] authorities wish to acquire the land the issue falls to be settled in accordance with the arrangements made for the settlement of disputes between the authorities in the county land acquisition and management scheme.[6]

The effect of a relevant date order is to place the authorities concerned under a positive duty to acquire all "outstanding material interests" in all land which, having regard to their land acquisition and management scheme,[6] is required for designated relevant development.

A "material interest" is defined as "the freehold or a lease the unexpired term of which, at the relevant time, is not less than seven years.[7] An "outstanding material interest" is one *not* owned by an

---

[1] The order appointing the Second Appointed Day cannot be made until all relevant development has been designated in all areas of Great Britain: Community Land Act 1975, s. 7(3)(a), pp. 305 *et seq, infra*. It would seem to follow, therefore, that regulations made after that date can amend earlier regulations so that development previously prescribed as "excepted development" becomes "relevant development". Cf. the express statutory provision in regard to post-2nd Appointed Day Use Classes Orders and General Development Orders, *ibid*, s. 25(4) and see note 9, p. 306, *infra*.

[2] An expression used for convenience; it is not used in the Act which refers to these orders as "orders under s. 18": Department of the Environment Circular 121/75 refers to them as "Duty Orders". As subsection (6) of section 18 defines the "Relevant Date" as the date on which such an order comes into force, "Relevant Date Order" would seem a more appropriate nomenclature.

[3] Community Land Act 1975, s. 18(3). Outstanding material interests are defined in *ibid*, s. 4(1): see below, and note 5, p. 299, *infra*.

[4] *Ibid*, s. 18(3).

[5] Where a New Town Corporation is involved there may be up to three claimants.

[6] Authorities were placed under a duty to compile a Land Acquisition and Management Scheme by 1 February 1976 (Department of the Environment Circular 121/75, para. 66): as to the purpose and requirements of these schemes, see Community Land Act 1975, s. 16 and Sch. 5.

[7] Community Land Act 1975, s. 6(1). In determining the unexpired term of a lease it is to be assumed that any option (other than one conferred by or under statute) to renew or extend is exercised and that options to terminate are not: *ibid*, s. 6(2).

authority, a Welsh local authority (which is not an "authority" under the Act[1]), a parish or community council or a charity.[2]

In the case of a charity, however, the material interest must have been owned by a charity, although not necessarily the same charity, continuously since 12 September 1974.[3]

It is, however, to be noted that in the case of material interests owned by a charity it (or some other charity) must have owned the same material interest throughout. Thus if a charity owns a leasehold interest on 12 September 1974 but after that date takes a new lease[4] or acquires the freehold, the latter interests will be "outstanding".

It is also to be noted that the Secretary of State may by order specify other material interests as outstanding.[5] Furthermore a material interest is to be treated as "owned" by any such body if at any time that body has entered into a binding contract for its acquisition or the body is or was entitled to the interest under a will and the vesting of the interest is subject only to completion of the administration of the deceased's estate.[6]

To this general duty to acquire all outstanding material interests in such land there are, however, the following four exceptions. Authorities are *not* under a duty to acquire:

(a) An outstanding interest in land which is not needed for designated relevant development within the ensuing ten years;[7]

(b) Outstanding interests in land in respect of which they have abandoned their power to acquire under the provisions governing suspension of planning permission;[8]

(c) An outstanding interest previously held by an authority but disposed of by them provided that immediately prior to the disposal no material interest was outstanding;[9] or

(d) Outstanding material interests in the operational land of statutory undertakers.[10]

[1] See note 4, p. 296, *supra*.

[2] *Ibid*, s. 4(1), and note that a charity in this context is a charity recognised as such for the purposes of the Income and Corporation Taxes Act 1970: Community Land Act 1975, s. 6(1).

[3] *Ibid*, s. 4(1)(b): i.e., the date of publication of the White Paper "Land", Cmnd, 5730, p. 22, *ante*.

[4] Unless the new lease is in the exercise of an option in the original lease: see note 7, p. 298, *supra*.

[5] Community Land Act 1975, s. 4(1)(c): Currently the Community Land (Outstanding Material Interests) Order 1976 adds material interests owned by: The Commission for New Towns; A co-operative housing association approved for the purposes of s. 341 of the Income and Corporation Taxes Act 1970; The Highlands and Islands Development Board; A housing association registered in accordance with s. 13(1) of the Housing Act 1974; The Housing Corporation; The Lee Valley Regional Park Authority; Letchworth Garden City Corporation; The North Eastern Housing Association; The Scottish Development Agency; The Scottish Special Housing Association; An unregistered self-build society as defined in s. 12 of the Housing Act 1974; The Welsh Development Agency.

[6] Community Land Act 1975, s. 4(2).

[7] *Ibid*, s. 18(4)(a). Note, however, that they have the power, though not the duty, to acquire the land which in their opinion is needed for any development (other than "exempted development" of Sch. 1) beyond the ten-year period.

[8] *Ibid*, s. 18(4)(b), and see pp. 300 *et seq*, *infra*.

[9] *Ibid*, s. 18(4)(c). But note the limitation upon revival of planning permission in such circumstances, p. 305, *infra*.

[10] *Ibid*, s. 18(4)(d). Note that the duty does not extend to non-operational land held by statutory undertakers: "operational land" is land used, and in which an interest is held, for the purpose of carrying on the undertaking: *ibid*, s. 5(2).

Suspension of planning permission

The provisions of the Act governing suspension of planning permission affect the compensation payable upon the compulsory acquisition of land to which a suspended planning permission relates in two respects. First, the carrying out of the development authorised by the permission, while that permission is suspended, may be penalised by a reduction in the compensation[1] that would otherwise be payable. Secondly, in valuing land for the purpose of assessing compensation after the Second Appointed Day, no account is to be taken of any planning permission which is, for the time being, suspended.[2]

These provisions for the suspension of planning permission differ according to whether the planning permission is granted before[3] or after the relevant date. The principal difference is that whereas in the former case the planning permission can revive in favour of a private applicant, it will not normally do so in the latter.

SUSPENSION OF PLANNING PERMISSION GRANTED BEFORE THE RELEVANT DATE

Planning permission granted[4] before the relevant date[5] is immediately and automatically suspended[6] until all the authorities in whose area is situated any part of the land to which the planning permission relates indicate that they do not intend to acquire the land[7] or until one of these authorities actually purchases.[8]

Following the grant (and automatic suspension) of planning permission it is for the authorities concerned to serve notice of their intention on the applicant and on any other person named in any certificate accompanying the application.[9] Such notices of intention are to be served "within the time allowed for giving notice to the applicant for planning permission of the manner in which his application has been dealt with, being the time prescribed by" the relevant order under

---

[1] See p. 303, *infra*.

[2] See pp. 306–307, *infra*.

[3] Although there are certain provisions for the optional suspension of planning permission granted before the relevant date but in pursuance of applications made before the First Appointed Day (Community Land Act 1975, s. 19), it being unlikely that any such applications are still outstanding, they are not dealt with in the text.

[4] Note that planning permission granted on appeal is deemed to be granted on the date of the decision appealed against: Community Land Act 1975, s. 6(3).

[5] I.e., any such grant of planning permission in pursuance of an application made after the First Appointed Day: see the previous note.

[6] Community Land Act 1975, s. 20.

[7] An authority may decide to purchase part only of the land concerned. *Ibid*, Sch. 7, para. 9, and see note 5, p. 301, *infra*.

[8] *Ibid*, para. 2.

[9] I.e., the certificates required by the Town and Country Planning Act 1971, s. 27: Community Land Act 1975, Sch. 7, para. 5. Note, however, that the Town and Country Planning Act 1971, s. 27(1)(a) which provides for a certificate to the effect that the applicant is either the owner of the fee simple or entitled to a tenancy in respect of the whole of the land is amended (by the Community Land Act 1975, s. 58(2) and Sch. 10, paras. 6(1)(a) and 7(1)(a)) to provide for "a certificate stating that at the beginning of the period of 21 days ending with the date of application, no person (other than the applicant) was the owner of any of the land to which the application relates." The Town and Country Planning Act 1971, s. 27(7), which defines "owner" for these purposes, is also amended to mean a person entitled to any material interest within the meaning of s. 6(1) and (2) of the Community Land Act 1975 (Community Land Act 1975, Sch. 10, paras 6(2) and 7(2).

the Town and Country Planning Acts.[1] In other words, they must serve the appropriate notice not later than the date by which the local planning authority is required to notify its decision on the planning application.

The duration of the suspension depends upon the reaction of the authorities having the power to acquire.

Authorities that state that they do not intend to acquire abandon their power to do so for a period of five years,[2] unless there is a breach of any condition[3] to which the notice of intention not to acquire was subject, in which case the power to acquire revives with effect from the date of breach: however, the planning permission does not thereby again become suspended. If none of the authorities concerned intend to acquire it follows that planning permission revives with effect from the date on which the last notice of intention was served and that the land cannot be acquired[4] under these provisions of the Act until the expiration of five years from the date of service of the first such notice.[5]

If, however, an authority serves a notice stating that it does intend to acquire it has twelve months in which to complete the "first step towards acquisition", i.e., the conclusion of a binding contract to purchase or, in the absence of agreement, the publication of notice of the making of a compulsory purchase order. If it fails in this requirement, not only does the planning permission revive, but the power to acquire is deemed to be abandoned as in the case of a notice of intention not to acquire. If, however, the compulsory purchase order is not confirmed or is quashed by the courts, it seems that planning permission revives with effect from the date of the decision of the Secretary of State or of the court, as the case may be, but that the authority's power to acquire is not formally abandoned on the same date.[6] Indeed,

---

[1] I.e., the Town and Country Planning (General Development) Order 1973 (SI 1973 No. 31), art. 7: made under the Town and Country Planning Act 1971, s. 31(1)(d): Community Land Act 1975, Sch. 7, para. 5(2). The time currently prescribed is "two months or such longer period as the parties may agree". It seems, therefore, that if the applicant agrees to an extension of time for consideration of the planning application, the time available to the authorities concerned to serve notice of their intention will be extended accordingly.

[2] Community Land Act 1975, Sch. 7, para. 1. They also abandon their powers of acquisition under the Town and Country Planning Act 1971 for the same period: Community Land Act 1975, s. 19(5).

[3] See Community Land Act 1975, Sch. 7, para. 8(1), for the types of condition that may be imposed; they are limited to such matters as confining the development to the terms of the planning permission, the time within which it must be begun or completed, etc., plus any other conditions specified in regulations made by the Secretary of State. The imposition of other types of condition is of no effect in this context, and a notice to which such a condition is attached is treated as being unconditional: Sch. 7, para. 7(2). A person wishing to challenge a condition as being without para. 8(1) above may, within six weeks of the service of the notice containing the condition, apply to the High Court (or Court of Session) for a determination: Sch. 7, para. 7(3) and (4). These regulations are subject to "negative" parliamentary procedure: Sch. 7, para. 8(6).

[4] Even by agreement, for it is the power to acquire that is abandoned and not merely the power to acquire compulsorily: Community Land Act 1975, Sch. 7, para. 1.

[5] An authority wishing to acquire only part of the land must attach to its notice a plan indicating the part or parts in question (*ibid*, para. 9(2)). It is not, however, absolved from its duty to serve notices *in toto* covering the whole of the land (para. 9(4)) so that if it fails to do so in respect of any part of the land within the time prescribed it will be taken to have abandoned its power to acquire such part.

[6] *Ibid*, Sch, 7, para. 2(2).

the fact that the compulsory purchase order is either not confirmed or quashed does not appear to have any immediate effect on the authority's power, although it does terminate the suspension of the planning permission. The authority will have completed the "first step towards acquisition"[1] within the twelve-month period and therefore retain its power. It has, however, a further hurdle to negotiate, for having completed this first step it has a further twelve months after the compulsory purchase order becomes operative in which to serve a notice to treat in respect of all "outstanding material interests"[2] in the land. This it clearly cannot do in the case of a quashed compulsory purchase order or one in respect of which the Secretary of State has notified his intention not to confirm. It seems, therefore, that in such cases the power to acquire is indefinitely retained. Thus, if the compulsory purchase order has been quashed on a technicality capable of rectification it seems that the authority may restart the operation; similarly in the case of a decision by the Secretary of State not to confirm because of some rectifiable defect or on grounds of prematurity. In other cases, however, it would seem that the power can be exercised only by agreement, thus leaving the owner or developer free to proceed.

If an authority having served a notice of intention to acquire subsequently changes its mind it must serve a further notice[3] on the applicant and, if it has already made a compulsory purchase order, on all persons on whom notice thereof is required to be served under the Acquisition of Land (Authorisation Procedure) Act 1946.[4]

If, however, an authority expresses an intention to acquire, makes a compulsory purchase order within twelve months from service of notice of such intention, obtains confirmation of such compulsory purchase order and serves notice to treat within twelve months from the date upon which it becomes operative,[5] planning permission revives when it actually purchases.[6] It is thus free to proceed with the permitted development itself or make the land available to others to do so, and the planning permission is taken into account in the assessment of compensation.[7] Upon the revival of planning permission any time limit attached thereto is extended for a period equal to the period of suspension.[8]

Finally, the Act provides that the blight notice provisions of the

---

[1] Defined as entering a binding contract or publishing notice of the making of the compulsory purchase order: Community Land Act 1975, Sch. 7, para. 1(5).

[2] For definition see p. 298, *supra*, and note 5, on page 299, *supra*.

[3] In the form to be prescribed by regulation: Community Land Act 1975, Sch. 7, para. 1(5). See now the Community Land (Prescribed Forms (England) Regulations 1976 (SI 1976 No. 320) and the corresponding Welsh Order.

[4] I.e., all owners, lessees or occupiers of the land except tenants for a month or less, but including statutory tenants.

[5] I.e., the date on which confirmation or, where a Minister is the acquiring authority, the making of the order is first published: Acquisition of Land (Authorisation Procedure) Act 1946, Sch. 1, paras 6 and 7(4).

[6] Or in Wales when the land is purchased by the local authority in whose area the land is situated: Community Land Act 1975, Sch. 7, para. 2(3).

[7] I.e., in accordance with the Land Compensation Act 1961, s. 14(2).

[8] Community Land Act 1975, s. 22(7), and note particularly the effect of this provision on the Town and Country Planning Act 1971, ss. 41 and 42.

Town and Country Planning Act 1971, ss. 192–207, shall apply to land in respect of which planning permission for relevant development is suspended.[1] The interest of anyone proposing to serve a blight notice must, of course, conform to the requirements of the Town and Country Planning Act 1971[2] but it is doubtful whether there would be anything to be gained by serving such a notice until it is known whether any authority is intending to acquire.[3]

Special provision is, however, made to cover the case of planning permissions granted upon an appeal against an enforcement notice.[4] In such cases the appellant is deemed to have made an application for the development to which the enforcement notice relates.[5] If the Secretary of State grants planning permission for that development the notices of intent under discussion must be served by the authorities concerned within three months after the grant of planning permission by the Secretary of State and must be served on all persons on whom the enforcement notice was served.[6] But if the planning permission granted differs from that for which the appellant is deemed to have applied, no notice can be served.[7]

Since suspension of a planning permission under these provisions lasts until all the authorities have abandoned their power to acquire, by serving notices to the effect that they do not intend to do so, or until an authority does in fact acquire (whichever is the earlier)[8] the effect of this provision must be to suspend the planning permission indefinitely if none of the authorities concerned in fact intends to acquire. The principle, presumably, is that a person should not gain by a breach of planning control if the Secretary of State does not feel justified in granting retrospective planning permission.

EFFECT ON COMPENSATION IF SUSPENSION IGNORED

If relevant development for which planning permission has been granted is proceeded with while planning permission is suspended, the suspended planning permission cannot be relied upon as a defence in

[1] Community Land Act 1975, s. 22(6). Land Acquisition and Management Schemes (see note 6, p. 298, *supra*) are required to specify which authority is the "appropriate authority" upon whom blight notices are to be served: Department of the Environment circular 121/75, para. 67(d) and see pp. 154 *et seq, ante*.

[2] See Town and Country Planning Act 1971, s. 192(3) and (5): pp. 131 *et seq, ante*.

[3] See para. (b), pp. 145–146, *ante*.

[4] I.e., under the Town and Country Planning Act 1971, s. 88.

[5] *Ibid*, s. 88(7).

[6] Community Land Act 1975, Sch. 7, para. 5(3).

[7] *Ibid*. Note that this prohibition is mandatory; its purpose, however, is not altogether clear, for the Secretary of State's powers to grant planning permission on an appeal against an enforcement notice are somewhat limited. Apart from granting planning permission for the development to which the notice relates, or discharging a condition attached to an earlier planning permission which is alleged to have been infringed, he can only impose conditions, including the substitution of more onerous conditions for any conditions discharged (Town and Country Planning Act 1971, s. 88(6)). Although such conditional grants of planning permission may not constitute grants "in accordance with the application" (Community Land Act 1975, Sch. 7, para. 5(3)) it is not very clear what is gained by removing the obligation imposed upon authorities to serve notices of intent.

[8] Community Land Act 1975, Sch. 7, para. 2(1).

enforcement proceedings.[1] Moreover, if an authority decides to acquire the land, any element of value attributable to such development is to be ignored in the assessment of compensation.[2] To this general rule there is an exception where development, having been initially carried out without any planning permission at all, is the subject of a subsequent planning permission either under the Town and Country Planning Act 1971, s. 32, or upon an appeal against an enforcement notice.[3] In such cases the local planning authority which granted the retrospective permission or the Secretary of State (in the case of a grant by him on appeal against an enforcement notice) may direct that full compensation shall be payable upon compulsory acquisition.[4]

SUSPENSION OF PLANNING PERMISSION GRANTED AFTER THE RELEVANT DATE

The general rule is that planning permissions for relevant development (or for development that includes relevant development)[5] granted[6] after the Relevant Date are automatically suspended irrespective of the date of the application.[7] Although the relevant section[8] is not in terms confined to planning permissions for *designated* relevant development[9] the date of the relevant date order[9] is the relevant date only in respect of the relevant development designated in that order.[10] It seems, therefore, that planning permission for relevant development that is not, at the time of the grant, designated relevant development is not caught by these provisions.[11]

To this general rule there are, however, the following exceptions:

(a) Where there are no outstanding material interests in the land *and* the development covered by the planning permission is carried out by or on behalf of an authority;[12]

(b) Where an authority has made a compulsory purchase order in respect of the land and the Secretary of State has served notice on the authority that he does not intend to confirm the compulsory

---

[1] Community Land Act 1975, s. 22(1).

[2] *Ibid*, s. 22(2).

[3] Under the Town and Country Planning Act 1971, s. 88.

[4] Community Land Act 1975, s. 22(4).

[5] *Ibid*, s. 6(4).

[6] Note that planning permission granted on appeal is deemed to be granted on the date of the decision appealed against; the date of planning permission granted by the Secretary of State on an appeal against a deemed refusal of planning permission under the Town and Country Planning Act 1971, s. 37, is the date on which notification of the decision is, in accordance with the section, deemed to have been received, i.e., on the expiration of the time allowed to local planning authorities to reach a decision: Community Land Act 1975, s. 6(3).

[7] *Ibid*, s. 21(1).

[8] *Ibid*, s. 21.

[9] See p. 297, *supra*.

[10] Community Land Act 1975, s. 18(6).

[11] Provided, however, that it is granted in pursuance of an application made after the First Appointed Day (see note 3, p. 300, *supra*) it will be suspended until one of the authorities within whose area the land is situated acquires, or all such authorities abandon their power to do so: pp. 300 *et seq*, *supra*.

[12] Community Land Act 1975, s. 21(2)(a).

purchase order (in so far as it affects the land in question) *and* directs that this exception shall apply;[1]

(c) Where a material interest in the land has been disposed of at a time when there were no material interests outstanding and the disposing authority has issued a certificate[2] in the prescribed form[3] to this effect and to the effect that it has approved the carrying out of the development in accordance with the planning permission.[4] If, however, the material interest has been disposed of before the First Appointed Day the certificate must also state that the authority has approved the interest as one appropriate for the purposes of these provisions.[5] In this connection it must be emphasised that we are concerned here only with planning permission granted after the Relevant Date and not, therefore, with a planning permission extant at the time at which the interest was disposed of or planning permission granted after the disposal but before the Relevant Date. In the former case there will be no further suspension, any suspension that there may have been having been terminated upon acquisition of all outstanding material interests by one or more authorities.[6] If in the latter case the planning permission was granted in pursuance of an application made on or after the First Appointed Day the appropriate suspension provision[7] will presumably (though it would seem somewhat unnecessarily) apply.

The "penalties" for carrying out development in respect of which planning permission has been granted but is suspended are common to all suspended planning permissions whether under these provisions or those already considered.[8]

A copy of the certificate referred to above must be sent to all other authorities[9] whose area includes any of the land[10] unless such other authority or authorities have given notice that they do not wish to receive such copies.[11]

THE SECOND APPOINTED DAY

The Second Appointed Day cannot be before all relevant development has been designated by Relevant Date Orders throughout Great

---

[1] Community Land Act 1975, s. 21(3).

[2] The certificate is conclusive evidence of the facts stated therein: Community Land Act 1975, s. 21(6).

[3] *Ibid*, s. 21(4). The form is to be prescribed by regulations under s. 53: *ibid*, s. 6(1).

[4] *Ibid*, s. 21(4).

[5] I.e., the provisions of s. 21: *ibid*, s. 21(5).

[6] Community Land Act 1975, Sch. 7, para. 2; it is possible, of course, for an authority to acquire a private leasehold interest in land in which the freehold is held by another authority.

[7] See pp. 300 *et seq*, *supra*.

[8] See pp. 303 *et seq*, *supra*.

[9] For the purpose of these provisions "authority" includes a Welsh local authority: Community Land Act 1975, s. 21(10).

[10] *Ibid*, s. 21(7).

[11] *Ibid*, s. 21(8).

Britain.[1] It must also be preceded by parliamentary approval of the draft regulations establishing financial hardship tribunals.[2] In itself, however, the appointment of this day has only one effect, albeit an important one, viz, to change the current full market value to current use value as the basis of compensation.[3] The change takes effect in relation to every compulsory acquisition[4] in pursuance of a notice to treat served on or after the Second Appointed Day[5] and applies in every "other case where compensation is payable pursuant to any provision contained in or made under any enactment and the amount of the compensation depends, directly or indirectly, on the value of any interest in land as at a date on or after the second appointed day".[6] The new current use value basis accordingly applies to acquisitions by agreement by bodies possessing compulsory powers, and it applies to compensation for severance and injurious affection and analogous claims in respect of depreciation in the value of land under the Land Compensation Act 1973, Part I, as it applies to compensation for the compulsory acquisition of any interest in land. This change is brought about by enacting that in assessing compensation it is to be "assumed that planning permission would not be granted for any development either on the land or any other land"[7] except:

(a) development of any of the classes specified in the Community Land Act 1975, Schedule 1, para. 1[8] ("exempt development"),[9] or in Town and Country Planning Act 1971, Schedule 8.[10]

(b) development for which planning permission is in force at the time and which is not then suspended.[11]

[1] Community Land Act 1975, s. 7(3)(a), and note that unless this provision is amended in connection with the current devolution proposals there cannot be different Second Appointed Days for England, Scotland and Wales.

[2] The establishment of these tribunals was promised in the White Paper of 1974, Cmnd. 5730, in recognition, no doubt, of the fact that land purchased in an open market and reflecting full development value, if compulsorily acquired at existing use value is bound to result in financial loss and hardship. Whether, after the Second Appointed Day, land will change hands in the open market at existing use value remains to be seen. If it does, this type of hardship will be confined to the acquisition of land from owners who purchased before the Second Appointed Day and will become progressively rarer with the passage of time. If it does not, and such hardship is to be avoided, these tribunals will have to become a permanent feature of the new scheme.

[3] Community Land Act 1975, s. 25.

[4] Except in certain cases where the land is acquired from a charity: see pp. 308 et seq, infra.

[5] Community Land Act 1975, s. 25(1)(a). It is therefore open to acquiring authorities to postpone service of notice to treat (within the permitted three years from date of confirmation) following a compulsory purchase order confirmed before the Second Appointed Day.

[6] Community Land Act 1975, s. 25(1)(b).

[7] Ibid, s. 25(3).

[8] Note that Sch. 1, paras. 2 and 3, are taken from the Town and Country Planning Act 1971, Sch. 8, paras. 4 and 5.

[9] See pp. 296–297, supra, and note that for the purposes of assessing compensation no account is to be taken of any changes in the types of development for which planning permission is granted by a general development order (see the Community Land Act 1975, Sch. 1, para. 1) made after the Second Appointed Day (or, in the case of an acquisition after that day, in pursuance of a compulsory purchase order made before it, of any such changes made after the making of or preparation of the draft of the order, was first published): Community Land Act 1975, s. 25(4)(b). Changes in the Town and Country Planning (Use Classes) Order affecting the need to obtain planning permission are treated in the same manner: Community Land Act 1975, s. 25(4)(a).

[10] Ibid, s. 25(3).

[11] It follows, therefore, that the rules governing compensation on the basis of equivalent reinstatement (Rule 5: pp. 239 et seq, ante) are unaltered.

Where a suspended planning permission has ceased to be suspended it is to be expected that in most cases the development will either have been carried out before the power of any authority to acquire revives, and will thus have become incorporated in the existing use value of the land, or the planning permission will have lapsed in accordance with the Town and Country Planning Act 1971, s. 41. This may not, however, be the case if the original planning permission was in outline only, with certain matters reserved for subsequent approval,[1] or in the cases mentioned in the preceding paragraphs where an authority has disposed of a material interest in the land and issued the requisite certificate, and the material interest is subsequently reacquired by the authority or acquired by some other authority in whose area the land lies.[2]

The principle apparently is that in such cases it would be unfair to deprive the landowner of the benefit of a planning permission when authorities have had every opportunity to acquire the land or, having done so, to retain all material interests therein. There is, moreover, the further consideration that if planning permissions falling into this category were not excepted, the way would be open to authorities to reopen decisions made before the Second Appointed Day so as to ensure the benefit of the lower level of compensation operating thereafter.

It follows that in any case in which compensation falls to be based on current existing use value (i.e., the vast majority of cases after the Second Appointed Day) development land tax will have no development value on which to bite and will therefore automatically cease to have effect: *aliter*, however, where a non-suspended planning permission is in force and falls to be taken into account in assessing compensation.

It also follows that in all cases in which the current existing use value basis of compensation applies, the planning assumptions of the Land Compensation Act 1961 cease to apply.[3] So too do any other provisions affecting compensation contained in any other enactment.[4]

To this, however, there is one general and one specific exception. The general exception is that these provisions of the Land Compensation Act 1961 and any other provisions affecting compensation in any other enactment will continue to be applied if to do so produces a lower level of compensation than results from applying the current existing use basis of the Act as described above.[5]

The special exception relates to land owned by charities and is dealt with hereunder.

---

[1] See the Town and Country Planning Act 1971, s. 42.

[2] Curiously enough, there is nothing in the Act to prevent such re-acquisition.

[3] I.e., those of the Land Compensation Act 1961, ss. 14–19; the Community Land Act 1975, s. 25(9).

[4] *Ibid*, s. 25(8).

[5] *Ibid*, s. 25(1). A knowledge of the existing code of compensation (i.e., that of the Land Compensation Act 1961) will therefore continue to be necessary in order to determine whether its application will produce a lower compensation figure than that of the Community Land Act 1975.

CHARITIES

It will already have been noted[1] that a material interest owned by a charity (but not necessarily the same charity throughout) during the whole of the period beginning with 12 September 1974 and ending with the "relevant time" is not an outstanding material interest.[2] In such cases charities will therefore be free to develop such land without the necessity (following the Relevant Date for the development and area in question) of the land first being acquired by an authority. That is not to say, however, that authorities will not have the power (as opposed to the duty) to acquire land belonging to charities, although the Secretary of State has intimated that he will not be inclined to confirm compulsory purchase orders in respect of such land "unless there are special planning reasons for doing so".[3]

For the purposes of compensation, after the Second Appointed Day interests in land held[4] by charities are divided into two distinct categories.

In the first category is an interest in land which itself is used "wholly or mainly for charitable purposes",[5] for example, a charity's offices, recreational land held in conjunction with a youth club, a church, the Library for the Blind, schools for the handicapped, British Legion workshops, etc.

If such land is compulsorily acquired,[6] compensation is to be based upon the assumption that planning permission would be granted for the prevailing development upon contiguous or adjacent land.[7] This general rule is, however, subject to two important provisos.

First, the interest must have been held by a charity, although not necessarily the same charity throughout, for a continuous period of seven years immediately preceding the date at which compensation is to be assessed. This may be either the date of entry or the date when the value falls to be agreed or assessed by the Lands Tribunal, whichever is the earlier.[8]

Secondly, this provision does not apply if the interest in the land has been held by a charity—again, not necessarily the same charity throughout—during the whole of the period beginning with 12 September 1974[9] and ending either on the date of notice to treat (provided it is served on or after the Second Appointed Day) or the date at which

[1] Pp. 299, supra.

[2] Community Land Act 1975, s. 4(1).

[3] Department of the Environment Circular 121/75, para. 51.

[4] An interest in land is treated as owned by a charity if they have entered into a binding contract for its acquisition or, if they are entitled thereto under the terms of a will, provided their entitlement is subject only to the completion of the administration of the deceased's estate: Community Land Act 1975, s. 25(7).

[5] Ibid, s. 25(5)(b).

[6] I.e., pursuant to a notice to treat served after the 2nd Appointed Day or in circumstances in which compensation falls to be assessed on the basis of values ruling after that date (ibid, s. 25(1))—e.g., where the 2nd Appointed Day intervenes between notice to treat and either the date of entry or the date on which the compensation falls to be determined: see note 8, infra.

[7] Ibid, s. 25(5): this is referred to in Circular 121/75, para 49(c) as "prevailing use value".

[8] Birmingham City Corpn v West Midlands Baptist (Trust) Association (Inc), [1970] AC 874; [1969] 3 All ER 172 [HL]; pp. 165 et seq, ante.

[9] I.e., the date of the White Paper "Land", Cmnd. 5730.

the value of the land falls to be assessed on or after the Second Appointed Day and that period is less than eleven years. In that case the interest falls into the second category (below).

Thus if, after the Second Appointed Day, notice to treat is served in pursuance of a compulsory purchase order and the interest has been held continuously by a charity or charities since 12 September 1974 for more than eleven years, the interest will fall into this first category and compensation will be assessed on the basis indicated above. That is, provided the land itself is used wholly or mainly for charitable purposes.

It is to be noted, however, that compensation for much of the land "used wholly or mainly for charitable purposes", e.g., a church, will, in appropriate cases, continue to be assessed on the equivalent reinstatement basis of Rule 5 of the Land Compensation Act 1961, s. 5,[1] which may well be a good deal higher than its value assessed on the above basis.

It must, moreover, be emphasised that these provisions apply only where the *same* interest in the land has been held throughout by one or more charities. Thus, if a charity, having previously owned only a leasehold interest, has acquired the freehold within the seven-year period, it will not, it seems, qualify for this special basis of compensation but will be treated in the same way as any other owner whose land is compulsorily acquired after the Second Appointed Day.[2]

The second category of interests held by charities includes interests in land which, though not itself used for charitable purposes, is nevertheless indirectly used for such purposes inasmuch as the rents and profits derived therefrom are devoted to charitable purposes.[3] This second category is, however, in all cases confined to land which has been continuously held by a charity, or by a succession of charities, throughout the period from 12 September 1974 to the date of notice to treat or the date at which the value of the land falls to be assessed, provided, in each case, that that date is on or after the Second Appointed Day and that that period does not exceed eleven years.[4] In such cases compensation is to be assessed without having to assume either that no planning permission would be granted for any development on the land (or any other land)[5] or that a suspended planning permission had not been granted.[6] In other words, compensation will be assessed on the basis of such of the assumptions of the Land Compensation Act 1961, ss.14–16, as may be applicable;[7] in addition, it will be open to the vendor charity in appropriate

[1] Pp. 239 *et seq, ante*: and see note 12, p. 306, *supra*.
[2] See pp. 306 *et seq. supra*.
[3] Cf. Community Land Act 1975, s. 25(5)(b) and s. 25(6)(a).
[4] *Ibid*, s. 26(6).
[5] The purpose of this provision (s. 25(2)) is to ensure that compensation discounts any betterment accruing from neighbouring land; it also, of course, discounts "worsenment": see pp. 217 *et seq, ante*.
[6] See pp. 306 *et seq, supra*.
[7] The Land Compensation Acts are not repealed and therefore remain operative except where expressly excluded, as in the generality of cases after the Second Appointed Day: see Community Land Act 1975, s. 25(1) and p. 306, *supra*.

cases to apply for a certificate of appropriate alternative development in accordance with s. 17 of that Act.[1]

Once again, in order to qualify for this concession the same interest must have been held throughout the relevant period.

It follows, therefore, that where the relevant period beginning on 12 September 1974 exceeds eleven years, an interest in land held by a charity or succession of charities purely as an investment will be acquired on the same basis as applies to interests in land owned by private persons—i.e., current existing use value.[2] That basis also applies, of course, where the interest in land which is itself used for charitable purposes has not, at the date when compensation falls to be assessed, been held by a charity or succession of charities for the minimum seven-year period unless it has been held continuously since 12 September 1974 for less then eleven years at the date of notice to treat or at the date when the value of the land falls to be assessed as described above.

The logic of these seven and eleven-year limits is not exactly self-evident. Presumably the latter is based upon the supposition that by the end of eleven years from 12 September 1974 (i.e., 11 September 1985) land compulsorily acquired will be replaceable at current existing values. Perhaps the underlying reason for the seven-year period is similar, namely that land purchased less than seven years prior to the Second Appointed Day will have been acquired at a price reflecting the overriding powers and duties of authorities to acquire all land having development potential within the ensuing ten years.

Finally, it is to be noted that development land tax applies to charities realising development value except where a charity develops land for its own use.[3]

Financial hardship tribunals

INTRODUCTION

Although the Secretary of State's discretionary powers to set up Financial Hardship Tribunals may be exercised at any time,[4] their purpose is to consider individual cases of financial hardship when all acquisitions by authorities come to be made at current use values,[5] i.e. after the Second Appointed Day. The constitution of these tribunals, and the criteria on which hardship is to be judged or extra compensation payable in respect of such hardship is to be assessed, remain to be laid down by regulations. The Second Appointed Day cannot be earlier than the date on which a draft of regulations establishing at least one financial hardship tribunal has been approved by resolution of each House of Parliament.[6] Pending such regulations (which seem unlikely

[1] As amended by the Community Land Act 1975, s. 47: see *ibid*, Sch. 9 and pp. 205 *et seq, ante*.
[2] Pp. 300 *et seq, supra*.
[3] Development Land Tax Act 1976, s. 25, and note the special provisions relating to land held by charities since before 12 September 1974: *ibid*, s. 24.
[4] Community Land Act 1975, s. 26.
[5] White Paper "Land", Cmnd. 5730, para. 46, September 1974.
[6] Community Land Act 1975, s. 7 (3)(b); alternatively the functions of a financial hardship tribunal may be conferred upon some existing body: *ibid*, s. 27(1).

to be available for some time) all that can be done at this stage is to consider those aspects on which guidance can be obtained from the relevant enabling provisions of the Act,[1] the White Paper,[2] and Ministerial statements of intent.

These can be divided into two groups: those relating to the establishment and constitution of these tribunals and those relating to the assessment of such extra payments as may be awarded: the latter are here referred to as "hardship payments".

It is the apparent intention that a number of tribunals shall be established so as to provide ready access in all parts of the country by anyone claiming to have suffered financial hardship.[3] The Act accordingly empowers the Secretary of State to make regulations constituting one or more such tribunals or conferring the requisite powers and duties upon one or more existing bodies.[4] Such regulations must provide for the appointment by the Secretary of State of chairmen and members, and may in addition provide for regulating future appointments and the tenure and vacation of office.[5] These regulations are required to be approved in draft by resolution of each House of Parliament (i.e., "positive" parliamentary procedure).[6] Further regulations which become effective subject to annulment by resolution of either House ("negative" procedure)[7] may be made in relation to the remuneration, pensions and allowances of members, officers and servants of tribunals, and the Secretary of State's decisions in these matters require the approval of the Minister for the Civil Service.[8]

HARDSHIP PAYMENTS

The Act provides that where a person claims that he has suffered financial hardship as a result of any of the changes in the law of compensation for compulsory acquisition coming into force on the Second Appointed Day[9] he may apply to a financial hardship tribunal[10] who will be required to consider the justification of the claim and, where appropriate, make an order specifying the amount of the hardship payment payable.[11] The claimant then has to serve a copy of the order upon the acquiring authority and the specified amount becomes due for payment three months from the date on which the copy order was served; if it is not then paid interest is payable from the date on which payment became due.[12]

Although the criteria by reference to which the tribunal is to decide

[1] Community Land Act 1975, s. 26.
[2] Cmnd. 5730, 1974.
[3] *Ibid*, paras. 46 and 47.
[4] Community Land Act 1975, s. 27(1).
[5] *Ibid*, s. 27(2).
[6] *Ibid*, s. 27(10).
[7] *Ibid*, s. 27(11).
[8] *Ibid*, s. 27(3).
[9] I.e., the changes effected by Community Land Act 1975, s. 25, pp. 305 *et seq, ante*.
[10] Community Land Act 1975, s. 27(4).
[11] *Ibid*, s. 27(5).
[12] Community Land Act 1975, s. 27(6) and (7). The rate of interest is that prescribed from time to time by orders under the Land Compensation Act 1961, s. 32. The current rate is $10\frac{1}{2}$%, Acquisition of Land (Rate of interest after Entry) (No. 4) Regulations 1977, SI 1977 No. 1656.

what constitutes hardship and the amount of any hardship payment remains to be laid down by regulations (the drafts of which require approval by both Houses of Parliament) the Act does specifically allow[1] for regulations providing that persons accepted by the tribunal as suffering financial hardship shall be entitled in appropriate cases to obtain certificates of appropriate alternative development under the Land Compensation Acts.[2] Such a concession may be of particular value to a landowner who has deliberately refrained from development in the interests of the general amenity of the area, e.g., by keeping a private park open to the public. There is, however, a statutory limit to the amount payable in respect of any one claim.[3]

Since the hardship must result from the reversion to current existing use value as the basis of compensation it is probably safe to assume that the more usual type of hardship that it is intended to cover is that which arises from the compulsory acquisition at current existing use value of land which was purchased by the claimant (or some person from whom he claims title other than by purchase) at a full market value that reflected substantial development potential. On this assumption it would seem likely that the criteria for assessing the amount of any hardship payment in the more usual cases will follow the lines of the "base values" on which development land tax is calculated.[4]

Other regulations laying down the procedure to be followed by financial hardship tribunals[5] or for dealing with claims by personal representatives of deceased persons who would have been entitled to apply to a tribunal had they survived[6] are subject only to negative parliamentary procedure.[7]

Acquisition of land belonging to authorities

As explained in chapter 1,[8] pending the Second Appointed Day the cost to authorities of acquiring land on a market value basis will be offset by purchasing net of development land tax. Since public authorities are not subject to tax, in the absence of special arrangements, authorities or Government Departments acquiring land from other public bodies would bear the full burden of compensation based on full market value. The Community Land Act 1975[9] accordingly provided for the modification, by order, of the Land Compensation Act 1961, s. 5,[10] where land is acquired from other authorities under the Act or from such other public bodies as may be specified in the order. The current order [11]

---

[1] Community Land Act 1975, s. 27(8).

[2] I.e., under Land Compensation Act 1961, Part III: pp. 163 et seq, ante.

[3] "£50,000 or such higher amount as may be prescribed by regulations" and approved by the Treasury: Community Land Act 1975, s. 25(9). Note, too, that any hardship payment awarded is in addition to the compensation payable under the Act.

[4] See pp. 97 et seq, supra.

[5] Community Land Act 1975, s. 27(8)(a).

[6] Ibid, s. 27(8)(c).

[7] Ibid, s. 27(1).

[8] Pp. 22 et seq, ante.

[9] S. 26.

[10] I.e., the "1919 Rules": pp. 163 et seq and 177 et seq, ante.

[11] Compulsory Acquisition by Public Authorities (Compensation) Order 1976 (SI 1976 No. 1218).

specifies five other public bodies,[1] and modifies Rule 2[2] so as to equate the compensation payable to that which would have been payable had the vendor been a private person subject to development land tax. In other words, compensation is to be the difference between market value assessed under Rule 2 and the development land tax payable by a private vendor on the assumption that he had himself purchased net of tax—i.e., the development land tax to be deducted is assessed on a base value[3] equivalent to the price paid by the vendor authority, reduced by the development land tax chargeable to the person from whom they acquired the land. It is to be noted, therefore, that if the vendor authority acquired before the Development Land Tax Act 1976 came into effect, so that no tax would have been chargeable to the then vendor, base value for the purpose of computing the notional tax to be deducted from market value will be the base value applicable under the ordinary rules.[3]

Acquisition of interests in Crown land

The similar problem facing authorities acquiring Crown land is dealt with somewhat differently, for instead of being able to modify the price payable, as explained above, the Secretary of State is only empowered to make a grant of such amount as may be approved by the Treasury having regard to the purchase price, rent or other payments made by the acquiring authority to the Crown.[4]

[1] The Highlands and Islands Development Board; The Lea Valley Regional Park Authority; the Scottish Development Agency; the Scottish Special Housing Association; and the Welsh Development Agency.

[2] I.e., the "1919 Rules": pp. 177 et seq, ante.

[3] See pp. 97 et seq, ante.

[4] Community Land Act 1975, s. 40. The Acquisition from the Crown (Grants) Order 1976 (SI 1976 No. 1219) adds to the authorities under the Act those bodies mentioned in note 1, supra, as bodies to whom such grants may be made. No order is required to authorise individual grants.

Compensation for Severance and Injurious Affection

1 INTRODUCTORY

As already indicated,[1] the Lands Clauses Acts provided for compensation for damage caused to other land in the same ownership as the land taken as a result of the severance therefrom of the land taken or of other "injurious affection" resulting from the compulsory acquisition. They also provided more limited rights to compensation for injurious affection to other neighbouring land in other ownership.

Both these rights are preserved.[2] Since they not only differ in substance and principle but also in their development, it will be convenient to consider them separately in sections 2 and 3A of this chapter. The latter rights have, however, been considerably extended in favour of a limited class of owners[3] by Part I of the Land Compensation Act 1973, the special provisions of which are considered under sub-head B of section 3.[4]

The Land Compensation Act 1973, Part II, confers powers upon acquiring authorities to mitigate the effect of public works upon neighbouring land and the exercise of these powers may affect the compensation payable in respect of injurious affection to such land. The relevant provisions are considered under sub-heading C of Section 3.[5]

2 COMPENSATION FOR SEVERANCE AND INJURIOUS AFFECTION OF LAND HELD BY THE VENDOR OF LAND COMPULSORILY ACQUIRED

The modern law on this subject stems from the Compulsory Purchase Act 1965, s. 7. It provides as follows:

"*Measure of compensation in case of severance*
    7. In assessing the compensation to be paid by the acquiring authority under this Act regard shall be had not only to the value of the land to be purchased by the

---

[1] See p. 3, *ante*: see also Chap. 5, pp. 158, *et seq, ante*.
[2] Compulsory Purchase Act 1965, s. 7 (below) and s. 10, p. 321, *infra*.
[3] Broadly "owner occupiers", including occupiers holding under a lease, and freehold reversioners of dwellings: see p. 315, *infra*.
[4] Pp. 328, *et seq, infra*.
[5] Pp. 340, *et seq, infra*.

acquiring authority, but also to the damage, if any, to be sustained by the owner of the land by reason of the severing of the land purchased from the other land of the owner, or otherwise injuriously affecting that other land by the exercise of the powers conferred by this or the special Act."

It is to be observed that it is this section that also provides for the payment of compensation in respect of the land actually taken; but whereas the basis on which such compensation is to be assessed is the subject of the detailed provisions of the Land Compensation Act 1961, Part II,[1] there are no corresponding statutory rules[2] in relation to the assessment of that element of the compensation payable[3] in respect of severance of the land taken from, or of injurious affection to, land remaining in the hands of the vendor.

Since, however, the Compulsory Purchase Act 1965, s. 7, is substantially a re-enactment of the Lands Clauses Consolidation Act 1845, s. 63, there is no lack of judicial authority. The basic principle is quite straightforward, the measure of compensation being the amount by which the land retained is reduced in value. The retained land need not be contiguous with the land taken,[4] used for the same purpose,[4] or held under the same title[5] it being enough "if unity of ownership conduces to the advantage or protection of the property as one holding",[6] provided that the claimant's interest in both the land taken and the land retained is such as to entitle him to compensation.[7]

Qualifying interests

Such interests are substantially the same as those that, in the case of acquisition, entitle the owner to receive notice to treat.[8] Both derive from the Lands Clauses Consolidation Act 1845, s. 18, which requires an acquiring authority not only to state that it is willing to treat for the purchase of the land to be acquired, but also "as to the compensation to be made to all parties for the damage that may be sustained by them by reason of the execution of the works".

---

[1] Chaps. 5 and 6, *ante*.

[2] See, however, Land Compensation Act 1973, Part I, pp. 328, *et seq, infra*.

[3] Note that compensation for severance and injurious affection is but an element in the overall purchase price and may, for example, be subject to capital gains tax: cf. the position in regard to compensation for disturbance, Chap. 9, p. 344, *post*; by the same token it will carry interest from the date of entry or the date on which compensation for the land taken falls to be determined: pp. 165, *et seq, ante*.

[4] *Cowper Essex* v *Acton Local Board* (1889), 14 App. Cas. 153.

[5] *Oppenheimer* v *Minister of Transport*, [1942] 1 KB 242, where the vendor had only an option to purchase the land taken which adjoined property of which he held the freehold.

[6] Per Lord Macnaghten in *Cowper Essex* v *Acton Local Board, supra*. Conversely unity of ownership is not in itself enough if the land is held in separate holdings: *Holditch* v *Canadian Northern Ontario Rly Co*, [1916] 1 AC 536 PC. Lord Macnaghten does not further define his concept of "one holding" except by adding "Otherwise the owner could hardly sustain injury by reason of the execution of works on the land taken". He seems merely to have been distinguishing the ownership of other separate estates so separated from that from which the land is taken as to be unaffected by its development.

[7] *Oppenheimer* v *Minister of Transport, supra*.

[8] I.e., all persons "interested" in the land: Lands Clauses Consolidation Act 1845, s. 18, and Compulsory Purchase Act 1965, s. 5; but this does not include persons holding under a tenancy of less than one year, from year to year or under a lease having less than one year unexpired: *Newham London Borough Council* v *Benjamin*, [1968] 1 WLR 694, CA, and see p. 369, *post*.

In this connection there is, however, "no material distinction between a legal interest in land and an equitable one".[1]

The "qualifying" interests thus include options to purchase leasehold as well as freehold interests;[2] easements and other rights appurtenant to land such as rights of light,[3] profits à prendre,[4] riparian rights,[5] rights of access,[6] and mortgage interests.[7] A purely personal right such as an unexercised right of pre-emption or a licence is not in itself sufficient although in the latter case it may affect the compensation payable. Thus in *Tull's Personal Representatives* v *Secretary of State for Air*[8] it was held that a person having a qualifying interest in the land may include in his claim for compensation, compensation for loss of profits derived from a licence to use the land in a particular way.[9] Similarly, although no right of privacy is known to the law,[10] loss of privacy may be taken into account in assessing compensation for injurious affection if the value of the claimant's interest in the land retained and in respect of which the claim is made is depreciated by the use to which the land taken is to be put.

Obviously, however, the compensation payable for severance or injurious affection will be limited to the value of the vendor's interests. Thus if the land taken is leasehold the reduction in the value of other land or other interests in other land held by the lessee will be limited to the unexpired term of the lease. Similarly, if the land taken was freehold and the retained land leasehold, compensation for severance and injurious affection will be limited to the effect on the value of the vendor's lease. Conversely, if the freehold owner of the land taken also owns other land subject to a lease, compensation under this head will be limited to the effect on the value of the freehold reversion of the land retained.

Severance

At this stage it is convenient to treat severance and injurious affection as two separate heads under which compensation may be claimed, for the nature of the injury to the retained land that falls to be taken into

---

[1] Per Asquith LJ in *Oppenheimer's* case, *supra*. See also *DHN Food Distributors Ltd.* v *Tower Hamlets London Borough Council*, [1976] 3 All ER 462, [1976] 1 WLR 852 for an equitable interest held sufficient to justify a claim for compensation for disturbance: p. 347, *post*.

[2] *Oppenheimer's* case, *supra*.

[3] *Metropolitan Board of Works* v *Metropolitan Rly Co* (1868), LR 3 CP 612.

[4] *Bird* v *Great Eastern Rly Co* (1865), 34 LJ CP 366, but shooting or fishing rights, etc., if not appurtenant to land may merely constitute a licence.

[5] See the cases cited in note 4, p. 324, *infra*. For a case in which flood prevention work carried out by a water authority gave rise to compensation for damage to fishing rights under the Land Drainage Act 1930, s. 34, see *Welsh National Water Development Authority* v *Burgess* (1974), 28 P & CR 378.

[6] See the cases cited in note 6, p. 324, *infra*.

[7] *R* v *Middlesex (Clerk of The Peace)*, [1914] 3 KB 259, but note the special provisions of the Lands Clauses Consolidation Act 1845, s. 112, in regard to a mortgagee's claim to compensation, p. 319, *infra*.

[8] [1957] 1 QB 523.

[9] Cf. the analogous position in relation to inclusion in a claim for interference with ancient lights of damages in respect of loss of light to other windows which were not ancient lights: *Re London Tilbury and Southend Railway and Gower's Walk Schools*, p. 327, *infra*.

[10] *Re Penny South Eastern Rly Co* (1857), 7 E & B 660.

account under each head is somewhat different. Compensation for severance, as the word implies, is limited to the effect on the retained land of the loss of the land taken. In the case of farm land, for example, the loss of essential farm buildings, although perhaps representing a negligible reduction in acreage, will clearly reduce the value of the remainder of the farm by the cost of their replacement, including, of course, the loss to cultivation of the land upon which the new buildings are to be built and any further loss that may be involved by having to relocate the new buildings in a less convenient position. Conversely, the loss of a substantial acreage may render the smaller holding retained very much less economical to run, perhaps further increasing the difficulties of the farmer by leaving him with buildings that can no longer be economically supported by the reduced acreage. Similarly, the farming operations may be rendered much less flexible by, for example, the division of the holding by a new road.[1]

The same principles, of course, apply to other types of property, for example, where a householder loses out-buildings or part of his garden or other amenity land; or where business premises are in any way severed. In this connection, however it is to be borne in mind that in appropriate circumstances vendors may require the acquisition of the entire holding.[2]

It is also to be noted in this context that the limitation of compensation for houses that are unfit for human habitation to the value of the cleared site[3] does not affect the assessment of compensation in respect of severance of such land from other land retained by the vendor. Thus, if the loss of the land taken (at cleared site value) prevents the intended expansion of adjoining business premises, the value of those premises will be reduced and compensation is payable accordingly.[4]

It is not, however, necessary that the damage to the land retained be immediate; it is sufficient if the loss of the land taken only renders abortive a proposed use of the land retained. Thus in *Ripley* v *Great Northern Railway*[5] compensation was awarded to the owner of a reservoir from which he proposed to supply water to cotton mills that he had hoped to build on the land taken. Similarly, prior to 1947[6] and post-1959[7] the potential development value of the land has to be taken into

---

[1] See for example *Cooke* v *Secretary of State for the Environment* (1973), 27 P & CR 234, note 6, p. 346, *post*.

[2] See pp. 108, *et seq*, *ante*.

[3] Housing Act 1957, s. 59, re-enacting the Housing Act 1936, s. 40(2). For compensation based on the value of the cleared site see pp. 255, *et seq*. *ante*.

[4] *Palmer & Harvey Ltd* v *Ipswich Corpn*, *(1953)*, 4 P & CR 5. In that case the authority relied upon a passage in the judgment in *Northwood* v *LCC*, (No. 2) [1926] 2 KB 411 where it was said that the "statute, by limiting the compensation to the selling value of the cleared site, excludes compensation for anything else" but it was held that the statutory provisions were not concerned with anything other than the compensation payable for the land acquired and that the Court in *Northwood*'s case were not considering any question of severance.

[5] (1875) 10 Ch. App. 435.

[6] For the situation under the Town and Country Planning Act 1947, see pp. 8, *et seq*, *ante*.

[7] If there is no planning permission for the development for which the land taken is claimed to be suitable the question of what development (if any) would be appropriate falls to be decided in accordance with the Land Compensation Act 1961, ss. 14–18 (re-enacting the Town and Country Planning Act 1959, ss. 2–6): pp. 185, *et seq*, *ante*: these assumptions do not apply to land retained: p. 181, *ante*..

account so that if the land retained cannot be developed[1] or becomes less suitable for development as a result of the severance, compensation will be payable on the basis of the resulting difference in development values.[2]

Injurious affection

The damage to retained land that gives rise to a claim to compensation on the ground of injurious affection is, however, very much wider, for it includes reductions in value attributable to the execution of works upon the land taken and the use to which that land is ultimately to be put.[3] The compensation for severance or injurious affection, being part of the overall compensation payable upon the compulsory acquisition of the land taken, has inevitably to be based upon the damage to the retained land that it is *anticipated*[4] will result from the construction or use of any works to be carried out on the land taken. It follows, therefore, that no further claim can be made for damage that arises later and which was foreseeable at the date on which compensation was agreed, or determined by the Lands Tribunal. It is, however, to be assumed that the use of the land taken will be in conformity with the statutory powers under which the works are to be constructed and operated. Damage caused by acts that are *ultra vires* or due to negligence or the exercise of statutory powers in a manner that is unnecessarily harmful to third parties[5] cannot be the basis of a claim for compensation related to the compulsory acquisition of the land on which the operation takes place; the remedy for such damage, on the contrary, is by action for damages and/or an injunction.[6]

Where, however, the damage is caused by works constructed partly on the land taken and partly on other land the claim for injurious affection can include the effect of the works as a whole and not merely the effect of that part of the works actually constructed on the land taken.[7]

Measure of compensation

The basic principle is that the compensation payable is to be equivalent to the amount by which the retained land has been reduced in value as a

---

[1] See, for example, *R* v *Brown* (1867), LR 2 QB 630.

[2] Subject, however, to the *Pointe Gourde* principle and the "set-off" provisions of the Land Compensation Act 1961, s. 6 and Sch. 1: pp. 217, *et seq, ante*, and see Measure of Compensation, below.

[3] I.e., including loss of amenity (e.g., increase in dust and noise consequent upon the use of a road constructed upon the land taken) and loss of privacy: see *Duke of Buccleuch* v *Metropolitan Water Board* (1872), LR 5 HL 418 and *R* v *Pearce ex parte London School Board* (1898), 67 LJ QB 842.

[4] *Rockingham Sisters of Charity* v *R.*, [1922] 2 AC 315.

[5] See, e.g., *Lagan Navigation Co.* v *Lamberg Bleaching Dyeing and Finishing Co.*, [1927] AC 226 per Lord Atkinson at p. 243.

[6] *Imperial Gas Light and Coke Co,* v *Broadbent* (1859), 7 HL Cas. 600; *Caledonian Railway* v *Colt* (1860), 3 Macq, 833; 3 LT 252.

[7] Land Compensation Act 1973, s. 44, thus overruling *Edwards* v *Minister of Transport,* [1964] 2 WLR 515, in which the compensation in respect of nuisance from a new road adjoining the claimant's property was held to be limited to the nuisance arising solely from the short length of the road actually constructed on land acquired from him.

result of the severance therefrom of the land taken and/or the injurious affection thereto resulting from the use to which the land taken is to be put. In this connection, however, the proper comparison is between the value of the retained land after taking account of the scheme[1] in pursuance of which the land taken is being acquired, and its value on the assumption that there is no such scheme. In *Clark* v *Wareham and Purbeck RDC*[2] land was acquired to construct a new sewage works to replace existing out-dated, inefficient and grossly overloaded works. The Lands Tribunal accepted the evidence of the acquiring authority that, but for the scheme, the old works would have been completely modernised. They rejected the authority's contention that the measure of damage to the land retained should be the difference between its value with the new works adjoining (the "with scheme world") and its value with the old works remaining unmodernised (the "real world") since to apply that difference would conflict with the *Pointe Gourde* principle[1] by bringing into account changes in value entirely due to the scheme. The proper yardstick for measuring injury to retained land was therefore held to be the difference between its value in the "with scheme world" and its value in the "no scheme world" as opposed to its value in the "real world". As this case demonstrates, the "no scheme world" will not necessarily be the same as the "real world", i.e., the state of affairs on the relevant date.

It is also to be noted that only what may be termed the "net depreciation" in the value of the land may be the subject of compensation. Thus, if the acquiring authority provide works designed to mitigate the nuisance, their effect in doing so must be taken into account.[3]

MORTGAGED LAND

Where part only of mortgaged land is acquired so that the land retained represents insufficient security for the principal money outstanding, the mortgagee is entitled to require the acquiring authority to pay to him such proportion of the compensation payable as is required to make good the deficiency, any dispute between mortgagee and mortgagor as to the appropriate amount being referable to the Lands Tribunal.[4] The same principle applies where mortgaged land is so injuriously affected as to reduce its value below that which is required to provide security for the loan.

Compensation for severance and injurious affection. Land retained by vendor of land compulsorily acquired: summary

1. If the owner of an interest in land compulsorily acquired has an interest or interests in other land which, together with the land taken

---

[1] Pp. 217, *et seq, ante.*
[2] (1972) 25 P & CR 423.
[3] See e.g. *Lord Breem's Executors* v *British Waterways Board* [1977] JPL 730 (unrestricted boating rights on canal replaced by a 20 year licence for a single boat) and see section 3B of this chapter, pp. 328, *et seq, infra.*
[4] Lands Clauses Consolidation Act 1845, s. 112. Compulsory Purchase Act 1965, s. 16.

formed a single holding,[1] he will be entitled to compensation in respect of any damage to the retained land that results from the severance therefrom of the land taken and/or from the use to which the land taken is to be put.[2]

2. The latter head of damage cannot include damage to a purely personal right unconnected with the land.[3] Nor can it include damage for which the appropriate remedy is an action for damages and/or an injunction, e.g., damage resulting from negligent or *ultra vires* actions on the part of the acquiring authority.[4]

3. Compensation may, however, be claimed in respect of interference with the enjoyment of the land retained, even though no legal right is infringed,[5] and if the works to be constructed on the land taken extend over other land not acquired from the claimant, damage resulting from the use of the works as a whole may be included.[6]

4. The measure of compensation in respect of both severance and injurious affection is the amount by which the value of the claimant's interest in the retained land is depreciated by the severance and/or the injurious affection resulting from the use to which the land taken is to be put.[7] In other words, the compensation payable is the difference between the value of the land retained, assuming no land is being taken, and its value after taking the acquisition into account.

5. In assessing the value of the retained land on this assumption, however, no account may be taken of any development potential arising solely from the scheme of development in pursuance of which the land taken is being acquired.[8]

6. If any of the land retained is increased in value by the scheme of development that increase must be deducted from the total compensation payable, i.e., in respect of injurious affection to other land retained together with that payable in respect of the land actually acquired.[9]

7. Subject to the above, the damage to the land retained for which compensation is payable includes all damage reasonably foreseeable as a result of the acquisition; no second claim can be accepted unless damage arises that could not reasonably have been foreseen.[10]

8. Compensation payable in respect of severance and injurious affection, being part of the total compensation in respect of the acquisition, may be liable to capital gains tax; it will, however, carry interest as from the date of entry or the date on which the compensation is determined, whichever is the earlier.[11]

---

[1] I.e., the interest in the retained land need not be the same interest throughout or the same as the interest in the land acquired: p. 315, *supra*.
[2] Compulsory Purchase Act 1965, s. 7, p. 314, *supra*.
[3] P. 316, *supra*.
[4] P. 318, *supra*.
[5] P. 316, *supra*.
[6] Land Compensation Act 1973, s. 44, p. 318, *supra*.
[7] P. 318, *supra*.
[8] *Clark* v *Wareham and Purbeck RDC* (1972), 25 P & CR 423: see p. 319, *supra*.
[9] Pp. 217, *et seq, ante*.
[10] P. 318, *supra*.
[11] P. 315, note 3, *supra*.

3 COMPENSATION FOR INJURIOUS AFFECTION TO LAND HELD BY THIRD PARTIES

A. The general law

Prior to the passing of the Land Compensation Act 1973 the right to compensation for injurious affection to land not held with the land acquired was extremely limited. It arose from the Lands Clauses Consolidation Act 1845, s. 68 which in essence merely provided a procedure for the settlement of claims to compensation in excess of £50 in respect of any lands injuriously affected by the execution of works. It has, however, been interpreted by the courts as establishing a right to compensation for the injurious affection of land not formerly held with the land acquired, and although s. 68 is not reproduced in modern legislation its judicial interpretation is specifically preserved.[1]

A claim arises whether the land on which the works giving rise to the injurious affection was purchased compulsorily or by agreement[2] but no claim arises if s. 68 (or Compulsory Purchase Act 1965, s. 10) is excluded by the special Act under which that land falls to be acquired.[3]

REQUIREMENTS

Subject to the above, a valid claim to compensation for injurious affection under this head must fulfil the following requirements:

(a) The injurious affection must result from the *execution* of the works and *not* from their use.[4] Although this requirement arises directly from the wording of the section the distinction between the two is not always as clear as at first appears. There seems little doubt, at any rate where the works are carried out on land acquired or appropriated for planning purposes under the Town and Country Planning Act 1971, that for this purpose "execution" includes works of maintenance for it is provided by the Town and Country Planning Act, 1971 that:

> "The erection, construction or carrying out, or maintenance, of any building or work on land which has been acquired or appropriated by a local authority for planning purposes, whether done by the local authority or by a person deriving title under them, is authorised by virtue of this section if it is done in accordance with planning permission, notwithstanding that it involves interference with an interest or right to which this section applies, or involves a breach of a restriction as to the user of land arising by virtue of a contract."[5]

Subsection (3) of s. 127 provides that compensation shall be payable in

---

[1] Compulsory Purchase Act 1965, s. 10, sub-s. (1) brings the procedure up to date by substituting determination by the Lands Tribunal for determination by an arbitrator or jury, and sub-s. (2) gives statutory recognition to "the right which s. 68 of the Lands Clauses Consolidation Act 1845 has been construed as affording."

[2] *Kirby* v *Harrogate School Board*, [1896] 1 Ch. 437.

[3] *Ferrar* v *London Sewers Comrs* (1869), LR 4 Ex. 227. *Jolliffe* v *Exeter Corporation*, [1967] 1 WLR 993.

[4] *Hammersmith City Rly Co* v *Brand* (1869) LR 4 HL 171, in which it was held that no claim for compensation for injurious affection arising from vibration etc., from locomotives using a railway line already completed could be sustained. See, however, p. 322, *infra*.

[5] Note, however, the proviso to s. 127(1) excluding interference with the apparatus, etc. of statutory undertakers. Section 127(2) applies this section to "any easement liberty, privilege, right or advantage annexed to land and adversely affecting other land, including any natural right of support".

respect of any interference or breach of contract authorised by sub-section (1) under the Lands Clauses Consolidation Act 1845, s. 63 or 68, or under the Compulsory Purchase Act 1965, s. 7 or 10, in the same way as compensation is payable for other injurious affection under those sections.

The leading case on this aspect of the law is *Fletcher* v *Birkenhead Corporation*,[1] where the sub-stratum beneath a house was described as a "wet running silt" the removal of which by the pumping of under-ground water in order to fill, and then keep full, a reservoir constructed by the respondent Corporation caused subsidence to the appellant's house.

Like s. 127 of the Act of 1971, the relevant statutory provision[2] also made specific reference to "maintenance". The appellant was held entitled to compensation for the damage to his house caused by the subsidence resulting from the removal of the silt along with the water, on the ground, *inter alia*, that a reservoir does not really come into existence as such until it is filled with water, but also on the ground that even if the pumping operations were not covered by the word "con-struction" they were clearly covered by the word "maintenance".[3]

This case was distinguished from the earlier case of *Hammersmith and City Rly Co* v *Brand* (*supra*)—a case involving the corresponding pro-visions of the Railway Clauses Consolidation Act 1845—on the grounds that there was no analogy between the running of locomotives on a railway line the construction of which had already been completed, and the pumping of water for the purpose of filling a reservoir and thereafter maintaining the water supply. There was the further dis-tinction, however, in that there is no mention of "maintenance" in the relevant section of the Railway Clauses Consolidation Act;[4] in that section, however, the word used is "construction" as opposed to "execution" of works and in following the Court of Appeal decision in *Fletcher*'s case in *re Simeon and the Isle of Wight RDC*[5] (also concerned with the extraction of underground water, in this case in breach of a restric-tive covenant) Luxmoore J appears to have taken the view that the drawing of the water from the land, as a prerequisite to its supply, is an "execution" of the works authorised, and that the words "execution of works" are wider than "construction of works" and "include the exer-cise that is the carrying out and the execution of the appropriate statutory powers".[6] As already suggested, since waterworks in effect cease to be waterworks unless continuously supplied with water there is clearly a case for regarding the requisite extraction as, in a sense, a continuing operation or "execution" but it is difficult to think of other public works to which such a principle can sensibly be applied, and it is submitted that Luxmoore J's extremely wide interpretation of the

[1] [1907] 1 KB 205.
[2] Waterworks Clauses Act 1847, s. 6.
[3] Collins, MR at p. 214. For a recent case involving a right of support see *Wilson's Brewery Ltd.* v *West Yorkshire Metropolitan County Council* [1977] JPL 667.
[4] S. 6.
[5] [1937] Ch. 525.
[6] Per Luxmoore J at p. 539.

words "execution of works" cannot be universally applicable to claims for compensation under the Lands Clauses Consolidation Act 1845, s. 68, or the Compulsory Purchase Act 1965, s. 10.[1]

The effect of this requirement is, however, somewhat modified by the Land Compensation Act 1973, Part I,[2] which provides for the payment of compensation to a limited category of owners[3] of neighbouring property which is depreciated by certain specified types of nuisance[4] arising from the use as opposed to the execution of public works, including such nuisance arising from a newly constructed or improved highway.

Furthermore, where the actual carrying out of such works so affects the enjoyment of any neighbouring dwelling that its continued occupation is not reasonably practicable, the appropriate authority[5] has a discretionary power to pay the extra costs[6] of the occupier in providing himself and his family with alternative accommodation for the whole or any part of the period during which the works are being carried out.[7] No payment may be made, however, except in pursuance of an agreement entered into between the claimant and the authority prior to the expenses being incurred.[8]

(b) The value of the *land or interest in land* must be directly affected by physical interference with some legal right[9] of which the claimant is entitled to make use in connection with his property.[10] This requirement also follows from the opening words of the Lands Clauses Consolidation Act 1845, s. 68, namely "if any party shall be entitled to any compensation in respect of any *land or interest in land* . . . etc". No compensation is therefore payable in respect of a purely personal right which is neither connected with, nor appurtenant to, land. For example, a right, albeit an exclusive right, to sell refreshments in a theatre is a licence unless some specific part of the premises is actually demised.[11] Similarly, there being no legal right to privacy or a view, loss of such amenities cannot be the basis of a claim to compensation under this head.

On the other hand, a right to take the products of land (as in the case of sporting rights)[12] may amount to a profit à prendre, and interference

---

[1] See, for example, the clear distinction between "construction" and "use" drawn by Lord Halsbury LC in *Cowper Essex* v *Acton Local Board* (1889), 14 App. Cas. 153 at p. 161, and by Lord Watson at p. 164, there being no distinction drawn between the words "construction" and "execution".

[2] See the next section of this chapter, pp. 328, *et seq, infra*.

[3] Broadly owner-occupiers: see pp. 330, *et seq, infra*.

[4] See pp. 329, *et seq, infra*.

[5] As to which see note 6, p. 335, *infra*.

[6] Land Compensation Act 1973, s. 28. Since only the extra costs are recoverable (*Ibid*, s. 28(3)) allowance has to be made for expenses that would in any case have had to be incurred had the claimant remained in his own home, e.g., costs of food, heat, light, any reduction in rates, etc.

[7] *Ibid*, s. 28(2).

[8] *Ibid*, s. 28(3).

[9] Interference giving rise to a claim to compensation may be to a public as well as to a private right, but in the former case the claimant must show special damage over and above that suffered by the general public: see para. (c), *infra*.

[10] *Ricket* v *Metropolitan Rly Co* (1867), LR 2HL, 175.

[11] *Frank Warr & Co. Ltd.* v *LCC*, [1904] 1 KB 713.

[12] *Bird* v *Great Eastern Rly Co* (1865), 34 LJCP 366; but shooting or fishing rights, etc. if not appurtenant to land may merely constitute a licence.

with profits à prendre or easements,[1] both of which are appurtenant to land, will give rise to a claim to compensation. Similarly, compensation will be payable in respect of a breach by the acquiring authority of a restrictive covenant benefiting and therefore running with the land and affecting its value,[2] but not in respect of a purely personal covenant for the convenience of the occupier. The breach must, however, result from the execution as opposed to the use of the works constructed under the statutory powers.[3]

Riparian rights of access to and use of a river[4] (as well as the right to an undiminished flow of water therein)[5] and the analogous right of access to and from a public highway[6] are equally legal rights, interference with which will give rise to claims to compensation under this head if the value of the land (or an interest therein) is thereby diminished. Where, however, the interference with a public right results in loss of profits, such damage is regarded as on the one hand too remote and on the other as not amounting to any physical interference with land or any interest in land, but only with the personal interests of the occupier resulting from the particular purpose for which he uses the land.[7]

Thus highway alterations making access to a public house less convenient and resulting in loss of custom and therefore profits cannot be the subject of a claim to compensation[7] and the same applies where the construction of a bridge prevents access of shipping to a wharf.[8]

On the other hand it seems that where such loss of profit affects the

---

[1] *Glover v North Staffs. Rly Co* (1851), 16 QB 912; *Furness Rly Co v Cumberland Co-op Building Society* (1884), 52 LT 144; *Barnard v Great Western Rly Co* (1902), 86 LT 798 (interference with private rights of way); *Eagle v Charing Cross Rly Co* (1867), LR 2CP 638; *Re London Tilbury and Southend Rly Co and Gower's Walk Schools* (1889), 24 QBD 326 (interference with ancient light); *Metropolitan Board of Works v Metropolitan Rly Co* (1868), LR 3CP 612 (interference with a right of support).

[2] *Long Eaton Recreation Grounds Co v Midland Railway*, [1902] 2 KB 574 (a decision of the Court of Appeal) in which the Railway Company erected an embankment in breach of a covenant restricting any building to a certain building line and restricted the type of building to the erection of private dwellings. For a method of assessing compensation for infringement of a restrictive covenant see *SJC Construction Ltd. v Sutton London Borough Council* (1974), 28 P & CR 200: p. 285, *ante*.

[3] In the *Long Eaton* case, *supra*, the judge of first instance (Lawrence J) thought otherwise, but the point was not raised in the Court of Appeal: see, however, para. (a), *supra*. In that case the question considered by the Court of Appeal was confined to whether the erection of the embankment constituted a breach of a covenant not to build. It was held that it did. The additional interference with the amenities of the dominant tenement by the use of the railway thereafter was not in issue, and would in any event be a matter going to the *quantum* of damages which was a question for the arbitrator. However, where a restrictive covenant restricts use of the servient land there is no reason why a public authority, unless specifically empowered to override such restrictions *without* paying compensation, should be in any better position in respect to damages than any other owner of the servient land.

[4] *Macey v Metropolitan Board of Works* (1864) 33 LJ Ch. 377: *Lyon v Fishmongers' Co* (1876), 1 App. Cas. 662. And the same principle applies to access to the sea: *Attorney-General of Straits Settlements v Wemyss* (1888), 13 App. Cas. 192.

[5] *Mortimer v South Wales Rly Co* (1859), 1 E & E 375: see, however, the Water Act 1945, for the code governing the abstraction of water by statutory water undertakers. See also note 5 on p. 316, *supra*.

[6] *Caledonian Rly Co v Walker's Trustees* (1882), 7 App. Cas. 259; access rendered steeper and less direct; *Chamberlain v West End of London and Crystal Palace Rly Co* (1863), 2 B & S 617: access partially obstructed; *R v St. Luke's Vestry* (1871), LR 7 QB 148: level of a footway lowered; *Metropolitan Board of Works v Howard* (1889), 5 TLR 732: highway no longer a thoroughfare due to closing of a bridge.

[7] *Ricket v Metropolitan Rly Co* (1867), LR 2 HL 175.

[8] *Hewett v Essex County Council* (1927), 97 LJ KB 249.

value of an interest in the land, compensation therefor may be claimed; thus in *Hewett*'s case[1] where the owners of a wharf were held not to be entitled to claim the cost of building a new wharf below a bridge that obstructed access to the original wharf, the extra cost of handling thereat, nor compensation for loss of traffic. They were, however, held to be entitled to compensation in respect of the depreciation in the value of the old wharf which would, of course, reflect increased handling costs and the volume of traffic using it. Similarly, where access from the main traffic flow to a car dealing business was permanently obstructed, it was held that although no compensation was payable in respect of the loss of profit, in so far as such loss depreciated the value of the plaintiff's interest (a tenancy from year to year) compensation was payable therefor.[2]

Thus, in the case of certain types of commercial premises, those of retailers, for example, where value has a direct relationship to profitability, its loss or reduction will in practice be recoverable, albeit indirectly, provided, of course, that the premises do not have as great or greater value for other purposes.

It is suggested, however, that a helpful distinction may lie in the fact that the profitability of a business is the basis of goodwill which attaches to the proprietor rather than to the land, and can, of course, be sold quite separately. Where, however, goodwill depends upon the location of the premises, reduction in its value due to reduced profits will clearly affect their value.

In summary, it may be said, as a general proposition, that the test is whether or not the market value of the claimant's interest in his land has been depreciated by the execution of the relevant statutory powers. This test, however, is not wholly comprehensive, for compensation has been awarded for interference with ancient lights despite the fact that the saleable value of the property was not affected.[3]

(c) The cause of injurious affection must be such that in the absence of statutory powers it would be actionable as a tort.[4] It is from this rule, which somewhat overlaps the previous rule, that it follows that interference with a public right can only found a claim for compensation where the claimant suffers some special damage other than that inflicted upon the general public.[5] Thus the narrowing of a stretch of road, though causing general inconvenience to the public may result in special damage to properties fronting thereon.[6] Similarly, the absence of a claim to compensation for loss of privacy or other intangible amenity may seem as much an example of the application of this requirement as of that described in the previous paragraph.

---

[1] *Hewett* v *Essex County Council*, *supra*.
[2] *Argyle Motors (Birkenhead) Ltd.* v *Birkenhead Corpn*, [1974] 2 WLR 71 HL.
[3] *Eagle* v *Charing Cross Rly Co* (1867), LR 2 CP 638.
[4] *Ricket* v *Metropolitan Rly Co*, *supra*: *Metropolitan Board of Works* v *McCarthy* (1874), LR 7 HL 243: it is from this rule that it follows that assessment of compensation under this head is subject to the same general rules as the assessment of damages in tort, *infra*. Note, however, the inclusion under this head of damages arising from breach of restrictive covenants: see p. 324, *supra*, and notes 2 and 3 thereon.
[5] P. 324, *supra*.
[6] *Beckett* v *Midland Rly Co* (1867), LR 3 CP 82.

(d) The act causing the damage must however be *intra vires* the statute: if it is *ultra vires* the remedy remains by action.[1] But where a claim to compensation has been made in such circumstances, the courts have shown considerable reluctance in accepting a defence founded by the responsible authority or undertakers on their own negligence or lack of statutory authority for the action giving rise to the injurious affection.[2] In such cases the authority is therefore in the somewhat invidious position of having to prove its own negligence or excess use of its powers.

Further claims. As in the case of claims to compensation for severance and injurious affection where land is retained by the vendor of land acquired[3] it seems clear that "a person seeking to obtain compensation under these Acts must once for all make one claim for all damages which can be reasonably foreseen".[4] But the Lands Clauses Consolidation Act 1845, s. 68, refers to land which "*has been* ... injuriously affected ..." and, although there appear to be no reported cases on this point, logic would seem to point to a further claim being permissible where, for example as a result of a change of plan by the authority concerned, damage occurs which could not have been foreseen at the date of the initial claim. There is, for example, no suggestion that an earlier claim for compensation would have affected the position in the *Long Eaton*[5] case which appears to have been brought after, rather than in anticipation of, the building of the embankment.

MEASURE OF COMPENSATION

It follows from para. (c), *supra*, that the assessment of compensation follows the same principles as are applicable to the assessment of damages in tort.[5] Since compensation under this head is payable only in respect of physical interference with rights appertaining to land or interests in land the rule of *restitutio in integrum* applies so that compensation falls to be assessed as the amount required to restore the claimant to the financial position in which he would have been had he not suffered the interference in question.[6]

It follows also that where in fact there is a common law right of property giving rise to an action without proof of damage, such as in the case of trespass to land, or interference with riparian rights,[7] rights of light[8] or rights of way[9] the same applies to claims to compensation.

---

[1] *Imperial Gas, Light and Coke Co.* v *Broadbent* (1859), 7 HL Cas. 600: *Caledonian Rly Co* v *Colt* (1860), 3 Macq. 833.
[2] *Uttley* v *Todmorden Board of Health* (1874), 44 LJCP 19: *Colac (President etc. of)* v *Summerfield*, [1893] AC 187 PC; *Welsh National Water Development Authority* v *Burgess* (1974), 28 P & CR 378.
[3] See p. 318, *supra*.
[4] Per Erle CJ in *Chamberlain* v *West End of London and Crystal Palace Rly Co* (1863), 2 B & S 617 at p. 638, a case under the Lands Clauses Consolidation Act 1845, s. 68.
[5] See notes 2 and 3, p. 324, *supra*.
[6] *Livingstone* v *Rawyards Coal Co.* (1880), 5 App. Cas. 25 per Lord Blackburn at p. 39; *Shearman* v *Folland*, [1950] 2 KB 43 per Asquith LJ at p. 49.
[7] *McCartney* v *Londonderry and Lough Swilly Rly Co*, [1904] AC 301: *Jones* v *Llanrwst UDC*, [1911] 1 Ch. 393.
[8] *Colls* v *Home & Colonial Stores*, [1904] AC 179: *Jolly* v *Kine*, [1907] AC 1; and see *Eagle* v *Charing Cross Rly Co*, p. 324 supra.
[9] *Kidgill* v *Moor* (1850), 9 CB 364.

In *Re London, Tilbury & Southend Railway and Gower's Walk Schools*[1] Lord Esher MR held that compensation arising from interference with ancient lights could include the additional loss of value resulting from interference with light to other windows which were not ancient lights, on the ground that even if such additional damage could not be recovered in an action in tort (which he thought would be the case) it could nevertheless be included in the compensation payable under the Railway Clauses Consolidation Act 1845, s. 16 thereby implying that the claim to compensation under that Act (similar in terms to the Lands Clauses Consolidation Act 1845, s. 68) is wider than the claim for damages sustainable in an action in tort. But in *Horton v Colwyn Bay UDC*[2] these views of Lord Esher's appear to have been accepted as a correct statement of the law in cases of tort rather than as an authority for the proposition that compensation under this head covers a wider range of injury than that for which damages can be claimed in tort. The principle is stated by Lord Esher thus:

"The plaintiff is entitled to recover for all the damage caused which was the direct consequence of the wrongful act, and so probable a consequence that, if the defendant had considered the matter, he must have foreseen that the whole damage would result from that act. If that be so, and a person puts up buildings, the inevitable consequence of their erection being to obstruct ancient and modern lights, should he not be taken to have foreseen that in obstructing the one he would obstruct the other? If that were proved in a common law action the plaintiff would be entitled to damages for the whole of the consequences of the wrongful act of obstructing ancient lights, which would include damage to the new as much as to the old lights."[3]

This principle is not, in tort,[4] confined to rights of light, but it is difficult to see to what physical interference with other rights enjoyed in connection with any interest in land it would be applicable.

In the same way, where, for example, the injury complained of is actual damage to a building the complainant cannot recover compensation for further damage resulting from his failure to act reasonably in mitigating the damage;[5] so far as he fails to do so he may be met by a plea of contributory negligence.[6] Conversely he may not increase his claim by including damage caused by his own unnecessary actions. Such damage may also, however, be said to be too remote as in the case where the injury complained of is the loss of profits.[7]

PAYMENT OF INTEREST

It is to be noted that compensation for severance and/or injurious affection where land has been acquired from the claimant, being part of the total compensation payable in respect of that acquisition carries

[1] (1889) 24 QBD 326.
[2] [1908] 1 KB 327.
[3] See also *Griffith v Richard Clay & Sons*, [1912] 2 Ch 291: *Wills v May*, [1923] 1 Ch. 317.
[4] For an application to a claim in respect of personal injuries see *Wormald v Cole*, [1954] 1 QB 614.
[5] *British Westinghouse Co. Ltd. v Underground Railways*, [1912] AC 673. But it has been held that it would be unreasonable to expect a plaintiff to destroy his own property in order to minimise the damages payable by the defendant: *Elliott Steam Tug Co. v Shipping Controller*, [1922] 1 KB 127, 140.
[6] *R A Brand & Co. v S. Barrow & Co.* (1965), 109 Sol Jo 834.
[7] *Ricket v Metropolitan Rly Co*, p. 324, *supra*.

interest in the same way as does the purchase money on a sale between individuals where there is delay upon the part of the purchaser.[1] There are in addition special provisions for the payment of interest where the acquiring authority enter before the compensation has been agreed or awarded where the eventual settlement carries interest from the date of entry.[2]

Hitherto there has been no provision for the payment of interest on compensation for injurious affection to land owned by third parties—indeed, there is no obvious date from which such interest ought to be payable. Since May 1973,[3] however, interest is payable from the date of claim.[4]

PRACTICE NOTE

The first essential to a claim for compensation, as for damages in tort, is for the claimant to show that the authority caused the injury complained of, at least in part. Similarly, if contributory negligence is pleaded it must be shown that the complainant's negligence is at least partly the cause of injury.[5]

In assessing the amount by which an interest in land has been depreciated by the acts complained of it is permissible to assume that the property can be placed upon the market in the manner most favourable to the owner. Thus, if the damage is to an agricultural estate which it is thought would command a higher price by sale in lots, the difference between the value of the land before and after the damage occurred may be calculated accordingly.[6] But whatever the method adopted it is almost always advisable to present expert evidence to support both the proposed method of sale and the relevant valuation.[7]

B. Compensation for injurious affection under Part I of the Land Compensation Act 1973

INTRODUCTION

The Land Compensation Act 1973, set out to alleviate the damage caused to neighbouring property in two ways. Part I of the Act considerably extends the rights of a limited class of owners of land from whom no land is acquired, but whose land is depreciated in value by specified "physical factors" caused by the *use* of public works on

---

[1] Re *Piggott & Great Western Railway* (1887), 18 Ch. D 146.

[2] Compulsory Purchase Act 1965, s. 11: for the prerequisite of such entry see p. 70, *ante*. The rate of interest is that prescribed from time to time by Treasury regulations made under the Land Compensation Act 1961, s. 32.

[3] Land Compensation Act 1973, s. 63.

[4] As to the rate of interest, see the current Acquisition of Land (Rate of Interest after Entry) Regulations.

[5] *Caswell* v *Powell Duffryn Associated Collieries Ltd.*, [1940] per Lord Atkin at p. 165.

[6] *Colman* v *Basingstoke RDC* (1966), 17 P & CR 270, LT.

[7] For cases in which lay evidence on behalf of a claimant has been dismissed as wholly inadequate to rebut the expert evidence called by the authority see, for example, the Lands Tribunal decisions in *King* v *West Dorset Water Board* (1962), 14 P & CR 166; *Lucey's Personal Representatives and Wood* v *Harrogate Corpn* (1963), 14 P & CR 377; and *Rush and Tomkins Ltd.* v *West Kent Main Sewerage Board* (1963), 14 P & CR 469.

neighbouring land. It is with these provisions that this section of this chapter is concerned. The second set of provisions in Part II of the Act increases the powers of public authorities, particularly highway authorities, by permitting the acquisition of land that is not actually required for roads or other public works but which may be adversely affected by the *construction or use* thereof,[1] and to use such additional land or any other land in their possession (including land forming part of a highway) for the carrying out of subsidiary works for the purpose of mitigating the effect of the main or original works on their immediate surroundings.[2]

Although these latter provisions are primarily concerned with conferring the requisite powers[3] upon highways etc., authorities, there are two sections of Part II of the Act[4] which deal with the insulation of buildings against noise caused by the construction or use of public works. In so far as they fit any of the conventional heads of compensation it would seem appropriate to consider these sections here, in part because they provide a specific remedy for injurious affection arising from noise, and in part because, once again, the mitigating effect of such insulation has to be taken into account in assessing compensation under Part I.[5] These provisions will be dealt with separately in the last section of this chapter.[6]

DAMAGE GIVING RISE TO A CLAIM TO COMPENSATION

Under Part I of the Act, compensation can be claimed in respect of the depreciation in the value of a qualifying interest[7] in land caused by noise, vibration, smell, fumes, smoke, artificial lighting or by the discharge on to the land of any substance, whether solid or liquid arising from the *use*[8] of certain public works,[9] provided that use commenced after 16 October 1969. The relevant public works are defined as any highway, aerodrome or any other works provided in the exercise of statutory powers on any land used in the exercise of such powers.[10] They include, moreover, any alteration to the carriageway of a highway;[11] any reconstruction, extension or other alteration to other

---

[1] Land Compensation Act 1973, Part II, ss. 22 and 26.

[2] *Ibid*, ss. 23 and 27.

[3] See note 1, p. 341, *infra*,

[4] *Ibid*, ss. 20 and 21.

[5] P. 338, *infra*.

[6] Pp. 340 *et seq*, *infra*.

[7] As to which see p. 330 *infra*.

[8] As opposed to their construction, as to which see p. 321 *supra*. Note, however, the powers conferred upon responsible authorities to pay the expenses of persons moving temporarily during the *construction* of works: Land Compensation Act 1973, s. 28, p. 323, *supra*.

[9] *Ibid*, s. 1.

[10] *Ibid*, s. 1(3): for example, land used as a refuse tip: see *Shepherd and Shepherd v Lancashire CC*, p. 333, note 6, *infra*.

[11] I.e., by realignment (horizontally or vertically), widening, or by provision of an additional carriageway; but in such cases compensation is only payable if the noise, vibration, etc., emanates from the actual length of carriageway altered, etc.: Land Compensation Act 1973, s. 9(5). In *Hickmott v Dorset County Council* (1975), 30 P & CR 237 (upheld on appeal [1977] JPL 715) it was held that increase in traffic and therefore of vibration alleged to have damaged the claimant's house reflected the general increase in traffic upon classified roads in the South West and could not be attributed to improving the alignment of the road in question within a relatively quiet village.

public works[1] or any change of use in respect of any public works other than a highway or aerodrome.[2] Although the source of the noise, vibration, etc. must be situated on or in the public works alleged to be their cause, an aircraft causing any of these nuisances on approach or departure is for this purpose deemed to be within the boundaries of the aerodrome in question.[3]

Moreover, since the object of these provisions is to provide a remedy where none otherwise exists, they do not extend to cases where an action lies in tort, so that no compensation can be claimed unless the aerodrome or other works are covered by some statutory immunity.[4]

Compensation does not, therefore, cover injurious affection arising from accidents to either aircraft or vehicles on a highway.[5]

QUALIFYING INTERESTS: GENERAL RULE

Dwellings

The interests in the land injuriously affected that give rise to a right to compensation[6] are closely similar to those which entitle an owner thereof to serve a blight notice.[7] That is to say, that they are confined in the case of a dwelling[8] to "an owner's interest", i.e., ownership of the freehold and/or of a leasehold interest for a term of years certain having at least three years unexpired at the date of the notice of claim,[9] provided that, if the interest carries the right of occupation, the owner of that interest must in fact occupy the dwelling as his residence.

---

[1] Note, however, that in the case of an aerodrome these provisions only apply to alterations to *runways* (by realignment, extension or strengthening, or provision of a new runway) or *aprons* (where the alteration must be designed to provide for an increased number of aircraft): Land Compensation Act 1973, s. 9(6).

[2] *Ibid*, s. 9(1): note, however, that such alterations must have taken place subsequent to the date on which the highway was first opened to the public or the date on which the public works were first used. Note also that a change of use does not include intensification of existing use: *ibid*, s. 9(7).

[3] *Ibid*, s. 1(5).

[4] *Ibid*, s. 1(6). In the case of aerodromes statutory immunity is provided by the Civil Aviation Act 1949, s. 41(2). Thus no claim to compensation arises in the case of aerodromes to which this section does not apply at the time when the nuisance arises. Application of this subsection is by Order in Council: see, for example, the Air Navigation Order, 1966, (SI 1966 No. 1184); the Civil Aviation Act (Isle of Man) Order 1952, (SI 1952 No. 1032), and the Civil Aviation Act (Channel Islands) Order, 1953, (SI 1953 No. 393), etc. Note, however, that the immunity created by this section does not prevent the granting of an injunction where there has been a breach of a condition of an aerodrome licence: *Bosworth-Smith* v *Gwynnes Ltd*. (1919), 89 LJ Ch. 368, following *Polsue and Alfieri Ltd*. v *Rushmer*, [1907] AC 121.

If, however, a claim to compensation under these provisions is resisted on the ground that no enactment relating to the works in question in fact confers immunity and no compensation is accordingly paid, it cannot afterwards be contended in defending a subsequent action that any enactment in force when the claim was resisted does, after all, afford protection from actions for nuisance; *ibid*, s. 17, and cf. the reaction of the Courts in similar circumstances in regard to claims for compensation under the Compulsory Purchase Act 1965, s. 10, p. 326, *supra*.

[5] Land Compensation Act 1973, s. 1(7).

[6] *Ibid*, s. 2. Note, however, that the interests must have been acquired *before* the "relevant date": see the heading *Qualifying Dates, infra*.

[7] Pp. 131 *et seq, ante*. The term "resident owner-occupier", in relation to the blight notice provisions, is, however, widened to include the reversioner of a dwelling occupied by a tenant.

[8] I.e., a building or part of a building occupied, or (if not occupied) last occupied or intended to be occupied, as a private dwelling and including any garden, yard, outhouses and appurtenances belonging to or usually enjoyed with that building: Land Compensation Act 1973, s. 87(1).

[9] See the heading *The Claim Period, infra*.

In short, except in the case of a freehold reversion subject to a lease or a leasehold subject to a sub-lease which in either case gives a right of occupation, compensation will only be payable to someone in residence.

Business Premises

In the case of non-residential premises a similar provision to those applicable to the service of a blight notice again applies. Thus no compensation is payable in respect of investment property. In the case of business property the land must at the date of service of the notice of claim, comprise or form part of a hereditament,[1] the annual value[1] of which does not exceed the amount currently prescribed by order under the Town and Country Planning Act 1971.[2] Again, the claimant must be in occupation of at least a substantial part of the land in right of an owner's interest, i.e., as freeholder, or leaseholder under a lease having not less than three years to run at the date of claim.[3]

Agricultural Land

In the case of an agricultural unit, however, the freeholder or lessee (again the lease must have three years unexpired) must occupy the whole unit although he need only occupy a part in right of an owner's interest. Thus a farmer who owns only part of his holding as freeholder or lessee, and has but a lesser interest in the remainder, may claim in respect of the whole.[4] It follows, therefore, that no compensation is payable in respect of injury to non-residential property (including a farm)[5] to the freeholder not in occupation. Moreover, the requirement that at least part of an agricultural unit must be occupied in right of an owner's interest is somewhat more restrictive than at first appears for it will rule out most agricultural holdings held under a tenancy, the normal tenancy in England and Wales being a tenancy from year to year. This seems anomalous for, because of the security of tenure provisions of the Agricultural Holdings Act 1948, such a tenant will usually have an expectation of continued possession considerably exceeding the minimum three-year period of future enjoyment laid down in the case of a lease.[6] There is the further anomaly arising from the fact that a tenant of an agricultural holding which is compulsorily

---

[1] As defined in the Town and Country Planning Act 1971, s. 207: Land Compensation Act 1973, s. 2(6): see p. 130, *ante*.

[2] The current limit is £2,250: Town and Country Planning (Limit of Annual Value) Order, 1973, (SI 1973 No. 425).

[3] Note that no account may be taken of any expectation of a renewal of the tenancy under the Landlord and Tenant Act 1954: cf. the contrary situation where leasehold business premises are compulsorily acquired: Land Compensation Act 1973, s. 47, p. 367, *post*.

[4] It should, however, be noted that a 364-day grazing tenancy is normally a licence and does not, therefore, constitute an interest in land.

[5] Which, in this context, includes the farm house or other dwelling if occupied by the tenant of the agricultural unit for the purpose of farming the land: Town and Country Planning Act 1971, s. 207(1); Land Compensation Act 1973, s. 87(1).

[6] If serious damage is suffered the landlord's interest will, of course, be affected since it will ultimately be reflected in the rent, which under the Agricultural Holdings Act 1948 may be submitted to arbitration at the instance of either party at intervals of not less than three years. If, therefore, serious damage is anticipated, landlords may in some cases be well advised to consider the granting of a lease (before the "relevant date", *infra*, but having at least three years to run thereafter) so that the tenant can claim compensation and the landlord can take it into account at the next rent review.

acquired is now entitled to compensation that takes his security of tenure into account.[1]

Rights under the Leasehold Reform Act 1967

In contrast, special provision is made to take account of a lessee's rights to acquire the freehold or an extended lease of a house by virtue of the Leasehold Reform Act 1967, Part I.[2] Where, before the "relevant date"[3] the lessee has given his landlord notice of his desire to obtain the freehold or an extended lease, his existing lease is to be treated as conferring an owner's interest even though it has less than three years to run. If, however, the claim is not made until after the freehold or an extended lease has been acquired, compensation is only payable in respect of his original interest.[4] Similarly, if, having acquired the freehold or extended lease, he disposes of it, he cannot thereafter claim compensation for the damage to his previous qualifying interest. He may, however, do so if he has merely contracted to sell the freehold or extended lease, provided the claim is made before the beginning of the "claim period".[5]

QUALIFYING INTERESTS: EXCEPTIONS TO THE GENERAL RULE

Trustees

To the general rule that claims to compensation are confined to persons within the above categories, exceptions are made in favour of a mortgagee of a qualifying interest, and of trustees where, under the terms of the trust a person beneficially entitled is entitled or permitted to occupy the land. In this latter case occupation by such a person is to be treated as occupation by the trustees in right of the interest vested in them.[6]

Mortgagees

A mortgagee of an interest may claim as if he were the person entitled to that interest but he may only claim in respect of the damage to the interest subject to the mortgage. Thus if he is mortgagee of the freehold of a hereditament or agricultural unit in the occupation of the mortgagor he may claim as if he himself were in occupation, but if the mortgagor has leased the property to a lessee in occupation, the mortgagee will have no claim. Moreover a claim by a mortgagee does not prevent a claim by the mortgagor, though the former's interest is protected by the provision that any compensation paid in respect of an interest subject to a mortgage is payable to him or, if there is more than one mortgagee, to the first mortgagee.[7]

QUALIFYING DATES

The general rule is that the "qualifying interest" must have been

---

[1] Land Compensation Act 1973, s. 48: p. 367, *post*.
[2] A lease carrying such a right is referred to in the Act as "a qualifying tenancy".
[3] See the heading *Qualifying Dates, infra*.
[4] Including, therefore, a leasehold interest having less than three years to run.
[5] See the heading *The Claim Period, infra*.
[6] Land Compensation Act 1973, s. 10(4). Note, however, that this does not apply where land is vested in a sole tenant for life within the meaning of the Settled Land Act 1925.
[7] Land Compensation Act 1973, s. 10(1).

acquired[1] before the relevant date,[2] that is to say, the date on which the public works giving rise to the injury are first used or, in the case of a highway, first open to the public.[3] As already indicated, no claim arises in respect of works, etc. already in use as at 16 October 1969.[4] If, however, the claim to compensation arises from the subsequent alteration of the carriageway of an existing highway; the reconstruction of or other alteration to other public works;[5] or any change of use of any public works other than a highway or an aerodrome, the relevant date is adjusted accordingly, and becomes the date on which the highway is re-opened to public traffic or the other works are first used after completion of the alterations. In the case of a change of use the relevant date is the date of such change.[6]

In this context a person who has acquired a qualifying interest after the relevant date but has done so by inheritance[7] from a person who had such an interest[8] before the relevant date is in effect deemed to have acquired his interest before that date.[9]

THE CLAIM PERIOD: GENERAL RULE

The relevant date is not only important as the first test as to whether an interest which would otherwise qualify the owner to claim compensation in fact entitles him to do so,[10] but also because it determines the period within which claims may be made. As a general rule the "claim period" is the two-year period beginning on the expiration of twelve months from the relevant date,[11] a provision which is presumably intended to ensure that there is some experience of the effect of

---

[1] For this purpose acquisition in pursuance of a contract dates from the date of the contract; Land Compensation Act 1973, s. 19(2).

[2] Ibid, s. 2(1).

[3] Ibid, s. 1(9).

[4] Ibid, s. 1(8).

[5] Note, however, that in the case of an aerodrome these provisions only apply to runway and apron alterations: ibid, s. 9(3). See note 1, p. 329, supra.

[6] Ibid, s. 9(1) and (2). The responsible authority (see note 6, p, 335, infra) is required, on demand, to furnish a written statement indicating the relevant date; in the case of a claim arising from runway or apron alterations on an aerodrome it is for the Secretary of State to certify the relevant date, but these provisions apply only where the relevant date falls after 23 June 1973: ibid, s. 15. In Shepherd and Shepherd v Lancashire County Council, [1977] JPL 106 (a claim in respect of nuisance arising from use of neighbouring land as a controlled refuse tip) the County Council unsuccessfully contended that the date on which the public works would be first used after completion (the relevant date) would not arise until tipping was completed and the land returned to agricultural use. The Lands Tribunal held that the relevant date was the date on which tipping began and that the claim period therefore commenced one year thereafter. It was also held, however, that since the depreciation in the value of the claimant's house resulting from proximity to the tip (which the Lands Tribunal accepted) could not be attributed to the specified physical factors (ibid, s. 1(2), p. 329, supra) no compensation was payable under these provisions.

[7] Apart from a specific testamentary disposition this expression includes devolution upon intestacy, or in the case of a former joint tenant, by survivorship, appropriation in lieu of any legacy or share in residue and inheritance by virtue of a settlement: Land Compensation Act 1973, s. 11.

[8] Or a greater interest out of which the claimant's interest is derived: ibid, s. 11(1).

[9] Ibid, s. 11.

[10] The Act includes the requirement that the interest must have been acquired before the relevant date, as part of the definition of a "qualifying interest". But as the date of acquisition cannot, in itself, be relevant to the definition of an interest in land it has been felt more appropriate to consider its significance separately under the head "relevant dates".

[11] Land Compensation Act 1973, s. 3(2).

the use of the highway or works before deciding whether injury in fact results, and if so, its extent. It follows that in the case of a leasehold interest having barely four years to run at the relevant date it will be of the utmost importance to make a claim as soon as the claim period begins, so that at least three years remain unexpired from the date when notice of claim is given, for it is that date from which the three-year period runs, and not the relevant date.[1] At the latter date, therefore, a leasehold interest on which the claimant relies to give him a qualifying interest must have over four years unexpired.

THE CLAIM PERIOD: EXCEPTIONS TO THE GENERAL RULE

Land subject to contract

To this general rule there are, however, three exceptions. In the first place a claim may be made *before* the commencement of the claim period if during the twelve months beginning on the relevant date the claimant has made a contract for disposing of his interest or, "in so far as it is an interest in land which is not a dwelling, for the grant of a tenancy of that land" and the claim is made before such disposal or grant of a tenancy.[2]

It must be emphasised, however, that these provisions apply only to the making of the claim; they do not affect the interest that the claimant is required to have possessed since before the relevant date. Thus a freeholder of an agricultural unit who has contracted to grant a tenancy will not thereby be entitled to make a claim unless he was previously in occupation. If, at the relevant date, his property had been let these provisions do not assist him. But the question arises whether, if he was in occupation and therefore has a claim, he must discount any damage inflicted upon any dwelling included in the tenancy to be occupied by the tenant and occupier of the agricultural unit. It is submitted, however, that the true contradistinction is between a *dwelling* owned or leased as such, and an *agricultural unit*, the definition of which includes a dwelling occupied by the occupier of the unit for the purpose of farming it,[3] so that a claim in respect of damage to such a unit is to be based upon the depreciation of the then occupier's interest[4] in the unit as a whole, including any such dwelling. In other words, for these purposes such dwellings are to be regarded as integral parts of the agricultural unit with which they are occupied, and not as dwellings *qua* dwellings.[5]

If the contract was made before the relevant date then the right to compensation, if any, will have passed to the new owner or lessee-

---

[1] Land Compensation Act 1973, *Ibid*, s. 2(4), p. 330, *supra*.

[2] *Ibid*, s. 3(3)(a). Note, however, that compensation is not payable until the claims period begins. Nor can any dispute arising from the claim be referred to the Lands Tribunal before that date: *ibid*, s. 16(2).

[3] See the definition of an agricultural unit in Town and Country Planning Act 1971, s. 207(1), incorporated by the Land Compensation Act 1973, s. 87(1), and see p. 130, *ante*.

[4] Which must, of course, have been either the freehold or a head lease having at least three years unexpired at the date of service of the notice of claim: Land Compensation Act 1973, s. 2.

[5] In practice noise or smell—and in most cases smoke—will depreciate the value of the holding only in so far as they cause nuisance to the occupiers of the farm house: on the other hand some fumes or discharges may affect productivity of the land.

occupier since acquisition of a qualifying interest dates from the date of any contract in pursuance of which the interest was created.[1] Even if anticipation of the damage has substantially reduced the purchase price or rent, the vendor or lessor has therefore no claim to compensation. Accordingly the latter's only remedy is to endeavour to persuade his purchaser or lessee to agree a price or rent that reflects the compensation ultimately payable.

By keeping alive the vendor's or lessor's claims where the contract is subsequent to the relevant date but prior to the commencement of the claim period these provisions preserve the protection afforded in respect of the properties concerned, which would otherwise be entirely lost. It is not, however, entirely clear why the claim must be lodged before the transaction is completed by conveyance or lease.

Highways not maintainable at public expense
The second exception to the general rule arises from the restriction of the definition of a highway for these purposes to a highway or part of a highway maintainable at public expense.[2] Where a highway is not so maintainable when first open to traffic (i.e. at the relevant date) but becomes so within three years thereafter the claim period is extended to one year after the date on which the highway becomes maintainable at public expense.[3] In such a case, therefore, the claim period may be of barely a year's duration.

Transitional Provisions
The third exception to the general rule arises from the transitional provisions of the Act[4] whereby the claim period, if having less than two years unexpired at the date of commencement of Part I of the Act (23 June 1973) was extended to 23 June 1975.

NOTICE OF CLAIM

Contrary to the more usual practice of leaving such details as the manner in which actual claims are to be made, and the information to be provided, to regulations, these requirements are incorporated in the Act[5] and the claimant is required to serve upon the responsible authority[6] a notice giving the particulars of:

"(a) the land[7] in respect of which the claim is made;

[1] *Ibid*, s. 19(2); but note that no claim will pass to the tenant-occupier of a non-residential hereditament or of an agricultural unit unless the tenancy is in the form of a lease having a minimum of three years to run when the claim is made. In other cases no compensation under these provisions is payable in respect of such properties: see p. 330, *supra*.
[2] As defined in the Highways Act 1959, s. 295(1): Land Compensation Act 1973, s. 19(1).
[3] This provision only applies where the claim period would otherwise have ended earlier, but this could only have occurred under the transitional provisions, *infra*, so that this qualification of Land Compensation Act 1973, s. 19(3), is now spent.
[4] *Ibid*, ss. 14(1) and 19(1).
[5] *Ibid*, s. 3(1).
[6] I.e., in the case of a highway, the appropriate highway authority, and in relation to other public works the persons managing those works: *ibid*, s. 1(4). The appropriate highway authority is the authority which constructed the highway in question or, as the case may be, carried out the alterations giving rise to the claim: *ibid*, s. 19(1).
[7] In the case of non-residential and non-agricultural property this should include the appropriate reference to the valuation list.

(b) the claimant's interest and the date on which and the manner in which it was acquired;[1]
(c) the claimant's occupation of the land (except where the interest qualifies for compensation without occupation);[2]
(d) any other interests in the land so far as known to the claimant;[3]
(e) the public works to which the claim relates;[4]
(f) the amount of compensation claimed;[5]
(g)[6] any land contiguous or adjacent to the land in respect of which the claim is made, being land to which the claimant is entitled in the same capacity[7] . . . on the relevant date."

Once a notice of claim has been served the responsible authority has a right, on giving reasonable notice, to authorise entry upon the premises in respect of which the claim is made for the purpose of survey and valuation.[8]

THE MEASURE OF COMPENSATION

Subject to the *de minimis* provisions that no compensation shall be payable unless the net amount due exceeds £50,[9] the basis of compensation under these provisions, as in other cases of injurious affection, is the depreciation in the value of the land affected.[10] The crucial date is the *first day of the claim period*, so that compensation can only be claimed in respect of depreciation that has either already arisen from the use of the works giving rise to the claim on that date or from

---

[1] Which of course must be prior to the relevant date except where the manner in which in the interest was acquired is by inheritance: see p. 333, *supra*. If the interest is that of a "qualifying tenancy" under the Leasehold Reform Act (p. 332, *supra*) this fact must be stated, and if the claim is made after the acquisition of the freehold or extended lease, sufficient details must be given to establish that the claimant is still entitled to claim: Land Compensation Act 1973, s. 12(6).

[2] I.e., in the case of a freeholder or superior lessee of a dwelling-house, other than one forming part of an agricultural unit: p. 331, *supra*.

[3] Where the interest is subject to a mortgage the responsible authority is under an obligation to pay any compensation arising in respect of that interest to the mortgagee. Note, too, that occupation, by a person beneficially entitled, of land held in trust (other than occupation by a sole tenant for life under the Settled Land Act 1925) is deemed to be occupation by the trustees, so that they, rather than the actual occupier, should lodge the claim: see p. 332, *supra*. Trustees for sale are required to deal with the compensation as if it were proceeds of sale arising under the trust, and Settled Land Act trustees are required to treat it as capital money: Land Compensation Act 1973, s. 10. In the case of land belonging to an ecclesiastical benefice of the Church of England ("church property") compensation is payable to the Church Commissioners: *ibid*, s. 13.

[4] If the claim is in respect of depreciation arising from an alteration of a highway; the reconstruction, extension or other alteration of public works; or a change of use (other than in respect of a highway or aerodrome) the alterations or change of use must be specified: *ibid*, s. 9(4).

[5] For the measure of compensation see below.

[6] This information is required to enable the responsible authority to set-off, against the compensation claimed, any "betterment" to adjoining land: pp. 339 *et seq, infra*.

[7] A person is deemed to be entitled to two interests in the same capacity if he is entitled to both beneficially; as trustee of the same trust; or as personal representative of the same person: *ibid*, s. 6(5). Note that this requirement is in contrast to that governing claims for compensation for injurious affection of land retained following acquisition of other land of the claimant: p. 315, *supra*.

[8] Wilful obstruction of the person so authorised is an offence punishable on summary conviction by a maximum fine of £20: Land Compensation Act 1973, s. 3(4).

[9] *Ibid*, s. 7.

[10] Note that the special rules for the assessment of the value of the claimant's interest which are here described apply only for the purpose of assessing depreciation to that interest. They do *not* apply where it is a question of assessing any offsetting increase in the value of that interest due to the works in question: *ibid*, s. 6(1), p. 339, *infra*.

intensification of use then reasonably foreseeable.[1] By the same token, assessment of compensation is by reference to prices then ruling.[2]

On the other hand the value of the interest in respect of which this claim is made is to be assessed by reference to the nature of the interest and the condition of the land as at the date of *service* of the notice of claim[3] subject however, to the proviso that no building or any improvement or extension to a building that is first occupied after the relevant date is to be taken into account, nor any change of use made after the latter date.[4]

If, however, "the interest is subject to a mortgage or to a contract of sale or to a contract made after the relevant date for the grant of a tenancy" compensation is to be assessed as if it were not subject to the mortgage or contract.[5] But in this connection it must be borne in mind that for the purpose of determining entitlement to compensation, disposal or acquisition in pursuance of a contract dates from the date of the contract[6] so that if a contract of sale is made *before* the relevant date only the prospective purchaser or tenant can claim. It is also to be noted that despite the general rule that once a claim is established no further claim in respect of the same land or any part thereof can be entertained[7] this does not prevent a claim being made by both the mortgagee of an interest and the person entitled to that interest.[8]

Subject to the above, the interest is to be valued in accordance with Rules 2 to 4 of the 1919 Rules[9] on the assumption that planning permission would be granted for development of the land in which the interest subsists within the classes of development specified in the 8th Schedule to the Town and Country Planning Act 1971[10] but for no other development.[11] This assumption as to planning permission is, however, subject to provisions designed to ensure that compensation shall not be payable twice over in relation to depreciation that in

---

[1] *Ibid*, s. 4(2). If intensification proves greater than anticipated on the first day of the claim period no further claim can be made: *ibid*, s. 8(1).

[2] *Ibid*, s. 4(1).

[3] *Ibid*, s. 4(4)(a), unless the claim is in respect of a "qualifying tenancy" (see p. 336 and note 1 thereon, *supra*) and is made after the claimant has acquired the freehold or an extended lease; in such a case the nature of the interest and condition of the land is to be assessed as at the relevant date: *ibid*, s. 12(6). In the normal case, however, a lessee should clearly submit his claim as soon as he is entitled to do so for the longer he delays the shorter his unexpired term and the less the compensation.

[4] *Ibid*, s. 4(5).

[5] *Ibid*, s. 4(4)(c).

[6] *Ibid*, s. 19(2).

[7] *Ibid*, s. 8(1).

[8] *Ibid*, s. 10(1). The latter person will, of course, generally be the mortgagor. The other exception to the general rule arises where both a lessee and a lessor hold qualifying interests: *ibid*, s. 8(1), and see p. 331, *supra*. Nor, of course, does the general rule apply if a subsequent alteration, extension of the works, or a change of use results in further depreciation: *ibid*, s. 9(4)(b).

[9] I.e., now the Land Compensation Act 1961. s. 5: Land Compensation Act 1973. s. 4(4)(b). For the 1919 Rules see p. 164, *ante*. Rules 1, 5 and 6 are, of course inapplicable where no land is actually acquired.

[10] Land Compensation Act 1973, s. 5. For the Town and Country Planning Act 1971, 8th Schedule, see p. 195, *ante*, and Appendix, p. 456, *post*.

[11] If planning permission for some other development has in fact been granted such permission is to be ignored except in so far as the development has been carried out: Land Compensation Act 1973, s. 5(4).

substance arises from the same cause.[1] Thus if compensation has become payable in respect of a refusal or in respect of a condition imposed on the grant of planning permission for a development within Part II of the Schedule,[2] or in respect of an order[3] requiring the removal of any building or any change of use, it is not to be assumed that planning permission will be granted for such development within Part II of the Schedule (or granted other than subject to the condition imposed, as the case may be) or for the reinstatement of any such building or resumption of any use the subject of the order.[4]

Effect of works etc. mitigating depreciation of claimant's interest

It must, however, be emphasised that only what may be termed the "net" depreciation can be considered.[5] In other words, if certain ameliorating measures have been taken they must be taken into account. Thus, if a highway authority has carried out works on land adjoining a highway for the purpose of "mitigating any adverse effect which the construction, improvement, existence or use of a highway has or will have" on its surroundings[6] regard must be had to the effect of such works.[7] Such works will, of course, frequently take the form of tree planting,[8] which by the nature of things will take some years to provide either a visual screen or a barrier against noise. In such cases it seems that it will be necessary to consider both the time lag until such planting can be expected to have a significant effect, and the extent to which it will ultimately provide an effective remedy. Thus, if, for example, the land in respect of which the claim is made is depreciated in value by such use of the highway as can be anticipated at the beginning of the claim period by, say, 20 % in annual value but by only 15 % after, say, 5 years and ultimately, after, say 15 years by only 5 %, compensation will have to be assessed accordingly.

Similarly, where, under certain enactments[9] a responsible authority

---

[1] Note also the "omnibus" provision of the Land Compensation Act 1973, s. 8(7), that compensation shall not be payable both under Part I, *ibid*, and under any other enactment in respect of the same depreciation.

[2] Compensation is payable in these cases under the Town and Country Planning Act 1971, s. 169: p. 405, *post*.

[3] I.e., an order under *ibid*, s. 51, requiring discontinuance of use or alteration or removal of buildings; in such cases compensation is payable under *ibid*, s. 170: p. 415, *post*.

[4] Land Compensation Act 1973, s. 5(3).

[5] But where compensation is payable the claimant is entitled to any reasonable valuation or legal expenses incurred in the preparation of his claim: *ibid*, s. 3(5): he is also entitled to interest from the date of service of the notice of claim or the beginning of the claim period, whichever is the later; *ibid*, s. 18(1).

[6] See *ibid*, ss. 23(1) and 27(2), which confer the necessary powers to carry out such works. *Ibid*, s. 22, defines the circumstances in which highway authorities may acquire land compulsorily for the purpose of mitigation, and *ibid*, s. 26, confers somewhat wider powers to acquire such land by agreement. *Ibid*, s. 24, empowers highway authorities to enter into agreements with neighbouring landowners to use their land for similar mitigating purposes. As to these powers see note 1, p. 341, *infra*.

[7] *Ibid*, s. 4(3)(b).

[8] *Ibid*, s. 23(2), specifically mentions "the planting of trees, shrubs or plants of any description and the laying out of any area of grassland" as works that can be carried out for this purpose (though without prejudice to the generality of such powers).

[9] I.e., under Land Compensation Act 1973, s. 20, or the Airports Authority Act 1965, s. 15, or any corresponding local enactment. The Land Compensation Act 1973, s. 20, empowers the Secretary of State to impose a duty on, or to empower responsible authorities (by regulation) to insulate buildings against noise arising from public works. The Airports Authority Act 1965, s. 15,

has a duty to insulate buildings against noise arising, or expected to arise, from either the construction or use of public works, or to make a grant to private owners towards the cost of such insulation, depreciation of the claimant's interest must be assessed accordingly.[1] In other words, where depreciation in the value of a dwelling-house results from noise and the above conditions apply, the extent of the depreciation will be assessed upon the assumption that the house was already insulated to the relevant extent. But even if the insulation (normally in the form of the double-glazing of windows)[2] is completely effective there may still be a claim for compensation if the noise is such that windows cannot be opened without serious inconvenience from noise, or the claimant's enjoyment of the garden[3] is seriously affected.

Set-off of increase in value of other land held by claimant

It must be borne in mind that any increase in the value of the claimant's interest in the land in respect of which the claim is made and of any interest he may have, in the same capacity[4] in any other land contiguous or adjacent thereto is to be set-off against the compensation otherwise payable.[5]

The assessment of any *increase* in the value of the claimant's interest either in the land the subject of the claim or in land contiguous or adjacent thereto to which he is entitled in the same capacity is not subject to any of the special provisions described above[6] in connection with the assessment of *depreciation* to the former interest.[7] It follows, therefore, that where there is enhancement of value of these interests their valuation is to be based upon the market's assessment as to what planning permission can reasonably be expected.[8] This is because the question whether or not adjacent public works confer an increase in value, and if so, to what extent, depends very largely upon the development potential of the land. A new highway, for example, may be a serious inconvenience to immediately adjacent houses, but a very valuable asset if it affords access to back-land with development poten-

---

similarly empowers the Secretary of State to issue regulations making a scheme under which the Airport Authority are required to make grants towards the cost of insulation (originally of dwellings only but now, by virtue of the Land Compensation Act 1973, s. 21, of such other classes of buildings as the Secretary of State may specify).

[1] *Ibid*, s. 4(3)(a): the same applies where an authority, having only a discretionary power in such matters, has either exercised its discretion in favour of the claimant or undertaken to do so.

[2] See the Airports Authority Act 1965, s. 15, note 8, p. 338, *supra*.

[3] A dwelling is defined as including "any garden, yard, outhouses, and appurtenances belonging to or usually enjoyed with that building": Land Compensation Act 1973, s. 87(1).

[4] See note 6, p. 336, *supra*.

[5] Land Compensation Act 1973, s. 6, provided, of course, that the increase in value results from the works in respect of which the claim is made or, in the case of a claim arising from alterations, extensions, or changes of use, results from such alterations or changes of use: *ibid*, s. 9(4). It can, for example, often happen that the nuisance caused by proximity to a new highway is offset by the value of better access.

[6] See pp. 336 *et seq*, *supra*.

[7] *Ibid*, s. 6(2), which specifically states that the special provisions of *ibid*, ss. 4 and 5, described above shall not apply to the assessment of any increase in the value of the interest in respect of which the claim is made. But it is only to that interest that these provisions apply; there is therefore no need specifically to exclude their application to the assessment of any increase in value of adjacent etc. land.

[8] The planning assumptions of the Land Compensation Act 1961, ss. 14–16 do not apply: see p. 181 *ante*.

tial for residential, commercial or industrial purposes. The same, of course, may apply in reverse: a sewage works, for example, is unlikely to be anything but a detriment to immediately adjacent residential land, though perhaps no great inconvenience to a neighbouring farmer. At first sight, therefore, it seems anomalous and unfair that the full development potential of the land is to be ignored when assessing depreciation. However, given the underlying principle of these provisions of the 1973 Act—increased protection for the owner-occupier—to do so is perfectly logical.

Adjustment of compensation where other land subsequently compulsorily acquired
Where a deduction is made from the compensation payable under these provisions by virtue of an offsetting increase in the value of an interest in contiguous or adjacent land, and that interest[1] is subsequently acquired, the amount of that deduction is to be taken into account when assessing the compensation or purchase price.[2] Similarly, where, after a claim has been made, the whole or part of the land in which the interest the subject of the claim subsists is compulsorily acquired, the compensation payable in respect of the claim is to be deducted from the compensation payable in respect of the acquisition if the latter compensation falls to be assessed without regard to such depreciation.[3] As already explained, the purpose of these provisions of the Land Compensation Act 1973 is to provide a remedy, where none previously existed, for injurious affection caused by the use of public works, to a certain restricted class of owners.[4] If the owner of the land acquired retains other land that is injuriously affected he has his remedy under the Lands Clauses Consolidation Act 1845, s. 63, or the Compulsory Purchase Act 1965, s. 7.[5] He cannot, therefore, claim compensation under the Act of 1973 once he has received notice to treat,[6] unless his claim arises from subsequent further depreciation of the land retained resulting from alterations, extensions, etc., of the works or a change of the use for which the land was acquired.[7]

C. Mitigation of injurious effect of public works: Part II of the Land Compensation Act 1973

As indicated in the introduction to this chapter, this Part[8] of the Act of 1973 is mainly concerned with provisions empowering authorities

---

[1] This provision applies where the interest acquired is the same as that in respect of which the deduction was made (whether or not the whole or only part of the land in which the interest subsists is acquired) or where the acquisition is from the claimant or a person deriving title from him: Land Compensation Act 1973, s. 6(4).

[2] *Ibid*, s. 6(3): a provision corresponding with that of Land Compensation Act 1961 s. 8, pp. 231 *et seq, ante.*

[3] *Ibid*, s. 8(6). Compensation will fall to be assessed without regard to the depreciation if, e.g., the acquisition is in pursuance of the same scheme as that encompassing the public works in question: see p. 217, *ante*. In such cases, therefore, in the absence of this provision the vendor would be doubly compensated for the effect of the works.

[4] As defined on pp. 330 *et seq, supra.*

[5] The Lands Clauses Consolidation Act 1845, and the Compulsory Purchase Act 1965, pp. 314 *et seq, supra.*

[6] Land Compensation Act 1973, s. 8(2).

[7] *Ibid*, s. 9(4)(b).

[8] *Ibid*, ss. 20–28.

responsible for the construction and operation of public works to carry out supplementary works (e.g., tree planting etc.) designed to mitigate the nuisance caused to neighbouring owners by the principal works and to acquire land on which to do so.[1]

These provisions do not, therefore, directly give rise to any claims for compensation, although, as explained in the previous section[2] they may have an indirect effect upon the amount of compensation payable under Part I of the Act by reducing the injurious affection (and therefore the compensation payable in respect thereof) caused by the principal works. The same applies to the provisions under which responsible authorities may insulate buildings or make grants to private owners towards the cost of such insulation.[3] But if in these cases the responsible authority has a duty to make such grants the owners of affected buildings will have a corresponding right to claim them; indeed it is important that people making claims under Part I of the Act should exercise that right, for the amount of the grant to which they are entitled will be taken into account in the assessment of compensation whether or not the grant is claimed.[4]

The provisions of the Act in this regard are, however, merely enabling provisions, it being left to the Secretary of State to issue regulations.[5] His powers are wide and he may impose a duty to insulate or pay grant, or merely confer a discretionary power. He may prescribe the classes of works in respect of which the duty or discretion is to be exercised; minimum noise levels above which insulation is to be provided; the nature and extent of the insulation work to be undertaken; the rate of grant; the area in which qualifying buildings must be situated, and the classes of persons entitled to claim.

The Secretary of State may also provide, in the case of buildings subject to a lease, that if a claim is made by either the landlord or tenant and consent of the other party to the tenancy to the execution of the requisite works is withheld, it may be dispensed with.[6] Where the responsible authority is not the local authority[7] the latter may be appointed agents of the former in operating the scheme.[8]

The schemes that will eventually emerge from these provisions will therefore inevitably tend to be highly localised in their operation and likely to differ in detail one from another.

[1] *Ibid*, s. 22 empowers highway authorities to acquire land for these purposes and s. 23 empowers them to carry out the relevant supplementary works: ss. 26 and 27 confer corresponding powers on other authorities in relation to other public works; s. 24 empowers highway authorities to enter into agreements with private landowners for the execution of supplementary works; and s. 25 extends the powers of the Secretary of State to advance money to highway authorities for these purposes.
[2] P. 338, *supra*.
[3] Land Compensation Act ss. 20–21.
[4] *Ibid*, s. 4(3).
[5] *Ibid*, s. 20, and note 9, p. 338, *supra*. Regulations are to be made by Statutory Instrument and the draft of the first set of regulations is subject to affirmative resolution in each House of Parliament. Subsequent regulations will only be subject to negative resolution of either House: see note 2, p. 342, *infra*.
[6] *Ibid*, s. 20(4).
[7] For example, the operation of an aerodrome.
[8] Land Compensation Act 1973, s. 20(5).

All that can be said here is that where owners of property suffer from excessive noise emanating from public works, particularly an aerodrome or urban highway, they will be well advised to ascertain whether any regulations (or in the case of an aerodrome, any scheme under the Airports Authority Act, 1965, s. 15[1]) apply.[2]

D. Compensation for injurious affection to land held by third parties: summary

1. The right of an owner of an interest in land to claim compensation for injurious affection to the land resulting from the use of neighbouring land compulsorily acquired depends upon the nature of his interest. Unless he has what may be broadly described as an "owner-occupier's interest"[3] compensation is payable only in respect of damage resulting from the execution of works (which includes their maintenance) on the acquired land; damage arising from the *use* of the acquired land cannot be the subject of compensation.[4]

2. The damage, moreover, must arise from interference with a private legal right[5] and in the absence of statutory protection of the responsible authority, must be actionable in tort.[6]

3. The measure of compensation follows the principle of *restitutio in integrum* as in tort; interest is payable from the date of claim.[7]

4. *Special provisions relating to owner-occupiers*——in this context an owner-occupier is a person in occupation by right of an owner's interest, that is, a freehold or leasehold having at least three years unexpired[8] at the "relevant date", i.e., the date on which the public works are first used or, in the case of a highway, first opened to the public.[9] In the case of business premises there is a limit to the rateable value[10] and in the case of an agricultural unit the claimant must occupy the whole unit and at least part of it by right of an owner's interest.[10] Such persons may, however, include trustees and mortgagees.[11]

---

[1] This section is amended to enable schemes thereunder to cover buildings other than dwellings: *ibid*, s. 21.

[2] The current regulations are the Noise Insulation Regulations 1975 (SI 1975 No. 1763). These regulations apply exclusively to the effect of noise generated by highways on residential property within 300 metres of the nearest point on the carriageway (Reg. 7). Reg. 3 imposes a duty on highway authorities (for whom local authorities may act as agents: Reg. 14) to insulate such buildings or make a grant therefor where the highway is first opened to the public after 16 October 1972; in other cases they have powers but not duties (Reg. 4). Reg. 5 extends these powers to insulation against construction noise. Specifications of insulation work are set out in Sch. 1.

[3] For definition see pp. 331 *et seq, supra* and para. 4, *infra*.

[4] P. 321, *supra*, but note the exception where that use is restricted by covenant: see note 3, p. 344, *supra*.

[5] P. 323, *supra*.

[6] P. 325, *supra*, and note that if there is no such protection, e.g., where the authority's actions are *ultra vires*, the remedy is by action and there is no claim to compensation: p. 326, *supra*.

[7] Land Compensation Act 1973, s. 63: p. 326, *supra*.

[8] P. 330, *supra*, and note that while account may be taken of a lessee-claimant's rights to an extended lease or acquisition of the freehold under the Leasehold Reform Act 1967 (p. 332, *supra*) no such account can be taken of the security of tenure provisions of either the Landlord and Tenant Act 1954 or the Agricultural Holdings Act 1948: see p. 331, *supra*.

[9] P. 333, *supra*.

[10] P. 331, *supra*.

[11] P. 332, *supra*.

5. The damage must arise from one or more of the specified "physical factors".[1] Except in the case of damage arising from a new or improved highway, no compensation is payable unless the operators have express or implied statutory immunity,[2] and no compensation is payable in respect of damage arising from accidents involving aircraft or vehicles on a highway.[3]

6. Claims to compensation must be made within the claim period, i.e., normally the two-year period beginning one year after the relevant date.[4]

7. The measure of compensation is the consequential depreciation in the value of the interest in the land as it exists at the date of the claim, but by reference to prices ruling on the first day of the claim period and the damage then suffered or foreseeable.[5]

8. In assessing compensation account must be taken of any measures taken by the responsible authority (or on its behalf) to mitigate the damage[6] and of any appreciation of other land held by the claimant resulting from the public works concerned.[7] Any deduction under the latter head is to be discounted if the land appreciated in value is subsequently compulsorily acquired.[8]

9. No compensation is payable if the net amount due is less than £50.[9]

10. Where a dwelling is rendered temporarily uninhabitable during construction of the works, the responsible authority has power to defray the additional expenses incurred by the occupier in accommodating himself and his family elsewhere, provided an agreement to that effect is concluded before any such expenses are incurred.[10]

---

[1] I.e., noise, vibration, smell, fumes, smoke, artificial lighting or the discharge on to the land of any solid or liquid substance: Land Compensation Act 1973, s. 1: p. 329, *supra*.

[2] *Ibid*, s. 1(6), p. 330, *supra*.

[3] *Ibid*, s. 1(7), p. 330, *supra*.

[4] Pp. 333 *et seq, supra*. Note particularly the exception to this rule where the land in respect of which the claim is made does not comprise a dwelling and is subject to a contract for sale entered into within the year following the relevant date: pp. 334 *et seq. supra*.

[5] Pp. 336 *et seq, supra*.

[6] Pp. 338 *et seq, supra*.

[7] Pp. 339 *et seq, supra*.

[8] Pp. 340 *et seq, supra*.

[9] P. 336, *supra*.

[10] Pp. 323, *supra*.

CHAPTER 9

Compensation for Disturbance

1 INTRODUCTORY

Compensation for disturbance falls to be considered under three distinct heads. The first and most usual case [1] is that which arises where the acquisition is either of a freehold interest or of a leasehold interest greater than that of a year or from year to year. As in the case of compensation for injurious affection where no land has been acquired from the claimant[2] there is no express statutory provision either conferring a right to compensation for disturbance or governing its assessment. In both cases the right to compensation is derived from the Act of 1845[3] under which, it will be recalled, the basis of compensation for land compulsorily acquired was its value *to* the owner. There being no assumption that he was a willing seller it follows that he would be unlikely to give up possession unless the compensation payable covered costs of removal. Hence the development of case law by which such costs were regarded as but an element in the total compensation as part of the value of the land to the owner.[4] Although Rule 2 of the 1919 Rules[5] established the concept of the market value obtainable by a willing seller as the basis of compensation for land compulsorily acquired, Rule 6 expressly provided that "this provision of Rule 2 shall not affect the assessment of compensation for disturbance or any

---

[1] Considered in the next section of this chapter under the heading "Compensation for Disturbance in the case of acquisition of a freehold or long leasehold"; p. 346, *infra*.

[2] Pp. 321 *et seq, ante*.

[3] Lands Clauses Consolidation Act 1845.

[4] P. 4, *ante*, note 2: cf. p. 315, *ante*, note 3. Note, however, that for tax purposes a distinction is to be drawn between that part of the compensation for disturbance that in effect represents reimbursement of out of pocket expenses and that which represents compensation for loss of profits or goodwill. While the latter is included in the total purchase price for the purpose of assessing capital gains or corporation tax (see p. 360, *infra*) it is not the practice of the Inland Revenue to include the former: see *Bostock, Chater & Sons Ltd.* v *Chelmsford Corpn* (1973), 26 P & CR 321, and the Board of Inland Revenue statements at page 348. In the later case of *Hobbs (Quarries) Ltd.* v *Somerset County Council* (1975), 30 P & CR 286, the parties jointly instructed revenue counsel to appear *amicus curiae* and accepted his submissions that (i) where the compensation is assessed by reference to loss of anticipated profits it must be reduced where tax would be payable on such profits in the hands of the recipient; (ii) the sum reduced should be grossed up by the amount of the extra tax payable; (iii) no deduction for tax should be made where compensation is based upon sale of a capital asset; (iv) if interest is awarded it should be awarded gross and the tax deducted and accounted for by the acquiring authority: *ibid* at p. 294.

[5] Acquisition of Land (Assessment of Compensation) Act 1919, s. 1, now the Land Compensation Act 1961, s. 5: see pp. 164 *et seq, ante*.

other matter not directly based on the value of land". Rule 6 does not, however, "confer a *right* to claim compensation for disturbance. It merely leaves unaffected the right which the owner would, before the Act of 1919, have had to claim that the compensation to be paid for the land should be increased on the ground that he had been disturbed".[1] It accordingly remains a prerequisite of a valid claim to compensation for disturbance that the loss must form part of the value of the land to the owner.

Although, as already indicated, that right is the product of the case law considered in Section 2 of this chapter, it is affected by the statutory provisions of Rule 6 to the extent that there being specific reference therein to compensation for disturbance it is now regarded as a specific head of compensation.[2] The right to compensation for disturbance may, however, be excluded either expressly or impliedly by the special or general Act by which the compulsory acquisition is authorised. It has, for example, been held[3] that the assessment of compensation for unfit, dangerous, etc. property on the basis of the value of the cleared site under the relevant provision of the Housing Act 1957[4] is intended to be inclusive and that therefore no additional payment can be claimed for disturbance.[5] The same applies where compensation is based upon the cost of equivalent reinstatement under Rule 5 of the 1919 rules,[6] for apart from the actual costs of removal (which are allowable as part of the cost of reinstatement) the occupier is, by definition, placed in an equivalent position after reinstatement to that in which he was at the time of the acquisition and it is on that basis that the compensation is assessed. A claim to compensation for other expenses resulting from the dispossession would therefore amount to a claim to have these expenses allowed twice over.

The second head under which compensation for disturbance falls to be considered arises from the special statutory provisions[7] governing the acquisition of interests of less than a year or from year to year. This is the subject matter of Section 3 of this chapter: "Compensation for disturbance in the case of the acquisition of short tenancies". The usual practice of acquiring authorities in such cases is, however, to acquire the freehold or superior leasehold, serve notice to quit in their capacity as landlord and postpone taking possession until the termination of the tenancy. The occupier will then have no interest in the land, and until the passing of the Act of 1973[8] would have had no claim to

---

[1] Per Lord Greene MR in *Horn* v *Sunderland Corpn*, [1941] 2 KB 26 at p. 34.

[2] See Denning LJ in *Harvey* v *Crawley Development Corpn*, [1957] 1 QB 485 at pp. 493–4; but see also *Healy or McArdle* v *Glasgow Corpn*, note 7, p. 350, *infra*.

[3] *Walkes-Hilliman* v *Greater London Council* (1969), 20 P & CR 736; and on the corresponding provisions of the Housing Act 1925, *Northwood* v *LCC*, [1926] 2 KB 411.

[4] Housing Act 1957, ss. 29 and 59. See pp. 255 *et seq, ante*.

[5] There may, however, be entitlement to a well-maintained allowance under *ibid*, ss. 30 and 60 (see pp. 262 *et seq, ante*) a home loss payment or disturbance payment under the Land Compensation Act 1973, Part III, pp. 372 *et seq, infra*.

[6] Pp. 239 *et seq, ante*.

[7] Lands Clauses Consolidation Act 1845, ss. 121 and 122, now Compulsory Purchase Act 1965, s. 20, pp. 365 *et seq, infra*.

[8] Land Compensation Act 1973, Part III.

compensation at all. Part III of that Act,[1] however, expressly provides for certain statutory payments analogous to compensation for disturbance where a person is displaced from his house or farm[2] and for "Disturbance Payments"[3] in certain other cases. These are considered in Section 4 of this chapter.

Part III of the Act of 1973 also confers powers upon acquiring authorities to help displaced resident owner-occupiers as well as imposing certain duties in regard to rehousing.[4] These too are provisions of which those concerned with cases of disturbance will require to have some knowledge, and although they do not confer rights to monetary compensation they are briefly considered in the final section of this chapter.[5]

2 COMPENSATION FOR DISTURBANCE IN THE CASE OF ACQUISITION OF A FREEHOLD OR LONG LEASEHOLD

The general rule

THE IMPORTANCE OF OCCUPATION

The general rule is "that any loss sustained by a dispossessed owner (at all events one who occupies his house) which flows from a compulsory acquisition may be properly regarded as the subject of compensation for disturbance provided, first, that it is not too remote and, secondly, that it is the natural and reasonable consequence of the dispossession of the owner".[6]

The caveat in relation to the claimant's occupation of his house is fundamental, for it is occupation rather than the nature of the property that is crucial. Thus, where an individual owned the premises being acquired and also owned, controlled and managed a company carrying on business therein, it was held formerly that only the company, as a separate *persona*, could claim compensation for disturbance.[7] But if the owner of the premises was itself a company and the occupying company was a wholly owned subsidiary, the directors and managers of which were appointed and entirely controlled by the parent company so that the former was merely the agent for the latter, the parent company

---

[1] "Provisions for Benefit of Persons Displaced from Land", *ibid*, ss. 29–43.
[2] Described in the Act as "Home and Farm Loss Payments" respectively: *ibid*, ss. 29–36.
[3] *Ibid*, ss. 37–38.
[4] *Ibid*, ss. 39–43.
[5] Section 5 of this chapter, p. 390, *infra*.
[6] Per Romer LJ in *Harvey* v *Crawley Development Corpn (supra)* at p. 494. Note, however, that no compensation is payable for disturbance where the disturbance has already been taken into account in assessing the compensation payable in respect of severance and injurious affection: *Cooke* v *Secretary of State for the Environment* (1973), 27 P & CR 234. In that case compensation was claimed under the head of disturbance on the ground that the severance of a farm by a major trunk road would make it impossible to drive cattle across the road and they would have to be transported. It was held that this inconvenience had already been reflected in assessing, in the compensation, the depreciation in the value of the land retained, under the head of severance and injurious affection: see pp. 314 *et seq, ante*, and cf. the position where compensation is based on the cost of equivalent reinstatement, p. 345, *supra*.
[7] *Taylor* v *Greater London Council* (1973), 25 P & CR 451. *Brain and Drive Yourself Car Hire Co.* v *LCC* (1957), 9 P & CR 113, LT.

may retain the right to compensation for disturbance.[1] The distinction evidently lies in the fact that in such a case the parent company in effect "employs" its subsidiary and those working for it, whereas the individual's control over his company normally derives not only from his shareholding but from his employment *by* the company as a director. If that be so, however, it would have seemed to follow that if the subsidiary company held the legal interest in premises occupied on a mere licence by the parent company, there could be no claim to compensation for disturbance under this head.[2] The Court of Appeal (overruling the Lands Tribunal) has, however, recently held that in such a case compensation for disturbance is nevertheless payable to the parent company,[3] the *ratio decidendi* being that since equity would never permit eviction of the parent company by its subsidiary the former has an equitable interest sufficient to maintain a claim for compensation for disturbance. But this decision was also held to be but a natural development of the growing tendency of the courts to ignore the separate legal entities of companies within a group in which the parent company completely controls the subsidiaries, and to look instead at the economic entity of this group as a whole. The courts will in short, lift the corporate veil and look at the substance of the matter.[4] It may be, therefore, that the distinction between an individual and a company wholly within his control can similarly be ignored, for the relationship between a company in occupation of the premises and a controlling director who is both its employee and its landlord is not easy to distinguish in this context from that between an occupying parent company and a wholly owned subsidiary holding the legal interest.[5]

Although the nature of the property acquired is second in importance to occupancy in considering compensation for disturbance, it may nevertheless affect the application of the underlying principle. For example, loss of profit or of goodwill may arise in the case of business premises, although clearly irrelevant to a dwelling. It will be convenient, therefore, to consider such special elements of compensation for disturbance separately.

The reason that occupation is crucial is that while the reinvestment of the proceeds of property held as an investment is a matter of choice[6] it

[1] *Smith, Stone, Knight Ltd.* v *The Lord Mayor, Aldermen and Citizens of Birmingham*, [1939] 4 All ER 116.
[2] The acquiring authority, after acquiring the legal interest, could, of course, terminate the licence.
[3] *DHN Food Distributors Ltd.* v *Tower Hamlets London Borough Council* [1976] 3 All ER 462, [1976] 1 WLR 852, CA.
[4] See Lord Denning MR at p. 467 and p. 860.
[5] In *Solomon Woolfson and Solfred Holdings Ltd.* v *Glasgow Corpn* (1975); 30 P & CR 505 the Lands Tribunal for Scotland followed *Taylor*'s case and the *Brain and Drive Yourself Car Hire Co.* case (note 7, p. 346, *supra*) and held that the occupying company had no claim to compensation for disturbance despite the fact that one of the joint owners of the premises held 999 out of a total of 1,000 shares and his wife held the remaining share. However, this case must now be looked at in the light of the *DHN* case, note 3, *supra*.
[6] The Scott Committee (1918) had, however, recommended that "where the claimant can prove that, acting reasonably, he is put to special expense for reinvestment, the cost of a single reinvestment should be allowed as an item of the claim".

is unreasonable not to recognise that an occupier's needs can often only be met by moving to alternative accommodation.[1]

RESIDENTIAL PREMISES

Thus, if a person, on being dispossessed from his house acquires another house, his entitlement to compensation for disturbance will include the cost of removing his furniture, of having his carpets and curtains altered to fit his new house as well as his travelling expenses, stamp duty, and legal and surveyors' fees in acquiring it[2] and these latter may also include abortive expenses reasonably incurred in the course of his search for alternative accommodation. Thus in *Harvey* v *Crawley Development Corporation* the claimant, Mrs Harvey, was allowed the fees of a surveyor employed to survey a house which she considered purchasing but which she subsequently turned down because of the unsatisfactory nature of the surveyor's report—and this in addition to the fees incurred in purchasing the house she later acquired[3] and the other items mentioned above.[4]

Losses excluded from Compensation for Disturbance

On the other hand it was pointed out that had the claimant not been in occupation and had she merely owned the house as an investment and reinvested the proceeds in stocks and shares or in another house as opposed to leaving them on deposit with her bank she could not claim the brokerage or the legal etc. fees on acquiring real property. Such costs of reinvestment would have been purely the result of her own choice of investment and too remote to be regarded as the result of the compulsory acquisition.[5] A dispossessed owner who decides not to

---

[1] The claimant in respect of a dwelling need not, however, occupy it as his permanent residence: *Venables* v *Department of Agriculture for Scotland*, 1932 SC 573 (acquisition, *inter alia*, of a shooting lodge).

[2] *Horn* v *Sunderland Corpn*, [1941] 2 KB 26; and *Harvey* v *Crawley Development Corpn (supra)*. See also *John Line & Sons Ltd.* v *Newcastle upon Tyne Corpn* (1956), 6 P & CR 466 in which the costs of altering stationery, of advertising and notifying customers of change of a business address were allowed.

[3] A person from whom land is compulsorily acquired is also entitled to the legal and surveyors' fees incurred in disposing of his property to the acquiring authority (including the reasonable costs of preparing his claim: *LCC* v *Tobin*, [1959] 1 WLR 354) but such expenses are claimable not as compensation for disturbance but as compensation for "any other matter not based directly on the value of the land" (see the Land Compensation Act 1961, s. 5(6), pp. 164 *et seq, ante*): *Minister of Transport* v *Lee*, [1965] 2 All ER 986 [CA], a case involving acquisition in response to a blight notice (see pp. 129 *et seq, ante*) in respect of which compensation for disturbance was, at the time, statutorily excluded by the Town and Country Planning Act 1962, s. 143(1)(b); see also *Redfield Hardware Ltd.* v *Bristol Corpn* (1963) 15 P & CR 47.

[4] In *Rutter* v *Manchester Corpn* (1974), 28 P & CR 443, LT a claim by a person rehoused by the local authority for increased costs of travel to work was allowed on the ground that such costs were "a natural and reasonable consequence" of the dispossession, and in the particular case were capable of quantification—the claimant had three years nine months to go before retirement; his claim was reduced, however, to take account of imponderables such as the possibility of early retirement, redundancy or obtaining work nearer his new home. **Note**: Lessees may also claim compensation for improvements or fixtures for which they would be entitled to compensation by their landlord upon the termination of their lease. Such entitlement may arise from the terms of the lease or, in the case of business or agricultural tenants, under the Landlord and Tenant Act 1927, (see p. 370, *infra*) or the Agricultural Holdings Act 1948 (p. 371, *infra*).

[5] Per Denning LJ in *Harvey* v *Crawley Development Corpn (supra)* at p. 493. Similarly, depreciation in the value of the owner's shares in a company occupying the land and controlled by him is also too remote: *Brain and Drive Yourself Car Hire Co.* v *LCC* (1957), 9 P & CR 113; *Roberts* v *Coventry*

purchase a new house is in a similar position, and if he decides instead to move into a guest house he can claim the actual costs of moving, but neither the cost of living in the guest house, nor the costs that would have been incurred if he had decided otherwise and purchased a new house in which to live.[1] In other words the costs must actually be incurred[2] or be genuinely anticipated.[3]

However, if the claimant is only able to find an alternative house at a higher price than that which he receives in compensation for the house acquired he cannot claim the difference since he is presumed to have got value for his money—i.e., a better house than the house acquired, for which he is also presumed to have obtained full market value. But if the dwelling acquired has been specially constructed or adapted to meet the needs of a disabled person (which would not necessarily enhance its market value) and is occupied by such a person at the date of entry (or was last so occupied) compensation may, if the claimant so desires, be assessed on the basis of equivalent reinstatement under Rule 5.[4]

Moreover, in the case of the relocation of businesses there may be a further exception to this rule in that if the rent[5] demanded for the only alternative premises reasonably available exceeds that previously paid, compensation may be payable in respect of an excess reflecting no advantage to the business: e.g., extra space which cannot be put to productive use or a more salubrious neighbourhood which is of no commercial advantage to the business in question.[6]

On the other hand, where structural additions and improvements to the new premises are carried out so that these premises are an improvement on the old and the cost of such alterations represents value for the extra money spent rather than replacement of facilities lost, the costs will be disallowed.[7] Similarly, where the new premises are leasehold and improvements are carried out under an express covenant

---

Corpn, [1947] 1 All ER 308. For other examples of expense being too remote to entitle a claimant to compensation for disturbance see *Re Clarke and Wandsworth District Board of Works* (1868), 17 LT 549; and *Re Tynemouth Corpn and the Duke of Northumberland* (1903), 89 LT 557. But see note 6, p. 347, *supra.*

[1] *Ibid*: but he may now be entitled to a Home Loss Payment under the Land Compensation Act 1973, s. 29, as to which see p. 372, *infra.* He would also be entitled to the losses incurred on the sale of surplus furniture, etc.: see *Venables v Department of Agriculture for Scotland* 1932 SC 573 p. 354, *infra.*

[2] Note, however, that if a dispossessed occupier of business premises unreasonably fails to mitigate his loss by failing to move into available alternative premises, compensation may be limited to what it would have been had he done so; see, for example, *Bede Distributors Ltd.* v *Newcastle upon Tyne Corpn* (1973), 26 P & CR 298 and pp. 353 *et seq, infra.*

[3] Thus, for example, compensation for anticipated loss of profits may be claimed: pp. 357, *et seq, infra.*

[4] Land Compensation Act 1973, s. 45; for Rule 5 and its application see pp. 239 *et seq, ante.*

[5] But if the "replacement premises" are *purchased* the "value for money" principle applies as with dwelling-houses.

[6] *Easton v Islington Corpn* (1952), 3 P & CR 145: *Greenberg v Grimsby Corpn* (1961), 12 P & CR 212; *WJ Mogridge (Bristol 1937) Ltd.* v *Bristol Corpn* (1956), 8 P & CR 78.

[7] *Smith v Birmingham Corpn* (1974), 29 P & CR 265. See also *Tamplin's Brewery Ltd.* v *County Borough of Brighton* (1971), 22 P & CR 746, where the subject land was part of the claimant's bottlery. The local authority had acquired other land which they sold to the Brewery to enable them to establish a much more modern plant. It was held that the basis of compensation should be the cost of replacement, less the saving in running costs attributable to the new equipment, multiplied by ten years' purchase. See also *Bibby & Sons Ltd.* v *Merseyside County Council* [1977] JPL 528.

in the lease, they again represent value for money and will not be allowed;[1] so also in the case of other improvements that add to the value of the lease and will give rise to a claim against the lessor upon its expiration.[2].

The general principle is, therefore, that although the claimant is entitled to be fully reimbursed for expenses reasonably incurred as a result of dispossession he is not entitled to make a profit. Thus in *Horn* v *Sunderland Corporation*[3] agricultural land was acquired as ripe for building and the purchase price fixed accordingly. It was held that, since the use to which the land was to be put and on which it was valued was wholly incompatible with its continued use for agriculture, no compensation for disturbance could be claimed except to the extent that the agricultural value of the land together with the compensation for disturbance therefrom might exceed the compensation payable on the basis of the land being building land. In other words, the claimant cannot sell (as a willing seller in the open market in accordance with Rule 2)[4] for a purpose that enhances the value of his land but which *ipso facto* involves dispossession and then claim compensation for the inevitable disturbance as well: *aliter* if, having taken into account the cost of acquiring and moving to another farm, he would have been better off as he was. In short, he can claim on whichever basis he prefers but he cannot have it both ways. He is entitled "to be put so far as money can do it, in the same position as if his land had not been taken from him. In other words, he gains the right to receive a money payment not less than the loss imposed upon him in the public interest, but on the other hand no greater".[5]

On the other hand compensation for disturbance can be claimed even though the use of the premises is limited by a temporary planning permission expiring at the date of acquisition where the time limitation would not have been imposed but for the proposed compulsory acquisition. This is because, in valuing the interest acquired, any effect on value resulting from the fact that acquisition is compulsory has to be ignored;[6] compensation therefore falls to be assessed upon the assumption that the property has the benefit of permanent planning permission. Since it follows that dispossession results from the acquisition and not from the termination of the temporary planning permission, compensation for disturbance is payable.[7]

---

[1] *Bresgall & Sons Ltd.* v *London Borough of Hackney* (1976), 32 P & CR 442.

[2] I.e., under the Landlord and Tenant Act 1927: see *Bresgall & Sons Ltd.* v *London Borough of Hackney, supra*.

[3] [1941] 2 KB 26.

[4] Land Compensation Act 1961, s. 5(2): pp. 164 *et seq, ante*.

[5] Per Scott LJ in *Horn's* case, *(supra)* at p. 42.

[6] Land Compensation Act 1961, s. 9: p. 176, *ante*.

[7] *Healey or McArdle* v *Glasgow Corpn* (1971), 24 P & CR 134: a Scottish Lands Tribunal decision in which it was unsuccessfully argued on behalf of the acquiring authority that the planning assumption of the Land Compensation (Scotland) Act 1963, ss. 22–24 (reproducing the Land Compensation Act 1961, ss. 14–16) applied only to "ascertaining the value of the relevant interest" and not to disturbance, being, under Rule 6 a "matter not directly based on the value of the land". It was held, however, that "the value of the relevant" interest included disturbance, claims for disturbance having been always treated as part of the value of the land.

Expenses incurred before Notice to Treat

It must, however, be emphasised that the losses incurred can only be the subject of compensation for disturbance if they are incurred as "the natural and reasonable consequence of the dispossession". Thus in *Webb* v *Stockport Corporation*[1] an owner, having been notified that the local authority were interested in acquiring his property, opened negotiations. No agreement, however, was reached, and in the meantime the local authority obtained a compulsory purchase order and served notice to treat. Up to the date of service of the notice to treat the owner had been a potential seller negotiating with the Corporation who, as a private treaty purchaser, could at any time have broken off negotiations without becoming responsible to the claimant for any loss or expenses involved. Legal and surveyors' fees incurred before the date of notice to treat (at which date the owner first technically became a claimant) could not therefore be included as an element in the compensation payable for disturbance; they did not arise "as a natural and reasonable consequence of the dispossession of the owner", which could only be put into effect after confirmation of the compulsory purchase order and service of the notice to treat.

This proposition that compensation for disturbance cannot include loss suffered or expenses incurred before notice to treat appears to have been adopted by the Lands Tribunal as a "normal" rule and in *Bostock, Chater & Sons Ltd.* v *Chelmsford Corpn*[2] the Tribunal quoted in their support the judgment of Danckwerts LJ in the *Square Grip Reinforcement* case[3] where he says[4] "It seems to me that the normal rule must apply unless some special reason can be found for disregarding it". But the issue in that case was the date on which the claimant's *interest* in the land fell to be valued for the purposes of compensation; compensation for disturbance as such was not in issue.[5] Moreover, although the Lands Tribunal followed the "rule" (without apparently even considering whether any special reason existed for disregarding it) in *G. E. Widden & Co. Ltd.* v *Kensington & Chelsea Royal London Borough*[6] they do not appear to have been entirely consistent. Even in *Bostock*'s case (*supra*) the decision seems to have turned more upon the conclusion that the claimant company's attempts to relocate could not, in the light of their financial position, be regarded as genuine, rather than upon the proposition that the costs incurred in relocation could not in any event have been allowed as an element in the compensation for disturbance because they were incurred before notice to treat.

In another case[7] the acquiring authority contested a claim based

---

[1] (1962) 13 P & CR 339.

[2] (1973) 26 P & CR 321.

[3] *Square Grip Reinforcement Co. (London) Ltd.* v *Rowton Houses Ltd. and the LCC* (1967), 18 P & CR 258.

[4] *Ibid* at p. 262.

[5] In this case it was unsuccessfully claimed that compensation should be assessed as at the date of entry: see now *Birmingham Corpn* v *West Midland Baptist (Trust) Association (Inc.)* (1969), 3 WLR 389 (HL); pp. 165 *et seq, ante*.

[6] [1970] RVR 160.

[7] *Bede Distributors Ltd.* v *Newcastle upon Tyne Corpn* (1973), 26 P & CR 298.

upon the claimant company's decision to go into voluntary liquidation on the ground that they could have mitigated their loss by relocating,[1] and that compensation should therefore be based upon the cost of doing so, including costs which would almost inevitably have had to be incurred before the date of notice to treat. That that would have been the correct basis of compensation, had it not been held (on other grounds) that in all the circumstances the company's action in going into voluntary liquidation was reasonable, was tacitly accepted by the Lands Tribunal.

The fact is that in many cases it is likely to take much longer to find and equip alternative business premises than is likely to be available between notice to treat and the date on which the acquiring authority require possession.[2] In such cases a claimant is in a dilemma. If he awaits notice to treat he increases the risk either of being forced to close down his business altogether or of incurring a delay between vacating the premises being acquired and his ability to reopen elsewhere, thereby suffering a loss of profit and increasing the compensation payable. Moreover to incur expenses before notice to treat, and even more so before confirmation of any relevant compulsory purchase order is in any event to take the risk that the property may not ultimately be acquired and the expenditure prove abortive. But if the property is in fact ultimately required and compulsorily purchased, and if relocation mitigates the loss, and therefore the compensation payable, it seems contrary to principle that the claimant should be penalised by inability to recover items of costs which are undoubtedly allowable if incurred after notice to treat.

Moreover, in most cases in which the property being acquired is a dwelling, and in many cases where it comprises business premises or agricultural land, the "owner-occupier" is now entitled to serve a blight notice as soon as a compulsory purchase order covering the property is made.[3] If the acquiring authority does not object to such a notice within two months it is then deemed to have served notice to treat and it seems more than a little anomalous and administratively cumbersome for it to be necessary for persons affected by a compulsory purchase order to serve a blight notice, if qualified to do so, in order to protect their right to such costs of relocation as may be incurred before the acquiring authority would otherwise in fact have served notice to treat.

If the device of a blight notice is used in order to bring forward the notice to treat it is, of course, of the utmost importance that the persons serving the notice should wait until there is a deemed notice to treat before either incurring expense in seeking alternative premises or otherwise changing their position to their possible detriment.

In the case of *Walters, Brett and Pack* v *South Glamorgan County Council*[4] the claimants were a firm of solicitors whose offices were the subject of a

---

[1] Where failure to mitigate loss is alleged by the acquiring authority the onus is upon them to prove it; *Roy* v *Westminster City Council* (1975), 31 P & CR 458.

[2] As to an acquiring authority's powers of entry before completion see p. 70, *ante*.

[3] Land Compensation Act 1973, s. 70, p. 137, *ante*.

[4] (1976) 238 Estates Gazette 733 LT.

compulsory purchase order made in June 1970 but not confirmed until January 1974. In August 1971 and again in November 1972 the acquiring authority had intimated that confirmation was imminent and suggested that the claimants should seek alternative accommodation. In October 1974 the claimants served a blight notice which became effective on acceptance by the County Council two months later. In the meantime, however, the claimants had vacated their offices in November 1974, but it was held that in assessing compensation regard had to be had to the state of the premises as at the date of the deemed notice to treat: on that date they were, of course, vacant. The *ratio decidendi* of this decision appears to have been that by serving the blight notice in these circumstances the claimants had taken themselves outside the scope of the compulsory purchase order and must accept the consequences, viz that the compulsory purchase order and the correspondence relating thereto had become inadmissible and irrelevant.

It would therefore be going too far, in the authors' view, to accept this case as authority for the proposition that where there has been no such overt action on the part of the claimants there are no circumstances in which expenses incurred in good faith before notice to treat can be included in a valid claim for compensation for disturbance. Although there is clearly a presumption against the inclusion of such expenses it is submitted that each case must be judged on the basis of whether or not there was a genuine attempt to mitigate the loss and if so, whether in doing so it was reasonable to incur expenses without waiting for the acquiring authority to serve notice to treat.[1] On this supposition it must be assumed that had the Lands Tribunal found that the claimant company in *Bostock*'s case (*supra*) had genuinely intended to relocate, or that to have done so would have reduced their losses, the decision would have been in their favour for, before incurring those expenses they had been quite specifically informed that the Minister intended to confirm the compulsory purchase order as it affected their premises. For reasons which had nothing to do with the claimant company, actual confirmation and therefore service of notice to treat was, however, considerably delayed.[2]

Duty to mitigate loss

Reference has been made to the duty to mitigate loss, but it is in essence no more than a duty to act reasonably for if loss arises from

[1] This supposition is not, of course, consistent with the bald statement of the presiding member of the Lands Tribunal in *Widden*'s case (*supra*) that "I do not accept that compensation may extend to cover reimbursement of losses incurred before the notice to treat". But nor, however, does that statement seem consistent with the arguments accepted by the Lands Tribunal in the *Bede* case (*supra*). For a case in which this question was in issue but in which legal and surveyors' fees, incurred before notice to treat, were allowed, see *Drake and Underwood* v *LCC* (1960), 11 P & CR 427, at p. 438.

[2] Moreover if the Lands Tribunal had accepted the statement in *Widden*'s case (see the previous note) as a correct statement of the law the prolonged consideration given to the Corporation's alternative method of assessment in the *Bede* case would appear to have been irrelevant. Nor does it follow that had no blight notice been served in the *Walters, Brett and Park* case, *supra*, and the acquiring authority had proceeded with the acquisition by serving notice to treat, the claimants' expenses incurred before notice to treat would necessarily have been disallowed.

unreasonable behaviour it cannot be said to be a natural and reasonable consequence of the dispossession and, in effect, becomes too remote. Thus, as has been seen in both *Bostock*'s case and the *Bede* case (*supra*), consideration must be given to such opportunities to relocate rather than doing nothing, waiting for the acquiring authority to take possession and claiming compensation for disturbance on the basis of the complete cessation of business.[1] In such cases the availability of alternative accommodation is always relevant and must be taken into account, but it will not be considered unreasonable to reject relocation if the available alternative premises are substantially more expensive than those from which the claimant is being displaced[2] or the cost of relocation is, at the time, beyond the claimant's resources.[3] Similarly, if the claimant's resources would not permit relocation, abortive costs in searching for alternative premises cannot be allowed.[4] On the other hand, although the financial resources available to a company may be relevant in deciding whether they acted reasonably in refusing to relocate, it is not relevant to a claim for removal expenses actually incurred. A company electing to relocate although operating at a loss remains, therefore, entitled to the reasonable costs of doing so.[5]

Further removal expenses allowable

Apart from the items already mentioned removal expenses may include losses on a sale of surplus furniture and equipment even if the latter is of a purely personal nature and readily portable. Thus in *Venables* v *Department of Agriculture for Scotland*[6] a dispossessed tenant of land with sporting rights successfully claimed compensation on losses incurred in the sale of a motor launch, a motor car and sporting equipment.

Other business losses

Similarly, losses upon the forced sale of business stock and equipment are claimable. It has thus been held that where articles of equipment, retained by the claimant on giving up the business, were valued on the basis of their value to a purchaser of the business as a going concern at £240, but only at £50 on the basis of the price they would be likely to fetch if separately auctioned, the claimant was held entitled to the difference (£190).[7]

Moreover, in assessing loss of profits, allowance may be made for the loss of time involved in searching for alternative premises.[8]

---

[1] P. 351, *supra*.

[2] *Knott Mill Carpets Ltd.* v *Stretford Borough Council* (1973), 26 P & CR 129. See also *Roy* v *Westminster City Council, supra*, in which a medical practitioner was upheld in his contention that the terms upon which the acquiring authority had offered alternative accommodation were unreasonably onerous.

[3] *Bede Distributors Ltd.* v *Newcastle upon Tyne Corpn (supra)*.

[4] *Bostock, Chater & Sons Ltd* v *Chelmsford Corpn (supra)*.

[5] *Burrow* v *Metropolitan Rly Co* (1884), *Times*, 22 November HL.

[6] 1932 SC 573.

[7] *Somers & Somers* v *Doncaster Corpn* (1965), 16 P & CR 323.

[8] *Smith* v *Birmingham Corpn* (1974), 29 P & CR 265, where compensation was based on complete closure of the business for a period which was extended by the Lands Tribunal to take account of the time spent in seeking new premises and the time taken in actual removal.

Fixtures

On the same principle damages resulting from disturbance include the cost of replacing fixtures attached to the freehold.[1]

Loss of profits and goodwill

Claims for loss of profits arise either where, as a result of dispossession the business has to be wholly closed down[2] or where, despite relocation, the move involves a curtailment of business which may be temporary or permanent. For example, it may have proved impossible for the new premises to be got ready for the resumption of business before the original premises have to be vacated; there may therefore either be a complete break[3] or if business can be immediately transferred at a reduced level pending completion of necessary alteration or installation of plant and equipment, only a partial break.

Alternatively, there may be a partial extinguishment, as for example where an engineering works comprising several lines of production cannot be reinstated in toto in the new premises; in such circumstances compensation may be payable on the basis of the total extinguishment of the part of the business that has to be abandoned; so too where a dispossessed mixed farmer has to abandon distinctive parts of his enterprise to which his new farm is unsuited.

Moreover, where a business is totally or partially extinguished and the land, whether comprising business premises or agricultural land, is leasehold it is not to be assumed, when assessing compensation for loss of profits, that the business will in any event be extinguished upon the termination of the lease. This is because account has to be taken of any expectation of renewal of the lease under the Landlord and Tenant Act 1954, in the case of business tenancies[4] or the security of tenure provisions of the Agricultural Holdings Act 1948 in the case of agricultural tenancies.[5] Since these provisions more frequently affect the assessment of compensation for disturbance in relation to tenancies of less than a year or from year to year their effect is considered in detail in the next section of this chapter.[6]

Goodwill

In this connection it is, however, necessary to distinguish claims for loss of goodwill. Goodwill may be defined as the value of that element of profitability that arises from specific business connections related to the location of the premises acquired or the personality of the proprietor. For example, that element of a retailer's trade that is predominantly local, and dependent upon custom that he will inevitably lose if he

---

[1] *Gibson* v *Hammersmith and City Rly Co* (1863), 32 LJ Ch. 337. Where there is no relocation the value of fixtures will be reflected in the valuation of the claimant's interest.

[2] Note that where the claimant is the proprietor of a business and is over the age of sixty he may be entitled to claim compensation for disturbance on the assumption that the business has been extinguished by the acquisition and cannot reasonably be relocated: Land Compensation Act 1973, s. 46, p. 361, *infra*. For the assessment of compensation for loss of profits upon extinguishment of a business see p. 360, *infra*.

[3] As in *Smith* v *Birmingham Corpn*, note 8, p. 354, *supra*.

[4] Land Compensation Act 1973, s. 47.

[5] *Ibid*, s. 48.

[6] See pp. 365 *et seq infra*, and in particular, pp. 370–372, *infra*.

moves out of the locality, represents his goodwill.[1] Similarly, where a solicitor's practice could be said to be largely dependent upon an established and locally well-known address, and likely to be adversely affected even by a move within the same neighbourhood, he was held entitled to compensation for goodwill.[2] On the other hand, a wholesale business, or one dependent upon customers from a wide area, though possessing goodwill of value to a purchaser of the business, is likely to be able to move within a fairly wide radius without loss of custom, in which case his loss of goodwill will be negligible and no claim therefor can be sustained. Similarly in the case of a retailer able to move within the immediate area.[3] But the proprietor of a business may have a claim for loss of goodwill, even though the business is being carried on at a loss, if he can establish that continued occupation of the acquired premises would have given him the opportunity to increase his goodwill and show a profit.[4]

The loss or diminution of goodwill which gives rise to a claim to compensation must therefore be a personal asset in the sense that it does not pass to the acquiring authority upon acquisition of the land, but in so far as it is not extinguished it remains the property of the trader. Difficulty may be encountered, however, in cases where the goodwill claimed arises purely from the situation and nature of the property, for in such circumstances the special trading value of a shop resulting from its situation in a busy and popular shopping centre is part of the value of the freehold rather than a personal asset of the trader. It is sometimes referred to as "non-personal goodwill" in contra-distinction to the personal goodwill which alone is relevant in the context of compensation for disturbance; but the former is not, strictly speaking, goodwill at all. This is not to say, however, that there cannot be goodwill attached to such a business if it can be shown that there is some particular and personal element in the management that has increased profitability beyond the inherent profitability of the site. For example, in the case of a public house the custom is deemed attributable to its existence as such and to arise, as in the case of a shop in a busy shopping area, from the mere habit of customers in resorting to that particular house or shopping area. The "goodwill" will therefore pass with the freehold.[5] But *aliter*, it is submitted, if the dispossessed landlord has, for example, established a personal catering enterprise attracting a more selective clientele.

In *Park Automobile Co. Ltd.* v *City of Glasgow Corporation*,[6] in which the land being acquired comprised a filling station, the acquiring authority

---

[1] *White* v *Public Works Commissioners* (1870), 22 LT 591: *John Line & Sons Ltd* v *Newcastle upon Tyne Corpn* (1956), 6 P & CR 466, in which goodwill (described in the head-note as the "positional trade", i.e., the trade related to the location of the acquired premises) was capitalised at five years' purchase.

[2] *R* v *Scard* (1894), 10 TLR 545. So too in the case of a medical practice: *Roy* v *Westminster City Council*, p. 357, *infra*.

[3] See the dictum of Bramwell LJ in *Re Bidder and North Staffordshire Rly Co* (1878) 4 QBD 412 at p. 432.

[4] *Burrow* v *Metropolitan Rly Co* (1884), *Times*, 22 November HL.

[5] *Re Kitchin ex parte Punnett* (1880), 16 Ch. D 226 at p. 233.

[6] (1975) 30 P & CR 491 (Lands Tribunal for Scotland).

sought to establish an analogy with licensed premises and a deduction from the compensation payable in respect of business retainable at the new premises. It was held, however, that there is no such analogy since, in the case of a filling station (and by inference, other trading establishments), there is no local monopoly such as is conferred by a liquor licence. Moreover, the proper basis of valuation of a filling station is its market value as a going concern, and it would be impossible to assess how much of the old business would be retained at premises on a different traffic route.

Assessment of compensation for loss of profits or goodwill

As far as compensation for loss of goodwill is concerned, it must be emphasised that it is not the market value of the claimant's local connection that has to be ascertained, but the *quantum* of loss suffered by him in having to sacrifice potential business arising from an established business or practice.[1] Thus although it is unlawful to sell the goodwill, or any part thereof, of a medical practice,[2] the fact that such goodwill therefore has no market value does not prevent a valid claim for compensation for loss of the goodwill of a medical practice if, as a result of the acquisition, the practice cannot be continued in the locality or is entirely extinguished.[3]

For the purpose of compensation, loss of profits as such and loss of goodwill are both normally calculated on the basis of the average profit over the previous three years multiplied by a multiplier expressed as so many "years' purchase".

There is, however, no hard and fast rule as to the appropriate number of years' purchase and even an average of three years' profits may in certain circumstances be inappropriate as a starting point. For example, profits during the previous three years may have been affected by special circumstances and require adjustment either directly,[4] or indirectly by altering the multiplier. But in so far as such special circumstances have depreciated profits they themselves must be the reasonable result of the dispossession. Thus, where failure to find alternative premises led to the proprietor's inability to offer security of employment, allowance has been made for the effect upon profits of the consequential loss of a key employee who testified to the effect that he would otherwise have continued in the firm's employment.[5] Similarly, an allowance has been made for inability fully to exploit a patent as a result of impending acquisition[6] and for loss of contracts, including, it seems, loss incurred in the carrying out of existing contracts.[7] On the other hand, in the first of these cases[8] a claim that demolition and

---

[1] *Remnant* v *LCC* (1952), 3 P & CR 185, 195; and *Somers and Somers* v *Doncaster Corpn* (1965), 16 P & CR 323.
[2] National Health Service Act 1946, s. 35(2).
[3] *Roy* v *Westminster City Council* (1975) 31 P & CR 458.
[4] See, for example, *Drake and Underwood* v *LCC* (1960), 11 P & CR 427, where an average of the previous five years' profits was employed.
[5] *G. E. Widden & Co.* v *Kensington & Chelsea Royal London Borough Council*, [1970] RVR 160.
[6] *Powner & Powner* v *Leeds Corpn* (1953), 4 P & CR 167.
[7] *W. Rought Ltd.* v *West Suffolk County Council* (1954), 4 P & CR 347.
[8] See *Widden's* case, *supra*.

redevelopment of neighbouring property by another authority had also depreciated profits was dismissed on the ground that such works were not the result of dispossession by the acquiring authority.[1]

Similarly, a decision not to proceed with plans to install labour-saving equipment owing to the threat of ultimate compulsory acquisition may at least be indirectly relevant.[2]

Conversely, where the profits have been increasing over the previous three or more years, and but for the dispossession would have been expected to continue to do so, this too can be taken into account by taking the last year's profits only as the basis of the calculation, by increasing the number of years' purchase, or by a combination of the two.[3]

Where a claim for loss of profits arises from a forced removal of a business, account may be taken of defects associated with the new premises which are likely adversely to affect the level of profits as compared with those earned at the original premises. Reference has already been made to allowances for unproductive increases in rent.[4] On the same reasoning increases in the cost of transport of men and materials[5] and of adaptation of the new premises[6] may be allowed, as also may the cost of running two sets of premises during the transition period.[7]

In assessing the number of years' purchase to be applied in the valuation of goodwill the Lands Tribunal tend to give the most weight to evidence derived from private sales of similar businesses in the open market, the multiplier being readily calculable where details of both profits and the premises, as well as the purchase price, are available.[2] In the absence of such information as to the behaviour of the market, reliance will be placed upon settlements of compensation reached between the District Valuer and owners of other similar businesses compulsorily acquired.

DEDUCTIONS FROM PROFITS

In calculating profits for this purpose certain deductions fall to be made from net profits deduced from the ordinary profit and loss account. The first such deduction is in respect of interest on the capital employed in

---

[1] But if the neighbouring redevelopment had been part of the scheme in pursuit of which the claimant's property was being acquired it would seem that the claim would have been allowable since in assessing the purchase price (of which compensation for disturbance forms a part) the effect of the scheme falls to be discounted: Land Compensation Act 1961, s. 6, pp. 220 *et seq, ante*, and cf. *Healey or McArdle* v *Glasgow Corpn*, [1971] JPL 708, p. 350, *supra*.

[2] See *Zarraga* v *Newcastle upon Tyne Corpn* (1968), 19 P & CR 609, p. 359, *infra*.

[3] *Somers and Somers* v *Doncaster Corpn* (1965), 16 P & CR 323: a case concerned with the valuation of goodwill, but this principle would appear to be equally applicable to claims for loss of profits.

[4] P. 349, *supra*.

[5] *W. Rought Ltd.* v *West Suffolk County Council*, [1955] 2 QB 338 CA: *Herrburger Brooks* v *St Pancras Corpn* (1960), 11 P & CR 390.

[6] But architects' and surveyors' fees will only be allowable in so far as they are incurred merely to replace facilities lost: to the extent that their work provides improved facilities they cannot be reimbursed: *ibid*. Cf. *W. J. Mogridge (Bristol 1937), Ltd.* v *Bristol Corpn* (1956), 8 P & CR 78 in which fees incurred in respect of a new building were allowed even although the proposal was ultimately abandoned.

[7] *Mogridge*'s case, *supra*.

the business, i.e., capital sunk in plant, vehicles, stock, and debtors (less creditors).

Secondly, since the rental value of the premises is reflected in the capital value, and therefore the compensation payable in respect of the land, a corresponding deduction has to be made from the profits: if the claimant is a tenant the rent payable will, of course, have appeared in the profit and loss account, but if this rent is less than the market rent a further deduction must be made equivalent to the difference, i.e., the "profit rent".

Thirdly, cases have occurred in which further deductions have been made in respect of the notional wages earned by the proprietor.[1] On the other hand, in *Perezic* v *Bristol Corporation*[2] such a deduction, in the case of a "one-man business" was held to be unjustified, and this is a view which certainly seems the more in accord with principle. The claimant does, after all, lose his job, and it does not follow that he can readily find employment elsewhere or in the same trade.

If such loss of employment (for which an employee of standing would normally qualify for redundancy pay) is to be excluded by calculating profits net of notional wages it would seem difficult to argue that the compensation he receives puts the claimant in as good a position financially as he would otherwise have been.[3]

In *Zarraga*'s case[4] the Lands Tribunal went further and dismissed the acquiring authority's submission that wages paid to the claimant's wife for part-time assistance in the business (a fish and chip shop) should be deducted from profits even though such payments had been allowed by the Inland Revenue for tax purposes. The Tribunal's decision rested in part upon evidence to the effect that in private sales of such "husband and wife" enterprises the market made no such deduction in valuing goodwill, and in part upon evidence that the claimant had intended to install labour-saving equipment (which would probably have made his wife's services unnecessary) but had been inhibited from doing so by the fore-knowledge of probable compulsory acquisition. Moreover, in *Nielson* v *Camden Borough Council*[5] the Lands Tribunal, in dismissing a claim by the acquiring authority to deduct a notional salary in respect of the claimant's managerial services, distinguished *Mathews*' case[6] on the ground that the question was not in issue, and *Speyer*'s case[6] on the ground of the special characteristics of the business and premises and, by implication, showed a preference for the reasoning of the earlier decision in *Pearce*'s case, *Perezic*'s case and *Drake & Underwood*'s case.[7] The Lands Tribunal further distinguished cases[8] in which the claimant

[1] *Mathews* v *Bristol Corpn* (1954), 4 P & CR 401; *Speyer* v *Westminster Corpn* (1958), 9 P & CR 478.
[2] (1955) 5 P & CR 237: see also *Pearce* v *Bristol Corpn* (1949), 1 P & CR 367 (a case involving a farmer): p. 366, *infra*.
[3] See the comments of Scott LJ in *Horn* v *Sunderland Corpn*, p. 350, *supra*.
[4] *Zarraga* v *Newcastle upon Tyne Corpn* (1967), 19 P & CR 609; and see p. 358, *supra*.
[5] (1968) 19 P & CR 801.
[6] *Supra*.
[7] *Infra*.
[8] *Shulman (Tailors) Ltd.* v *Greater London Council* (1966), 17 P & CR 244: *Noeltex Ltd.* v *Westminster City Council*, [1964] Estates Gazette Digest 138.

was a limited company in which there was formal separation of ownership and management. Similarly, they quoted with approval a case of a "family" company in which directors' fees were shown as a deduction in arriving at net profits for the purpose of assessing compensation.[1]

The situation in regard to a partnership appears to be somewhat different for in *Drake and Underwood* v *LCC*[2] a distinction was drawn between a whole-time partner in respect of whose services no deduction was made and a part-time partner (who *inter alia* kept the accounts) apparently on the ground that the latter's services were "not entirely indispensable" since a large proportion of his work for the partnership "could have been and in fact was done by a paid secretary or clerk",[3] employed by an associated business the management of which constituted the part-time partner's principal employment.

Finally, it has been held that, if the compensation payable for temporary loss of profits will not be taxable in the hands of the recipient, a deduction must be made equivalent to the tax that would have been payable had the profits been actually earned.[4] However, the present position appears to be that the compensation is included as part of the consideration for the disposal for the purposes of capital gains tax or of corporation tax as chargeable gains so that "any reduction of the compensation to take account of the tax which might have been chargeable on the lost profits" becomes inappropriate.[5]

TOTAL EXTINGUISHMENT OF BUSINESS

Where, as a result of compulsory acquisition, it proves impracticable to relocate, and the business is therefore totally extinguished, the assessment of compensation follows the same principles as those already discussed: abortive costs in searching for alternative premises, losses resulting from forced sale of stock and equipment, the value of fixtures etc., all being allowable where relevant. When it comes to assessing compensation for goodwill or loss of profits, however, such losses are, of course, both permanent and total. In such cases the Lands Tribunal has held[6] that the proper approach is not to attempt to multiply average profits by an inevitably somewhat arbitrary number of years' purchase

---

[1] *Lewis' Executors and the Palladium Cinema (Brighton) Ltd.* v *Brighton Corpn* (1956), 6 P & CR 318. Note that in *Nielson*'s case, *supra*, it was unsuccessfully argued on behalf of the Corporation that the size of the business was relevant, it being accepted that in that case it was such that the most likely purchaser in the market would have been a fairly large limited company.

[2] (1960) 11 P & CR 427. The partnership was an informal one by which profits were divided as to 60% to the full-time partner and 40% to the other partner.

[3] Cf. *Zarraga*'s case, p. 359, *supra*: in that case the claimant's wife also kept the accounts as well as occasionally helping in the shop. Assuming *Drake*'s case to have been rightly decided the distinction is apparently two-fold, viz that a "husband and wife" business (if regarded as such in the market) is to be treated differently from other informal partnerships and that in *Zarraga*'s case the wife's services might not have been required if the claimant had not been inhibited by the pending acquisition from installing labour-saving equipment.

[4] *West Suffolk County Council* v *W. Rought Ltd.*, [1957] AC 403 6 P & CR 362.

[5] See *Bostock, Chater & Sons Ltd* v *Chelmsford Corpn* (1973), 26 P & CR 321, and the Board of Inland Revenue Statements at p. 348. But see also *Hobbs (Quarries) Ltd.* v *Somerset County Council* (1975), 30 P & CR 286, at p. 294, note 4, p. 344, *supra*. See also *Wood Mitchell & Co.* v *Stoke-on-Trent City Council* [1977] JPL 315.

[6] *W. Clibbett Ltd.* v *Avon County Council*, [1975] RVR 131, per the President, Douglas Franks QC.

but to follow the principles adopted by the courts in assessing damages for total loss of earnings, an appropriate allowance being made for the risks of business and taxation; in other words, the amount that would produce an equivalent income on investment, or by way of purchase of an annuity, must be reduced to take account of such factors.[1]

SPECIAL PROVISIONS RELATING TO ELDERLY PROPRIETORS OF SMALL BUSINESSES

In order to ameliorate the problems of an elderly proprietor of a small business faced, as a result of the compulsory acquisition of his premises, with having to re-establish himself elsewhere for the few remaining years before retirement, the Act of 1973[2] provides that where, on the date on which the acquiring authority require possession of the land on which the trade or business is carried on, the owner[3] is over the age of sixty[4] he may claim compensation for disturbance on the basis of the complete extinction of his business,[5] irrespective of the availability of suitable alternative accommodation. Since the age of the proprietor is much less relevant, if indeed relevant at all, in the case of larger businesses employing labour this concession is confined to the small business defined by reference to "annual" value.[6] It is accordingly provided that at the date on which the proprietor is required to give up possession, the land in question must either be, or form part of, a hereditament the annual value of which does not exceed the amount from time to time prescribed by order.[7] It is a further prerequisite that the acquiring authority shall have both compulsorily acquired[8] and

---

[1] The amount awarded in respect of loss of profits in *Clibbett*'s case in fact represented three years' purchase of average profits, the unexpired term of the lease being about four and a half years. Compensation fell to be assessed after the coming into force of the Land Compensation Act 1973, s. 47, but the report does not reveal to what extent any expectation of a further renewal of the lease under the Landlord and Tenant Act 1954, Part II, affected the assessment of compensation for loss of profits. The inference to be drawn from the amount of the award, as well as from the agreed value of the lease (£275), would seem to be that there was, in the circumstances, little expectation of renewal. See pp. 367 *et seq, infra*.

[2] Land Compensation Act 1973, s. 46.

[3] That is, a person claiming compensation for the acquisition of his interest in the land (whether or not that interest exceeds an interest for a year or from year to year): *ibid*, s. 46(1). Note, however, that these provisions also apply to the assessment of disturbance payments under *ibid*, ss. 37 and 38: as to which see pp. 385 *et seq, infra*. For the special requirements where the owner is a partnership firm or company see p. 367, *infra*.

[4] In other words, statutory recognition is given to the *personal* circumstances of the claimant—but only in regard to age. In *Bailey* v *Derby Corpn*, [1965] 1 WLR 213 the Court of Appeal held that compensation on the basis of total extinguishment of a business could not be allowed on the grounds of the claimant's ill-health. Although in that case ill-health developed after entry by the acquiring authority, there is an implication in the judgment of Russell LJ (at p. 221) that the decision would have been the same if illness had developed prior to the acquisition. The question whether such personal circumstances are relevant to this question therefore remains uncertain. See "Compensation for Compulsory Acquisition" published by *Justice* (1973), para. 41.

[5] See p. 360, *supra*.

[6] Cf. for example, the identical criterion adopted in relation to blight notices, pp. 130 *et seq, ante*.

[7] Land Compensation Act 1973, s. 46(1)(b): the current limit of annual value is £2,250: Town and Country Planning (Limit of Annual Value) Order 1973 (SI 1973 No. 76). For definition of "hereditament" see note 5, p. 130, *ante*.

[8] These provisions do not, therefore, apply as such to acquisition by agreement so that in such cases the vendor should insist upon a price fully reflecting the value of the business as a going concern.

required possession of, the whole of the land on which the trade or business is carried on.[1]

Furthermore, since the object of these provisions is to provide full compensation for the goodwill of the business they will not apply where the proprietor has disposed of the goodwill of the whole of his trade or business[2] or unless he gives an undertaking that he will not dispose of his goodwill (or that part of it which he has retained) and will not engage in, or have any interest in, any similar business within such period of time and within such area as the acquiring authority may require.[3] If either of these undertakings is broken the acquiring authority may recover the difference between the compensation paid and the compensation that would have been payable without regard to these provisions.[4]

Thus, if the owner of the business in fact breaks the second of these undertakings he could be significantly worse off than if he had opted for compensation to be assessed in the ordinary way. There are two reasons why this might be so. In the first place there is no limit to either the area or period within which the acquiring authority may require him to refrain from re-establishing his business; it does not therefore follow that the goodwill of his former business would have any value. Secondly, cases in which ability to acquire an interest, especially a fairly minor one, in another established business within the same trade which would, of itself, affect the assessment of compensation for disturbance are difficult to visualise and must in any event be rare. It follows, therefore, that where it can be shown that the business cannot reasonably be relocated somewhere where the goodwill of the former business will be preserved and the owner is at all likely to wish to retain an interest in his trade or business in the same locality, it is wiser to rely on the ordinary law than to invoke these special provisions.

Where the acquired business is carried on by a partnership all the partners must be over the age of sixty and the undertakings mentioned above apply as if subscribed to by each partner individually.[5] Thus breach of such undertakings by a single partner entitles the acquiring authority to recover the whole of the compensation attributable to these provisions from the firm rather than from the partner in breach and, moreover, not merely the share of that partner. Where there is a number of partners, and the amount involved is substantial[6] it may therefore be provident to require each partner to subscribe to a deed of indemnity.

Similar provisions apply to the shareholders where the business is

---

[1] Land Compensation Act 1973, s. 46(1). As to the rights of owners to require acquiring authorities, desirous of acquiring only part of their property, to acquire the whole see pp. 108 *et seq*, *ante*.

[2] He cannot, of course, claim compensation in respect of any portion of his goodwill of which he has disposed: *ibid*.

[3] *Ibid*, s. 46(1) and (3).

[4] *Ibid*, s. 46(4).

[5] *Ibid*, s. 46(5).

[6] It must be borne in mind that "annual value" of the premises can only constitute a very rough and ready guide to the profitability of, and therefore the goodwill appurtenant to, the trade or business for which they are used.

operated by a limited company; in such a case, however, a person holding less than 50 % of the shares[1] (a minority shareholder) need not be over sixty years of age provided he (or she) is the spouse of a shareholder who has attained that age. The provisions relating to the requisite undertakings apply to each shareholder as they apply to partners: they also apply to the company.[2] It is to be noted, however, that although there is no specific provision to this effect the clear implication is that the relevant shareholding position, along with the age of the shareholders, is the position ruling as at the date on which the company gives up possession. There seems, therefore, nothing to prevent younger shareholders from transferring their shares to their more senior colleagues prior to that date, thus obtaining for the company the full advantages of these provisions while freeing themselves from any restrictions arising from the undertakings. Presumably, by withdrawing from a partnership before the firm is required to give possession, junior partners can obtain similar advantages.[3]

Compensation for disturbance payable to dispossessed owners:[4] Summary

1. No compensation for disturbance is payable:

(a) To owners not in occupation of the property acquired except where owner and occupier are companies within the same group;[5]

(b) where compensation has been assessed on the basis of the cost of equivalent reinstatement under Rule 5;[6]

(c) Where the acquisition is under the Housing Acts and compensation falls to be assessed on the basis of the value of the cleared site;[6]

(d) Where the acquisition is in pursuance of a blight notice and the compensation claimed is in respect of expenses incurred prior to the date of the deemed notice to treat;[7]

2. In all other cases the basis of compensation is the loss sustained by the dispossessed owner which flows from the compulsory acquisition provided it is the natural and reasonable consequence of the dispossession and is not too remote.[8] There is, however, a presumption against the inclusion of expenses incurred before the date of notice to treat.[9]

---

[1] "Shareholders" for this purpose include only holders of shares carrying voting rights: Land Compensation Act 1973, s. 46(6).

[2] *Ibid.*

[3] Note, however, that whereas ibid, s. 46(6)(a) (the "company" provisions) requires an amendment to subs. (1)(a) (which expressly refers to the date of giving possession) where the business is operated by a company, sub-s. (5) (the partnership provisions) is in purely general terms and applies to s. 46 as a whole.

[4] I.e., freeholders and leaseholders having at least twelve months unexpired. See *Newham London Borough Council* v *Benjamin*, [1968] 1 WLR 694 (CA): for compensation for disturbance, if any, available to those with lesser interests see pp. 365 *et seq, infra.*

[5] Pp. 346 *et seq, supra.*

[6] P. 345, *supra.*

[7] Pp. 352 *et seq, supra.* In these cases, however, a home loss payment will normally be available: see pp. 372 *et seq, infra.*

[8] Pp. 346 *et seq, supra.*

[9] Pp. 351 *et seq, supra.*

3. In all cases recoverable expenses include the actual costs of removal, and, provided the lost property is replaced, travelling expenses incurred in searching for alternative accommodation,[1] surveying fees rendered abortive by the unsatisfactory nature of the surveyor's report,[1] legal and surveying fees incurred in acquiring alternative accommodation and stamp duty upon the conveyance.[2] Losses resulting from the enforced sale of surplus furniture, equipment and business stock may also be included.[3]

   (a) In the case of a dwelling-house[4] being compulsorily acquired, other items of expenditure that may be covered include the cost of refitting curtains and carpets,[5] the extra cost of travel to work (if quantifiable)[6] and the cost of replacing fixtures.[7]

   (b) In the case of business premises there may be included a claim for loss of goodwill;[8] loss of profits (whether temporary as a result of disruption caused by the move or permanent as a result of the alternative premises being less suitable to the conduct of the business);[9] cost of adapting the new premises;[10] reprinting of stationery;[11] replacement of fittings and immoveable plant;[7] loss of key staff;[12] and the increased cost of transport of men and materials.[13]

4. Expenses which cannot be claimed include the amount by which the cost of the new premises exceeds the value of the old[10] (except where additional rent of new business premises reflects aspects of no productive use in carrying on the business);[14] the costs of any improvements to the new premises which provide facilities lacking in the old; the costs of improvements carried out in pursuance of an express term of the lease of the new premises or in respect of which a claim can be made against the lessor upon its termination.[15]

5. Where a business cannot be relocated, compensation may be claimed on the basis of its total extinguishment.[16]

---

[1] Pp. 348 *et seq, supra*. In principle it would seem that these expenses will be recoverable if, as a result of genuine inability to find alternative accommodation, the claimant changes his mind and decides not to replace his lost property, e.g. if dispossessed from his home he decides to live in an hotel, or if dispossessed from his business, he is forced to wind it up: see *Bede Distributors Ltd*. v *Newcastle upon Tyne Corpn*, pp. 351 *et seq, supra*.

[2] Pp. 348 *et seq, supra*.

[3] P. 354, *supra*.

[4] And note the option open to a handicapped person displaced from a house specially adapted to ameliorate his disability, to have compensation assessed on the equivalent reinstatement basis of Rule 5: pp. 349, *supra*, and 239 *et seq, ante*.

[5] P. 348, *supra*.

[6] See note 4, p. 348, *supra*.

[7] P. 355, *supra*.

[8] Pp. 355, *et seq, supra*.

[9] P. 355, *supra*; and note that the profits as shown in the Profit and Loss Account may be subject to deductions: pp. 358, *et seq, supra*.

[10] P. 349, *supra*.

[11] P. 348, note 2, *supra*.

[12] P. 357, *supra*.

[13] P. 358, *supra*.

[14] P. 349, *supra*.

[15] Pp. 349–350, *supra*.

[16] P. 360, *supra*, and note the option available in this regard where the proprietors of a small business are over sixty years of age: pp. 361 *et seq, supra*.

3 COMPENSATION FOR DISTURBANCE ARISING FROM THE ACQUISITION OF SHORT TENANCIES

Where a person is in occupation of land but has no greater interest than as tenant for a year[1] or from year to year an authority requiring the property and possessing powers of compulsory acquisition will inevitably require the freehold and/or any superior leasehold interest. Normally therefore the acquiring authority will either induce the landlord to give to the tenant notice to quit, or itself acquire the landlord's interest, give notice to quit, and in either case await determination of the tenancy before taking possession. By that time the occupying tenant will have ceased to hold any interest in the property and, prior to the Act of 1973[2] would therefore have had no entitlement to compensation.[3] In such cases, however, this Act changed the position in two ways. In the first place it confers an entitlement to certain statutory payments variously described as Home or Farm Loss Payments in the case of a house or farm and as Disturbance Payments in other cases. Farm Loss and Disturbance Payments cannot be made if the claimant is otherwise entitled to compensation in respect of the disturbance. There is, however, no such restriction upon Home Loss Payments which (provided the claimant fulfils the requisite qualifications[4]) may therefore be claimed in addition to compensation for disturbance in accordance with the provisions described in this and the preceding section of this chapter. For convenience all these payments are dealt with in the next following section.

Secondly, the Act of 1973 provides in effect that in assessing compensation due to a tenant of business premises or agricultural land account is to be taken of the security of tenure afforded under the Landlord and Tenant Act 1954 and the Agricultural Holdings Act 1948 respectively.[5] The effect of these provisions in relation to compensation for disturbance is explained below.

It may be, however, that the acquiring authority requires possession before the date on which the tenancy can be determined by notice to quit. In that event it may, if it is unable to obtain the tenant's consent, serve notice of entry and take possession.[6]

In such cases the displaced tenant has an express statutory right to "compensation for the value of his unexpired term or interest in the land, and for any just allowance which ought to be made to him by an

---

[1] Including a leasehold interest for a term of years certain which at the relevant date has less than a year unexpired: *Newham London Borough Council* v *Benjamin*, [1968] 1 WLR 694 (CA), p. 366, *infra*.

[2] Land Compensation Act 1973, Part III, pp. 372 *et seq*, *infra*.

[3] I.e., other than under the terms of the lease or statutory provisions applicable thereto, e.g., in the case of business tenancies the Landlord and Tenant Act 1954, or in the case of agricultural tenancies the Agricultural Holdings Act 1948 or the Agriculture (Miscellaneous Provisions) Act 1968, and see also p. 369, *infra*.

[4] See pp. 374 *et seq*, *infra*.   [5] P. 355, *supra*, and pp. 366 *et seq*, *infra*.

[6] For the provisions governing entry without consent and before compensation has been agreed see p. 70, *ante*.

incoming tenant, or for any loss or injury he may sustain".[1] Although these statutory provisions are exclusive and do not afford a mere alternative to compensation under the Compulsory Purchase Act 1965,[2] it seems that the same heads of compensation for disturbance as under that section, as derived from case law, (and considered in the previous section of this chapter) apply so far as they may be appropriate.

Subject to his prospects of obtaining a renewal of a business lease[3] or continued security of tenure of agricultural land,[4] a short-term tenant has, by definition, but a very limited expectation of continued enjoyment. Compensation for disturbance must therefore be assessed accordingly. Thus, while compensation for loss of profits, for example, will be limited to that period it will seldom be possible to claim that expenses incurred in searching for and moving to alternative premises arise from the compulsory acquisition of the interest, as opposed to its determination by effluxion of time.[5].

The general rule in such cases is that entry operates, in effect, as a "deemed" notice to quit given on the date of entry so that the unexpired term or interest runs to the date on which such a notice would operate to terminate the tenancy.[6] But the value of that interest will depend upon whether, but for the compulsory acquisition and the scheme[7] in pursuit of which it is effected, the claimant could have expected to remain in possession.

Agricultural tenancies: special considerations

Thus in *Pearce* v *Bristol Corporation*[8] it was held that since the claimant farmer holding under a yearly tenancy[9] was ejected from his land as a result of notice of entry, the acquiring authority could not call in aid the

[1] Compulsory Purchase Act 1965, s. 20, re-enacting the Lands Clauses Consolidation Act 1845, s. 121.

[2] S. 7, replacing the Lands Clauses Consolidation Act 1845, s. 63: *Newham London Borough Council* v *Benjamin*, [1968] 1 WLR 694 and [1968] 1 All ER 1195.

[3] Under the Landlord and Tenant Act 1954: pp. 370 *et seq, infra*.

[4] Under the Agricultural Holdings Act 1948: pp. 371 *et seq, infra*.

[5] But where the acquired land comprises a house in respect of which compensation is payable on the basis of the value of the cleared site (as to which see pp. 255 *et seq, ante*) the tenant, not being entitled to an owner-occupiers allowance, may qualify for a disturbance payment covering costs of removal: Land Compensation Act 1973, s. 37(2), pp. 385 *et seq, infra*.

[6] *Newham London Borough Council* v *Benjamin, supra*, and *Greenwoods Tyre Service Ltd.* v *Manchester Corpn* (1971), 23 P & CR 246, in which the Lands Tribunal also relied upon *Birmingham Corpn* v *West Midlands Baptist (Trust) Association*, [1970] AC 874, *supra*. Note, however, that in *Greenwoods'* case the issue was whether the "deemed" notice to quit operated from the date of actual entry or from an earlier date specified for the giving of possession in the notice of entry. It is doubtful whether the *West Midlands Baptist* case can have any application in deciding from what date expenses incurred in seeking to relocate can be included in compensation for disturbance: see pp. 351 *et seq, supra*.

[7] As to the effect of the "scheme" see pp. 217 *et seq, ante*.

[8] (1950) 1 P & CR 367, followed in *Wakerley's* case, note 2, p. 367, *infra*. Cf. this case with *Rugby Joint Water Board* v *Shaw-Fox* , [1972] 2 WLR 757 (HL) (p. 171, *ante*) where the issue was somewhat different, viz whether the planning permission for a non-agricultural use granted before notice to treat had enabled the landlords to serve an effective notice to quit under the Agricultural Holdings Act 1948. It was held that it did. Note, too, that *Pearce's* case preceded the *West Midland Baptist* case so that it was the position as at the date of notice to treat that would have been crucial, and not the position at the date of entry.

[9] Note that in England and Wales the usual agricultural tenancy is one from year to year; a term of years certain, common in Scotland, is unusual.

provisions of the Agricultural Holdings Act 1948 whereby, not-withstanding the security of tenure conferred thereby, a valid and effective notice to quit may be served where the land is required for non-agricultural purposes.[1] Consequently the value of the unexpired term or interest fell to be assessed on the assumption that the claimant would otherwise have remained undisturbed subject only to the speculative possibility of those conditions arising in which, under the Act, the landlord would be able to serve a valid notice to quit and might be expected so to do.

The principle underlying this decision has now been extended so as to apply even where an acquiring authority serves a notice to quit.[2] Consequently, unless there are other grounds on which an effective[3] notice to quit can be given and expected, compensation for disturbance, and for loss of profit in particular, falls to be assessed upon the assumption that, but for the acquisition, the tenant could have expected to remain in possession indefinitely.

Business tenancies: special considerations

Under the Landlord and Tenant Act 1954 business tenancies[4] are protected in two ways. In the first place such tenancies can only be terminated by notice to quit even on the expiration of a term of years certain or where a tenant holds over thereafter. Secondly, the tenant has a right to apply for a new lease. There is a limited number of grounds on which a landlord may object[5] to the grant of such a lease and in the case of dispute it is for the Court to decide whether the landlord's objection should be upheld and to determine the terms on which any new lease should be granted. It was, however, specifically provided that in the event of compulsory acquisition of the premises, compensation[6] was to be assessed without regard to the right of the tenant to apply for a grant of a new tenancy.[7] This provision has now been reversed and it is specifically provided that such rights are to be taken into account.[8]

Although thus put on to a broadly comparable footing, the business

---

[1] Agricultural Holdings Act 1948, ss. 24(2)(b) and 25(1)(e).

[2] Land Compensation Act 1973, s. 48: see the first case under s. 48, *Wakerley* v *St. Edmonsbury Borough Council* [1977] JPL 455 LT. Note, however, that if the compensation payable under the Agriculture (Miscellaneous Provisions) Act 1968, s. 12, exceeds the compensation thus payable the claimant may opt for the latter: see pp. 371 *et seq, infra*, as to the special provisions governing compensation for tenanted agricultural land.

[3] I.e., in this context a notice given on one of the grounds specified in the Agricultural Holdings Act 1948, s. 24(2). Under *ibid*, s. 23, notice to quit terminating the tenancy not less than twelve months from the end of the current year of the tenancy, although perfectly valid, will only be effective if within one month of the service of such notice the tenant fails to serve a counter-notice under *ibid*, s. 24(1), or if the tenant's right to serve such a counter-notice is excluded by *ibid*, s. 24(2).

[4] Broadly, tenancies exceeding three months' duration of any premises in which a trade or business is lawfully carried on: see Landlord and Tenant Act 1954, s. 23. The Act does not, however, cover agricultural or mining leases, controlled tenancies under the Rent Restriction, etc., Acts, tenancies of licensed premises, etc.: *ibid*, s. 43.

[5] *Ibid*, s. 30.

[6] That is, Compensation under the Lands Clauses Consolidation Act 1845, s. 121, or now, Compulsory Purchase Act 1965, s. 20.

[7] Landlord and Tenant Act 1954, s. 39(1). As to the rights of renewal see *ibid*, ss. 24–26.

[8] Land Compensation Act 1973, s. 47.

tenant's position is in this respect not quite as favourable as that of the agricultural tenant, for one of the grounds on which a landlord of business premises can object to the grant of a new lease is that he intends to demolish or reconstruct the premises, either in whole or in part, or carry out substantial work of construction which he cannot reasonably do without obtaining possession.[1] The probability of an objection being upheld remains, therefore, to be taken into account whereas the right of a landlord of agricultural land to serve a notice to quit on the ground that the land is required for development is now expressly to be ignored.

In this connection, therefore, a difficulty may arise from the fact that the acquiring authority have either acquired the landlord's interest under the same compulsory powers or already own the property.

In the former case, however, it would seem that since the making of a compulsory purchase order covering the property constitutes a clear indication that the "land is, or is likely, to be acquired by an authority possessing compulsory purchase powers" any redevelopment proposal that arises solely from the scheme, the execution of which is the purpose of the compulsory purchase order, is to be ignored.[2] Unless, therefore, there is some reason to anticipate that the original landlord would have sought to redevelop,[3] irrespective of the compulsory acquisition, the tenant's compensation would seem to be assessable on the assumption that a new lease would have been granted.

But a different situation arises where the acquiring authority's ownership of the landlord's interest is of longer standing. For example, it may own property, leased to a business tenant, which it requires to redevelop in conjunction with an adjoining clearance area in respect of which it has made a compulsory purchase order in which it has included such property in added lands "reasonably necessary for the satisfactory development or use of the cleared area".[4]

In such a case the acquiring authority does not, of course, require to use compulsory powers either to acquire the tenant's interest or to redevelop its own property since by definition a short tenancy can be terminated within any period in which the compulsory purchase order is likely to be confirmed.[5] The question therefore arises whether the acquiring authority can successfully plead that its ability, as landlord, to object to an application for a new lease on the grounds of intended redevelopment nullifies the tenant's expectations of continued possession. The answer to that question, it is submitted, depends upon whether the property is capable of satisfactory redevelopment as a

---

[1] Landlord and Tenant Act 1954, s. 30(1)(f). Other grounds of objection are broadly similar to those upon which a valid notice to quit may be given to an agricultural tenant, although they also include a right to object on the ground that the landlord himself desires to occupy the premises or terminate sub-tenancies of part of the holding in order more profitably to let the premises as a whole: *ibid*, s. 30(1)(a) to (g).

[2] Land Compensation Act 1961, s. 9, p. 176, *ante*.

[3] Or be likely to resist a new lease on one of the other grounds of objection specified in the Landlord and Tenant Act 1954, s. 30(1).

[4] Housing Act 1957, s. 43: see pp. 260 *et seq*, *ante*.

[5] In the authors' experience, however, such properties are nevertheless sometimes included in the compulsory purchase order.

single entity and if so whether, apart from the scheme of the compulsory purchase order, there have been any proposals (which will normally be ascertainable from the Minutes of the appropriate local authority committee) to do so.

It should, however, be noted that the occupier holding a "short" tenancy is not entitled to a notice to treat[1] and if he receives one it does not confer a right to claim compensation because it will not, at that stage, be known whether the acquiring authority will in fact require possession before termination of the tenancy in pursuance of a notice to quit.[2] A right to compensation under this section[3] only arises, therefore, upon service of notice of entry or upon entry by agreement. Thus where a tenant having less than a year of his lease unexpired at the date of confirmation of the compulsory purchase order, received notice to treat and submitted a claim to compensation without waiting for notice of entry, it was held that his claim was premature.[4]

By analogy, therefore, it would seem to follow that in so far as the date of service of notice to treat is of importance[5] in determining what expenses may be included in a claim for compensation for disturbance under the previous section of this chapter,[6] it is the date of entry in the case of short tenancies. There is, however, a purely practical objection to such a conclusion since by the terms of the Landlord and Tenant Act 1954, short tenancies can be determined by as little as six months' notice,[7] which in many cases would make relocation virtually impossible.[8]

Furthermore, the acquiring authority is liable to pay such compensation for improvements carried out by the tenant as would have been payable by any other landlord upon the termination of the lease under the Landlord and Tenant Act 1927, s. 1. Under that section compensation for improvements[9] is not to exceed either the net addition in the value of the holding directly attributable to the improvement, or the cost of carrying out the improvement at the termination of the tenancy, less the cost of any work necessary to bring the improvement

[1] Lands Clauses Consolidation Act 1845, s. 18, and its successor, the Compulsory Purchase Act 1965, s. 5, require the service of notice to treat to all persons "interested in" the land. Such persons are not, however, further defined.

[2] *Newham London Borough Council* v *Benjamin*, [1968] 1 WLR 694 (CA).

[3] I.e., the Compulsory Purchase Act 1965, s. 20.

[4] *Benjamin*'s case, *supra*.

[5] See pp. 351 *et seq, supra*.

[6] Or the Lands Clauses Consolidation Act 1845, s. 63.

[7] Landlord and Tenant Act 1954, s. 25. In *Alexandre Ltd.* v *Cambridge City Council* (1975), 31 P & CR 444, however, it was held that notwithstanding this provision a quarterly tenancy may be determined upon giving three months' notice since the Landlord and Tenant Act 1954, s. 39, specifically provides that the extensions of time conferred by *ibid* ss. 24 and 25 shall not affect the operation of the Lands Clauses Consolidation Act 1845, s. 121 (now the Compulsory Purchase Act 1965, s. 20).

[8] In practice, of course, the prospects of reasonable relocation depend very largely upon the state of the property market at the time—a further factor which would seem to support the authors' contention at pp. 351 *et seq, supra*, that the test must be what is reasonable in all the circumstances of the particular case rather than whether expenses were incurred before or after the date of notice to treat or notice of entry, as the case may be.

[9] Note that compensation is only payable in respect of improvements effected within three years of the termination of the tenancy: Landlord and Tenant Act 1927, s. 2. The claim for compensation must be made within a month of the date of the notice terminating the tenancy: *ibid*, s. 1(1)(a).

into a reasonable state of repair.[1] In assessing the compensation payable, however, account has to be taken of the effect upon the additional value attributable to the improvement, of any proposals to demolish, alter or change the use of the premises, and the length of time likely to elapse between the termination of the tenancy and the demolition, alteration or change of use.[2] Since the purpose of compulsory acquisition of a tenant's interest is generally to expedite demolition, alteration or change of use, this proviso is likely to reduce the compensation payable in respect of improvements very significantly.[3] Where, but for the acquisition, the tenant would have had a reasonable expectation of a renewal of his tenancy, the value of improvements will, of course, be included in the valuation of his interest.

Compensation under the Landlord and Tenant Act 1954

In this context it is important to consider the compensation which would be available under the Landlord and Tenant Act 1954 if the tenancy had been allowed to run its course because if such compensation (which may be either one or two years' rateable value of the premises, as explained below) exceeds the compensation payable under s. 20 of the Act of 1965 (supra) the claimant is entitled to the higher sum.[4]

Where the landlord objects to an application for a new lease on any of the grounds specified in s. 30(1) of the Act of 1954 and establishes such ground to the satisfaction of the court, the court is precluded from awarding a new tenancy. If the landlord's ground of objection is that he intends demolition or reconstruction,[5] that he wishes to terminate sub-tenancies in order to let the premises as a whole at a rent exceeding the aggregate of the rents of the parts,[6] or that he requires the premises for his own occupation,[7] the tenant will be entitled to compensation.[8] These are the grounds on which the landlord can object which may be said to lie wholly outside the control of the tenant. The other grounds of objection are based either upon default by the tenant,[9] or an unreasonable refusal by him to accept alternative accommodation offered by the landlord:[10] hence the exclusion of compensation.

If, during the whole of the previous 14 years the premises had been occupied for a business carried on by the occupier[11] the compensation

---

[1] Landlord and Tenant Act 1927, s. 1(1).

[2] Ibid, s. 1(2).

[3] Where the Lands Tribunal determines that no compensation be payable, or that the compensation be reduced because of intended demolition, etc., it may, however, authorise a further claim to be made if the intention is not put into effect within a prescribed period: ibid, s. 1(3).

[4] Landlord and Tenant Act 1954, s. 39(2), as amended by the Land Compensation Act 1973, s. 47(3).

[5] Landlord and Tenant Act 1954, s. 30(1)(f): pp. 367–8, supra.

[6] Ibid, s. 30(1)(e).

[7] Ibid, s. 30(1)(g). But note that a landlord cannot object on this ground if his interest has been acquired less than five years prior to the termination of the current tenancy: ibid, s. 30(2).

[8] Ibid, s. 37(1).

[9] Ibid, s. 30(1)(a), (b) and (c).

[10] Ibid, s. 30(1)(d).

[11] Ibid, s. 27(2) and (3). This provision equally applies where during the 14 preceding years there has been a change of occupier and the current occupier succeeded to the business: ibid, s. 27(3)(b).

payable will be twice the rateable value of the holding: in other cases it will be the rateable value.[1]

Compensation under the Agriculture etc. Acts

Since 1948[2] a tenant whose tenancy is determined by notice to quit has had a statutory right to compensation for disturbance.[3] Such compensation is in respect of expenses or loss directly attributable[4] to the quitting of his holding unavoidably incurred in connection with the sale or removal of his household goods, fixtures, produce and live or dead stock (i.e., implements etc.) The amount of compensation is normally one year's rent and it is payable without proof of actual loss.[5] The tenant may, however, claim a greater sum (up to a maximum of two years' rent) provided he notifies his landlord in writing of his intention to do so at least a month before the termination of the tenancy and provided, before the sale of his stock, produce, etc., his landlord is given an opportunity to make a valuation.

Compensation for disturbance is, of course, in addition to compensation for certain improvements,[6] for the continuous adoption of a special system of farming that enhances the value of the holding[7] and for the tenant right.[8] These matters are, however, outside the scope of this work and are mentioned here only to draw attention to the somewhat specialised nature of the law and valuation practice relating to agricultural holdings.

In addition to compensation for disturbance, as outlined above, the agricultural tenant in possession (or entitled to possession) is also entitled, if his interest is compulsorily acquired, to a further payment equivalent to four years' rent,[9] except where the land is acquired for an agricultural purpose.[10]

Where, however, the tenancy is for a term of two years or more the amount payable by the acquiring authority under this provision is limited to the amount by which, if any, the total amount payable by

---

[1] *Ibid*, Rateable value is to be determined in accordance with s. 27(5): *ibid*, s. 27(5).

[2] Prior to the coming into force of the Agricultural Holdings Act 1948 the compensation payable to agricultural tenants on quitting their holdings was, in the absence of written agreement, governed by "the custom of the country", i.e., local custom.

[3] Agricultural Holdings Act 1948, s. 32. Unless the grounds of the notice to quit include default on the part of the tenant, e.g., failure to comply with a notice to pay arrears of rent or to remedy a breach of the tenancy agreement; or where a certificate of bad husbandry has been obtained: *ibid*, s. 34(1).

[4] As to the words "directly attributable" see, for example *Re Evans and Glamorgan County Council* (1912), 76 JP 468.

[5] Agricultural Holdings Act 1948, s. 34(2).

[6] See *ibid* ss. 35, 36 and 46, and *Halsbury's Laws*, 4th Edition, Vol. I, paras. 1095, *et seq.*

[7] *Ibid*, s. 56.

[8] I.e., growing crops, unexhausted manurial equivalents, etc.

[9] Agriculture (Miscellaneous Provisions) Act 1968, ss. 9–12. Note that this "reorganisation compensation" is also payable, under certain circumstances, by a private landlord: *ibid*, ss. 9 and 10.

[10] For example, for the purposes of agricultural research, experimentation or demonstration; for the provision of small holdings or where the Minister acquires the land to ensure its efficient use for agriculture: *ibid*, s. 12(1).

way of compensation exceeds the amount that would have been payable had the tenancy been from year to year.[1]

Thus, in the case of the acquisition of a leasehold interest compensation under this sub-head is reduced by the amount by which compensation for the unexpired term exceeds the compensation that would have been payable in the case of a tenancy from year to year. Accordingly if such excess is greater than the sum equivalent to four years' rent the tenant derives no benefit from these provisions. In other words, entitlement to this latter element of compensation can be regarded as a recognition of the effect of the security of tenure provisions of the Act of 1948 in conferring upon the tenant an expectancy of continued occupancy analogous to that of a tenant holding a leasehold interest. It is not, therefore, applicable where there is in fact such an interest which entitles the tenant to at least the same amount of compensation.

4 HOME, FARM LOSS AND DISTURBANCE PAYMENTS UNDER PART III, LAND COMPENSATION ACT 1973[2]

1 Home loss payments[3]

(i) INTRODUCTORY

As the words imply, the purpose of a home loss payment is to provide some limited monetary compensation to those who, as a result of compulsory acquisition of an interest in the dwelling concerned, or as a result of certain other related actions of a local authority,[4] are displaced from a home[5] which has been occupied as such for a minimum period by virtue of certain interests or rights.

(ii) REQUIREMENTS

There are two main prerequisites to entitlement. First there must be the requisite acquisition of an interest in the dwelling;[6] such other of the actions by local authorities as are specified;[7] or improvement by a housing association.[8] Where the displacement results from the actual

---

[1] Agriculture (Miscellaneous Provisions) Act 1968, ibid, s. 12(2).

[2] As amended by the Housing Act 1974: see Sch. 13, para. 38.

[3] Land Compensation Act 1973, ss. 29–33.

[4] Or of certain housing associations, infra.

[5] I.e., either a dwelling or a caravan (as to which see p. 376, infra). For definition of a "dwelling" see p. 330, note 8, ante. Note also that temporary displacement during the execution of works of improvement or redevelopment does not qualify for a home loss payment: ibid, s. 29(3A), inserted by the Housing Act 1974, Sch. 13, para. 38(2).

[6] Ibid, s. 29(1)(a), but not including acquisition in response to a blight notice or notice under the New Towns Act 1965, s. 11, requiring acquisition of land within the designated area of a New Town which an owner may serve if the land remains unacquired seven years after designation (see p. 81, supra): Land Compensation Act 1973, s. 29(5).

[7] Land Compensation Act 1973, s. 29(1), as amended by the Housing Act 1974, para. 38, 13th Sch.; and see p. 373, infra.

[8] I.e., a registered housing association within the meaning of the Housing Act 1974, or an unregistered housing association falling within s. 18(1)(a) of that Act, i.e., an association for the time being specified in an order under the Housing Finance Act, 1972, s. 80: Land Compensation Act 1973, s. 29(1)(d); (inserted in that Act by the Housing Act 1974, Sch. 13, para. 38).

acquisition, that acquisition must have been compulsory,[1] but the displacement will only be deemed to result from the acquisition if the claimant is still in occupation when the acquisition is authorised; it is not, however, necessary, thereafter, for the acquiring authority to have required possession.[2] But if land is held by an authority possessing compulsory purchase powers for some future redevelopment or improvement[3] and the occupiers of any dwellings thereon are permitted to remain in occupation in the meantime so that the immediate cause of the displacement is the carrying out of that development or improvement[4] it matters not that the original acquisition was by agreement;[5] similarly, where the displacement results from the appropriation by a local authority of land which it already holds[6] or from redevelopment or improvement of their property by a registered Housing Association.[7] Thus a person who is displaced by the acquisition of his own interest by agreement loses his entitlement, although the acquiring authority has a discretionary power to pay to him the sum to which he would have been entitled had the acquisition been compulsory.[8] On the other hand acquisition of an interest by agreement does not affect the right of any other person to a home-loss payment[9] so that, for example, the acquisition by agreement of the freehold or superior leasehold will not affect the rights of tenants.

Reference has already been made to the carrying out of redevelopment or improvements by a housing association; apart from the appropriation of land already held by them, the other actions of local authorities that may give rise to a home-loss payment are as follows:

(a) The making of a "housing order",[10] i.e., a demolition, closing or clearance order under the Housing Acts.

(b) The service of an improvement notice within the meaning of Part VIII of the Housing Act 1974[11] in respect of the dwelling.[12]

(c) The carrying out of an improvement of the dwelling or of redevelopment of land previously acquired or appropriated and

---

[1] Land Compensation Act 1973, s. 29(6).

[2] *Ibid*, s. 29b(3).

[3] Improvement includes alteration and enlargement and redevelopment includes a change of use: *ibid*, s. 29(7A), as inserted by the Housing Act 1974, Sch. 13, para. 38(3).

[4] I.e., pursuant to an improvement notice under the Housing Act 1974, Sch. 13, para. 38(1)(b) and see para. (ii) of the text, and notes 11 and 12, below.

[5] *Ibid*, s. 29(1)(c).

[6] *Ibid*.

[7] Housing Act 1974, Sch. 13, para. 38(1)(b).

[8] Provided the acquisition was authorised before the vendor relinquished possession. Note, too, that the discretion extends only to the payment of a sum equivalent to the home-loss payment and not, it seems, to any lesser sum: Land Compensation Act 1973, s. 32(7). See, however, Compensation for unfit houses under the Housing Acts, pp. 255, *et seq, ante*.

[9] Land Compensation Act 1973, s. 29(6).

[10] *Ibid*, s. 29(1)(b).

[11] Broadly speaking an improvement notice requires the owner of a dwelling without one or more of the standard amenities which can be provided at reasonable expense to make provision accordingly. But the powers of a local authority to serve such a notice are limited to dwellings which came into existence prior to 3 October 1961 and which are either within an area declared to be a "general improvement area" within the Housing Act 1969, Part II, or an area declared to be a "housing action area" within the Housing Act 1974, Part IV.

[12] Land Compensation Act 1973, s. 29(1)(b), as amended by the Housing Act 1974, Sch. 13, para. 38(1)(a).

for the time being held for the purpose for which it was acquired or appropriated.[1]

This latter provision gave rise to some difficulty in *R* v *Corby District Council ex parte McLean*.[2] In that case the claimant occupied a temporary local authority bungalow (one of the post 1939–45 war "pre-fabs") that had become unfit for human habitation. The local authority wished to redevelop the land on which this and a number of similar dwellings stood, but refused a home-loss payment on the ground that the displacement arose from the unfitness of the bungalow and not from the proposal to redevelop. The claimant successfully applied for an order of *mandamus*, it being held that the word "redevelopment" in this context must be given its ordinary meaning (i.e., to include the requisite preliminary demolition) and that there was no case for distinguishing between local authority tenants and tenants of privately owned property displaced because of unfitness, who would most certainly qualify for a home-loss payment in similar circumstances under para. (a) above.

(iii) THE CLAIMANT'S QUALIFICATION

The second set of requirements prerequisite to entitlement to a home-loss payment relate to the nature of the claimant's occupancy and the rights or interests from which it arises. These requirements are as follows:

(a) The claimant must, at the date of the displacement, have been occupying the dwelling or a substantial part thereof as his only or main residence.[3]

(b) Subject to the next following paragraph, he must either have been in occupation for at least the previous five years or be the immediate successor of a person or persons who have so occupied the dwelling. In other words, the dwelling must have been continuously occupied as the sole or main residence of the person in occupation at all times during that five-year period.[4]

(c) Where, however, the dwelling comprises a room or rooms not constructed or structurally adapted as a separate dwelling, the claimant will not be disqualified by reason of occupation of that "dwelling" for less than five years if, during the remainder of that period he has occupied other "dwellings" within the same building.[5] *Aliter*, it seems, if he has been in occupation of a series of dwellings within the same building for a period of less than five years, but there has been no previous occupancy of any of the dwellings he has occupied, as somebody's sole or main residence, sufficient to make up the requisite five years.

(d) The claimant must be in occupation of the dwelling as of right,

---

[1] Land Compensation Act 1973, s. 29(1)(c).

[2] [1975] 2 All ER 568.

[3] Land Compensation Act 1973, s. 29(2)(a).

[4] This appears to be the combined effect of *ibid*, s. 29(2)(a) and s. 32(3)—a peculiarly striking example of clumsy draftsmanship.

[5] *Ibid*, s. 32(5), which provides that the dwelling from which he is displaced shall be regarded as "the same dwelling" as those previously occupied by him in the same building.

that is to say, he must either have an interest[1] in the dwelling (including a right or permission to occupy under the terms of a trust by which the legal interest in the dwelling is held by the trustees[2]); be in occupation under a contract of employment;[3] or in right of a statutory tenancy within the meaning of the Rent Act 1968[4] or a contract covering a furnished letting to which Part VI of that Act applies.[5]

(e) Where a person entitled to a home-loss payment dies before the expiration of six months from the date of displacement (the period in which the claim must be made[6]) without having submitted his claim, a claim may still be made within that period by any person (other than a minor) who has himself resided in the dwelling, or a substantial part of it, as his sole or main residence throughout the five-year period ending with the date of displacement, provided he is "entitled to benefit" as a surviving joint tenant on the death of the original occupier or under a testamentary disposition or intestacy taking effect on that person's death.[7]

The case of a surviving joint tenant is straightforward, but that of a person "entitled to benefit" from a testamentary disposition or intestacy is complicated by the fact that the Act contains no indication of the manner in which such a person must benefit. Had the intention been to confine the benefit to an interest in the dwelling of which the testator had power to dispose, or which passed under the terms of a trust to this other person, the Act would presumably have said so. But in ordinary language a person may be said to be "entitled to benefit by virtue of testamentary dispositions taking effect . . . on the death of the deceased" if he does so from a legacy, be it never so small, or the bequest of a single chattel of small value, for "disposition" includes both a bequest of personalty and a devise of realty. It is hard to believe, however, that such an entitlement to such minor "benefit" is intended as a qualification unless, but for the acquisition, this other person would, as a result of the death of the deceased former occupier, have been entitled to remain in occupation, e.g., under the Rent Acts, the terms of a trust or, of course, if the deceased had an interest, where he has inherited that interest or such share therein as would have entitled or permitted him to have remained in occupation. The difficulty is particularly well illustrated in the case of a service tenancy. A contract of employment is personal to the employee. A lodger, whether relative or not, who has

---

[1] *Ibid,* s. 29(4)(a).

[2] *Ibid,* s. 29(8). This subsection, however, expressly excludes an interest vested in a trustee who is a sole tenant for life under the Settled Land Act 1925 presumably because under that Act such a person, as beneficial owner, is to all intents and purposes himself the owner of the interest; but the provision is so worded as to imply that he is not to be regarded as in occupation by virtue of an interest in the dwelling: a proposition for which there would appear neither rhyme nor reason.

[3] Land Compensation Act 1973, s. 29(4)(d).

[4] *Ibid,* s. 29(4)(b).

[5] Or would apply but for the provisions of the Rent Act 1968, s. 70(3)(a) (exclusion of leases held under the Crown) or s. 71 (exclusion of dwellings above a specified rateable value): Land Compensation Act 1973, s. 29(4)(b).

[6] Land Compensation Act 1973, s. 32(1).

[7] *Ibid,* s. 32(4).

resided with the deceased for the previous five years would have no rights to continued occupation as against the landlord-employer[1] and may well have no qualifications for the particular employment. It may be equitable, within the underlying philosophy of these provisions to compensate him for loss of his home but it remains something of a mystery why his entitlement should depend upon either the deceased's will or his position under an intestacy, neither of which can confer on him any right to a third person's property. Nevertheless, the Act clearly contemplates a multiplicity of claims arising under these provisions, for in providing criteria for the division of the home-loss payment between several claimants in respect of the same dwelling the Act expressly refers to joint occupiers *and* persons entitled by virtue of these provisions.[2]

Moreover, these provisions seem unhappily framed in another respect, viz that this other person still has to make his claim within the six months from the date of displacement[3] even where the deceased's death is sudden, wholly unexpected and takes place immediately prior to the expiration of the six-month period; the provisions in this regard are quite specific in *prohibiting* payment "except on a claim made in that behalf by the person entitled thereto before the expiry" of that period.[4]

(iv) CARAVANS

The provisions relating to home-loss payments apply, in effect, as if in the above explanation the words "caravan on a caravan site"[5] were substituted for the word "dwelling".[6] In other words the claimant must be displaced from the site and not merely from the caravan, but he will only receive a home-loss payment if there is no suitable alternative site available on which he can station his caravan on reasonable terms.[7] Conversely, the requirement of five years of occupation relates to the site as a whole and not to any particular caravan or plot thereon.[8] But where the claimant has not himself been in occupation for the full five-year period preceding displacement he can only rely upon previous continuous occupation of a caravan by others (as their sole or main residence) who have occupied the same "plot", though not necessarily the same caravan.[9]

---

[1] Other than such very limited rights to further temporary occupation as may be awarded by the court in an action by the landlord for possession.

[2] Land Compensation Act 1973, s. 32(6), p. 376, note 1, *infra*.

[3] *Ibid*, s. 32(4).

[4] *Ibid*, s. 32(1).

[5] "Caravan site" is defined as "land on which a caravan is stationed for the purpose of human habitation and land which is used in conjunction with land on which a caravan is so stationed": *ibid*, s. 33(7). This is the same definition as that of Caravan Sites and Control of Development Act 1960, s. 1(4), and incorporated (by s. 290(1)) in the Town and Country Planning Act 1971. In other words, in the case of land accommodating a number of caravans it is what is normally referred to as a single "plot" as opposed to the whole area or site to which the site licensing provisions of Part I of the Act of 1960 in practice normally apply.

[6] Land Compensation Act 1973, s. 33.

[7] *Ibid*, s. 33(2).

[8] *Ibid*, s. 33(5)(c), and see note 5, *supra*.

[9] *Ibid*, s. 32(3), as modified by *ibid*, s. 33(5)(a). Cf. the similar restrictions to the actual dwelling as opposed to any dwelling within the same building, p. 374, para. (c), *supra*.

The claimant must occupy the site or "plot" as of right, i.e., by virtue of the same interests or rights (in so far as they are applicable) as entitle a displaced occupier of a dwelling to a home-loss payment. Thus, since the Rent Acts have no application to caravans, he must have an interest in the land, including a right or permission to occupy under the terms of a trust, or must occupy by right of a "service" tenancy.

(v) THE AMOUNT OF HOME-LOSS PAYMENTS

The amount of a home-loss payment is to be the rateable value multiplied by a multiplier that may be altered from time to time by orders made by the Secretary of State,[1] which may also alter the maximum and minimum amounts payable. The current amount laid down in the Act itself[2] is three times the rateable value subject to a maximum of £1,500 and a minimum of £150.

Where the dwelling is an hereditament for which a rateable value is shown in the valuation list current at the date of the displacement no difficulty arises and the rateable value is that shown.[3] But where the dwelling either forms only part of an hereditament, or forms part of more than one hereditament, the Act provides[4] for an apportionment and/or aggregation to be made by the valuation officer,[5] and the certification by him of the amount properly attributable to the dwelling.

In other cases the valuation officer is required to determine the rateable value *de novo*[6] in accordance with the normal principles of the General Rate Acts.[7]

In the case of a claim in respect of a caravan the relevant rateable value is that of the caravan site (or plot) together with the caravan.[8] Where a single caravan is located on an isolated site or plot, the site and caravan are likely to appear in the current valuation list as a single hereditament, but where a number of caravans is accommodated on a large "site" the entry may be in respect of the whole area, the occupier being the site operator rather than the individual caravan residents.[9] In such a case the valuation officer must value the particular site (or plot) together with the caravan and certify accordingly; he cannot apportion the rateable value of the larger site.[10]

Where there is more than one person entitled to claim in respect of the same dwelling the amount of each claim is to be the total

[1] Under Land Compensation Act 1973, s. 30(2), such orders are made by Statutory Instrument subject to negative procedure, i.e., effective unless annulled by resolution of either House within the prescribed period of 40 sitting days.

[2] *Ibid*, s. 30(1).

[3] *Ibid*, s. 30(3)(a).

[4] *Ibid*, s. 30(3)(b).

[5] As defined in the General Rate Act 1967.

[6] Land Compensation Act 1973, s. 30(3)(c).

[7] I.e., the Acts of 1967 and 1970.

[8] Land Compensation Act 1973, s. 33(4)(b).

[9] Where the caravans are occupied as permanent residences they and the land on which they stand are rateable individually: *Field Place Caravan Park Ltd.* v *Harding (Valuation Officer)*, [1966] 3 All ER 247 (CA). But where caravans are let for short periods to holidaymakers or are frequently moved within the overall site or park the operator of the park will be the "rateable occupier: but note the valuation officer's discretion in this regard: Rating (Caravan Sites) Act 1976, s. 1."

[10] Land Compensation Act 1973, s. 33(4)(a).

payable in respect of the dwelling divided equally between the persons so entitled.[1]

(vi) PROCEDURE

As already indicated, a claim for a home-loss payment must be made within a six-month period beginning on the date of the displacement; claims made after the expiry of that period cannot be met.[2] On the other hand there is nothing to prevent the making of a claim before the actual date of displacement provided it is then known that possession will in fact be required and, in the case of displacement resulting from the acquisition of an interest in the dwelling, provided the acquisition has been authorised.[3] Moreover, since it is expressly provided that in the latter case, a person does not lose his entitlement by vacating after authorisation of the acquisition but before being required to do so[4] it follows, by analogy, that once a local authority's requirement of possession has been notified, occupiers are free to move without awaiting notification of a date by which possession will be required and without loss of entitlement,[5] even though such early vacation has enabled them to find a satisfactory alternative house.[6]

The claim must, however, be made in writing and must include or be supplemented by such particulars as the authority responsible for making the payment may reasonably require in order to establish its validity.[7] If in doubt as to what particulars may be relevant the claimant should therefore notify the authority of his claim and at the same time enquire what further particulars are required. Since the submission of such particulars may be "supplemental" to the claim the formal submission of the notice of claim within the six-month period will be sufficient to ensure that the claim is "in time" even if the particulars cannot be provided until after the expiration of that period. This may be a particularly valuable "concession" to a person whose claim arises only at a late stage as a result of the death of the original claimant shortly before the period expires.[8]

---

[1] Land Compensation Act 1973, *ibid,* s. 32(6). This subsection expressly contemplates a multiplicity of claims, in addition to claims arising from joint occupation, arising from the provisions of s. 32(4). In regard to claims by third persons following the death of the original claimant, see p. 375, *para,* (e), *supra.*

[2] *Ibid,* s. 32(1). There was an exception to this rule in the case of displacement taking place before the passing of the Act in which case the "claim period" was six months thereafter (i.e. from 23 May 1973), a provision which is no longer of importance.

[3] *Ibid,* s. 29(3). Since a person vacating before authorisation loses his entitlement, a claim made before authorisation could only be dealt with thereafter because only then would it be known that the claimant was still in occupation on the date of authorisation; there would, however, be nothing to prevent the acquiring authority acquiring by agreement and agreeing to make an equivalent payment to a person wishing to vacate earlier: see p. 373, *supra.*

[4] *Ibid.*

[5] Indeed, the lodging of claims before the date of displacement is expressly contemplated by the Act, s. 32(2), *infra.*

[6] Cf. the position of a caravan resident able to find a suitable alternative site, *ibid,* s. 33(2), and p. 376, *supra.* The distinction presumably arises from the fact that a home-loss payment is, at least in part, compensation for adaptations to suit the particular requirements of the occupier but which do not add to the value of his interest or give a right to compensation from his landlord; a caravan dweller takes his "home" together with such adaptations, to his new site.

[7] *Ibid,* s. 32(1).

[8] See p. 376, *supra.*

The claim must, of course, be made to, and paid by the authority responsible for the displacement, i.e., if the displacement results from acquisition, the acquiring authority; if from the making of an order, resolution, the carrying out of improvements, or other event, the authority making the order or executing the works of improvement, etc.[1]

Payment of the claim must be made on or before the expiration of three months from the making thereof or from the date of displacement, whichever is the later.[2] The act provides no special means either of arbitration in the event of disagreement or of enforcement, thus leaving such matters to the courts in an action for civil debt.

2 Farm loss payments[3]

(i) REQUIREMENTS

Entitlement to a farm-loss payment is very much narrower than entitlement to a home-loss payment. Not only are the provisions confined to displacement from an agricultural unit resulting from an acquisition of an interest therein,[4] but the acquisition must be of the occupier's own interest in the whole of the agricultural unit and must result in his displacement from the whole of the unit.[5] Moreover the occupier must have an "owner's interest",[6] that is to say, a freehold interest or a tenancy granted or extended for a term of years certain of which at least three years remain unexpired on the date of displacement.[7]

As with home-loss payments there is no entitlement to a farm-loss payment where the acquisition is by agreement. The acquiring authority has, however, power to make an *ex gratia* payment of the equivalent amount even where the acquisition is prior to authorisation; in that case the authority is deemed to have been authorised as at the date of the agreement.[8] It follows, therefore, that an acquiring authority may undertake to make such a payment as part of the agreement and should, where possible, be required to do so.

Furthermore, a farm-loss payment is only payable where the displaced occupier resumes farming within three years of displacement on another agricultural unit and, when he begins to farm it, he is in occupation of the whole[9] in right either of a freehold interest or a

[1] Land Compensation Act 1973, s. 29(3A), as amended by the Housing Act 1974, Sch. 13, para. 38(1)(c).
[2] Land Compensation Act 1973, s. 32(2).
[3] *Ibid*, ss. 34–36.
[4] Other than in response to a blight notice or notice under the New Towns Act 1965, s. 11: see note 6, p. 372, *supra*.
[5] Land Compensation Act 1973, s. 34(1).
[6] *Ibid*, thus ruling out the ordinary agricultural tenant who in England and Wales normally holds from year to year. Compensation payable to such a tenant, however, will now normally take account of his security of tenure under the Agricultural Holdings Act 1948: see the Land Compensation Act 1973, s. 48 and pp. 265, *et seq*, *supra*, and note 2, p. 367, *supra*.
[7] *Ibid*, s. 34(2).
[8] *Ibid*, s. 36(4): but see the corresponding provisions of *ibid*, s. 32(7), relating to home-loss payments note 8, p. 373, *supra*.
[9] This requirement seems likely to give rise to some difficulty. There is no attempt in the Act to define what constitutes "beginning" to farm the new unit and it is a very common practice for purchasers or tenants designate of agricultural holdings, particularly when possession is given on

tenancy.[1] But an agricultural unit in which the displaced occupier acquires a freehold interest or tenancy in anticipation of dispossession from his original holding, before the acquisition of his original unit has been finally authorised, is not a "new agricultural unit" for this purpose.[2] In other words there must be a replacement of the lost unit after authorisation, which entitles the dispossessed farmer to farm the new unit within the three-year period. But, in the sense that the new unit need in no way be equivalent to the original unit, replacement may be little more than nominal. Thus a farmer farming several distinct units who is displaced from one such unit, albeit a small and unimportant one in relation to his farming operations as a whole, will be entitled to a farm-loss payment provided he acquires another holding in accordance with the above provisions; similarly, if he loses a very large unit replacement by a very small holding will be sufficient.[3] But a farmer who loses a major part of a large holding will have no such entitlement even though acquisition of a new holding is essential if what remains to him of his original holding is to be economically operated.[4] Although a farm house, if occupied by the farmer for the purpose of farming his land, is part of the agricultural unit it also falls within the definition of a "dwelling".[5] It seems, therefore, that a displaced farmer is entitled to a home-loss payment irrespective of whether he acquires another agriculture unit, and also becomes entitled to a farm-loss payment. Similarly, his employees occupying service cottages will also qualify for home-loss payments even where the farmer is the legal occupier, for persons occupying a dwelling under a contract of service are specifically included under the provisions governing home-loss payments.[6]

Again, a farm-loss payment is excluded where the person displaced is entitled to any payment under the Agriculture (Miscellaneous Provisions) Act 1968, s. 12, as a consequence of the acquisition of the farmer's interest or the taking possession of his land.[7] There is no corresponding provision excluding a home-loss payment where other forms of compensation are available under other enactments even where compensation is available on an equivalent reinstatement basis[8]

Lady Day (25 March) to be permitted to enter and cultivate parts of the holding during the preceding autumn and winter months. Why such an eminently sensible arrangement should deprive the farmer of a farm-loss payment is anything but clear.

[1] I.e., including a tenancy from year to year; cf. the leasehold interest in the original unit required to establish entitlement to a farm-loss payment.

[2] Land Compensation Act 1973, s. 34(4). A farmer having the opportunity to secure another farm before authorisation will therefore be very well advised to try to postpone completion.

[3] But in such cases the amount of the farm-loss payment may be significantly reduced: Land Compensation Act 1973, s. 35(6) and (7), pp. 382–383, infra.

[4] Compensation for his interest, however, will of course take such factors into account; see pp. 316, et seq, ante, and note his right to require acquisition of the whole in pursuance of a blight notice. See Land Compensation Act 1973, ss. 79–80, pp. 144 and 148, ante, respectively.

[5] Land Compensation Act 1973, s. 87(1).

[6] Ibid, s. 29(4)(d), p. 375, supra.

[7] Ibid, s. 35(5); under s. 12 of the Act of 1968 the tenant of a farm compulsorily acquired may, upon being required to give up possession by the acquiring authority, be entitled to up to four times the annual rental value of the land taken: see p. 371, supra.

[8] I.e., under Rule 5: Land Compensation Act 1961, s. 5(5); pp. 239, et seq, ante.

and therefore takes account of special adaptations to a dwelling for the convenience of the particular occupier.[1]

Finally, it is to be noted that a person is only regarded as "displaced" from an agricultural unit if he gives up possession on being required to do so by the acquiring authority; on completion of the acquisition; or upon the expiration of any licence[2] under which the authority, having acquired the land, permits him to remain in possession.[3] While it logically follows, as provided,[3] that for the purposes of these provisions the date of displacement should be the date on which the person concerned gives up possession, the addition of the words "as aforesaid", i.e., in accordance with the above provisions, has the effect of precluding a farm-loss payment where, for example, the occupier holds over after completion and only gives up possession following an order of the Court. He would not then be giving up possession either on being required to do so by the acquiring authority or on completion of the acquisition; *aliter*, of course, if he holds over with permission since such permission would constitute a licence. Once again there is no corresponding provision in regard to home-loss payments for entitlement arises purely from the fact of displacement which is neither further defined nor (once the acquisition has been authorised, etc.)[4] related to the circumstances in which possession is surrendered.

(ii) THE AMOUNT OF FARM-LOSS PAYMENTS

The amount of a farm-loss payment is the average annual profit derived from the land (after deducting letting value and profits) from any activity for the loss of which compensation is payable under the head of disturbance.[5] A further proportionate deduction falls to be made where the value of the new unit exceeds that of the unit acquired and the farm-loss payment is limited to the amount, if any, by which it, together with the value of the interest acquired, exceeds the compensation actually payable upon the acquisition of the interest.[6]

The average annual profit is the average of the last three years' profits from the use of the land for agricultural purposes unless the claimant has been in occupation for less than three years, in which case the average annual profit is to be calculated for the actual period of occupation.[7] Normally the three years will be the three accounting[8] years ending within the twelve-month period immediately preceding the date of displacement.[9] But if no accounts have been made up they are to be compiled for this purpose for the three years ending with the date of displacement.[10]

---

[1] E.g. under the Land Compensation Act 1973, s. 45, where a dwelling has been specifically adapted for a disabled occupier, p. 361, *supra*.

[2] Or under a tenancy which does not make the occupier a tenant as defined by the Agricultural Holdings Act 1948: Land Compensation Act 1973, s. 34(3)(c).

[3] *Ibid*, s. 34(3).

[4] See pp. 378, *et seq, supra*, but note the effect of acquisition by agreement, pp. 373, *et seq, supra*.

[5] See pp. 366 and 371, *et seq, supra*.

[6] *Ibid*, s. 35(8): see p. 383, *infra*.

[7] *Ibid*, s. 35(1).

[8] I.e., the twelve-month period for which the claimant's accounts are normally compiled.

[9] Land Compensation Act 1973, s. 35(2).   [10] *Ibid*, s. 35(1).

Where, however, the claimant holds over under a licence or tenancy[1] so that the date of displacement is the date of termination of that licence or tenancy he may elect to compute his average annual profits from the three accounting years ending on or after the date of completion of the acquisition. Similarly, where no accounts are available such accounts as are required may be made up for a three-year period ending on, or on any convenient date after, the date of completion of the acquisition.[2]

The rent to be deducted from profits is "the rent that might reasonably be expected to be payable in respect of the agricultural land acquired if it were let for agricultural purposes to a tenant responsible for rates, repairs and other outgoings".[3] If the claimant is a tenant paying rent on some other basis then the above rent is to be substituted in accounts prepared for this purpose, for that which is actually paid.[4]

As has been explained earlier in this chapter[5] compensation may be payable for loss of profits as part of the compensation for disturbance if, for example, in this connection, it is not possible to continue the activity concerned on the new unit and no other suitable alternative unit was reasonably available. Thus if a general farmer were unable to continue to run a dairy herd on his new unit and successfully claimed compensation for loss of profits thereon as an item in his claim for compensation for disturbance, he must exclude his dairying activities from his accounts in assessing his profits under these provisions for the purposes of substantiating a claim for a farm-loss payment.[6]

Once the annual average profit is determined a deduction therefrom will have to be made if the agricultural value of the land[7] acquired exceeds the agricultural value of the land comprised in the new agricultural unit.[8] In comparing values the agricultural land in each unit is to be valued in accordance with Rules 2 to 4[9] and in each case without regard to the principal dwelling thereon, the valuation of the acquired land being made as at the date of displacement and of the new agricultural unit as at the date on which the claimant began to farm it.[10] The deduction is to be "proportionate" so that if, for example, the value of

---

[1] I.e., a tenancy such as that described in note 2, p. 381, *supra*.

[2] Land Compensation Act 1973, s. 35(3). I.e., if his licence or tenancy permits him to remain in possession for more than a year after completion of the acquisition he can exclude from his calculations profits made in years subsequent to the accounting year that ends within the twelve-month period following completion. This may very well be to his advantage if the conditions in which he remains in possession are inimical to profitable farming as a result, for example, of the development of neighbouring land which may result in interference with drainage, trespass, etc. On the other hand his ability to "rob" the land without fear of the longer term consequences may make his years of occupancy under licence his most profitable.

[3] *Ibid*, s. 35(4), i.e., the rent that will be reflected in the compensation for the land acquired.

[4] *Ibid*.

[5] Pp.355, *et seq*, *supra*, and particularly p. 360, *supra*.

[6] Land Compensation Act 1973, s. 35(5). This does not, of course, mean an accurate cost-accounting exercise (a peculiarly difficult operation in relation to farm products), merely that he cannot take any particular elements in his profits into account in calculating both compensation and farm-loss payment. For the latter purpose, therefore, he simply has to deduct the profits of the activity concerned which have been accepted as ranking for compensation for disturbance.

[7] I.e., its value "as land used solely for agriculture": *ibid*, s. 35(7).

[8] *Ibid*, s. 35(6).

[9] I.e., Land Compensation Act 1961, s. 5(2) to (4): see pp. 164 and 177, *et seq*, *ante*.

[10] Land Compensation Act 1973, s. 35(7); see also note 9, p. 379, *supra*.

the land acquired exceeds that of the new unit as assessed as above by 10 %, the farm-loss payment is reduced by 10 %.

The purpose of this provision is presumably to discourage a purely nominal relocation (e.g., by a substantial farmer taking a small holding), as a means of securing a farm-loss payment, where the claimant is to all intents and purposes retiring and perhaps purchasing a holding at a price reflecting the value of the house rather than of the land.[1] But if this is so it seems a curiously "hit and miss" method of going about it. The fact that the agricultural value of the new unit is substantially less than that of the old may merely reflect poorer quality land, or a smaller acreage, solely due to the claimant's inability, in a competitive market, to find a new unit roughly comparable in size with the old. In such cases there seems little logic in reducing the farm-loss payment where the acquisition results in the claimant moving to an inferior farm.

Finally, the limit placed upon the amount of a farm-loss payment is the amount by which the farm-loss payment, as calculated in accordance with the above provisions "together with compensation for the acquisition of the interest in the land acquired assessed on the assumption mentioned in the Land Compensation Act 1961, s. 5(2), (3) and (4)[2] (including compensation for disturbance), exceeds the compensation actually payable for the interest."[3]

The effect of this somewhat convoluted formula is not immediately self-evident. The essential point, however, is that a distinction is drawn between the compensation for the interest assessed under the Land Compensation Act 1965, s. 5 (the 1919 Rules) and the compensation payable therefor under the Land Compensation Act 1965, Part II, taken as a whole. In assessing the price in the open market under s. 5 ("the s. 5 valuation") the market will, of course, reflect the chances of obtaining planning permission for development (i.e., "hope" value) but where there is significant doubt whether such development value will in fact be realisable by the actual grant of planning permission, the market's assessment of value will clearly be less than that which arises when compensation comes to be assessed on the basis that planning permission that has not actually been granted (and might well not be granted) is nevertheless to be assumed. For example, agricultural land bordering a built-up area but shown as "white land" in the development plan will probably command a higher price in the market than is justified purely by its agricultural or "existing use" value because of the hope that planning permission will some time in the future be available; but the market price will not be as high as it would be if the land were already the subject of planning consent for, say, residential development. But if the local authority acquire such land for housing purposes, compensation falls to be assessed as if planning permission for such development had actually been granted.[4]

In such cases the compensation actually payable (the "Part II

[1] See p. 380, *supra.*
[2] See pp. 177, *et seq, ante.*
[3] Land Compensation Act 1973, s. 35(8).
[4] Land Compensation Act 1961, s. 15, p. 191, *ante.*

valuation") may exceed the "s. 5 valuation". If the farm-loss payment together with the compensation for disturbance added to the latter more than offsets the difference, the formula will operate to limit the farm-loss payment. Thus if, for example, the excess of the "Part II valuation" over the "s. 5 valuation" is £5,000, but compensation for disturbance comes to £3,000 and the farm-loss payment to £2,500, the farm-loss payment will be limited to £500.

It may be, however, that the "s. 5 valuation" will exceed the "Part II valuation". This may occur where the compensation payable is reduced by virtue of the effect of the overall scheme of acquisition[1] in respect of which a purchaser in the open market (Rule 2) is unlikely to expect any such allowance in agreeing a price. In such circumstances the excess will be further increased by the addition of the compensation for disturbance and the farm-loss payment, so that the limit on the latter cannot apply. In other words, as far as entitlement to a farm-loss payment is concerned, the farmer is not to be prejudiced by the effect of the scheme upon the assessment of compensation for his interest.

(iii) PROCEDURE

As in the case of claims for home-loss payments, claims for farm-loss payments can only be met if made within the prescribed period, i.e., before the expiration of one year beginning on the date on which the claimant begins to farm the new unit.[2] The claimant must provide such details as are reasonably necessary to determine the amount of the farm-loss payment to which he is entitled (if any) but these details need not accompany the claim; they are supplemental thereto rather than an integral part thereof and need not therefore be submitted within the prescribed period.[3] Where a person entitled to a farm-loss payment dies before the expiration of the claim period having failed to submit a claim, the right to do so devolves upon his personal representatives provided they can register the claim before the expiration of the claim period.[4]

Where the agricultural unit acquired is farmed by a partnership it is the firm (rather than individual partners) which is the occupier and any interest in the land of any of the partners is to be treated as an interest of the firm. On the other hand, the requirements relating to the new unit

---

[1] As to which see pp. 217, et seq, ante. Compensation for the interest may also be reduced as a result of any enhancement in value of land retained, but since it is a prerequisite to entitlement to a farm-loss payment that the farmer be displaced from the whole of the agricultural unit (p. 379, supra.) such a reduction is likely to be applicable only where the farm is part of a larger estate in the same ownership but farmed in separate units.

[2] Land Compensation Act 1973, s. 36(1), but note the requirement that the claimant must have started to farm the whole of the new unit, and the difficulties to which this may give rise: note 9, p. 379, supra.

[3] Land Compensation Act 1973, s. 36(1).

[4] Ibid, s. 36(3). Cf. the corresponding provision governing home-loss payments, p. 375, supra. In the case of farm-loss payments the lack of provision for the extension of the claim period is, however, much less likely to cause hardship for by definition a deceased person entitled to such a payment will have acquired, and been in sufficiently good health to have started to farm, his new unit; either he or his personal representatives can therefore be expected to have had time for submission of the claim.

are fulfilled provided any one of the partners secures such a unit and begins to farm it within the three-year period following displacement.[1]

A successful claim to a farm-loss payment carries with it the right to reimbursement of the reasonable valuation and legal expenses incurred in its preparation and presentation[2] and the right to interest[3] thereon at the currently prescribed rate[4] from the date of expiration of the claim period.[5]

Disputes as to the amount of a farm-loss payment are to be referred to the Lands Tribunal[6] but no specific provision is made in regard to disputes as to entitlement. In such cases it will be for the claimant to refer his claim to the Lands Tribunal together with an application for the matter in issue to be treated as a preliminary point of law.[7]

3 Disturbance payments[8]

(i) PRELIMINARY REQUIREMENTS

Disturbance payments are designed to meet cases in which people who are displaced from land, including houses or other buildings situate thereon, would not qualify for compensation for disturbance due to having no interest in the land, or would not qualify for a home-loss payment, either because they fail to fulfil the occupancy requirements or simply because it is not their "home" from which they are displaced.

Although displacement from land used for agriculture[9] is expressly excluded, disturbance payments are of considerably wider application than either home- or farm-loss payments. They will, for example, include displacement from a farm house,[10] from buildings used exclusively for trade or commerce, and from land without buildings used for such purposes, e.g., a scrap yard.

With one significant difference the actions of local authorities, or of housing associations, that give rise to a claim for a disturbance payment are the same as those that give rise to a home-loss payment.[11] The difference is that, whereas the latter refer to displacement from, and the acquisition of, an interest in a *dwelling*, the corresponding provisions governing disturbance payments refer to displacement from, and

---

[1] *Ibid*, s. 36(2).

[2] *Ibid*, s. 36(5), but without prejudice to the powers of the Lands Tribunal in respect of costs and expenses.

[3] *Ibid*, s. 36(6).

[4] I.e., the rate from time to time prescribed by Treasury regulations made under the Land Compensation Act 1961, s. 32. The current rate of interest at the time of going to press is 10½%: Acquisition of Land (Rate of Interest after Entry) (No. 4) Regulations 1977 (SI 1977 No. 1656).

[5] I.e., the period of one year from the date on which the claimant began to farm the new unit: Land Compensation Act 1973, s. 36(1).

[6] *Ibid*, s. 35(9).

[7] Lands Tribunal Rules 1963 (SI 1963 No. 483), Rule 48.

[8] Land Compensation Act 1973, ss. 37 and 38.

[9] *Ibid*, s. 37(1).

[10] Note that *ibid*, s. 37(7), expressly excludes "land which is used for the purposes of agriculture" rather than "land which forms part of an agricultural unit" which would include the farm house: see pp. 131, *ante*.

[11] Land Compensation Act 1973, s. 37(1); as to the housing associations to which these provisions apply, see note 8, p. 372, *supra*.

acquisition of, *land*. They also refer to housing orders, resolutions or undertakings affecting a *house or building on the land* or an improvement order affecting a *house* thereon. The home loss provisions on the other hand use the word "dwelling" in place of the words in italics.

The use of the word "house" instead of "dwelling" raises the question whether a housing order etc., in respect of a single dwelling (which for the purposes of the home-loss payment provisions includes a room or rooms not structurally adapted as a single dwelling[1]) can be said to be an order in respect of the house or other building (e.g., a block of flats). In this respect the word "dwelling" is very much wider than the word "house" but some indication that dwellings which are not also houses are intended to be covered can be derived from the special provision for persons displaced from a "dwelling" adapted to meet the needs of a disabled occupier.[2] This is, however, the only use of the word "dwelling" in the sections of the Act covering disturbance payments, and there is no reference to parts of houses or buildings. But if it be the intention that dwellings that are not also houses should be covered it seems curious that, having so carefully referred only to dwellings in the section dealing with home-loss payments, and having made special provision for dwellings comprising a room or rooms not structurally adapted as a single dwelling[1] the draftsmen should switch to the narrow word "house"[3] if a contrast with dwelling were not intended. The conclusion to which one is forced, therefore, is that the narrower interpretation must be accepted, although provided the order etc., is made in respect of the house or building and the occupier of a dwelling within it is thereby displaced his claim to a disturbance payment will not be affected; *aliter* it seems if the order etc. is in respect only of the dwelling (assuming, of course, that it does not comprise a house).

(ii) QUALIFICATIONS

The crucial qualifications entitling a person (hereafter referred to as a "claimant") to a disturbance payment and the manner in which they differ from those giving entitlement to a home-loss payment may be summarised as follows:

(a) The claimant must be in lawful occupation of the land.

(b) He must, however, have no interest in the land which would entitle him to compensation for disturbance. To this general rule, however, there are two exceptions. First, he may have an interest in land acquired by a housing authority in circumstances in which compensation falls to be assessed, under the Housing Acts, on the basis of site value[4] provided that that interest does not entitle him to an "owner-occupier supplement";[5] Secondly, where the authority is the

---

[1] Land Compensation Act 1973, s. 87(1), and see also s. 29(5), and p. 374, *para*, (c) *supra*.
[2] *Ibid*, s. 38(3).
[3] "House" is not in fact defined in the Act except in relation to Scotland: *ibid*, s. 87(1).
[4] I.e., under the Housing Act 1957, ss. 29(2) or 59(2); Land Compensation Act 1973, s. 37(2)(b) and (c): pp. 255 *et seq*, *ante*.
[5] I.e., payments under the Housing Act 1957, Sch. 2, Part II, and the Housing Act 1969, Sch. 5: see pp. 265, *et seq*, *ante*.

landlord (having previously acquired the freehold or superior leasehold) of business premises and the occupier, upon determination of his interest by notice to quit is entitled to compensation under the Landlord and Tenant Act 1954, s. 37,[1] he may elect whether to take that compensation or a disturbance payment.[2]

(c) In the case of displacement resulting from the acquisition of the land in question the claimant must have been in lawful occupation when the notice of the making of the compulsory purchase order was first published,[3] or in the case of an order not requiring confirmation,[4] on the date on which the preparation of the draft order was first notified to the public.[5] Where the land is acquired under an Act of Parliament that designates it as subject to compulsory acquisition the corresponding date is that of the publication of the Parliamentary Bill.[6] Where the acquisition is by agreement[7] that date is the date of the agreement.[8]

(d) Similarly where a housing order has been made, a resolution passed, an undertaking accepted or an improvement notice served[9] in respect of the house or building upon the land there will be no entitlement to a disturbance payment unless the claimant was in occupation at the time the order was made, the resolution passed, the undertaking accepted or the improvement order served.[10]

However, even if these requirements are not fulfilled the responsible authority[11] has discretionary powers to make an equivalent payment.[12]

(iii) THE AMOUNT OF DISTURBANCE PAYMENTS

The amount of a disturbance payment is to be the sum required to meet the reasonable expenses of the claimant in moving from the land from which he is displaced.[13] In the case of a person carrying on a trade or business he is also entitled to be reimbursed for the trading losses[14] he will sustain in having to quit the land,[13] and in the assessment of such

---

[1] As to which see pp. 370, et seq, supra.
[2] Land Compensation Act 1973, s. 37(4).
[3] Ibid, s. 37(3)(a).
[4] For example, an order made by the Secretary of State.
[5] Land Compensation Act 1973, s. 37(3)(a).
[6] Ibid, s. 37(3)(b).
[7] Note the contrast with home-loss payments where acquisition by agreement bars entitlement: ibid, ss. 29(1) and 32(7), pp. 373, et seq, supra.
[8] Presumably upon completion of the contract of sale.
[9] As to which see note 11, p. 373, supra.
[10] Land Compensation Act 1973, s. 37(3).
[11] As to which see p. 379, supra.
[12] Land Compensation Act 1973, s. 37(5); as to whether this discretion permits the payment of any lesser amount, see note 8, p. 373, supra.
[13] Land Compensation Act 1973, s. 38(1): "The reasonable expenses of the person entitled to the payment in removing from the land from which he is displaced" (Ibid, s. 38(1)(a) and Land Compensation (Scotland) Act 1973, s. 35(1)(a)) have been held by the Lands Tribunal for Scotland as capable of including costs incurred by a protected tenant in redecorating the house vacated: Anderson v Glasgow Corpn [1974] RVR 398. The reason for this decision, viz that such redecoration by a tenant would not be reflected in the fair rent and would not therefore be covered by the compensation payable to the landlord, does not, however, appear to have very much relevance to an assessment of expenses incurred in removing.
[14] As to the assessment of trading losses, see pp. 357, et seq, supra.

losses account is to be taken of the availability of suitable alternative accommodation and of his previous expectation of continued occupation of the premises from which he has been displaced.[1]

Where displacement is from a dwelling adapted for the special needs of a disabled person (who need not be the claimant or person entitled to the disturbance payment) then if an authority having functions under the National Assistance Act 1948, s. 29[2] has, or if requested to do so, would have, provided assistance in such adaptation, the disturbance payment will include the reasonable expenses incurred by the claimant in making comparable modifications to any dwelling to which the disabled person moves.[3]

Disturbance payments carry interest from the date of displacement[4] and disputes as to the amount thereof are referable to the Lands Tribunal.[5]

4 Compensation for disturbance payable to short-term tenants and to those having no legal interest in the land acquired

SUMMARY

1. In this context those holding under "short-term" tenancies include occupiers with no greater interest than as tenant for a year or from year to year, and leases having less than a year of their lease unexpired.[6]

2. The procedure normally adopted by acquiring authorities in these cases is to acquire the freehold (or superior leasehold) and terminate the tenancy (or await the expiration of the lease).[6] In these circumstances the compensation will be confined to such payments as are applicable under the relevant statutes, viz:

   (a) In the case of acquisition of a dwelling, a home-loss payment,[7] or if this is something for which the claimant fails to qualify, a disturbance payment.[8]

   (b) Also if the dwelling is a caravan and its site is acquired, the person dispossessed may be entitled to a home-loss payment.[9]

   (c) In the case of acquisition of agricultural land such compensation as is payable by a landlord under the Agricultural Holdings Act 1948 and the Agriculture (Miscellaneous Provisions) Act

---

[1] Land Compensation Act 1973, s. 38(2). Note, however, that where the displaced person is aged over sixty the special provisions described on pp. 361, et seq, supra, apply to the calculation of disturbance payments in like manner as they apply to compensation for disturbance where that person has an interest in the land which is the subject of compulsory acquisition: ibid, s. 46(7).

[2] The National Assistance Act 1948, s. 29, confers powers upon local authorities to make arrangements for promoting the welfare of the disabled; a local authority for this purpose is the council of a county, county district, metropolitan borough or the Common Council of the City of London: ibid, s. 65(1).

[3] Land Compensation Act 1973, s. 38(3).

[4] Ibid, s. 37(6), and see note 4, p. 385, supra.

[5] Ibid, s. 38(4) and see p. 385, and note 7, supra.

[6] P. 365, supra.

[7] Under the Land Compensation Act 1973, ss. 29–32, pp. 372, et seq, supra.

[8] Under ibid, ss. 37–38, pp. 385, et seq, supra.

[9] Under ibid, s. 33, p. 376, supra.

1968.[1] The tenant may also qualify for a home-loss payment.[2]

(d) In the case of acquisition of business premises such compensation as is payable by a landlord under the Landlord and Tenant Acts 1927 and 1954.[3] Since, under these circumstances, the tenant will have no interest in the land he may also qualify for a disturbance payment.[4]

3. Where the acquiring authority requires possession before the termination of the tenant's interest it may, after serving notice of entry, take possession. In such cases compensation is payable:

(a) For disturbance which, where relevant in the particular circumstances, may include such items of expenditure resulting from the disturbance as are allowable where the occupier either holds the freehold or a long lease.[5] In these cases, however, the notice of entry takes the place of notice to treat so that there is a presumption against the payment of compensation in respect of expenses incurred before the date of notice of entry.[6]

(b) Under the statutory provisions mentioned in paragraph 2 above, except that a business tenant will not qualify for a disturbance payment, since by definition, he still has, at the date of notice of entry, an interest in the land.[7]

5 Rehousing obligations of local etc. authorities

The general principle of the rehousing provisions of the Act of 1973[8] is that where a person is displaced from his home, whether it be a dwelling or a caravan, as a consequence of any of the actions of public authorities which give rise to a right to a home-loss payment,[9] and suitable alternative accommodation is not available on reasonable terms, and no advance has been made to that person towards the acquisition of alternative accommodation[10] the local authority[11] has an obligation to rehouse him. This obligation also arises, however, upon acquisition by agreement: it is not confined to persons having the rights of occupation that are a prerequisite to a home-loss payment, and thus extends

---

[1] P. 371, *et seq, supra*, and note that assessment of compensation for the tenant's interest must take into account his expectation, but for the acquisition, of continued security of tenure.

[2] Under *ibid*, ss. 29–32, pp. 372, *et seq, supra*, and note that a farm-loss payment is only available to those holding a freehold interest, or a leasehold having at least three years unexpired, p. 379, *supra*. Farm tenants are also wholly excluded from eligibility for disturbance payments in respect of their land, though not in respect of the farm house, p. 385, *supra*.

[3] Pp. 370, *et seq, supra*.

[4] Pp. 385, *et seq, supra*.

[5] P. 366, *supra*, and see section 2 of this chapter, pp. 346, *et seq, supra*. In assessing such compensation account must of course be taken of the limited period of further occupation which, by definition, such a tenant could have expected to enjoy: p. 366, *supra*.

[6] Pp. 366, *et seq, supra*.

[7] Pp. 386, *et seq, supra*.

[8] Land Compensation Act 1973, s. 39, as amended by the Housing Act 1974, Sch. 13, para. 40.

[9] Pp. 373, *et seq, supra*.

[10] That is, under the Land Compensation Act 1973, s. 41, or under the Small Dwellings Acquisition Acts 1899 to 1923; Housing (Financial Provisions) Act 1958, s. 43; or by a development corporation or the Commission for the New Towns otherwise than under the Land Compensation Act 1973, s. 41: *ibid*, s. 39(4).

[11] Where displacement results from acquisition or development by a development corporation the obligation to rehouse rests with that corporation. Similarly if it results from development by the Commission for the New Towns it rests with the Commission: *ibid*, s. 39(8).

to any person in lawful occupation (i.e., other than a trespasser) other than persons who have merely a temporary permission of residence pending demolition.[1] It does not, however, extend to displacement resulting from compulsory acquisition in response to a blight notice[2] nor to any acquisition of land in relation to which the Secretary of State had decided (before the passing of the Act),[3] in accordance with the relevant provisions of the Housing Act 1957,[4] that a housing scheme is not necessary.[5]

Finally, where the displacement results from the acquisition or development of land following appropriation for that purpose, of land previously acquired, the obligation to rehouse is limited in exactly the same way as are the powers of acquiring authorities to defray expenses incurred by persons having no interest in the property acquired, in acquiring an alternative dwelling.[6] That is to say, the person concerned must have been in occupation of the accommodation from which he is displaced when the intention of the acquiring authority was first publicised or agreement to acquire was reached as explained under subheading (c) above.[7] Similarly, if he has been displaced in consequence of a housing order, resolution, undertaking or improvement notice he must have been in occupation at the time when the order was made, the resolution passed, the undertaking accepted or the notice served.[8]

5 OTHER PROVISIONS FOR THE BENEFIT OF DISPLACED RESIDENTIAL OCCUPIERS UNDER PART III, LAND COMPENSATION ACT 1973

1 Introductory

In addition to the obligations which it imposes upon acquiring authorities in relation to home loss, farm loss and disturbance payments, Part III of the Act of 1973 also confers upon such authorities discretionary powers to grant loans to displaced residential owner-occupiers and to defray the expenses incurred by persons not entitled to compensation for disturbance[9] in acquiring alternative accommodation. The Act also substantially increases the obligation of local authorities to rehouse persons displaced in circumstances similar to those that give rise to claims to home-loss payments. Although these powers and duties cannot be regarded as falling strictly within the law

---

[1] Land Compensation Act 1973, s. 39(3).

[2] *Ibid*, s. 39(2). As to blight notices see pp. 129, *et seq, ante*. Cf. the home-loss payment provisions which, in addition, exclude acquisitions in response to notices under the New Towns Act 1965, s. 11: note 6, p. 372, *supra*.

[3] 23 May 1973.

[4] The Housing Act 1957, Sch. 9, para. 1, prohibits undertakers empowered to acquire dwellings housing 30 or more persons from taking possession until the Secretary of State has either approved a rehousing scheme or decided that such a scheme is unnecessary.

[5] Land Compensation Act 1973, s. 39(5).

[6] Pp. 391, *et seq, infra*.

[7] Land Compensation Act 1973, s. 39(6); cf. the similar provisions of s. 37(3); see para. (c) p. 387, *supra*.

[8] *Ibid*.

[9] See Section ss. 2 and 3 of this chapter, pp. 346 and 365, *et seq, supra*.

of compensation for compulsory acquisition, they so closely affect the position of persons displaced from their homes as a result of such acquisition or those other actions of public authorities (or certain housing associations) which entitle them to home loss or disturbance payments that it seems appropriate to consider such matters in this chapter.

2 Defrayment of expenses in acquiring alternative accommodation

As has been explained in section 2 of this chapter the compensation payable to an owner-occupier of a dwelling compulsorily acquired includes reimbursement of reasonable expenses incurred in finding alternative accommodation. These include reasonable travelling expenses incurred in finding an alternative dwelling, fees reasonably incurred in having possible properties surveyed (even if as a result of the surveyor's report the property proves unsuitable) and legal and surveyor's fees in connection with the new acquisition.[1]

The Act of 1973[2] now confers powers on acquiring authorities to defray such expenses (not, of course, including the purchase price of the new dwelling)[3] in cases where in consequence of the compulsory acquisition of any land[4] a resident occupier having either no legal interest or no greater interest than one of a year or from year to year is displaced.

There are, however, three qualifications to the exercise of these powers.

In the first place, they cannot be exercised in favour of a person only permitted to occupy the dwelling acquired pending its demolition, or whose occupation amounts to trespass.[5]

Secondly, where the land is acquired under a compulsory purchase order the person displaced must have been in occupation at the time when notice of the making of the order was first published or, in the case of a compulsory purchase order not requiring confirmation, when the draft order was first published.[6] Similarly, where the acquisition is in pursuance of an Act of Parliament specifying the land as subject to compulsory acquisition the person displaced must have been in occupation when the Parliamentary Bill was first published.[7] Where acquisition is by agreement the relevant date is the date of the agreement.[8]

---

[1] *Harvey* v *Crawley New Town Development Corpn*, [1957] 1 QB 485, pp. 348, *et seq*, *supra*.

[2] Land Compensation Act 1973, s. 43.

[3] *Ibid*, s. 43(1).

[4] Or of any of the other actions mentioned in *ibid*, s. 39(1) which in effect is an adaptation of the actions giving rise to a home-loss payment (*ibid*, s. 29(1)): see p. 373, *supra*.

[5] *Ibid*, ss. 39(3) and 43(4).

[6] *Ibid*, ss. 39(6)(a) and 43(4).

[7] *Ibid*, ss. 39(6)(b) and 43(4). If the land is not so specified in the original Bill but by subsequent amendment, the relevant date is the date of publication of the amendment: *ibid*, s. 39(6)(b).

[8] *Ibid*, ss. 39(6)(c) and 43(4). There must, it seems, be a binding agreement, though not necessarily an agreement as to the purchase price if it is agreed that that should be fixed in accordance with ordinary rules governing compensation for compulsory acquisition. But an agreement merely to negotiate is not, it is submitted, enough to prevent these powers being exercised in favour of a person whose occupation commences in the course of such negotiations and before any binding agreement has been reached.

Thirdly, no payment can be made under these provisions unless the new dwelling is acquired[1] not later than a year after the displacement and is reasonably comparable to the dwelling from which the claimant has been displaced.[2]

3 Loans for the acquisition or construction of alternative dwellings

Where an owner-occupier[3] of a dwelling is displaced either as a result of its compulsory acquisition or of any of the other actions of local authorities (or improvement by a housing association) which gives rise to claims for home-loss payments,[4] local authorities[5] have power to advance money to such owner-occupier to enable him to acquire or construct[6] another dwelling.[7] Although the exercise of these powers is subject to such conditions as may be approved by the Secretary of State,[8] local authorities have a wide discretion as to the terms on which such advances are made.[9] The principal sum may be as much as the full value of the borrower's interest in the dwelling he acquires or constructs; it must, however, be secured by a mortgage of that interest.[10]

---

[1] In this context it is sufficient if a contract for the purchase of the new dwelling is entered into within this period: Land Compensation Act 1973, s. 43(3).

[2] *Ibid*, s. 43(2).

[3] That is, a person in occupation in right of a freehold interest or a term of years certain of which not less than three years remain unexpired either on the date of displacement or, in the case of displacement resulting from the carrying out of development on land previously acquired or appropriated, on the date of acquisition or appropriation: *ibid*, s. 41(9).

[4] See pp. 373, *et seq, supra*.

[5] In London either the London Borough or the Greater London Councils; elsewhere County District Councils: *ibid*, s. 39(7) and 41(1).

[6] "Construction of a dwelling" includes acquisition of a building for conversion into a dwelling or conversion of a building previously acquired: *Ibid*, s. 41(10).

[7] *Ibid*, s. 41(1).

[8] *Ibid*, s. 41(2).

[9] *Ibid*, s. 41(3)(a), provides that the advance *shall* be made on terms providing for the repayment of the principal either at the end of a fixed period (with or without provision for extension) or upon notice, subject in either case to a provision for earlier repayment upon the happening of a specified event. S. 41(3)(b), however, provides that the advance *shall* be made on such other terms as the authority thinks fit. Although s. 41(3) contains no indication as to whether para. (b) is an alternative or an addition to para. (a), it is submitted that it is the latter and that whatever other terms are imposed the terms of the advance must include provision for repayment of the principal in one or other of the ways set out in para. (a).

[10] *Ibid*, s. 41(5). An advance for the construction of a dwelling may be made by instalments as the work proceeds: *ibid*,s. 41(4).

CHAPTER 10

Compensation in Respect of Certain Planning Decisions

1 INTRODUCTION

The Town and Country Planning Act 1971 draws a distinction between classes of development falling within the 8th Schedule[1] thereto and all other development. The latter is termed "new" development.[2] The first general rule is that no compensation is payable in respect of a refusal or conditional grant of planning permission for any new development unless the land in question has an "unexpended balance of established development value";[3] in that case although compensation may be claimed for the depreciation in the value of the land resulting from such refusal or conditional grant of planning permission, it cannot exceed the unexpended balance. These cases are dealt with in the next section of this chapter. The second general rule is that no compensation is payable in respect of any refusal or conditional grant of planning permission for any development falling within Part I of the 8th Schedule;[4] to this there is no exception. And the third general rule is that compensation is normally payable where the value of the subject land is reduced or the owner is put to expense as a result of planning decisions that prevent him from developing or using his land in a manner that would otherwise be perfectly legitimate. For example, an established existing use or a planning permission not specifically expressed as personal to the occupier or limited in time enures for the permanent benefit of the land.[5] Thus if an order is made to discontinue an established use or demolish an existing building which had not been erected in contravention of planning control[6] or to revoke or modify an existing planning permission;[7] or if planning permission for development of a class falling within Part II of the 8th Schedule to the Act of

---

[1] For Sch. 8 to the Town and Country Planning Act 1971 see Appendix, p. 456, *post*.

[2] *Ibid*, s. 22(5).

[3] For explanation see p. 394, *et seq*, *infra*.

[4] Somewhat anomalously, where land is compulsorily acquired compensation therefor is assessed upon the assumption (*inter alia*) that planning permission would be available for any development falling within either Part I or Part II of the 8th Schedule of the Act of 1971 (the Land Compensation Act 1961, s. 15(3): p. 196, *ante*); no compensation is payable, however, where planning permission is refused or granted subject to onerous conditions for development falling within Part I as opposed to Part II of the Schedule: Town and Country Planning Act 1971, s. 169.

[5] Town and Country Planning Act 1971, s. 33.

[6] I.e., an order under *ibid*, s. 51.

[7] I.e., an order under *ibid*, s. 45.

1971 is refused or granted only subject to onerous conditions, compensation will normally be payable.

Similarly, where the value of land is reduced or the owner is put to expense by the imposition of special obligations such as those which may arise in connection with listed buildings,[1] building[2] and tree[3] preservation orders or tree planting requirements[4] compensation may be payable.[5]

These cases, together with the rather special case of compensation arising from the service of a stop notice[6] are the subject of Part VIII of the Act of 1971 and are dealt with in Sections 3 *et seq* of this chapter.

2 COMPENSATION FOR PLANNING DECISIONS RESTRICTING NEW DEVELOPMENT

As has been explained in the sections 4 and 5 of chapter 1, the basis of the Town and Country Planning Act 1947 was the nationalisation of the potential development value of all land with total compensation limited to a global sum of £300 million. Thereafter, future developers would be required not only to obtain planning permission but also, so to speak, to buy back the development value of the land concerned by paying an equivalent development charge. Compensation for compulsory acquisition of land was accordingly restricted to "existing use" value.

In 1952, however, while retaining existing use value as the basis of compensation for compulsory acquisition of land, the Government decided[7] to abolish the development charge and distribute the £300 million fund, not in a single operation (which it was thought would be inflationary) but as and when those who had established claims thereon sought and were refused planning permission (or were granted planning permission subject to conditions sufficiently restrictive to reduce the full development value of the land). In other words, established claims were to be irrevocably attached to the land concerned. If the owner of such land were granted planning permission for the full development of his land he would, of course, suffer no loss and his claim would be extinguished; if, on the other hand, planning permission for any development was refused he would be able to claim compensation to the extent of his established claim. These changes were effected by the Town and Country Planning Acts of 1953 and 1954, the latter containing provisions of considerable complexity whereby the estab-

---

[1] I.e., where an application for listed building consent under Town and Country Planning Act 1971, s. 55 is refused.

[2] I.e., orders under *ibid*, s. 58.

[3] I.e., orders under *ibid*, s. 60.

[4] I.e., orders under *ibid*, s. 59.

[5] See the Town and Country Planning Act 1971, s. 176, for compensation where regulations restricting the display of advertisements made under *ibid*, s. 63 adversely affect land used for such display before 1 August 1948 (i.e., the relevant appointed day under the Town and Country Planning Act 1947). Since the lapse of almost 30 years makes it so unlikely that many such cases will arise in the future, it seems hardly necessary to consider these provisions further.

[6] I.e., a notice under the Town and Country Planning Act 1971, s. 90: see p. 441, *infra*.

[7] See the White Paper, Cmnd. 8699, November 1952: p. 10, *ante*.

lished claims were to be annexed to the land[1] (and thereafter termed "claim holdings"), adjusted to take account of multiplicity of interests and of acquisitions, dispositions and development already effected and apportioned where the land in respect of which the claim was originally made (the *claim area*) had subsequently been dealt with in separate lots. Having made these adjustments the balance of any particular claim holding still outstanding immediately before the commencement of the Act of 1954 is known as the *original unexpended balance of established development value*.[2]

Over the years these "claim-holdings" (and therefore the occasions on which compensation can be claimed for refusal or conditional grant of planning permission for "new" development) have lost much of their importance and value. In the first place, much of the land in respect of which claims were established has since been developed. Secondly, most owners of land for the development of which planning permission is unlikely to be forthcoming (e.g., land in a Green Belt, land reserved for agriculture, etc.) and in respect of which a claim was established will have long since submitted planning applications in order to claim such compensation for refusal of planning permission to which their established claims entitled them. Thirdly, inflation has so depreciated the value of the original and now purely notional £300 million fund, let alone of any individual claim, that in many cases, particularly where there has been subdivision of the claim holdings, the compensation now available will be little more than derisory.

For these reasons it has not been thought justifiable in this work to devote the considerable space that is required for a full explanation of these matters. They are therefore dealt with only in fairly broad outline.[3] In particular, it is not proposed to consider the means by which the *original* unexpended balance of established development value is arrived at for even where there is an unexpended balance entitling a disappointed applicant for planning permission to claim compensation all that is normally necessary is to ascertain whether there is such a balance attached to the land, and if so, its amount. This can be done simply by applying to the Secretary of State[4] for a certificate[5] stating whether the land in question has an original unexpended balance. If it has, the certificate must also contain a general statement as to the accepted state of the land on 1 July 1948[6] for the purpose of determining the claim for loss of development value under the Town and Country

---

[1] Previously such claims had been disposable as personal property: see p. 12, *ante*.

[2] Established development value is sometimes alternatively referred to as "the established claim under Part VI of the Town and Country Planning Act 1947" since it is from this claim that the various claim holdings were initially derived.

[3] They are now covered by the Town and Country Planning Act 1971, Part VII and Schs. 15, 16 and 17, re-enacting the relevant provision of the Town and Country Planning Act 1954. For a further explanation of these provisions see *Corfield on Compensation and the Town and Country Planning Act 1959*, Solicitors Law Stationery Society, 1961, pp. 35 *et seq*.

[4] Originally the function of the Central Land Board (Town and Country Planning Act 1954, s. 48) which was, however, dissolved on 1 April 1959, its outstanding functions being transferred to the Minister of Housing and Local Government and thence to the Secretary of State.

[5] Town and Country Planning Act 1971, s. 145(1). Such a certificate may also be issued on the initiative of the Secretary of State himself.

[6] The "appointed day" under the Town and Country Planning Act 1947.

Planning Act 1947, part VI, and must state that balance.[1] The Secretary of State may, although he is not obliged to, include in the
certificate additional information in regard to more recent acts or
events[2] which necessitate further adjustment of the original unexpended balance in order to arrive at the actual unexpended balance at
the date of the application.[3] On the other hand, where an acquiring
authority which has served a notice to treat with a view to the compulsory acquisition of an interest in land, applies for a certificate in
respect of that land the Secretary of State is required to show, not the
original unexpended balance, but the actual balance if any, immediately
prior to the notice to treat,[4] i.e., taking into account any adjustments
necessitated by acts or events since the computation of the original
balance.

It follows that where a landowner wishes to know the current unexpended balance and the Secretary of State's certificate merely states the
original unexpended balance it may be necessary to know whether,
since the original balance was computed, any planning permission has
been granted for development the value of which in whole or in part
absorbs the unexpended balance; whether any compensation has
already been paid in respect of a previous refusal or conditional grant of
planning permission; or whether, as a result of some later planning
permission all or any of that compensation has been, or has become
liable to be repaid. Normally this will present no difficulty; in the
former two cases the relevant development value or the compensation
paid falls to be deducted from the original balance, and in the latter case
compensation repaid falls to be added back.

Difficulty may arise, however, where the land the subject of the
planning decision in respect of which the owner of an interest therein
wishes to claim compensation does not exactly coincide with any
particular claim area. In that event an apportionment will be required
for which purpose it will be necessary to delineate the relevant claim
areas on a map. The various areas wholly within any of the lines so
drawn will, unless the relevant claim holdings have been extinguished,
have "unexpended balances",[5] though it may still be necessary to ascertain their amount by preliminary apportionment if they form only part
of any particular claim area; in such cases the "unexpended balance"

---

[1] Although the Secretary of State is required only to state the balance "subject to any outstanding claims under Part I or Part V of the Act of 1954" it seems inconceivable that any such claims will still be outstanding.

[2] For example, planning decisions which have already resulted in payment of compensation or, if compensation has been paid and planning permission subsequently granted, the refunding of such compensation: see p. 404, *infra*.

[3] Town and Country Planning Act 1971, s. 145(2).

[4] *Ibid*, s. 145(3).

[5] The Town and Country Planning Act 1954, s. 17(1) enacted that "land shall be taken to have an unexpended balance of established development value immediately after the commencement of this Act if there are then subsisting one or more claim-holdings whose area consists of that land, or includes that land together with other land, and there is not then subsisting any claim-holding whose area consists of part only of that land, whether with or without other land". This latter requirement necessitates the delineation explained in the text: the sub-division and apportionment explained avoids perpetuating situations in which claim-holdings and "land having an unexpended balance" do not coincide.

will then be the aggregate of the apportioned amounts, plus the value of any claim holding whose area wholly coincides with the area concerned multiplied by eight-sevenths. Thus, in simple diagrammatic form, if the land with which one is concerned is a simple rectangle A B C D falling

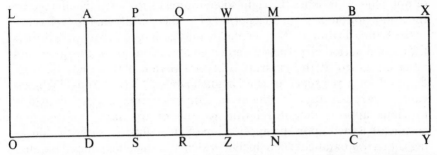

partially within two rectangular claim areas, W X Y Z and L M N O, and wholly containing a third, P Q R S, it will be necessary first to consider the land in five parts; A P S D, to which will be allocated the appropriate fraction of the claim holding whose area is L M N O; P Q R S, which is itself a claim area entitled to the whole of the relevant holding plus the appropriate part of the holding corresponding to L M N O; Q W Z R, to which, like A P S D, will be allocated a fraction of L M N O only; W M N Z, to which will be allocated apportioned parts of both L M N O and W X Y Z; and M B C N entitled to a part of W X Y Z only. The unexpended balance attributable to A B C D will thus be eight-sevenths of the aggregate.[1] Occasionally it may happen that a claim-holding cannot reasonably be apportioned in strict compliance to the ratio that the area of the part bears to the area of the whole; this will be so where it has not hitherto been necessary to make an apportionment or sub-division, but had one been necessary a greater proportion of the value of the holding would have attached to one part of the claim area than to others; in such cases it will be necessary to sub-divide the claim area accordingly before attempting to assess the unexpended balance.

If the issue of a certificate involves any new apportionment[2] or a deduction from the balance outstanding in respect of planning decisions, the certificate[3] may only be issued upon the application of a person having an interest[4] in the land in question and notice of the effect of the proposed apportionment or deduction must be given[5] to all persons whose interests are likely to be substantially affected, and such

---

[1] The unexpended balance was increased by one-seventh in order to take account, somewhat approximately, of the capital value of the interest, less income tax at the standard rate from 1 July 1948 (the appointed day of the Act of 1947) and which would have been payable if the £300 million fund had been distributed in accordance with the Act of 1947.

[2] A new apportionment is defined as any apportionment relating in whole or in part to matters in respect of which there has been no previous apportionment: Town and Country Planning Act 1971, s. 145(10).

[3] Other than in the case of a certificate issued by the Secretary of State on his own initiative, without any application therefor.

[4] Which must be either an interest in fee simple or a tenancy of the land: Town and Country Planning Act 1971, s. 134(4), and see note 6, p. 401, infra.

[5] By the Secretary of State: ibid, s. 145(4).

persons may object and may appeal to the Lands Tribunal.[1] The notice must state that objections or other representations may be made within 30 days, and no certificate may be issued until that period has expired. If objections are received from any person, whether he has been notified or not, who establishes the right to an interest substantially affected by the apportionment, a further period of 30 days is allowed for reference to the Lands Tribunal. The certificate may be issued at any time during the second period of 30 days if and when objections are withdrawn, and must be issued at the expiration of that period if there has been no demand for a reference to the Lands Tribunal. The Lands Tribunal cannot vary an apportionment in a manner inconsistent with any previous apportionment relating to any of the same matters.[2] A certificate issued upon the application of an acquiring authority showing the *current* balance is conclusive evidence of the unexpended balance shown, but a certificate relating to the original unexpended balance and which may also, at the discretion of the Secretary of State, contain additional information regarding any further deduction to be made therefrom for the purpose of determining the current balance is only sufficient proof of the facts stated unless the contrary is shown.[3] In the case of the latter type of certificate a fee of 25 pence is payable upon application and a further fee of 75 pence when a new apportionment is involved.[4]

Exclusion and modification of compensation in certain cases

Compensation for refusal or conditional grant of planning permission is excluded where the application is in respect of certain types of development;[5] if the decision is made on certain grounds;[5] if certain other development is permitted in lieu; or if the land has been acquired or appropriated by a body possessing compulsory powers.[6] It may also be varied if upon submission of the claim to the Secretary of State he decides to grant a more favourable permission than that proposed by the local planning authority.[7] These exceptions to the general rule[8] may be summarised as follows:

(i) Refusal[9] of an application involving a "material change[10] in the use of any buildings or other land".[11] This and the next following

---

[1] Town and Country Planning Act 1971, s. 145(5).
[2] *Ibid*, s. 145(6).
[3] *Ibid*, s. 145(7).
[4] *Ibid*, s. 145(9).
[5] *Ibid*, s. 147.
[6] *Ibid*, s. 149.   [7] *Ibid*, s. 148(3).
[8] If planning permission is refused it is not necessary, in order to establish a claim for compensation, to prove that the relevant development would in fact have been carried out had it been granted: *Overland v Minister of Housing and Local Government* (1957), 8 P & CR 389 (LT).
[9] For the purpose of paras. (i) to (vii) above (i.e., the Town and Country Planning Act 1971, s. 147) a grant of planning permission subject to a condition prohibiting development upon a specified part of the land is treated as a refusal with respect to that part of the land: *ibid*, s. 147(6).
[10] Note that certain changes in user, though material, do not require permission. See *ibid*, s. 23(2) to (5). As to what change of user involves development, see *ibid*, s. 22(1) and the Town and Country Planning (Use Classes) Order 1972, (SI 1972 No. 1385).
[11] The Town and Country Planning Act 1971, s. 147(1)(a). Cf. the similar words used in the definition of development in *ibid*, s. 22(1).

exceptions were said to be made on the ground that the restriction imposed would be in conformity with the ordinary obligations of "good neighbourliness".[1] Normally the word "land" in Acts of Parliament includes "buildings" and is expressly so defined in the Act of 1971.[2] In the interpretation of this subsection, however, the insertion of the word "other" before "land" appears to have been intended to denote that the expressions "any buildings" and "other land" are to be interpreted as mutually exclusive.[3] In other words, the subsection defines two categories of development: material change in the use of a building and a material change in the use of land, other than buildings. In such cases compensation is excluded. "What is not excluded is development which involves the change from one category to another—from the category of the use of land to the category of use of building. That is included".[4] No doubt this interpretation must be accepted; otherwise one would indeed "get the most absurd position"[4] but it is still not altogether clear why refusal of planning permission for development involving material change in user should imply that the proposed change must necessarily have involved "bad neighbourliness".

(ii) Any decision upon an application for consent to the display of advertisements.[5]

(iii) The imposition of conditions with regard to the density, lay-out, construction, design and use of buildings, the lay-out of land for the purpose of development, the construction, design or lay-out of any access[6] to a highway or the working of minerals.[7]

(iv) The application to any planning permission of conditions limiting its duration in accordance with sections 41 and 42 of the Act.[8]

(v) The application to any planning permission of conditions attached to industrial development certificates or office development permits.[9]

(vi) Refusal of planning permission on the ground that the application is premature either because of the priorities envisaged in the development plan, or because of anticipated delay in the provision of adequate water supplies or drainage facilities. A subsequent refusal

[1] Cmd. 8699, November 1952. The Town and Country Planning Act 1932, s. 19, permitted the inclusion of somewhat similar provisions in a planning scheme, but contained a number of qualifications and safeguards which are not repeated in subsequent Acts. See also the Town and Country Planning Act 1971, s. 26, providing for the advertisement of planning applications and the consideration of objections where the development concerned might be regarded as infringing "good neighbourliness".
[2] Town and Country Planning Act 1971, s. 290(1).
[3] The same words appear in ibid, s. 22(1).
[4] Speech by the Solicitor-General, House of Commons Official Report, 22 November 1954, at cols. 842–848. See also 189 House of Lords Official Report, at col. 1514.
[5] I.e., under regulations made under the Town and Country Planning Act 1971, s. 63: ibid, s. 147(1)(b).
[6] Not including a service road: ibid, s. 147(2).
[7] Ibid.
[8] Ibid, s. 147(5).
[9] I.e., by virtue of ibid, ss. 71 or 82: ibid, s. 147(3).

on any of the same grounds does not, however, exclude compensation if at least seven years have elapsed since the original decision.[1]

(vii) Refusal on the ground that the land concerned is unsuitable for the proposed development by reason of its liability to flooding or subsidence.[2]

(viii) Refusal of planning permission where there is already a grant of permission (subject to no condition other than of the type enumerated in para. (iii) above) for any development of a residential, commercial or industrial character consisting wholly or mainly of the construction of houses, flats, shops, office premises, industrial buildings (including warehouses) or any combination thereof.[3] Such permission may have been granted on an application by another person, or it may arise from a direction or an undertaking by the Secretary of State that such permission shall be granted.[4]

(ix) Where the land concerned has been compulsorily acquired; purchased by agreement by an authority possessing compulsory powers; appropriated by a local authority for a purpose for which it could have acquired the land compulsorily; become operational land of statutory undertakers; or is held for certain purposes by the National Coal Board, no compensation is payable either to the authority concerned or to persons deriving title from them, in respect of any planning decision made after the date of the notice to treat, contract of sale, appropriation, etc. Note, however, that, in the case of statutory undertakers' operational land and National Coal Board land, the exclusion of persons deriving title from the authorities concerned does not operate if the relevant disposition of the interest in the land by these authorities took place before 1 January 1955;[5] in the case of acquisitions (compulsory or otherwise) it operates where the disposition took place subsequent to 30 June 1948, and in the case of appropriation, where the appropriation took place after that date.[6]

(x) No compensation is payable under this Part of the Act where it can be claimed under the Town and Country Planning Act 1971, s. 165, in respect of a planning decision which follows withdrawal of permission granted by a development order.[7]

Claims for compensation must be submitted on the prescribed form within six months of the planning decision concerned[8] to the local planning authority, who must transmit them to the Secretary of State[8] who, unless the claim is withdrawn,[9] must give notice thereof to any

[1] Town and Country Planning Act 1971, s. 147(4).
[2] Ibid, s. 147(5).
[3] Ibid, s. 148.
[4] Ibid, s. 148(2).
[5] I.e., the date of commencement of the Town and Country Planning Act 1954.
[6] Town and Country Planning Act 1971, s. 149.
[7] Ibid, s. 149(4).
[8] Ibid, s. 154, subject to the power of the Secretary of State to allow an extension of time (ibid, s. 154(2)). For the prescribed form and regulations governing the submission of claims see the Town and Country Planning (Compensation and Certificates) Regulations 1974 (SI 1974 No. 1242).
[9] If the Secretary of State considers that compensation is excluded under any of the provisions of the Town and Country Planning Act 1971, ss. 147 and 148; or that the development is not "new" development; or that the land has no unexpended balance of established development value he must notify the claimant accordingly and invite him to withdraw his claim: ibid, s. 154(5)(a).

persons appearing to him to have an interest in the land to which the decision relates.[1] The Secretary of State may then review the decision; if the original decision was that of the local planning authority, and he is of the opinion that had the application been referred to him he would himself have made a decision more favourable to the applicant, he may, if the decision amounted to a refusal, substitute one granting permission with or without conditions and applicable to the whole or any part of the land; and if the original decision resulted in conditional permission he may remove the conditions imposed or substitute less onerous ones.[2]

Alternatively, the Secretary of State may, if appropriate, substitute some other form of development, and this procedure is available to him not only where the original decision was made by a local planning authority as in the previous paragraph, but also where he made it himself either under the Town and Country Planning Act 1971, s. 35, or upon appeal under s. 36.[3] The Secretary of State may direct that his final decision shall either take effect as if the original application included an application for permission for the development substituted by him and the original decision had included the grant of permission therefor; or as if the original decision had been his own and had included an undertaking to grant permission for the relevant alternative development.

Before any such direction is given, however, the Secretary of State must notify the local planning authority concerned, and any persons who had submitted, and not withdrawn, a claim, of his intended decision. Such claimants then have 30 days in which to submit a modified claim and the Secretary of State may consider such proposals before making his final direction, whereafter the claim has effect as if it had been made on the basis of the Secretary of State's direction and the compensation is calculated accordingly.[4]

The measure and determination of compensation

Subject to the cases already considered in which compensation is excluded, the right to compensation for refusal or conditional grant of planning permission is conferred upon all persons who, at the time of the decision[5] are entitled to an interest in land[6] to which the decision

---

[1] *Ibid*, s. 154(5)(b).

[2] *Ibid*, s. 155. As to the Secretary of State's powers to review planning decisions the subject of claims for compensation see *ibid*, ss. 38 and 39.

[3] *Ibid*, s. 38. Cf. *ibid*, ss. 35 and 36, under which, in contrast to the powers considered here, the Secretary of State's decisions must be confined to the terms of the application: he cannot grant planning permission for some other development.

[4] *Ibid*, s. 155.

[5] Where there has been an appeal, the relevant time remains the date of the original decision by the local planning authority: *ibid*, s. 290(4)(d).

[6] I.e., either an interest in fee simple or a tenancy; *ibid* s. 134(4). By virtue of s. 290(1) "tenancy" has the meaning assigned thereto by the Landlord and Tenant Act 1954, viz: "A tenancy created either immediately or derivatively out of the freehold, whether by a lease or underlease, by an agreement for a lease or underlease or by a tenancy agreement or in pursuance of any enactment (including this Act), but does not include a mortgage term or any interest arising in favour of a mortgagor by his attorning tenant to his mortgagee, and references to the granting of a tenancy and to demised property shall be construed accordingly."

relates, which is depreciated in value thereby and which is land having an unexpended development value.[1] If the interest concerned extends to other land, the right to compensation arises only from the depreciation of that interest in so far as it subsists in the land to which the planning decision relates; no rights under this Part of the Act arise in respect of any other land even though its value may be affected.[2]

Where there is only a fee simple interest in possession, the assessment of compensation on the basis of the amount by which the value of the land has been depreciated subject to the limits imposed by the current unexpended balance of established development value is relatively straightforward. The amount by which the value is depreciated is the difference between the value which would have been attributable to the land had the permission been granted, and the lower value which results from the refusal of planning permission or the imposition of conditions. The latter value is to be calculated as at the date of the relevant planning decision which may have been made on some other application[3] or in the exercise of the Secretary of State's powers of review;[4] and on the assumption that, apart from the effect on any of these decisions, only Schedule 8 development would be permitted.[5] The value which the land would have had but for the planning decision is to be calculated on the assumption that the decision was to the "contrary effect".[5] That is to say, if planning permission was refused this valuation will be made on the assumption that it was granted subject only to such of the conditions mentioned in s. 147(2) of the Act[6] as might reasonably be expected to be imposed. Where planning permission was granted conditionally the valuation will be made on the assumption that only those conditions mentioned in s. 147(2) above[6] were imposed.[7] The amount by which this latter exceeds the former will, of course, be the amount by which the value of the land has been depreciated as a result of the planning decision; if it is *less* than the unexpended balance of established development value, it will represent the compensation payable; if it is not, the compensation will be equivalent to the unexpended balance.[8] For the purpose of any future transaction the unexpended balance will, in the former case, be reduced by the amount of the compensation (i.e., in that case the depreciation in value) and, in the latter case, will be extinguished.[9]

[1] Town and Country Planning Act 1971, s. 134(2). The requirement that the land must have an unexpended balance of course follows from the basis of compensation; if there is no unexpended balance there can be no compensation.

[2] *Ibid*, s. 152(2).

[3] Or, for example, granted by development order under *ibid*, s. 24. In *Hanily* v *Minister of Local Government and Planning*, [1952] 2 QB 444: [1952] 1 All ER 1293 it was held that any person with a genuine hope of acquiring an interest in the land might apply for planning permission without informing the owner; see now, however, the Town and Country Planning Act 1971, s. 27, re-enacting the Town and Country Planning Act 1959, s. 37 requiring such applications to be accompanied by a certificate to the effect that the owners of the land have been notified. Although submission of a certificate which the applicant knows to contain false information constitutes an offence a planning permission bona fide granted upon such an application probably remains valid.

[4] P. 401, *supra*.

[5] Town and Country Planning Act 1971, s. 153(1).

[6] I.e., the conditions mentioned in para. (iii) on p. 399, *supra*: *ibid*, s. 153(5)(a).

[7] *Ibid*, s. 153(5)(b).   [8] *Ibid*, s. 152(1).   [9] *Ibid*, s. 140(1).

Similar calculations will be made in each case where there is more than one interest subsisting in the land but in such a case, if the aggregate of the amount by which the various interests are depreciated in value exceeds the unexpended balance, the unexpended balance must be allocated between them in proportion to the respective amounts by which they have been depreciated in value; the compensation payable in respect of each interest will then be the appropriate portion of the unexpended balance.[1] Thus, to take a very simple example, if the unexpended balance is, say, £500 and there is both a fee simple and a leasehold interest[2] and the depreciation attributable is calculated at, say, £800 and £200 respectively, it will be necessary to reduce these latter sums by one-half; the compensation payable will, therefore, be £400 and £100 respectively, the unexpended balance being accordingly extinguished.

Rather more difficulty arises, however, where the land as a whole has no specific unexpended balance or where the interests affected by the planning decision do not coincide, as to area, with the land in respect of which the planning decision has been given. In these cases it is first necessary to calculate the depreciation of the value of each interest; it is then necessary to divide the land to which the decision relates into "qualified"[3] land and unqualified land, and to superimpose the areas covered by the interests concerned. There will then be a delineation of a number of areas which, in the first place, will be either qualified or unqualified, and in the second place will be areas in the whole of which an interest (or apportioned part of such an interest) subsists.[4] The depreciation of the value of the interests can thereafter be apportioned between these areas according to the nature of the areas and the effect of the planning decision in relation to each of them. Compensation will first be assessed in relation to each of these sub-divisions of the land to which the decision applies; in the cases of areas of unqualified land there will, of course, be no compensation; in other cases the compensation will be whichever is the less of the unexpended balance attaching to the area or the depreciation in value of the interest concerned; if any area includes more than one interest, the respective depreciation in values must be aggregated; if the aggregate exceeds the relevant unexpended balance, each must be reduced *pro rata*.[5] The total compensation payable is thus the aggregate of the compensation attributable to the parts.[6]

In such cases, however, for the purpose of ascertaining the unexpended balance of established development value on some future occasion, each part of the land that has had to be considered separately will remain permanently as an area to be considered on its own, and will

---

[1] *Ibid*, s. 152(3).
[2] In valuing a tenancy the date of expiration of which is uncertain, that date is to be taken as that which appears reasonable and probable in the interests of the person in whose favour any right of determination or option operates: *ibid*, s. 163(2).
[3] I.e., land having an unexpended balance of established development value.
[4] Cf. the calculations for determining unexpended balance, p. 396, *supra*.
[5] Town and Country Planning Act 1971, ss. 152(4) and (5); see *ibid*, s. 152(3).
[6] *Ibid*, s. 152(5).

have attached to it the appropriate unexpended balance; the land taken as a whole will cease to be regarded as "qualified" land and future determination of compensation or adjustment to the unexpended balance will be calculated by reference to the parts into which it has been divided.[1]

Claims for compensation under this Part of the Act are determined by the Secretary of State.[2] If the compensation exceeds £20 he must, if he considers it practicable to do so, make an apportionment between different parts of the land in so far as the planning decision does not affect the land uniformly but affects such parts differently.[3]

Both the compensation itself and any apportionment are subject to appeal to the Lands Tribunal;[4] details must therefore be notified to claimants and, where there is an apportionment, to all other persons entitled to interests in the land which may be substantially affected thereby. In addition, where the Secretary of State has determined that compensation exceeding £20 is payable, a "compensation notice", giving details of the planning decision, the land to which it relates, the amount of compensation and any apportionment, must be deposited with the council of the local authority in whose area the land is situated and with the local planning authority. These notices must be registered in the register of local land charges and the compensation is considered as distributed rateably according to area over the land as a whole, or, if an apportionment has been made, over the relevant parts of the land.[5]

If on some future occasion any new development is contemplated despite the fact that compensation has been paid in respect of a past planning decision, the compensation will in most cases be recoverable, and must be paid or secured to the satisfaction of the Secretary of State before the proposed development is carried out.[6] With the exception of the development specified in the Town and Country Planning Act 1971[7] and development that consists of the winning and working of minerals, however, the liability to refund the compensation depends upon the decision of the Secretary of State; that decision depends on whether or not, having regard to the probable value of the development, he considers it reasonable that such recovery should be made. If he does not, he may be required to issue a certificate to that effect.[8] The amount to be recovered is the amount of the compensation specified in the compensation notice, unless the area to be developed neither coincides with nor is wholly included in the area to which the notice relates; in that event the compensation must first be apportioned accordingly.[9] Once a repayment has been made no further recovery is possible in

---

[1] Town and Country Planning Act 1971, Part V and Sch. 15.
[2] Ibid, ss. 154(4) and 156(1). Town and Country Planning (Compensation and Certificates) Regulations 1974 (SI 1974 No. 1242).
[3] Town and Country Planning Act 1971, s. 158(1).
[4] Ibid, s. 156.
[5] Ibid, s. 158(6).
[6] Ibid, s. 159(1).
[7] S. 159(2)(a): see para. (viii), p. 400, supra.
[8] Town and Country Planning Act 1971, s. 159(3).
[9] Ibid, s. 160(1).

respect of any subsequent development on the same land[1] except in so far as, and to the extent that, the Secretary of State may have remitted[2] any portion of the amount to be recovered, in which case he must ensure that the amount remitted is entered upon the original compensation notice.

The Secretary of State's power to remit arises where he is satisfied that the development concerned is desirable for the proper development of the land but owing to its value would not be likely to be carried out unless he makes a remission in whole or in part of the amount recoverable.[3]

The effect of recovery on the unexpended balance is to add back the compensation recovered.[4]

3 OTHER RESTRICTIONS ON DEVELOPMENT OR USE OF LAND

The Town and Country Planning Act 1971, Part VIII, deals with the right to compensation in respect of various restrictions on the development or use of land, which may be imposed under other provisions of the Act. The matters covered by Part VIII can be categorised as follows:
 (i)   Restrictions on development other than new development;[5]
 (ii)   Revocation and discontinuance orders;[6]
 (iii) Buildings of special architectural or historic interest;[7]
 (iv)   Trees;[8]
 (v)   Advertisements;[9]
 (vi)   Stop notices.[10]

1 Restrictions on development other than new development

(i) INTRODUCTORY

The Town and Country Planning Act 1971, s. 169, deals with compensation for refusal of development within Part II of the 8th Schedule:[11] such development is in a special category as regards

---

[1] *Ibid*, s. 160(3).
[2] Cf. the Secretary of State's power under *ibid*, s. 159(3), to certify that he is of the opinion that the section should not apply at all; if that power is exercised the whole of the compensation specified in the compensation notice remains available for recovery in the event of subsequent development. Under *ibid*, s. 162(2), he may remit the whole or part of the amount recoverable.
[3] *Ibid*, s. 162(2).
[4] *Ibid*, s. 161.
[5] Town and Country Planning Act 1971, s. 169.
[6] *Ibid*, ss. 164–168, 170.
[7] *Ibid*, ss. 171–173. Compensation under the Ancient Monuments Acts 1913–1953 is also dealt with under this head.
[8] Town and Country Planning Act 1971, ss. 174–5. Compensation for refusals of felling licence under the Forestry Act 1967, s. 11, are also dealt with.
[9] Town and Country Planning Act 1971, s. 176.
[10] *Ibid*, s. 177.
[11] Town and Country Planning Act 1971, Sch. 8, Part II is set out in full in the Appendix at p. 456, *post*.

compensation. This is the only case in which, apart from the somewhat obsolete provisions relating to "unexpended balances",[1] compensation is payable merely for refusal of permission or the imposition of conditions on a planning permission. In the case of any other development, including development within Part I of the 8th Schedule, refusal or the imposition of conditions gives rise to no special rights, unless it results in the land becoming incapable of reasonably beneficial use, in which case it may be possible to serve a purchase notice.[2]

The distinction between Part I and Part II of the 8th Schedule has already been noted.[3] The most important practical difference is in the treatment of works to buildings.[4] Works involving the *rebuilding* of a building which was in existence on 1 July 1948[5] or on a "material date"[6] would be within Part I of the Schedule[7] (provided the works are within the applicable floorspace and cubic content limitations).[8] On the other hand, works to the same building amounting only to *enlargement, improvement or other alteration* of the building (subject to the same limitations) would be within Part II.[9] Thus in the former case no compensation would be payable on a refusal of planning permission. In the latter case compensation could be claimed. Therefore it is of considerable importance to distinguish "rebuilding" from "alteration". This is a question of fact. A proposal which involves the complete replacement of one building by another would clearly not fall within Part II.[10] On the other hand a proposal to take down and re-erect one wall of a building would be within Part II,[10] and, if permission is refused, could give rise to a claim to compensation. The test in practice will be whether the identity of the building is retained.[11] The wording of the application for planning permission will not necessarily be conclusive,[12] and one must look at the substance of what is proposed.[13]

It will be noted that there is considerable overlap between the

[1] See pp. 395 *et seq, supra*.
[2] For a detailed treatment of purchase notices see p. 114, *ante*.
[3] See p. 393, *supra*.
[4] The term "building" includes "part of a building": s. 290(1). But otherwise it is used in its ordinary sense and may, for example, relate to a building comprising more than one dwelling-house, whether divided horizontally or vertically: see *Green* v *Birmingham Corporation* (1951), 2 P & CR 220 at 224 LT.
[5] 1 July 1948 is the "appointed day" as defined by the Town and Country Planning Act 1971, s. 290(1). This is referred to as "the appointed day" because it was the day appointed for the corresponding provisions of the Town and Country Planning Act 1947 to come into effect.
[6] "A material date" means either "the appointed day" or "the day by reference to which the schedule falls to be applied in the particular case in question": Sch. 8, para. 12. In practical terms this means that the relevant building must have been in existence either on 1 July 1948 or at the date when the claim was made: see *Moxey* v *Hertford RDC* (1973) 27 P & CR 274 LT. However, if an enforcement notice has been served before the date of the claim and subsequently becomes effective, no claim can be based on the existence of the building at the date of the claim: Sch. 8, para. 12 proviso.
[7] Sch. 8, para. 1.
[8] See p. 409, *infra*.
[9] Sch. 8, para. 3.
[10] *Sainty* v *Minister of Housing and Local Government* (1964), 15 P & CR 432 DC.
[11] Cf. *City of London Real Property Co. Ltd.* v *War Damage Commission* [1956] 1 Ch. 607 and the discussion of the expression "war damage ... made good by works which include *alterations or additions* ..." in the War Damage Act 1943, s. 8.
[12] *National Provincial Bank* v *Portsmouth Corpn* (1959), 11 P & CR 6 CA.
[13] *Ibid*, and see also *Burman* v *St. Albans Corpn* (1961), 12 P & CR 360 LT.

categories of development contained in Part II of the 8th Schedule and those for which permission is granted by the General Development Order.[1] Thus, for example, the General Development Order grants permission for "enlargement improvement or other alteration of a dwelling-house" subject to certain limits as to cubic content and height, etc. Such development would often also fall within para. 3 of the 8th Schedule. In this case therefore no question of compensation under Part VIII of the Town and Country Planning Act 1971 will normally arise because permission is granted automatically. However, if the General Development Order[1] permission is withdrawn by, for instance, an Article 4 direction,[2] and permission is subsequently refused for the same development, a claim will arise under s. 169, and not in respect of the withdrawal of the General Development Order permission.[3]

(ii) RIGHT TO COMPENSATION[4]

A claim arises under s. 169 when on an application for permission for development within Part II of the 8th Schedule,[5] it is refused or granted subject to conditions by a decision of the Secretary of State.[6] To establish a right to compensation the claimant must show that the value of his interest in the relevant land is less than it would have been if permission had been granted, or had been granted unconditionally. The compensation is an amount equal to the difference between those two values.[7] In assessing the value of the land without permission or subject to the conditions as the case may be, it is assumed that any subsequent application would be dealt with in the same way.[8] However, if the Secretary of State undertakes,[9] when refusing permission, to

---

[1] Town and Country Planning General Development Order 1977 (SI 1977 No. 289) as to which see p. 414, *infra*.

[2] For the nature and effect of an Article 4 direction see p. 414, *infra*.

[3] For claims in respect of withdrawals of General Development Order permissions see p. 419, *infra*. It is assumed in relation to such claims that permission would be granted for 8th Sch. development: s. 164(4). There is therefore no overlap with compensation for refusal of development within Part II of the 8th Schedule.

[4] For the assessment of compensation see also p. 446, *infra*, and for procedure see p. 448, *infra*.

[5] The Schedule is set out in full in the Appendix at p. 456, *post*.

[6] Town and Country Planning Act 1971, s. 169(1). Note that in this case, unlike that relating to claims under Part VII (see p. 395, *supra*) a claim cannot be made in respect of the decision of a local planning authority. The decision must be that of the Secretary of State on appeal or on a called-in application.

[7] Town and Country Planning Act 1971, s. 169(2).

[8] *Ibid*, s. 169(3)(a).

[9] There are other provisions in the Town and Country Planning Act 1971 which refer to the Secretary of State's "undertaking" to grant permission: see, for example, s. 180(1)(c). However it is difficult to see how such an undertaking could be given without offending the principle that the Secretary of State cannot fetter his discretion in relation to the consideration of future applications: see e.g. *Lavender & Son Ltd* v *Minister of Housing and Local Government*, [1970] 1 WLR 1231. In practice the Secretary of State will not go further than to indicate that his decision is "without prejudice" to a further application, possibly indicating the changes that might be made. This could not be said to be an "undertaking". However, unless the subsequent application is for "the like permission" and therefore excluded by s. 169(3)(a), the prospect of obtaining permission following a "without prejudice" refusal would be reflected in the market value of the land after the refusal, and therefore would be taken into account indirectly in assessing compensation. It is thought that the expression "the like permission" would be narrowly construed in the context of s. 169(3)(a), so that, only if the subsequent application is for precisely the same development, is it to be assumed that the same decision would be given on a renewed application.

grant permission for some other development on the same land, that undertaking must be taken into account in assessing the value.[1] Compensation cannot be claimed under this section if a purchase notice[2] is served.[3]

The claim may arise not only from the refusal of permission, but also from the imposition of conditions which affect the value. However no claim can arise out of the imposition of the statutory time-limits relating to the submission of details and commencement of development,[4] nor of conditions contained in an Industrial Development Certificate[5] or Office Development Permit.[6] Furthermore when conditions are imposed regulating the design or external appearance of buildings or the size or height of the buildings, the Secretary of State may, if it appears to him reasonable to do so having regard to local circumstances,[7] direct that such conditions shall be disregarded, wholly or partly, in assessing compensation.[8]

Although the claim normally arises in relation to a decision of the Secretary of State on an actual application, it may also arise where an application is of no effect through the lack of an Industrial Development Certificate. In most areas[9] an application for industrial development[10] above certain floor space limits is of no effect unless supported by an Industrial Development Certificate issued by the Secretary of State certifying that the development can be carried out consistently with the proper distribution of industry.[11] If an application is made unsupported by the necessary Industrial Development Certificate the local planning authority must consider whether they would have refused permission for the whole or part of the development in any event.[12] If they would have refused permission they must serve a notice to that effect on the applicant.[12] If such a notice is served in respect of an application for development within Part II of the 8th Schedule a claim under s. 169 for compensation will arise as though there had been an actual refusal of the application by the Secretary of State.[13] Since compensation will be based on a comparison of the actual value of the

---

[1] Town and Country Planning Act 1971, s. 169(3)(b).

[2] For purchase notices see p. 114, ante.

[3] Town and Country Planning Act 1971, s. 169(8). The service of a purchase notice by itself rules out the payment of compensation under s. 169, whether or not the notice is accepted or confirmed. Furthermore it appears that the service of a purchase notice even after the s. 169 claim has been submitted will defeat the claim unless payment has already been made.

[4] I.e., under the Town and Country Planning Act 1971, ss. 41–42: ibid, s. 169(7).

[5] See the Town and Country Planning Act 1971, s. 72.

[6] See ibid, s. 82; also s. 169(7).

[7] It is not clear in what respect "local circumstances" should be regarded by the Secretary of State as relevant to whether an entitlement to compensation should arise from the imposition of conditions. The theory behind s. 169 has nothing to do with actual circumstances, but is based on the purely notional assumption implicit in the Town and Country Planning Act 1947 that certain categories of limited development should be treated as within the "existing use" of land: see pp. 6–9, ante.

[8] Town and Country Planning Act 1971, s. 169(4).

[9] Other than those areas excluded from control by the Secretary of State by regulations made under s. 68(2).

[10] As defined by the Town and Country Planning Act 1971, s. 67(1)(a), (b).

[11] Ibid, s. 67(1).

[12] Ibid, s. 72(1).

[13] Ibid, s. 169(5). Note that in this case the decision of the local planning authority is sufficient.

land with the value it would have had if permission had been granted,[1] the applicant will in effect receive the benefit of development value which could never have been realised in practice without an Industrial Development Certificate.

The categories of development within Part II of the 8th Schedule may be summarised[2] as follows:

(a) Alterations to existing buildings[3]

A claim may arise out of the refusal by the Secretary of State, or grant subject to conditions, of permission for the enlargement, improvement or alteration of a building which was in existence at a material date,[4] or building erected in substitution for such a building.[5] The erection of an additional building on land in the same curtilage[6] to be used in connection with the original building is treated as an enlargement.[7] If the building was in existence on 1 July 1948 the cubic content of the original building must not be increased by more than one-tenth, or in the case of a dwelling-house, by more than 1,750 cubic feet if that would be more than one-tenth.[8] If there are several buildings in the same curtilage used for the purposes of an institution or undertaking their cubic content may be aggregated for these purposes.[9] In the case of a building erected after 1 July 1948 (even if in substitution for a building in existence on that day) the cubic content must not be increased at all.[10] Furthermore, in assessing compensation no account is to be taken of any prospective use which would offend the floorspace limitations imposed by the 18th Schedule.[11] The effect of this is that in addition to the cubic content limitation, compensation cannot be claimed in respect of refusal of planning permission for any increase of more than 10 % in the gross floor space used for any purpose.[12]

The operation of these provisions in relation to the alteration of buildings can be illustrated by considering the following different situations which might arise:

(a) If the works of alteration are interior works which do not affect the external appearance, no permission is required and no question of compensation will arise.[13] The same will apply if the work is covered by a General Development Order permission.

---

[1] See p. 407, *supra*. Since permission could not have been granted without an IDC the assumption that permission is granted makes it necessary to assume also the grant of an IDC.

[2] They are set out in full in the Appendix at p. 456, *post*.

[3] Sch. 8, para. 3.

[4] See notes 5 and 6 on p. 406, *supra*.

[5] By rebuilding work complying with Sch. 8, para. 1.

[6] For the meaning of "curtilage" see *Sinclair Lockhart's Trustees* v *Central Land Board* (1950) 1 P & CR 195, 204.

[7] Sch. 8, para. 11(a).

[8] Sch. 8, para. 3(a), (b).

[9] Sch. 8, para. 11(b).

[10] Town and Country Planning Act 1971, s. 169(6)(a).

[11] *Ibid*, s. 169(3)(c).

[12] See *ibid*, Sch. 18, set out in full in the Appendix at p. 458, *post*. Gross floorspace is assessed by external measurement, and floorspace shared between different uses in the same building is apportioned between them: *ibid*, Sch. 18, para. 4. In the case of a building erected since 1 July 1948 resulting from the rebuilding within the scope of Sch. 8, para. 1, no floorspace increase is allowed: Sch. 18, para. 2.

[13] In this case there is no development: Town and Country Planning Act 1971, s. 22(2)(a).

(b) If the work is to a building which was in existence on 1 July 1948 and involves an increase of no more than one-tenth in either the existing cubic content[1] or the existing floorspace used for any purpose,[2] then on refusal of permission by the Secretary of State compensation will be payable. The measure will be the difference between the value of the land as it is, and as it would have been if permission had been granted.[3]

(c) The same will apply in the case of a new building erected after 1 July 1948, but in this case the work must involve no increase in cubic content.[4] The floorspace may still be increased by one-tenth unless the new building was the result of the rebuilding of a previous building within the scope of the 8th Schedule, para. 1, in which case no increase in floorspace is permitted.[5]

(d) If the work involves an increase of cubic content greater than one-tenth in the case of a building in existence on 1 July 1948, or any increase in the case of a building erected since that date, then the development is outside the scope of s. 169 altogether,[6] and no claim will arise.

(e) If, on the other hand, the increase in cubic content would be within the applicable limits, but the floorspace used for any purpose would be increased beyond the limits imposed by the 18th Schedule, then a claim to compensation may arise. However in assessing compensation the value of the land with the permission will be assessed as though the floorspace used for any purpose would be restricted to the 18th Schedule limits.[7]

(b) Agricultural or forestry buildings[8]

If land was used for agriculture or forestry[9] at a material date,[10] compensation can be claimed for the refusal or grant subject to conditions by the Secretary of State of permission for building or other operations required for the purposes of the use. However, this does not apply if the operations involve the erection or alteration of a dwelling-house, or of buildings used for the purpose of market gardens, nursery grounds or timber yards, or for other purposes not connected with general farming operations or with the cultivation or felling of trees. Thus a claim for compensation for refusal of permission for a broiler

---

[1] Town and Country Planning Act 1971, Sch. 8, para. 3.

[2] *Ibid*. Sch. 18, para. 1.

[3] *Ibid*, s. 169(2).

[4] *Ibid*, s. 169(6)(a).

[5] *Ibid*, Sch. 18, para. 2, which applies where the building to be altered is not "the original building". In the case of a building resulting from rebuilding within Sch. 8, Part I, the original building is the earlier building and therefore para. 2 of Sch. 18 rather than para. 1 applies: Sch. 18, para. 5.

[6] Town and Country Planning Act 1971, s. 169(1).

[7] *Ibid*, s. 169(3)(c).

[8] Town and Country Planning Act 1971, Sch. 8, para. 4: set out in full in the Appendix at p. 458, *post*.

[9] "Agriculture" is defined in s. 290(1). Note that it does not include the breeding or keep of livestock other than for the production of food, wool, skins or fur or for use in farming. Thus land used for the breeding of race-horses or dogs would not be within the paragraph: see *Belmont Farm Ltd.* v *Minister of Housing and Local Government* (1962), 13 P & CR 417. "Forestry" is not defined.

[10] See note 6, p. 406, *supra*.

house was disallowed, because that was not regarded as a "purpose connected with general farming operations".[1]

(c) Minerals required for agricultural use[2]

Refusal or grant subject to conditions by the Secretary of State of an application for permission for the winning and working of minerals for agricultural use may attract a claim for compensation. However the application must have related to land held or occupied with land used for agriculture and the minerals must be required for the purpose of that use, for example, for use in fertilising the land, or in connection with the maintenance or improvement or alteration of buildings or works occupied or used for agriculture.[2]

(d) Uses within the same Use Class[3]

A claim may arise if permission is refused, or granted subject to conditions, by the Secretary of State for the change of use of a building to a use within the same class specified in the Use Classes for Third Schedule Purposes Order 1948.[4] The proposed use must be within the same class as the use at "a material date" i.e., either at 1 July 1948 or at the date of the claim. If the building has been unoccupied since 1 July 1948, the comparison may be made with the last previous use provided there has been some use since 7 January 1937.[3] In many cases such a change of use will not require permission in any event, because if it is a change to a use within the same class of the Use Classes Order (made for the purposes of s. 22 of the Act)[5] no development is involved. However, although the classes specified in the Use Classes for Third Schedule Purposes Order are similar in many respects to those specified in the Use Classes Order, there are important differences. In particular, the Use Classes for Third Schedule Purposes Order has not been amended since 1948 to reflect the various changes made in the Use Classes Orders current since that date. Thus, for example, until 1972 both the Use Classes for Third Schedule Purposes Order and the Use Classes Order included restaurants in the same class as shops.[6] No permission was therefore needed for a change from an ordinary shop to a restaurant and no claim for compensation under s. 169 would have arisen. However, from 1972 restaurants were excluded from the definition of a shop in the Use Classes Order,[7] but the Use Classes for Third Schedule Purposes Order was not altered. Thereafter permission was required for a change from a shop to restaurant. However if it were refused by the Secretary of State, or granted subject to conditions, a

---

[1] *Moxey* v *Hertford RDC* (1973), 27 P & CR 274. Note that there is no similar limitation in the general permission granted for agricultural buildings by the General Development Order (though there is a limitation on floor area) so that an alternative claim might have been possible under s. 165: see p. 419, *post*.

[2] Town and Country Planning Act 1971, Sch. 8, para. 5. In this case use for forestry is excluded.

[3] *Ibid*, Sch. 8, para. 6.

[4] Town and Country Planning (Use Classes for Third Schedule Purposes) Order 1948, SI 1948 No. 955.

[5] Under the Town and Country Planning Act 1971, s. 22(2)(f). The current order is the Town and Country Planning Use Classes Order 1972, SI 1972 No. 1385.

[6] Compare Class I in the Use Classes for Third Schedule Purposes Order 1948 and in the Use Classes Order 1963, SI 1963 No. 606 (repealed) taken with the definition of "shop" in each order.

[7] Use Classes Order 1972 (*supra*), Art. 2(2).

claim for compensation would arise if it could be shown that the value would have been enhanced by the permission. Other examples of cases where a claim might arise are refusals of permission for a change from general shop to a shop for the sale of motor vehicles,[1] or to a launderette,[2] or a change from a dance hall to bingo.[3]

(e) Minor extension of use[4]

The fifth category of development within the 8th Schedule, Part II, relates to any building (other than a building erected since 1 July 1948)[5] or land which was used as to part only for a particular purpose on a material date.[6] The extension of that use so that, in the case of a building, the cubic content, or, in the case of other land, the area used for that purpose, is not increased by more than one-tenth is within Part II of the Schedule.[4] It is difficult to envisage a claim to compensation arising frequently under this head, since the extension of one constituent use within a planning unit is unlikely by itself to amount to a material change of use.[7] However, if a claim were to arise in the case of a building, the compensation would be subject to the floorspace limitations imposed by the 18th Schedule.[8] It must be remembered that the use of land for building or other operations is excluded from the statutory definition of "use",[9] so that, for example, this category cannot be used to base a claim for refusal of permission to extend mineral workings.[10]

(f) Mineral waste[11]

The last category of development within Part II of the 8th Schedule is the deposit of waste material or refuse reasonably required in connection with the working of minerals on land comprised in a site which was being used for that purpose at a material date.[6] This would often be within the permission granted by the General Development Order for the tipping of waste by mineral undertakers.[12]

(iii) TIME LIMITATIONS

Generally all the categories of development within the 8th Schedule represent minor alterations or additions to existing buildings, oper-

---

[1] Excluded from Class I of the Use Classes Order by the Town and Country (Use Classes) (Amendment) No. 2 Order 1960, SI 1960 No. 282, but still within Class I of the Use Classes for Third Schedule Purposes Order 1948.

[2] Specifically excluded from the definition of "shop" in the Use Classes Order 1972, but regarded as within the corresponding definition of the Use Classes for Third Schedule Purposes Order 1948 as a use "for other purposes appropriate to a shopping area".

[3] In the 1948 Order, Class XXI included "use as a dance hall" and "use ... for indoor games". In the Use Classes Order 1972 the corresponding class (Class XVIII) substitutes "use ... as a gymnasium or sports hall" instead of "use ... for indoor games ...". Bingo therefore would no longer qualify.

[4] Town and Country Planning Act 1971, Sch. 8, para. 7.

[5] *Ibid*, s. 169(6)(b).

[6] For the meaning of a "material date" see note 6, p. 406, *supra*.

[7] See e.g., *Wood v Secretary of State* (1973), 25 P & CR 303.

[8] See p. 409, *supra*.

[9] Town and Country Planning Act 1971, s. 290(1).

[10] See *Stokes v Secretary of State for War* (1950), 1 P & CR 118.

[11] Sch. 8, para. 8.

[12] Town and Country Planning General Development Order 1977, SI 1977 No. 289, Class XIX 3.

ations or uses. If the existing buildings or uses are subject to a condition in a planning permission limiting the period for which they are permitted, the 8th Schedule development for which compensation is claimed will be treated as subject to the same limitation.[1]

2 Revocation and Discontinuance Orders

(i) INTRODUCTORY

This section is concerned with three different classes of restriction which may be imposed on development or uses of land which would otherwise be lawful. The three classes are:

(i) Orders revoking or modifying existing permissions granted on application. These will be referred to generally as "section 45 orders".[2]

(ii) Restrictions imposed on permissions previously granted by development orders ("Development Order restrictions").

(iii) Orders requiring the discontinuance of a use of land or the alteration or removal of buildings or works ("section 51 orders").[3]

(a) Section 45 Orders

The Town and Country Planning Act 1971, s. 45, confers on a local planning authority the power to make an order revoking or modifying a planning permission granted on an application under Part III of the Act.[4] Generally such an order does not take effect unless confirmed by the Secretary of State,[5] who must, if requested, give any persons affected an opportunity to appear before and be heard by a person appointed for the purpose.[6] However if all those who in the authority's opinion are affected by the order have notified the local authority that they do not object,[7] an expedited procedure is provided whereby the order can take effect at the end of a specified period without the need for confirmation.[8]

Where the permission relates to buildings or other operations, the power to revoke or modify may be exercised at any time before the operations have been completed.[9] However the revocation or modification will not affect so much of the operations as have been pre-

---

[1] Sch. 8, para. 10.

[2] Town and Country Planning Act 1971, s. 45(1).

[3] *Ibid*, s. 51.

[4] I.e., a permission granted by the local planning authority or the Secretary of State pursuant to an application as opposed to, for example, a permission granted by a development order (see p. 414, *infra*) or one granted by the Secretary of State in lieu of confirming a purchase notice (see p. 123, *ante*). A section 45 order may also be made in respect of permission granted by a section 51 order in connection with the discontinuance etc. required thereby: s. 51(2); see p. 415, *infra*.

[5] Town and Country Planning Act 1971, s. 45(2).

[6] *Ibid*, s. 45(3). The Secretary of State's decision can only be challenged by an application to the High Court under s. 245: *ibid*, s. 242(1), (2)(a).

[7] *Ibid*, s. 46(1) as amended by the Local Government Act 1974, Sch. 6.

[8] Town and Country Planning Act 1971, s. 46(5). The expedited procedure is not applicable to an order affecting a permission granted by the Secretary of State or to one modifying time-limit conditions imposed by virtue of ss. 41–2: *ibid*, s. 46(6).

[9] Town and Country Planning Act 1971, s. 45(4)(a). Provided the operations have not been completed at the date when the order is made by the authority it does not appear to matter if the building is subsequently completed before confirmation of the order by the Secretary of State. This is because s. 45(4) refers to the time when the "power conferred by this section ... is exercised". This is clearly a reference to the power conferred on the authority by s. 45(1), which is "exercised"

viously[1] carried out.[2] Where permission relates to a change of use the power must be exercised before the change has taken place.[3]

(b) Development Order restrictions

Planning permissions may be granted directly by development orders made by the Secretary of State[4] without any need for a specific application to the local planning authority. The most familiar and important example is the General Development Order[5] which grants permissions for a number of classes of development, such as minor works within the curtilage of a dwelling-house, temporary uses of land, agricultural buildings and works,[6] etc. Such permissions are applicable to all land subject to the limitations laid down in the order.[7]

These permissions cannot be revoked or modified by a section 45 order, since that power is limited to permissions granted on an application.[8] However, the Secretary of State can vary or revoke the General Development Order including any planning permissions granted by it, by a subsequent development order.[9] Furthermore, Article 4 of the current General Development Order enables the Secretary of State or the appropriate planning authority to direct that any permission granted by the order is not to apply to a particular development or class of development or within a particular area.[10] Except in certain specified cases[11] such a direction made by a local planning authority requires the approval of the Secretary of State.[12]

---

when the order is made. Although as stated above, the order does not ordinarily take effect "unless" confirmed by the Secretary of State (s.45(2)), his act of confirmation cannot be said to be an "exercise" of the power to revoke. If the order takes effect without confirmation (under s. 45(5)), the point is even clearer. For a contrary view see [1950] JPL 24. A comparison may also be drawn with *Earl of Iveagh* v *Minister of Housing and Local Government*, [1964] 1 QB 395, where it was held that a building preservation order under the Town and Country Planning Act 1947, s. 29, was not "effectively made" until confirmed by the Minister (at p. 407). However, that case turned on the construction of the Town and Country Planning Act 1959, s. 31, and "should not assist an argument under any other statute that an order made without being confirmed is not an order made" (per Russell LJ at p. 408). The argument in the *Iveagh* case may have been assisted by the fact that under s. 29(3) of the 1947 Act a building preservation order did not take effect "*until*" confirmed by the Minister. This may be contrasted with the use of the word "unless" in s. 45(2) of the 1971 Act.

[1] I.e., previous to the making of the order by the authority; see note 9, *supra*. Work carried out between the making of the order and its confirmation could be the subject of a claim for compensation: see p. 417, *infra*.
[2] Town and Country Planning Act 1971, s. 45(4) proviso.
[3] *Ibid*, s. 45(4)(b). Again, the relevant date appears to be the making of the order, not its confirmation: see note 9, *supra*.
[4] Town and Country Planning Act 1971, s. 24(1), (2).
[5] The current order is the Town and Country Planning General Development Order 1977, SI 1977 No. 289. The permissions are granted by Article 3, and the 1st Schedule to the order. Other "special" development orders have been made granting permissions in respect of particular areas or categories of development; see e.g., the Town and Country Planning (Ironstone Areas Special Development) Order 1950, (SI 1950 No. 1177).
[6] Within Classes I, IV and VI respectively of the 1st Schedule to the General Development Order 1977.
[7] Town and Country Planning Act 1971, s. 24(3).
[8] *Ibid*, s. 45(1).
[9] *Ibid*, s. 287(3).
[10] Town and Country Planning General Development Order 1977, Art. 4(1).
[11] *Ibid*, Art. 4(3).
[12] *Ibid*, Art. 4(2).

For the purpose of the entitlement to and assessment of compensation the withdrawal of a development order permission by the revocation or amendment of the order itself or by a direction made under it is treated in the same way as the revocation of a permission by a section 45 order.[1]

(c) Section 51 Orders

The Town and Country Planning Act 1971, s. 51, enables a local planning authority to make an order discontinuing a use of land or imposing conditions upon its continuance, or requiring steps to be taken for the alteration or removal of buildings or works.[2] The order may itself grant permission for any development of the relevant land,[3] including permission for the retention of buildings or works or the continuance of a use.[4] The order does not take effect unless confirmed by the Secretary of State with or without modifications.[5] Provision is made for persons affected to be heard by a person appointed by the Secretary of State before the order is confirmed.[6] If the requirements of the order will involve the displacement of residential occupiers, the authority must ensure that suitable alternative accommodation is provided, if not otherwise available to them.[7] Non-compliance with the requirements of a section 51 order is an offence.[8] In addition, if the requirements include steps for the alteration or removal of buildings or works the authority may, after the time specified for compliance in the order, itself carry out the necessary work.[9]

It may be noted that a section 51 order may be used where a planning permission has been fully implemented and where, therefore, a section 45 order is not possible.[10] Alternatively it might be used in conjunction with a revocation order in relation to a building permission which has been partly implemented, in order both to remove the work already carried out and to revoke the remainder of the permission. However, the use of the section 51 order is not limited to cases where permission has been granted. An order may be made in respect of uses or works for which no permission was required[11] or which have become immune

---

[1] See further p. 419, *infra*.

[2] Town and Country Planning Act 1971, s. 51(1). The expression "buildings or works" includes waste materials, refuse and other matters deposited on land: *ibid*, s. 290(1).

[3] *Ibid*, s. 51(2).

[4] *Ibid*, s. 51(3).

[5] *Ibid*, s. 51(4), (5).

[6] *Ibid*, s. 51(6). The Secretary of State's decision can only be challenged by an application to the High Court under s. 245 of the Act: *ibid*, s. 242(1), (2)(b). For an example of an unsuccessful challenge see *Re Lamplugh* (1967), 19 P & CR 125.

[7] Town and Country Planning Act 1971, s. 51(8).

[8] *Ibid*, s. 108(1).

[9] *Ibid*, s. 108(2). The authority is not able to recover the cost of this work from the owner (cf. s. 91 relating to enforcement notices). Any material removed from the site and not claimed within three days may be sold, but the proceeds must be paid to the person to whom the materials belonged before removal: Public Health Act 1936, s. 276, applied by the Town and Country Planning Act 1971, s. 108(2).

[10] Town and Country Planning Act 1971, s. 45(4).

[11] E.g., development carried out before the Town and Country Planning Act 1947 came into effect, or development permitted by a development order (see p. 414, *supra*) or even uses or works which do not amount to development.

from enforcement action[1] or as an alternative to an enforcement notice in the case of development carried out in breach of planning control.[2]

(ii) RIGHT TO COMPENSATION[3]

(a) Section 45 Orders

When a planning permission is revoked or modified by a section 45 order a claim may be made by any person who has an interest in the land who can show that either:

(a) he has incurred expenditure in carrying out work which is rendered abortive by the revocation or modification; or

(b) he has otherwise sustained loss or damage which is directly attributable to the revocation or modification.[4]

It seems that compensation should be assessed as at the date when the order takes effect.[5]

Abortive expenditure. Under this head the claim must relate to expenditure on physical work carried out on the land.[6] Such matters as the cost of leasing the land and raising capital would not be included.[6] Nor would costs incurred in objecting to the revocation order.[7] However, any expenditure incurred in the preparation of plans or in other preparatory matters for the purposes of the work is treated as expenditure incurred in carrying out the work;[8] and for this purpose it is not necessary that work on the land should have been carried out.[9] The expression "preparatory matters" in this context is probably limited to "other matters *ejusdem generis* with plans and . . . directly associated with physical work on the site".[10] "Clearly the cost of general inquiries before the stage is reached when a specific project emerges as likely to be successful should be ruled out, but thereafter . . . the test to be applied is whether the preparatory matters . . . are such that without

---

[1] Under the Town and Country Planning Act 1971, s. 87(1) or (3).

[2] See, e.g., *Blow and Blow* v *Norfolk County Council* (1965), 16 P & CR 342 LT at p. 345. Although a section 51 order, unlike an enforcement notice, involves compensation (see p. 421, *infra*), the compensation is unlikely to be more than minimal if the use or works can be shown to have been unlawful. The section 51 order has the advantage that the authority can use it to grant permission for some alternative development without having to wait for an application: see note 4, p. 415, *supra*. The authority (unlike the Secretary of State) has no corresponding power to grant permission in conjunction with an enforcement notice. Thus section 51 orders may be a flexible and convenient means of discontinuing unlawful uses of land. One drawback is that the question of unlawfulness or the extent of any liability to compensation will not normally be determined until after the order has been confirmed.

[3] For assessment of compensation see also p. 446, *infra*.

[4] Town and Country Planning Act 1971, s. 164(1). Note that in certain cases compensation is repayable on subsequent development: See p. 421, *infra*.

[5] I.e., the date of confirmation, or if the order takes effect without confirmation, the end of the specified period after publication under s. 46: see p. 413, *supra*. This was the date taken in *Hobbs (Quarries) Ltd.* v *Somerset County Council* (1975), 20 P & CR 286 LT, and it is consistent with the general principle (see *Birmingham Corpn* v *West Midland Baptist Trust*, [1970] AC 874) that compensation should be assessed as at the date at which the loss is incurred.

[6] *Southern Olympia Ltd.* v *West Sussex County Council* (1952), 3 P & CR 60 LT.

[7] *Evans* v *Cheshire County Council* (1952), 3 P & CR 50 LT, at p. 56.

[8] Town and Country Planning Act 1971, s. 164(2).

[9] *Holmes* v *Bradfield RDC*, [1949] 2 KB 1; [1949] 1 All ER 381 DC.

[10] *Southern Olympia Limited* v *West Sussex County Council supra* at p. 67, and see *Evans* v *Cheshire County Council* note 7, *supra*, at p. 57.

them an architect would lack the necessary information to carry out his instructions".[1]

Except for expenditure on plans or other preparatory matters, the work must not have been carried out before the grant of planning permission.[2] Furthermore, it is likely that a claim for work carried out after the grant of permission would be disallowed if it is not carried out in accordance with the permission, for example if detailed approval is required before work is commenced and has not been obtained.[3] Otherwise the claim may be made for any expenditure which has actually been incurred even though the work could have been done more cheaply.[4] However, credit must be given for such value derived from the work as is not affected by the revocation or modification.[5] It appears to be irrelevant that the expenditure was incurred after the making of the revocation order, provided it is incurred before the order takes effect.[6] Until then the owner has no choice but to proceed on the basis that the permission is still effective, since, if he stops work pending a decision on the revocation order and it is then not confirmed, there is no right to compensation for the delay.[7]

Other loss or damage. Provided the loss is "directly attributable" to the revocation or modification, there is no limitation on the categories of loss for which compensation may be claimed. Thus the claim may be for depreciation in the value of the relevant land caused by the revocation[8] or modification[9] of the permission. Such depreciation may include not only the loss of the value inherent in the permission itself, but also the loss of the prospect of further permissions which might have been expected to follow if that permission had not been revoked.[10] In calculating depreciation in the value of land it is to be assumed that planning permission would be granted for development of any class specified in the 8th Schedule to the Act.[11] Thus the claim will represent the difference between, on the one hand, the value of the land with the benefit not only of the relevant permission but also of an assumed

[1] *Evans* v *Cheshire County Council, supra,* at p. 57. Thus in that case it was held that the claim could include under this head "proper recompense for [the claimants'] time and out-of-pocket expenses incurred in collecting all the information necessary to the submission of a planning application". It was also held to include legal costs in connection with a conditional contract to purchase, but this is doubtful: see the *Southern Olympia* case, note 6, *supra.*

[2] Town and Country Planning Act 1971, s. 164(3).

[3] In that case the work would be "unlawful"; see *LTS Print and Supply Services Ltd* v *London Borough Council of Hackney* (1975), 31 P & CR 133 CA. The section must be construed as applying only to work lawfully carried out: cf. *Glamorgan County Council* v *Carter*, [1963] 1 WLR 1.

[4] *Evans* v *Cheshire County Council, supra,* at p. 55.

[5] See *ibid,* at p. 59.

[6] Whether on confirmation by the Secretary of State under s. 45(3) or as an unopposed order under s. 46.

[7] See *K and B Metals Ltd.* v *Birmingham City Council*, [1976] JPL 760 LT, a case relating to a discontinuance order. There is no provision corresponding to the Acquisition of Land (Authorisation Procedure) Act 1946, 2nd Schedule, para. 8, which requires the exclusion of value attributable to work done with a view to increased compensation: see p. 69, *ante.*

[8] See e.g., *Upperton* v *Hampshire County Council* (1965), 16 P & CR 333.

[9] See e.g., *Wilson* v *West Sussex County Council*, [1963] 2 QB 764.

[10] See *Laing* v *Buckinghamshire County Council* (1960), 11 P & CR 114.

[11] Town and Country Planning Act 1971, s. 164(4). For the full terms of the 8th Schedule see the *Appendix, post.* For these purposes the application of the 8th Schedule is subject to the modifications specified in the Town and Country Planning Act 1971, s. 278 (in particular the limitations contained in Sch. 18: see p. 458, *post*).

permission for 8th Schedule development, and, on the other hand, its value without the relevant permission but still with the assumed permission for 8th Schedule development.

Since the claim is for loss or damage sustained by the claimant and is not confined to damage referable to the particular land, it may include loss in respect of other land owned by the claimant which is directly attributable to the revocation.[1] A claim may also be based in appropriate circumstances on the loss of prospective profits which would have accrued from the implementation of the permission.[2] Such a claim may be disallowed if it is too speculative or remote,[3] but the mere fact that the business has not been commenced at the time of the revocation should not rule out a claim if in the circumstances the extent of the likely loss can be adequately established.[4] On the other hand, in so far as the anticipation of increased profits is reflected in the value of the land it will be compensated in the claim for depreciation of the land, and it cannot be separately claimed under the heading of loss of profits.[5] Thus in *Oxshott Garages Ltd. v Esher Urban District Council*[6] the claim related to the revocation of a planning permission granted to an established garage to develop adjoining land as a petrol station. A claim based on the prospect of increased petrol sales was disallowed since this would be reflected in the claim for depreciation in the value of the land. On the other hand, the established car showroom business would also have become more convenient and profitable on the removal of the existing petrol pump to the new site. A claim in respect of this element was allowed since it would not have been reflected in the value of the new petrol station site. In *Hobbs (Quarries) Ltd. v Somerset County Council*[7] it was held that a claim in respect of the revocation of a permission for working a quarry would be based on loss of profits *as an alternative* to a claim for depreciation in the value of the land, because there was no evidence that there was another quarry available to be bought at market value which could have been used to earn the same profit.[8] It appears therefore that the ordinary basis of the claim will be for the depreciation of the land, and this will be assumed to reflect any prospect of increased profits, unless there are special circumstances which make that assumption unrealistic.

Special considerations apply to a claim in respect of mineral operations. In such cases no claim may be entertained in respect of build-

---

[1] Such a claim would be assessed in the same way as a claim for injurious affection: cf. Compulsory Purchase Act 1965, s. 7, and see Chap. 8.

[2] *Hobbs (Quarries) Ltd.* v *Somerset County Council* (1975), 30 P & CR 286 LT; *Oxshott Garages Ltd.* v *Esher UDC*, [1964] RVR 440 LT; cf. *Bollans* v *Surrey County Council* (1968), 20 P & CR 745 LT.

[3] See *Halford* v *Oxfordshire County Council* (1951), 2 P & CR 358 LT distinguished in *Bollans* v *Surrey County Council*, *supra*.

[4] *Hobbs (Quarries) Ltd.* v *Somerset County Council*, *supra*.

[5] *Collins* v *Feltham UDC*, [1937] 4 All ER 189; *Wimpey & Co. Ltd.* v *Middlesex County Council*, [1938] 3 All ER 781; applied in *Oxshott Garages Ltd.* v *Esher UDC*, *supra*. Cf. *D. McEwing & Sons Ltd* v *Renfrew County Council* (1959), 11 P & CR 306, 311.

[6] [1964] RVR 440.

[7] (1975) 30 P & CR 286 LT.

[8] A similar argument was adopted in *Bollans* v *Surrey County Council*, *supra*.

ings, plant or machinery unless the claimant can prove that he is unable to use them except at the loss claimed.[1]

(b) Development Order restrictions

Compensation may be payable where a permission granted by a development order is withdrawn.[2] To establish a claim to compensation three conditions must be fulfilled:

(i) planning permission for development must have been granted by a development order;

(ii) the permission must have been withdrawn, either by revocation or amendment of the order, or by the issue of a direction under the Order; and

(iii) an application must have been made for planning permission for the same development and have been refused or granted subject to conditions other than those imposed by the development order permission.[3]

Compensation cannot be claimed under this provision in relation to permission for the development of operational land of statutory undertakers[4] or for the imposition of conditions pursuant to an industrial development certificate or office development permit.[5] In practice the most common situation in which a claim to compensation is likely to arise is where a direction is made restricting the scope of a general permission granted by a development order.[6] This power has been frequently used, for example, to restrict the general permission for agricultural buildings[7] in areas of scenic importance.[8] In such a case a claim for compensation will arise if, following the direction, permission is refused or granted conditionally for a development which would previously have been within the scope of the development order permission. It should be noted, however, that for the claim to be established the circumstances must have been such that advantage could have been taken of the development order permission before the direction was made. Otherwise it cannot be said that permission was ever granted for the particular development and the first of the conditions set out above would not be fulfilled. Thus, for example, if the particular land only began to be used as an agricultural holding after the making of the direction it would never have qualified for the unrestricted permission granted by Class VI of the order, and compensation cannot be claimed for its withdrawal.

Although the right to compensation most commonly arises following the making of a direction under the development order, it may also arise out of the amendment or revocation of the order itself.[9] Since the

---

[1] Town and Country Planning (Minerals) Regulations 1971, SI 1971 No. 756, reg. 5.

[2] See p. 414, *supra.*

[3] Town and Country Planning Act 1971, s. 165(1).

[4] *Ibid*, s. 165(3).

[5] *Ibid*, s. 165(4). A condition imposed by an industrial development certificate or office development permit is automatically included in the subsequent permission: *ibid*, ss. 71, 82.

[6] Under the Town and Country Planning (General Development) Order 1977, Art. 4(1): SI 1977 No. 289.

[7] *Ibid*, Class VI.

[8] See Ministry of Housing and Local Government Circular 39/67, paras. 3–6.

[9] See p. 414, *supra.*

enactment of the corresponding provisions of the Town and Country Planning Act 1947, the General Development Order has been amended on a number of occasions, and on four occasions has been revoked and replaced by a completely new order.[1] To give rise to a claim for compensation it appears to be sufficient if the development applied for was at some time in the past permitted by a development order and at that time the circumstances were such that the particular land could have benefited from that permission. If restrictions introduced by subsequent orders or subsequent amendments to the order have removed that permission there is the basis of a claim for compensation.

Although the section refers to the permission being "withdrawn" by a subsequent revocation or amendment,[2] it is thought that this would be apt to cover the situation where the permission as expressed in the development order is limited by the imposition of a further condition. An example of this was the floorspace limitation imposed on agricultural buildings, by amendment in 1960[3] to the then current General Development Order.[4] Previously the permission for agricultural buildings granted by the order was unlimited in relation to floor space.[5] The 1960 amendment added a condition to the permission in effect limiting the floorspace to be provided under the permission to 5,000 square feet every two years. Although this was expressed as a limitation on the existing permission rather than a revocation of the permission itself, it nonetheless operated as a *withdrawal* of permission for any development outside the limit.[6]

The withdrawal of the development order permission for any development does not itself give rise to a claim. This only arises if an application is subsequently made for permission for that development and is refused or is granted subject to conditions. The compensation provisions relating to a revocation or modification order are then applicable as though the development order permission had been granted by the local planning authority under Part III of the Act and had been revoked or modified by the decision on the planning application.[7] The compensation is therefore assessed according to the same principles as outlined above, by reference to values as at the date of the decision of the planning authority. It should be noted that if the development in question also comes within the Town and Country Planning Act 1971, 8th Schedule, Part II, no compensation will be payable under these provisions because it is assumed that permission

---

[1] The following is the sequence of orders: (1) SI 1948 No. 958: operative 1 July 1948; (2) SI 1950 No. 728: operative 22 May 1950; (3) SI 1963 No. 709: operative 1 May 1963; (4) SI 1973 No. 31: operative 1 March 1973; (5) SI 1977 No. 289: operative 29 March 1977.

[2] Town and Country Planning Act 1971, s. 165(1)(b).

[3] Town and Country Planning General Development (Amendment) Order 1960, SI 1960 No. 283.

[4] Town and Country Planning General Development Order 1950, SI 1950 No. 728.

[5] *Ibid*, Class VI 1.

[6] Cf. *Garland v Minister of Housing and Local Government* (1968), 20 P & CR 93, CA, in which it was held that when an extension to a house exceeded the limits set out in Class I of the General Development Order the whole extension was carried out without permission and was not to be regarded merely as in breach of a limitation in the permission.

[7] Town and Country Planning Act 1971, s. 165(2).

would be granted for any development within the 8th Schedule.[1] In such a case the claim should be made under s. 169.[2]

(c) *Section 51 Orders*

Where a section 51 order is made, any person who shows that he has suffered damage in consequence of the order, either by depreciation of the value of his interest in the land, or by being disturbed in his enjoyment of the land, is entitled to compensation.[3] The value of any permission granted by the order must, of course, be taken into account in assessing the depreciation caused by the order, but there is no provision requiring it to be assumed that permission would be granted for development within the 8th Schedule.[4] The claim in respect of disturbance will be assessed in accordance with the ordinary rules applicable to such claims in respect of the acquisition of land.[5] No claim will be allowed in respect of uses or works which are unlawful, for example if they are in breach of a condition in a planning permission.[6] Similarly, if there is doubt about the legality of a use this will be reflected in the market value of the land on which a claim to depreciation is based.[7] The date in relation to which compensation is to be assessed is the date when the order takes effect and a claim is not excluded because it relates to expenditure incurred between the making of the order and its confirmation.[8]

(iii) REGISTRATION AND REPAYMENT OF COMPENSATION

In making a claim for compensation in respect of a revocation or modification order[9] or a development order restriction[10] (but not a discontinuance order)[11] it is important to bear in mind that the compensation may have to be repaid if planning permission for valuable development is subsequently granted and implemented.[12] This may apply whether or not the later permission is the same as that revoked, and even if the value of the later permission is less than the compensation awarded the whole of the compensation may still be repayable. Therefore before making a claim under those provisions it is desirable to consider the likelihood of any planning permission being applied for in the future, and if so, the consequences with regard to repayment of compensation.

The provisions only apply where compensation paid for a revocation

---

[1] *Ibid*, s. 164(4).
[2] As to which see p. 405, *supra*. For an example of such a claim see *Fry* v *Essex County Council* (1962), 11 P & CR 21 LT.
[3] Town and Country Planning Act 1971, s. 170(1).
[4] Cf. s. 164(4) relating to section 45 orders: see p. 417, *supra*.
[5] As to which see Chap. 9.
[6] See, e.g., *Harrison* v *Gloucestershire County Council* (1953), 4 P & CR 99 LT.
[7] See, e.g., *Blow and Blow* v *Norfolk County Council*, [1966] 3 All ER 579, [1967] 1 WLR 1280, CA.
[8] *K and B Metals Ltd.* v *Birmingham City Council*, [1976] JPL 760 LT, distinguishing *Blow and Blow* v *Norfolk County Council*, *supra*.
[9] See p. 416, *supra*.
[10] See p. 419, *supra*.
[11] See *supra*.
[12] Town and Country Planning Act 1971, ss. 166–168.

or modification order or a development order restriction includes an amount in respect of the depreciation in the value of an interest in land exceeding £20.[1] In such a case the local planning authority responsible for the claim[2] must first, so far as is practicable, make apportionment[3] of this amount between different parts of the land, by dividing the land into parts and distributing the amount between those parts according to the extent to which each part is affected by the order or refusal.[4] They must give particulars of the apportionment to the claimant and to any other person with an interest in the land which appears to be substantially affected by the apportionment.[5] The apportionment may be challenged, by any person who is given particulars, or claims that he is substantially affected, by reference to the Lands Tribunal.[6] Notice of reference must be given within 30 days of the issue of the particulars.[7] Any person who has an interest substantially affected by the apportionment may be heard on the reference.[8]

Once the apportionment has been made the authority must give notice to the Secretary of State, specifying both the amount of the compensation for depreciation and its apportionment.[9] He will in turn cause a notice of the fact (referred to as a "compensation notice") to be deposited with the London Borough or County District in which the land is situated,[10] who will then be responsible for registering the notice in the register of local land charges.[11]

The object of the apportionment and registration is to ensure that if any valuable development is carried out on the same land an appropriate proportion of the compensation is repaid.[12] The duty to make a repayment does not arise unless and until it is proposed to carry out "new development" within certain categories. "New development" is any development not included in the 8th Schedule.[13] The categories in respect of which a payment may become due are:

"... *any new development*

(a) ... *which is development of a residential, commercial or industrial character which consists wholly or mainly of the construction of houses, flats, shops or*

---

[1] Town and Country Planning Act 1971, s. 166(1) and (6). The interest must be either the fee simple or a tenancy: *ibid*, s. 166(6). "Tenancy" is defined as in the Landlord and Tenant Act 1954, s. 69(1): Town and Country Planning Act 1971, s. 290(1).

[2] See p. 452, *infra*.

[3] For an example of an apportionment by the Lands Tribunal (under the Town and Country Planning Act 1954, s. 28) see *Eales Johnson v Minister of Housing and Local Government* (1958), 9 P & CR 350.

[4] Town and Country Planning Act 1971, s. 166(1) and (2).

[5] *Ibid*, s. 166(1); "Interest" is again limited to a fee simple or tenancy: s. 166(6).

[6] *Ibid*, s. 166(3), applying with appropriate modifications *ibid*, s. 156(2) and the Town and Country (Compensation and Certificates) Regulations 1974, SI 1974 No. 1242, reg. 7.

[7] SI 1974 No. 1242, reg. 7(1).

[8] *Ibid*, reg. 7(3).

[9] Town and Country Planning Act 1971, s. 166(5).

[10] *Ibid*, s. 158(4), applied by s. 166(5).

[11] *Ibid*, s. 158(5), applied by s. 166(5). See Local Land Charges Rules 1966, SI 1966 No. 579, r. 8.

[12] Town and Country Planning Act 1971, s. 168, applying *ibid*, ss. 159–160, as to which see p. 404, *supra*.

[13] *Ibid*, s. 22(5) and see p. 393, *supra*. Sch. 8 for these purposes is applied subject to the modifications made by s. 278(2) and Sch. 18: see s. 168(4).

office premises, or industrial buildings (including warehouses),[1] *or any combination thereof: or*

(b)   *... which consists in the winning and working of minerals; or*

(c)   *... to which, having regard to the probable value of the development, it is in the opinion of the Secretary of State reasonable that this section should apply".*[2]

In a case which might come within category (c) a developer may protect himself by applying for a certificate from the Secretary of State to the effect that having regard to the probable value of the development the section will not be applied to it.[3]

Before any development within these categories is carried out[4] the recoverable amount must be paid or secured to the satisfaction of the Secretary of State. In the simplest case, that where the land on which the development is to be carried out ("the development")[5] includes the whole of the land comprised in the compensation notice, the recoverable amount will be the whole of the compensation.[6] As already stated, this applies whether or not the new development is the same as that for which compensation was paid, and whether or not the value of the new development is as much as the compensation.

If only part of the land subject to the compensation notice is included in the land on which the new development is to be carried out, the recoverable amount will be so much of the compensation as is attributable to that part. If that part coincides with an area or areas for which a share has been registered under the apportionment, that share will be the recoverable amount. If it is part of an area for which a share has been apportioned, the registered share will be treated as distributed rateably over that area.[6] If there has been no apportionment, the compensation as a whole will be treated as distributed rateably over the whole area subject to the compensation notice, and the recoverable amount will be related to the proportion which the development area bears to the area subject to the compensation notice.[7]

If the development is initiated[8] before the required payment has been made or secured, the Secretary of State may serve a notice on the developer specifying the amount appearing to him to be recoverable, and requiring him to pay it within a specified period of not less than three months.[9] It will be payable as a single capital payment, unless the

---

[1] None of these categories is defined for the purpose of this section, save that "building" is defined as including "any structure or erection, and any part of a building as so defined but ... not ... plant or machinery comprised in a building": *ibid*, s. 290(1).

[2] Town and Country Planning Act 1971, s. 159(2).

[3] *Ibid*, s. 159(3).

[4] This does not apply if the compensation notice relates to compensation paid under a modification order (as to which see p. 413, *supra*) and the only new development is development in accordance with the modified permission: *ibid*, s. 168(1), proviso.

[5] It is not clear how the "development area" is defined, but it is likely to be related to the area defined in the preceding application for planning permission as the site of the development. In cases affected by these provisions the definition of the application site should be made with the terms of the registered apportionment in mind.

[6] Town and Country Planning Act 1971, s. 160(1)(a).

[7] *Ibid*, s. 160(1)(b). See further the illustration of these provisions at p. 397, *supra*.

[8] I.e., in the case of operations when it is "begun": s. 290(5).

[9] Town and Country Planning Act 1971, s. 160(6).

Secretary of State directs that part or all is to be payable in instalments,[1] in which case the payment must be secured as directed by the Secretary of State.[2] The Secretary of State may remit the whole or part of the amount if he is satisfied that, having regard to the value of "any proper development" of the land, no such development is likely to be carried out if the full amount is recoverable.[3]

Once the compensation under the compensation notice has been repaid, no further amount is recoverable in respect of any subsequent development.[4] But if the Secretary of State remits all or part of the amount[5] the amount of the remission will remain payable on subsequent development and the Secretary of State will amend the register if necessary to show the amount outstanding.[6]

Any sum recovered by the Secretary of State under these provisions will be repaid by him to the local planning authority who paid the compensation in the first place, but having deducted any contributions or grants[7] which were made by him towards that compensation.[8]

3 Buildings of special architectural or historic interest and ancient monuments

(i) INTRODUCTORY

Compensation under the Town and Country Planning Act 1971, Part VIII in respect of buildings of special architectural or historic interest may arise in three cases:

(i) Compensation for refusal of consent to alteration or extension of a listed building;[9]

(ii) Compensation for revocation or modification of a listed building consent;[10]

(iii) Compensation for loss or damage caused by service of a listed building preservation notice.[11]

The duty to prepare lists of buildings of special architectural or historic interest (referred to as "listed buildings") is imposed on the Secretary of State by the Town and Country Planning Act 1971, s. 54. It is an offence to execute any works for the demolition of a listed building[12] or for its alteration or extension in any manner which would

---

[1] Town and Country Planning Act 1971, s. 160(5)(a).

[2] *Ibid*, s. 160(5)(b).

[3] *Ibid*, s. 160(2).

[4] *Ibid*, s. 160(3). Note that this may also occur where the land is sold to an authority possessing compulsory purchase powers (see s. 257) and in that case no further repayment is due: *ibid*, s. 160(4).

[5] See note 3, *supra*.

[6] Town and Country Planning Act 1971, s. 160(2), (3).

[7] Under s. 167 or under Part XIII of the 1971 Act, as to which see p. 454, *infra*.

[8] *Ibid*, s. 168(3). If the compensation is recovered in instalments the deductions will be apportioned by the Secretary of State: *ibid*, s. 168(3), proviso.

[9] Town and Country Planning Act 1971, s. 171.

[10] *Ibid*, s. 172.

[11] *Ibid*, s. 173.

[12] In this context ecclesiastical buildings used for ecclesiastical purposes and buildings included in a scheme or order covering, or a list of, ancient monuments for the time being in force under enactments relating to ancient monuments are excluded: see *ibid*, s. 56(1).

affect its character as such,[1] unless those works are authorised by the grant of listed building consent.[2] Listed building consent may be granted by the local planning authority or by the Secretary of State.[3] Like a planning permission,[4] a listed building consent may be revoked or modified by an order made by the local planning authority[5] or by the Secretary of State.[6] If the order is made by the authority it requires confirmation by the Secretary of State,[7] unless it takes effect under an expedited procedure laid down for unopposed orders which do not involve payment of compensation.[8]

Where there is a threat to a building which is not listed but which the local planning authority considers to be of special architectural or historic interest, it may secure interim protection by the service of a "building preservation notice".[9] This will remain in force for six months unless before the end of that period the Secretary of State makes a decision as to whether or not to include the building in the statutory list.[10] While the notice is in force, it is treated for all purposes as a listed building.[11]

For convenience the provisions for compensation in respect of ancient monument control will also be dealt with in this section.[12]

(ii) RIGHT TO COMPENSATION[13]

(a) Refusal of consent to alteration or extension

Where alterations or extensions are made to a listed building development will normally be involved, and planning permission may be required in addition to listed building consent. However, there may be works which require listed building consent, because they affect the character of a building as a building of special architectural or historic interest,[14] but which do not require planning permission. Thus, for instance, works which affect important architectural features in the interior of the building would require listed building consent, but would not involve development unless the external appearance of the building is affected.[15] Alternatively, even if the exterior of the building

---

[1] *Ibid*, s. 55(1).

[2] *Ibid*, s. 55(2)(a). In the case of demolition notice must also be given to the Royal Commission on Historical Monuments (England) or the Royal Commission on Ancient and Historical Monuments (Wales and Monmouthshire) as the case may be; access must be given to the appropriate Commission for the purpose of recording the building: s. 55(2)(b).

[3] For the procedure see *ibid*, Sch. 11, Part I.

[4] See p. 413, *ante*.

[5] Town and Country Planning Act 1971, Sch. 11, para. 10(1).

[6] *Ibid*, para. 11.

[7] *Ibid*, para. 10(2).

[8] *Ibid*, para. 12. This is analogous to the procedure where revocation or modification orders are unopposed, although in such cases compensation may arise: see *ibid*, s. 46, p. 413, *supra*.

[9] *Ibid*, s. 58(1).

[10] *Ibid*, s. 58(3).

[11] *Ibid*, s. 58(4).

[12] See p. 427, *infra*.

[13] For assessment of compensation see also p. 446, *infra*, and for procedure see p. 448, *infra*.

[14] See p. 424, *supra*.

[15] Town and Country Planning Act 1971, s. 22(2)(a).

is affected the works may not require a specific planning permission because they are permitted by the general development order.[1]

A claim for compensation arises where listed building consent is refused by the Secretary of State, or granted by him subject to conditions,[2] for works of alteration or extension which either do not amount to development or are permitted by a development order.[3] Compensation is payable if it is shown that the value of an interest in the land is less than it would have been if consent had been granted or had been granted unconditionally.[4] For this purpose it is assumed that a subsequent application for the like consent would be determined in the same way, but an undertaking by the Secretary of State to grant some other consent for works to the building must be taken into account.[5] No compensation is payable under this section if a purchase notice is served in respect of the land.[6] A claim may be made in relation to a building protected by a building preservation notice,[7] but it will only be payable if and when the building is in fact listed.[8] If it is not listed compensation will be payable in respect of any loss or damage directly attributable to the effect of the notice.[9]

It may be noted that the right to compensation under this section is similar in many respects to the claim for refusal of planning permission for development within the 8th Schedule.[10] However, the interaction between the two is not entirely satisfactory. For instance, if planning permission and listed building consent are refused for works to a listed building which are not permitted by the General Development Order, no claim will arise under the Town and Country Planning Act, s. 172 in respect of the refusal of listed building consent.[11] On the other hand, although a claim could in theory arise in respect of the refusal of development within Part II of the 8th Schedule,[12] in practice the value of the land is unlikely to be affected by the refusal of permission for works which cannot be carried out without listed building consent. It is difficult to see any logical reason for giving a right to compensation for refusal of listed building consent in cases where planning permission is granted by a development order, and not, for instance, in cases where planning permission is granted on an application[13] but cannot be implemented without listed building consent.

---

[1] E.g., alterations to a dwelling-house permitted by Class I of the Town and Country Planning General Development Order 1977 (SI 1977 No. 289).

[2] Either on appeal or on a reference to him of an application for listed building consent: see Town and Country Planning Act 1971, Sch. 11, paras. 8 and 4 respectively.

[3] *Ibid*, s. 171(1).

[4] *Ibid*, s. 171(2).

[5] *Ibid*, s. 171(3). See the comments on the similar provisions of s. 169(3)(a), (b), at p. 407, notes 8–9.

[6] *Ibid*, s. 171(4). This applies whether the purchase notice is a listed building purchase notice (under s. 190) or a purchase notice served in respect of the refusal (s. 180) or revocation of planning permission (s. 188). For a discussion of purchase notices generally see pp. 114, *et seq*, *ante*.

[7] See p. 425, *supra*.

[8] Town and Country Planning Act 1971, s. 173(2).

[9] *Ibid*, s. 173(3).

[10] I.e. under *ibid*, s. 169, as to which, see p. 405, *supra*.

[11] See *ibid*, s. 172(1)(a).

[12] I.e., under *ibid*, s. 169.

[13] In principle there is no difference between a permission granted by a development order, and one granted under a development order on a specific application: see *ibid*, s. 24(2).

(b) Revocation or modification of listed building consent

The provisions for compensation in respect of an order revoking or modifying a listed building consent[1] are similar to those relating to revocation or modification of a planning permission.[2] Compensation is payable for loss or damage arising out of expenditure on abortive works[3] or which is otherwise directly attributable to the revocation or modification.[4] Apart from work on plans and similar preparatory matters[5] no compensation is payable in respect of works carried out before the grant of permission.[6]

(c) Loss or damage caused by service of a building preservation notice

As noted above,[7] a building preservation notice is a means by which interim protection can be secured for a listed building pending a decision by the Secretary of State whether or not to include it in the statutory list. The protection cannot last longer than six months.[8] If, within that time, the building is listed, no compensation is payable. However, if the six months expires without the building being listed, any person who had an interest in the land at the time when the notice was served is entitled to compensation in respect of any loss or damage directly attributable to the effect of the notice.[9] Such a claim may include a sum payable in respect of any breach of contract caused by the necessity of discontinuing or countermanding works to the building.[10]

(iii) ANCIENT MONUMENTS

(a) Introductory

Ancient monuments are protected by a separate system of control operated by the Secretary of State under the Ancient Monuments Acts 1913 to 1953.[11] The expression "ancient monument" is widely defined.[12] It includes, but is not limited to, monuments which were specified in the Schedule to the Ancient Monuments Protection Act 1882 and those listed under the Ancient Monuments Consolidation and Amendment Act 1913, s. 12.[13] A monument may be any "building or structure or other work whether above or below the surface of the land ... and any cave or excavation".[14] A monument is an ancient monument if in the opinion of the Secretary of State it is "of a like character"

[1] *Ibid*, s. 172.
[2] See p. 416, *supra*, and the notes thereto which apply *mutatis mutandis* to claims under *ibid*, s. 172.
[3] *Ibid*, s. 172(1)(a).
[4] *Ibid*, s. 172(1)(b).
[5] *Ibid*, s. 172(2).
[6] *Ibid*, s. 172(3).
[7] See p. 425, *supra*.
[8] See p. 425, *supra*.
[9] Town and Country Planning Act 1971, s. 173(3).
[10] *Ibid*, s. 173(4).
[11] This is the collective title given to what remains of the Ancient Monuments Consolidation and Amendment Act 1913, the Ancient Monuments Act 1931 and the Historic Buildings and Ancient Monuments Act 1953: see the 1953 Act, s. 22(2).
[12] Ancient Monuments Act 1931, s. 15(1).
[13] *Ibid*, s. 15(2)(b)(i), (ii).
[14] *Ibid*, s. 15(1)(a). Ecclesiastical buildings for the time being used for ecclesiastical purposes are excluded: *ibid*.

to a scheduled or listed ancient monument, or if in his opinion its preservation is a matter of public interest "by reason of the historic, architectural, traditional, artistic or archaeological interest attaching thereto".[1]

There may be an overlap with listed building control since a building may qualify both for listing under the Town and Country Planning Act and also for scheduling under the Ancient Monuments Acts. However, in practice most listed buildings are occupied, whereas the great majority of listed ancient monuments are archaeological sites, ruins or structures for which there is no present-day use.[2]

The Secretary of State has a duty to prepare and publish lists of ancient monuments.[3] Before listing any monument he must serve a notice of intention to list on the owner and occupier.[4] Anyone who is served with a notice of intention to list or with notice that a building is already listed[5] must give to the Secretary of State three months' notice before carrying out any work for the purpose of demolishing, removing or repairing any part of the monument or of making any alterations or additions to it.[6] This period gives the Secretary of State an opportunity to serve an "Interim preservation notice".[7] If such a notice is served, it becomes an offence to demolish or alter the monument without the written consent of the Secretary of State.[8] An interim preservation notice lasts at the most for 21 months.[9] If more lasting protection is required for a monument in relation to which an interim preservation notice is in force a "preservation order" may be made by the Secretary of State,[10] following a procedure which provides for objections from interested persons to be considered[11] and for special parliamentary procedure.[12] Once a preservation order takes effect the monument is permanently[13] protected against demolition or alteration without the consent of the Secretary of State.[14]

If a monument which is subject to an interim preservation notice or a preservation order appears to the Secretary of State to be liable to fall into decay due to neglect, he may make a "guardianship order", constituting himself the guardian of the monument.[15] No special procedure is laid down for making such an order and there is no provision

---

[1] Ancient Monuments Act 1931, s. 15(1)(b)(iii).

[2] See Department of the Environment Circular 23/77, para. 21.

[3] Ancient Monuments Consolidation and Amendment Act 1913, s. 12(1).

[4] Ancient Monuments Act 1931, s. 6(1).

[5] *Ibid*, s. 6(5).

[6] *Ibid*, s. 6(2).

[7] Historic Buildings and Ancient Monuments Act 1953, s. 10.

[8] *Ibid*, s. 12(1).

[9] *Ibid*, s. 10(3).

[10] *Ibid*, s. 11(1).

[11] *Ibid*, Sch. The procedure is similar to that applying to confirmation of compulsory purchase orders: (see p. 34, *ante*) except that if the order is confirmed by Act of Parliament it may be challenged in the High Court by an aggrieved person who claims to have been substantially prejudiced by a failure to comply with the statutory requirements: *ibid*, Sch., para. 5(1), and cf. p. 52, *ante*.

[12] Historic Buildings and Ancient Monuments Act 1953, s. 11(1). For special parliamentary procedure see p. 51, *ante*.

[13] Unless the order is revoked: *ibid*, s. 11(2).

[14] *Ibid*, s. 12(1).   [15] *Ibid*, s. 12(5).

for objections to be considered. Once the order is made the Secretary of State takes on the duty of maintaining the monument, and he has wide powers to do whatever is necessary for its maintenance and for its proper control and management, including the right to access and the right to open up the monument or make excavations.[1]

(b) Right to Compensation

It will be noted that the mere listing of an ancient monument imposes no restrictions apart from the requirement for notice of any works to be given. This contrasts with the listed building procedure under which it is an offence to carry out works to a building as soon as it is included in the statutory list.[2] The compensation provisions are also more favourable to owners of ancient monuments than of listed buildings. As has been seen,[3] the latter have very limited rights to compensation for the loss caused by the listing.[4] In the case of an ancient monument, however, any person who has an interest in the whole or part of the monument is entitled to compensation payable by the Secretary of State[5] if his interest is injuriously affected by the service of an interim preservation notice or by the coming into operation of a preservation order,[6] or if he suffers damage or incurs expenditure in respect of his interest in consequence of the refusal or grant subject to conditions of a consent required because of the notice or order.[7]

The right is to receive "such compensation as may be appropriate in the circumstances".[8] Where a preservation order is made, any question as to the right to compensation or its assessment in respect of both the order itself and the superseded interim preservation notice, is determined in accordance with the provisions of the preservation order.[9] Where no order is made the compensation due in respect of the interim preservation notice is to be determined in default of agreement by the Lands Tribunal "as may appear to the Tribunal to be just".[10]

From the wording of these provisions it appears that a claim cannot be made until either a preservation order has been made or the interim preservation notice has lapsed through revocation or the expiration of the 21-month period. Until that time it is not known whether the claim is to be determined in accordance with the provisions of a preservation order or not.

In assessing compensation normally it will be reasonable to assume that the effect of the making of a preservation order will be to secure the monument permanently against substantial demolition or alteration,

---

[1] *Ibid*, s. 12(5), applying Ancient Monuments Consolidation and Amendment Act 1913, s. 4, and Ancient Monuments Act 1931, s. 3.

[2] See p. 424, *supra*.

[3] See p. 426, *supra*.

[4] The loss in value may be very substantial: see, e.g., *Amalgamated Investment and Property Co. Ltd.* v *John Walker and Sons Ltd*, [1976] JPL 308.

[5] Historic Buildings and Ancient Monuments Act 1953, s. 13(4).

[6] *Ibid*, s. 12(2)(a).

[7] *Ibid*, s. 12(2)(b).

[8] *Ibid*, s. 12(2).

[9] *Ibid*, s. 12(3)(a). For an example of such provision made by a preservation order, see *Hoveringham Gravels Ltd.* v *Secretary of State*, [1975] 1 QB 754 at p. 762.

[10] Historic Buildings and Ancient Monuments Act 1953, s. 12(3)(b).

even though the Secretary of State has power to grant consent for such works.[1] Thus in *Hoveringham Gravels Ltd.* v *Secretary of State*[2] compensation was awarded on the basis that the making of the preservation order took away permanently the right to exploit the land. It was not thought necessary to wait until consent had in fact been refused. Even where compensation has been claimed and paid in respect of the making of the order, it seems that a further claim could be made on a specific refusal of consent to works. However, in considering what compensation is "appropriate in the circumstances"[3] the Tribunal will no doubt take into account the basis on which the compensation for the preservation order was assessed. If it was based on the assumption that no exploitation would ever be allowed, it is difficult to envisage a further claim being accepted for the refusal of consent for some form of exploitation.

It is possible that consent might be granted to works which do not seriously prejudice the historic value of the building, but subject to conditions requiring expenditure. In that case a claim based on the expenditure could be made.[4] If compensation is paid in respect of a preservation order on the basis of permanent sterilisation and consent is subsequently granted for some form of exploitation, there is no provision for requiring any repayment.[5]

In practice the value of this right to compensation will depend largely on what, apart from the ancient monuments control, could be done with the land without planning permission. In the *Hoveringham Gravels* case[6] a claim was made in relation to a site comprising an iron-age fort which was listed as an ancient monument. The site contained valuable deposits of gravel. A preservation order was made and the owners claimed compensation based on the value of the land for gravel-working. Planning permission for gravel-working had in fact been refused on the ground that the site was an ancient monument which ought to be permanently preserved. The Court of Appeal held in these circumstances that the loss of the right to work the land for gravel was caused by the refusal of planning permission rather than by the making of the preservation order.[7] The ground of refusal would have been perfectly proper even if the preservation order had not been made,[8] and on the basis of the history of the case there was no reason to anticipate that planning permission would in those circumstances have been granted.[9] Accordingly compensation was awarded of £100,[10] based on

---

[1] Historic Buildings and Ancient Monuments Act 1953, s. 12(1).
[2] [1975] 1 QB 754.
[3] Historic Buildings and Ancient Monuments Act 1953, s. 12(2).
[4] *Ibid*, s. 12(2)(b).
[5] Cf. the position when a planning permission is revoked: p. 421, *supra*.
[6] See note 2, *supra*.
[7] *Hoveringham Gravels Ltd.* v *Secretary of State*, [1975] 1 QB 754 at p. 763 A–E per Lord Denning MR.
[8] See *ibid*, at p. 771 per Scarman LJ applying Lord Reid's dictum in *Westminster Bank Ltd.* v *Minister of Housing and Local Government* [1971] AC 508, 529.
[9] *Hoveringham Gravels Ltd.* v *Secretary of State*, [1975] 1QB 754 at p. 772 per Scarman LJ.
[10] The Lands Tribunal had awarded £57,000 on the basis of use for gravel-working: see (1974) 14 RVR 153.

the agricultural uses to which the land could have been put without planning permission,[1] or for which permission would have been available under the General Development Order.[2]

If planning permission has in fact been granted for works to the monument, the value of the permission can be taken into account since the preservation order will have been the sole cause of sterilisation. In other cases, although in theory it will be open to a claimant to attempt to show that planning permission would have been granted,[3] it is difficult to envisage circumstances in which such an attempt would succeed in practice. Thus the claim will generally be limited to such value as could be realised without the need to apply for planning permission.[4] In the case of buildings this may depend on whether or not the building could be demolished without planning permission. The demolition of a house is not normally regarded as development,[5] but the demolition of a fort or castle would almost certainly be an engineering operation and therefore require permission.[6] In the former case, but not the latter, compensation could be assessed on the basis of what could be done on the cleared site.

Compensation is also payable by the Secretary of State where an interest in the whole or part of an ancient monument is injuriously affected by the making of a guardianship order.[7] If this is made during the currency of a preservation order, compensation will be determined in accordance with the provisions of the guardianship order itself. If the guardianship order is made while an interim preservation notice is in force, compensation will be assessed either under the subsequent preservation order, if one is made, or otherwise in default of agreement, by the Lands Tribunal on such terms "as may appear to the Tribunal to be just".[8] Compensation under this head will not, of course, include damage already compensated for under the interim preservation notice or the preservation order. However, if additional injurious affection is caused by the control exercised by the Secretary of State or, for

---

[1] Town and Country Planning Act 1971, s. 22(2)(e).

[2] See the Town and Country Planning General Development Order 1977 (SI 1977 No. 289) Sch. 1, Classes VI–VII. In fact by implementing these permissions the owners could have destroyed the value of the site as an ancient monument and therefore have removed the only reason for refusing permission for gravel-working (see [1975] 1 QB at p. 760–761). However, the Court of Appeal rejected the argument that the compensation should for this reason include loss of the right to commercial exploitation. This was because (per Lord Denning at pp. 760–761) the latter was not directly "caused by" the order, or because (per Orr LJ at p. 767) in practice the General Development Order permission would have been taken away by an Article 4 direction (as to which see p. 414, *supra*). The second reason is with respect unsatisfactory, because if an Article 4 direction had been made, compensation would have been payable under the Town and Country Planning Act 1971, s. 165, for any loss "directly attributable" to the direction (see p. 419, *supra*). Therefore a similar argument could have arisen that this compensation should be based on value for gravel-working. The Court would ultimately have been driven back to Lord Denning's imprecise but convenient test of remoteness.

[3] See [1975] 1 QB 754 at p. 772D per Scarman LJ.

[4] I.e., matters which either do not constitute development (Town and Country Planning Act 1971, s. 22) or which are permitted by the General Development Order.

[5] See *Iddenden v Secretary of State*, [1972] 1 WLR 1433: [1972] 3 All ER 883.

[6] See *Coleshill and District Investment Co. Ltd. v Minister of Housing and Local Government*, [1969] 2 All ER 525 [1969] 1 WLR 746.

[7] Historic Buildings and Ancient Monuments Act 1953, ss. 12(6), 13(4).

[8] *Ibid*, s. 12(6)(a)–(c).

example, by excavations carried out by him,[1] this would be a proper basis for a claim for compensation.

4 Trees

(i) INTRODUCTORY

A tree preservation order is an order made by a local planning authority[2] with a view to protecting trees or woodlands in their area in the interests of amenity.[3] Normally the order requires the confirmation of the Secretary of State.[4] Such an order may prohibit the cutting down, topping, lopping, uprooting, wilful damage or wilful destruction of trees except with the consent of the local planning authority, and it may also make provision for securing replanting of any part of a woodland which is felled in the course of forestry operations.[5] The Act only provides the framework of the system of protection; the detail is filled in by the tree preservation order itself, the form of which must follow or substantially follow[6] the form of order set out in the regulations made under the Act.[7]

The prescribed form of order makes provision for applications for consents required by the order to be made to the local planning authority, who may grant or refuse consent, or grant it subject to conditions.[8] There is a right of appeal to the Secretary of State against the authority's decision or failure to make a decision, and a consent once granted may be revoked or modified by an order analogous to a section 45[9] order.[10] When a consent is granted to fell any part of a woodland, the authority must normally give a direction specifying its requirements for replanting.[11] However, such a direction is not given if the consent is for thinning in the interests of sound silvicultural practice, or is granted for the purpose of enabling development to be carried out in accordance with a planning permission already granted; and in other cases the authority may dispense with the replanting requirement with the approval of the Secretary of State.[11]

---

[1] See Ancient Monuments Act 1931, s. 3(1).

[2] The Secretary of State has a reserve power to make an order under the Town and Country Planning Act 1971, s. 276(1)(c).

[3] Town and Country Planning Act 1971, s. 60(1). See generally the Memorandum on the Preservation of Trees and Woodlands (2nd Edition 1966) issued by the Ministry of Land and Natural Resources. There is no statutory definition of a "tree" or a "woodland". However, it has been suggested that in this context "... in woodland a tree should be something of 7 or 8 inches in diameter" (*Kent County Council* v *Bachelor*, [1976] JPL 254, per Lord Denning MR).

[4] Town and Country Planning Act 1971, s. 60(4).

[5] *Ibid*, s. 60(1)(a), (b).

[6] SI 1969 No. 17, reg. 4(1).

[7] Town and Country Planning (Tree Preservation Order) Regulations 1969, SI 1969 No. 17 as amended by SI 1975 No. 148 (made under the Town and Country Planning Act 1971, s. 60(5)).

[8] Town and Country Planning (Tree Preservation Order) Regulations 1969, Sch., Form of Order, Art. 3.

[9] I.e., Town and Country Planning Act 1971, s. 45, as to which see p. 413, *supra*.

[10] *Ibid*, Sch., Form of Order Sch. 3, applying the relevant provisions of the Town and Country Planning Act 1962, Part III.

[11] Town and Country Planning (Tree Preservation Order) Regulations 1969, Sch., Form of Order, Art. 6.

This system of control must be looked at in conjunction with the control exercised by the Forestry Commissioners under the Forestry Act 1967. A felling licence granted by the Commissioners is generally required for the felling of growing trees, but this is subject to a number of important exceptions.[1] For example, a felling licence is not required for trees growing in an orchard, garden, churchyard or public open space.[2] Nor is a licence needed if the aggregate cubic content of the trees felled and that of the trees sold in any quarter do not exceed 825 cubic feet and 150 cubic feet respectively.[3]

Where a tree subject to a tree preservation order is proposed to be felled in circumstances such that a felling licence is also required, the local planning authority cannot consider the matter until an application has been made to the Forestry Commissioners for a felling licence.[4] There are three possible courses open to the Forestry Commissioners.[5] They may refuse a licence, in which case that will be the end of the matter, and the local planning authority will have no jurisdiction in the matter.[6] Secondly, they may propose to grant a licence, in which case they must notify the local planning authority.[7] If the authority object the matter is referred to the Secretary of State,[8] who will deal with it as though it were an application for a consent under a tree preservation order.[9] If he grants consent, then the requirement for a felling licence is dispensed with.[10]

The alternative is that the Commissioners, "having presumably decided that no forestry considerations are involved,[11] may, without expressing a view, refer the application to the local planning authority for them to deal with.[12] In this case the authority will deal with it as though it were an application for a consent under a tree preservation order,[13] whereupon the requirement for a felling licence will cease to apply so long as the tree preservation order remains in force, whether or not the authority grant the particular application.[14]

(ii) RIGHT TO COMPENSATION[15]

A claim to compensation under these provisions may arise in three cases:

    (i) where a felling licence is refused;

---

[1] Forestry Act 1967, s. 9(2)–(4).
[2] Ibid, s. 9(2)(b).
[3] Ibid, s. 9(3)(b).
[4] Ibid, s. 15(5).
[5] See the discussion of the corresponding provisions of the Forestry Act 1951, s. 13, in Cardigan Timber Co. v Cardiganshire County Council (1957), 9 P & CR 158 LT at p. 181.
[6] Forestry Act 1967, s. 15(1)(b).
[7] Ibid, s. 15(6).
[8] Ibid, s. 15(2)(a).
[9] Ibid, s. 15(2)(a) and Sch. 3.
[10] Ibid, s. 15(2)(b).
[11] Cardigan Timber Co. case (supra) at p. 182.
[12] Forestry Act 1967, s. 15(1)(b).
[13] Ibid, s. 15(3)(a) and Sch. 3.
[14] Ibid, s. 15(3)(b).
[15] For procedure, see p. 448, infra.

(ii) where consent under a tree preservation order is refused, granted subject to conditions, or revoked or modified;

(iii) where a replanting direction is made which frustrates the commercial use of the land for growing timber or forest products.

(a) Refusal of felling licence

If a felling licence is refused and the quality of the timber deteriorates as a result, compensation is payable by the Forestry Commissioners to the owner of the trees under the Forestry Act 1967.[1] The measure of compensation is the depreciation, if any, in the value of the trees which is attributable to the deterioration in quality of the timber resulting from the refusal.[2] After a licence is refused, claims may continue to be made from time to time in respect of continuing deterioration,[3] but no claim may be made for deterioration which occurred more than ten years before the date of the claim.[4] When the trees are eventually felled, any claim in respect of previous deterioration must be made within one year of the felling.[5] In calculating compensation the trees are valued on the basis of prices current at the date of the claim.[6] No account is to be taken of deterioration which is attributable to neglect of the trees after the refusal of the licence.[7] If, having refused a licence, the Commissioners subsequently give notice to the owner that they are prepared to grant a licence, the claim will be limited to deterioration which occurred before the giving of the notice.[8]

It will be noted that the claim is limited to the effects of physical deterioration in the quality of the timber. It cannot include any claim for loss caused by a fall in market prices.[9] Nor apparently will it include loss due to extraneous causes, such as storm or fire.[10] If the claim is in respect of deterioration up to the date of the claim, the measure will be the difference between the value of the trees having regard to the quality of the timber at the date of the claim and the value they would have had at that date if the quality of the timber had not deteriorated since the date of the refusal. If the period for which compensation can be claimed does not extend up to the date of the claim—for instance if the trees have been felled or if a notice has been given indicating that a licence would be granted—then the measure will be based on a comparison of the quality of the timber at the beginning and at the end of that period, but the valuation will be based on prices current at the date of the claim.[11]

---

[1] Forestry Act 1967, s. 10(4). This does not apply in the exceptional case where a licence for felling in accordance with an approved plan is refused for reasons of national interest and the owner is enabled to require the Commissioners to purchase: see *ibid*, s. 14.

[2] *Ibid*, s. 11(1).

[3] *Ibid*, s. 11(3).

[4] *Ibid*, s. 11(3)(a).

[5] *Ibid*, s. 11(3)(b).

[6] *Ibid*, s. 11(4)(b).

[7] *Ibid*, s. 11(4)(a).

[8] *Ibid*, s. 11(5). For an example of a claim in these circumstances, see *Winders* v *Forestry Commission* (1958), 9 P & CR 500 LT.

[9] *Winders* v *Forestry Commission* (*supra*) at p. 502.

[10] *Cardigan Timber Co.* case (*supra*) at p. 184.

[11] See *Winders* v *Forestry Commission* (*supra*) at p. 504.

(b) Refusal of tree preservation order consent
The Town and Country Planning Act 1971, s. 174, enables provision to
be made in a tree preservation order for payment of compensation on
refusal of consent or grant of consent subject to conditions.

Under the prescribed form of order[1] compensation is payable for loss
or damage suffered in consequence of a refusal of consent or a grant
subject to conditions.[2] For this purpose the revocation or modification
of a consent is treated as a refusal[2] and compensation may accordingly
be claimed. However, the authority may exclude a claim for compensation if, at the same time as making their decision on the application they certify that they are satisfied either that the refusal or
condition is in the interests of good forestry, or, in relation to trees
which are not comprised in woodlands, that they have an outstanding
or special amenity value.[3] Such a certificate may be appealed against to
the Secretary of State in the same way as a refusal of consent.[4] Where a
certificate is given no compensation is payable in respect of the trees
affected by the certificate.[5]

The ambit of the claim is not specifically restricted, as in the case of
the refusal of a felling licence.[6] Nor is it limited to the owner of the trees.
Any person who has suffered loss or damage directly attributable to the
refusal may make a claim. It has been said that the claim is analogous to
a claim in respect of loss or damage attributable to a revocation order.[7]
If the claim is made by the owner he will ordinarily be entitled to loss of
the capital value of the trees.[8] But if the circumstances are such that
ultimately clear-felling will probably be permitted, an award of the
whole capital value may be inappropriate, and the compensation may
be based on loss of profit caused in respect of those trees by the
postponement of felling.[8] The claimant may also have suffered loss of
profits which he would have made from the use of the land following
clearance. Compensation can be paid in respect of such loss provided it
can be satisfactorily proved and is not purely speculative.[9] These
principles will apply where consent is refused under the tree preservation order purely on amenity grounds rather than on forestry
grounds. If it can be shown by the compensating authority that, quite
apart from the tree preservation order, a felling licence would have been
refused on forestry grounds,[10] the proper measure of the loss will, it

[1] Town and Country Planning (Tree Preservation Order) Regulations 1969, SI 1969 No. 17,
Sch.
[2] *Ibid*, Sch., Form of Order, Art. 9.
[3] *Ibid*, Sch., Form of Order, Art. 5.
[4] *Ibid*, Sch., Form of Order, Art. 8 and Sch. 3.
[5] *Ibid*, Sch., Form of Order, Art. 9 proviso.
[6] See p. 434, *supra*.
[7] *Bollans* v *Surrey County County Council* (1968), 20 P & CR 745 LT at p. 754. For compensation for
revocation orders see p. 416, *supra*.
[8] *Cardigan Timber Co.* v *Cardiganshire County Council* (1957), 9 P & CR 158 LT at p. 183.
[9] *Bollans* v *Surrey County Council* (1968), 20 P & CR 745 LT at p. 754, distinguishing *Halford* v
Oxfordshire County Council (1952) 2 P & CR 358 LT.
[10] See p. 433, *supra*. In such cases the Forestry Commissioners could refuse a licence without
referring it to the local planning authority, and if so, a claim would only arise under the Forestry
Act 1967, s. 11. However, they may refer it to the local planning authority even in cases in which
they would refuse a licence.

seems, be the amount which would have been awarded for deterioration under the Forestry Act.[1]

Account must be taken of any compensation which has been previously paid in respect of the same trees under a tree preservation order or under corresponding provisions[2] of previous legislation.[3] Furthermore, if the value of any other land of the owner would have been reduced by the felling of the trees for which consent was refused, that must be taken into account.[4] Costs incurred in contesting the tree preservation order or the refusal of consent will not be allowed as part of the claim.[5]

(c) Replanting requirements

As indicated above,[6] where consent is granted for the felling of part of a woodland the authority must, except in three sets of circumstances,[7] issue a direction specifying the matter in which, and the time within which, the land is to be replanted.[7] Before 1968 no claim could be made for loss or damage arising out of such a direction.[8] However, the Countryside Act 1968[9] introduced a right to compensation where the effect of the direction was to frustrate commercial forestry. This is now reproduced in the Town and Country Planning Act 1971, s. 175.

A claim will only arise if the Forestry Commissioners

    (a) have decided not to make any advance under the Forestry Act 1967[10] in respect of the replanting; and

    (b) have made that decision on the ground that the direction frustrates the use of the woodland area for the growing of timber or other forest products for commercial purposes and in accordance with the rules or practice of good forestry.[11]

The Forestry Commissioners may be required by the claimant to give a certificate stating their decision and the grounds for it.[12] If the requirements for a claim are satisfied, the local planning authority will be liable to pay compensation in respect of any loss or damage caused or incurred in consequence of compliance with the direction.[13]

The purpose of this provision is clearly to ensure that owners are not

---

[1] *Cardigan Timber Co.* case (*supra*) at p. 183.

[2] I.e., either an interim preservation order made under the Town and Country Planning (Interim Development) Act 1943, s. 8, or any provision relating to the preservation of trees or protection of woodlands contained in an operative scheme under the Town and Country Planning Act 1932.

[3] Town and Country Planning (Tree Preservation Order) Regulations 1969, SI 1969 No. 17, Sch., Form of Order, Art. 10(a).

[4] *Ibid*, Art. 10(b).

[5] *Bollans v Surrey County Council* (*supra*) (1968), 20 P & CR 745 LT at p. 756.

[6] P. 432, *ante*.

[7] Town and Country Planning (Tree Preservation Order) Regulations 1969, Sch., Form of Order, Art. 6. The exceptions are (1) where the consent is for silvicultural thinning; (2) where it is granted to enable a planning permission to be implemented; and (3) where the Secretary of State agrees to the requirement being dispensed with: *ibid*.

[8] See Memorandum on the Preservation of Trees and Woodlands, (2nd Edition 1966), *supra*, at para. 20.

[9] Countryside Act 1968, s. 25: see Ministry of Housing and Local Government Circular 44/68.

[10] S. 4, which empowers the Commissioners to make advances by way of grant or loan to owners of land who carry out afforestation including replanting.

[11] Town and Country Planning Act 1971, s. 175(2).

[12] *Ibid*, s. 175(3).

[13] *Ibid*, s. 175(4).

penalised by being required for amenity reasons to carry out planting in a way which is not consistent with commercial forestry practice. Logically, therefore, the compensation should represent the difference between the value of the land as replanted in accordance with the direction and its value as it would have been if replanted in accordance with ordinary commercial practice (in addition to the value of any advance which could reasonably have been expected towards such replanting from the Forestry Commissioners). However, the section does not specifically limit the claim to loss caused by the method of replanting imposed by the direction. Compensation is payable for any loss caused "in consequence of compliance with the direction". This would appear to enable a comparison to be made between the value of the land subject to the direction and its value without any direction and therefore without any replanting requirement. Thus a comparison could be made with its value as cleared land, available, for example, for agriculture.

5 Advertisements

(i) INTRODUCTORY

Control of advertisements[1] is effected by regulations[2] made under the Town and Country Planning Act 1971, s. 63. The regulations apply to all advertisements subject to certain specified exceptions, such as, for example, advertisements displayed on enclosed land and not readily visible from outside,[3] advertisements displayed on vehicles,[4] etc. No advertisement to which the regulations apply may be displayed unless consent has been expressly granted ("express consent") or is deemed to be granted ("deemed consent").[5] The regulations set out a number of circumstances in which express consent is not required and consent is therefore deemed to be granted.[6] In particular, express consent is not required for advertisements falling within six "specified classes".[7] In most of these cases the deemed consent is subject to the power of the local planning authority to discontinue the display by a "discontinuance notice".[8] Additional restrictions, both on deemed consents

[1] An "advertisement" means "any word, letter, model, sign, placard, board, notice, device or representation, whether illuminated or not, in the nature of, and employed wholly or partly for the purposes of advertisement, announcement or direction (excluding any such thing employed wholly as a memorial or as a railway signal) and (without prejudice to the preceding provisions of this definition) includes any hoarding or similar structure used, or adapted for use, for the display of advertisements, and references to the display of advertisements shall be construed accordingly": Town and Country Planning (Control of Advertisements) Regulations 1969, SI 1969 No. 1532, reg. 2(1). The definition in the Act is the same except for the omission of the words "(excluding ... railway signals)": Town and Country Planning Act 1971, s. 290(1).
[2] Town and Country Planning (Control of Advertisements) Regulations 1969, SI 1969 No. 1532, as amended by SI 1972 No. 479, SI 1974 No. 185 and SI 1975 No. 898.
[3] *Ibid*, reg. 3(1)(a).
[4] *Ibid*, reg. 3(1)(c).
[5] *Ibid*, reg. 6(1).
[6] *Ibid*, regs. 6(2), 9–14. Additional restrictions apply in areas of special control: regs. 26–27, see *infra*.
[7] *Ibid*, reg. 13.
[8] *Ibid*, reg. 16.

and on the advertisements for which express consent may be given, apply in "areas of special control".[1] One case in which deemed consent is enjoyed, except in areas of special control,[2] (and subject to the power of discontinuance) is for the continuing display of an advertisement which was being displayed on 1 August 1948,[3] or the continuing use of a site for the display of advertisements which was being so used on that date.[4] This is the only case in which a right to compensation arises on the discontinuance of a display which enjoys deemed consent.

In those cases which do not enjoy deemed consent, express consent must be obtained from the local planning authority or the Secretary of State.[5] Normally consent is granted for a five-year period only.[6] An express consent may be revoked or modified by an order made by the local planning authority[7] subject to confirmation by the Secretary of State.[8] The procedure is similar to that applicable to an opposed revocation order under section 45 of the Act.[9] Where the consent relates to a display involving the carrying out of building or similar operations, the power to revoke or modify[10] must be exercised before the operations have been completed and the order will not affect operations previously carried out.[11] In other cases the power must be exercised before the display is begun.[12]

(ii) RIGHT TO COMPENSATION[13]

The only case in which the Act itself provides for compensation is where, for the purpose of complying with the regulations, works are carried out either:

[1] I.e., areas defined pursuant to the Town and Country Planning Act 1971, s. 63(3)(b) as being "either rural areas or areas other than rural areas which appear to the Secretary of State to require special protection on the grounds of amenity". The procedure and the restrictions are set out in the 1969 regulations, regs. 26–27.

[2] Ibid, reg. 27(1).

[3] The commencement date of the first Control of Advertisement Regulations (SI 1948 No. 1613). See also SI 1969 No. 1532, reg. 11(1).

[4] SI 1969 No. 1532, reg. 11(3), subject to there being no substantial increase in the extent, or alteration in the manner of the use of the site: reg. 11(3)(a).

[5] For the procedure, see SI 1969 No. 1532, regs. 17–22.

[6] SI 1969 No. 1532, reg. 20.

[7] It seems that the Secretary of State may also make such an order under his reserve powers: see the Town and Country Planning Act 1971, s. 276(2)(a), which applies to orders made under the provisions of ibid, s. 45, as applied by regulations under Part IV of the Act (such as SI 1969 No. 1532, reg. 24).

[8] Town and Country Planning (Control of Advertisements) Regulations 1969, reg. 24. The statutory basis for this power is the Town and Country Planning Act 1971, s. 63(2)(c), which authorises the application of the provisions of the Act mentioned in s. 60(2). These provisions include s. 45 (revocation etc. orders), which is applied subject to modifications by reg. 24 (see 1969 regulations, reg. 33(1) and Sch. 4).

[9] See p. 413, supra. There is no provision for an expedited procedure in the case of unopposed orders.

[10] This applies to the making of the order, not its confirmation: see the comments on s. 45(4) at p. 413, supra.

[11] As to operations carried out between the making of the order and its confirmation see p. 417, supra.

[12] Town and Country Planning (Control of Advertisements) Regulations, SI 1969 No. 1532, reg. 23(3).

[13] For procedure, see p. 448, infra.

  (a) for removing an advertisement which was being displayed on
      1 August 1948; or
  for discontinuing the use, for the display of advertisements, of a
  site used for that purpose on that date.[1]

As we have seen,[2] the current regulations only require such removal or
discontinuance either in areas of special control if no express consent is
given,[3] or in other areas if a discontinuance order is made.[4] The
expenses reasonably incurred in carrying out such works may be
recovered on a claim made to the local planning authority.[5] No compensation is payable under this section for any other loss as, for
instance, the depreciation in the value of the site.

  The control of Advertisements Regulations[6] also provide for the
recovery of compensation on the revocation or modification of an
express consent under regulation 24.[7] The statutory basis for the payment of compensation in this case is not clear. The Town and Country
Planning Act 1971, s. 63,[8] enables the regulations to incorporate,
subject to certain exceptions, the provisions of Part III[9] and Part IX[10]
of that Act. Part III includes the provisions relating to the revocation
and modification of planning permissions (ss. 45–46). However, the
provisions relating to compensation for revocation and modification
orders (ss. 164, 166–168) are in Part VIII of the Act, and there is no
express authorisation for any provisions of Part VIII of the Act to be
incorporated in the Control of Advertisement Regulations. Furthermore, it is difficult to argue that the incorporation of s. 45 carried with
it, by implication, the compensation provisions since, in other cases
where it is intended that a section is to apply in such circumstances, the
Act contains specific provision to that effect.[11] Thus, although the 1969
Regulations purport to apply the compensation provisions relating to

---

[1] Town and Country Planning Act 1971, s. 176.
[2] See p. 438, *supra*.
[3] Express consent in areas of special control may only be given in specified circumstances: SI
1969 No. 1532, reg. 27(2).
[4] SI 1969 No. 1532, regs. 11, 16.
[5] Town and Country Planning Act 1971, s. 176.
[6] SI 1969, No. 1532.
[7] SI 1969 No. 1532, reg. 25.
[8] S. 63(2)(c), applying s. 60(2), which makes similar provisions in relation to tree preservation
orders.
[9] S. 60(2)(a) refers to the "provisions of Part III of this Act relating to planning permission and
to applications for planning permission". This wording is derived from the Town and Country
Planning Act 1947, s. 28(1)(c), in which the provisions relating to planning permissions and those
relating to special control (trees, advertisements, etc.) were in the same part of the Act. The latter
provisions are now in Part IV of the 1971 Act and it is not clear which, if any, of the provisions of
Part III are intended to be excluded, apart from those specifically referred to. In any event there is
no difficulty in treating the revocation order provisions as being "provisions ... relating to
planning permission ...".
[10] Part IX contains provisions relating to purchase notices etc.: see p. 119, *ante*.
[11] See, e.g., s. 164(5), which provides that a reference to a section 45 order (as to which see p.
413, *supra*) is to "include a reference to an order under the provisions of that section as applied by
s. 51(2) of this Act" (as to s. 51(2) see note 3 on p. 415, *supra*), and cf. s. 276(2) which refers to
"orders under s. 45 of this Act, *or under the provisions of that section as applied by ... any regulations made
under Part IV of this Act*". A similar wording would be expected in s. 164 if it had been intended to
apply it to s. 45 orders made under the Control of Advertisements Regulations.

section 45 orders,[1] it does not appear that there is any statutory basis for that provision.[2]

Turning to the substance of the compensation provisions of the Regulations (on the assumption that they are *intra vires*), the right given is analogous to the right given by s. 164 in the case of the revocation or modification of a planning permission.[3] If it is shown that any person has incurred expenditure[4] in carrying out, in connection with the display in question, work which is rendered abortive by the revocation or modification, or has otherwise sustained loss or damage which is directly attributable to the revocation or modification, the authority must pay compensation in respect of that expenditure, loss or damage.[5] In this case, however, unlike an order relating to a planning permission, no compensation is payable for loss or damage consisting of the depreciation in value of any interest in the land.[6] Nor is any compensation payable for work carried out before the grant of consent or for any other loss or damage arising out of anything done, or omitted to be done, before the grant of consent, other than expenditure on preparation of plans or similar preparatory works.[7]

The exclusion of compensation for depreciation of the value of land will cause difficulty in practice. Apart from any specific expenditure, the damage will normally consist of the loss of the use of the advertisement or the site during the period for which the consent would have lasted.[8] The most obvious way in which to put a value on the right to such use is to estimate the rent which the market would pay for such a right.[9] However it appears that this will only be appropriate if it can be shown that such a rent would in fact have been received. If the advertisement would in fact have been displayed for the claimants' own purpose, he cannot claim the loss of notional rent as depreciation in the value of the land and his claim will be limited to such other loss as can be satisfactorily proved, notwithstanding the practical difficulty of proving, for instance, the extent of any additional business which would have been attracted by the advertisement.

[1] See Town and Country Planning (Control of Advertisements) Regulations 1969, SI 1969 No. 1532, reg. 33(1) and Sch. 4, applying the Town and Country Planning Act 1962, s. 118 (which corresponded to what is now s. 164 of the Town and Country Planning Act 1971). For provisions relating to compensation on s. 45 orders, see p. 416, *supra*.

[2] Under the corresponding provisions of the Town and Country Planning Act 1947 the compensation provisions (s. 22) were contained in the same part of the Act as those relating to the making of the order (s. 21), and as such were clearly incorporated in the provisions relating to advertisement control (s. 31(1)(c)). However, when the compensation provisions were put into a different part of the 1962 Act (Part VII of that Act) no corresponding adjustment was made to the advertisement provisions (s. 34(2)(c)).

[3] Town and Country Planning Act 1971, s. 164: see p. 416, *supra*.

[4] This may include expenditure incurred in the preparation of plans and other similar preparatory work, whether incurred before or after the grant of the consent: SI 1969 No. 1532, reg. 25(2).

[5] SI 1969 No. 1532, reg. 25(1).

[6] SI 1969 No. 1532, reg. 52(1) proviso. This exclusion is derived from the Town and Country Planning Act 1947, s. 22(1), and has survived in the regulations, notwithstanding the amendment of *ibid*, s. 22 (to include compensation for depreciation) by the Town and Country Planning Act 1954, s. 38 (see now the Town and Country Planning Act 1971, s. 164).

[7] SI 1969 No. 1532, reg. 25(2).

[8] Normally five years from the date of the consent: *ibid*, reg. 20, p. 438, *supra*.

[9] Cf. *Wrotham Park Estate Co. Ltd. v Parkside Homes Ltd.*, [1974] 1 WLR 798, 815.

6 Stop notices

(i) INTRODUCTORY

The means by which authorities can take action to remedy a breach of planning control is the service of an "enforcement notice",[1] which will specify the steps required to remedy the breach, and the time within which they are to be effected. The notice is served on the owner and occupier of the land on which the alleged breach has taken place and on any other person having an interest which is materially affected.[2] The breach in question may involve the carrying out of development without planning permission, that is, the making of a material change in the use of the land or the carrying out of building or other operations;[3] alternatively, it may involve a failure to comply with conditions or limitations imposed on a permission already granted.[4] Where the breach involves the carrying out of operations, or a change in the use of any building to use it as a dwelling-house, the notice must be served within four years of the breach.[5] Otherwise the notice may be served at any time provided the breach occurred since the end of 1963.[6] The notice will not take effect until a date specified in the notice, which must be at least 28 days from the date of service.[7] During that time there is a right of appeal to the Secretary of State against the enforcement notice,[8] and until the appeal is finally determined the operation of the notice is suspended.[9] The grounds on which an appeal may be brought are listed in the Town and Country Planning Act 1971, s. 88(1), under paragraphs (a) to (g), and it is normal to refer to them by the appropriate paragraph letter. They are as follows:

"(a) that planning permission ought to be granted for the development to which the notice relates, or as the case may be, that a condition or limitation alleged in the enforcement notice not to have been complied with ought to be discharged;

(b) that the matters alleged in the notice do not constitute a breach of planning control;[10]

(c) in the case of a notice which, by virtue of s. 87(3)[11] of this Act, may be served only within the period of four years from the date of the breach of planning control to which the notice relates, that that period has elapsed at the date of service;

(d) in the case of a notice not falling within paragraph (c) of this subsection, that the breach of planning control alleged by the notice occurred before the beginning of 1964;

[1] Town and Country Planning Act 1971, s. 87.
[2] Ibid, s. 87(4).
[3] Ibid, s. 22(1).
[4] Ibid, s. 87(2).
[5] Ibid, s. 87(3).
[6] Ibid, s. 87(1).
[7] Ibid, s. 87(8).
[8] Ibid, s. 88(1).
[9] Ibid, s. 88(2).
[10] Either because the matters alleged in the notice have not occurred, or, if they have, because they do not amount in law to a breach: see Jeary v Chailey UDC (1973), 26 P & CR 280.
[11] See note 5, supra.

(e) that the enforcement notice was not served as required by s. 87(4) of this Act;[1]

(f) that the steps required by the notice to be taken exceed what is necessary to remedy any breach of planning control;

(g) that the specified period for compliance with the notice falls short of what should reasonably be allowed."

On an appeal the Secretary of State may quash the enforcement notice, or vary it in favour of the appellant and in addition he has power to grant planning permission for the development to which the notice relates.[2]

The effect of an enforcement notice may be suspended for a considerable period while an appeal is heard and determined. The "stop notice" procedure[3] is designed to fill this gap, by enabling authorities, in appropriate cases, to prohibit the continuation of the offending operations pending the determination of an appeal.

A stop notice can only be served[4] when an enforcement notice has already been served, and it must be directed to activities which are alleged in the enforcement notice to constitute a breach of planning control or to activities which are included in the matters alleged by the enforcement notice to constitute the breach of planning control.[5] The stop notice will prohibit the carrying out or continuance of the activities described in the notice from the date specified for it to take effect, which must be not less than 3 and not more than 28 days from the day of service.[6] While the stop notice is in operation it is an offence to carry on the prohibited activities.[7]

The stop notice procedure was only available where the breach in question involved the carrying out of operations. In the context of the Act this means "building, engineering, mining or other operations", which together constitute the first limb of the definition of "development" in s. 22(1). It has now been extended to cases where the breach consists of a use of land, whether without planning permission or in contravention of a condition.[8] However, only in cases involving operations or the deposit of refuse or waste materials on land, can the procedure be used to prohibit activities which began over twelve months earlier.[9] A stop notice will cease to operate as soon as the enforcement notice comes into effect. However, the stop notice may

---

[1] An appeal on this ground may be disregarded if there has been no substantial prejudice: s. 88(4)(b).

[2] Town and Country Planning Act 1971, s. 88(5), (7).

[3] Ibid, s. 90. The procedure was first introduced by the Town and Country Planning Act 1968, s. 19. Section 90 has now been amended by the Town and Country Planning (Amendment) Act 1977, s. 1.

[4] It may be served by the local planning authority (s. 90(1), or by the Secretary of State under his reserve powers (s. 276(5)).

[9] Town and Country Planning Act 1971, s. 90(1), as substituted by the Act of 1977 s. 1(1).

[6] Ibid, s. 90(1), (3), as substituted by the Act of 1977.

[7] Ibid, s. 90,(7), as substituted by the Act of 1977.

[8] By the Act of 1977. Some residential uses are excluded: ibid. s. 90(2).

[9] Town and Country Planning Act 1971, s. 90(2).

itself be withdrawn before that time by the authority,[4] and it will also cease to operate if the enforcement notice on which it depends is withdrawn or quashed on appeal.[2]

(ii) RIGHT TO COMPENSATION[3]

In certain cases loss caused by the service of a stop notice may be the subject of a claim to compensation.[4] A distinction is drawn between those cases in which the charges alleged in the enforcement notice are upheld or admitted, and those cases where the charges are not substantiated. In the former case no right to compensation in respect of the stop notice is given. Thus, there is no right to compensation when the enforcement notice is upheld on appeal, or when it is not contested. Similarly, no right to compensation arises where an appeal succeeds on grounds (a), (f) or (g).[5] In those cases the validity of the charges in the enforcement notice is not contested; the issue is whether the breach should be put right by grant of an appropriate planning permission (ground (a)) or, if not, whether the requirements of the notice for remedying the breach should be varied (grounds (f) and (g)).

The circumstances in which a right to compensation is given are[6] when:

"(a) the enforcement notice is quashed on grounds other than those grounds mentioned in s. 88(1)(a), of this Act;[7]
(b) the enforcement notice is varied, otherwise than on the grounds mentioned in that paragraph, so that the matters alleged to constitute a breach of planning control cease to include one or more of the activities prohibited by the stop notice;
(c) the enforcement notice is withdrawn by the local planning authority otherwise than in consequence of the grant by them of planning permission for the development to which the notice relates or for its retention or continuance without compliance with a condition or limitation subject to which a previous planning permission was granted;
(d) the stop notice is withdrawn."

The first situation (s. 177(2)(a)) will be the most common in practice. If, for instance, an enforcement notice is served in relation to the building of an extension to a house, a stop notice could be served to prevent further work while the enforcement notice is pending. An appeal might be lodged against the enforcement notice on the grounds that the extension is development permitted by the General

---

[1] Town and Country Planning Act 1971, s. 90(4), as substituted. Note that such a withdrawal is without prejudice to the powers of the local authority to serve a further notice: *ibid*, s. 90(6). There is no provision for the Secretary of State to withdraw a notice served by him; but it could be withdrawn by the local authority, since a notice served by him has the "like effect" as one served by the authority: *ibid*, s. 276(5).

[2] *Ibid*, s. 90(4), as substituted.

[3] For procedure, see p. 448, *infra*.

[4] Town and Country Planning Act 1971, s. 177, as amended by the Act of 1977, s.2.

[5] See p. 447, *supra*.

[6] Town and Country Planning Act 1971, s, 177(2), as amended by the Act of 1977, s. 2.

[7] Grounds (f) and (g) would not lead to the notice being quashed, but only to the requirements or time limits being varied. No question of compensation will arise on appeal limited to those grounds.

Development Order.[1] This ground of appeal would fall under ground (b) of s. 88(1).[2] If the Secretary of State allowed the appeal on this ground, the enforcement notice would be quashed and the stop notice would fall with it. Compensation would be payable for the loss caused by the prohibition of work in the interim. If the Secretary of State decided that the extension was not within the General Development Order permission,[3] he might nonetheless decide to grant planning permission and allow the appeal under ground (a).[4] In that case the stop notice would lapse on the quashing of the enforcement notice but no compensation would be payable.

The second situation (s. 177(2)(b)) is concerned with cases where an appeal succeeds in part. For instance, an enforcement notice might be served in relation to the deposit of waste in a specified area. If it were shown on appeal under ground (b)[5] that part of the area was covered by a planning permission, the enforcement notice could be varied to exclude that part of the area, but confirmed in respect of the remainder. If a stop notice had been served relating to that part which is ultimately excluded on appeal, a claim to compensation would arise, because the enforcement notice would have been varied so as to exclude an activity prohibited by the stop notice.[6] On the other hand, if the stop notice was confined to that part in relation to which the enforcement notice was confirmed, no claim would arise.

Similarly, an enforcement notice might include a number of different uses of the same land in the allegation of breach of planning control, and a stop notice might be served prohibiting all those uses. If an appeal were made under ground (d)[7], it might be established that some of those uses began before 1964 and were therefore immune from enforcement action, but that others began more recently. In that case the enforcement notice would be varied so as to exclude the uses which began before 1964 but upheld in relation to the remainder. A claim to compensation would arise in respect of the loss flowing from the prohibition of the uses excluded from the enforcement notice, but not the others.[8] This would be so, apparently, even if it were shown that the other uses began more than one year before the stop notice, and thus that the stop notice should never have been served.[9] In that case there is no specific right to compensation, although there would be a good defence to a prosecution for failing to comply with the stop notice.

The third situation in which a claim can be made (s. 177(2)(c)) arises where the enforcement notice is withdrawn voluntarily by the local

---

[1] See the Town and Country Planning General Development Order 1977, SI 1977 No. 289, Class 1.

[2] Town and Country Planning Act 1971, s. 88(1)(b): see p. 441, *supra*.

[3] Note that, in such a case, the whole of the extension is treated as development without permission, not merely the excess over the General Development Order limits: see *Garland v Minister of Housing and Local Government* (1968), 20 P & CR 93.

[4] Town and Country Planning Act 1971, s. 88(1)(a): see p. 441, *supra*.

[5] See note 1, *supra*.

[6] Town and Country Planning Act 1971, s. 177(2)(b), as substituted.

[7] *Ibid*, s. 88(1)(d): see p. 441, *supra*.

[8] *Ibid*, s. 177(1) as substituted.

[9] See p. 442, *supra*.

planning authority before it takes effect,[1] with the result that the stop notice also lapses[2] without the allegations in the enforcement notice having been tested. If, however, the enforcement notice is withdrawn only because the local planning authority decide to grant planning permission for the offending operations, no claim to compensation arises. This can only happen if an application is made for the necessary planning permission. The assumption appears to be that the making of an application by an owner implies an acceptance of the validity of the allegations in the notice, so that the position is analogous to that in which an appeal is upheld on ground (a).[3] However, the exception could give rise to injustice where there is more than one person interested in the land. One of them might be content to avoid the expense of an appeal by accepting a planning permission, even though forfeiting a possible right to compensation under the stop notice. By applying for and receiving planning permission (which would normally enure for the benefit of the land)[4] he would also preclude any claim being made in respect of the stop notice by the other interested persons, whether or not they were parties to the application.

The fourth situation (s. 177(2)(d)) is that in which the stop notice itself is withdrawn[5] voluntarily by the authority. In that case a claim arises whether or not the enforcement notice is subsequently upheld. However, in assessing the claim it will be relevant to consider whether or not the enforcement notice would have been upheld, because, if the operations were in fact unlawful, apart from the prohibition in the stop notice, compensation could not be claimed for their temporary disruption.[6]

Compensation is payable by the local planning authority[7] and may be claimed by any person who, at the time when the stop notice was first served, had an interest[8] in the land to which it relates.[9] Thus, if a person sells his interest in the land during the currency of the stop notice, the purchaser has no entitlement to compensation unless he had an interest in the land at the time when it was served. If, however, he had any interest, for example an option to purchase, at the date when the stop notice was served, the compensation is not apparently limited to loss attributable to that interest. He can claim for any loss suffered by him even if his interest changes.[10]

[1] An enforcement notice cannot be withdrawn after it has taken effect: see Town and Country Planning Act 1971, s. 87(9).

[2] *Ibid*, s. 90(4)(c), as substituted by the Act of 1977, s. 1.

[3] *Ibid*, s. 88(1)(a): see p. 441, *supra*.

[4] *Ibid*, s. 33(1).

[5] The withdrawal of a stop notice does not prevent a further stop notice being served subsequently under the same enforcement notice: *ibid*, s. 90(6), as substituted.

[6] See *Higham v Havant and Waterloo UDC* [1951] 1 KB 50 DC, affd. [1951] 2 KB 527 CA.

[7] See p. 452, *infra*.

[8] There is no definition of "interest" in this context.

[9] Town and Country Planning Act 1971, s. 177(1). The reason for this limitation is presumably that it is thought unnecessary to compensate a person who bought with knowledge of the stop notice. Although this will make it less easy for the existing owner to sell, any resulting loss to him can be compensated.

[10] The claim is for "any loss or damage directly attributable to the prohibition ...": s. 177(1). A person's interest in the land, therefore, is relevant to his right to compensation, but not to the measure of compensation once his right is established.

The measure of compensation is the "loss or damage directly attributable to the prohibition contained in the notice".[1] In cases relating to building operations, for example, this will normally be made up of any additional building costs attributable to the delay caused by the stop notice and loss of value attributable to the postponement of completion and occupation. Where the prohibited operations were being carried out by a contractor, under a contract entered into before the end of 1969, the stop notice is treated, in the absence of specific provision in the contract, as though the operations had been countermanded or discontinued in breach of contract,[2] and any sum payable in respect of that breach can be recovered as part of the compensation.[3]

In other cases the measure of damage will depend upon how serious is the effect of a temporary disruption of operations in a particular case. For instance, in the case of waste disposal, the organisation of the owner might be sufficiently flexible to enable the temporary loss of the use of one site to be made good elsewhere without significant disruption to the business as a whole. In that case the loss suffered by him might be negligible. On the other hand, even temporary loss of one site might cause serious loss if, for example, it deprived him of the chance to secure a valuable waste disposal contract. In that case substantial compensation could be payable.[4]

7 General provisions as to assessment of compensation

The 1971 Act[5] provides that in all but three cases compensation in respect of the depreciation of an interest in land under the provisions of Part VIII, which have been considered above, shall be assessed in accordance with the rules set out in the Land Compensation Act 1961, s. 5.[6] The exceptions are the two sets of provisions relating to trees,[7] and those relating to stop notices.[8] In other cases under Part VIII[9] the rules will only apply if and so far as any part of the compensation awarded is attributable to depreciation of the value of an interest in land. They will have no application if, for example, it is considered appropriate to assess the compensation on the basis of loss of potential profits.[10] The

---

[1] Town and Country Planning Act 1971, s. 177(1). Account must be taken of the extent to which the loss is attributable to his failure to respond to a notice requiring information under *ibid* s. 284: *ibid* s. 177(b) as substituted.

[2] *Ibid*, s. 90(8).

[3] Town and Country Planning Act 1971, s. 177(5). These special provisions relating to pre-1970 contracts are repealed in relation to stop notices served after the commencement date of the Act of 1977 (22 August, 1977).

[4] Cf. *Hobbs (Quarries) Ltd.* v *Somerset County Council* (1975), 30 P & CR 286 LT, in which compensation in respect of the revocation of a permission for gravel working was based on the loss of a contract connected with a particular road construction project. It would have been different if the loss of the particular permission could have been made good by acquiring another site in the right locality (see *ibid*, at p. 291).

[5] Town and Country Planning Act 1971, s. 178(1), (2). This section does not apply in any event to the two cases considered in this chapter which are not covered by Part VIII of the 1971 Act, i.e., compensation under the Forestry Act 1967 (p. 434, *supra*), and the Ancient Monuments Acts (p. 427, *supra*).

[6] These rules are set out and discussed at p. 164, *ante*.

[7] Town and Country Planning Act 1971, ss. 174, 175: see p. 432, *supra*.

[8] *Ibid*, s. 177; see p. 441, *supra*. In the cases relating to advertisements compensation will not in any event include depreciation in the value of land: see p. 440, *supra*.

[9] I.e., ss. 164–165 (p. 416, *supra*), s. 169 (p. 407, *supra*) s. 170 (p. 421, *supra*), ss. 171–173 (p. 426).

[10] As in *Hobbs (Quarries) Ltd.* v *Somerset County Council* (1975), 30 P & CR 286 LT; see p. 418, *ante*).

application of the Land Compensation Act 1961 is in any event limited to the rules set out in s. 5 of that Act.[1] The subsequent provisions of that Act,[2] including the various statutory assumptions that are required to be made as to grant of planning permission, are not applied to assessment of compensation under Part VIII.[3] In considering the market value of any land it will be necessary, therefore, to apply the common law principle that land is to be valued "not ... merely by reference to the uses to which it is being put at the time at which its value has to be determined, but also by reference to the uses to which it is reasonably capable of being put in the future".[4] Thus, for example, if the value of the land is enhanced by the likelihood of obtaining a planning permission for some valuable use, this "hope value" can be taken into account, since it would be reflected in the market value.[5] The difference is that in this case (unlike cases to which the Land Compensation Act assumptions apply) the hope value will be discounted to reflect the risk of not obtaining permission: when a statutory assumption is applied, there is no such risk, because the permission is assumed.

Special considerations apply subject to the same exceptions[6] where the interest in question is subject to a mortgage.[7] Although a claim in respect of the depreciation in the value of the interest may be made by either the mortgagee or the mortgagor,[8] in either case[9] the assessment of compensation is based on the mortgagor's interest valued as though it were not subject to a mortgage,[10] but the resulting compensation is paid to the mortgagee.[11] He is then required to apply it as if it were

---

[1] See note 6, *supra*.

[2] For a description of these provisions see p. 185, *ante*.

[3] See *Burlin* v *Manchester City Council*, [1976] RVR 119 LT, in which it was held that the provisions of the Land Compensation Act 1961, ss. 14–16, were not applicable to assessment of compensation under the Town and Country Planning Act 1971, s. 164, in respect of a revocation order (as to which see p. 416, *supra*). Although the reasoning of the Tribunal was directed to the particular terms of s. 164, the same conclusion is implicit in the wording of s. 178(1) itself, when read with the Land Compensation Act 1961, s. 5. Section 5 draws a distinction between the "rules" (which are those set out under paragraphs (1) to (6) in the section) and the "following provisions of this Part of this Act" (i.e., ss. 6–16) which are also applied to the assessment of compensation for compulsory acquisition. S. 178(1) of the 1971 Act refers only to the "rules". Had it been intended to apply the other provisions of Part II of the 1961 Act one would have expected specific provision similar to that in s. 5 itself. Therefore it seems that the conclusion reached in the *Burlin* case (*supra*) is equally applicable to other cases to which s. 178(1) applies, and is not limited to revocation orders.

[4] *Vyricherla* v *Revenue Divisional Officer, Vizagapatam*, [1939] AC 302 PC at p. 313. The value of those potentialities will, of course, depend in particular on the prospect of the removal of restrictions (e.g., by grant of planning permission): see *Corrie* v *MacDermott*, [1914] AC 1056 PC at pp. 1063–1064.

[5] In the case of compensation under ss. 164–165 (i.e., revocation orders and development order restrictions: see p. 416, *supra*) the value of "hope" of obtaining planning permission will generally be negligible, because the market will take account of the fact that, if any new development is carried out, the compensation will have to be repaid (see p. 421, *supra*). Thus in almost every such case it will be right to compare the value of the land before revocation with its value without any permission other than permission for 8th Schedule development: see *Burlin* v *Manchester City Council*, [1976] RVR 119.

[6] See notes 7–8, *supra*.

[7] Town and Country Planning Act 1971, s. 178(2).

[8] *Ibid*, s. 178(2)(b).

[9] *Ibid*, s. 178(2)(c).

[10] *Ibid*, s. 178(2)(a).

[11] The first mortgagee, if there is more than one: Town and Country Planning Act 1971, s. 178(2)(d).

the proceeds of sale.[1] This will not affect the mortgagor's personal entitlement to compensation for other loss suffered by him apart from depreciation in the value of his interest.[2]

Thus, for example, assume that A owns a site with planning permission for industrial development. The permission is revoked by a revocation order after A has spent £2,000 on preparatory works. The value of the land with the permission is £20,000, and without permission £1,000. It is subject to a mortgage in favour of B for £15,000. A may claim compensation in respect of the depreciation in the value of the land and in respect of abortive expenditure. The former will be based on the value of his interest as though it were not subject to the mortgage (i.e., £20,000−£1,000=£19,000) and this will be paid to B as mortgagee whether or not he has made a claim. He will then apply it in satisfaction of the debt and pay the surplus to A. The abortive expenditure claim (£2,000) will be paid direct to A.

Interest

There is no statutory provision for interest to be awarded in respect of the period between the date on which the claim arises and the date of the award. Accordingly, interest can only be awarded from the date when compensation is assessed or agreed.[3]

8 Procedure

(i) CLAIMS OTHER THAN FOR LISTED BUILDINGS, TREES OR ADVERTISEMENTS

These claims relate respectively to:

(a) revocation and modification orders (s. 45 orders);[4]
(b) development order restrictions;[5]
(c) restriction on development within Part II of the 8th Schedule;[6]
(d) discontinuance orders (s. 51 orders);[7]
(e) stop notices.[8]

Procedure for making a claim is governed by the Town and Country Planning General Regulations 1976.[9] The claim must be made in writing and be served on the relevant authority[10] by delivering it at their offices or sending it by pre-paid post.[11] It must be served within six months of the date of the "decision" in respect of which the claim is made,[12] unless the time is extended by the Secretary of State.[13]

---

[1] Town and Country Planning Act 1971, s. 178(2)(d). As to application of proceeds of sale, see *Halsbury's Laws*, (3rd Edn.) Vol. 27, pp. 309–311.

[2] *Ibid*, s. 178(2)(b).

[3] *Hobbs (Quarries) Ltd.* v *Somerset County Council* (1975) 30 P & CR 286; see p. 86, *ante*.

[4] See p. 416, *supra*.

[5] See p. 419, *supra*.

[6] See p. 407, *supra*.

[7] See p. 421, *supra*.

[8] See p. 443, *supra*.

[9] SI 1976 No. 1419, reg. 14.

[10] I.e., the authority which is liable to pay (see p. 452, *infra*).

[11] SI 1976 No. 1419, reg. 14(1).

[12] *Ibid*, reg. 14(2)(a).

[13] *Ibid*, reg. 14(2), proviso.

The use of the word "decision" in this context gives rise to difficulty since it will not always be clear which decision is the relevant one. The position is further obscured by the fact that the time of a "planning decision" in the case of an appeal is specifically defined in the Act[1] as the time of the decision of the local planning authority, not that of the Secretary of State. Notwithstanding this, it is thought that in the case of a claim for refusal of permission under Part II of the 8th Schedule[2] the relevant decision must be that of the Secretary of State, for that is the only decision in respect of which the claim can arise,[3] and the time of the local planning authority's decision (if any) is irrelevant.[4]

In the case of a revocation or modification order[5] or a discontinuance order[6] confirmed by the Secretary of State, the relevant decision should in principle be the confirmation rather than the making of the order by the authority, since, again, that is the time when the claim arises.[7] However, the same reasoning cannot apply when the revocation or modification order takes effect without confirmation,[8] since the only "decision" is that of the authority making the order. In that case, therefore, it seems that the claim should be made within six months of the local planning authority's decision to make the order.[9]

In the case of development order restrictions[10] the relevant decision would appear to be that of the local planning authority, even where there is an appeal against the decision. In this case a decision of the Secretary of State is not necessary to give rise to a claim.[11] Furthermore, the section specifically relates the right to compensation to the "*planning decision* whereby the planning permission in question is refused".[12] One must therefore have regard to the definition of "planning decision".[13] Thus even where the refusal is confirmed by a decision of the Secretary of State on appeal the "time" of the planning decision will still be the time of the authority's decision.[14] In the case of such claims therefore the claim should be made within six months of the local planning authority's decision[15] even if there is an appeal. If the application is

---

[1] Town and Country Planning Act 1971, s. 290(4)(d).

[2] I.e., a claim under *ibid*, s. 169 (see p. 407, *supra*).

[3] See p. 407, *supra*, note 6.

[4] The relevant section (s. 169) does not specifically use the expression "planning decision", and therefore it is possible to disregard the definition of that expression in s. 290(4) in considering which is the relevant "decision" for these purposes.

[5] I.e., a claim under the Town and Country Planning Act 1971, s. 164 (see p. 416, *supra*).

[6] I.e., a claim under *ibid*, s. 170 (see p. 421, *supra*).

[7] It is of interest to note that in the analogous provisions of the Town and Country (Control of Advertisements) Regulations 1969, SI 1969 No. 1532, reg. 25(1), the time is expressly made to run from the date of confirmation of the order.

[8] Under the Town and Country Planning Act 1971, s. 46; see p. 413, *supra*.

[9] The decision will be the relevant resolution of the authority: see the Local Government Act 1972, Sch. 12, para. 39(1).

[10] I.e., claims under the Town and Country Planning Act 1971, s. 165 (see p. 419, *supra*).

[11] See p. 419, *supra*.

[12] Town and Country Planning Act 1971, s. 165(2).

[13] See note 1, *supra*.

[14] Town and Country Planning Act 1971, s. 294(4)(d).

[15] Where there is an appeal in default of decision (under s. 37) the relevant time is the end of the period within which the notification of the decision of the authority should have been given: *ibid*, s. 290(4)(d) and s. 37.

called in for decision by the Secretary of State[1] the relevant decision will be his. In the case of a stop notice[2] the relevant decision will be either the decision of the authority to withdraw the stop notice or the enforcement notice on which it depends, or alternatively, the decision of the Secretary of State on appeal quashing or varying the enforcement notice.[3]

(ii) CLAIMS IN RESPECT OF LISTED BUILDINGS[4]

In these cases similar provision is made by the Town and Country Planning (Listed Buildings etc.) Regulations.[5] The claim must be made in writing and served on the relevant authority (addressed to the Clerk) by delivering it at their offices or by sending it by pre-paid post. It must be made within six months of the decision in respect of which the claim is made, unless the Secretary of State allows a longer period.[6] Here again, the word "decision" gives rise to problems. In the case of refusal of consent to alterations the claim arises out of a decision of the Secretary of State[7] and time will run from that decision. When the claim arises out of a listed building consent revocation or modification order[8] the same considerations will apply as to an order revoking a permission.[9] In the case of a building preservation notice,[10] the claim arises when the notice "ceases to have effect without the building having been included" in the statutory list.[11] If this results from the notification of the decision of the Secretary of State not to list the building,[12] that will presumably be the relevant "decision" for the purpose of the claim. But it may also happen if a six-months' period elapses without a decision having been made.[12] In that case there is no positive decision from which the time under the regulations can run, except for the original decision of the local planning authority to serve the building preservation notice.[13] However, that cannot be the relevant decision, since, if it were, a notice of claim would have to be served before the claim had arisen.[14] The only sensible way in which the regulations can be applied to this situation is by regarding the Secretary of State as having notionally made a decision at the end of the six-month period to allow the building preservation notice to lapse by taking no action. The time for service of the claim will thus run from the end of that period. However, as a precautionary measure in such circumstances, it would be prudent

[1] I.e., under *ibid*, s. 35. In such a case the local planning authority does not make any formal decision.
[2] I.e., claims under *ibid*, s. 177 (see p. 443, *supra*).
[3] See p. 444, *supra*.
[4] I.e., under the Town and Country Planning Act 1971, ss. 171–173 (see p. 425, *supra*).
[5] SI 1977 No. 228, reg. 7.
[6] *Ibid*, reg. 7(1), (2).
[7] See p. 425, *supra*.
[8] See p. 427, *supra*.
[9] See p. 449, *supra*.
[10] See p. 427, *supra*.
[11] Town and Country Planning Act 1971, s. 173(2).
[12] *Ibid*, s. 58(3); see p. 425, *supra*.
[13] *Ibid*, s. 58(1); see p. 425, *supra*.
[14] The six-month period allowed by SI 1977 No. 228, reg. 7, for service of the claim would expire at the same time as the notice ceasing to have effect under s. 58(3).

to ask the Secretary of State to allow an extension of time under the regulation if and so far as necessary to validate the claim.[1]

Ancient monuments

There are no specific provisions in the Ancient Monuments Acts governing the procedure for claims in respect of notices or orders under those Acts, but when a preservation order or guardianship order has been made the terms of the order will govern the manner in which the claim is to be made.[2]

(iii) TREES

For compensation for refusal of consent under a tree preservation order the claim must be made in the manner provided by the order. The prescribed form of order[3] requires the claim to be in writing and to be served on the authority which made the order by delivering it at their offices or sending it by pre-paid post.[4] In this case the claim must be made within a period of twelve months from the date of the decision of the authority or of the Secretary of State, as the case may be, or, if there is an appeal, from the date of the Secretary of State's decision on the appeal.[5] This wording is not readily applicable to a claim in respect of the revocation or modification of consent (which is treated as a refusal for these purposes).[6] However, by analogy, it seems that, where the order is confirmed by the Secretary of State, his decision will be the relevant one; but if it takes effect as an unopposed order the relevant decision will be that of the authority making the order. In this case there is no provision for the time to be extended.

A claim in respect of a replanting direction[7] must be served on the relevant authority within twelve months of the date on which the direction was given or, if there is an appeal, from the date of the Secretary of State's decision. In either case the authority may extend the time.[8]

A claim under the Forestry Act 1967 must be made in the manner prescribed by regulations under that Act.[9]

(iv) ADVERTISEMENTS

A claim for expenses for the removal or discontinuance of a 1948 display[10] must be made by a claim in writing to the relevant authority

---

[1] It is most unfortunate that the regulation (SI 1977 No. 228, reg. 7) is not drafted so as to relate more closely to the provisions giving rise to the claim. In this, as in the other cases, the right to compensation is dependent upon a claim being made "within the time … prescribed by regulations" (s. 173(3) etc.), and it is therefore a matter of considerable importance to ensure that the time limits are observed.

[2] See the Historic Buildings and Ancient Monuments Act 1953, s. 12(3), (6) and p. 429, *supra*.

[3] Town and Country Planning (Tree Preservation Order) Regulations 1969, SI 1969 No. 17, Sch.; see p. 432, *supra*.

[4] *Ibid*, para. 11(1).

[5] *Ibid*, para. 11(2).

[6] *Ibid*, para. 9.

[7] Town and Country Planning Act 1971, s. 175(4).

[8] See p. 436 *supra*.

[9] Forestry Act 1967, ss. 11(2), 35. See Forestry (Felling of Trees) Regulations 1951, SI 1951 No. 1726, reg. 5, preserved by Sch. 6, para. 1(1) of the 1967 Act.

[10] I.e., under the Town and Country Planning Act 1971, s. 176; see p. 438, *supra*.

within six months after completion of the works giving rise to the claim. The claim must contain sufficient information to enable the authority to give it proper consideration, and the authority may call for further particulars if necessary.[1] A claim for compensation on revocation or modification of a consent must be made in writing to the relevant authority, addressed to the Clerk, and served on the authority by delivering it at their offices or by sending it by pre-paid post. It must be made within six months after confirmation of the order.[2]

(v) DETERMINATION OF CLAIMS

Any question of disputed compensation under Part VIII of the Town and Country Planning Act 1971 is determined by the Lands Tribunal, except in so far as is otherwise provided by any tree preservation order or by regulations under the Act.[3] The provisions of the Land Compensation Act 1961, ss. 2–4 (which govern procedure and costs),[4] are specifically applied to determination of such claims.[5] Compensation under the Forestry Act 1967 and the Ancient Monuments Acts will also normally be assessed by the Lands Tribunal under the relevant provisions of those Acts.[6]

9 Who is liable to pay compensation?

(i) OUTSIDE GREATER LONDON

Liability to pay compensation under Part VIII of the Town and Country Planning Act 1971[7] will fall on either the county planning authority or the district planning authority.[8] The choice between the two authorities in most cases[9] is governed by the Local Government Act 1972.[10] The first question is: "who took the action by virtue of which the claim arises?" If it was a local authority, that authority will be liable to

---

[1] Town and Country Planning (Control of Advertisements) Regulations 1969, SI 1969 No. 1532, reg. 30.

[2] Town and Country Planning (Control of Advertisements) Regulations 1969, SI 1969 No. 1532, reg. 25(1), (3).

[3] Town and Country Planning Act 1971, s. 179(1). There is no contrary provision in the current form of tree preservation order (see p. 432, supra) or in any of the relevant regulations (see p. 448 or p. 450, supra). This provision gives the Lands Tribunal exclusive jurisdiction over all matters incidental to the assessment of compensation: see Harrison v London Borough of Croydon, [1968] Ch. 479.

[4] See p. 83, ante.

[5] Town and Country Planning Act 1971, s. 179(2).

[6] Forestry Act 1967, ss. 31(1)(a), s. 11(6); Historic Buildings and Ancient Monuments Act 1953, ss. 12(b), (c). The 1953 Act does not itself give the Lands Tribunal jurisdiction where a preservation order or guardianship order is made, but the order itself will normally make such provision (see, for example, the provisions cited in Hoveringham Gravel Co. Ltd. v Secretary of State (1974), 27 P & CR 549 LT at 552).

[7] See p. 405, supra.

[8] That is, the county council or the district council for the area concerned: see the Town and Country Planning Act 1971, s. 1(1), as amended by the Local Government Act 1972, s. 182(1). Special provisions apply to National Parks: see the Local Government Act 1972, Sch. 17.

[9] Compensation under ss. 174–175 (trees) is covered by para. 35 of the same Schedule: see p. 454, infra. In the case of compensation for revocation of a consent under the Control of Advertisement Regulations, the compensation will be paid by the district planning authority: see the amendments made by SI 1975 No. 185.

[10] Sch. 16, para. 34.

pay compensation.[1] Thus if the claim arises out of a refusal by an authority of a permission or consent, a revocation order made by an authority, or a notice served by an authority, the liability to compensation will fall on that authority.

If the action was taken by the Secretary of State the position is more complicated. If it was a decision by him on an application referred to him[2] by a local authority or on an appeal[3] from an authority, the liability will fall on the authority who made the reference or from whom the appeal was made.[4] If it was action taken by him under his reserve powers,[5] the authority liable to compensation will be the "appropriate authority",[6] which expression can be considered under three categories:

(a) *Revocation or modification orders*.[7] Where the claim arises out of a revocation or modification order made by the Secretary of State (whether relating to a planning permission or to a listed building consent) the liability falls on the local planning authority which granted the permission or consent affected by the order.[8] Where the permission or consent in question was granted before 1 April 1974,[9] the liability will apparently fall on the authority which has inherited[10] the relevant liabilities of the predecessor authority which granted the permission or consent. It is not clear what happens if the permission or consent was granted by the Secretary of State. This appears to be a *lacuna* in the Schedule. Possibly the intention of the draftsman can be divined by referring back to paragraph 34(1), so that, where the grant was made by the Secretary of State, the relevant authority will be "the local planning authority from whom the appeal was made to him or who referred the matter to him".[11]

(b) *Building preservation notices*[12] *and advertisements*.[13] In these cases the liability, where the relevant action is taken by the Secretary of State, falls on the district planning authority.[14]

---

[1] Local Government Act 1972, Sch. 16, para. 34(1).

[2] Under the Town and Country Planning Act 1971, s. 35 (planning permission) or Sch. 11, para. 4 (listed building consent).

[3] Under *ibid*, s. 36, 27, or Sch. 11, paras. 8–9.

[4] Local Government Act 1972, Sch. 16, para. 34(1). Although applications will in general be made in the first instance to the district planning authority, the responsibility for deciding the application will depend on the nature of the application (see *ibid*, Sch. 16, paras. 15, 25). The detailed arrangements as between authorities will be found in the "development control scheme" for the particular county (see Department of the Environment Circular 74/73, Annex 2).

[5] Town and Country Planning Act 1971, s. 276 (headed "Default powers of Secretary of State") gives the various powers to take action in cases where the local authority has failed to do so.

[6] Local Government Act 1972, Sch. 16, para. 34(2).

[7] The Schedule also includes in this category compensation for refusal of permission for development previously covered by a development order permission (Town and Country Planning Act 1971, s. 165). However, in such cases the claim arises by virtue of a refusal of permission (see p. 419, *supra*), not by virtue of any action which the Secretary of State can take under s. 276 (see note 5, *supra*). Its inclusion in this category therefore appears to be otiose.

[8] Local Government Act 1972, Sch. 16, para. 34(2)(a).

[9] I.e., the date when the Local Government Act 1972 came into effect.

[10] Under the Local Government Act 1972, s. 254(2)(a).

[11] Local Government Act 1972, Sch. 16, para. 34(1).

[12] Town and Country Planning Act 1971, s. 173: see p. 427, *supra*.

[13] *Ibid*, s. 176: see p. 438, *supra*.

[14] Local Government Act 1972, Sch. 16, para. 34(2)(b).

(c) *Discontinuance orders*[1] *or stop notices*.[2] In these cases if the Secretary of State makes the order or notice under s. 276 the authority responsible for compensation should be named by him in the order or notice.[3]

Trees

When the claim relates to a refusal of consent or to a replanting direction made under a tree preservation order, the liability to pay compensation falls on the authority which made the tree preservation order or, if it is made by the Secretary of State, the authority named in the order.[4]

Reimbursement and contributions

In all the above cases (apart from the provisions relating to trees) the Secretary of State may, after consultation, direct, in any case or class of case, that the whole or a specified proportion of the compensation to which an authority is liable shall be reimbursed by another authority.[5] This is in addition to the general power of the Secretary of State in any case (including those relating to trees) to require a contribution from an authority which derives benefit from the action giving rise to the claim.[6] Where the action is taken wholly or partly in the interest of a service provided by a Government Department, the cost of which is defrayed out of moneys provided by Parliament, the Minister responsible for the service may make a contribution of an amount determined by him with the consent of the Treasury.[7] In relation to claims in respect of revocation orders or development order restrictions[8] there is also provision for the Secretary of State to make a contribution to compensation where he would have been liable to a claim under Part VII in respect of an unexpended balance of established development value.[9]

(ii) WITHIN GREATER LONDON

In Greater London the functions of the local planning authority which could give rise to a claim for compensation under Part VIII (except for building preservation notices) rest with the Greater London Council[10] which will be the authority responsible for compensation. In relation to building preservation notices the Greater London Council and the relevant Borough Council exercise concurrent functions, and compensation will be payable by the authority which served the notice.[11] However, in any of the cases to which Part VIII applies, the Greater London Council may delegate its functions to the relevant Borough Council with the consent of the Secretary of State, or may be required

---

[1] Town and Country Planning Act 1971, s. 170: see p. 421, *supra*.

[2] *Ibid*, s. 177: see p. 443, *supra*.

[3] Local Government Act 1972, Sch. 16, para. 34(2)(c).

[4] *Ibid*, Sch. 16, para. 35. For the provisions of Tree Preservation Orders see p. 432, *supra*.

[5] *Ibid*, Sch. 16, para. 34(3).

[6] See the Town and Country Planning Act 1971, s. 255(3). Local authorities or statutory undertakers may also make voluntary contributions: *ibid*, s. 255(2).

[7] *Ibid*, s. 254.

[8] See pp. 416, 419, *supra*.

[9] *Ibid*, s. 166. See pp. 394 *et seq*, *supra*.

[10] Town and Country Planning Act 1971, Sch. 3, para. 3(1), and Town and Country Planning (Local Planning Authorities in Greater London) Regulations 1965, SI 1965 No. 679, reg. 3.

[11] Town and Country Planning Act 1971, Sch. 3, para. 4.

by him to do so.[1] In such cases the two authorities may agree to the transfer of liability to compensation arising out of the exercise of those functions to the Borough Council.[2] The provisions as to contributions by other authorities[3] or Ministers[4] apply in Greater London as well as outside.

[1] *Ibid*, Sch. 3, para. 5.
[2] *Ibid*, Sch. 3, para. 6.
[3] See note 6, *supra*.
[4] See note 7, *supra*.

Appendix

TOWN AND COUNTRY PLANNING ACT 1971

SCHEDULE 8
Sections 22, 43, 164, 169, 180 and 278

DEVELOPMENT NOT CONSTITUTING NEW DEVELOPMENT
PART I
DEVELOPMENT NOT RANKING FOR COMPENSATION UNDER S.
169

1. The carrying out of any of the following works, that is to say—
  (a) the rebuilding, as often as occasion may require, of any build-
    ing which was in existence on the appointed day, or of any
    building which was in existence before that day but was
    destroyed or demolished after 7 January 1937, including the
    making good of war damage sustained by any such building;
  (b) the rebuilding, as often as occasion may require, of any build-
    ing erected after the appointed day which was in existence at a
    material date;
  (c) the carrying out of works for the maintenance, improvement
    or other alteration of any building, being works which affect
    only the interior of the building, or which do not materially
    affect the external appearance of the building and (in either
    case) are works for making good war damage,
so long as (in the case of works falling within any of the preceding
sub-paragraphs) the cubic content of the original building is not
exceeded—
  (i) in the case of a dwelling-house, by more than one-tenth or
    1,750 cubic feet, whichever is the greater; and
  (ii) in any other case, by more than one-tenth.
2. The use as two or more separate dwelling-houses of any building
which at a material date was used as a single dwelling-house.

PART II
DEVELOPMENT RANKING FOR COMPENSATION UNDER S. 169

3. The enlargement, improvement, or other alteration, as often as
occasion may require, of any such building as is mentioned in paragraph 1 (a) or (b) of this Schedule, or any building substituted for such a

building by the carrying out of any such operations as are mentioned in that paragraph, so long as the cubic content of the original building is not increased or exceeded—

(a) in the case of a dwelling-house by more than one-tenth or 1,750 cubic feet, whichever is the greater; and

(b) in any other case, by more than one-tenth.

4. The carrying out, on land which was used for the purposes of agriculture or forestry at a material date, of any building or other operations required for the purposes of that use, other than operations for the erection, enlargement, improvement or alteration of dwelling-houses or of buildings used for the purposes of market gardens, nursery grounds or timber yards or for other purposes not connected with general farming operations or with the cultivation or felling of trees.

5. The winning and working, on land held or occupied, with land used for the purposes of agriculture, of any minerals reasonably required for the purposes of that use, including the fertilisation of the land so used and the maintenance, improvement or alteration of buildings or works thereon which are occupied or used for those purposes.

6. In the case of a building or other land which, at a material date, was used for a purpose falling within any general class specified in the Town and Country Planning (Use Classes for Third Schedule Purposes) Order 1948, or which having been unoccupied on and at all times since the appointed day, was last used (otherwise than before 7 January 1937) for any such purpose, the use of that building or land for any other purpose falling within the same general class.

7. In the case of any building or other land which, at a material date, was in the occupation of a person by whom it was used as to part only for a particular purpose, the use for that purpose of any additional part of the building or land not exceeding one-tenth of the cubic content of the part of the building used for that purpose on the appointed day, or on the day thereafter when the building began to be so used, or, as the case may be, one-tenth of the area of the land so used on that day.

8. The deposit of waste materials or refuse in connection with the working of minerals, on any land comprised in a site which at a material date was being used for that purpose, so far as may be reasonably required in connection with the working of those minerals.

PART III
SUPPLEMENTARY PROVISIONS

9. Any reference in this Schedule to the cubic content of a building shall be construed as a reference to that content as ascertained by external measurement.

10. Where, after the appointed day, any buildings or works have been erected or constructed, or any use of land has been instituted, and any condition imposed under Part III of this Act, limiting the period for which those buildings or works may be retained, or that use may be continued, has effect in relation thereto, this Schedule shall not operate except as respects the period specified in that condition.

11. For the purposes of paragraph 3 of this Schedule—

(a) the erection, on land within the curtilage of any such building as is mentioned in that paragraph, of an additional building to be used in connection with the original building shall be treated as the enlargement of the original building; and

(b) where any two or more buildings comprised in the same curtilage are used as one unit for the purposes of any institution or undertaking, the reference in that paragraph to the cubic content of the original building shall be construed as a reference to the aggregate cubic content of those buildings.

12. In this Schedule "at a material date" means at either of the following dates, that is to say—

(a) the appointed day; and

(b) the date by reference to which this Schedule falls to be applied in the particular case in question:

Provided that sub-paragraph (b) of this paragraph shall not apply in relation to any buildings, works or use of land in respect of which, whether before or after the date mentioned in that sub-paragraph, an enforcement notice served before that date has become or becomes effective.

13.—(1) In relation to a building erected after the appointed day, being a building resulting from the carrying out of any such works as are described in paragraph 1 of this Schedule, any reference in this Schedule to the original building is a reference to the building in relation to which those works were carried out and not to the building resulting from the carrying out of those works.

(2) This paragraph has effect subject to section 278 (4) of this Act.

SCHEDULE 18
Sections 168, 169, 180 and 278

CONDITION TREATED AS APPLICABLE TO REBUILDING AND ALTERATIONS

1. Where the building to be rebuilt or altered is the original building, the amount of gross floorspace in the building as rebuilt or altered which may be used for any purpose shall not exceed by more than 10 % the amount of gross floorspace which was last used for that purpose in the original building.

2. Where the building to be rebuilt or altered is not the original building, the amount of gross floorspace in the building as rebuilt or altered which may be used for any purpose shall not exceed the amount of gross floorspace which was last used for that purpose in the building before the rebuilding or alteration.

3. In determining under this Schedule the purpose for which floorspace was last used in any building, no account shall be taken of any use in respect of which an effective enforcement notice has been or could be served or, in the case of a use which has been discontinued, could have been served immediately before the discontinuance.

4. For the purposes of this Schedule gross floorspace shall be ascertained by external measurement; and where different parts of a

building are used for different purposes, floorspace common to those purposes shall be apportioned rateably.

5. In relation to a building erected after the appointed day, being a building resulting from the carrying out of any such works as are described in paragraph 1 of Schedule 8 to this Act, any reference in this Schedule to the original building is a reference to the building in relation to which those works were carried out and not to the building resulting from the carrying out of those works.

Index

ACQUISITION OF LAND. *See also* COM-
PULSORY ACQUISITION; COMPULSORY
PURCHASE
Assessment of Compensation Act 1919 ... 4,
163
Authorisation Procedure Act, 1946
Community Land Act 1975 ... 74
compulsory purchase orders, 2, 30, 32 *et
seq*
former severance provisions, 108
historical background, 2
incorporation into special Acts, 30

ACTION AREA
compensation for land in—
planning permission to be assumed, 198,
199, 202–204, 207
SCHEME OF DEVELOPMENT, EFFECT, 224,
225, 236

ADVERTISEMENTS,
areas of special control, 438, 439
consent for display, 437, 438
discontinuance notice, 437, 438, 439
planning refusal, no compensation, 399
revocation or modification of, 438, 453
compensation, 439, 440, 452
control of, 437
compensation, right to, 438
Regulations, 439, 440
purchase notice, 115, 119
meaning, 437*n.*
removal of 1948 display, 438, 439
compensation, 438, 451

AERODROMES,
alterations, etc., injurious affection, 329, 330

AGRICULTURAL UNIT. *See also* AGRICUL-
TURE
blight notice, 17, 131, 156, 352
affected area, remainder uneconomic, 144
objection notice, 148, 149
objection notice, 145, 148, 149
partnership, 133, 156
farm loss payment, 160, 379–385
amount, 381–384
displacement, meaning, 381
other compensation excluded, 380
partnership, 384
procedure, 384

AGRICULTURAL UNIT—*contd.*
meaning, 111*n.*, 131
public works, use affecting, 331, 334, 342
severance, counter-notice, 111–113, 114

AGRICULTURE,
agricultural land, severance, 110, 114
agricultural tenancy—
compensation—
assessment, 182
disturbance, for, 355, 365, 366, 371,
380, 388
farm loss payment, 379–385
planning restrictions, compensation—
buildings for purpose of, 410
General Development Order, 414, 420
minerals for use in, 411, 457

ANCIENT MONUMENTS,
compensation, right to, 429
claims, 451
compulsory purchase, 50
guardianship order, 428, 431
interim preservation notice, 428, 429
list, 428
listed building control and, 428
meaning, 427
preservation order, 428, 429, 430
protection, 427–429

APPEAL. *See* LANDS TRIBUNAL

BETTERMENT,
compensation, set-off, 4–6, 16, 217
1961 Act, under, 220 *et seq*, 233
scheme of development, 217, 218, 220 *et
seq*, 231–234, 236
development land tax, 25. *See also* DEVELOP-
MENT LAND TAX
floating value, meaning, 7
historical survey, 4–7
levy, 19–21, 29
abolition, 21, 29
meaning, 5
shifting value, meaning, 7
Uthwatt Report, 6

BLIGHT NOTICE,
acceptance, 144, 155

BLIGHT NOTICE—*contd.*
agricultural unit, 17, 131, 156, 352
affected area, remainder uneconomic, 144
objection notice, 148, 149
partnership, 133, 156
appropriate authority, 154
appropriate enactment, 155
blighted land, categories, 66–67, 133, 156
Community Land Act 1975, under, 142
Land Compensation Act 1973, under, 137
Act authorising compulsory acquisition, 138
clearance area, 140
general improvement area, 138
new street order affecting, 140–142
New Town order, 139
notice to treat not served, 138
planning resolution as to, 138, 155
slum clearance resolution, 140
Town and Country Planning Act 1971,
under, 133–137
development plan—
certain land, 135, 155
highway, land for, 135
meaning, 139
highway purposes, for, 136, 137, 155
local plan, allocated in, 134, 155
notice to treat not served, 137
special road, land connected with, 136,
137
structure plan, indicated in, 133, 134,
155
trunk road, land connected with, 136,
137
Community Land Act 1975, under, 142, 188,
302, 303
corporate body, 133
counter-notice of objection, 144, 145–153,
and see objection notice, *infra*
hereditament—
dwelling, occupied as, 130, 156, 352
part only to be acquired, objection, 148
small business, 130, 131, 156
inability to sell, 142–144, 156
interest qualifying, 131, 156
limits of remedy, 129, 130
listed building deliberately neglected, 276,
277
mortgagee, by, whether, 132, 133, 156
notice to treat deemed served, 144, 157, 240
objection notice, 144, 145–153, 157
acquisition not proposed, 145
within 15 years, 150
claimant not entitled to interest, 151
inability to sell not shown, 152
interest not qualifying, 151
land outside specific categories, 145
Lands Tribunal, reference to, 145 *et seq*,
157
onus of proof, 153
new street order, where, 147
no acquisition within 15 years, 150
part only, acquisition proposed, 147–150
period for service, 144, 155, 157
extension, 154

BLIGHT NOTICE—*contd.*
relevant date, 153
slum clearance resolution, where, 147
substitution of second, 152
withdrawal, 152
occupation, beneficial, 131
owner-occupier, 129, 132
personal representative, by, 133
planning blight, 17, 107, 129 *et seq*, 156
planning permission suspended, 142, 188,
302, 303
procedure, 144 *et seq.*
property qualifying, 130, 156
qualifying interest, 131, 156
qualifying property, 130, 156
requirements, 130
blight, what constitutes, *see* blighted land,
categories, *supra*
inability to sell, 142–144, 156
qualifying interests, 131, 156
qualifying property, 130, 156
requisite legal interests, 132
resident owner-occupier, 17, 129, 130, 132,
156
small business premises, 17, 130, 131, 156,
352
summary, 156
withdrawal, 153

BUILDINGS,
architectural or historical interest, of—
building preservation notice, 425
compensation, 424, 426, 427
assessment, 446
authority liable to pay, 452, 454
claims, 450, 452
listed building. *See* LISTED BUILDING.
blight notice, objection, 148
change of use—
enforcement notice, 441
whether permission needed, 194, 411, 457
clearance area, compulsory purchase,
77–80, 257, 260
minor extensions of use, 412, 457
noise insulation grants, 329, 341, 342, 343
obstructive, demolition, 260
operations in breach of planning control,
441. *See also* STOP NOTICE.
planning refusal—
compensation—
agricultural etc. buildings, 410, 457
alteration etc., for, 406, 409, 456
change of use within same Class, 411,
412
no compensation—
conditions as to lay-out etc., 399, 409
material change in use, 398
rebuilding, 406, 456
severance, counter-notice, 108, 113
unfit, acquisition, 77–80, 257, 260. *See also*
UNFIT HOUSING.
use not constituting development, 194
work not constituting—
development, 194
new development, 456

BUSINESS LOSSES,
disturbance payments, 387
freehold etc. interest, disturbance, 354
business totally extinguished, 360, 364
deductions from profits, 358–360
elderly proprietors, 361
fixtures, 355
goodwill, 163, 355, 360
partnership profits, deduction, 360
profits, 163, 355–360
assessment, 357
deductions from, 358
relocation, 351–354

BUSINESS PREMISES,
blight notice, small business, 17, 130, 131,
156, 352
public works, use, affecting, 331
tenancy, compensation—
disturbance, for, 355, 365, 367–369, 389
land taken, for, 182
unfit, owner-occupier's allowances, 269, 272

CAPITAL GAINS TAX,
compensation, deduction from, 29
injurious affection, for, 320
severance, 320

CARAVANS,
home loss payments, 376, 377, 388
reforming of displaced persons, 389

CERTIFICATE OF APPROPRIATE
ALTERNATIVE DEVELOPMENT. *See*
COMPENSATION FOR LAND TAKEN

CHARITY,
Community Land Act 1975, 307, 308
compensation, 25, 308–310
material interests, 299, 308
development land tax, 310

CLEARANCE AREA,
blight notice, 140
compulsory purchase, 3, 30, 32, 77–80, 259
compensation, 260
confirmation, 79
constructive entry, 80
housing authority powers, 77
inquiries or hearings, 79
unfit houses, 259
adjoining land, power to acquire, 56, 58,
260
clearance orders, 260
compensation, 260, 271
compulsory purchase, 77–80, 257, 260
well-maintained allowance, 262, 263, 272

CLEARANCE ORDER,
disturbance payment, 385, 386
home loss payment, 373
unfit houses, 260

CLOSING ORDER.
disturbance payment, 385, 386
home loss payment 373

COMMON(S),
compulsory acquisition, 49, 277
certificates as to, 49, 50, 51, 277
compensation—
commoners, procedure, 280, 281, 282
owner, 278
rights appurtenant, 280, 281
rights in gross, 280, 281
enclosed land, 280
exchange land, 49, 50, 277, 279
freehold in soil, of, 278
compensation, 278
statutory limitations on use, 279
special parliamentary procedure, 49, 277
meaning, 49n., 277n.
registration of ownership and rights, 278

COMMUNITY LAND,
Act of 1975 ... 23–25. *See also* COMMUNITY
LAND ACT 1975.
Scheme, 22–28, 98
criticisms, 25–28
Development Land Tax Act 1976 ... 25,
98. *See also* DEVELOPMENT LAND TAX
White Paper "Land", 1974 ... 22

COMMUNITY LAND ACT 1975,
authorities for purposes of, 23n., 296n.
acquisition of—
Crown land, 313
land from other public bodies, 312
blight notice under, 142
charities, 307, 308
compensation, 25, 308–310
material interests, 299, 308
compulsory purchase, 31, 74. *See also* COM-
PULSORY PURCHASE
development land, 23
excepted development—
compulsory purchase, 75, 76, 77
meaning, 75n., 297
exempt development, 306
meaning, 75n., 296
financial hardship tribunals, 24, 306, 310
hardship payments, 311
First Appointed Day, 23
development land, power to acquire after,
23
land acquisition and management scheme,
298
material interest—
meaning, 298
outstanding, 74n., 298, 299
duty to acquire, 298, 299
planning permission suspension, 304,
305 .
purpose, 191, 296
relevant date, 297
duty orders, 24, 298, 305
relevant development—
designated, 298
meaning, 23, 296
Second Appointed Day, 23, 305
charities, compensation, 308–310
development land tax, 307

COMMUNITY LAND ACT, 1975—_contd._
existing use value after, 6, 23, 29, 159, 161, 306
financial hardship tribunals, 24, 306, 310
summary, 23–25
suspension of planning permission, 24, 186, 300
assumptions as to permission, effect on, 186, 188
blight notice, 142, 188, 302, 303
development ignoring, 304
duration, 301
enforcement notices, 303, 304
granted after relevant date, 304
granted before relevant date, 300
notices of intention, 300–303
revival, 301, 302
unoccupied office premises, 286 _et seq._ _See also_ UNOCCUPIED OFFICE PREMISES

COMPENSATION,
assessment—
historical summary, 28
land taken, for. _See_ COMPENSATION FOR LAND TAKEN
planning permission, refusal of, 29
unfit housing. _See_ UNFIT HOUSING
betterment, set-off, 4–6, 16, 217
1961 Act, under, 220 _et seq_, 233
capital gains tax, deduction from, 29
check list, basic questions, 162
conveyance, costs of, 93
determination of, 83
absent and untraced owners, 88
development land tax, deduction of, 25, 29, 97 _et seq. See also_ DEVELOPMENT LAND TAX
development of law of, 1 _et seq_
disturbance, for. _See_ DISTURBANCE
easements, extinguishment or acquisition, 283, 284, 285
existing use value, 28
Community Land Act, under, 6, 23, 29, 159, 161, 306
guidance note, 161
injurious affection, for. _See_ INJURIOUS AFFECTION
Land Clauses Acts, 2, 3, 4, 28
Land Compensation Act 1961. _See_ LAND COMPENSATION ACT 1961
Land Compensation Act 1973. _See_ LAND COMPENSATION ACT 1973
land taken, for, 158 _et seq. See also_ COMPENSATION FOR LAND TAKEN
Lands Tribunal. _See_ LANDS TRIBUNAL
lease, rent, apportionment, 93
listed building. _See_ LISTED BUILDING
new development restricted. _See_ NEW DEVELOPMENT
1919 Rules, under, 4, 163, 164, 239
notice of claim, 83
notice to treat. _See_ COMPULSORY PURCHASE
obstructive building, demolition, 260
payment—
absent and untraced owners, 88

COMPENSATION—_contd._
advance, 95
ecclesiastical property, 94
failure by owner to convey, 89
mortgage, 90–92
advance payment, 95
omitted interests, 89
persons under disability, 94
rentcharge, 92
principles, 161
profits à prendre, extinguishment or acquisition, 283
restrictive covenants, breaches, 283, 285
severance, for. _See_ SEVERANCE
stop notice, 443–446. _See also_ STOP NOTICE
tax, deductions for, 25, 29, 97 _et seq_
unfit housing. _See_ UNFIT HOUSING
unoccupied office premises, acquisition, 293

COMPENSATION FOR LAND TAKEN,
assessment—
compulsory acquisition, no allowance for, 164, 177
equivalent reinstatement, cost of, 164, 165, 239 _et seq_
historical summary, 28
Land Compensation Act 1961 . . . 219, 220 _et seq_
market value, 28, 164, 180
agricultural tenancy, 182
business premises, 182
business tenancy, 182
lease, 182, 183, 184
planning assumptions, 15, 162, 180–182, 185 _et seq_
valuation procedures, 183
neighbouring land, effect of development, 217 _et seq_, 235
1919 Rules, 163, 164
no market demand, where, 164, 165, 239 _et seq_, 249
planning assumptions, 15, 162, 180–182, 185 _et seq_
Pointe Gourde principle, 178, 218, 219, 222, 223, 236
prospect of compulsory acquisition, effect, 176, 177
reinstatement basis, on, 164, 165, 239 _et seq_, 249
relevant date, 165
date compensation agreed, 167, 175
date compensation falls to be determined, 166, 167–169, 174
determination of interests to be valued, 169
entry, date of, 166, 167, 169–174
insurance, 169
interest, 169, 175
interests affected by notice to treat, 174, 175
Lands Tribunal award, 167, 168, 175
notice to treat, whether, 165, 169–174
summary, 174
tenant rehoused by authority, 166.

COMPENSATION FOR LAND TAKEN—*contd.*

scheme of development, effect, 171, 172, 178, 217 *et seq*, 235

special purpose for which no market, 164, 165, 239

special value to particular purchaser excluded, 164, 178

use a nuisance or illegal, 164, 179, 180

assumptions as to planning permission, *see* planning permissions assumed

certificate of appropriate alternative development, 15, 18, 204 *et seq*, 217

appeals, 210

applicants, 207

application, 208

consent of other party, 207

requirements prerequisite to, 205

Community Land Act 1975, effect, 211

copies, service of, 209, 210

development plan, certain areas excluded, 206, 207

effect, 213

failure to issue, 210

"nil" certificate, 209, 210, 214

change in development plan after, 214–216

"positive" certificate, 208, 209, 213

procedure, 208

proposal for compulsory acquisition, 205, 206

check list, basic questions, 162

contiguous land, effect of development, 217 *et seq*, 235

savings for local Acts, 234, 236

equivalent reinstatement, basis of, 164, 165, 239 *et seq*

churches, 242, 243, 245

continuance of use intended, 240, 243, 244, 249

cost wholly disproportionate, 241, 250

discretionary assessment, 241, 250

disturbance, claim for, ineligible, 345, 363

improbability of finding purchaser, 241, 242, 249

intention bona fide, 240, 243–245, 250

date intention formed, 245

1919 Rules as to, 164, 165, 239

no general demand or market, 164, 165, 239 *et seq*, 249

purchase notice, effect of, 242, 249

purpose, nature of, 241

general or localised, 246, 247, 250

purpose-built, need not be, 245–247, 249

relevant date, 240

replacement, type and cost, 248

requirements, 239

restricted use of land, 248

specialised buildings or equipment, 242

temporary use for another purpose, 243, 249

voluntary use by claimant, 245, 249

generally, 158

Land Compensation Act 1961 ... 218 *et seq*

COMPENSATION FOR LAND TAKEN—*contd.*

corresponding enactments, savings for, 234, 235

local Acts, savings in respect of, 234, 236

Pointe Gourde principle, 178, 218, 219, 222, 223, 236

listed building, 274–277

minerals, 238, 273

neighbouring land, effect of development, 217 *et seq*, 235

savings for local Acts, 234, 236

1919 Rules, 4, 163

text, 164

no general demand or market, 164, 165, 239, 249, *see also* equivalent reinstatement, basis of, *supra*

planning permissions assumed, 15, 162, 180–182, 185 *et seq*

certificate of appropriate alternative development, 15, 18, 204 *et seq*, 217, *and see* certificate of appropriate alternative development, *supra*

development plan, conforming with, 15, 185, 196–204

Action Area, 198, 199, 202–204, 217

amendment pending, 197, 198

Comprehensive Development Area, 198, 199, 202–204, 217

particular purpose, allocation for, 198, 199

specific user, allocation for range of, 201, 202

specified use, area allocated for, 199–201

existing planning permission, 15, 185–190, 216

deemed planning permission, 186–189

duration, 186

lapse, 190

personal permission, 186–189

planning authority, personal to, 186–189

subsequent grant, development on, effect, 185, 186

suspension under 1975 Act, 186, 188

time limit, 190

in force at date of notice to treat, 15, 185–190, 216

land applicable to, 181

not derived from development plans, 191

change of use within Use Classes Order, 194, 196

development for which land to be acquired, 15, 191–193, 216

existing use development, 194–196, 216, 217

sch. 8 developments, 15, 195, 196, 216, 217, 456

restrictions, cost of remedying, 188

summary, 216

Pointe Gourde principle, 178, 218, 219, 222, 223, 236

1961 Act provisions compared, 218 *et seq*

principles, 161

COMPENSATION FOR LAND
    TAKEN—*contd.*
purchase notice, 126, 168, 240
reinstatement basis, on, *see* equivalent rein-
    statement, basis of, *supra*
s. 17 certificate , *see* certificate of appropriate
    alternative development, *supra*
scheme of development, effect, 171, 172, 178,
    217 *et seq*, 235
    action area, land in, 224, 225, 236
        relevant date, 230
    betterment, set-off, 217, 218, 220 *et seq*,
        232, 233, 236
        double   recoupment,   avoidance,
            231–234
    comprehensive development area, land in,
        224, 225, 236
        relevant date, 230
    decrease in value, ignored, 223, 232, 233,
        236
    enhancement in value ignored 221–223,
        232, 233, 236
        double recoupment avoided, 231–234
    injurious affection, 218, 236, 319, 320
        avoidance of double compensation, 231
    Land Compensation Act 1961 ... 219 *et seq*
    meaning of scheme, 220 *et seq*, 235
    new town extension, 224, 225, 227–229,
        236
        direction order, 228, 229
        relevant date, 230
    new town site, designation, 224, 225–229,
        236
        direction order, 228, 229
        relevant date, 230
    Pointe Gourde principle, 178, 218, 219, 222,
        223, 236
        1961 Act provisions compared, 218 *et seq*
    several ownerships, land in, 220–224
    summary, 235
    town development area, 224, 225, 227
        relevant date, 230
statutory undertakers, from, 238, 250–255.
    See also STATUTORY UNDERTAKERS

COMPREHENSIVE   DEVELOPMENT
AREA,
    compensation for land in—
        planning permission to be assumed, 198,
            199, 202–204, 217
        scheme of development, effect, 224, 225,
            236
    meaning, 198*n*.

COMPULSORY ACQUISITION. *See also*
    COMPULSORY PURCHASE
commons. *See* COMMON(S)
compensation. *See* COMPENSATION; COM-
    PENSATION FOR LAND TAKEN
historical background, 1
land, of. *See* COMPULSORY PURCHASE OF LAND
provisional order procedure, 2, 3
unoccupied office premises, 286 *et seq*. *See also*
    UNOCCUPIED OFFICE PREMISES

COMPULSORY PURCHASE,
    Act of 1965 ... 31, 66
    bond by authority for entry, 71
    clearance area, 3, 30, 32, 77–80, 259
        compensation, 260
        confirmation, 79
        constructive entry, 80
        housing authority powers, 77
        inquiries or hearings, 79
        procedure, 77
    Community Land Act 1975, under, 31, 74
        confirmation without inquiry, 76
        excepted development, 75, 76, 77
        1946 Act, modifications to, 74
        objections disregarded, 75, 77
        powers of acquisition, 74
        unnecessary or inexpedient, 75, 77
    compensation. *See* COMPENSATION; COM-
        PENSATION FOR LAND TAKEN
    confirmation to entry, 66 *et seq*
        general vesting declaration, 31, 66, 71–74
        notice to treat, 31, 66, 67–69
    conveyance—
        costs of, 93
        failure by owner, 89
    ecclesiastical property, 94
    entry on land, 66, 70
        alternative procedure for, 70
        possession before conveyance, 70
        survey, for purposes of, 70
        unauthorised, 71
    general vesting declaration, 31, 66, 71–74
    Housing Act 1957, Part III, under, 3, 30, 32,
        77–80, 257, 260, *and see* clearance area,
        supra
    local authority, by, *see* 1946 Act procedure,
        infra
    mortgaged land, 90–92
    New Towns Act 1965, under, 31, 80–82
        development corporations, 80
        inquiry, 82
        powers of acquisition, 81
        procedure, 81
    1946 Act procedure, ... 2, 30, 32 *et seq*
        ancient monuments, 50
        certificate, 50, 51
        application of Act, 32
        challenge in Courts, 52
            action for declaration, 65
            aggrieved person, 52–54
            authorisation not empowered, 54, 56,
                57, 61
            certiorari, 65
            conclusions not supported by evidence,
                57–59
            errors of law, 57, 60
            grounds, 54 *et seq*
            material   and   immaterial   con-
                siderations, 57, 59
            procedural defects, 57, 61
                substantial prejudice to applicant,
                    56, 61
            procedure under para. 15 ... 63–65
            quashing of order, 65
            reasons, failure to give adequate, 57, 62

COMPULSORY PURCHASE—*contd.*
>requirements not complied with, 54, 56, 57, 61
>six-week period, 54
>special procedure, 52
>suspension of order, 64
>ultra vires authorisation, 54, 56, 57, 61
>validity of order, 52 *et seq*
>commons and open spaces, 49, 277
>>certificates as to, 49, 50, 51, 277
>Community Land Act 1975 … 74
>Government Department purchase, 46–48
>>hearing, 47
>>inquiry, 47
>>1967 Rules, 47
>>procedure, 46
>land, meaning, 33
>local authority purchase, 2, 32
>>confirmation, 34–37
>>>after inquiry or hearing, 36
>>>notice, 36, 37
>>>objections, 34
>>>without inquiry or hearing, 35
>>hearing, 36, 45
>>>confirmation of order without, 35
>>>inquiry distinguished, 45
>>>procedure after, 36, 37
>>inquiry procedure, 37 *et seq*
>>>attendance, 39
>>>COSTS, 44
>>>evidence, 39, 40, 41
>>>Government Department, representation, 40
>>>hearing distinguished, 45
>>>1976 Rules, 37
>>>notice of decision, 44
>>>notice of inquiry, 37
>>>procedure after inquiry, 42
>>>procedure at inquiry, 39
>>>reopening inquiry, 43
>>>Secretary of State's decision, 42
>>>site inspection, 42
>>>statement of reasons, 38
>>>statutory objector, meaning, 38*n.*
>>>statutory requirements, 37
>>>witnesses, 40
>>making of order, 32
>>notice, 33, 34
>National Trust land, 48
>severance provisions, former, 108
>special parliamentary procedure, 51
>>ancient monuments, 50
>>commons and open spaces, 49, 277
>>National Trust land, 48
>statutory undertakers land, 48, 250
>>certificate of Minister, 49, 51, 251
>unoccupied office premises, 294, 295
>notice to treat, 31, 66, 67–69
>>blight notice, deemed service after, 144, 149, 157
>>contents, 67*n.*, 83
>>effect, 68
>>entry after, 66, 70
>>new interests, creation of, 68, 69

COMPULSORY PURCHASE—*contd.*
>notice of claim, 83
>part of property, as to, 106. *See also* PURCHASE NOTICE; SEVERANCE
>period for service, 67
>persons to be served, 68
>purchase notice deemed to be—
>>Housing Acts, under, 129
>>planning Acts, under, 122, 125
>owner, compensation, payment—
>>absent and untraced, 88
>>disability, under, 94
>>failure to convey, 89
>part of property, of, 106 *et seq. See also* PURCHASE NOTICE
>payment into court for entry, 70
>persons under disability, from, 94
>purchase notice. *See* PURCHASE NOTICE
>rentcharge, land subject to, 92
>slum clearance, 3, 30, 32, 77–80

CROWN LAND,
>Community Land Act 1975, acquisition under, 313

DEED POLL,
>vesting of land by—
>>agricultural unit, severance, lessee, 112
>>disability, under, 95
>>mortgage, 91
>>owner—
>>>absent or untraced, 88
>>>failure to convey, 90
>>rentcharge, 92

DEMOLITION ORDER,
>disturbance payment, 385, 386
>home loss payment, 373
>obstructive building, 260

DEVELOPMENT,
>Community Land Act 1975. *See* COMMUNITY LAND ACT 1975
>gains tax, 21, 29
>land tax. *See* DEVELOPMENT LAND TAX
>new. *See* NEW DEVELOPMENT
>operations not constituting, 194
>planning permission. *See* PLANNING PERMISSION
>Town and Country Planning Act, 1971, sch. 8 … 15, 195, 196, 405 *et seq*, 456
>use of land not constituting, 194

DEVELOPMENT GAINS TAX,
>historical summary, 21, 29

DEVELOPMENT LAND TAX,
>Act of 1976 … 25, 28, 98
>charities, 310
>commencement of project of material development, on, 98
>compensation, deducted from, 25, 29, 97 *et seq*
>>advance payments, 103
>>Commissioners—
>>>action by, 100–103
>>>formula deduction, 102, 103

DEVELOPMENT LAND TAX—*contd.*
　liability to tax, 101
　no liability to tax, 100
　notices to, 99
　specific deduction, 101, 102
　subsequent procedure, 104
　mortgage before 12 May 1976 ... 104
　payments into court, 104
　procedure, 99 *et seq*
　subsequent to, 104
development value—
　charged on realisation, 22, 98
　meaning, 22, 98
liability to, 98
public authorities—
　acquisitions by, net of, 22, 98, 312
　deduction of tax by, 25, 99
　land acquired by—
　　Crown, from, 313
　　public bodies, from, 312, 313
　meaning, 99
realised development value, on, 98
Second Appointed Day, after, 307

DEVELOPMENT ORDER,
listed building, compensation, 274, 276, 426
planning permission withdrawn, 414, 419,
　420
　compensation, 419–421
　　repayment, 421–424
　General Development Order, 407, 414
　direction as to particular development,
　　414, 415, 419

DEVELOPMENT PLAN,
blight notice, 135, 155
certificate of appropriate alternative
　development, 206, 207
meaning, 139
planning permission assumed, 15, 185,
　196–204

DISABILITY, PERSON UNDER,
compulsory purchase, from, 94

DISABLED PERSON,
dwelling adapted for—
　disturbance, compensation for freehold
　　etc., 349
　disturbance payment, 388

DISTURBANCE,
compensation, 163, 164, 165, 272, 344
　Act of 1965, s. 20, under, 369, 370
　agricultural tenancy, 355, 365, 366
　　Agriculture etc. Acts, under, 371, 380,
　　　388
　　farm loss payment, 379–385
　business tenancy, 355, 365, 367, 389
　　improvements, 369
　　new lease, right to, 367, 368
　　notice of entry, 369, 389
　equivalent reinstatement claim and, 345,
　　349, 363
　farm loss payments, 160, 379
　　amount, 381–384
　　claim, period for, 384

DISTURBANCE—*contd.*
　displacement, meaning, 381
　other compensation excluded, 380
　partnership, 384
　procedure, 384
freehold or long leasehold, 344
　blight notice, expenses, 352, 353, 363
　business losses, 354
　　deductions from profits, 358–360
　　elderly proprietors, 361
　　fixtures, 355
　　goodwill, 163, 355, 360
　　partnership profits, deduction, 360
　　profits, 163, 355–360
　　relocation, 351–354
　business totally extinguished, 360, 364
　companies within group, 346, 347, 363
　expenses incurred before notice to treat,
　　351–353, 363
　fixtures, 355
　improvements disallowed, 349, 350, 364
　losses excluded, 348, 364
　mitigate loss, duty to, 353, 354
　occupation, 346–348
　removal expenses, etc., 348, 354, 364
　residential premises, 348
home loss payments, 160, 239, 372–379,
　388
　amount, 377
　caravans, 376, 377, 388
　claim, time for, 375, 378
　claimant's qualification, 374–376
　dwelling, occupation of, 374, 385, 386
　period of occupancy, 374
　procedure, 378
　requirements, 372–374
Landlord and Tenant Act 1954, under,
　370, 389
licensed premises, 159, 160
long leasehold, *see under* freehold, *supra*
short tenancies, 345, 365 *et seq*
　acquisition, method of, 365, 388
　Land Compensation Act 1973 ... 345,
　　365
　meaning, 365, 388
site value of unfit house, excluded in, 345,
　363
payments, 385–388
　amount, 387
　compensation, not entitled to, 386
　house or land, affecting, 386
　occupation of claimant, 387
　qualifications, 386
　requirements, 385
　trading losses, 387
rehousing obligations of local etc.
　authorities, 346, 389
residential owner-occupiers, 346, 390
　alternative accommodation, expenses,
　　390, 391, 392
　loans, alternative dwellings, for, 390, 392

DWELLING,
blight notice, 130, 156, 352
change of use in building to use as, 441

DWELLING—*contd.*
home loss payment, 374, 385, 386
single used as two or more separate, 194, 456
unfit, owner-occupier's allowance, 265–269, 272
use not requiring planning permission, 194
works, injurious, affecting, 330, 334
temporary accommodation, 323, 343

EASEMENTS,
acquisition, 283
compensation, 284, 285
extinguishment, 283
injurious affection—
third party, land held by, 323–325, 342
vendor, land retained by, 315, 316
severance, 315, 316

ECCLESIASTICAL PROPERTY,
churches, equivalent reinstatement, 242, 243, 245
compensation, payment, 94

ENFORCEMENT NOTICE,
planning control, breach of, 441
stop notice pending appeal, 441

ENTRY,
clearance area, constructive, 80
compensation, assessment, relevant date, 166, 167, 169–174
notice to treat, after, 66, 70
survey, for, 70
unauthorised, 71

EQUIVALENT REINSTATEMENT,
basis of compensation. *See* COMPENSATION FOR LAND TAKEN

EXISTING USE,
planning permission assumed, 194–196, 216, 217
Second Appointed Day, valuation after, 6, 23, 29, 159, 161, 306

FARM LOSS PAYMENT. *See under* AGRICULTURAL UNIT

FIELD GARDEN ALLOTMENT. *See also* COMMON(S)
meaning, 49*n.*, 277*n.*

FIXTURES,
disturbance, compensation for, 355

FORESTRY,
buildings for, planning restrictions, compensation, 410
use of land for, 194

FUEL ALLOTMENT. *See also* COMMON(S)
meaning, 49*n.*, 277*n.*

GARDEN,
blight notice, objection, 148, 150
severance, counter-notice, 108, 113

GENERAL DEVELOPMENT ORDER,
permission, granting—
agricultural buildings and works, 414, 420
direction as to particular development, etc., 414, 415, 419
listed building works, 426
waste, tipping of, 412
withdrawn, 414

GENERAL IMPROVEMENT AREA,
blight notice, 138

GENERAL VESTING DECLARATION,
compulsory purchase, 31, 66, 71–74
severance, counter-notice, 109

GOODWILL,
disturbance, compensation for loss, 163, 355, 360

GOVERNMENT DEPARTMENT,
compulsory purchase under 1946 Act—
local authority, by—
representation at inquiry, 40
statement of reasons to, 38
Minister, by, 46–48

HEARING. *See also* PUBLIC LOCAL INQUIRY
compulsory purchase—
Housing Act, Part III, under, 79
1946 Act, under—
Government Department, by, 47
local authority, by, 36, 37 *et seq*

HIGHWAY,
access, construction, planning restriction, no compensation, 399
blight notice—
appropriate authority for, 154
development plan, land for, 136, 137, 155
construction and use, injurious affection, 136, 329, 330, 335
maintenance and improvement not development, 194

HOME LOSS PAYMENT,
disturbance, compensation for, 160, 239, 372–379, 388
amount, 377
caravans, 376, 377, 388
claim, time for, 375, 378
claimant's qualification, 374–376
dwelling, occupation of, 374, 385, 386
period of occupancy, 374
procedure, 378
requirements, 372–374

HOUSING,
accommodation, provision of, 56, 59, 257
Act of 1957, unfit housing. *See* UNFIT HOUSING
Acts, purchase notice under, 128
association, improvements by—
disturbance payment, 385, 386
home loss payment, 372, 373
order—
disturbance payment, 385, 386

HOUSING—*contd.*
   home loss payment, 373
   rehousing obligations of local etc.
      authorities, 346, 389
   unfit for human habitation. *See* UNFIT HOUS-
      ING

IMPROVEMENT,
   disturbance, compensation, disallowed, 349,
      350, 364
   disturbance payment, 385, 386
   home loss payment, 372, 373

IMPROVEMENT NOTICE,
   disturbance payment, 385, 386
   home loss payment, 372, 373
   purchase notice following, 128

INDUSTRIAL DEVELOPMENT,
   certificate, 408
     claim unsupported by, notice of deemed
       refusal, 408, 409
     conditions—
       no compensation, 399, 408, 419
       purchase notice, 118
   refusal, purchase notice, 115, 116

INJURIOUS AFFECTION,
   compensation, 233, 314
     aerodromes, alterations etc., 329, 330
     ancient monument, guardianship order,
       431, 432
     highway, construction and use, 136, 329,
       330
     Land Compensation Act 1973—
       Part I, 323, 328 *et seq*
       Part II, 329, 340–342
     land held by third parties, 321
      execution of works, 321–323, 342
      further claims, 326, 342
      interest, 328, 342
      land or interest in land, 323–325, 342
      maintenance of works, 321–323, 342
      negligent or *ultra vires* acts, 326, 342
      practice note, 328
      private legal right, interference with,
       323–325, 342
      requirements, 321
      restitutio in integrum, 326, 342
      tort, actionable in, 325, 342
     land retained by vendor, 233, 314
      capital gains tax, 320
      further claim, 318, 320
      interest, 320, 327
      measure of compensation, 318
      mortgaged land, 319
      nature of injury, 318
      negligent or *ultra vires* acts, 318, 320
      qualifying interests, 315, 316
      scheme of development, 218, 231, 236,
       319, 320
      summary, 319
   noise insulation grants, 329, 341, 342, 343
   public works, mitigation of injurious
      effects, 340–342

INJURIOUS AFFECTION—*contd.*
   temporary accommodation during works,
      323, 343
   use of public works, 329
     agricultural unit, 331, 334, 342
     business premises, 331
     claim period, 333–335, 343
      contract, land subject to, 334
      highway not maintainable, 335
      transitional provisions, 335
     contract, land subject to, 334, 337
     dwellings, 330, 334
     Leasehold Reform Act 1967, rights, 332
     measure of compensation, 336, 343
     mitigation of damage, 338, 339, 341,
      343
     mortgagee, claim by, 332
     notice of claim, 335
     owner-occupier's interest, 330–332, 342
     physical factors causing damage, 329,
      343
     planning assumptions, 337
     qualifying dates, 332
     qualifying interests, 330
     set-off of increase, 339, 343
     subsequent compulsory acquisition,
      adjustment, 340, 343
     trustees, claims by, 332, 342
     works mitigating depreciation, 338,
      339, 343

INQUIRY. *See* PUBLIC LOCAL INQUIRY

LAND,
   clearance area, in, compulsory purchase,
      77–80, 257, 260
   compensation for land taken. *See* COM-
      PENSATION FOR LAND TAKEN
   layout, no compensation for planning
      restriction, 399
   meaning, 33
   undeveloped, severance, 110, 114
   use of. *See* USE OF LAND

LAND CLAUSES ACTS,
   assessment of compensation, 2, 3, 4, 28
   severance, counter-notice, 108, 110

LAND COMMISSION,
   Act of 1967 ... 19–21
     betterment levy, 19–21, 29
     abolition, 21, 29
   Crownhold, 19
   functions, 19

LAND COMPENSATION ACT 1961,
   betterment, 16, 220 *et seq*, 233
   certificate of appropriate alternative
      development, 15, 18, 204 *et seq*, 217
   compensation, determination of, 83, 161
     Second Appointed Day, after, 307, 309
     Town and Country Planning Act, Part
      VIII, 446
   criticisms, 17
   historical summary, 14–18, 28, 29

LAND COMPENSATION ACT 1961—*contd.*
Lands Tribunal. *See* LANDS TRIBUNAL
1919 Rules, 163
modification of, 16
planning assumptions, 15, 162, 180–182, 185 *et seq*
scheme of development, 219 *et seq*
set-off, 6, 16, 221, 222
summary, 14–18

LAND COMPENSATION ACT 1973,
blight notices, 137, *and see* BLIGHT NOTICE
severance, counter-notice, 106, 111

LANDS TRIBUNAL,
appeal, 87
interlocutory matters, 84
planning decision restricting new development, 404
award, 86
interest, 86, 96
blight notice objection, reference to, 145 *et seq*, 157
case stated, 87
compensation, determination of, 31, 83
absent and untraced owners, 88
clearance area, 78
general vesting declaration, 73
land taken, for, relevant data, 167, 168, 175
rent, apportionment, 93
costs, 86
decision, 86
disturbance payments, 388
jurisdiction, 83
1975 Rules, 83
procedure, 83–86
discovery, 84
evidence, 85
expert witnesses, 86
interlocutory matters, 84
notice of claim, 83
reference to, 84
severance, counter-notice—
agricultural units, 112
buildings, parks, gardens, 109, 113, 114

LEASE,
compensation for land taken, 182, 183, 184
relevant date, 166
injurious affection, 315, 316
public works, by, 1967 Act, under, 332
long, disturbance, 344
rent, apportionment by Lands Tribunal, 93
severance, 315, 316

LICENSED PREMISES,
disturbance, compensation for, 159, 160

LISTED BUILDING,
building preservation notice prior to listing. *See* BUILDINGS.
compensation, 274–277
alter or extend, consent refused, 274, 424, 425, 426
assessment, 446

LISTED BUILDING—*contd.*
authority liable to pay, 452, 453, 454
reimbursement and contributions, 454
claims, 450, 452
interest, 448
consent, revocation or modification, 274, 276, 424, 427
assessment, 446
authority liable to pay, 452, 453, 454
reimbursement or contributions, 454
claims, 450, 452
interest, 448
deliberate neglect, acquisition where, 274–276, 277
blight notice, 276, 277
direction for minimum compensation, 276, 277
summary, 276, 277
meaning, 424
planning permission, whether affecting, 274, 425, 426
purchase notice, 115, 116, 118, 426
form, 121
repairs notice, service where, 121
Secretary of State, powers, 122

LOCAL LAND CHARGE,
registration—
compensation, advance payment, 96
compensation notice, 404
development order restriction, 422
revocation or modification order, 422

LOCAL ACTS,
contiguous land, enhanced value, savings for, 234, 236

LOCAL AUTHORITY,
authorities for purpose of—
blight notice, 154
Community Land Act 1975 . . . 23*n.*, 296*n.*
purchase notice, 114, 121, 122, 127
compulsory purchase by, 2, 32. *See also* COMPULSORY PURCHASE
meaning, 32

LOCAL INQUIRY. *See* PUBLIC LOCAL INQUIRY

LOCAL PLAN,
blight notice, land allocated in, 134, 155

MANUFACTORY,
blight notice, objection, 148

MARKET VALUE,
compensation for land taken, 28, 164, 180
agricultural tenancy, 182
business premises, 182
business tenancy, 182
lease, 182, 183, 184
planning assumptions, 15, 162, 180–182, 185 *et seq*

MINERALS,
compensation for land taken, 238, 273
working—
deposit of waste on land, 412, 457
planning restrictions, no compensation, 399
MORTGAGE,
blight notice by mortgagee, 132, 133, 156
objection notice, 151, 152
compensation, payment, 90–92
advance, 95
compulsory purchase, 90–92
development land tax, 104
injurious affection—
land of vendor, 315, 316, 319
public works, use of, 332
meaning, 104
planning restrictions, compensation, 447
severance, 315, 316, 319

NATIONAL TRUST,
land, compulsory purchase, 48
NEW DEVELOPMENT,
meaning, 195, 393
planning restrictions, compensation for, 13, 29, 392, 394
claim holdings, 395
claimants, 401
claims, submission, 400
compensation notice, 404
determination, 401–405
established claims, provision for, 11–13, 394
exclusion, 398–401
measure, 401–405
qualified areas, interests, apportionment, 403
modification, 398–401
Secretary of State, powers, 400, 401, 404
subsequent development, recovery on, 404, 405
unexpended balance of established development value, 13, 395
certificate as to, 395–398
claim area, apportionment, 396–398
NEW STREET,
order, land affected, blight notice, 140–142
objection notice, 147
NEW TOWN,
corporation—
Community Land Act 1975 authority, 23n., 296n.
compulsory purchase, 80
order, land affected, blight notice, 139
scheme of development—
extension, 224, 225, 227–230, 236
site, designation, 224, 225, 227–230, 236
NOISE,
insulation grants, 329, 341, 342, 343
public works, injurious use, 343

NOTICE TO TREAT,
compensation, assessment relevant date, 165, 169–174
compulsory purchase. See COMPULSORY PURCHASE
deemed service—
blight notice, 144, 157, 240
purchase notice, 122, 125, 129

OBJECTION NOTICE. See BLIGHT NOTICE
OFFICE DEVELOPMENT,
permits, conditions—
no compensation, 399, 408, 419
purchase notice, 118
OFFICE PREMISES,
unoccupied. See UNOCCUPIED OFFICE PREMISES
OPEN SPACE. See also COMMON(S)
meaning, 49n., 277n.
OWNER,
compensation, payment—
absent, 88
failure by, to convey, 89
untraced, 88
owner-occupier. See OWNER-OCCUPIER
OWNER-OCCUPIER,
allowance, unfit house. See UNFIT HOUSING
blight notice, 17, 129, 130, 132, 156
residential—
disturbance, 346, 390–392
public works, injurious, 330–332, 342

PARK,
blight notice, objection, 150
severance, counter-notice, 108, 113
PARTNERSHIP,
agricultural unit, 133, 156
disturbance, compensation for—
business losses, 360, 362
farm loss payment, 384
PAYMENT INTO COURT,
compensation—
agricultural unit, 112
development land tax, deduction of, 104
mortgage, 91
owner—
absent or untraced, 88, 104
disability, under, 94
failure to convey, 90, 104
rentcharge, 92
PERSONAL REPRESENTATIVE,
blight notice by, 133
objection notice, 151, 152
PLANNING BLIGHT. See BLIGHT NOTICE
PLANNING CONTROL,
breach of, enforcement notice, 441
stop notice pending appeal. See STOP NOTICE

PLANNING PERMISSION,
assumptions as to, for compensation for land taken. *See* COMPENSATION FOR LAND TAKEN
conditional grant—
  breach of conditions, 441
  new development, compensation. *See* NEW DEVELOPMENT
  purchase notice, 115, 116, 117, 406
  sch. 8, Part I development, 195, 406, 456
    no compensation, 195, 406, 456
  sch. 8, Part II development, 195, 406, *and see* sch. 8, Part II, under, *infra*
development order restrictions, 413, 414, 415
  compensation notice, 422–424
  compensation, right to, 419–421
    assessment, 448
    authority liable to pay, 452, 454
    claims, 448, 452
  registration, 421–424
  repayment of compensation, 421–424
  subsequent "new development", 421–424
discontinuance order, 393, 415, *and see* s. 51 order, *infra*
listed building, affecting, 274, 425, 426
modification order—
  purchase notice, 115, 116
    compensation, 126, *and see* s. 45 order, *infra*
refusal of—
  compensation—
    new development. *See* NEW DEVELOPMENT
    purchase notice, 126, 127
  purchase notice, 114, 115, 117, 406
  sch. 8, Part I development, 195, 406, 456
    no compensation, 195, 406, 456
  sch. 8, Part II development, 195, 406, 456, *and see* sch. 8, Part II, under, *infra*
revocation order—
  purchase notice, 115
    compensation, 126, *and see* s. 45 order, *infra*
sch. 8, Part II, under, 195, 406, 456
  compensation for restriction, 196, 405 *et seq*
    assessment, 446
    authority liable to pay, 452, 454
      reimbursement and contributions, 454
    claims, 448, 452
    interest, 448
    right to, 407
    time limitations, 412
s. 45 order, 413
  compensation notice, 422–424
  compensation, right to, 416
    abortive expenditure, 416
    assessment, 446
    authority liable to pay, 452, 453
      reimbursement and contributions, 454
    claimant, 416, 418
    claims, 448, 452

PLANNING PERMISSION—*contd.*
  date for assessment, 416
  interest, 448
  loss or damage, categories, 417
  other land, loss in respect of, 418
development order permission, after withdrawal of, 420
  registration, 421–424
  repayment of compensation, 421–424
  subsequent "new development", 421–424
s. 51 order, 393, 415
  compensation, right to, 421
    assessment, 446
    authority liable to pay, 452, 454
      reimbursement and contributions, 454
    claims, 448, 452
    interest, 448
suspension of. *See under* COMMUNITY LAND ACT 1975

POINTE GOURDE,
  principle of assessment, 178, 218, 219, 222, 223, 236

PROFITS À PRENDRE,
  acquisition, 283
  compensation, 284
  extinguishment, 283
  injurious affection—
    third party, land held by, 323–325, 342
    vendor, land retained by, 315, 316
  severance, 315, 316

PUBLIC AUTHORITY,
  Community Land Act 1975 ... 23*n.*, 296*n.*
  development land tax. *See* DEVELOPMENT LAND TAX

PUBLIC LOCAL INQUIRY,
  compulsory purchase—
    Community Land Act 1975, under, 76
    Housing Act, Part III, under, 79
    New Towns Act 1965, under, 82
    1946 Act, under—
      aggrieved person, 53
      commons and open spaces, 50
      Government Department, by, 47
      local authority, by, 36, 37 *et seq*

PURCHASE NOTICE,
  Housing Acts, under, 128
    deemed notice to treat, 129
  severance, counter-notice of objection, 106. *See also* SEVERANCE
  Town and Country Planning Act 1971, under, 107, 114
    compensation, 126, 168, 240
    deemed notice to treat, 122, 125
    Industrial Development Certificate, conditions, 118
    industrial development, planning refusal, 115
    local authority, service on, 114, 127
      action by authority, 122, 127
      time for, 121, 127
      unwilling to accept, 122, 128

PURCHASE NOTICE—*contd.*
Office Development Permit, conditions, 118
planning decisions, application, 114
procedure, 121
reasonably beneficial use—
land incapable of, in existing state, 114, 115, 127, 242, 249, 406
matters to be considered, 116
new development possibility ignored, 116
what constitutes, 119
requirements, 114
Secretary of State—
decision, quashing of, 125, 128
default, deemed confirmation on, 125, 128
powers of, 122–125, 128
summary, 127

REFUSE,
deposit on land—
mineral working, in connection with, 457
stop notice, 442, 444, 446

RENTCHARGE,
compensation, payment, 92

RESTRICTIVE COVENANTS,
interference with, 283
compensation, 285
injurious affection, 324

SEVERANCE,
compensation, 314
land retained by vendor, 233, 314
capital gains tax, 320
interest, 320, 327
measure of compensation, 318
mortgaged land, 319
nature of injury, 316–318
qualifying interests, 315, 316
summary, 319
counter-notice of objection, 106
agricultural, etc., land, 110, 114
agricultural unit, 111–113, 114
lessee, acquiring authority as, 112
procedure, 112
tenant for less than year, 113
buildings, parks, gardens, 108, 113
general vesting declaration, 109
Land Clauses Consolidation Act 1845 ... 108, 110
Land Compensation Act 1973 ... 106, 111
Lands Tribunal, reference to, 109, 112, 113, 114
summary, 113
underdeveloped land, 110, 114
notice to treat, *see* counter-notice of objection, *supra*
purchase notice, 106, 107, 114 *et seq. See also* PURCHASE NOTICE

SLUM CLEARANCE. *See also* CLEARANCE AREA; UNFIT HOUSING
compulsory purchase, 3, 30, 32, 77–80, 257, 271
resolution, land affecting, blight notice, 140
objection notice, 147

SPECIAL PARLIAMENTARY PROCEDURE,
ancient monument, preservation order, 428
compulsory acquisition, 51
ancient monuments, 50
commons, 49, 277

STATUTORY UNDERTAKERS,
compulsory purchase from, 48, 250
certificate of Minister, 49, 51, 251
compensation, 238, 250–255
apparatus, interference with, 253–255
certificate of appropriate Minister, 250, 252, 254
direction that payment unreasonable, 254, 255
extinguishment of rights, 253–255
no certificate issued, 251, 252, 255
summary, 255
easements, acquisition of, 283
meaning, 49n., 250n.
purchase notice served on, 122
works not requiring planning permission, 194

STOP NOTICE,
compensation, right to, 443–446
authority liable to pay, 445, 452, 454
claimants, 445
claims, 448, 452
grounds for, 443–445
measure of, 446
payment, 445, 452, 454
reimbursement and contribution, 454
enforcement notice—
appeal partly successful, 444
breach of planning control, 441
pending appeal on, 442
grounds of appeal, 441
planning permission, grant on appeal, 442
suspended, 303, 304
quashing on appeal, 443, 444
withdrawal, 443
compensation, 444, 445
procedure, 442

STRUCTURE PLAN,
blight notice, land indicated in, 133, 134, 155

TOWN AND COUNTRY PLANNING,
Act of 1947—
Central Land Board, 8, 9
criticisms, 10, 11
development charge, 9, 11, 21, 394
existing use value, 6, 394
1919 Rules, application of, 4, 9
purchase notice, 107, 114
summary, 8–10
Uthwatt Committee recommendations, 6, 8

TOWN   AND   COUNTRY   PLAN-
NING—*contd.*
  Act of 1953—
    development charge, abolition, 11
    historical background, 10–14
  Act of 1954—
    criticisms, 13, 14
    established claims, provisions for, 11–13,
      394
    historical background, 10–14
    1919 Rules, application of, 4
    unexpended balance of established
      development value, 13, 395
  Act of 1959—
    criticisms, 17
    historical summary, 14–18
  Act of 1968, general vesting declaration, 31,
    66, 71
  Act of 1971—
    blight notice, 133–137
    compensation for certain planning deci-
      sions, 393, 394
    purchase notice, 115. *See also* PURCHASE
      NOTICE
  blight. *See* BLIGHT NOTICE
  new development. *See* NEW DEVELOPMENT
  planning permissions. *See* PLANNING PER-
    MISSIONS

TOWN DEVELOPMENT AREA,
  scheme of development, compensation, 224,
    225, 227, 230

TREES,
  felling licence, 433
    refusal, compensation, 433, 434, 451
  preservation orders, 432
    consent, 432
      refusal, compensation, 435, 451, 452,
        454
  meaning, 432
  purchase notice, 115, 119
  replanting, direction, 432
    compensation, 436, 451, 454

TRUSTEES,
  injurious affection, use of public works,
    claims, 332, 342

UNFIT HOUSING,
  clearance area, 259
    adjoining land, power to acquire, 56, 58,
      260
    clearance orders, 260
    compensation, 260, 271
    compulsory purchase, 77–80, 257, 260
    well-maintained allowance, 262, 263, 272
  compensation, 255 *et seq*, 271
    clearance area, 260, 271
      retail shop, discretionary payment, 270,
        271
    obstructive building, 260, 261
    owner-occupier's allowances, 265, 272
      business premises, 269, 272
      continuous occupation, 266

UNFIT HOUSING—*contd.*
    minimum qualifying period, 265, 266,
      268, 272
    partial occupation, 266–268
    private dwellings, 265–269, 272
    repayment, 270
    temporary vacancy or absence, 268
    tenancy, effect of, 266–268
  partially well-maintained allowance, 264,
    272
  severance, 317
  site value, based on, 238, 255, 271
    additional allowances, 256, 257, 271,
      272
    disturbance, no additional payment,
      345, 363
    inapplicable, where, 261
  summary, 271–273
  unfit house incapable of being rendered
    fit, 258, 259, 271
  well-maintained allowance, 262, 264, 269,
    272
    repayment, 270
  Housing Act 1957 ... 257, 271
    displacement, discretionary payment, 270
    owner-occupier's allowance, 265, 272
    Part II ... 258, 271
      compensation, 258, 259, 271
    Part III, clearance areas, 3, 30, 32, 77–80,
      257, 271
      compensation, 260, 271
      well-maintained allowance, 262, 263, 272
  notice to do work, 258
  obstructive buildings, demolition, 260
  undertaking to do work, 258

UNOCCUPIED OFFICE PREMISES,
  acquisition, powers of, 286
    agreement, by, 288, 293
    compensation, 293
    compulsory purchase procedure, 294
    conditions, 287
    letting, attempts at, 287
    other land, 288
    partial occupation, 287
    scope of, 287
  Community Land Act 1975 ... 286 *et seq*
    completion date, 289
    compensation assessable at, 293, 294
    completion notice, 289
      several recipients, 289, 290
      subsequent notice, withdrawal by, 290,
        291
    rating assessment, based on, 289, 291
  compulsory purchase procedure, 294
  entry, powers of, 289, 292
  information as to, power to require, 289, 291
  notices, service of, 293
  occupation, 288

USE OF LAND,
  change of—
    breach of planning control, 441
      stop notice, whether applicable, 442
    within same Class, 411, 457
      planning permission assumed, 194, 196

USE OF LAND—*contd.*
  discontinuance, 393
    purchase notice, 115
    s. 51 order, 415
      compensation, right to, 421
  minor extensions of, 412, 457

WASTE,
  deposit on land—
    mineral working, in connection with, 412, 457
    stop notice, 442, 444, 446

WORKS,
  injurious affection—
    execution of works, 321–323, 342
    public works, use of, compensation, 329.
     See also INJURIOUS AFFECTION

WORSENMENT,
  injurious affection, 5. *See also* INJURIOUS AFFECTION